The Economics of Happiness

Mariano Rojas

Editor

The Economics of Happiness

How the Easterlin Paradox Transformed Our
Understanding of Well-Being and Progress

 Springer

Editor
Mariano Rojas
FLACSO-México & UPAEP
Tlalpan, Ciudad de México, Mexico

ISBN 978-3-030-15834-7   ISBN 978-3-030-15835-4   (eBook)
https://doi.org/10.1007/978-3-030-15835-4

This Springer imprint is published by the registered company Springer Nature Switzerland AG.
The registered company address is: Gewerbestrasse 11, 6330 Cham, Switzerland

Foreword: Happiness or GDP?

Since World War II, happiness has moved into the social sciences. Nearly all of the prior literature is in the humanities, going all the way back to Aristotle, though psychology, as in Abraham Maslow's "hierarchy of needs," has its foot in the door. This work typically takes off from preconceived ideas about what *should* make people happy—what makes for "*the Good Life*." On this, there are almost as many judgments as judges. Although there is much thought-provoking wisdom in this literature, there is no real evidence about how happy people really are and what *does* make them happy, which is what the social scientist seeks to know. We now have well-tested data on people's happiness that provide the basis for scholarly research, as exemplified by the work in this book.

I cannot do justice to the depth and breadth of the many fine contributions here. Let me simply say that I am humbled, honored, and grateful to each of the authors. I owe special thanks to Mariano Rojas whose time-consuming efforts brought the volume into existence.

In these brief remarks I would like to address an issue of growing urgency as measures of happiness gain increasing attention among policy-makers: Which is a better measure of society's well-being and guide to public policy – Happiness or GDP?

My answer is *Happiness*. Here is why.

First and foremost, happiness is a much more comprehensive measure than GDP. As a measure of well-being, GDP, in per capita terms, at best approximates the average change in people's real incomes, that is, in the quantity of goods and services produced and, for the most part, consumed by society. Happiness, in contrast, registers the effect on well-being not only of income, but also of developments in other aspects of people's lives, most importantly, health and family circumstances. GDP is about the economic side of life, focusing solely on output and income; happiness summarizes the degree to which the many concerns of everyday existence are satisfied.

China's experience transitioning from socialism to capitalism provides an acid test of the merits of GDP versus happiness as a summary measure of well-being, because GDP and happiness move in opposite directions. In the period since 1990 GDP goes up at perhaps the highest rate ever observed, while happiness goes down. Which measure, GDP or happiness, better captures what is happening to people's lives, to their well-being?

The answer is easily happiness. China's policy of "economic restructuring," though it raised markedly the growth rate of GDP, involved major collateral damage – massive unemployment and dissolution of the social safety net. The result, for those still employed as well as the unemployed, was new and pressing worries about jobs and income security, family life, and health. These concerns, which are central to people's feelings of well-being, are not reflected in GDP, but they are in self-reported happiness. No wonder that social policy expert Gerard Lemos concludes in a 2012 book titled *The End of the Chinese Dream: Why the Chinese People Fear the Future*, that "the Chinese people are deeply insecure about themselves and their future" (p. 3). In promoting the expansion of output, what was happening to people's lives as a whole was being neglected.

There is a curious contradiction in economics. There is recognition that many activities like loss of a job and migration have not only pecuniary effects like gain or loss of income but also nonpecuniary consequences, particularly psychological effects such as increased anxiety or stress. Yet, when it comes to evaluating society's overall well-being, the principal criterion is GDP per capita, which totally omits nonpecuniary effects. If the focus is exclusively on output, then the fact that the same policies that produce more output result simultaneously in serious side effects is totally overlooked. How can one justify ignoring the far-reaching psychological consequences for people's lives of massive unemployment and destruction of the social safety net?

In addition to its greater scope, there are other reasons for preferring happiness to GDP. For one thing, happiness is a measure with which people can personally identify. The man in the street reads the headline, "GDP Up by 5 Per Cent," yawns, and quickly turns to the sports pages. But when the headline proclaims, "Happiness Up by 5 Per Cent," he reads on. People can understand happiness; in contrast, GDP is to most persons a remote and meaningless concept. When I ask my class "What does GDP measure?" I am met with mute silence – and this is a group of advanced undergraduates majoring in economics.

Another reason for preferring happiness is that the judgment of well-being is made by the individuals whose well-being is being assessed, not by outsiders. In the case of GDP, the determination of people's well-being is made by so-called experts, the statisticians who put the numbers together. Some economists like to think of GDP as a "hard" statistic like the output of iron ore, in contrast to supposedly "soft" survey data expressing people's views and feelings. This distinction is a hangover from the twentieth-century behaviorist era of economics when it was an article of faith that what people said was not to be trusted.

In fact, there is no single "hard" figure for GDP. In measuring it, numerous judgments are required about what to include, as Simon Kuznets, the pioneer in GDP measurement, repeatedly pointed out. Should unpaid homemakers' services like childcare, preparing meals, and housecleaning be included in GDP? (They are not, but the same services, if performed by hired employees are included.) How about the production of food produced by farm families for their own consumption? (In) Gambling, alcoholic beverages, narcotics, and prostitution – in or out? (Depends chiefly on legal status, which differs among and within countries, and changes over time.) What about defense spending – are Americans better off by the amount of their country's huge military outlays (which are included in GDP) than Costa Ricans who do not even have a standing army? Questions like these on what to include must be faced in constructing an estimate of GDP. They illustrate that GDP is not a "hard," objective, measure and that its scope is determined by subjective judgments made by persons other than those whose well-being is being evaluated. In contrast, happiness is what people themselves tell us about their well-being.

Some scholars object to the idea of happiness as an official metric of well-being claiming that people might then falsify their reported happiness. Others complain that the measure gives too little importance to systemic considerations like political and civil rights. These are reasonable concerns, but their proponents offer no alternative summary measure of well-being, leaving us where we are now, with GDP. Happiness may not be the last word in the measurement of well-being, but it is better than GDP.

Others criticize happiness measures because they have an upper bound, while GDP does not. This is a curious complaint. It implies that society's goal should be unattainable – in particular, that we can never have enough output – and that it would be unfortunate if we were ever to reach an upper bound. By contrast, one might argue that a society where each person reports for their happiness the maximum value of 10 is precisely what we would like to achieve – everyone completely happy. For those worried about reaching utopia anywhere in the near future, let me note that we are still considerably short everywhere of the upper limit – according to the *World Happiness Report* where 10 is the top score, the highest countries average around 7.5 and the lowest, 3.0.

It is encouraging to see that both the United Nations and OECD are now advocating for happiness as a policy objective. Their proposals, however, are not that GDP should be abandoned, but that happiness should be considered as a supplement to GDP. Indeed, some analysts even propose a "dashboard" of measures, perhaps 10 or more. Such proposals are a step in the right direction, because they lessen the importance of GDP. But having two or more criteria of well-being runs into the problem of how much importance should be attached to each item? What if some metrics move in one direction and others, the opposite way, as did GDP and happiness in the recent experience of China? How does one decide what has happened to well-being? Which measure(s) is the better guide to policy? Clearly there is need for a primary measure that resolves such conflicts. I believe that measure is Happiness.

For over half a century, real GDP per capita has reigned as the principal gauge of societal well-being. If happiness were to supplant GDP, public policy would be moved in a direction more meaningful to people's lives. Whereas output has heretofore been the primary focus, jobs and job security would move center stage.

I have noted how China's experience demonstrates the serious human costs of
sacrificing jobs for output. Even as I write, ongoing developments in the United
States provide yet another example. A 35-day partial shutdown of the United States
government starting in December 2018 led to the layoff of hundreds of thousands of
federal government employees and federal contract workers. Commenting on reports
of the stress and suffering being felt by these workers, Secretary of Commerce
Wilbur Ross said:

> Put it in perspective. You're talking about 800,000 workers. And while I feel sorry for the
> individuals that have hardship cases, even if all those workers were never paid again, you're
> talking about a third of a per cent of our GDP, so it's not like it's a gigantic number overall.

Here we have GDP weighed directly against the lives of thousands of workers,
and GDP wins out – a striking illustration of how preoccupation with GDP leads to
minimizing the human side of economic activity. In contrast, happiness would put
the workers and their experience first.

This is not to say that we should throw GDP away, but its role becomes
secondary. If one wants to know specifically about the economy's output, GDP is
a useful tool. Similarly, if one wants a summary measure of health, life expectancy is
appropriate. A dashboard of measures can be informative about the various conditions impacting people. But if one wants a summary measure of people's overall
well-being and a clear-cut guide to policy, then happiness is the answer, because
happiness measures what really matters in people's lives. It reports directly on the
circumstances of ordinary people everywhere in the world.

University Professor Emeritus of   Richard A. Easterlin
Economics
University of Southern California
Los Angeles, CA, USA

Contents

Contributors

Stefano Bartolini University of Siena, Siena, Italy

Tony Beatton The Institute for Social Science Research, The University of Queensland and the Queensland University of Technology (QUT), Brisbane, QLD, Australia

Martin Binder Bard College Berlin, Berlin, Germany
Levy Economics Institute of Bard College, Blithewood, Annandale-on-Hudson, NY, USA

David G. Blanchflower Dartmouth College, Hanover, NH, USA
University of Stirling, Stirling, Scotland
NBER, Cambridge, MA, USA

Andrew E. Clark Paris School of Economics – CNRS, Paris, France

Jan-Emmanuel De Neve University of Oxford, Oxford, UK

Ada Ferrer-i-Carbonell Institute for Economic Analysis (CSIC), Barcelona, Spain

Paul Frijters London School of Economics, London, UK

Carol Graham Brookings Institution, Washington DC, USA
University of Maryland, College Park, MD, USA

Arthur Grimes School of Government, Victoria University of Wellington, Wellington, New Zealand
Motu Research, Wellington, New Zealand

John F. Helliwell Vancouver School of Economics, University of British Columbia, Vancouver, BC, Canada

Johannes Hirata Hochschule Osnabrück, University of Applied Sciences, Osnabrück, Germany

Haifang Huang University of Alberta, Edmonton, AB, Canada

Caspar F. Kaiser Nuffield College, Oxford University, Oxford, UK
DSPI, Oxford University, Oxford, UK

Christian Krekel London School of Economics, London, UK

Lucía Macchia City, University of London, London, UK

Chloe Michel University of Zurich, Zurich, Switzerland

Gabriel Leite Mota Independent researcher, Porto, Portugal

Max B. Norton Vancouver School of Economics, University of British Columbia, Vancouver, BC, Canada

Andrew J. Oswald University of Warwick, Warwick, UK
IZA Institute for the Study of Labor, Bonn, Germany

Sergio Pinto University of Maryland, College Park, MD, USA

Anke C. Plagnol City, University of London, London, UK

Eugenio Proto Centre for Economic Policy Research, London, UK
University of Bristol, Bristol, UK
IZA Institute for the Study of Labor, Bonn, Germany

Maurizio Pugno Department of Economics and Law, University of Cassino, Cassino, Italy

Xavier Ramos Departament d'Economia Aplicada, Universitat Autònoma de Barcelona, Barcelona, Spain

Marc Reinhardt University of Bologna, Bologna, Italy

Mariano Rojas FLACSO-México & UPAEP, Tlalpan, Ciudad de México, Mexico

Francesco Sarracino Institut National de la Statistique et des Etudes Economiques du Grand-Duché du Luxembourg (STATEC), Luxembourg City, Luxembourg
LCSR National Research University Higher School of Economics, Moscow, Russia

Michelle Sovinsky University of Mannheim, Mannheim, Germany
Centre for Economic Policy Research, London, UK

Maarten C. M. Vendrik Department of Macro, International and Labour Economics (MILE), SBE, Maastricht University, Maastricht, The Netherlands
ROA, SBE, Maastricht University, Maastricht, The Netherlands
IZA, Bonn, Germany
EHERO, Erasmus University, Rotterdam, The Netherlands

Shun Wang KDI School of Public Policy and Management, Sejong, South Korea

George Ward Massachusetts Institute of Technology, Cambridge, MA, USA

Rainer Winkelmann University of Zurich, Zürich, Switzerland

List of Figures

List of Tables

Part I
Introduction

Chapter 1
The Relevance of Richard A. Easterlin's Groundbreaking Work. A Historical Perspective

Mariano Rojas

Abstract The Easterlin Paradox emerged within a particular historical context; economics moved from an early interest in happiness during the eighteenth and nineteenth centuries to its complete neglect during the first decades of the twentieth century. Due to this neglect economics faced serious limitations to address well-being issues and to contribute to happiness in societies. The chapter presents the evolution of economics in order to show why Richard A. Easterlin's pioneer work in happiness and economics is groundbreaking; in fact, it constitutes the foundation of a new area in economics: Happiness economics. The chapter analyzes the emergence of happiness economics as well as its consequences and contributions to economics.

It has been more than 40 years since Richard A. Easterlin published his groundbreaking work on happiness and economics. His contribution entitled *Does Economic Growth Improve the Human Lot? Some Empirical Evidence* was published in 1974 and constitutes the first empirical study on the relationship between economic growth and happiness. This contribution introduced what is now widely known as the Easterlin Paradox: In the long run economic growth does not increase people's happiness, even when there is a positive association between the two variables in cross-section studies. As time went on the paradox attracted the attention of economists and triggered a vast research agenda which nowadays constitutes the foundation of the economics of happiness.

It is necessary to recognize that the interest in the study of happiness was not new in economics; as a matter of fact, early economists considered that the study of happiness was central to economics. For example, in his *An Essay on the Principle of Population* (1798) Robert Malthus expressed: "*The professed object of Dr. Adam Smith's inquiry is the nature and causes of the wealth of nations. There is another inquiry, however, perhaps still more interesting, which he occasionally mixes with it, I mean an inquiry into the causes which affect the happiness of nations*". As a matter of fact, Malthus was referring to the main theme addressed by Adam Smith in his

M. Rojas (✉)
FLACSO-México & UPAEP, Tlalpan, Ciudad de México, Mexico

© Springer Nature Switzerland AG 2019
M. Rojas (ed.), *The Economics of Happiness*,
https://doi.org/10.1007/978-3-030-15835-4_1

book entitled *The Wealth of Nations*; however, it is worth to recognize that Smith was always very attentive to the study of happiness, as it is shown by some references to the subject in *The Wealth of Nations* and, primarily, by his many reflections on the topic in his previous work entitled *The Theory of Moral Sentiments*. It is important to remark that Smith, like many other economists afterwards, was also highly skeptical about the capacity of economic growth to generate happiness.

It was during the first decades of the twentieth century that economics abandoned its interest in happiness in order to focus on the study of choice. The emphasis on economic goods – those that must be purchased – led to the centrality of the budget constraint in economics and, with some disregard for the study of people's well-being, the raise income emerged as the main area of study in economics. Economic growth models acquired greater relevance during the following decades. By neglecting the study of happiness, economists were basing their policy recommendations on a major presumption: that people's well-being increases with the expansion of the consumption possibilities; unfortunately, there was no interest in corroborating this presumption. It was really astonishing for a discipline so proud of adopting the scientific method to be so weak in scientifically addressing one of its foundational premises: Is it really true that happiness increases with the expansion of income?

Richard Easterlin's 1974 work addressed a central but neglected issue in economics. What is the relationship between economic growth and happiness? The question was frequently asked in the past; however, rather than relying on presumptions or on ethical and moral considerations, Easterlin followed the scientific method to come out with an answer. His contribution shifted economics away from the path of uncorroborated presumptions as well as from relying on ethical and doctrinal considerations to address well-being issues. It also provided a simple but clever methodology to deal with Jeremy Bentham's main concern: the measurement of people's happiness. The method followed by Easterlin recognizes that happiness is an experience people have and not a construct to be defined by experts; in consequence, it also recognizes that every person is the authority to judge her life. The incorporation of subjectivity in the study of happiness moves economics from its focus on the realm of objects to that on the realm of people, and it allows for better understanding of people's lives. It also provides insight to reconsider the unfruitful path of expanding consumption possibilities without knowing what its well-being impact is.

Richard A. Easterlin's groundbreaking work is clearly the foundation of happiness economics, which nowadays is a vibrant branch within economics. Groundbreaking work necessarily questions basic postulates of its academic field, and it also opens new paths for its development; hence, to fully understand the significance of Easterlin's work it becomes necessary to review the historical context within which this work emerged.

1.1 The Historical Context

1.1.1 Early Economists Were Interested in Happiness

Adam Smith, considered by many as the father of economics, was as concerned about happiness as he was about material wealth. Being a professor of moral philosophy, Smith borrowed from ethical and moral doctrines to address the relationship between material wealth and happiness. In fact, in his Theory of Moral Sentiments (1759) Smith articulates his doubts about the role that material wealth plays in generating happiness; for example, he states that "wealth and greatness are mere trinkets of frivolous utility, no more adapted for procuring ease of body or tranquillity of mind than the tweezer-cases of the lover of toys". Thus, he affirms that "in what constitutes the real happiness of human life, they are in no respect inferior to those who would seem so much above them. In ease of body and peace of mind, all the different ranks of life are nearly upon a level, and the beggar, who suns himself by the side of the highway, possesses that security which kings are fighting for." The primacy that Smith gives to happiness is evident when he sustains that "All constitutions of government, however, are valued only in proportion as they tend to promote the happiness of those who live under them. This is their sole use and end."

Smith's view on happiness was clearly influenced by his background in moral philosophy, and his disdain for material wealth borrows from a long-standing tradition in philosophy that associates happiness to tranquility and virtue in life. Indeed, Smith believed that the pursuit of happiness through the accumulation of material wealth could be a trap leading to hard-working but not happier people. In his Theory of Moral Sentiments Smith states that "We are then charmed with the beauty of that accommodation which reigns in the palaces and economy of the great; and admire how everything is adapted to promote their ease, to prevent their wants, to gratify their wishes, and to amuse and entertain their most frivolous desires. If we consider the real satisfaction which all these things are capable of affording, by itself and separated from the beauty of that arrangement which is fitted to promote it, it will always appear in the highest degree contemptible and trifling"; he then ads that "It is this deception which rouses and keeps in continual motion the industry of mankind". Smith and many of his contemporary scholars believed that material wealth was an important topic for economists to study, but they were careful enough not to associate the raise in material wealth with greater happiness. Unfortunately, during the following centuries – and especially during the twentieth century – many economists made the mistake of associating the wealth of nations with the happiness in nations.

It is necessary to remark that most of the early economists had a background in ethics and moral philosophy which inclined them to be interested in people's happiness; however, this same background distanced them from following the scientific method in the study of happiness.

1.1.2 Early Economists Followed the Ethical Tradition When Addressing Happiness

For centuries the study of happiness was the exclusive playground of philosophers and moralists. How a person ought to live her life and what principles should regulate it were fundamental questions in ethics and morality. Not surprisingly, criteria provided by philosophers and moralists constituted the basis for judging goodness and badness in a person's life, while no authority was recognized to people in judging their life. Thus, happiness – or the good life – ended up being assessed by a third person on the basis of criteria provided by experts.

The ethical tradition relied on the method of discernment; this is: intellectual reasoning was used to identify the relevant criteria. The criteria to judge a person's happiness was usually presented as a list of attributes which a person's life ought to satisfy and which had to be observed by a third-party; some threshold levels were proposed. Persuasive rhetoric was used by scholars to justify their view due to the lack of research-based evidence supporting the main arguments and the proposed criteria. There were no hypotheses to be tested but assertions to be accepted. There was no interest in studying what people were experiencing and what they thought about their life. People's own assessments were usually demeaned on the basis of arguments such as people having incomplete or incorrect information or lacking the appropriate knowledge to make a good judgment. It was common for scholars working within this ethical tradition to assume that people were not in a good position to judge their life.

Within the ethical tradition happiness became an academic construct which ended up being delineated by scholars and where people's own experience of being well was irrelevant.

1.1.3 Jeremy Bentham and Happiness as an Experience People Have

Jeremy Bentham's ideas were influenced by the Enlightenment as well as by important political changes that took place at the end of the eighteenth century and the beginning of the nineteenth century, such as: the American Revolution, the French Revolution, the decline of absolutist monarchies and of the Catholic Church's power, and the rise and fall of Napoleon. Bentham lived in an age where the political power of some ordinary citizens was increasing while that of the traditional monarchic and religious groups was declining; and he was interested in social reforms and public actions that contributed to citizens' well-being. Bentham was not so much interested in the promotion of particular policies but in the development of a method to determine which policies contributed the most to the human lot. He believed that happiness as it is experienced by people – rather than abstract and morally-inspired definitions of the good life – should guide public policy and social reform.

Bentham approached happiness as an experience that happens to people and not as a theoretical construct to be defined by philosophers and moralists. In this way Bentham shifted the substrate of information to judge people's lives as good or bad from the realm of objects to the realm of experiences, and he shifted the authority to make this judgment from experts to people themselves. Rather than entertaining himself in theoretical speculations and doctrinal postulates, Bentham believed that it was necessary to rely on people's experience of being well in order to find whether some policies were doing goodness or not. Bentham knew that a measurement of happiness was needed, but he did not go as far as asking people about their experience of being well; instead, he proposed the *felicific calculus*, which aimed at measuring happiness on the basis of a sophisticated computation of pleasurable and painful experiences, and which also took different attributes of these experiences into consideration.

In Bentham's conception, happiness was an experience that happens to people and, consequently, the role of experts was not to define it but to study it. He was uneasy with experts' inclination of superimposing their own values and judgements to those of people.

The shift in the focus of attention from academic discussions on constructs of the good life to people's experience of being well was conceptually revolutionary; but the computation proposed by Bentham was highly complex, partial, and unpractical. Bentham believed that the experience of happiness could be compared across human beings and that it constituted a good framework to guide public police; however, his proposed computation was very difficult to perform.

It is also important to remark that in Bentham's view happiness was not only an experience that happens to people, it was also an important source of motivation: people aim for happiness. Hence, Bentham combined the study of happiness with the study of human behavior. The search for greater happiness is intrinsically good; in addition, it motivates – and explains – human action.

1.1.4 Utilitarianism Gets into Economics

The ideas of Bentham were incorporated into economics, mostly through the work carried out during the second half of the nineteenth century by economists such as Stanley Jevons, Carl Menger, and Leon Walras. These economists set the foundations for the Theory of Utility and for the Subjective Theory of Value. They wanted to explain the determination of prices of commodities, but their theory laid on the idea that people's happiness is the factor that, in the end, explains prices and supports all economic decisions.

Alfred Marshall was the central figure in the development of the analytical tools used by microeconomic theory in the twentieth century; with this analytical toolbox economics focused on the study of markets, supply and demand, and equilibrium prices and quantities. However, the agent who is behind these markets and whose behavior is crucial in determining the equilibrium prices in the Marshallian analyses continued to be an agent who experienced happiness and whose actions aimed for happiness. In his *Principles of Economics* (1890) Marshall makes several references to happiness; for example: *"the spirit of the age induces a closer attention to the question whether our increasing wealth may not be made to go further than it does in promoting the general wellbeing; and this again compels us to examine how far the exchange value of any element of wealth, whether in collective or individual use, represents accurately the addition which it makes to happiness and wellbeing"*. Marshall goes as far as to recognize that the association between material wealth and happiness may be weak; he states that *"Not only does a person's happiness often depend more on his own physical, mental and moral health than on his external conditions: but even among these conditions many that are of chief importance for his real happiness are apt to be omitted from an inventory of his wealth"*.

Thus, when the economists of the late nineteenth and early twentieth century embarked on the study of prices, quantities, and markets they knew that, in the end, they were addressing a deeper and more relevant issue: human happiness.

1.1.5   Economics Focuses on Explaining Choice While Marginalizing People's Happiness

The complicated and clearly unpractical method proposed by Bentham to compute happiness persuaded many scholars that it was a futile aim to look for a measure of people's experience of being well. During the last decade of the nineteenth century Irving Fisher expressed his skepticism on the practical possibility of measuring utility; it is important to remark that Fisher was not objecting to the existence of a utility which had well-being substance, but he considered its measurement to be impracticable. As a matter of fact, Fisher stated that *"the 'utility standard' [for measuring the change in the value of money] is. . .impracticable, even if the theory of such a standard were tenable"*. Fisher argued that happiness – as cardinal utility – was not necessary to address exchange considerations and that it sufficed to work with an ordinal ranking of options. In consequence, he concentrated his effort in the study of prices, under the assumption that they provided information on people's well-being. It is needless to state that the prices of goods are easily observable and measurable.

Wilfredo Pareto showed that the ordinal ranking of commodity bundles suffices to deal with issues of choice; hence, in a discipline that was bending towards the explanation of choice it became evident that happiness had no instrumental value; it was possible to explain choice without making use of happiness. Like Fisher, Pareto did not rule out the validity of Bentham's utility proposal; he was not rejecting the existence of people's experience of being well nor the role it plays in motivating people. However, Pareto argued that the conception of a utility function with happiness substance was not necessary to develop a framework explaining choice; it was sufficient to assume a utility function that allowed for the ordering of options.

In consequence, the meaning of utility as an indicator of people's happiness ceased to be relevant, and the notion of utility lost its happiness foundation to become no more than a simple device to order options, which are usually expressed in the realm of objects. Pareto made of utility just a plain number that had no happiness substance at all.

The new theory of utility abandoned its original conception based on the experience of happiness people have in order to focus on the explanation of consumer decisions. The first half of the twentieth century saw enormous progress – made by economists such as J.R. Hicks, R.G.D Allen, and Paul Samuelson – in the development of ordinal utility theory, preference theory, and the theory of value. Economists who were trained in the first half of the twentieth century learned almost nothing about people's happiness; instead, they mastered a highly sophisticated framework to study people's decisions and to explain market-equilibrium quantities and prices.

Welfare economics relied on Pareto-optimality concepts, and on the basis of welfare theorems economists promoted competitive markets and rejected interventions that could distort prices. On the basis of their theoretical framework economists assumed that the promotion of competitive markets suffices to reach optimality; however, they could say nothing about what was happening to people's experience of being well. In strict sense, economics could not even confirm that people are happier with greater income or with lower inflation rates. The well-being foundations of economics were weak and the discipline could not provide an answer to some simple questions which ordinary people are interest in, such as: How much additional happiness is obtained from a 10% increase in income? How unhappy are low-income people? How much unhappiness does unemployment generate? Does migration increase happiness?

Due to the lack of research on people's well-being economists were forced to rely on uncorroborated assumptions to provide public-policy advice. Economists of the mid-twentieth century had no choice but to assume – without any proof – that people's happiness is strongly associated with the consumption of commodities and that by producing more everyone will be better off. The emphasis that economics placed on the study of choice could only lead to one major recommendation: expand the space of choice.

1.1.6   The Emphasis on Consumption. The Realm of Objects

The adoption of ordinal utility and of preference theory also provoked a shift in the focus of attention of economists: from people to the realm of objects. Utility was defined in a space of commodities rather than in the realm of people's experiences of being well.

Two major trends influenced economics during the late years of the nineteenth century and the first decades of the twentieth century: Formalization and objectivism. Scholars with a philosophical background – such as Adam Smith, Jeremy Bentham, and Karl Marx – who were predominant in the original stages of the economics were slowly replaced by those with backgrounds in physics, mathematics, and engineering. It suffices to state that Pareto had formal training in mathematics and physics and worked as a civil engineer for many years before getting involved in the study of sociology and economics. Irving Fisher wrote his dissertation under the advice of the mathematician and prominent thermodynamic engineer Willard Gibbs, who also was the thesis advisor of the renowned mathematician Edwin Wilson. Wilson himself was the advisor of Paul Samuelson's PhD dissertation; in fact, Samuelson borrows from Gibbs' thermodynamics models to develop his economic-system ones.

The inspiration that economics got from physics and engineering was also accompanied by the interest economists had in following the methods of the so-called hard sciences; a scientific approach was introduced into economics and economists started thinking in terms of theories, hypotheses and corroborations. However, physics and engineering are disciplines that focus on the study of objects rather than persons, and their methodology relies on using indicators of objects – the so-called objective indicators – rather than on indicators of the experiences people have – which are considered as subjective. It comes as no surprise that economists in the twentieth century were inclined to marginalize the subjective conception of utility in order to concentrate in the study of objective variables, such as bundles of commodities, income, prices, and observed decisions. For example, revealed-preference theory advocates that economics should study what people do rather than what they experience or report.

The introduction of objectivism into the social sciences generated some debate; for example, during the first half of the twentieth century the philosopher Edmund Husserl argued in his book entitled *The Crisis of the European Sciences* that science – in particular social sciences – had forgotten the world of life (*lebenswelt*) and its inherent subjectivity. Husserl stated that by focusing too much on objects – and indicators of objects – science had become insensitive to the sense of being, this is: to the experiences that human beings have.

1.1.7   Progress as Economic Growth. The Increasing Relevance of GDP

Economics as a science of choice focused on explaining consumption and production decisions. However, rather than explaining how preferences were formed, economists concentrated in the study of ways and policies to expand the space of choice. In consequence, the variable occupying the site of honor in the discipline was income and, in particular, its rate of growth. Greater income was associated to more options to choose from and, thus, to a greater utility – in its ordinal sense. Some economists argued that by having more income people could satisfy more needs and, it was assumed, this converted into greater well-being. There was no direct observation of people's experience of being well, but it was assumed that more income was always better.

The national accounting system was developed during the first half of the twentieth century, and the Gross Domestic Product (GDP) acquired relevance. The effort to develop a measure of the aggregate income in societies was headed by Simon Kuznets in the 1930s; this effort led to the creation of the GDP indicator. After World War II the United Nations Statistical Office adopted and further developed the standard methodology of national production and income accounts. This methodology was adopted by the majority of the member countries of the United Nations Organization and, with this, GDP gained enormous importance as an aggregate indicator of production and availability of goods and services.

In the post Second World War period and the beginning of the Cold War one the United States had geopolitical motivations to implement a technical assistance program reaching many countries in the world. It is within this particular context that the concepts of development and underdevelopment were introduced in a speech made by the President of the United States Harry S. Truman in the late 1940s. GDP per capita became a major indicator to assess the degree of development, and its rate of growth became an indicator of progress. In 1960 W.W. Rostow published his book entitled *The Stages of Economic Growth*; the book inspired the highly influential development-aid programs promoted by western countries, and it clearly defined the route that underdeveloped countries ought to follow in order to become developed. The last stage proposed by Rostow – that which defined the final aspiration which agencies of international development should pursue for all countries benefiting from foreign aid – was called the age of high mass consumption. For Rostow, as well as for the many agencies and international organizations promoting development, the uncorroborated assumption that people's well-being was strongly associated to their capacity to purchase more commodities seemed obvious.

In the mid years of the twentieth century economists also became interested in constructing theoretical models to understand and explain differences in GDP across countries and over time. As time went on, models of economic growth evolved from the simple Harrod-Domar and Solow-Swan models to the highly sophisticated models of the present. New capital concepts were also introduced; terms such as human and social capital were incorporated into the old models that relied on physical and natural capital. The importance that income acquired also reflected in related concepts, such as poverty – which ended up being associated to low income- and social classes – which were mostly defined in terms of income and ownership of assets.

1.1.8 Does Economic Growth Improve the Human Lot? Some Doubts Existed

Economic growth and other income-related concepts came to be the major preoccupation of international organizations, development agencies, national governments and most economists; however, it is important to recognize that doubts about its capacity to generate well-being were always present. For example, John

Maynard Keynes believed that income was just a necessity but not something of major value. For Keynes, the value of income does not go as far as having the material means to survive; once the economic problem is solved human beings will have more important issues to focus on. In his preface to Essays in Persuasion – written in 1931- Keynes stated that "the day is not far off when the Economic Problem will take the back seat where it belongs, and that the arena of the heart and head will be occupied, or re-occupied, by our real problems—the problems of life and of human relations . . ."

In 1934, while he was leading the effort to construct the income and production accounting system, Simon Kuznets manifested that "The welfare of a nation can scarcely be inferred from a measurement of national income". Moses Abramovitz also expressed his doubts in 1959 by stating that "we must be highly skeptical of the view that long-term changes in the rate of growth of welfare can be gauged even roughly from changes in the rate of growth of output".

The speech delivered by Senator Robert F. Kennedy at the University of Kansas in 1968 is well known: "But even if we act to erase material poverty, there is another greater task, it is to confront the poverty of satisfaction – purpose and dignity – that afflicts us all. Too much and for too long, we seemed to have surrendered personal excellence and community values in the mere accumulation of material things. Our Gross National Product. ... counts air pollution and cigarette advertising, and ambulances to clear our highways of carnage. It counts special locks for our doors and the jails for the people who break them. It counts the destruction of the redwood and the loss of our natural wonder in chaotic sprawl. It counts napalm and counts nuclear warheads and armored cars for the police to fight the riots in our cities. It counts Whitman's rifle and Speck's knife, and the television programs which glorify violence in order to sell toys to our children. Yet the gross national product does not allow for the health of our children, the quality of their education or the joy of their play. It does not include the beauty of our poetry or the strength of our marriages, the intelligence of our public debate or the integrity of our public officials. It measures neither our wit nor our courage, neither our wisdom nor our learning, neither our compassion nor our devotion to our country, it measures everything in short, except that which makes life worthwhile."

Doubts about the capacity of GDP to measure progress in societies were not rare in the twentieth century; of course, these doubts extended to the capacity of income to generate well-being. However, economic theory was not in a position to address these doubts because the discipline had abandoned its original interest of measuring and studying people's happiness. Economic-growth models could explain, with limited degree of accuracy, which were the main factors leading to rapid growth and how they worked; however, they could say nothing on whether economic growth could increase the human lot.

1.2   Groundbreaking Work by Richard A. Easterlin

It will take a revolutionary approach to shake the foundations of economics in order to provide an empirical answer to the existing doubts. In 1974 Richard A. Easterlin published his work entitled *Does Economic Growth Improve the Human Lot? Some Empirical Evidence*. Easterlin followed a scientific approach to address the question he posed in the title of his contribution. Before getting into the study of Easterlin's contribution it is important to know a little bit more about the person who is behind this groundbreaking work.

1.2.1   Richard A. Easterlin: Pioneer in Happiness Research

After receiving an undergraduate degree in mechanical engineering Richard A. Easterlin had a fairly orthodox economic education at the University of Pennsylvania in the late 1940s and early 1950s. As a student he was exposed mainly to Keynesian theory and to the epistemological foundations of economics. As he describes in his book entitled *The Reluctant Economist*, during his PhD studies in economics he learned the beliefs and culture of the profession: he learned that economics is the queen of the social sciences, that this status comes from its inclination to use formal theoretical models, that people's tastes and preferences are static and exogenous, that economists do research on the basis of so-called hard data, that neither the report from the person nor the information that comes from opinion surveys is admitted, that reading articles published in inter and extra-disciplinary journals is of little utility, and that measurement without theory is irrelevant. Easterlin states that it took him several years to question some of the beliefs that were instilled in him during his doctorate studies.

As the title of his book clearly reveals, Easterlin is an economist, but he is a reluctant one. He belongs to a small group of scholars who are humble enough to recognize the limitations of their discipline and to be open to new ideas and approaches as long as scientific rigor is not sacrificed. The circumstances allowed him to channel his interests in a creative and productive way. At the end of his doctoral studies, Easterlin was invited to join a research project headed by his thesis supervisor, the economist Simon Kuznets – the same one who led the construction of the income and production accounting system – and by the demographer Dorothy Thomas. Easterlin learned in this research project that knowledge of history and demography is crucial to understand long-term economic trends. Kuznets' work made him recognize the value that empirical research has in the generation of knowledge as well as the important knowledge that can be obtained by taking advantage of all sources of information. Easterlin also understood the limitations of a discipline that relied too much on the construction of theoretical models while neglecting the value of available information. The circumstances inclined Easterlin to do empirical research with a long-run perspective; in the long-run preferences are no longer given and frames of reference are expected to change; hence, the traditional assumptions of economic theory do not sustain.

It is not surprising then that Easterlin showed great curiosity and a lot of courage to risk doing research with data reported by people (the so-called subjective data) He used the scarce information available in the 1970s to conduct research on the relationship between income and happiness. The report from his research was published in the chapter entitled *Does Economic Growth Improve the Human Lot? Some Empirical Evidence*; this work was groundbreaking, and it had consequences for economic theory that went beyond the particular findings which are reported. A previous work by Easterlin entitled *Does Money Buy Happiness?* and based on the same research was published in *The Public Interest* in 1973.

1.2.2   The Empirical Evidence: The Easterlin Paradox

In the early 1970s Richard Easterlin was invited by economists Paul David and Melvin Reder (Easterlin's former professor of microeconomics at the University of Pennsylvania) to make a contribution to a book in honor of Moses Abramovitz. The book was addressing economic-growth issues.

It was during his stay at the Center for Advanced Studies in Behavioral Sciences of Stanford University that Easterlin became aware of the existence of some databases containing information on people's happiness and life evaluation. This information came from questions made directly to people thanks to the pioneering public-opinion work conducted by Hadley Cantril and by the Gallup Company during the period from 1946 to 1966; the information comprised a total of 29 surveys applied in 19 countries. Although very limited, the information allowed Easterlin to have a historical perspective on what was happening in several countries which had very different socio-economic conditions. With great curiosity, great confidence in the value of empirical work, and against the predominant dogma in the economics discipline – which recommended *'paying attention to what people do and not to what they say'*- Easterlin decided to use these databases to provide an empirical answer to the recurrent question: Does economic growth improve the human lot? His main finding is widely known as the Easterlin Paradox. Easterlin found that at a given moment in time and in a particular country, high-income people tend to report higher levels of happiness than low-income people. A similar result is obtained when working with country averages at a given moment in time: Those countries with higher per capita income tend to report higher average levels of happiness. However, when he followed a historical time-series perspective Easterlin found that there are no significant changes in people's happiness when income grows over time. Similarly, average happiness in countries did not increase over time as economic growth took place. Easterlin concluded that in the long run there is no relationship between income and happiness; although at a given moment in time people with higher income report higher levels of happiness. In consequence, the answer to the question posed in the title of his contribution was that economic growth does not improve the human lot; this was an unexpected finding which also seemed paradoxical to many economists trained in a discipline inclined to magnify the importance of income and the necessity of economic growth.

1.2.3 Immediate Impact of Easterlin's Research

In one way or another some major economists and social thinkers quickly echo Easterlin's findings; such is the case of Tibor Scitovsky's *The Joyless Economy*, Fred Hirsch's *Social Limits to Growth*, Robert Heilbroner's *The False Promise of Growth*, and even Erich Fromm's *To have or to Be*. However, these scholars did not produce original research in the subject. The vast majority of economists of the 1970s were trained in a discipline that assumed that income was enormously important for people's well-being, that their relationship was plain and straightforward, and that this was so evident that there was no need of corroboration. These economists were also immersed in a paradigm of progress as economic growth; the paradigm assumed that the promotion of economic growth was one of the main duties of international organizations, foreign aid agencies, and national governments. It should come as no surprise that many researchers simply clung to their theoretical models while pointing to the subjective nature of the information used by Easterlin. These economists went on doing what they had been doing for decades: building more sophisticated models to explain economic growth, developing new concepts of capital to better explain income differences across countries, working on more accurate measures of income, and making policy recommendations to generate rapid economic growth.

It took almost two decades for some economists to realize the importance of Richard A. Easterlin's groundbreaking work and to develop research agendas on happiness and economics; many of these early researchers are contributors to the present book. Since then, research on happiness and economics has grown exponentially. Some researchers have directly addressed the existence of the paradox and have provided different explanations, but most of the researchers have used happiness data to deal with many other issues in economics. Researchers are benefiting nowadays from the easy availability of information on people's happiness. This shows that the contribution made by Richard A. Easterlin to economics goes far beyond the specific finding on the relationship between economic growth and happiness. The pioneer work by Easterlin opened a new area of research by provided the method to scientifically study people's happiness.

1.3   The Economics of Happiness

When Richard A. Easterlin decided in the early 1970s to use some available databases containing information on reported well-being to explore the long-run relationship between happiness and economic growth he did not only shake the foundations of economics but he also initiated a new field in economics.

1.3.1   Happiness Is Back into Economics

Economics used to be an academic discipline interested in the study of people's happiness. Early economists such as Adam Smith and Thomas Malthus were as concerned about people's happiness as they were about material wealth. Bentham made it clear that social and economic reform should be guided by the principle of increasing people's happiness. Jevons, Walras, and Menger recognized that the (subjective) experience of being well was both a final aim and a central motivation which explained people's behavior. Even Alfred Marshall was clear about the importance for economics of studying happiness.

Unfortunately, during the first decades of the twentieth century economics opted to concentrate in the study of choice while marginalizing the study of happiness. The consequence was a shift of focus from people's happiness to the expansion of the space of choice; economists placed their attention in the realm of objects while neglecting the realm of experiences of being well people have. The expansion of the production and consumption of commodities became the main concern of many economists.

The return of the study of happiness increases the potential of economics to contribute to the well-being in societies. It is now possible for economists to test their assumptions regarding the nature and strength of the relationship between income and happiness, as well as to do research on the importance of other variables, such as inflation and unemployment. Happiness research has provided a lot of evidence on the nature of the relationship between economic variables and people's well-being; for example, it has shown that the plain and straightforward relationship between income and well-being that many economists implicitly assumed was not correct; it has also shown that unemployment has substantial non-pecuniary costs.

1.3.2   People's Reports Provide Useful Information Not Available Everywhere

Easterlin took a bold decision in the 1970s when he used reports to well-being questions to study the relationship between economic growth and people's happiness. He decided to rely on people's own assessments regarding their happiness; in fact, he worked with the following two questions: a happiness one (*"In general, how happy would you say that you are – very happy, fairly happy, or not very happy?"*) and a life-evaluation (the well-known Cantril ladder question) This decision was taken at a time when the vast majority of economists believed that their field should focus only on what people do and not on what they say.

By neglecting people's own assessments economists were missing important information which could not be obtained from other sources. Variables of objects do not provide information on feelings, frustrations, achievements, joy, pain, pleasure and other experiences of being well people have; and any association which economists make between these variables and people's well-being requires strong and unrealistic assumptions. Reported well-being also incorporates information on the values, beliefs and life trajectories that intervene in how people understand their context and their place in it. Well-being is not really about a set of objects in the space of choice but about how people make sense of them. So called hard-data can provide a lot of information but cannot provide information on how people experience their world and make sense of them given their particular situation.

Nowadays subjective well-being questions are frequent in national and global surveys, and many national statistical offices and international organizations gather information on people's satisfaction with life, emotions, life evaluations, and so on. This information has forced economists to focus on the realm of experiences – where happiness takes place – rather than on the realm of objects.

1.3.3   The Importance of Subjectivity

Well-being is inherently subjective because the experience of being well cannot take place without the presence of concrete persons – of flesh and blood and who are in their specific life circumstance. It would possible to conceive a world full of objects and with no persons; it would be impossible to conceive the existence of well-being in this kind of world because persons are necessary for the experience of being well to exist. Objects (merchandize, commodities, assets) may trigger experiences of being well in persons, but these experiences do not exist in the realm of objects. It requires real persons for happiness to take place, and these persons live within a specific culture and have their own values, beliefs, life trajectory, nurturing conditions, aspirations and so on. Subjectivity – the specific life situation of a real person – is inherent to happiness; hence, it is not correct to talk about objective happiness or about objective well-being.

Practically all economists recognize that utility is subjective, this is: that person-specific values and standards play an important role in utility. However, the adoption of objectivism shifted the focus of attention in economics from concrete human beings to objects and commodities. Economists became accustomed to work with so-called objective variables, and some of them went as far as to defend the existence of an objective well-being which is defined in terms of lists of objective variables. Rather than recognizing the theoretical and methodological limitations which are faced when a set of objective variables are used to attempt measuring something that is inherently subjective many economists preferred to reject people's reports and to cling to the situation portrayed by the objective income data when the Easterlin Paradox was presented.

By working with happiness reports Easterlin introduced subjectivism back into economics. Subjectivism also allows for the incorporation of cultural diversity as well as differences across persons in values, beliefs, standards of evaluation and so on. Happiness economics recognizes that well-being is inherently subjective and it is well positioned to address well-being issues in a multicultural world.

1.3.4 The Person as Authority to Judge Her Life

In times when the political power seemed to be moving from monarchs to citizens Jeremy Bentham cautioned about the *ipsedixitists*; as Collard states *"Bentham insisted that the measurement of well-being should be firmly based on the concerns and subjective valuations of those directly concerned. Those who wished to super-impose other judgements were dismissed as 'ipsedixitists'"*. Collard concludes his work with the following recommendation: *"Beware of the ipsedixitists: don't allow a few people (even important people) to dictate what is to be included or excluded."* Unfortunately, for decades no voice was given to people, and indicators of well-being were based merely on criteria proposed by scholars, experts, and politicians. Public policy and development strategies were designed on the basis of criteria where the experience of being well of those directly concerned played little role and where the values and judgments of experts and organizations prevailed.

When Richard A. Easterlin decided to use happiness reports to proxy the human lot he was also recovering and putting into practice a basic principle in economics: the authority to judge a person's life rests exclusively on the person herself. Economists of the twentieth century stressed this principle when talking about consumer sovereignty but neglected it when designing well-being indicators on the basis of income, possession of durable goods, financial assets and other observable variables. The work of Easterlin made it clear that the using of external criteria proposed by experts should never supplant people's own evaluation of their life, and that the role of the expert is not to judge a person's life but to understand it. Happiness economics transfers the authority in evaluating life from *ipsedixitists* to people, and this clearly empowers them.

1.3.5 Working with Concrete Human Beings

Economists got used to work with highly simplified agents, such as consumers and producers. These simplified agents had specific functions, such as purchasing goods or allocating resources to the production process; they did also have specific behavioral routines which made it easy to formalize their conduct. It is widely recognized that models are simplified versions of reality, but most economists defended their usefulness and many of them accepted the conclusions obtained from these theoretical models. Discipline-based well-being concepts emerged in economics – as well as in other social sciences; for example, it became common to talk about consumer well-being, which was immediately and straightforwardly associated to people's purchasing power or to the possession of durable goods.

By working with simplified agents economists got a partial and incomplete view of the well-being situation of concrete human beings. Economic agents, such as the consumer, do not reproduce the richness of concrete human beings, and this reflects in very limited conceptions of well-being economists work with. Richard A. Easterlin decided to work with reports made by human beings; these reports were not made by simplified consumers or by producers but by persons of flesh and blood. By doing this Easterlin forced economists to work again with concrete human beings and to understand them in their particular life situation which goes, by far, beyond their economic situation.

Happiness research has shown that the so-called consumer well-being is a very limited concept which cannot proxy the human well-being one. It has also shown that economic theories – which are mostly designed to address issues of consumers and which tend to magnify the importance of income – are very limited to address well-being issues of concrete persons. It has become clear that there is more to life than income and that for many persons there are more important aspects in life. It is also clear that Robert F. Kennedy had a point when he argued that many things that make life worthwhile are not associated to income.

1.3.6   New Directions in Welfare Economics

There is not much about well-being in welfare economics; in fact, it is mostly about choice. Ordinal utility and preference theory were used to explain human behavior, but the formation of preferences remained *terra incognita* in economics. In fact, economists are trained to consider preferences as a primitive notion – in its mathematical understanding; preferences are used to explain choice but they are seldom explained. Economists were not interested in studying preferences but in using them to explain behavior; hence, they assumed that preferences were given, exogenous, and stable. George Stigler and Gary Becker argued that *de gustibus non est disputandum*, and Milton Friedman argued that the realism of assumptions was not a relevant issue to be discussed. However, without a clear understanding of how preferences emerge, of the factors that shape them, and of how preferences change over time people's behavior cannot be fully understood. Happiness research does not question people's tastes and preferences but it allows for a better understanding of human behavior by recognizing that people prefer what they expect to make them happier and that the pursuing of happiness is a main motivation for human action. Economics has a greater potential of understanding people's behavior by studying their happiness. The work of Easterlin makes economics recover what Bentham and other early economists knew: that it is essential to combine the study of human behavior with that of happiness.

Welfare economics was very weak in addressing well-being issues; for example, it could not tackle basic well-being questions such as what is the happiness benefit from an increase in income or the happiness cost of unemployment. For decades economics measured the value of things in monetary terms while dodging the fundamental question of what is the worth of money. Happiness research allows for finding the value of money as well as for studying how and why this value changes along people, across cultures, and over time.

It is important to recognize that some economists were disappointment with welfare economics due to its limitations to address fundamental well-being questions. However, many disappointed economists opted to bring back ethical considerations into economics; unfortunately, the ethical tradition places the authority in judging goodness in a person's life in the hands of experts, and it has limited capacity to address well-being issues in a multicultural world where values, aspirations and norms of evaluation change across cultures and even along persons. Richard A. Easterlin's groundbreaking work shifts away from a willingness-to-pay understanding of value while still recognizes that people have the authority to judge their life, it also shifts away from the ethical understandings of value that places the authority in an external agent.

1.3.7   On the Notion of Progress

Progress as economic growth was the mantra of the twentieth century; in an opposite way to what Keynes imagined in the 1930s, it was postulated that societies should aspire to an age of high mass consumption. Within the progress as economic growth paradigm the increasing of productivity was a main social objective and working hard and harder was postulated as a virtue. The concept of human capital equated human beings to machines, and the concept of social capital made of human relations a mere instrument in the procurement of economic growth. Leisure was considered as unproductive and work as an inherently unsatisfactory activity whose only purpose was to obtain the income which would allow purchasing the commodities that – it was claimed – would generate well-being. The planet was no more than natural capital whose role was to provide the raw materials used to produce the affluence of commodities to be massively consumed. The Easterlin Paradox directly addressed the foundations of the progress as economic growth mantra and it showed that social progress must not be equated to economic growth.

Nowadays, in the beginning of the twenty-first century, there are several social and academic movements asking for a reconsideration of what progress is and what societies should aim for; local and regional initiatives proliferate calling for new measures of progress in societies, going beyond GDP, and even calling for de-growth. In 2012 the United Nations General Assembly approved a resolution entitled "*Happiness: towards a holistic approach to development*" which explicitly stated that "*the pursuit of happiness was a fundamental human goal,* (and) *recognized that the gross domestic product (GDP) indicator was not designed to and did not adequately reflect the happiness and well-being of people*".

A new conception of progress as happiness is emerging. It is expected for this new understanding of progress to foster the development of a new national accounting system based on people's experiences of being well. A reconsideration of public policy and development strategies is also expected to take place once the final aim shifts from economic growth to people's happiness.

1.3.8 Doing Research on Happiness

Happiness economics is not about introducing a new dogma, relying on uncorroborated assumptions, and replacing current *ipsedixitists* by new ones. It is about doing scientific research to understand people's happiness in order to design better policies and development strategies. Richard Easterlin's 1974 paper addressed a fundamental question: *Does economic growth improve the human lot?* Besides this question, the title of his contribution also included the phrase *Some empirical evidence*. This expression is crucial because it showed that the study of happiness should not be dominated by doctrines, ideologies, grand theories, and dogmas but by scientific research. Theories should lead to hypotheses to be tested, rigorous methodologies must be implemented, sound data is required, and theories must be reviewed on the light of findings. Debate and dialogue is necessary and peer review of research reports is valuable. Nowadays there are thousands of papers in academic journals reporting happiness research; the number of published papers has been growing exponentially during the past two decades. There are many academic journals focused on happiness research as well as academic societies and organizations that make of happiness research their central topic. As Richard A. Easterlin showed, this is the way of enriching knowledge and increasing the possibilities for economics of making a positive contribution to the happiness in societies.

1.4 The Following Chapters

The 19 chapters that follow illustrate the richness of happiness economics and the fruitfulness of Richard A. Easterlin's pioneer work. The book is organized in five sections: Income and Happiness, Happiness in Welfare Economics, Applications of Happiness in Economics, Happiness in Development, and Happiness along the Life Course and the Social Context. Of course, these five sections do not exhaust all areas where Easterlin's work has had an influence in economics.

Many of the chapters were written by early happiness economists who started doing happiness research in the 1990s. Some chapters are written by young scholars and others by young scholars in collaboration with early happiness economists. The participation of young scholars shows that one can expect a fertile and prolific future for happiness research.

Acknowledgements I would like to acknowledge the assistance of Humberto Charles Leija in reviewing and editing all chapters in the book.

General References

Abramovitz, M. (1959). The welfare interpretation of secular trends in national income and product. In *The allocation of economic resources: Essays in honor of Bernard Francis Haley* (pp. 1–22). Stanford: Stanford University Press.

Allen, R. G. D. (1933). On the marginal utility of money and its application. *Economica, 40*(May), 186–209.

Allen, R. G. D. (1935). A note on the determinateness of the utility function. *Review of Economic Studies, 2*, 155–158.

Aristotle. (2009). *The Nichomachean ethics*. Oxford: Oxford University Press.

Bentham, J. (1780). *An introduction to the principles of morals and legislation*. Mineola: Dover Publications.

Bharadwaj, K. (1972). Marshall on Pigou's wealth and welfare. *Economica, 39*(153), 32–46.

Bruni, L. (2006). *Civil happiness, economics and human flourishing in historical perspective*. London: Routledge.

Bruni, L., & Guala, F. (2001). Vilfredo Pareto and the epistemological foundations of choice theory. *History of Political Economy, 33*, 21–49.

Collard, D. (2003). *Research on well-being: Some advice from Jeremy Bentham* (WeD Working paper 02). University of Bath, United Kingdom.

Coyle, D. (2015). *GDP. A brief but affectionate history*. Princeton: Princeton University Press.

Easterlin, R. A. (1973). Does money buy happiness? *The Public Interest, 30*, 3–10.

Easterlin, R. (1974). Does economic growth improve the human lot? Some empirical evidence. In P. A. David & M. W. Reder (Eds.), *Nations and households in economic growth* (pp. 89–125). New York: Academic.

Easterlin, R. (2001). Income and happiness: Towards a unified theory. *Economic Journal, 111* (473), 465.484.

Easterlin, R. (2004). *The reluctant economist: Perspectives on economics, economic history, and demography*. New York: Cambridge University Press.

Easterlin, R. (2010). *Happiness, growth, and the life cycle*. New York: Oxford University Press.

Edgeworth, F. Y. (1881). *Mathematical psychics: An essay on the application of mathematics to the moral sciences*. London: C. Kegan Paul & Co.

Edwards, J. M. (2009). Joyful economists: Remarks on the history of economics and psychology from the happiness studies perspective. *Journal of the History of Economic Thought, 32*(4), 611–613.

Fisher, I. (1892). Mathematical investigations in the theory of value and prices. *Transaction of the Connecticut Academy, 9*, 1–124.

Fisher, I. (1911). *The purchasing power of money: Its determination and relation to credit interest and crises*. New York: MacMillan Co.

Friedman, M. (1953). The methodology of positive economics. In *Essays in positive economics*. Chicago: University of Chicago Press.

Fromm, E. (1976). *To have or to be*. New York: Harper & Row.

Heilbroner, R. L. (1977, March 3). The false promise of growth. *New York review of books*.

Hicks, J. R. (1939). The foundations of welfare economics. *The Economic Journal, 49*(196), 696–712.

Hicks, J. R., & Allen, R. G. D. (1934). A reconsideration of the theory of value. Parts I & II. *Economica, 1*, 52–76; 2: 196–219.

Hirsch, F. (1976). *Social limits to growth*. Cambridge: Harvard University Press.

Hobson, J. A. (1929). *Wealth and life: A study in values*. London: Macmillan.

Jevons, W. S. (1871). *The theory of political economy*. London: Macmillan.

Kaldor, N. (1939). Welfare propositions of economics and inter-personal comparisons of utility. *Economic Journal, 49*(195), 549–552.

Keynes, J. M. (1931). *Essays in persuasion*. London: Macmillan.

Knight, F. H. (1944). Realism and relevance in the theory of demand. *Journal of Political Economy, 52*, 289–318.

Kuznets, S. (1948). National income: A new version. *The Review of Economics and Statistics, 30* (3), 151–179.

Lange, O. (1934). The determinateness of the utility function. *Review of Economic Studies, 1*, 218–225.

Malthus, T. (1798). *An essay on the principle of population*. London: J. Johnson.

McMahon, D. (2006). *Happiness: A history*. New York: Grove Press.

Pareto, V. [1909] (1971). *Manual of political economy*. New York: Kelley.

Pasinetti, L. (2005). Paradoxes of happiness in economics. In L. Bruni & P. L. Porta (Eds.), *Economics & happiness: Framing the analysis* (pp. 336–343). Oxford: Oxford University Press.

Pigou, A. C. (1912). *Wealth and welfare*. London: MacMillan & Co.

Pigou, A. C. (1920). *The economics of welfare*. London: MacMillan and Co.

Robbins, L. (1932). *An essay on the nature and significance of economic science*. London: MacMillan & Co.

Rojas, M. (2017). The subjective object of well-being studies. In G. Brulé & F. Maggino (Eds.), *Metrics of subjective well-being: Limits and improvements* (pp. 43–62). Cham: Springer.

Rojas, M., & Veenhoven, R. (2013). Contentment and affect in the estimation of happiness. *Social Indicators Research, 110*(2), 415–431.

Samuelson, P. A. (1937). A note on measurement of utility. *Review of Economic Studies, 4*, 155–161.

Samuelson, P. A. (1938a). The empirical implications of utility analysis. *Econometrica, 6*, 344–356.

Samuelson, P. A. (1938b). The numerical representation of ordered classifications and the concept of utility. *Review of Economic Studies, 6*, 65–70.

Samuelson, P. A. (1947). *Foundations of economic analysis*. Cambridge, MA: Harvard University Press.

Samuelson, P. A. (1950). Probability and the attempts to measure utility. *Economic Review, 1*, 167–173.

Schmidt, T., & Weber, C. E. (2008). On the origins of ordinal utility: Andreas Heinrich Voigt and the mathematicians. *History of Political Economy, 40*, 481–510.

Scitovsky, T. (1976). *The joyless economy: An inquiry into human satisfaction and consumer dissatisfaction*. London: Oxford University Press.

Sim, B., & Diener, E. (2018). Accounts of psychological and emotional well-being for policy purposes. In E. Diener, S. Oishi, & L. Tay (Eds.), *Handbook of well-being*. Salt Lake City: DEF Publishers.

Smith, A. [1759] (1767). *The theory of moral sentiments*. Edinburgh: A. Miller/A. Kincaid/J. Bell.

Smith, A. [1776] (1937). *An inquiry into the nature and causes of the wealth of Nations*. New York: Modern Library.

Stigler, G. (1950). The development of utility theory I. *The Journal of Political Economy, 58*(4), 307–327.

Stigler, G. J., & Becker, G. S. (1977). De Gustibus non est Disputandum. *The American Economic Review, 67*(2), 76–90.

van Praag, B. M. S., & Frijters, P. (1999). The measurement of welfare and well-being; the Leyden approach. In D. Kahneman, E. Diener, & N. Schwarz (Eds.), *Foundations of hedonic psychology: Scientific perspectives on enjoyment and suffering* (pp. 413–433). New York: Russell Sage Foundation.

Viner, J. (1925). The utility concept in value theory and its critics. *The Journal of Political Economy, 33*(6), 638–659.

Voigt, A. [1893] (2008). Number and measure in economics. In T. Schmidt, & C. E. Weber (Eds.), *On the origins of ordinal utility: Andreas Heinrich Voigt and the Mathematicians*, History of Political Economy, *40*, 502–504.

Walsh, C. M. (1901). *The measurement of general exchange-value*. New York: MacMillan Co.

Wolfe, A. (1931). On the content of welfare. *American Economic Review, 21*(2), 207–221.

Zeuthen, F. (1937). On the determinateness of the utility function. *Review of Economic Studies, 4*, 236–239.

Part II
Income and Happiness

Chapter 2
Different Versions of the Easterlin Paradox: New Evidence for European Countries

Caspar F. Kaiser and Maarten C. M. Vendrik

Abstract According to the Easterlin Paradox, richer people are happier than poorer people, but when a country becomes richer over time, its people do not become happier. There is debate on whether this paradox holds. To shed light on this controversy, we distinguish between five different versions of the paradox. They apply to either groups of countries or individual countries, and to either the long or the medium term. We argue that the long term is most appropriate for testing the paradox, and that tests of the paradox should control for an autonomous time trend. We conduct such tests by estimating country-panel equations for mean life satisfaction in 27 European countries that include trend and cyclical components of per capita GDP as regressors. Concerning groups of countries, we find a robust confirmation of the long- and medium-term versions of the paradox for a group of nine Western and Northern European countries. Moreover, we obtain a non-robust rejection of the medium-term variant of the paradox for a set of 11 Eastern European countries. Regarding individual countries, the medium-term variant of the paradox holds for the nine Western and Northern European countries, but is rejected for Greece, Ireland, Italy, Spain, Bulgaria, Lithuania, and Poland.

This is an abridged version of a longer working paper with the same title (see Kaiser and Vendrik 2018)

C. F. Kaiser
Nuffield College, Oxford University, Oxford, UK

DSPI, Oxford University, Oxford, UK

M. C. M. Vendrik (✉)
Department of Macro, International and Labour Economics (MILE), SBE, Maastricht University, Maastricht, The Netherlands

ROA, SBE, Maastricht University, Maastricht, The Netherlands

IZA, Bonn, Germany

EHERO, Erasmus University, Rotterdam, The Netherlands
e-mail: m.vendrik@maastrichtuniversity.nl

© Springer Nature Switzerland AG 2019
M. Rojas (ed.), *The Economics of Happiness*,
https://doi.org/10.1007/978-3-030-15835-4_2

2.1 Introduction

It has been more than 40 years since Easterlin published his path-breaking study
"Does economic growth improve the human lot: Some empirical evidence" (1974).
In that and later papers (Easterlin 1995, 2005, 2017), he showed that while at a point
in time individual happiness is positively correlated with individual income in the
USA and other countries, over time average happiness in these countries does not
trend upward as average income continues to grow. This seemingly contradictory
pair of findings has become famous as the "Easterlin Paradox". Although these
paradoxical findings have been confirmed for several other developed countries by
other happiness researchers (e.g., Layard et al. 2010; Clark et al. 2014), there are also
happiness scientists (e.g., Stevenson and Wolfers 2008; Sacks et al. 2012, 2013;
Veenhoven and Hagerty 2006; Veenhoven 2011; Veenhoven and Vergunst 2014;
Diener et al. 2013a) who have presented counterevidence to the Easterlin Paradox.
Although Easterlin (2017) has convincingly pointed out several shortcomings in the
contestants' studies, this still raises the question as to who is right.

In this study we investigate this issue both on a conceptual level and by
conducting our own estimations on country panel models that are similar to those
of Layard et al. (2010) and Sacks et al. (2013), using updated life satisfaction data
from the Eurobarometer surveys. On a conceptual level we show that in the debate
on the Easterlin Paradox at least two distinct versions of this paradox are discussed.
The first version refers to individual countries and has been formulated above. The
second version of the paradox extends the first part of the paradox to the positive
correlation between average happiness and GDP per capita across countries (see, e.
g., Deaton 2008, Easterlin 2017) and contrasts it with a zero cross-country correlation between (annual) rates of change in average happiness and GDP per capita over
time. This seems like a mere cross-sectional reformulation of the paradox for groups
of countries. However, there is an essential difference compared to time-series
regressions that test whether individual countries with a positive rate of economic
growth also experienced a positive time trend in happiness. In the cross-country
regression, average annual rates of change in SWB are not only regressed on average
annual rates of economic growth, but also on a constant (see, e.g., Easterlin 2017,
Table 1). This constant picks up drivers of (linear) trends in SWB other than
economic growth that are common to all countries (e.g., trends in marriage and
divorce rates, social capital, trust, aging, and income inequality; see Angeles 2011;
Bartolini and Sarracino 2014; Bartolini et al. 2013a, b; Gruen and Klasen 2013).

On the level of individual countries, this suggests that when a time-series
regression of SWB of a specific country with positive economic growth reveals a
significant positive time trend in SWB, this trend could be driven by trends in other
determinants of SWB than economic growth (see also Clark 2011, p. 259). In such a
case the positive time trend in a country's SWB does not imply a non-spurious
positive correlation between SWB and long-term economic growth in that country.
Therefore, a reliable test of the paradox should in our view at least control for
possible spuriousness arising from time trends in other determinants of SWB. Hence,

to reliably test the Easterlin Paradox for individual countries, one should regress SWB in a country on the long-term economic growth trend while controlling for a country-specific autonomous time trend. Unfortunately, this is not possible due to perfect collinearity of such a time trend with the time-linear long-term economic growth trend. Thus, reliable tests of the Easterlin Paradox for separate individual countries do not seem possible.

However, there are two partial ways out of this problem. First, instead of controlling for a country-specific autonomous time trend, one may control for specific other determinants of SWB. But such an approach raises the thorny question which other determinants of SWB are predetermined with respect to per capita GDP, and hence should be controlled for ("good" controls in the terminology of Angrist and Pischke 2009), and which determinants are mediating the effect of per capita GDP on SWB, and hence should not be included when wishing to estimate the total correlation of per capita GDP and SWB over time ("bad" controls). Moreover, the selected good control variables may not capture all autonomous determinants of SWB that vary in a linear-trend-like fashion. To circumvent these problems, one may adopt a country-panel approach to testing the Easterlin Paradox as introduced by Layard et al. (2010) and also used by Sacks et al. (2013). In this approach, which we follow in the present study, real GDP per capita (GDPpc) data are corrected for short-term business cycle effects[1] by means of a Hodrick-Prescott (HP) filter (Hodrick and Prescott 1997), and the resulting GDPpc trend and cyclical components are used as regressors in panel regressions for the average SWB in countries. In this study we use two variants of the HP filter: The first one sets the parameter λ of the HP filter to its conventional value 6.25 for annual data (see Ravn and Uhlig 2002), which is also used by Sacks et al. (2013).[2] This filters out fluctuations in GDPpc due to business cycles of up to about 8 years of length (as defined by Burns and Mitchell 1946; see, for example, Fig. 2.1 (left) for the Netherlands).[3] In our second HP filter, we set $\lambda = \infty$. This filter is equivalent to the least-squares fit of a linear trend model for GDPpc with a slope coefficient given by the average growth rate of GDPpc over the whole estimation period (see Fig. 2.1 (right)). This filter also corresponds to the average growth rate used as regressor in the SWB regressions of Easterlin (2017) and Veenhoven and Vergunst (2014) and filters out all cyclical fluctuations within the estimation period. In particular, in the case of the transition of ex-communist countries from communism to capitalism, the linear trend filter filters out contraction-expansion cycles, which may take up to 20 years, and hence last

---

[1]See Easterlin's (2017 Sect. 2) distinction between short-term fluctuations and long-term trends in GDPpc.

[2]Layard et al. (2010) adopt a value of 9.5 for λ, but mention in their note of Table 6.5 that setting $\lambda = 6.25$ produces similar results.

[3]Hamilton (2017) criticizes the HP filter for introducing spurious dynamic relations in the cyclical component that have no basis in the underlying data-generating process. However, for our purposes of regressing SWB on primarily an appropriate GDPpc trend measure, the HP filter seems more suitable than the alternative filter that is presented by Hamilton (2017). Moreover, this alternative filter generates similar results. See Kaiser and Vendrik (2018) for further discussion of this.

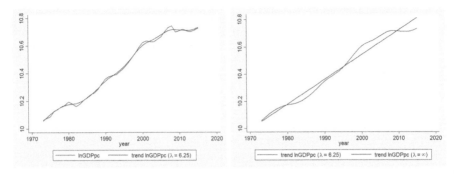

Fig. 2.1 Time paths for the Netherlands of: (left) lnGDPpc vs. trend lnGDPpc for $\lambda = 6.25$, and (right) trend lnGDPpc for $\lambda = 6.25$ vs. trend lnGDPpc for $\lambda = \infty$

much longer than the usual business cycles. Easterlin (2017) makes the point that for allowing the average growth rate GDPpc to filter out such transition cycles, the estimation period should be long enough, i.e. at least roughly 20 years for transition countries. Generally, in order to test for a long-term correlation between SWB and GDPpc in countries over time, the most appropriate filter of GDPpc is one that corrects for all cyclical fluctuations - no matter their duration. Such a filter is the linear trend filter of GDPpc with $\lambda = \infty$, which thus seems more suitable for this purpose than HP filters of GDPpc with lower values of λ as used by Layard et al. (2010) and Sacks et al. (2013).

We distinguish between tests of the paradox that apply to groups of countries and tests that apply to individual countries. Unfortunately, the linear time trend filter can only be used for testing the Easterlin Paradox for groups of countries. In the case of tests for individual countries, one cannot control for an autonomous time trend when using such a filter due to perfect collinearity of the time trend with the filtered GDPpc series. However, a HP filter of GDPpc with $\lambda = 6.25$ can be used since it is not perfectly collinear with a linear time trend. Because a HP filter of GDPpc with $\lambda = 6.25$ only corrects for business cycle fluctuations up to about 8 years of length, we refer to estimations with such a filter as tests of a medium-term version of the paradox. Thus, we conceptually distinguish between long-term and medium-term variants of the paradox.

Therefore, combining all the distinctions made above, we can distinguish the following five variants of the Easterlin Paradox:

EPgl: Whereas at a point in time happiness varies positively with income both among and within countries, over time countries with a higher long-term rate of economic growth in a certain group of countries do not exhibit a more positive change in average happiness when controlling for a common time trend (Easterlin 2017, p. 316; Veenhoven and Vergunst 2014).

EPgm: Whereas at a point in time happiness varies positively with income both among and within countries, over time countries with a higher medium-term rate of economic growth in a certain group of countries do not exhibit a more positive change in average happiness when controlling for a common time trend (Layard et al. 2010; Sacks et al. 2013).

EPi0: Whereas at a point in time happiness varies positively with income within countries, over time average happiness in a particular individual country does not trend upward as average income trends upward (Easterlin 1974).[4]

EPil (not testable!): Whereas at a point in time happiness varies positively with income within countries, over time a higher long-term rate of economic growth in a particular individual country is not associated with a more positive change in average happiness when controlling for a country-specific time trend.

EPim: Whereas at a point in time happiness varies positively with income within countries, over time a higher medium-term rate of economic growth in a particular individual country is not associated with a more positive change in average happiness when controlling for a country-specific time trend.

We test these different versions of the Easterlin Paradox except the non-testable EPil for European countries by estimating country-panel equations for mean life satisfaction that include long- or medium-term trend and cyclical components of GDPpc and country dummies as regressors. Throughout, we take the first parts of the paradox' variants (*i.e.* correlations of happiness and income within and among countries) for granted because their validity has been confirmed in numerous empirical studies (e.g., Deaton 2008; Sacks et al. 2012, 2013). To account for heterogeneity in the correlations of mean life satisfaction and trend GDPpc between different country groups, we partition our total sample of 27 countries into sub-samples consisting of Western and Northern European, Southern European, and Eastern European countries.

Our main results are as follows. Concerning groups of countries, we find a clear and robust confirmation of the paradox for the long as well as medium term for a group of nine Western and Northern European countries. Moreover, we obtain a non-robust rejection of the paradox for the medium term for a set of 11 Eastern European countries. Concerning individual countries, the medium-term version of the paradox (EPim) clearly holds for the nine Western and Northern European countries, but is significantly rejected for Greece, Ireland, Italy, and Spain. Thus, in the latter four as opposed to the former nine countries, economic growth was positively associated with changes in life satisfaction in the medium term. Regarding the individual Eastern European countries, this also holds for Bulgaria, Lithuania, and Poland, but for the other EE countries results are unreliable, partially due to the limited length of the time series (11 years).

The remainder of this paper is organized as follows. Section 2.2 reviews the state of the debate on the Easterlin Paradox in the literature. In Sect. 2.3 the estimation equations for the tests of the different versions of the paradox are explained. Section

---

[4]We do not follow Easterlin (2017, p. 312) in extending the formulation of variant EPi0 to also include the variation of happiness with income across countries. This is because EPi0 only concerns the variation of happiness with income *within* countries. The same holds for the individual-country variants EPil and EPim.

2.4 presents the data and descriptive statistics. Then, Sect. 2.5 discusses the estimation results for groups of countries and individual countries, respectively. Finally, Sect. 2.6 draws some general conclusions.

2.2 State of the Debate

Variant EPi0 (non-positive time trend in average happiness) of the Easterlin Paradox has been tested and confirmed by Easterlin (1974, 1995, 2017) for the USA, by Easterlin (1995, 2005) and other happiness researchers (e.g., Layard et al. 2010, and Clark et al. 2014) for many other developed countries, and by Easterlin (2009) for several transition countries. On the other hand, Veenhoven (2011) has estimated trends in mean life satisfaction for 15 developed countries over the period 1970–2010 and has found significant positive trends for seven of these countries. As GDPpc trended upwards in the period considered in all the 15 countries, Veenhoven's results imply a rejection of EPi0 for the seven developed countries with significant positive trends in life satisfaction. Similarly, Sacks et al. (2012) report that six out of nine European countries in the period 1973–1989 show a significantly positive regression relationship between average life satisfaction and ln (GDPpc) (see their Fig. 6). Because GDPpc trended upward in all the nine countries, these regressions may be interpreted as tests of EPi0, with the important limitation that these tests do not correct for business-cycle fluctuations in GDPpc. However, as argued above, EPi0 is not an appropriate version of the Easterlin Paradox and should be replaced with the country-specific medium-term variant EPim of the paradox, as this controls for an autonomous time trend, and hence for possible spuriousness driven by trends in other determinants of happiness.

Most tests of the Easterlin Paradox in the literature are tests of EPgl and EPgm on the level of groups of countries. The long-term version EPgl has been tested using cross-country regressions of average rates of change in SWB on average growth rates of GDPpc by Easterlin, Veenhoven, and their co-workers. On the one hand, Easterlin and colleagues (see, e.g., Easterlin et al. 2010; Easterlin and Sawangfa 2010; Easterlin 2015, 2017) consistently find confirmations of EPgl for groups of developed countries, developing countries, transition countries, and all countries taken together. On the other hand, Veenhoven and Vergunst (2014) find a rejection of EPgl for a large combined data set of countries and attribute the differences of their results with those of Easterlin et al. (2010) to the comparatively much larger size of their data set. Furthermore, they find that the correlation between happiness and economic growth is quite strong in the 20 lower-income nations in their data set and relatively small in the high-income nations (Table 4b). However, Veenhoven and Vergunst's approach is extensively criticized by Easterlin (2017).

Layard et al. (2010) and Sacks et al. (2013) also test the Easterlin Paradox on the level of groups of countries using country-panel regressions. However, they test the time-series correlation of SWB with (less appropriate) medium-term rather than long-term trends in GDPpc because they use HP filters with $\lambda = 9.5$ and 6.25, respectively. Employing Eurobarometer data for average life satisfaction in a group of 16 mainly Western European countries over the period 1973–2007, Layard et al. (2010) find insignificant coefficients of medium-term trend GDPpc in panel regressions of average life satisfaction while controlling for country-fixed effects, a time trend or year dummies, the cyclical GDPpc component, the unemployment rate, and the inflation rate. In our terminology, they thus test for and confirm EPgm for this group of Western European countries. However, the control for the unemployment rate may cause underestimation of the total effect of medium-term trend GDPpc, as parts of that effect may run via induced medium-term changes in the unemployment rate. Contrariwise, Sacks et al. (2013), using several data sets for average SWB in groups of countries all over the world and estimating country-panel regressions of average SWB on medium-term trend GDPpc similar to those of Layard et al., find significant positive correlations of SWB and trend GDPpc in most of their data sets for the world as a whole. Moreover, when using Eurobarometer data for average life satisfaction (in a group of 30 European countries over the period 1973–2009), they find a significant positive correlation of SWB and trend GDPpc as well. However, they do not find significant correlations for their Gallup World Poll data set for a "ladder-of-life" version of SWB in a world-wide group of 141 countries in the period 2005–2011 and for Latinobarometro data for average life satisfaction in 18 Latin American countries in the period 2001–2010.

An interesting study by Proto and Rustichini (2013) moves the analysis forward by analysing the relation between GDPpc and life satisfaction without imposing a functional form on the term for GDPpc. They specify the variation of GDPpc in terms of quantiles and run micro-macro-panel regressions of life satisfaction data from the World Values Survey and Eurobarometer on the GDPpc quantiles while controlling for country- and year-fixed effects, individual employment status, and personal income. These regressions reveal a non-monotonic relation between GDPpc and life satisfaction which is significantly positive for poorer countries and regions, but becomes insignificant for richer countries/regions, and even turns significantly negative for the richest countries/regions. This suggests a rejection of the medium-term variant EPgm of the Easterlin Paradox for poorer countries and regions, but not necessarily of the more appropriate, long term variant EPgl because the time series for the poorer countries and regions are too short for that. Another limitation of these tests is that the use of controls for individual employment status and personal income may either lead to an overestimation of the medium-term effects of GDPpc since effects of country-specific business cycles other than on individual employment status and personal income are not controlled for, or lead to an underestimation of the total medium-term effects of GDPpc since parts of that effect may run via induced medium-term changes in individual employment status and personal income. This ambiguity makes the use of these controls problematic.[5]

---

[5]Beja (2014) and Opfinger (2016) also test for the Easterlin Paradox, but in our view the dynamic model of Beja is mis-specified (missing levels of lnGDPpc), and Opfinger only uses the last two waves of the WVS, which implies an estimation period of 5–7 years that is much too short to test the Easterlin Paradox in a reliable way. Furthermore, there is no control for cyclical fluctuations in GDPpc.

2.3   Estimation Strategy

In this paper we focus on estimations that use the long-term HP filter (with $\lambda = \infty$) for groups of countries and the medium-term HP filter (with $\lambda = 6.25$) for individual countries as these most closely correspond to the two most appropriate testable versions of the paradox (EPgl and EPim; see Sect. 2.1). See Kaiser and Vendrik (2018) for extensive discussion of our estimation strategy and results when using the medium-term filter for groups of countries (corresponding to EPgm) and the long-term filter for individual countries (corresponding to EPi0).

2.3.1   Estimation Equations for Testing the Country-Group Variants of the Easterlin Paradox

We begin with our approach to testing the long-term group variant EPgl of the Easterlin Paradox. The baseline equation has the form

$$LS_{ct} = \beta \ trend \ \ln GDPpc_{ct} + \gamma \ cyclical \ \ln GDPpc_{ct} + \sum_{t'} \delta_{t'} d_{t'}$$
$$+ \sum_{c'} \alpha_{c'} d_{c'} + \varepsilon_{ct}, \tag{2.1}$$

where LS_{ct} is mean life satisfaction in country c in year t, $trend \ \ln GDPpc_{ct}$ and $cyclical \ \ln GDPpc_{ct}$ are the long-term ($\lambda = \infty$) trend and cyclical components of $\ln GDPpc_{ct}$, $d_{t'}$ and $d_{c'}$ represent year and country dummies, and ε_{ct} is the error term. The year and country dummies account for, respectively, year-specific country-invariant determinants like differences in survey design across waves and common time trends and shocks, and country-specific time-invariant determinants like institutions and cultural differences in SWB scale use. The error term is clustered over countries to account for heteroscedasticity and serial correlation, which both occur in our estimations (Angrist and Pischke 2009, Ch. 8).

To test for EPgl[6] we then conduct two-tailed t tests of a null hypothesis of equality to zero of the parameter β of $trend \ \ln GDPpc_{ct}$ against the alternative hypothesis of non-equality of β to zero. If such tests fail to reject the null hypothesis or if the sign of β is negative, EPgl is confirmed. If the null hypothesis is rejected and the sign of β is positive, EPgl is rejected. Alternatively, we conduct one-tailed tests of the null hypothesis $\beta \leq 0$ against the alternative hypothesis $\beta > 0$. If such tests fail to reject the null hypothesis, EPgl is confirmed, whereas a rejection of the null hypothesis implies a rejection of EPgl. As p values in one-tailed tests are half of those in the

---

[6]When using an HP filter with $\lambda = \infty$ for an estimation period of much less than 20 years (see Sect. 2.1), the following applies to the medium-term version EPgm.

two-tailed tests, EPgl will more easily be rejected at conventional significance levels by the one-tailed tests than by the two-tailed tests.

The estimate of β is only driven by cross-country variation in the trend GDPpc growth rates, since trend GDPpc growth rates in individual countries are constant over time (see Fig. 2.1 (right)). These trend GDPpc growth rates correspond to the average long-term GDPpc growth rates that are used as regressor in regressions of average annual SWB changes in the methodology of Easterlin et al. and Veenhoven and Vergunst (2014). However, a difference with our approach is that Easterlin et al. and Veenhoven and Vergunst follow a two-step procedure in which they first estimate long-term average rates of changes in mean SWB and GDPpc (in percentages) and then regress these average rates of change on each other, whereas we directly regress mean SWB levels in the countries on long-term trend lnGDPpc over time. A disadvantage of Easterlin's and Veenhoven and Vergunst's procedure is that the estimated average rates of change in mean SWB tend to be unstable (i.e. sensitive to adding or dropping observations) in samples with few observations per country (e. g. the WVS). According to a conventional rule of thumb in econometrics, stable estimates of regression coefficients require an amount of observations which is at least ten times the number of explanatory variables in the regression. Although the resulting measurement error in SWB trends may be random in large country samples, it may raise standard errors in the regression coefficients of the long-term GDPpc growth rate and therefore decrease the chances of rejecting EPgl. In the country-panel approach of Layard et al. (2010) and Sacks et al. (2013) that we follow, this complication is avoided by directly regressing SWB levels in countries on trend lnGDPpc over time with enough panel observations to get stable, and hence reliable, estimates of coefficient β of *trend* $\ln GDPpc_{ct}$ in Eq. 2.1.

A concern in our country-panel approach is that with a clustered error term, the asymptotic standard errors of the regression coefficients need to be corrected for the low number of clusters, i.e. countries, in the sample and subsamples that we use (from 4 to 27; about 50 is the minimal required number of clusters, see Cameron and Miller 2015, Section VI). Therefore, we employ the command *regress y x, vce (cluster)* in Stata, which includes a finite-sample adjustment of the cluster-robust standard errors and uses a T distribution with G-1 degrees of freedom instead of a standard normal distribution for t-tests based on these standard errors (G denotes the number of clusters). However, even with both adjustments, Wald tests tend to over-reject (op. cit.). For us, the remaining downward bias in the cluster-robust standard errors will lead to too high a likelihood of rejection of the null hypothesis (either h$_0$: $\beta = 0$ or h$_0$: $\beta \leq 0$) of *trend* $\ln GDPpc_{ct}$ in Eq. 2.1, and hence rejection of the paradox. Therefore, we need a more reliable test, which we obtain by correcting for the first-order serial correlation over time more directly than by clustering standard errors over countries. Such correlation signals the joint effect on life satisfaction of lags of trend and cyclical lnGDPpc and lags of and serial correlation in time-varying omitted variables (see Vendrik 2013, and Angrist and Pischke 2009, Sect. 8.2.2), which implies that Eq. 2.1 represents a dynamically incomplete model. The serial correlation, and hence the resulting downward bias in the standard errors of the parameter estimates, can be largely reduced by making Eq. 2.1 dynamically more complete with the addition of one-year lagged mean life satisfaction to the right-hand side of Eq. 2.1.[7] This yields

$$LS_{ct} = \beta \ trend \ \ln GDPpc_{ct} + \gamma \ cyclical \ \ln GDPpc_{ct} + \sum_{t'} \delta_{t'} d_{t'}$$

$$+ \varphi LS_{ct-1} + \sum_{c'} \alpha_{c'} d_{c'} + \varepsilon_{ct}. \tag{2.2}$$

The lagged life satisfaction term picks up the joint effect of lags of trend and cyclical lnGDPpc and lags of and serial correlation in time-varying omitted variables. As the estimate of parameter φ turns out to be significantly positive in our estimations, the initial effect[8] $\beta \ \Delta trend \ \ln GDPpc_{ct}$ of a change in $trend \ \ln GDPpc_{ct}$ in year t on life satisfaction is reinforced in year $t + 1$ by $\varphi\beta \ \Delta trend \ \ln GDPpc_{ct}$, in year $t + 2$ by $\varphi^2\beta \ \Delta trend \ \ln GDPpc_{ct}$ etc. In the end, this reinforcement process will converge to a total long-run effect $\frac{\beta}{1-\varphi} \Delta trend \ \ln GDPpc_{ct}$ of the change in $trend \ \ln GDPpc_{ct}$ in year t on life satisfaction (see Vendrik (2013) for more complete dynamics[9]). In this case, EPgl is tested via a null-hypothesis of equality to zero or non-negativity of the long-run effect $\frac{\beta}{1-\varphi}$ of $trend \ \ln GDPpc_{ct}$.

The dynamic-model concept of a long-run effect should be distinguished sharply from the concept of a long-term effect in the macro-economic time series context of the analysis of the Easterlin Paradox. Whereas 90% convergence to a long-run life satisfaction equilibrium usually takes place within a range of 1–11 years[10], the expression "long term" refers to time periods of at least 20 years or so. In the presence of country-fixed effects our estimate of φ in Eq. 2.2 will suffer from a downward Nickell bias. To correct for this Nickell bias, we apply a bias-corrected least squares dummy variables (BCLSDV) estimator in Stata to correct for the Nickell bias in the coefficient of lagged life satisfaction (see Bruno 2005a), for the underlying econometrics). The command for this estimator calculates bootstrap standard errors of the parameter estimates of Eq. 2.2, which are sufficiently reliable

---

[7]Because our regressors are likely not strictly exogenous, eliminating the serial correlation by a Prais-Winston or Cochrane-Orcutt transformation of the error term would not lead to consistent and efficient standard errors of the parameter estimates (Wooldridge 2003, Sects. 12.3 and 12.5).

[8]We here use the term "effect" rather than "correlation" because a dynamic model like Eq. 2.2 usually presupposes causality from the right-hand-side variables to the left-hand-side variable of the equation. Although testing of the Easterlin Paradox only involves correlations, dynamic-model concepts like short and long-run effects are more generally applicable to correlations as well.

[9]In that analysis adaptation of individual life satisfaction to income changes is modelled. In the simplified dynamics in the present paper such adaptation is implicitly and partially incorporated in the contemporaneous effects of the trend and cyclical lnGDPpc variables. See, however, the end of the next section for an extension that explicitly models adaptation of life satisfaction to medium-term changes in lnGDPpc.

[10]The number of years τ within which convergence for 90% takes place can be calculated as $\varphi^\tau = 1 - 0.9 = 0.1$ or $\tau \ln \varphi = \ln 0.1$ or $\tau = \ln 0.1/\ln \varphi$. For estimates of φ between 0.1 and 0.8 this yields $1.0 < \tau < 10.3$ (cf. Vendrik, 2013).

when the remaining serial correlation of the error term of Eq. 2.2 turns out to be weak.

In line with Easterlin (2017), we apply two criteria for including countries in our tests of the Easterlin Paradox. First, to obtain a less heterogeneous sample in terms of population size, countries must have more than one million inhabitants. Second, the available surveys for average life satisfaction in a country should minimally span 10 years and at least one complete cycle of GDPpc.

2.3.2 Estimation Equations for Testing the Individual-Country Variants of the Easterlin Paradox

Apart from our above argument that variant EPi0 of the Easterlin Paradox is not an appropriate version of this paradox, a limitation in the estimation of time trends in average happiness in individual countries as conducted in the literature (see Sect. 2.2), is that these estimations do not control for differences in survey design across waves. It is not possible to obtain reliable estimates of time trends of average happiness in individual countries from separate regressions while controlling for wave or time-fixed effects because such fixed effects then pick up part of the time trend. A partial solution to this problem is offered by Easterlin (2017, p. 319). He estimates time trends of average happiness in individual countries by adding inter-actions between country dummies and year to a country-panel regression of average happiness on year while controlling for country-fixed effects as well as two dummies for specific changes in survey design.

To test medium-term variant EPim[11] of the Easterlin Paradox for individual countries separately, we extend this approach in several directions. Firstly, we replace in Eq. 2.1 the main effects of *trend* ln $GDPpc_{ct}$ and *cyclical* ln $GDPpc_{ct}$, for $\lambda = 6.25$ by their interactions with country dummies, and add interactions of a time trend with the country dummies. Secondly, we drop the year-fixed effects as they would otherwise pick up part of the time trend for the reference country of the country dummies. Thirdly, since standard errors of the interaction coefficients based on clustered error terms implode as the effective number of clusters for each country-specific coefficient estimate is only one, the serial correlation in the error terms is now controlled for by adding interactions of one-year lagged life satisfaction (cf. Eq. 2.2) with the country dummies to Eq. 2.1. Fourthly, to control for different preceding questions affecting responses to the life satisfaction equation, we select waves such that the number of distinct preceding questions across time is minimised. We then include dummies for the remaining different preceding questions in our estimation equations. Because the number of these dummies is still large (ten), insignificant dummies are dropped from the regressions (see footnote 26 for more details).

---

[11] See Kaiser and Vendrik (2018) for our similar approach to testing EPi0.

Implementing all these modifications results in an estimation equation of the form

$$LS_{ct} = \sum_{c'} [\beta_{c'} d_{c'} \, trend \, \ln GDPpc_{c't} + \gamma_{c'} d_{c'} \, cyclical \, \ln GDPpc_{c't} + \delta_{c'} d_{c'} \, year$$
$$\times \, + \varphi_{c'} d_{c'} LS_{c't-1} + \alpha_{c'} d_{c'}] + \sum_{p} \delta_p d_p + \varepsilon_{ct},$$

$$(2.3)$$

where d_p represents dummies for different preceding questions. The interaction coefficients indicate country-specific correlations of mean life satisfaction with *trend* $\ln GDPpc_{c't}$, *cyclical* $\ln GDPpc_{c't}$, *year*, and lagged mean life satisfaction, respectively. Analogously to Eq. 2.2, country-specific long-run correlations of mean life satisfaction with *trend* $\ln GDPpc_{c't}$, *cyclical* $\ln GDPpc_{c't}$, and *year* are given by $\beta_{c'}/(1 - \varphi_{c'})$, $\gamma_{c'}/(1 - \varphi_{c'})$, and $\delta_{c'}/(1 - \varphi_{c'})$, respectively. Here we have no downward Nickell bias in the country-specific estimates of $\varphi_{c'}$ as these estimates are only driven by the single cluster of observations for the specific country and Nickell bias only occurs with more than one cluster. Given the implosion of clustered standard errors, merely heteroscedasticity-robust or bootstrap standard errors can be used when serial correlation is small. We give preference to the type of standard errors which tend to be larger, as these seem to suffer less from finite-sample bias. For the bootstrap estimation of standard errors we chose to draw samples independently for each country, as this seems to be the appropriate method for the interaction coefficient estimates and since sampling across all countries broke down.

Because the number of country-specific observations may be too low for a number of countries, in some robustness regressions we replace the country-specific interactions of cyclical $\ln GDPpc_{c't}$ and/or $LS_{c't-1}$ with their main effects. To correct for the Nickell bias in the non-country-specific coefficient of $LS_{c't-1}$ we again apply the BCLSDV estimator of Bruno (2005a, b). However, now we do not use the bootstrap standard errors of the other coefficient estimates of Eq. 2.3 from this estimator, but calculate bootstrap-with-strata standard errors in a regression of Eq. 2.3 where the coefficient of $LS_{c't-1}$ has been fixated on the bias-corrected BCLSDV estimate. We follow this procedure because the required strata option for the interaction coefficient estimates (see above) is not available in the calculation of the bootstrap standard errors of the BCLSDV estimator. This specification is also our baseline for the Eastern European countries, where we only have 12 available observations per country. We then further run a robustness regression in which the interaction term for *year* has been replaced by its main effect. However, the latter regression is not very reliable as a test of the Easterlin Paradox for individual countries because country-specific correlations of mean life satisfaction with trend GDPpc are then only controlled for by a common time trend. Because of this concern, the much shorter time series, and the different levels and development of GDPpc of East as compared with Western European countries, we estimate the various variants of Eq. 2.3 for subgroups of Western and Eastern European countries separately.

A final concern is that country-specific estimates of $\varphi_{c'}$ and standard errors of all coefficient estimates are still biased for countries for which, after the addition of the interactions of one-year lagged life satisfaction, significant serial correlation in the error term continues to exist. In robustness checks and to diminish this serial correlation, we add country-specific interactions of one-year lagged *trend* $\ln GDPpc_{c't-1}$ to the above variants of Eq. 3.3 for the Western European countries. For countries for which the estimate of the interaction coefficient $\beta_{c'}$ of *trend* $\ln GDPpc_{c't}$ is significant and positive and the estimate of the interaction coefficient $\beta_{-1c'}$ of *trend* $\ln GDPpc_{c't-1}$ is significant and negative, the latter coefficient estimate can be interpreted as modelling adaptation of life satisfaction to medium-term changes in GDPpc. For all countries, long-run correlations of mean life satisfaction with *trend* $\ln GDPpc_{c't}$ are given by $(\beta_{c'} + \beta_{-1c'})/(1 - \varphi_{c'})$.[12]

2.4 Data and Descriptive Statistics

We use data from the nationally representative Eurobarometer surveys, ranging from 1973 to 2015. To elicit responses on life satisfaction, respondents are typically asked the following question: *"On the whole, are you very satisfied, fairly satisfied, not very satisfied or not at all satisfied with the life you lead?"* with response options: *"Very satisfied (1), fairly satisfied (2), not very satisfied (3), not at all satisfied (4)".* In most years more than one EB survey took place. In order to obtain country-year averages of life satisfaction, we take the mean of all responses in a given year and country.

For our estimations concerning groups of countries to test EPgl, we include all waves apart from those in which the set of response options or question format deviate from the format given above. We exclude these waves because such framing effects can have substantial effects on response patterns (Diener et al. 2013b). Henceforth, we will refer to this set of waves as "EB Standard". Since we cannot use year-fixed effects in our country-specific estimations that test EPim (see Sect. 2.3.2), it is even more crucial for our purposes that country-year means of life satisfaction remain comparable over time. However, questions that immediately precede the life satisfaction question may impact answers to the life satisfaction question (see, e.g., Easterlin 2017). For our estimations in Sect. 2.5.2, we therefore select waves such that the number of distinct preceding questions across time is minimised, while continuing to have at least one EB wave available per year. This allows us to use dummies for preceding questions without them being collinear with the time trend of the reference country. We will call this set of waves "EB Restricted". In total, "EB Standard" and "EB Restricted" cover 35 countries for the years 1973 to 2015. Of these we exclude Cyprus, Luxembourg, and Malta

---

[12]This expression follows from noting that in the long-run equilibrium current and past values of all variables are equal to each other.

because their populations do not exceed our threshold of one million inhabitants. We additionally exclude Albania, Iceland, Macedonia, Montenegro, Norway, and Serbia because they are observed for fewer than 10 years (see Sect. 2.3.1). This leaves us with 27 countries in total.

We use real and PPP-adjusted data on GDP per capita (GDPpc) for all estimations (in constant 2010 international $). We primarily rely on data from the OECD (2017). Since not all European countries and years are covered by this data set, we supplement it with various other sources. We thus mainly use constant GDPpc data from the World Bank (2017) for Bulgaria, Croatia, and Romania. We also use this data for Ireland in 2015 because the OECD data for Ireland shows an implausible growth rate of 22% in that year.[13] The OECD does not provide data on GDPpc for West and East Germany separately. For all years prior to 1991, we therefore use UNCTAD (2017) data for West Germany and data from Henske (2009) for East Germany. For years since 1991 we use data from Destatis (2017a). In cases where the OECD data does not extend far enough into the past, we use data from Penn World Tables (expenditure-side real GDP) (Feenstra et al. 2015). Finally, to minimize end-point problems in the estimation of the Hodrick-Prescott filter with $\lambda = 6.25$, we use GDPpc projections by the IMF (2016) for the years 2016–2021. As this series is expressed in current prices, we convert this series into constant prices using the inflation projections from the IMF for these years. For some robustness tests we include the unemployment and the inflation rate to our estimations. We source this data from the OECD and secondarily the World Bank. We additionally use data from the German Bundesagentur für Arbeit (2017) and DeStatis (2017b) to have distinct series for West and East Germany.

In our analyses we distinguish between Eastern and Western European countries because of their very different levels of GDPpc, the fact that most Eastern European countries went through an economic transition from communism to capitalism, and the much different observation windows we have available for each group.[14] Mean levels of life satisfaction and GDPpc in the period 2004–2015 are clearly higher amongst Western than amongst Eastern European countries (3.07 *vs.* 2.68 and $38,017 *vs.* $21,762, respectively). However, the subset of Southern European countries (Spain, Greece, Italy, Portugal) falls short of that tendency and has a mean LS (= 2.61) and a mean GDPpc (= $30,386) closer to the Eastern European countries.

---

[13]This extreme growth was largely driven by an accounting trick of a number of multinational companies (Inman, 2016). Therefore, this change in GDPpc is unlikely to have had an impact on living standards. The World Bank data set records a growth of only 7%.

[14]Mean T is 35 for the Western European countries and 13 for the Eastern European countries.

2.5   Results

2.5.1   Results for Groups of Countries

In this section we present the results for groups of countries[15] when using the HP
filter with $\lambda = \infty$, which is suitable for testing the long-term version EPgl of the
paradox. However, the estimation period is too short for the Eastern European
countries to actually allow for tests of the long-term version of the paradox. When
we present results for this group alone, we therefore label these results as results
about the medium-term variant EPgm of the paradox.[16]

We begin with presenting the estimation results for Eq. 2.1. First, we estimate this
equation for the group of all 27 European countries selected in Sect. 2.4. Figure 2.2
(left) presents a scatterplot for this country group in which residuals from regressing
Eq. 2.1 without trend lnGDPpc are plotted against residuals from regressing
trend ln $GDPpc_{ct}$ on the country and year dummies. The linear regression fit of
this cloud of data points is rising, but only slightly and the slope as given by the
coefficient estimate 0.10 of trend lnGDPpc in column (1) of Table 2.1, turns out to be
strongly insignificant. However, a striking feature in the scatter diagram in Fig. 2.2
(left) is that the data points for Ireland (as indicated by red dots) are outliers with
extremely low and high values of the residual of trend lnGDPpc (which represents
the double difference of trend lnGDPpc with respect to its time and country means).
This raises the question on the impact of these outliers, which becomes visible in
Fig. 2.2 (right) where we drop Ireland. This leads to a remarkably strong rise in the
slope of the regression line, which is reflected in a marginally ($p = 0.10$) significant[17]
and much larger coefficient estimate of 0.62 for trend lnGDPpc in column (2) of
Table 2.1. The result of column (1) was hence largely driven by the outlier Ireland.
Therefore, we drop Ireland from the subsequent regressions in this section.

Thus, for our sample of 26 European countries without Ireland the long-term
variant of the Easterlin Paradox is marginally rejected. However, Proto and
Rustichini (2013) found a non-monotonic relation between GDPpc and life satisfaction, which is significantly positive for poorer countries/regions, but insignificant or
significantly negative for richer countries/regions. This suggests that our rejection of
the paradox may be driven by the subgroup of the 13 less developed Eastern
European countries with their lower mean GDPpc. Therefore, in column (3) we
drop these countries from the regression, leaving us with 13 mainly Western

---

[15]Here we use "EB-Standard" data.

[16]In Kaiser and Vendrik (2018) we extensively discuss the results of our tests when setting $\lambda = 6.25$
which more closely corresponds to tests of EPgm. These results are very similar to those for $\lambda = \infty$,
the main difference being slightly more reliably significant coefficients for sets of Eastern European
countries.

[17]In this study we call an estimate (strongly) significant when its p-value in a two-tailed t test is
below 0.05 (0.01), and marginally significant when its p value in a two- or one-tailed t test is higher
than 0.05, but lower than 0.10. In the latter case we mention the p value in parentheses, which refers
to a two-tailed t test unless it is explicitly stated that it refers to a one-tailed t test.

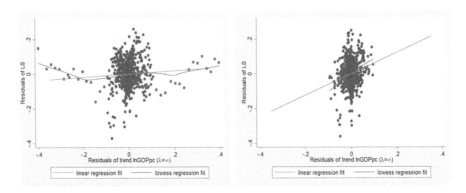

Fig. 2.2 Scatterplots of residuals of regression of Eq. 2.1 for the long term without *trend* ln $GDPpc_{ct}$ against residuals of regression of *trend* ln $GDPpc_{ct}$ on year and country dummies for all countries with Ireland marked in red (left) and when omitting Ireland (right)

Table 2.1 Baseline Results for Eq. 2.1 for the Long Term

	(1)	(2)	(3)	(4)	(5)	(6)
	All	All, no IE	EU-13	EU-9	SE	EE
Trend LnGDPpc	0.095	0.616*	0.783	0.014	1.425	0.477*
	(0.125)	(0.356)	(0.762)	(0.556)	(1.250)	(0.228)
Cyclical LnGDPpc	0.765***	0.782***	0.872***	0.159	0.527	0.832**
	(0.137)	(0.150)	(0.176)	(0.324)	(0.413)	(0.275)
R-squared	0.943	0.945	0.931	0.934	0.885	0.938
Number of Countries	27	26	13	9	4	13
Number of Observations	666	624	454	315	139	170

Note: Estimated with Stata's 'regress' command. Country and year dummies included. Country-clustered standard errors in parentheses. Significance levels: for two-tailed t test: +: $p < 0.20$, *: $p < 0.10$, **: $p < 0.05$, ***: $p < 0.01$; for one-tailed t test: +: $p < 0.10$, *: $p < 0.05$, **: $p < 0.025$, ***: $p < 0.005$

European countries without Ireland (EU-13). For this EU-13 the coefficient estimate is insignificant, but surprisingly it is even larger in size than for the total group of 26 European countries without Ireland (0.78 *vs.* 0.62). The large standard error (0.76) of this estimate may be due to strong heterogeneity in the effects of differences in long-term economic growth on life satisfaction across different (groups of) EU-13 countries. Given the strong sensitiveness of mean life satisfaction in the Southern European (SE) countries Greece, Italy, Spain, and Portugal to the recent Euro crisis and their lower mean GDPpc, the large size of the coefficient for the EU-13 may be driven by this group of four SE countries. This is also suggested by the scatter diagram for the EU-13 in Fig. 2.3 (left) in which the data points for the four SE countries are indicated by red dots. Dropping these data points from the regression, we obtain Fig. 2.3 (right) with a slope that is virtually flat. This is reflected by the strongly insignificant and very small coefficient 0.01 of trend lnGDPpc in the regression for the nine remaining Western and Northern European countries in

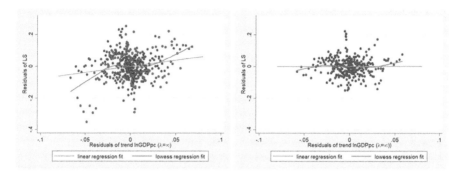

Fig. 2.3 Scatterplots of residuals of regression of Eq. 2.1 for the long term without *trend* ln *GDPpc_ct* against residuals of regression of *trend* ln *GDPpc_ct* on year and country dummies for the group of EU-13 countries with Southern European countries marked in red (left) and when omitting Southern European countries (right)

column (4) of Table 2.1. Thus, in this subgroup of highly developed countries (EU-9) a higher long-term growth of GDP per capita was not associated with a more positive change in average life satisfaction. So, the group of these nine Western and Northern European countries clearly satisfies the long-term-variant EPgl of the Easterlin Paradox.[18]

Figure 2.3 also suggests that when we restrict the regression to the four Southern European countries, the coefficient of trend lnGDPpc will be significant, positive, and large. However, column (5) of Table 2.1 shows that although this coefficient is indeed large and positive, it is not statistically significant (p = 0.34). The large standard error that drives this (1.25) seems to be due to the coefficient of trend lnGDPpc being identified by only three[19] differences in country-specific observations for the average growth rate of GDPpc. Finally, column (6) shows that for the group of 13 Eastern European (EE) countries the coefficient of trend lnGDPpc is marginally (p = 0.06) significant, positive, and large. Thus, in this group of countries (with their short estimation period) a higher *medium*-term growth of GDP per capita was associated with a more positive change in average life satisfaction. This implies a marginal rejection of the medium-term-variant EPgm of the Easterlin Paradox for this group of countries. Because these countries had a lower mean GDP per capita than the Western and Northern European countries, this is in line with the significantly positive relation between GDPpc and life satisfaction for poorer countries and European regions as found by Proto and Rustichini (2013).

However, especially the last result may be biased due to the small number (13) of country clusters. Clustered standard errors of the parameter estimates then tend to be

---

[18]The coefficient of cyclical lnGDPpc is insignificant for this group of countries as well, so even cyclical fluctuations in GDPpc were not associated with changes in average life satisfaction in these countries.

[19]Given this extremely low number of effective observations, we also run a robustness regression of Eq. 2.1 for this group of countries without cyclical lnGDPpc. This yields a coefficient of 1.66 with a standard error of 1.11 (p = 0.23), which is close to marginally significant in a one-tailed t test.

underestimated (see Sect. 2.3.1). In our case this downward bias in the standard errors is likely to be especially strong as tests for first and second-order serial correlation of the error term (see Wooldridge 2003, pp. 399–402) in Eq. 2.1 show strong positive first-order serial correlation (in the order of 0.50–0.70).[20] We therefore reduce this first-order serial correlation by adding one-year lagged mean life satisfaction to Eq. 2.1, yielding Eq. 2.2. Table 2.2 presents estimation results for Eq. 2.2 for the same groups of countries as those distinguished in Table 2.1 for Eq. 2.1. Now, the long-run effects of trend lnGDPpc and cyclical lnGDPpc are the relevant estimates that can be compared with the coefficient estimates in Table 2.1.[21]

For the total sample of all 27 European countries, column (1) of Table 2.2 shows a strongly significant and large bias-corrected coefficient of 0.81 for lagged life satisfaction, which implies a strong persistence of mean life satisfaction. This persistence does not only reflect a possible direct effect of lagged life satisfaction on current life satisfaction, but also reinforcement of the effects of trend and cyclical GDPpc, and those of omitted variables (*e.g.*, health)[22] on life satisfaction. A serial correlation test for Eq. 2.2 shows that, as a result of the addition of the lagged life satisfaction term, all first-order and second-order serial correlation is eliminated (i.e. becomes insignificant) except for marginally (p = 0.08) significant, negative, and small (−0.05) first-order serial correlation for the EU-13 countries. Hence, the bootstrap standard errors of the parameter estimates calculated by the BCLSDV estimator in Stata (see Sect. 2.3.1) are more reliable than those obtained from the estimation of Eq. 2.1. The coefficient estimates for trend lnGDPpc and cyclical lnGDPpc in column (1) of Table 2.2 can be interpreted as short-run effects of these variables (see footnote 8 in Sect. 2.3.1), which is insignificant for trend lnGDPpc but significant for cyclical lnGDPpc. The reinforcement of these effects results in much larger long-run (LR) effects, which are nevertheless insignificant for trend lnGDPpc, but significant for cyclical lnGDPpc. The size and standard error of the long-run effect of trend lnGDPpc in Table 2.2 are both about twice as large as their equivalents in Table 2.1. In general, the much larger standard errors of the long-run effects in Table 2.2 not only reflect the downward bias of the standard errors estimates in Table 2.1 due to the low number of clusters (13), but also the partial control for serially correlated and time-varying omitted variables via the added lagged life satisfaction term. Therefore, the estimates for Eq. 2.2 in Table 2.2 seem more reliable than those for Eq. 2.1 in Table 2.1.

For the sample of 26 European countries without Ireland, column (2) of Table 2.2 shows a long-run effect of trend lnGDPpc, which is again somewhat larger than the

---

[20]The second-order serial correlation is significant for most groups, but relatively small (at most 0.16). We do not explicitly correct for that in the following.

[21]In time-series analysis a static equation like Eq. 2.1 is interpreted as the long-run-equilibrium equation that corresponds to a dynamic equation like Eq. 2.2 (cf. Vendrik, 2013).

[22]In Eq. 2.2 such omitted variables work via changes in the error term which in the next year are reinforced via the lagged life satisfaction term. This reinforcement also picks up the effects of positive serial correlation in time-varying omitted variables. See Vendrik (2013) for a deeper dynamic analysis.

Table 2.2 Baseline Results for Eq. 2.2 for the Long Term

	(1)	(2)	(3)	(4)	(5)	(6)	(7)
	All	All, no IE	EU-13	EU-9	SE	EE	EE-11
L.Life Satisfaction	0.805***	0.806***	0.850***	0.716***	0.795***	0.668***	0.527***
	(0.033)	(0.035)	(0.037)	(0.049)	(0.091)	(0.080)	(0.102)
Trend LnGDPpc	0.039	0.170+	0.250+	−0.092	0.484	0.097	0.225+
	(0.045)	(0.111)	(0.184)	(0.173)	(0.511)	(0.171)	(0.162)
Cyclical LnGDPpc	0.146**	0.170**	0.079	0.053	0.049	0.595**	0.614**
	(0.060)	(0.068)	(0.098)	(0.111)	(0.205)	(0.211)	(0.216)
LR effect of Trend LnGDPpc	0.198	0.877+	1.665+	−0.323	2.363	0.291	0.476+
	(0.235)	(0.568)	(1.199)	(0.618)	(2.344)	(0.504)	(0.319)
LR effect of Cyclical LnGDPpc	0.748**	0.875**	0.528	0.188	0.238	1.790**	1.297**
	(0.310)	(0.364)	(0.659)	(0.386)	(1.012)	(0.802)	(0.556)
Number of Countries	27	26	13	9	4	13	11
Number of Observations	631	591	434	300	134	157	121

Note: Estimated with 'xtlsdvc' command, written by Bruno (2005b). Country and year dummies included. Bootstrapped (400 replications) standard errors in parentheses. Significance levels: for two-tailed t test: +: $p < 0.20$, *: $p < 0.10$, **: $p < 0.05$, ***: $p < 0.01$; for one-tailed t test: +: $p < 0.10$, *: $p < 0.05$, **: $p < 0.025$, ***: $p < 0.005$. R-squareds are not reported by the 'xtlsdvc' command

coefficient in column (2) of Table 2.1, but which is now only marginally ($p = 0.06$) significant in a one-tailed test. Hence, the marginal rejection of the Easterlin Paradox for this group of countries in Table 2.1 is now ambiguous in Table 2.2. We also find such weak evidence for a rejection of EPgl for the group of 13 mainly Western European countries without Ireland (EU-13) in column (3) of Table 2.2 (one-tailed $p = 0.08$), which is in contrast with the insignificant result in Table 2.1 and which is due to the much larger size of the long-run effect of trend lnGDPpc. However, when we drop the four Southern European countries in column (4) of Table 2.2, the long-run effect of trend lnGDPpc is again strongly insignificant and even negative, implying a clear confirmation of the long-term variant EPgl of the Easterlin Paradox for this group of nine highly-developed Western and Northern-European countries (EU-9).

For the group of four Southern European countries column (5) of Table 2.2 shows an insignificant long-run effect of trend lnGDPpc as well, which is consistent with the result in column (5) of Table 2.1. However, for the group of 13 Eastern European countries the strongly insignificant long-run effect of trend lnGDPpc in column (6) is inconsistent with the marginally significant effect of trend lnGDPpc in column (6) of Table 2.1. This is due to a much lower size as well as much larger standard error of the estimate in Table 2.2. Especially the much smaller size of the latter estimate is puzzling and may be driven by one or more outlier countries. Such outliers may be Turkey because it is not an ex-communist country like the other EE countries, and East Germany because it has been integrated with highly developed West Germany since 1990 and has a much longer time series for life satisfaction in our dataset than the other EE countries (since 1990 *vs.* 2004). When we drop these two countries from the group of EE countries, the long-run effect of trend lnGDPpc as shown in column (7) of Table 2.2 becomes much larger and marginally significant in a one-tailed t test ($p = 0.07$). In addition, an estimation of Eq. 2.1 for the remaining subgroup of 11 EE countries yields a significant coefficient of trend lnGDPpc (with size 0.568). We thus obtain weak evidence of a rejection of the medium-term variant EPgm of the Easterlin Paradox for this group of 11 Eastern European countries (EE-11).

We performed a number of checks to assess how robust these results are to dropping or adding relevant control variables (particularly the unemployment and inflation rate) and to restricting the estimation period. See Kaiser and Vendrik (2018) for an extended discussion. Our estimates are qualitatively robust to most of these checks. However, the weak rejection of the paradox for the group of EE-11 countries turns out to be driven by an associated decline in the inflation rate and its positive effect. Since long-term changes in the inflation rate should be considered a good control in the sense of Angrist and Pischke (2009),[23] the rejection of the Easterlin paradox in our baseline regressions for this set of countries should be viewed as possibly spurious.

---

[23]For example, economic reforms in a country and globalization may lead to both higher long-term economic growth and lower inflation.

In sum, for the group of Northern and Western European countries (EU-9) we have obtained a clear and unambiguous affirmation of the long-term version of the Easterlin Paradox. Moreover, we have obtained weak and non-robust evidence for a rejection of EPgm for the set of Eastern European countries without Turkey and East Germany. As explained earlier, the estimation period for the 11 Eastern European countries is only 11 years (2004–2015), which includes short-term, but not medium-term cycles of GDPpc that tend to last between roughly 15 and 30 years (see Sect. 2.1). Hence in the case of the EE-11 countries, the HP filter with $\lambda = \infty$ may only provide us with tests of the medium-term version of the paradox.[24] For a genuine test of the more appropriate long-term variant EPgl for this country group longer time series are needed.

2.5.2   Results for Individual Countries

In this section we present the results of testing the medium-term variant EPim[25] of the Easterlin Paradox for individual countries. Here we use "EB-restricted" data. Our discussion starts with the groups of Western European countries and then moves on to the group of Eastern European countries.

We estimate Eq. 2.3[26] for the group of 14 WE countries plus East Germany (WE$^+$).[27] Column (1) of Table 2.3 presents the long-run effects of trend lnGDPpc and cyclical lnGDPpc for all individual WE$^+$ countries. The long-run effect of trend lnGDPpc is (marginally) significant and positive for Greece (1.14), Ireland (0.26; $p = 0.07$), Italy (1.49), and Spain (0.86) in a two-tailed t test, and marginally significant and positive for Portugal (0.58) only in a one-tailed t test ($p = 0.10$).

---

[24]When using an HP filter with $\lambda = 6.25$ we obtain somewhat larger and slightly more significant estimates for this group of countries. Our rejection of EPgm is nevertheless non-robust in this case, too. See Kaiser and Vendrik (2018) for an extended discussion.

[25]In Kaiser and Vendrik (2018) we also present tests of EPi0 (non-positive long-term time trend in happiness) for Western European countries (plus East Germany). There we show that EPi0 is robustly confirmed for Austria, Belgium, Greece, the Netherlands, Portugal, and West Germany, but robustly violated for Denmark, Finland, France, Great Britain, Italy, and Sweden. For the other countries the results are not robust. In the case of the Eastern European countries the limited observation period does not allow for reliable tests of a long-term non-positive time trend in happiness. Among these countries, we obtain (marginally) significant and positive medium-term time trends for Bulgaria, Hungary, Lithuania, Latvia, Poland, and Romania.

[26]These regressions include only two significant dummies for the preceding questions. The first dummy controls for a question on which political party the respondent supports (1979 and 1983 waves). The second dummy concerns a question on the share of friends appreciating talk about politics (1998 wave). These dummies have long-run effects averaged across countries of -0.06 and -0.07, respectively.

[27]We include East Germany here because East Germany has an estimation period that is much closer to the Western European country group. See Kaiser and Vendrik (2018) for more explanation.

Table 2.3 Baseline Results for Eq. 2.3 for WE⁺ Countries and the Medium Term

		(1)		(2)		(3)	
		Standard		Main effect of Cyclical LnGDPpc		Main effects of Cycl. LnGDPpc and L.Cycl. LnGDPpc, interactions of L.Trend LnGDPpc	
		Effect	SE	Effect	SE	Effect	SE
Austria	LR effect of Trend LnGDPpc	-1.362^{***}	(0.490)	-1.427^{***}	(0.468)	-1.450^{***}	(0.515)
(T = 20)	LR effect of Year	0.013^{**}	(0.006)	0.014^{**}	(0.006)	0.015^{+}	(0.009)
Belgium	LR effect of Trend LnGDPpc	0.442	(1.339)	-0.016	(1.029)	-0.146	(1.307)
(T = 40)	LR effect of Year	-0.007	(0.022)	0.000	(0.016)	0.003	(0.024)
Denmark	LR effect of Trend LnGDPpc	-0.120	(0.211)	-0.174	(0.196)	-0.240^{+}	(0.175)
(T = 40)	LR effect of Year	0.006^{*}	(0.003)	0.007^{**}	(0.003)	0.009^{***}	(0.002)
East Germany	LR effect of Trend LnGDPpc	-2.373^{**}	(1.062)	-2.475^{***}	(0.951)	-2.357^{**}	(1.108)
(T = 25)	LR effect of Year	0.057^{***}	(0.020)	0.058^{***}	(0.019)	0.056^{***}	(0.021)
Finland	LR effect of Trend LnGDPpc	0.403	(0.378)	0.311	(0.325)	0.285	(0.348)
(T = 20)	LR effect of Year	0.001	(0.004)	0.003	(0.004)	-0.000	(0.011)
France	LR effect of Trend LnGDPpc	-0.154	(0.396)	-0.153	(0.364)	-0.264	(0.368)
(T = 40)	LR effect of Year	0.008^{+}	(0.005)	0.008^{+}	(0.005)	0.011^{*}	(0.006)
Great Britain	LR effect of Trend LnGDPpc	-0.585^{***}	(0.157)	-0.580^{***}	(0.154)	-0.547^{***}	(0.156)
(T = 40)	LR effect of Year	0.016^{***}	(0.003)	0.015^{***}	(0.003)	0.015^{***}	(0.003)
Greece	LR effect of Trend LnGDPpc	1.141^{***}	(0.349)	1.154^{***}	(0.351)	0.853^{***}	(0.221)
(T = 34)	LR effect of Year	-0.030^{***}	(0.006)	-0.030^{***}	(0.006)	-0.023^{***}	(0.003)

(continued)

Table 2.3 (continued)

		(1)		(2)		(3)	
		Standard		Main effect of Cyclical LnGDPpc		Main effects of Cycl. LnGDPpc and L.Cycl. LnGDPpc, interactions of L.Trend LnGDPpc	
		Effect	SE	Effect	SE	Effect	SE
Ireland	LR effect of Trend LnGDPpc	0.255*	(0.139)	0.310**	(0.152)	0.269⁺	(0.166)
(T = 40)	LR effect of year	−0.007⁺	(0.005)	−0.010⁺	(0.006)	−0.008	(0.006)
Italy	LR effect of Trend LnGDPpc	1.490***	(0.141)	1.479***	(0.133)	1.455***	(0.171)
(T = 40)	LR effect of Year	−0.018***	(0.002)	−0.018***	(0.002)	−0.017***	(0.004)
Netherlands	LR effect of Trend lnGDPpc	−0.445⁺	(0.338)	−0.351	(0.367)	−0.302	(0.383)
(T = 40)	LR effect of year	0.009⁺	(0.006)	0.007	(0.006)	0.007	(0.007)
Portugal	LR effect of Trend LnGDPpc	0.577⁺	(0.449)	0.556	(0.512)	0.727⁺	(0.499)
(T = 29)	LR effect of Year	−0.023**	(0.009)	−0.023**	(0.010)	−0.011	(0.025)
Spain	LR effect of Trend LnGDPpc	0.863**	(0.420)	0.996**	(0.428)	0.805**	(0.379)
(T = 29)	LR effect of Year	−0.015*	(0.007)	−0.018**	(0.008)	−0.006	(0.008)
Sweden	LR effect of Trend LnGDPpc	0.189	(0.439)	0.137	(0.383)	0.065	(0.373)
(T = 20)	LR effect of Year	0.004	(0.006)	0.005	(0.005)	0.004	(0.004)
West Germany	LR effect of Trend LnGDPpc	−0.861	(0.932)	−0.851	(0.901)	−0.438	(0.697)
(T = 40)	LR effect of year	0.014	(0.013)	0.014	(0.013)	0.011	(0.010)
Number of Observations:		497		497		497	

Note: Estimated with Stata's 'regress' command, controlling for country-specific or main effects of cyclical lnGDPpc, PQDs, and country dummies. T now indicates the number of effective observations that identifies the interaction coefficient for a particular country. Strata bootstrapped (400 replications) standard errors in parentheses. Significance levels: for two-tailed t test: +: $p < 0.20$, *: $p < 0.10$, **: $p < 0.05$, ***: $p < 0.01$; for one-tailed t test: +: $p < 0.10$, *: $p < 0.05$, **: $p < 0.025$, ***: $p < 0.005$

Interestingly, these are precisely the countries that suffered most from the recent Eurocrisis. Thus, for these countries the medium-term variant EPim of the Easterlin Paradox for individual countries is violated. Note that the positive long-run effects of trend lnGDPpc for these countries go together with (marginally) significant negative time trends. For the other countries the long-run effect of trend lnGDPpc is either insignificant or (marginally) significantly negative (for Austria, East Germany, Great Britain, the Netherlands, one-tailed $p = 0.09$). Thus, for these individual countries the medium-term variant EPim of the Easterlin Paradox is confirmed.

For countries with less than 40 observations (Austria, East Germany, Finland, Greece, Portugal, Spain, and Sweden) the number of observations may be too low to lead to stable, and hence reliable, estimates of the four interaction terms for each country in Eq. 2.3 (see Sect. 2.3.2). In column (2) of Table 2.3 we therefore replace the interaction terms for cyclical lnGDPpc with its main effect. This yields qualitatively robust results except for insignificant effects of trend lnGDPpc for Portugal and the Netherlands.

We observe (marginally) significant first-order serial correlation in the error terms of the regressions in columns (1) (Greece, Spain, West Germany) and (2) (additionally Denmark and Ireland). As explained above, this may result in a downward bias to our standard errors. To reduce this serial correlation, we add country-specific interaction terms for one-year-lagged *trend* ln $GDPpc_{ct-1}$ and a main effect of one-year-lagged *cyclical* ln $GDPpc_{ct-1}$ to the regression in column (2). This yields the estimates in column (3) of Table 2.3. These estimates are similar to those in column (2), with again a rejection of the Easterlin paradox for Greece, Ireland, Italy, and Spain, but now also marginally for Portugal. We further observe (marginally) significant partial adaptation to medium-term changes in GDPpc for Greece, Ireland, Portugal, and Spain, as well as full adaptation for West Germany.

The estimates of column (3) may again not be robust due to too few observations for some countries.[28] We therefore conducted a robustness test in which we used the main effect of lagged life satisfaction instead of country-specific interactions. Our results are robust to this test, except that we no longer find a significant rejection for Ireland (this is likely driven by Ireland's strong deviation from the uniform coefficient of lagged life satisfaction). We also tried dropping the interactions of lagged *trend* ln $GDPpc_{ct-1}$ and the main effect of *cyclical* ln $GDPpc_{ct-1}$ from the previous regression, which showed no qualitative change in the estimates. Finally, we also checked for robustness against the impact of the recent Great Recession by restricting the estimation period to the period before 2008, which again yielded rejections of EPim for the same set of countries.

Overall, we conclude that the medium-term variant EPim of the Easterlin Paradox is robustly violated for Greece, Ireland, Italy, and Spain, but robustly confirmed for the nine Western and Northern European countries (EU-9). The latter confirmation is consistent with the confirmation of EPgl for the EU-9 as a group of countries.

We now turn to Eastern Europe. For these countries, column (1) of Table 2.4 shows the long-run effects of trend lnGDPpc and year from a regression of Eq. 2.3,

---

[28]See Kaiser and Vendrik (2018) for a more extensive discussion of these robustness results.

Table 2.4 Baseline Results for Eq. 2.3 for Eastern European Countries and the Medium Term

		(1)		(2)	
		Standard		Main effect of Year	
		Effect	SE	Effect	SE
Bulgaria	LR effect of Trend LnGDPpc	1.516	(2.155)	0.957**	(0.412)
(T = 11)	LR effect of Year	−0.018	(0.051)	−0.003	(0.006)
Croatia	LR effect of Trend LnGDPpc	1.011	(2.108)	1.335	(1.708)
(T = 11)	LR effect of Year	0.004	(0.012)	−0.003	(0.006)
Czech Republic	LR effect of Trend LnGDPpc	−1.253	(4.130)	0.421	(0.993)
(T = 11)	LR effect of Year	0.020	(0.035)	−0.003	(0.006)
Estonia	LR effect of Trend LnGDPpc	1.787	(1.740)	0.828	(0.684)
(T = 11)	LR effect of Year	−0.018	(0.029)	−0.003	(0.006)
Hungary	LR effect of Trend LnGDPpc	3.527	(3.997)	3.530	(2.853)
(T = 11)	LR effect of Year	−0.000	(0.027)	−0.003	(0.006)
Latvia	LR effect of Trend LnGDPpc	−0.855	(1.531)	1.045*	(0.582)
(T = 11)	LR effect of Year	0.042^{+}	(0.032)	−0.003	(0.006)
Lithuania	LR effect of Trend LnGDPpc	1.540	(1.931)	0.895***	(0.324)
(T = 11)	LR effect of Year	−0.024	(0.063)	−0.003	(0.006)
Poland	LR effect of Trend LnGDPpc	1.037	(2.987)	0.434*	(0.244)
(T = 11)	LR effect of Year	−0.024	(0.101)	−0.003	(0.006)
Romania	LR effect of Trend LnGDPpc	0.246	(3.138)	0.922^{+}	(0.691)
(T = 11)	LR effect of Year	0.019	(0.080)	−0.003	(0.006)
Slovakia	LR effect of Trend LnGDPpc	1.124	(4.495)	0.220	(0.315)
(T = 11)	LR effect of Year	−0.033	(0.116)	−0.003	(0.006)
Slovenia	LR effect of Trend LnGDPpc	−0.170	(1.194)	−0.483	(0.979)
(T = 11)	LR effect of Year	−0.009^{+}	(0.006)	−0.003	(0.006)
Turkey	LR effect of Trend LnGDPpc	2.823	(7.908)	−0.595	(0.760)
(T = 11)	LR effect of Year	−0.086	(0.201)	−0.003	(0.006)
Number of Observations:		132		132	

Note: Estimated with Stata's 'regress' and Bruno's 'xtlsdvc' command, controlling for main effect of cyclical lnGDPpc and country dummies. T now indicates the number of effective observations that identifies the interaction coefficient for a particular country. Strata bootstrapped (400 replications) standard errors in parentheses. Significance levels: for two-tailed t test: +: $p < 0.20$, *: $p < 0.10$, **: $p < 0.05$, ***: $p < 0.01$; for one-tailed t test: +: $p < 0.10$, *: $p < 0.05$, **: $p < 0.025$, ***: $p < 0.005$

using main effects instead of interactions for both cyclical lnGDPpc and lagged life satisfaction. In this regression all dummies for different preceding questions have been dropped because they were jointly insignificant. Strikingly, the long-run effects of trend lnGDPpc are (strongly) insignificant for all EE countries. This is unexpected in view of the marginally significant long-run effect of trend lnGDPpc for the group of EE countries without East Germany and Turkey in column (7) of Table 2.2. Our result may be due to too little variation in medium-term economic growth rates of the EE countries over the short estimation period of 11 years. Therefore, column (2) shows the long-run effects of trend lnGDPpc while controlling for a common time trend instead of country-specific time trends. Now for five out of 12 countries these long-run effects are (marginally) significant and positive, namely for Bulgaria, Lithuania, Latvia (p = 0.08), Poland (p = 0.06), and Romania (one-tailed p = 0.09). However, the control for a common instead of country-specific time trends makes the results of this test dubious for Latvia and Romania as the marginally significant and positive long-run effects of trend lnGDPpc for these countries in column (2) of Table 2.4 apparently pick up the positive country-specific long-run time trends found in column (1) (see also the discussion in Sect. 2.1). For the other three countries, i.e. Bulgaria, Lithuania, and Poland, the country-specific long-run time trends in column (1) are more negative than the common long-run time trend, and hence cannot account for the (marginally) significantly positive long-run effects of (mainly positive) changes in trend lnGDPpc in column (2). Thus, we conclude that the medium-term variant EPim of the Easterlin Paradox for individual EE countries is only rejected for Bulgaria, Lithuania, and Poland. For a reliable test of whether this variant of the Easterlin Paradox is also rejected for other EE countries, longer time series than those currently available are needed.

2.6   Conclusions

Our starting point was the argument that reliable tests of the Easterlin Paradox should control for the possibility of spuriousness of the correlation between average happiness and long-term economic growth by means of common or country-specific time trends. This led to a distinction between five variants of the paradox along the two dimensions of groups of countries *versus* individual countries and the long *versus* medium-term. We further argued that the long-term version of the paradox for groups of countries and the medium-term version for individual countries are the most appropriate testable versions of the paradox. We found a clear and robust confirmation of the long-term version (as well as the medium-term version) of the paradox for a group of nine Western and Northern European countries. Moreover, we obtained a non-robust rejection of the medium-term variant of the paradox for a set of 11 Eastern European countries. On the level of individual countries, the Easterlin Paradox for the medium term turned out to clearly hold for the nine Western and Northern European countries, but to be consistently rejected for Spain, Greece, Ireland, and Italy. Thus, in the latter four as opposed to the former nine countries, economic growth was positively associated with the development of life satisfaction in the medium term. In the case of the individual Eastern European countries, this was also found to hold for Bulgaria, Lithuania, and Poland, but for the other EE countries the test results are unreliable, partially due to the limited length of the time series (only 11 years).[29] Note that our results for individual European

---

[29]Note that this limitation also holds for other international data sets for life satisfaction and happiness. Examples are the World Values Survey (up to six observations) and the Gallup World Poll (13 observations for 2005–2017).

countries in the medium term are largely consistent with our findings for the groups of countries to which the individual countries belong.

We thus give a nuanced picture of the empirical validity of the Easterlin Paradox. On the one hand, we show that the paradox is confirmed for Western and Northern European countries, both as a group and individually. On the other hand, our results imply a rejection of the medium-term version of the paradox for three individual Southern European countries and Ireland, and at least suggest a rejection of the paradox for Eastern European countries in the medium term. Because the Western and Northern European countries have a high per capita GDP as compared to that of Southern and Eastern European countries and (initially) Ireland, our results are in line with those of Proto and Rustichini (2013), who find a non-monotonic relation between per capita GDP and life satisfaction over time. Thus, on the one hand and in line with Proto and Rustichini and Veenhoven and Vergunst (2014), but contrary to Easterlin (2017), we have obtained evidence that suggests that, at least in the (less appropriate) medium term, the Easterlin Paradox does not hold for lower-income European countries. On the other hand, and in line with Proto and Rustichini and Easterlin (2017), but contrary to Sacks et al. (2013) and Veenhoven and Vergunst (2014), we have found evidence that strongly suggests that, over the last 40 years, economic growth did not raise average life satisfaction in the long and medium term in higher-income European countries. Thus, in response to the title of Easterlin's 2016 paper: although the "blissful paradise" of universal validity of the paradox may have been lost, the paradox itself is not!

Acknowledgements We thank Erik de Regt for econometric advice, Marta Golin for advice on using Stata, Guy Mayraz and Ruut Veenhoven for sending us their data sets, Daniel Sacks and Justin Wolfers for information about their research, and John Barkley Rosser Jr., Robert Dur, Richard Easterlin, Ari Kapteyn, Maurizio Pugno, Mariano Rojas, Francesco Sarracino, and other participants of the International Conference on Policies for Happiness and Health in Siena, March 19–21, 2018, and the USC Happiness Conference at the occasion of the retirement of Richard Easterlin in Los Angeles, April 6, 2018, for helpful comments.

References

Angeles, L. (2011). A closer look at the Easterlin Paradox. *The Journal of Socio-Economics, 40*, 67–73.

Angrist, J. D., & Pischke, J. S. (2009). *Mostly harmless econometrics: An empiricist's companion.* Princeton: Princeton University Press.

Bartolini, S., & Sarracino, F. (2014). Happy for how long? How social capital and economic growth relate to happiness over time. *Ecological Economics, 108*(Suppl. C), 242–256.

Bartolini, S., Bilancini, E., & Pugno, M. (2013a). Did the decline in social connections depress Americans' happiness? *Social Indicators Research, 110*, 1033–1059.

Bartolini, S., Bilancini, E., & Sarracino, F. (2013b). Predicting the trend of well-being in Germany: How much do comparisons, adaptation and sociability matter? *Social Indicators Research, 114* (2), 169–191.

Beja, E. L. (2014). Income growth and happiness: reassessment of the Easterlin Paradox. *International Review of Economics, 61*(4), 329–346.

Bruno, G. S. (2005a). Approximating the bias of the LSDV estimator for dynamic unbalanced panel data models. *Economics Letters, 87*(3), 361–366.

Bruno, G. S. F. (2005b). *XTLSDVC: Stata module to estimate bias corrected LSDV dynamic panel data models, Statistical Software Components S450101, revised 08 Sep. 2005*. Boston: Boston College Department of Economics.

Bundesagentur für Arbeit. (2017). *Arbeitslose und Unterbeschäftigung*. Retrieved November 10, 2017, from https://statistik.arbeitsagentur.de/nn_217700/Statischer-Content/Rubriken/Arbeitslose-und-gemeldetes-Stellenangebot/Arbeitslose/Arbeitslosigkeit-in-Deutschland-seit-1950-Monats-Jahreszahlen.html

Burns, A. F., & Mitchell, W. C. (1946). *Measuring business cycles*. New York: National Bureau of Economic Research.

Cameron, A. C., & Miller, D. L. (2015). A practitioner's guide to cluster-robust inference. *The Journal of Human Resources, 50*(2), 317–372.

Clark, A. E. (2011). Income and happiness: Getting the debate straight. *Applied Research in Quality of Life, 6*, 253–263.

Clark, A. E., Flèche, S., & Senik, C. (2014). The great happiness moderation. In A. E. Clark & C. Senik (Eds.), *Happiness and economic growth: Lessons from developing countries* (pp. 32–139). Oxford: Oxford University Press.

Deaton, A. (2008). Income, health, and well-being around the world: Evidence from the Gallup World Poll. *Journal of Economic Perspectives, 22*(2), 53–72.

Destatis. (2017a). *Bruttoinlandsprodukt, Bruttowertschöpfung in den Ländern*. Retrieved July 2, 2017, from https://www.destatis.de/DE/Publikationen/Thematisch/Volkswirtschaftliche Gesamtrechnungen/VGRderLaender/VGR_LaenderergebnisseBand1.html

Destatis. (2017b). *Publikation – Preise – Verbraucherpreisindex für Deutschland – Lange Reihen ab 1948*. Retrieved November 10, 2017, from https://www.destatis.de/DE/Publikationen/Thematisch/Preise/Verbraucherpreise/VerbraucherpreisindexLangeReihen.html

Diener, E., Inglehart, R., & Tay, L. (2013a). Theory and validity of life satisfaction scales. *Social Indicators Research, 112*(3), 497–527.

Diener, E., Tay, L., & Oishi, S. (2013b). Rising income and the subjective well-being of nations. *Journal of Personality and Social Psychology, 104*(2), 267–276.

Easterlin, R. A. (1974). Does economic growth improve the human lot? Some empirical evidence. *Nations and Households in Economic Growth, 89*, 89–125.

Easterlin, R. A. (1995). Will raising the incomes of all increase the happiness of all? *Journal of Economic Behavior & Organization, 27*(1), 35–47.

Easterlin, R. A. (2005). Feeding the illusion of growth and happiness: A reply to Hagerty and Veenhoven. *Social Indicators Research, 74*(3), 429–443.

Easterlin, R. A. (2009). Lost in transition: Life satisfaction on the road to capitalism. *Journal of Economic Behavior & Organization, 71*(2), 130–145.

Easterlin, R. A. (2015). Happiness and economic growth: The evidence. In W. Glatzer, L. Camfield, V. Møller, & M. Rojas (Eds.), *Global handbook of quality of life* (pp. 283–299). International Handbooks of Quality-of-Life. Dordrecht: Springer.

Easterlin, R. A. (2017). Paradox lost? *Review of Behavioral Economics, 4*(4), 311–339.

Easterlin, R. A., & Sawangfa, O. (2010). Happiness and economic growth: Does the cross section predict time trends? Evidence from developing countries. In E. Diener & D. Kahneman (Eds.), *International differences in well-being* (pp. 166–216).

Easterlin, R. A., McVey, L. A., Switek, M., Sawangfa, O., & Zweig, J. S. (2010). The happiness-income paradox revisited. *Proceedings of the National Academy of Sciences, 107*(52), 22463–22468.

Feenstra, R. C., Inklaar, R., & Timmer, M. P. (2015). The next generation of the Penn World Table. *The American Economic Review, 105*(10), 3150–3182.

Gruen, C., & Klasen, S. (2013). Income, inequality, and subjective well-being: an international and intertemporal perspective using panel data. *Jahrbuch Für Wirtschaftsgeschichte / Economic History Yearbook, 54*(1), 15–35.

Hamilton, J. D. (2017). Why you should never use the Hodrick-Prescott filter. *Review of Economics and Statistics*, Just accepted MS, available online, https://doi.org/10.1162/REST_a_00706, 1–25.

Heske, G. (2009). Volkswirtschaftliche Gesamtrechnung DDR 1950-1989. Daten, Methoden, Vergleiche. *Historical Social Research/Historische Sozialforschung, Supplement, 21*, 1–356.

Hodrick, R. J., & Prescott, E. C. (1997). Postwar U.S. business cycles: An empirical investigation. *Journal of Money, Credit and Banking, 29*(1), 1–16.

IMF. (2016). *World economic outlook database*. Retrieved July 2, 2017, from http://www.imf.org/external/pubs/ft/weo/2016/02/weodata/index.aspx

Inman, P. (2016, July 12). Irish economy surges 26% as revised figures take in foreign investment. *The Guardian, Business*. Retrieved June 29, 2017, from https://www.theguardian.com/business/2016/jul/12/irish-economic-growth-revised-figures-foreign-investment-aircraft

Kaiser, C. W., & Vendrik, M. C. M. (2018). *Different versions of the Easterlin Paradox: New evidence for European countries*. IZA DP No. 11994. Bonn: IZA.

Layard, R., Mayraz, G., & Nickell, S. J. (2010). Does relative income matter? Are the critics right? In E. Diener, J. Helliwell, & D. Kahneman (Eds.), *International differences in wellbeing* (pp. 139–165). Oxford: Oxford University Press.

OECD. (2017). *Level of GDP per capita and productivity*. Retrieved July 2, 2017, from https://stats.oecd.org/Index.aspx?DataSetCode=PDB_LV#

Opfinger, M. (2016). The Easterlin paradox worldwide. *Applied Economics Letters, 23*(2), 85–88.

Proto, E., & Rustichini, A. (2013). A reassessment of the relationship between GDP and life satisfaction. *PLoS One, 8*(11), 1–10.

Ravn, M. O., & Uhlig, H. (2002). On adjusting the Hodrick-Prescott filter for the frequency of observations. *The Review of Economics and Statistics, 84*(2), 371–376.

Sacks, D. W., Stevenson, B., & Wolfers, J. (2012). Subjective well-being, income, economic development and growth. In P. Booth (Ed.), *The pursuit of happiness: Well-being and the role of government* (pp. 59–97). London: The Institute of Economic Affairs.

Sacks, D. W., Stevenson, B., & Wolfers, J. (2013). *Growth in income and subjective well-being over time*. Mimeo.

Stevenson, B., & Wolfers, J. (2008). Economic growth and subjective well-being: Reassessing the Easterlin Paradox. *Brooking Papers on Economic Activity, 2008*(1), 1–87.

UNCTAD. (2017). *Gross domestic product: Total and per capita, current and constant (2005) prices, annual, 1970–2015*. Retrieved July 2, 2017, from http://unctadstat.unctad.org/wds/TableViewer/tableView.aspx?ReportId=96

Veenhoven, R. (2011). Trend average happiness in nations 1946–2010: How much people like the life they live. *Trend Report Average Happiness*. World Database of Happiness, Happiness in Nations. Rotterdam: Erasmus University.

Veenhoven, R., & Hagerty, M. (2006). Rising happiness in nations 1946—2004: A reply to Easterlin. *Social Indicators Research, 79*(3), 421–436.

Veenhoven, R., & Vergunst, F. (2014). The Easterlin illusion: economic growth does go with greater happiness. *International Journal of Happiness and Development, 1*(4), 311–343.

Vendrik, M. C. M. (2013). Adaptation, anticipation and social interaction in happiness: An integrated error-correction approach. *Journal of Public Economics, 105*, 131–149.

Wooldridge, J. M. (2003). *Introductory econometrics; A modern approach* (2nd ed.). Mason: South-Western Thomson Learning.

World Bank. (2017). *World Development Indicators*. Retrieved July 2, 2017, from http://databank.worldbank.org/data/reports.aspx?source=2

Chapter 3
Lottery Wins and Satisfaction: Overturning Brickman in Modern Longitudinal Data on Germany

Andrew J. Oswald and Rainer Winkelmann

Abstract Paradoxically, the published literature on the psychological consequences of lottery wins has found almost no evidence that winners become happier. This famous puzzle was originally documented by the psychologist Philip Brickman and colleagues. Using new German panel data, we offer results that are more in accord with common sense and economic theory. We have been particularly influenced by the pioneering work of Richard Easterlin: in this paper we explicitly consider the idea of 'domain' satisfaction levels. First, our estimates show that lottery wins raise people's satisfaction with their overall income. Second, lottery wins' increase people's satisfaction with life. The effects documented here are, as might be expected, especially pronounced for big wins. One of the advantages of our data set is that it allows access to a greater number of large winners than has typically been possible in the published literature.

3.1 Introduction

This paper reconsiders the evidence on the effect of winning the lottery on individual income satisfaction and happiness. It thereby ties in to several key contributions of Richard Easterlin's work: that material means and happiness are not necessarily the same thing; that it is possible to measure happiness (and therefore perhaps also utility as used by economists); that the study of domain satisfaction (for example, Easterlin and Swafanga (2009)) in addition to overall happiness can provide fruitful insights; and that empirical facts and data rather than normative judgments can be used to answer questions about the determinants of individual happiness.

A. J. Oswald
University of Warwick, Warwick, UK

IZA Institute for the Study of Labor, Bonn, Germany
e-mail: andrew.oswald@warwick.ac.uk

R. Winkelmann (✉)
University of Zurich, Zürich, Switzerland
e-mail: rainer.winkelmann@econ.uzh.ch

© Springer Nature Switzerland AG 2019
M. Rojas (ed.), *The Economics of Happiness*,
https://doi.org/10.1007/978-3-030-15835-4_3

Specifically, Easterlin (1973, 1974) pointed out that despite of a positive cross-sectional correlation between income and happiness at the individual level, no such correlation shows up in aggregate data on national income and happiness over time or across countries: raising the income of all seems not to increase the happiness of all. The co-existence of a positive relationship between income and happiness at the individual level and no such relationship at the aggregate level is referred to as the Easterlin paradox.

Quite soon after Easterlin's pioneering work, Brickman et al. (1978) questioned the evidence on the first part of the paradox, the nature of the cross-sectional relationship itself, by studying lottery winners. In principle, a positive association between individual income and happiness could result from confounders (such as health) or reversed causality (happier people are more productive and have therefore higher incomes) and hence not be truly causal. Winning in the lottery might provide exogenous variation in income, and therefore allow identifying the effect of material means on happiness.

Other papers have followed (e.g., Kuhn et al. 2011), and this literature has produced another kind of paradox, as it has failed to provide persuasive evidence that winners become happier. This could mean that the typical cross-sectional result of a positive effect of income changes on happiness is biased upward, due to omitted variables, such as prestige and status associated with higher income, to give one example. Or else, the entire idea of using income shocks from lottery events may not be useful for identifying the effect of other income, in particular earned income, since the psychological consequences may differ by source of income.

Yet another possibility, and the one we focus on in our paper, is that the absence of clear evidence for a positive effect of lottery wins on happiness, rather than indicating "evidence of absence", is related to data limitations of previous studies, in particular low power due to a shortage of observations of people with large wins. Our contribution is therefore twofold. First, we provide a detailed review of the aforementioned literature that studies lottery winnings to estimate the effect of exogenous income shocks on wellbeing. Second, using new German panel data, we reinvestigate the link between lottery winnings and life satisfaction, offering results that are more in accord with common sense and economic theory. We obtain statistically significant effects that are especially pronounced for large winners.

3.2   Summary of the Main Lottery Literature

The modern empirical literature begins with a famous paper by Brickman and colleagues in 1978. Brickman et al.'s (1978) investigation consists of two parts centered on testing the claims of the adaptation level theory using interviews. Adaptation-level theory states that, because of two effects (so-called 'contrast' and 'habituation'), individuals with very positive life events should not feel a lot happier. Essentially, when there is a major positive event in one's level, 'contrast' kicks in by reducing the pleasure from ordinary events, since the individual contrasts the ordinary event with the major positive event. Hence, the individual is not stimulated by mundane pleasures in the way he or she was before the win. Moreover, 'habituation' erodes the pleasure from the major event that occurred, since the thrill of winning the lottery erodes gradually over time. Thus, the individual's level of happiness does not change significantly from before the win. Similarly, these adaptation effects hold in the downward direction for individuals who face a traumatic experience.

The Brickman et al. results, first, supported the hypothesis that the people with major positive events were not happier than others; their pleasure from ordinary events was significantly lower compared to the others. Second, the authors argued that these results were not due to pre-existing personality types or the interview setting. Third, their study indicated a contrast effect in people with a traumatic life experience (accident disability) which idealized the past rather than enhanced their present pleasures.

The first study within the Brickman paper interviews three samples of people: a sample of paralyzed accident victims, a sample of lottery winners, and a control sample who were neither winners nor victims. The sampled numbers were small at 29, 22, and 22, respectively. The accident victims were interviewed as part of an earlier study with a response rate of 85%. They were all personally interviewed, face-to-face, by a female graduate student. The winners were selected with preference to larger amounts won and proximity to other winners to reduce travel-time for interviewers. The response rate was 52%. The names of the control sample were shortlisted from 88 people living approximately in the same areas as the lottery winners. Out of 58 attempted contacts, the response rate was 41%. The winner and control sample were interviewed by 11 two-person teams. Three teams consisted of 2 males, three consisted of a male and a female, and five consisted of 2 females. Each team interviewed 2 winners and 2 control respondents. Four of the controls and 6 of the winners were interviewed face-to-face, and the rest in each category were interviewed over the phone. The authors (Brickman et al. 1978) suggest that a breakdown of their data found no differences between the two methods of interviewing. The participation letter sent to each of the respondents before the interview differed between winners and controls, since, for controls, the letter did not state that the interview was about lottery research.

All respondents were asked their age, occupation, race, religion, and level of schooling. Winners were asked whether their life had changed since they won and, if so, how it had changed. Winners and victims were asked if they thought they deserved what happened, and also whether they ask themselves 'why me?'. They were asked to divide 100% across 4 potentially causal factors: themselves, others, the environment, and chance; and also asked to rate their win and accident, respectively, on a scale anchored by the best and worst things that happened in their lifetime. All respondents were required to rate how happy they felt at this stage of their life and how happy they expected to be 2 years further on. Also, for winners/victims, they were asked how happy they were before the win/accident, and, for controls, how happy they were 6 months ago. Respondents were asked to rate how pleasant they found each of seven activities or events: talking with a friend, watching television, eating breakfast, hearing a funny joke, getting a compliment, reading a magazine, and buying clothes, on a scale which ranged from 0 (lowest pleasure) to 5 (highest). The victims were not asked the last item on the list.

As for the background information, the victims were significantly younger than the other two groups with a p-value ≤ 0.001; otherwise, the samples were not different statistically. On a scale of 0–5 with 2.5 as the 'natural' neutral point, winners rated their win at 3.78 and victims their accidents at 1.78, p-value ≤ 0.001, distributed symmetrically around the mean. Winners found ordinary pleasures significantly less enjoyable than control groups with a p-value $= 0.011$. The authors suggested that victims also found ordinary pleasures less enjoyable although this was not significant at the 5%. This might be because of missing data points and a comparison category for the victims. Lottery winners and controls were not significantly different in their ratings of how happy they were now, before winning (or, for controls, 6 months ago), and as expected in a couple of years. The victims experienced a nostalgia effect where the past happiness was significantly higher than the controls, p-value ≤ 0.001. The current happiness of victims was significantly lower than the control group, p-value ≤ 0.01. Although the authors suggest that future happiness exhibited no significant differences, this may be due to age variation in the sample size. Younger respondents probably had better hope for the future than older ones; this can be supported by the fact that the paraplegics' current happiness, despite what happened to them, was still higher than the midpoint.

In the second study within the Brickman et al. (1978) paper, the authors argued that the results in the first part were not due to pre-existing personality differences between interviewees or interviewers. Given the fact that gamblers (lottery ticket buyers) are more optimistic and confident than non-buyers, one purpose of the second study was to ensure that the results in the first study were not because of such personality differences. Also, the emphasis on the lottery winners' win in study 1 might cause them to use their win as reference for comparison to ordinary pleasures when asked about it. As a result, a further aim of study 2 was to assess the effects on respondents' self-ratings of mentioning the lottery in the interview.

Out of a sample of 156 people who were approached, 86 responded. Randomly, 44 were assigned to the lottery scenario and 42 to the everyday-life scenario. Interviewers were teams of two, one male and one female, with interviews held over the phone. Each team interviewed an equal number of participants from each scenario. Questions were identical to those in study 1, except that respondents were asked to indicate if and how frequently they bought lottery tickets, when their most recent purchase had been, and how much money they won.

In the sample, 59 of the 86 bought a lottery ticket – indicating that the majority of the control group who were also drawn from the same population were mostly buyers. The authors (Brickman et al. 1978) suggest this as a reason to suppose initially that there are no personality differences across the controls and the winners. There were no significant differences across groups based on background measures. Also, buyers and non-buyers' differences in happiness (before, now and in the future) were not significant. Moreover, there was no significant relationship between ticket buying and type of cover story for any dependent measure and so is the case when using number of tickets bought (more or less than once a month) and how recent was the last purchase. The authors also showed that it was difficult for the differences in cover stories to alter the results in the first study.

In explaining the implications of their results, Brickman et al. (1978) advocate adaptation-level theory, as described above, with a slight modification. Instead of the accident victims gaining more happiness from ordinary pleasures as a result of contrast, the victims lose happiness due to a 'nostalgia' effect, by which they idealize their past. The authors acknowledge the very restricted size of their sample and that no serious attempt was made to control for background information. This study should, as a result, be viewed with caution.

Brickman and colleagues argue that past research has suggested that winning the lottery can strain relationships and be stressful. However, they say that lottery winners described winning as one of the best things that could happen and on top they did not like any non-social activity (e.g. reading a book) over a social one (talking to a friend). Another possibility is that lottery winners reported less pleasure to appear modest. However, lottery winners would have then mentioned the negatives of winning the lottery rather than reporting lower pleasurableness in ordinary day-to-day events. A third possibility is that the lottery win provided an extreme endpoint that changed the winners' pleasure ratings rather than the actual experience of winning. This seems doubtful because neither victims nor winners rated the accident/win as the worst/best thing that could happen to them. Thus, the authors conclude that what happens is not an alteration of the subjective scale but rather the contrast with previous experience.

To sum up, Brickman et al. (1978) advocated an adaptation-level interpretation of pleasure and happiness ratings by subjects who faced a major positive/negative event in their life. Although their sample size is too small to allow definitive conclusions, the study is suggestive. It has garnered a huge ensuing literature.

Gardner and Oswald (2007) analyse the effect of a monetary stimulus on the mental wellbeing of a typical individual. They use longitudinal data on a random sample of Britons who receive medium-sized lottery wins (as exogenous income shocks) of between 1000 and 120,000 pounds. Their results suggest that when compared to two control groups, one with no wins and the other with small wins, the winning individuals eventually exhibit significantly better psychological health. After 2 years, the average measured improvement in mental wellbeing is 1.4 GHQ points.

The authors use the British Household Panel Survey (BHPS), a nationally representative sample of more than 5000 British households, with more than 10,000 adults (above 16), interviewed yearly from 1991. The BHPS contains an internationally used indicator by researchers called the General Health Questionnaire (Likert scale which ranges between 0 and 36 with 0 as highest well-being and 36 as clinical depression). Medical opinion holds that healthy individuals normally score 10–13. Data on lottery winnings were also available. After adjusting for inflation using the consumer price index, and converting monetary amounts into 1998 pounds, the authors have data on lottery winnings and GHQ-scores between 1996 and 2003. To allow for lags, they use wellbeing data over 1998–2001.

Of 33,605 person-years observations, they divide their sample into people who have no wins (26,646 observations), small-size wins (4822 observations), and medium-size wins (137 observations). Comparing people on their levels of GHQ, they (Gardner and Oswald 2007) find that individuals who have no wins have a higher mean GHQ distress score of 11.23 when compared to those with small wins, who in turn have a worse GHQ score of 10.94, compared to those people with medium-sized wins, who have a GHQ score of 10.73. However, they suggest that it is more natural to compare on changes, rather than levels, to difference out individual fixed effects.

Given the small number of medium-size lottery win observations (137), and that there is some random fluctuation in GHQ scores, Gardner and Oswald suggest that it is not sensible to put a lot of weight on a complex statistical structure. Hence they start by examining the longitudinal changes graphically. First, and although the standard errors are large, when comparing medium-size winners' change in happiness (year before lottery win to year of lottery win) to small-size winners and non-winners, the authors find that mental stress is initially about 0.5 GHQ points greater in medium-size winners. Second, when comparing by using the change of GHQ score between the year before and the year after the lottery win, they conclude that individuals with medium-size wins have a decrease in their mental stress, while the other two groups are indistinguishable from each other. Third, when comparing using the change of GHQ score between 2 years before and after the lottery win, the authors show that people with no wins have a significant increase of 0.19 GHQ points, interpreted as an underlying rise in stress in Great Britain. The authors also find that people with small wins have an average change of 0.18, thus indistinguishable from non-winners. The key Gardner-Oswald finding is that people with medium-size wins have an average wellbeing improvement of 1.22 GHQ points. This holds in approximately the same way for both sexes.

This paper's result is thus in contrast with adaptation-level theory. Gardner and Oswald suggest that the time delay might be explained by the fact that what matters is spending the money (not saving it) and that most people save an income shock. Another interpretation is that, at the start of the income shock, individuals find it harder to concentrate on whatever they are doing – which is one of the criteria within the GHQ questions – because they are thinking of their win. As time passes, the individual becomes more focused on what they do, since they are not thinking of their win.

The authors (Gardner and Oswald 2007) then proceed to use regression analysis. They draw the conclusion that, after the addition of controls (gender, age, race, family status, employment and educational status and regional dummies) and using a balanced sample size of 25,902 observations, the reduction in mental stress after winning the lottery is still a significant 1.4 points approximately, using 2-years-before and 2-years-after the lottery win. They estimate another regression with the level of GHQ three periods ago as an extra regressor to control for habituation effects and with a smaller sample size of 18,104 observations. On doing so, the effect-size rises slightly to 1.8 GHQ points. Although the sample size is smaller, the t-statistic is above 3. Moreover, on dividing the sample size into two groups, the authors find the same effect manifesting itself, and hence the effect appears not to be a random occurrence in a small data set. The authors highlight one limitation of the dataset – a lack of information on how often people participate in the lottery – although they also argue that the similar results between the small-wins group and no-wins group indicate that there is perhaps little difference in the unobservable characteristics across participants and non-participants.

To conclude, Gardner and Oswald (2007) suggest that, in contrast to adaptation-level theory, individuals with medium-sized lottery wins' experience reduced mental stress as compared to people with small or no wins. They accept that their effective sample size is small (137 observations), but wish to argue that the effect is robust to controls and to different sub-samples. Hence, Gardner and Oswald conclude that income has positive consequences for the wellbeing of individuals. The authors do not attempt to estimate the income-shock effect on the different components of the GHQ questions.

Apouey and Clark's (2015) study has the aim of singling out the general self-assessed, mental and physical health effects of income. In doing so, the authors point to the puzzling nature of the possible causality between income and health. They discuss two issues with cross-sectional regression analysis in this context. First, they point out that there is a problem of reverse causality. Poorer health directly causes lower income through less working time, for example. Second, they argue that there might be a problem of endogeneity of income where variables such as the genetic endowment of an individual affects both that individual's income and health in a simultaneous way. Apouey and Clark propose a solution to this issue. Lottery winnings, which are exogenous positive income shocks, are used by the authors to investigate the income effect on self-assessed mental and physical health, as well as the effect of lottery winnings on risky behaviours, including smoking and social drinking.

The Apouey and Clark paper concludes that positive income shocks cause a significant mental-health improvement but a rise in risky behaviours – whereas no significant impact is seen on general self-assessed health. This suggests that the studies which showed higher income lead to better health likely suffer from endogeneity. Also, the results constitute a puzzle in that self-assessed general health is likely to be a function of both physical and mental health. The authors suggest that positive income increases from lottery winnings lead to an increase in people's smoking and social drinking, and this in turn has negative consequences for physical health. Thus, the net effect on health is insignificant.

Apouey and Clark (2015) use a British household panel survey, BHPS, which has approximately 16,000 individuals in recent waves. Households can enter and exit the survey, thus leading to an unbalanced data set. The authors use health data in waves 6–18 (1996–2008) and lottery data in waves 7–18 (1997–2008). BHPS includes information about individual and household demographics, mental and physical health, labour-force status, employment, and values. Using this information, the authors construct a set of measures that include the following.

First, BHPS has a number of health variables which facilitate the estimation of the effects of income on general, mental, physical health and health behaviours. The four main measures, used in the analysis, are: (a) a dummy taking the value 1 if individual reports that he is in 'excellent' general health, over the last 12-months when compared to people in the same age group, from a set of possible responses including 'excellent', 'good', 'fair', 'poor', and 'very poor'; (b) a measure of mental health given by a reversed Likert GHQ score where higher scores indicate higher levels of wellbeing on a scale of 0–36; (c) a dummy variable taking the value 1 when individual reports a specific physical health problem; and d) physical health behaviour is measured using three variables, the first is a binary variable taking the value 1 if individual is a current smoker, the second states the number of cigarettes smoked per day and the third is an ordinal variable describing the frequency with which individual drinks at a pub or a club.

Second, the lottery data appear, as noted earlier, in waves 7–18. Having adjusted for inflation via the consumer price index, and reported lottery winnings in 2005 pounds, the three measures used, by the authors, for lottery winnings are: (a) a dummy variable taking the value 1 if the individual achieved any lottery win since the previous year; (b) a dummy variable taking the value 1 if the individual achieved a lottery win over 500 since the previous year; and (c) demeaned logarithm of lottery prize.

The authors (Apouey and Clark 2015) suggest that although the use of BHPS lottery winnings data in studying effect of positive income shocks on health measures is advantageous due to the latter's considerable exogeneity, BHPS provides no direct information to distinguish between non-players and unsuccessful players, along with lacking the amount that was gambled by winners and playing non-winners. Such information is crucial in ensuring the statistical exogeneity of lottery winnings. That is because the underlying assumption is that players and non-players (and winners and non- winners) have the same characteristics. This assumption is potentially unrealistic since non-players are likely more risk-averse than players, or perhaps come from a particular religious' background. In both cases, these unobservable characteristics could influence health, and thus lead to endogeneity.

Third, and conforming to the existing literature, the authors use age, education, labour-market and marital status, logarithm of household income, regions and waves variables as controls in their regression models.

Three econometric strategies were employed by the authors to estimate the effect of lottery wins on health variables. Given the access to a panel dataset, all of the strategies included individual fixed effects to address the endogeneity of lottery winnings due to the lack of information on player participation. This controls for time-invariant sample heterogeneity.

The first regression type compared winning against non-winning observations after controlling for time-invariant sample heterogeneity and other individual characteristics. The regression took the format: $H_{it} = \alpha + \beta AnyWin_{i, t-k, t} + \gamma X_{i, t-k, t} + v_i + e_{it}$ with $k \geq 0$, where H_{it} is the health outcome at time t, $AnyWin_{i, t-k, t}$ is a dummy for winning any prize between $t - k$ and t, $X_{i, t-k, t}$ are the control variables measured before the win and v_i are individual fixed effects. The second regression compared larger winnings against smaller ones by including an extra dummy, $BigWin_{i, t-k, t}$. The coefficient on this dummy is thus the effect of a win above £500 over and above the effect of a win. The author's suggested that given the average wins are very small to impact health, if β persists in having a significant effect then this would mean that there are time variant sample heterogeneity which are not controlled for in the model. The third regression omitted the term in the former specification and included an interaction term, $AnyWin_{i,\ t\ -\ k,\ t} \times \log(prize)_{i,\ t\ -\ k,\ t}$. In all the specifications, the author's regressed health outcomes at t on the sum of prizes received between $t - k$ and t. The models were estimated for $k = 0$ to capture the immediate effect on health and for $k = 1, 2$ to allow time for the health investments to manifest. The number of observations in regressions of general, mental and physical health range between 80 K and 107 K approximately depending on the value of k used, however, the regressions which use risky behaviours including smoking and social drinking fall down to 18 K and 26 K approximately observations depending on the value of k used.

Across the different specifications and values of k, the effect of lottery wins on self-assessed general health was found to be insignificant and, in most cases, negative. This result was robust to alternative definitions of the dependent variable. The authors appeal to Ruhm's (2000) argument that self- assessed general health likely consists of physical and mental elements that can sometimes work in opposite direction to produce a net insignificant effect. Thus, they estimate the impact of lottery wins on mental and physical health as well as on risky behaviour.

The effect of the logarithm of the prize on the reversed Likert GHQ is shown to be positive. In other words, there is a benefit from winning. Moreover, for $k = 2$, greater wins have a statistically significant impact on individuals' mental wellbeing. This result is consistent with Gardner and Oswald (2007), and shows the robustness of the latter's results to number of waves, different specifications, and more control variables. Having decomposed the Likert GHQ into its separate indices, Apouey and Clark find that the impact in particular is more positive when the question relates to happiness. There is some evidence that there is a positive effect on sleep quality and absence of pressure when $k = 1, 2$ and ability to concentrate when $k = 0, 1$. Another overall life satisfaction score was used to check for robustness; the logarithm of the lottery winnings showed a significant effect between the logarithm of lottery winnings and overall life satisfaction. Contemporaneously, a one percentage point change in the prize winnings led to an approximately 0.02-point increase on a scale of 0–7.

The authors (Apouey and Clark 2015) find no significant effect on physical health, which may be because it is hard for money to change a long term disability or illness. With that in mind, the authors suggest that lottery wins can affect lifestyle choices, including participating in risky behaviour such as smoking and social drinking. Although their empirical results seem to suggest that lottery winnings do in fact increase smoking and social drinking, since the coefficients are positive and significant, they find a number of coefficients on $AnyWin_{i,t-k,t}$ to be significant.

To sum up, Apouey and Clark (2015), by building partially on the work of Ruhm (2000), perhaps demonstrate that health should not be aggregated into one index, since health outcomes are many and sometimes opposing. It finds empirically that self-assessed general health and physical health are not influenced by income shocks, whereas mental health is affected by income shocks. It argues that an explanation for the apparent paradox of the positive impact on mental health and no impact on self-assessed health is due to an increased participation rate in risky behaviours.

In a creative research paper, Kuhn et al. (2011) exploit a natural experiment in the Netherlands. The Dutch Postcode lottery (PCL) uses random selection of a weekly postal code, and distributes cash and a new BMW to participants in the winning postcode. In this way, the authors study the causal consequences of an income shock upon winners' and their neighbours' behaviour. Economic theory offers predictions concerning the effects of such shocks on household behaviour. First, the permanent income hypothesis suggests that agents should save most of their windfall income. Second, classical theory predicts that households who receive in-kind transfers (like motor cars) should treat them as cash. Third, one interpretation of the Easterlin hypothesis suggests that positive shocks to neighbours' incomes should reduce one's happiness. Lastly, Veblen effects suggests that shocks to neighbour's incomes should affect one's own consumption. Traditionally, these theories have typically been tested without access to natural experimental designs.

The Kuhn et al. results suggest that, consistent with the life-cycle hypothesis, the effect on winners' consumption is largely confined to cars and other durables. Also, consistent with the theory of in-kind transfers, the vast majority of BMW winners liquidate their BMWs. Lastly, PCL nonparticipants who have winning neighbours have significantly higher levels of car consumption than other non- participants.

The approach of Kuhn et al. (2011) in effect uses the PCL as an exogenous income shock to scrutinize the predictions of these theories. The authors argue that participants in non-winning postcodes are a valid counterfactual to participants in winning codes. Given that assumption, this allows them to test for the effect of temporary income shocks on winners' consumption and happiness. Similarly, non-participants in non-winning postcodes are then a valid counterfactual to non-participants in winning postcodes, which allows the authors to test for 'social' effects (what might be called relativity or envy effects) of income shocks on non-participating households' consumption and happiness. However, this approach implicitly assumes that participants and non-participants do not chose their postcodes on the basis of neighbours in the area. With this assumption, they suggest that their study of social effects has a partial-population design as opposed to a group-changing intervention which is contaminated by possible causal consequences of mobility.

The authors' study uses the weekly street prize, which is one of the prizes awarded by the PCL. Once a postcode is selected, a net-tax amount of Euro 9375 is awarded to the winner. Out of the winners, one is randomly selected to win a BMW. The number of tickets bought does not affect the probability of winning the monetary amount. However, the probability of winning a BMW is influenced by the number of tickets bought. The data were collected from September 2003 to July 2006 through surveys sent to all addresses of winning postcodes 6 months after winning and selected one or more neighbouring control postcodes who were asked to fill the same survey. 419 postcodes were surveyed with an average of 19 households per postcode. The survey contained questions on household composition, demographic variables, education, labour supply, happiness, car ownership, large expenditures, income and lottery participation. For some of the questions, households provided information on their behaviour before and after winning the prize. Participants were not told that the study is on post-PCL behaviour, but rather were told that it was a general expenditure and income study on Dutch households. Households were offered 7.5 euros to complete the survey. The response rate was 32.7%, and thus the final sample contains 2011 household observations. Of these, 510 were completed via telephone.

The data of the authors (Kuhn et al. 2011) do not make it possible to identify the average treatment effect for participants exactly, since it is impossible to observe a winner's potential consumption in the winning postcode area if there is no treatment (lottery win). Thus, the authors assume that potential consumption in the case of a winning postcode with no treatment is the same as in losing participant households. They rely on a similar assumption for the indirect treatment effect in the case of non-participant households. Since the survey is hosted 6 months after the win, the authors examined the Cadastre and Public Register Agency data on house sales to ensure that there are no significant differences in the number of home sales after the PCL prize draw between winning and non-winning addresses. To distinguish between winners and non-winners, the authors accessed more data from the PCL administration to identify non-respondent winners. In finding social effects, they identify neighbours using postcode units and other proximity measures (in meters) using the spatial (x, y) coordinates.

After ensuring the random selection of winning postcodes, and absence of response or recall bias using preliminary analysis and linear probability models, the authors find, with regards to participant households, significantly higher levels of awareness of winners in winning postcodes than in non- winning postcodes of winners – thus implying some social effects. Consistent with liquidity-constrained versions of the life-cycle consumption model, the authors (Kuhn et al. 2011) find that participants in winning codes are 4.5 times more likely to initiate major exterior home renovations and spent over 500 euros more on non-car durables than participants in non-winning codes. Also, the main cars of winning codes' participants are 13 months newer than non-winning participants. This is surprising since the average main difference is more than 6 months (the time of winning the lottery) implying that the difference between winning and non-winning is not the only factor which determines the age of the main car.

Although the authors (Kuhn et al. 2011) suggest that statistically-speaking BMW ownership is not different between the two groups, implying that BMW prizes were sold after the win, and thus treated it as cash, which is consistent with the theory of in-kind transfers, there is no data on whether non-winning participants had more BMWs than winning participants ex ante. In fact, lower car expenditure amongst the non-winning participants after the lottery as compared to the winning participants might even imply that they do not need to spend as much on a car. Also, although this behaviour of selling the BMWs that were won might reflect the theory of in-kind transfers, it might be a manifestation of a preference for other cars over BMWs across the Dutch public.

The authors (Kuhn et al. 2011) also document the fact that nonparticipant winners' neighbours acquired significantly more cars than other nonparticipants, own more cars, and have more total car-efficiency units. Also, after addressing endogeneity bias in the living-in-very-close-proximity to winners, they find that car-efficiency units are higher in houses within two doors from a winner as compared to more than two doors from a winner (though only at the 10% level).

Kuhn et al.'s (2011) regression analysis uses the equation $c_i + \alpha + \beta Winner_i + \gamma Winners$ $proximity + e_i$ with included code-group fixed effects and other household characteristics differences. Beta is thus the own effect of consumption and Gamma is the social effect of consumption (including the winners). The average treatment effect is a linear combination of gamma and beta. Also, the effect of the neighbours (an indirect income effect) is proportional to gamma. This framework allows for the testing of simple theoretical hypotheses.

The regression results reveal that the average treatment effect of winning 10,000 Euros in the PCL postcode lottery reduces the average age of a household's main car by 0.4 years and also raises expenditure on non-car durables. Intriguingly, the authors find that winning the PCL has no effect on a household's reported happiness 6 months after the event. This therefore appears to match ideas of adaptation-level theory and the empirical conclusions of Brickman et al. (1978). Nonetheless empirically, it is not compatible with Gardner and Oswald (2007). This might be explained by either the cultural differences between the Dutch and the Britons, or that Gardner and Oswald's BHPS data surveyed a longer time-frames than this study.

Perhaps the most surprising result in Kuhn et al. is that living in a winning postcode has no effect on household happiness. In particular, relative income differences do not have large effects on happiness. Similarly, and consistent with indirect treatment effects' results, regression estimates suggest that the social effects are in the two most visible areas of consumption to the neighbour: exterior home renovations and car consumption.

To conclude, Kuhn and colleagues (2011) used PCL data to find the own and social effects of a lottery income shock – one equal to 8 months of household income – on households' behaviour and self-assessed happiness in a natural-experiment setting. Their results seem to support the life-cycle income hypothesis in that people adjust the time of buying durables to smooth their consumption – and that BMW winners sell their BMWs according to the theory of in-kind transfers. They find positive robust social effects (what might be called Keeping up with the Joneses effects) on the car consumption of winners' neighbours. Lottery winning does not affect winners' happiness, nor does it affect their neighbours' happiness. The approach's advantage is the exogeneity of the income shock. The disadvantages are the lack of the data on household ownership and consumption before the lottery and the interpretation of some results like selling-BMWs behaviour since it might be a reflection of preference over cars. Their approach, however, suggests significant social-multiplier effects that can in principle be used by governments as an economy stimulus along with lines of the standard Keynesian multiplier.

Raschke (2015), like Apouey and Clark (2015), investigates the causal impact of large unexpected lottery income shocks on individual mental health, and physical health, as well as health behaviours. However, Raschke (2015) uses an individual-level panel dataset of lottery winners from Germany between 2000 and 2011, as opposed to the British data used by Apouey and Clark (2015). His contribution is to focus on mental health outcomes – previous research argues that it responds positively to income shocks – and to consider whether there are potential educational and financial-literacy biases in lottery analysis.

Raschke (2015) draws the conclusion that, first, mental health declines immediately after winning a large prize. This result, he argues, is driven by individuals with low education and low levels of financial literacy. Winners with little education, although they report being happier, experience increased role limitations, are more anxious, and have less energy after the win. The result is robust, statistically and economically significant, and persists for up to 2 years after the win. Interestingly, this finding, as the author suggests, is driven by an index relating to focusing on work in the mental health survey. This conclusion seems inconsistent with our interpretation of the results of Gardner and Oswald (2007).

Second, highly educated and financially literate lottery winners have mental and physical health levels that are not affected by their win. Lastly, winning the lottery is estimated to have no impact on individuals' health behaviour such as smoking and alcohol consumption, and to have no influence on physical health measures such as doctor visits, hospital stay or illness-related work absences.

Since lottery participation is endogenous, Raschke (2015) focusses only on winners, who are, by definition, also lottery participants. Using a nationally representative survey, he follows individuals over several years and observes when they win a substantial lottery prize, and their characteristics before and after the windfall. Assuming that the propensity to participate in the lottery over time is constant, the identified effect controls for time-invariant sample heterogeneity that might otherwise lead to endogeneity problems. Thus, he estimates $Outcome_{i,\,t} = \alpha_i + \beta Lottery_{i,\,t-1} + \delta x_{i,\,t} + \tau_t + \varepsilon_{it}$ where αi are individual fixed effects, $Lottery_{i,\,t-1}$ is dummy variable which is 1 if individual i won the lottery the year prior to the survey year, t, and zero otherwise. $x_{i,\,t}$ is a vector of time variant sample heterogeneity such as marital and employment status, household size and income, state-level unemployment rate, dummy for if country was in recession during year t, year dummies, τ_t, and month of interview in all specifications. It is important to note that year dummies are perfectly collinear with the recession dummy. He estimates the models collectively for all winners' data, as well as separately by high-education and low-education winners. He also examines the models separately for those who owned financial assets, such as stocks, before winning the lottery, as a proxy for financial literacy.

Raschke (2015) uses the German Socioeconomic Panel (SOEP) over the years 2000–2011. For the lottery data, respondents are asked whether they won an amount worth more than 2500, measured in year-2005 Euros, in a lottery context and are asked to specify the amount they won. There are between 13 and 28 lottery winners each year in the sample. The average amount won is 19,800 Euros, which is six times the average net monthly household income. Depending on the variables of interest, his regression equations are estimated for sample sizes between 250 and 2000 observations.

For the health outcome variables, the first measure is self-reported health status, using a 5-point scale from "Very Bad" to "Very Good". The author constructed two different variables for this measure; the first was a dummy for "Good" or "Very Good" (Good health) and the second was a dummy for "Bad" or "Very Bad" (Bad health). Since 2002, SOEP added a version of the 12- question Short Form Health Survey (SF-12) in every other survey year about current physical and mental health. Two summary measures are computed from the SF-12 responses: The Mental Component Scale (MCS) and the Physical Component Scale (PCS). Each is standardized to have a mean of 50 and a standard deviation of 10 with higher values of the MCS and PCS indicating a better state of mental and physical health. Third, several objective-health measures are used, including a dummy for the individual staying in hospital for any reason within the calendar year prior to the survey, the total number of nights stayed in the hospital, and the total number of doctor visits in the weeks before the interview.

Smoking behaviour is measured. It is captured by a value of one if individual regularly smokes cigarettes, pipes or cigars at the time of the interview, and zero otherwise. The data on this variable are not available for the years 2003, 2005, 2007, 2009 and 2011. Alcohol consumption is available for 2006, 2007 and 2010 as measured with a question on the frequency of respondents' alcohol consumption, with possible answers being "Never", "Sometimes" and "Frequently". Raschke (2015) creates a dummy variable which takes the value 1 for frequent alcohol consumption and zero otherwise.

Lottery wins and objective health measures are reported in the year before the survey win. General self-reported health, SF-12 questions and health behaviour questions correspond to the current situation of the respondent.

On estimating a linear probability model with the dependent variable of Good Health or Bad Health, Raschke (2015), first, finds no statistically significant effect of winning the lottery on reporting being in good health in the self-assessed health measure. This is consistent with Apouey and Clark (2015). However, second, winning the lottery increases the likelihood of a person reporting being in bad health, by around 8 percentage points, statistically significant at the 1% level. This result is inconsistent with Apouey and Clark (2015). Although it might reflect a reporting problem among the lottery winners, the second result documented by Raschke suggests that the mental component score (MCS) of the SF-12 declines immediately after winning the lottery, is statistically significant, and is equal to a 22 percentage reduction of a standard deviation. This implies that individuals who win the lottery face reduced mental health immediately after their win. The particular components in the mental scale which are affected are the vitality component, which relates to respondents' energy levels, and the mental health component, which relates to feeling run-down and melancholy.

To understand the apparent decline of mental health immediately following a lottery windfall, Raschke (2015) estimates the same equation after dividing the sample into two subgroups: high educational level (at least t Fachhochschulreife) and low educational level (at most Realschulabschluss). He finds that the negative impact of winning the lottery on self-reported general health and mental health is statistically significant only for low-education individuals. The high-education individuals have neither statistically nor economically significant estimates on their coefficients. A similar pattern to the initial result is noted when dividing the components of SF-12 between higher and lower educational groups with lower educational groups having negative significant estimates when the dependent variable is vitality, role emotional problems, and mental score. This is interpreted as the worry associated with winning the prize particularly among groups who do not know how to use it. This is particularly evident when using the financial asset ownership proxy for financial literacy. The group of people who do not own financial assets have a statistically significant 56 percentage of a standard deviation reduction in mental wellbeing and a statistically significant 10 percentage points increase in the likelihood of reporting being in bad health. The group who owned financial assets prior to winning show no statistically significant impacts of income shock on self-reported general health or the mental component score.

Third, Raschke (2015) finds that the effect of winning the lottery on the objective measures of health are all not statistically different from zero. Also, as expected due to weakness of the health behaviour variables, there is no statistically significant impact on smoking or drinking.

To check for robustness, Raschke (2015) estimates the first regression but considering the effect of winning the lottery on health outcomes at any time within the previous k year. He adopts this based on the preferred strategy of Apouey and Clark (2015). He considers the values of k equal to 1, 2 and 3. He documents that the effect of lottery winning on bad self-reported health, although significant at the 5%, declines within 3 years from around 8 percentage points to 4.4 percentage points. Across mental component score, the effect disappears in 3 years from a statistically significant 22% of a standard deviation to statistically being not different from zero. Thus, he says, the mental health effect of a lottery win disappears within 3 years of the lottery win.

In summation, Raschke (2015) exploits lottery data in Germany to assess the impact of exogenous income variation on self-reported general health, mental and physical health and health behaviours. His findings are that there is a negative impact of a lottery win on mental health, which contradicts the literature on British data. This is particularly true, he says, in the case of low-education individuals and the financially illiterate. Like Apouey and Clark (2015), he detects no significant impact of lottery winnings on objective health outcomes, and, using a particular specification for health behaviours, he draws the conclusion that there are no significant consequences of lottery winnings for health behaviours.

Cesarini et al. (2016) use administrative data on Swedish lottery players. The authors estimate the causal impact of substantial wealth shocks on players' own wellbeing and their children's health. Their study makes three methodological contributions to the literature: first, they observe factors conditional on which lottery wealth is randomly assigned and thus can extract the exogenous shocks alone; second, the size of the prize pool is almost $1 Billion, which is some orders of magnitude higher than any other lottery study; third, they can observe a large set of outcomes, some of which are realized over 20 years after the event, with arguably no missing observations.

Their results suggest that: first, in adults, there is no evidence that wealth influences mortality or health-care utilization, except that there is a reduction in the consumption of mental-health drugs. Second, their wealth- mortality estimates are one-sixth as large as the cross-sectional wealth mortality data. Third, in the intergenerational analyses, they find that wealth increases children's health-care utilization in the years following the lottery win; that it may reduce obesity risk; and that it has no other significant impact on children's outcomes. Lastly, their findings imply that in a country with an extensive social safety-net the causal effects of wealth are neither a major source of wealth-mortality gradients nor of the observed relationship between child developmental outcomes and household income.

Within the paper, Cesarini et al. (2016) conduct two analyses. In the adult analysis, the outcomes of interest are total and cause-specific mortalities. They report the impact of wealth on a number of hospitalization and drug prescription variables. The authors include some outcomes to address channels that have been hypothesized by epidemiologists on how low income can affect health, and in particular, cardio-vascular and mental health. In their intergenerational analyses, they study how wealth affects infant and child-health characteristics. They also examine scholastic achievement, cognitive and non-cognitive skills, and compare their results to cross-sectional estimates.

The authors' data are based on a pooled sample of lottery players. Their dependent variables are date and cause of death (for up to 24 years' post-lottery), cognitive and non-cognitive skills, BMI, GPA, and test score in mathematics, English and Swedish, in grade 9, inpatient hospitalization data, and drug purchases. They hold constant demographic variables including a third-order age polynomial, female dummy, born in a Nordic country dummy, income, college completion dummy, and marital and retirement status as controls. To compare their results to cross-section data they use wealth and income data.

They have three different kinds of lottery data. The first is on prize-linked savings accounts which hold draws for winners instead of paying interest, and give two types of prizes, one dependent on account balance and one independent of that. Data on it are available from 1986 to 1994. Second, there is the Kombi lottery, which is hosted by the Swedish Social Democratic Party, available since 1998. Thus, the sample is not nationally representative. However, its data has 40,336 observations with up to 46,024 controls and 462 large prizes. Lastly, the Triss lottery, run by the government, which gives out two types of prizes, one won in a lump-sum and one given monthly in 1994–2010. The authors also control for the randomization process through which the lottery assignment took place by adding cell fixed-effects in the regression for winners. Overall, their adult sample size is 439,234, including data from the various lotteries; and their children sample-size ranges between 20,000 and 100,000 approximately. Prize data are from below 10,000 SEK with 404,165 observations to above 1 million SEK with 2140 observations. $Z_{i, t-1}$.

In the adult analysis, they (Cesarini et al. 2016) run a regression of the post-lottery outcome variable of interest, $Y_{i, t}$, against the prize won in millions SEK, $P_{i, 0}$, a vector of cell fixed effects, $x_{i, 0}$, and a set of controls in the previous time period, $Z_{i, t-1}$, according to this equation $Y_{i, t} + \alpha_t P_{i, 0} + \beta_t x_{i, 0} + \gamma_t Z_{i, t-1} + e_{i, t}$ using OLS. In the intergenerational analysis, they estimate a similar regression distinguishing between children born pre-lottery and post-lottery, and restrict their sample to pre-lottery children only, since otherwise the effect of the lottery on fertility might affect their results.

Before running the regressions, the authors adjust the standard errors for independence. Although the approach they rely on has potential imperfect, by running Monte Carlo simulations they check, and argue, that it works appropriately. The authors find no evidence that lotteries were not randomly assigned. After adjusting for age, the authors argue that the sample contained in their data is nationally representative.

The adult results suggest that, in a cross section, estimates across time of the effect of wealth on mortality give negative coefficients; however, using the lottery data in a panel analysis, leads to a positive estimate of wealth on mortality when estimating the regression in 2001–2010. Also, over time the gradients in cross-section fall while in panel analysis the gradients rise. This implies that the unobservable that stops us from identifying the true effect of wealth on health is on the rise. When the authors (Cesarini et al. 2016) divide the mortality into different causes they find a significant impact at the 5% level only for the following causes: alcohol, circulatory disease, diabetes, ischemic heart disease, other, and respiratory disease. Their results are robust to different sub-populations and removing extreme prizes. On estimating the proportional hazard model for efficiency of the estimators, they find a similar pattern.

With regards to health-care utilization, Cesarini et al. (2016) use inpatient care (available from 1987 onwards) and consumption of prescription drugs (available in 2006–2010). They have a number of variables including hospitalization for at least one night, a health index (predicts 5-year mortality risk, ranges between 0 and 100, higher values imply poorer health), total drug consumption, and drug consumption due to mental health. Only the latter outcome variable, drug consumption due to mental health, registered a significant negative wealth effect at the 5% level. Greater wealth due to exogenous lottery shocks reduced consumption of mental health-related drugs.

In the intergenerational analysis, Cesarini et al. (2016) show that, out of 18 health outcomes for children, including infant health data, body mass data, drug consumption data and hospitalization data, only one measure of BMI is potentially influenced by lottery shocks, at the 5% level. This does not survive sensitivity analysis. Thus, it is interpreted with caution – as a 1 million SEK lottery win increases the probability the child of the winner is obese by 2.1 percentage points approximately. The effect of lottery shocks on drug consumption of children in four categories (ADHD, asthma and allergy, mental health and all drugs less the first three categories and contraceptives) is statistically not different from zero. Similar to adults, using inpatient data due to a number of diseases for being hospitalized for at least 1 day, these are repeated for being hospitalized for at least 1 week. The results imply that a 1 million SEK positive wealth shock leads to a 2.1% increase in hospitalization within 2 years and 3.4% increase within 5 years.

With regards to developmental outcomes, the authors report six outcome variables: cognitive and non-cognitive skills, GPA in grade 9 and grade 9 tests in mathematics, Swedish and English. The effect of a wealth shock on all these variables is insignificant statistically, with the exception of cognitive skills which is affected by wealth income shock which is very slightly significant. In all the cases, the household health-wealth gradient seems to be exaggerated. However, health effects of wealth are substantially lower in their study. They suggest that this is because of a number of reasons including heterogeneity, estimating difficult-to-model substitution effects instead of true ones, and smaller prizes.

To sum up, Cesarini et al. (2016) use lottery-winners' data from Sweden to try to discover the effect of exogenous wealth shocks upon players' own health and upon their children's health and developmental outcomes. The authors' methodological contribution is to control for the lottery assignment and thus be able to leverage exogenous shocks in their analyses. Their excellent data source seems to point to a direction for further research, perhaps for a heterogeneous sample of countries. The study's results suggest that there is barely any income effect on health of children, and that, amongst adults, lottery wins appear only to reduce the consumption of mental-health-related drugs.

3.3 New Empirical Evidence on the Link Between Lottery Wins and Wellbeing

In the following, we provide new empirical evidence on the effect of winning in the lottery on well- being. The empirical specification is similar to the ones employed earlier by Gardner and Oswald (2007), Apouey and Clark (2015), and Raschke (2015). As in the latter, we use data from the German Socio-Economic Panel. However, we deviate from the previous literature in a number of ways: our outcome variable is "financial satisfaction" and not just overall "life satisfaction". We have access to more winners with economically substantial winning amounts than almost any other study before us. And we can bring to the table evidence from a supplementary survey that allows us to analyse how people self-select into lottery play.

3.3.1 Data

The empirical analysis is based on two types of sub-samples from the German Socio-Economic Panel (SOEP). First, we use longitudinal information on lottery winnings from the core survey, for the period 2000–2014. In 2000, the SOEP started including a question asking whether the household had received a lottery win during the previous year. The reporting threshold was initially set at DM 5000 or above (corresponding to 2500 Euros). In 2005, it was lowered to 500 Euros.

During the period 2000–2014, there were 617 people living in a household where such a win was reported at least once. In an earlier stage of this project (reported in Oswald and Winkelmann 2008), we had only access to data up to 2007. The additional 7 years of data allow us to report much more precise estimates here.

This arguably is the best dataset to date to study the effect of lottery windfalls on satisfaction: it is a longitudinal, representative household survey, and thus allows implementing an estimation strategy based on within-subject variation. Moreover, it has a sizeable number of large wins. For example, 67 people experienced a lottery win of a size exceeding the average net annual household income in the sample.

However, there are also some shortcomings.

- Selection into playing: we know who wins but we do not know who plays. In the main analysis, we focus on the time path of life satisfaction of individuals in households with at least one registered win. For these household, we know for sure that they participated in the year where they won. But neither do we know whether this was the case also in the other years, nor do we know how much money was spent on lottery tickets.
- We study life satisfaction of individuals but observe wins for households. Under the assumption that resources are equally shared within the household, it should not matter, who within the household actually played and won, but we do not have any direct evidence regarding the validity of this assumption.
- We do not know the exact date of the lottery win, only the year when it took place. In year t, respondents are asked to report lottery wins during the last calendar year, $t-1$. Thus, depending on the day and month of the interview, a considerable amount of time (in theory between 1 and 23 months) can have passed since the actual event and the reporting of life satisfaction.

In sum, there are a number of factors suggesting that measurement error may be relevant. Combined with small sample sizes, this will make it difficult to detect true effects of lottery wins on life satisfaction, if there were any. Perhaps this is one reason why prior studies have been inconclusive.

Our response is that, first, we can now benefit from a sample that has become bigger over time, as additional waves of the SOEP have added lottery winnings every year. Second, we provide supplementary evidence on potential non-random selection into playing from a secondary data source, the 2014 innovation sample of the SOEP. This is a cross-section survey where a special sub-module on lottery play was included. Questions asked were the frequency at which individuals participate in lotteries (at least once a week; at least once or twice per month; only a few times per year; never), the amount spent on buying tickets during the previous month, and whether they ever won a prize of at least 1000 Euros. In total, we have this purely cross-sectional information for 5868 persons.

3.3.2 The Sample of Winners

To construct the sample of winners, we proceed in two steps. First, we identify all households with a reported lottery win in any of the years under consideration, between 2000 and 2014. The exact wording of the question is as follows: "Did you or another member of the household receive a large sum of money or other assets (car, house, etc.) as an inheritance, gift, or lottery winnings last year?". Second, we extract information on all adult respondents in that household, in the year of reporting a win as well as for the years before and after. Information includes standard socio-economic indicators as well as two outcome measures, satisfaction with household income as well as overall life satisfaction.

Table 3.1 shows selected summary statistics for the sample of winning households in the year of their reported win. In total, there were 617 lottery wins reported in the 15-year period. In a few instances, the same winning amount was reported in two consecutive years, likely an instance of recall error, and we kept only the first of the two. In other cases, the respondents declared multiple windfalls in the same year (from winning the lottery, gifts as well as inheritances). These observations were dropped because it would not be possible to single out the lottery effect, if any, in such cases.

The second column shows that the number of observed lottery wins is reduced to 342 if only winning amounts above 2500 Euros are considered. This information comes from 166 households, with an average of 2.1 responses per household.

Table 3.1 Sample composition and descriptive statistics

Year	Number of person	amount > 2500 euros[a]	Number of households	Average amount	Average annual household income[a]
2000	36	34	16	9881.30	31,973.10
2001	18	18	9	7539.90	32,251.10
2002	25	20	9	99,992.50	38,693.30
2003	42	34	15	21,043.40	37,336.40
2004	25	20	8	5502.40	37,012.00
2005	43	25	13	8350.90	35,840.60
2006	58	33	14	10,117.00	34,907.60
2007	43	23	10	5169.00	34,690.10
2008	53	17	8	11,293.40	34,464.50
2009	32	17	10	6631.10	34,354.00
2010	40	17	9	21,205.80	34,159.00
2011	58	23	13	69,342.00	34,054.20
2012	38	22	11	10,457.90	34,324.40
2013	44	17	8	5810.50	33,649.10
2014	62	22	13	19,255.80	34,512.70

Source: German Socio-Economic Panel 2000–2014

[a]Income excludes lottery wins, inheritances and gifts. All amounts are in real (2010 = 100) Euros

From Table 3.1, we see that the average winning amount was above 20,000 Euros. Although this is far below the million dollar wins one typically associates with winning "big" in the lottery, it does constitute a significant fraction of average annual income, slightly under 60% for our sample of households.

The total estimation sample is larger, as we include also the non-winning years for all individuals living in a household with at least one win. This allows us to implement a within-subject research design. We determine the effect of winning in the lottery by following these individuals' life satisfaction before and after the win, in the spirit of an event-history-analysis. While the sample of winners is selected (as not everyone in the population plays the lottery and thus can be observed as a winner), the event of winning per-se is presumably random. In our estimation sample, individuals in a winning household are present in our dataset for an average of 9.7 years, leading to a total of 3305 (342 × 9.7) person-year observations. In regressions with a lag structure, the number of available observations is reduced accordingly.

3.3.3 The Decision to Play

Our secondary dataset allows us to provide some suggestive evidence on the selection into lottery participation from a cross-sectional point of view. Of the 5858 respondents, 75.2% and thus the vast majority never play in the lottery (see Table 3.2). Among the remaining quarter, the distribution of intensity is bimodal: 11.8% of the population, or 42% of players, participate at high frequency, at least once per week, 4.2% at least once or twice per month and the remaining 8.8% only a few times per year.

The frequency of play is also mirrored in the average amount spent on lottery tickets in the last month. This amount is 34 Euros in the high frequency group, falling to 19.5 in the medium frequency and to an average of 6 Euros in the low frequency group. Finally, and as expected, past winnings correlate with the frequency of play. 23% of respondents in the high frequency group report having won

Table 3.2 Descriptive statistics (n = 5858)

Frequency of playing lottery	%	% ever won	Amount spent last month
At least once a week	0.118	0.229	34.41
		(0.016)	(1.57)
At least once or twice per month	0.042	0.082	19.50
		(0.018)	(1.37)
Only a few times per year	0.088	0.072	6.09
		(0.011)	(0.42)
Never	0.752	0.022	0
		(0.002)	

Source: German Socio-Economic Panel, Innovation Sample 2014

Table 3.3 Socio-economic characteristics by frequency of play

	Weekly	Sometimes	Never
Household net monthly income	2811.9	2623.9	2764.1
	(59.15)	(50.35)	(25.14)
Male	0.586	0.562	0.448
	(0.019)	(0.018)	(0.007)
Age	61.17	50.87	50.4
	(0.506)	(0.560)	(0.286)
Employed	0.446	0.629	0.533
	(0.019)	(0.018)	(0.008)
Unemployed	0.026	0.062	0.051
	(0.006)	(0.009)	(0.003)
School grade: low	0.418	0.294	0.292
	(0.019)	(0.017)	(0.007)
School grade: intermediate	0.303	0.311	0.302
	(0.018)	(0.017)	(0.007)
School grade: high	0.060	0.064	0.064
	(0.009)	(0.009)	(0.004)
School grade: university entrance	0.147	0.181	0.205
	(0.013)	(0.014)	(0.006)
German nationality	0.972	0.926	0.946
	(0.006)	(0.009)	(0.003)
Married	0.634	0.536	0.527
	(0.018)	(0.018)	(0.008)
Satisfaction with household income	6.936	6.343	6.714
	(0.084)	(0.085)	(0.035)
Satisfaction with life	7.581	7.367	7.463
	(0.062)	(0.058)	(0.026)
Observations	689	761	4408

more than 1000 Euros at some point in the past. This proportion falls to 8% among the less frequent players and to 2% among those who (currently) do not play.

Given that most people do not play the lottery, one would expect that the group of players might be distinct, in terms of socio-economic characteristics, from those who do not play. Table 3.3 compares the means of standard socio-economic control variables for the two groups of the population. Mainly, those who play in the lottery are older, more likely to be male, more likely to be married and have somewhat less education than those who do not participate in lottery play.

The average household income does barely differ between the two groups, nor does average life satisfaction or satisfaction with household income. We take this as evidence that conditional on age, gender and education, there may not be much additional selection on unobservables. A more formal analysis based on a multivariate life satisfaction regression follows below, but we first sketch out our empirical framework.

3.4 Econometric Specification and Results

Consider the following specification for estimating the impact of winning the lottery on (financial or life) satisfaction:

$$S_{it} = \theta_t + \delta lottery\ win_{i,t-1} + \gamma \log house\ income_{i,t-1} + \beta x_t + \alpha_i + \varepsilon_{it} \qquad (3.1)$$

Here, lottery win can be either a binary dummy variable ($yes = 1$) or a set of dummies interacting the win with amount brackets (under 10 K, 10–40 K, 40–100 K, above 100 K). x_{it} is a vector of time varying individual characteristics such as marital status, employment status, and self-rated health. The specification also includes year dummies. Standard errors are clustered at the individual level.

In Eq. (3.1), δ is the effect of interest. It is the effect of winning for the sub-population of those who play in the lottery. After all, it is logically impossible to win in the lottery without first participating in it. Identification of δ requires the absence of selection effects. While winning in the lottery conditional on participation, and on intensity of play, is random, the act of taking part in lottery gambles, and the amount of tickets bought, may be endogenous and correlated with other unobserved determinants of life satisfaction.

With panel data we can control for time-invariant confounders. For example, if lottery players were intrinsically less happy than non-players, we could identify δ from a within-subject design, where the life satisfaction in a year following a win is compared to the life satisfaction in a year without one, all for the same individual.

However, confounding may be time-varying as well. For instance, a negative life event in $t - 1$ may prompt people to start playing in the lottery, increasing their chances to draw a winning ticket. With some persistence in the negative event, $Win_{i,\ t-1}$ and ε_{it} can be negatively correlated, leading to an underestimation of the effect of a win on life satisfaction.

A similar, and potentially important, bias would result if people consider the money spent on tickets as a negative (see Kim and Oswald 2017). A higher amount of spending will, of course, increase the chances of an actual win, again leading to a negative correlation between $Win_{i,\ t-1}$ and ε_{it} unless the unobserved amount spent is constant over time.

On the other hand, it seems plausible that the very act of buying tickets has a consumption value. Otherwise, it would be hard to explain why so many people take part in lotteries although the expected return is known to be negative. In that case, a larger amount (or at least a non-zero amount) spent on tickets, while increasing the chances of a win, might actually have a direct positive effect on life satisfaction, in terms of excitement and anticipation. If a person has not bought a ticket, that person cannot dream of a Ferrari or a round-the-world trip.

Yet another explanation for a positive correlation would be that there is an unobserved confounder rooted in personality, call it "optimism", which correlates positively both with life satisfaction and with participation in lotteries.

3.4.1 Life Satisfaction and Lottery Participation

One way to address the case for or against selection bias uses our cross-sectional data to estimate the association of intensity of play with life satisfaction.

Table 3.4 shows results from three regressions, one without controls, just frequency of play (this essentially reproduces the mean life satisfaction values of Table 3.3), a second one with controls, and a third one with controls and the amount of money spent on tickets added. Life satisfaction is the dependent variable.

Suppose that winning the lottery is considered the "treatment". Then Table 3.4 provides the "intention-to-treat" (ITT) effects. The difference between ITT and actual treatment is determined by luck, but a more intensive "intention" will make it more likely that a win occurs. Of course, that is where the analogy to typical RCTs ends, because we obviously do not claim that the assignment to intensity is necessarily random, nor do we rule out a-priori that the assignment per-se can have an effect on satisfaction (like a placebo would have).

In fact, winning (and in particular winning "big") is such a rare event that any ITT almost surely stems from reasons other than actual winning, i.e., from selection or direct effects. While the point estimates seem to suggest that those who play weekly are positively selected, or have a direct utility from doing so, and thus report a higher life-satisfaction, the observed differences turn out to be within the normal margin-of-error.

The last row shows the p-values of the F-statistic for the null hypothesis that lottery participation has no effect on life satisfaction. Based on the models with individual characteristics, the null hypothesis of no ITT cannot be rejected. There is some selection on observables: age, education and gender do matter for life satisfaction, and also for lottery participation. Keeping these factors constant, there is not much left, and we are led to conclude that from the point of view of playing and life satisfaction, selection is not a first-order issue in models that include these controls.

Table 3.4 Life Satisfaction and Frequency of Play (OLS)

Frequency of play (reference: weekly)	(1)	(2)	(3)
Once or twice per month	−0.211 (0.1211)	−0.1236 (0.1229)	−0.1533 (0.1233)
A few times per year	−0.214 (0.0939)	−0.1418 (0.0931)	−0.2034 (0.1017)
Never	−0.117 (0.0672)	−0.0710 (0.0684)	−0.1516 (0.0822)
Value			−0.0023 (0.0014)
Individual characteristics	No	Yes	Yes
Observations	5855	5519	5491
Prob > F	0.0975	0.4628	0.2669

Source: German Socio-Economic Panel, Innovation Sample 2014. Robust standard errors in parentheses

3.4.2 Winning in the Lottery and Satisfaction with Income

Main results on the effects of lottery wins on income satisfaction are shown in Table 3.5. All effects of interest are statistically significant. The log income coefficient is close to unity. Including fixed effects reduces the lottery coefficient by one third from 0.30 to 0.19, but it remains statistically significant. According to this model, a lottery win in year $t-1$ is thus worth about the same as a 20% increase in income.

From Table 3.1, we know that the average winning amount is about 60% of average annual income. Not surprisingly, the model predicts a larger income-satisfaction boost from a 60% income increase than from winning the same amount in the lottery. For one, lottery wins are one-off payments, whereas household income, as far as it comes from labour earnings or government transfers, is more permanent. Second, and relatedly, the win occurred during the previous year, and part of the income windfall has likely already been spent and is no longer being felt at the time of the interview.

The last column of Table 3.5 splits the effect by size of the win. This split trades off precision of estimates with additional information on effect heterogeneity. For

Table 3.5 Effect of lottery winnings on satisfaction with income

	(1)	(2)	(3)	(4)
Lottery win$t-1$	0.298	0.188	0.202	
	(0.105)	(0.089)	(0.09)	
Lottery win$t-2$			0.139	
			(0.088)	
Amnt$t-1 \leq 10000$				0.148
				(0.106)
$10,000 <$ Amnt$t-1 < 40,000$				0.294
				(0.181)
$40,000 <$ Amnt$t-1 < 100,000$				−0.051
				(0.333)
Amnt$t-1 \geq 100,000$				1.203
				(0.365)
Log household income$t$	1.085	0.993	0.981	0.984
	(0.181)	(0.141)	(0.142)	(0.142)
Number of observations	2970	2970	2970	2970
Fixed effects	No	Yes	Yes	Yes
Further individual characteristics	Yes	Yes	Yes	Yes

Source: German Socio-Economic Panel, own calculations. Cluster robust standard errors in parentheses. Individual controls include employment status, marital status, self-assessed health, and household size; "Amnt" is the reported size of the win

The third column of Table 3.5 probes into the longer-term effects of a lottery win, by including information regarding a lottery win 2 years ago. The $t-1$ effect increases slightly in size, and remains statistically significant, whereas the $t-2$ effect, while also positive, is smaller in magnitude and not statistically significant, providing evidence, also not really surprising, that the positive effect of winning in the lottery fades away with time

instance, the point estimate for a winning amount below 10 K is close to a tenth of effect of winning more than 100 K (no win at all is the reference). The former effect is insignificant, the latter statistically significant at conventional levels. Hence, there is evidence, as to be expected, that the overall effect is driven by those individuals who won a large amount of money in the lottery. Also, this pattern may help to explain why previous studies with data on mainly small winnings had difficulties to find reliable effects.

3.4.3   Winning in the Lottery and Life Satisfaction

Results for overall life satisfaction are shown in Table 3.6. The patterns remain similar, although magnitudes tend to be smaller. This is most pronounced for the estimated effect of household income: it is close to unity in the domain satisfaction equation and now drops below 0.2 in the life satisfaction equation. These point estimates, here marginally significant, are similar to those reported in the previous literature.

The consequences of winning in the lottery are reduced much less, to about 0.14 in the models with fixed effects, with a t-ratio of about 2. Thus, in relative terms, the lotto effect gains in prominence relative to the estimated effect of earned and transfer income. When splitting the effect up by amount, we find a monotonic relationship: the biggest effect is present for people who won an amount of 100 K or above in the previous year. Their reported life satisfaction is estimated to be increased by 0.5 on

Table 3.6 Effect of lottery winnings on overall satisfaction with life

Lottery win_{t-1}	0.182	0.145	0.135	
	(0.082)	(0.071)	(0.073)	
Lottery win_{t-2}			0.139	
			(0.088)	
$Amnt_{t-1} \leq 10000$				0.097
				(0.085)
$10,000 < Amnt_{t-1} < 40,000$				0.217
				(0.169)
$40,000 < Amnt_{t-1} < 100,000$				0.321
				(0.228)
$Amnt_{t-1} \geq 100,000$				0.502
				(0.204)
Log household income$_t$	0.262	0.171	0.179	0.167
	(0.148)	(0.105)	(0.106)	(0.105)
Number of Observations	3000	3000	3000	3000
Individual fixed effects	No	Yes	Yes	Yes
Further socio-economic characteristics	Yes	Yes	Yes	Yes

Notes: see Table 3.5

the 0–10 scale relative to non-winners. These results highlight the importance of having access to data that include large lottery wins. Lacking such a sample, it is not surprising that most of the previous literature has been inconclusive, although the findings of Brickman et al. (1978) remain a puzzle. It may be that Brickman and colleagues simply did not get a representative set of lottery winners.

3.5 Summary and Conclusions

We hope that this paper may offer a partial solution to the famous empirical puzzle that lottery winners do not seem to be happier than non-winners. Our results are consistent with the first part of the Easterlin paradox – that individual with higher financial means are happier in the cross-section, and also over time, in a longitudinal perspective.

Having established in this analysis a positive effect of lottery winnings, at least sizeable ones, on life satisfaction a year later, it would be useful for future research to focus more on the dynamic effect of the lottery win. For this, more precise information on the time of the win would be required, in addition to sampling winners' information at different periods post-lottery, ideally at a sub-annual frequency, to try to disentangle the players' slow changes in mental health and wellbeing. Also, due to the participation bias that arises in lotteries, the effects that all the previous papers estimate relate to lottery participants. This might be unrepresentative. Thus, other natural experiments must eventually be explored to ensure the robustness of the results presented in this line of research.

References

Apouey, B., & Clark, A. E. (2015). Winning big but feeling no better? The effect of lottery prizes on physical and mental health. *Health Economics, 24*(5), 516–538.

Brickman, P., Coates, D., & Janoff-Bulman, R. (1978). Lottery winners and accident victims: Is happiness relative? *Journal of Personality and Social Psychology, 36*(8), 917–927.

Cesarini, D., Lindqvist, E., Ostling, R., & Wallace, B. (2016). Wealth, health, and child development: Evidence from administrative data on Swedish lottery players. *Quarterly Journal of Economics, 131*(2), 687–738.

Easterlin, R. A. (1973). Does money buy happiness? *The Public Interest, 30*(3), 3–10.

Easterlin, R. A. (1974). Does economic growth improve the human lot? Some empirical evidence. In P. A. David & M. W. Reder (Eds.), *Nations and households in economic growth: Essays in honour of moses Abramovitz* (pp. 89–125). New York: Academic.

Easterlin, R. A., & Swafanga, O. (2009). Happiness and domain satisfaction: New directions for the economics of happiness. In A. K. Dutt & B. Radcliff (Eds.), *Happiness, economics and politics: Towards a multi-disciplinary approach* (pp. 70–94). Cheltenham: Edward Elgar.

Gardner, J., & Oswald, A. J. (2007). Money and mental well-being: A longitudinal study of medium-sized lottery wins. *Journal of Health Economics, 26*(1), 49–60.

Kim, S., & Oswald, A. J. (2017). *Does winning the lottery make people happier?* Unpublished paper, Singapore Management University.

Kuhn, P., Kooreman, P., Soetevent, A., & Kapteyn, A. (2011). The effects of lottery prizes on winners and their neighbors: Evidence from the Dutch Postcode Lottery. *American Economic Review, 101*(5), 2226–2247.

Oswald, A. J., & Winkelmann, R. (2008). *Delay and deservingness after winning the lottery* (Working paper No. 0815). Socioeconomic Institute, University of Zurich.

Raschke, C. (2015). *Unexpected windfalls, education, and mental health: Evidence from lottery winners in Germany* (Working paper). Sam Houston State University.

Ruhm, C. (2000). Are recessions good for your health? *Quarterly Journal of Economics, 115*(2), 617–650.

Chapter 4
Relative Income, Subjective Wellbeing and the Easterlin Paradox: Intra- and International Comparisons

Arthur Grimes and Marc Reinhardt

Abstract We extend the Easterlin Paradox (EP) literature in two key respects. First, we test whether income comparisons matter for subjective wellbeing both when own incomes are compared with others within the country (intra-national) and with incomes across countries (inter-national). Second, we test whether these effects differ by settlement-type (rural through to large cities) and by country-type (developed and transitional). We confirm the intra-national EP prediction that subjective wellbeing is unchanged by an equi-proportionate rise in intra-country incomes across all developed country settlement-types. This is also the case for rural areas in transitional countries but not for larger settlements in those countries. International income comparisons are important for people's subjective wellbeing across all country-settlement-types. Policy-makers must therefore consider their citizens' incomes in an international context and cannot restrict attention solely to the intra-national income distribution.

4.1 Introduction

The issue of inter-personal comparisons affecting people's utility has long been a vexed one in economics (Veblen 1899; Duesenberry 1949). Easterlin (1974) brought the issue of inter-personal comparisons to the forefront, providing evidence that an increase in a single citizen's income increases his or her welfare, while a proportionate increase in all citizens' incomes leaves all welfare levels unchanged. This 'Easterlin Paradox' implies that policies that strive to increase the incomes of all citizens by an equal proportion is up against a 'Prisoners Dilemma' in which people

A. Grimes (✉)
School of Government, Victoria University of Wellington, Wellington, New Zealand

Motu Research, Wellington, New Zealand
e-mail: arthur.grimes@motu.org.nz

M. Reinhardt
University of Bologna, Bologna, Italy

© Springer Nature Switzerland AG 2019
M. Rojas (ed.), *The Economics of Happiness*,
https://doi.org/10.1007/978-3-030-15835-4_4

strive to increase their income but the end result is to leave all citizens no better off in welfare terms.

Much of the work on the Easterlin Paradox, however, ignores two important aspects that we address. First, only rarely do studies address the issue of whether people also form relativistic comparisons against citizens in other countries. Second, only rarely do studies differentiate according to the size of settlement within a country. One branch of the wellbeing literature studies whether rural residents are happier than city residents, ceteris paribus, but these studies do not take account of relative income issues.[1]

We bridge these two branches of the literature, testing whether rural attitudes to relative incomes differ from urban attitudes, both for within and across country relativities. At a theoretical level, it may be that rural residents are happier than their urban counterparts because their isolation means that they are less negatively affected by the (higher) incomes of others either within the country or across countries. Conversely, urban residents in mobile societies may become happier by observing others' higher incomes if it provides a signal that they too may aspire to higher incomes as a result of the opportunities that a vibrant urban centre affords (a phenomenon known as the 'tunnel effect').

Using European and World Values Survey data, we confirm that individuals' life satisfaction (subjective wellbeing) rises as their personal income rises and falls as the incomes of similar individuals within their own country rise. This occurs across all settlement-types (rural through to large city) and for both country-types considered (developed and transitional). The intra-national predictions of the Easterlin Paradox are confirmed for all developed country settlement-types plus transitional country rural areas, but not for non-rural settlement-types in transitional countries. Notably, we find that inter-national income comparisons are important for individuals' subjective wellbeing across all country- and settlement-types. This extends the findings of Becchetti et al. (2013) who found a similar result but just for developed countries and without testing for settlement-type. We show that while inter-national income comparisons are important across all country and settlement types, the effect is smaller for transitional country large cities, consistent with a type of tunnel effect. Finally, when we include a full set of controls, we find no differences in life satisfaction across settlement sizes in either country-type, consistent with the presence of spatial equilibrium.

This set of results takes both the Easterlin Paradox literature and the rural-urban life satisfaction literature in new directions, highlighting factors that need to be considered in evaluating how incomes affect life satisfaction at the levels of the individual, the settlement and the country. Section 4.2 provides a brief review of relevant literature and, based on this literature, outlines our testing methodology. In Sect. 4.3 we detail our data. Section 4.4 provides the results of our tests, while Sect.

---

[1]A related area of research examines spatial patterns in regional wellbeing outcomes (Okulicz-Kozaryn 2011). We do not do so since, while our data indicates settlement size of respondents, it does not identify respondents' specific regions.

4.5 discusses the implications of our results for the complex relationships between income and personal wellbeing across settlement and country types.

4.2   Related Literature and Methodology

4.2.1   Life Satisfaction and Subjective Wellbeing

It is now widely accepted that policy-makers' objective functions should incorporate broad measures of wellbeing when making policy choices (Stiglitz et al. 2009; Easterlin 2010; Layard 2011; Helliwell et al. 2013). One such measure – that we use in this study as an indicator of subjective wellbeing – is life satisfaction.

The psychological literature has long used subjective wellbeing measures as valid indicators of human happiness (Diener et al. 1999; Di Tella and Macculloch 2006; Kahneman and Krueger 2006; Clark et al. 2008; Dolan et al. 2008). Economists' increasing acceptance of subjective wellbeing as a valid outcome measure rests, in part, on the correlation between subjective wellbeing and objective measures of wellbeing and utility such as migration flows and health outcomes (Deaton 2008; Oswald and Wu 2010; Grimes et al. 2014). There is also support for the validity of subjective wellbeing measures from neuroscience studies (Ekman et al. 1990; Frey and Stutzer 2002; Kahneman and Krueger 2006; Layard 2011) while tests of measurement consistency across people and across time validate use of life satisfaction scores as a (noisy) measure of subjective wellbeing (Frey and Stutzer 2002; Layard et al. 2008; Krueger and Schkade 2008). Given this evidence, life satisfaction of individual i (LS_i) is typically treated as a function of (unobserved) utility u_i plus a random additive term, v_i.

4.2.2   Easterlin Paradox

Easterlin (1974) found a paradox in the relationship between GDP, income and subjective wellbeing: (i) within countries, richer people are more satisfied with their lives than are poorer people; (ii) richer countries tend to be, on average, happier than poorer countries; however, (iii) over time, subjective wellbeing at the national level does not rise with income. The Easterlin Paradox implies that if each individual in society becomes richer by the same degree then no individual is any better off (in subjective wellbeing terms) than they were prior to their income increasing.

One possible explanation of the paradox is a process of adaptation to income over time whereby increased income increases aspirations commensurately so that income does not increase happiness in the long run (Duesenberry 1949; Brickman and Campbell 1971; Di Tella et al. 2010). A second explanation is the 'Relative Income Hypothesis' by which people derive utility from income in relation to other groups (Duesenberry 1949; Van Praag and Kapteyn 1973; Kapteyn et al. 1978;

Luttmer 2005). The importance of choosing an appropriate reference group is highlighted by a range of studies starting with Festinger (1954). Commonly, the average income for people with a given set of characteristics shared by the individual is used as the appropriate relative income (y^*) in the utility function. Thus life satisfaction may be modelled as Eq. (4.1):

$$LS_{it} = u_i(y_{it}, y^*_{it}, \mathbf{x}_{it}) + v_{it} \tag{4.1}$$

where y_{it} is person i's own income, y^*_{it} is person i's reference group income, and $\mathbf{x}_{it}$ is a vector of other (non-pecuniary) determinants of utility (for example age, gender, marital status) of person i, each in period t.

Depending on the nature of the environment, reference groups may not always impose a negative effect on subjective wellbeing. Senik (2008) found that in stagnant and immobile countries ('old Europe'), higher relative income has negative effects whereas in countries with higher degrees of mobility (e.g. post-transition European countries), reference income signals potential future income gains and so is viewed positively.

Stevenson and Wolfers (2008, 2013) find that income is correlated with life satisfaction at all income levels, and find evidence that the gains are larger at higher income levels. Furthermore, they find that similar coefficients are shared by the relationship between income and life satisfaction at the cross country and at the domestic level, and find that changes in economic growth are (positively) associated with changes in subjective wellbeing. (For a contrary view, see Layard et al. 2009; Helliwell et al. 2013) The Stevenson and Wolfers results, if taken at face value, suggest another hypothesis: that relative income effects might operate at both the national and the international level. The extension of reference income to other nations was suggested by Clark et al. (2008, equation 3, p. 102). The literature on the importance of inter-national relative income is sparse despite evidence that macroeconomic variables have real effects on individuals' subjective wellbeing (Di Tella et al. 2003). One study that explicitly tests the hypothesis that other countries' national income can have reference group effects is Becchetti et al. (2013). They find that people in developed European countries compare their material standard of living with living standards in other countries; the closer the country, the greater is the (negative) effects on own life satisfaction of an increase in other countries' incomes. Two natural extensions of Becchetti et al. are to test firstly whether inter-country comparison effects are similar for developed countries versus transitional economies, and secondly whether the social comparison effects are similar across the type of settlement (rural through to large city) within countries.

4.2.3 Rural Versus Urban Life Satisfaction

A growing body of work investigates how life satisfaction varies between rural and urban areas but there is, as yet, no consistent set of established findings. Cantril

(1965), and subsequently Veenhoven (1994), established that life satisfaction was approximately equal in rural and urban areas of developed countries; however, in developing countries, life satisfaction in urban areas exceeded that in a country's rural areas. Berry and Okulicz-Kozaryn (2009) contrasted rural locations against large cities finding that rural and urban life satisfaction was approximately equal in a group of ('Latin') developed countries whereas Anglo-Saxon developed countries showed higher rural than urban life satisfaction. Individuals in developing Asian cities experienced higher life satisfaction than their rural counterparts but in other developing countries, there was no significant difference between rural and urban life satisfaction. Morrison (2011) found results consistent with those of Berry and Okulicz-Kozaryn for New Zealand (an Anglo-Saxon developed country), but Kettlewell (2010) found a contrary result for Australia where female (but not male) rural-to-urban-movers experienced an increase in life satisfaction up to 4 years following their move. Easterlin et al. (2011), using Gallup Poll data, found substantially greater life satisfaction in urban relative to rural areas within developing countries but found that these differences disappear in developed countries. They show that the rural-urban life satisfaction divide in developing countries can largely be explained by differing occupation structures, incomes and education levels. In contrast, Drichoutis et al. (2010), using data for non-Anglo-Saxon European countries, found that both happiness and life satisfaction is higher in rural than in urban locations.

Two lacunae are apparent in this range of spatial studies. First, as suggested by Morrison (2014), internal migration should play a spatial arbitrage role in evening out life satisfaction differences across settlement types within countries. The reasons why this may not occur are still at issue (Glaeser et al. 2014). Second, given the large literature on interpersonal comparisons, life satisfaction differences between rural and urban areas may reflect differing emphases placed on income (or other) relativities in different areas. For instance, one may hypothesise that if rural areas are more immobile than urban areas, then rural residents may be more prone to making interpersonal comparisons than their urban counterparts who may be more likely to have positive tunnel effects. This may be the case both for within and across country comparisons. Conversely, the paucity of close neighbours in rural areas may reduce the salience of social comparisons relative to the situation in urban areas. We bring the inter-personal relativity effects (at both intra-national and inter-national levels) face-to-face with the rural-urban wellbeing literature to test whether the strength of inter-personal comparisons differs across spatial types, distinguishing between developed country versus transitional economy responses.

4.2.4 Methodology

We adopt an encompassing theoretical framework in which we start with an extended form of the generic utility function in Eq. (4.1). Specifically, we hypothesise that life satisfaction of individual i in settlement-type s (discussed further below) within country j at year t (LS_{isjt}) is a function of their own real (CPI-adjusted) income ($OwnIncome_{isjt}$), the mean income of a reference group within their own country in the same year ($RelGNDI_{isjt}$), and the per capita (PPP-adjusted) Gross National Disposable Income (GNDI) of their country relative to a mean of comparator country GNDI ($RelGNDI_{jt}$), plus a vector of personal characteristics (x_{isjt}),[2] country fixed effects (β_j) and wave fixed effects (τ_t).

The country fixed effects account for the effect of (unchanging) country institutions (Veenhoven 2009) and for any systematic tendency to report higher or lower life satisfaction based on country of residence. Wave fixed effects refer to the specific wave of the World Values Survey. Each of $OwnIncome_{isjt}$, $RefIncome_{isjt}$ and $RelGNDI_{jt}$ is expressed in natural logarithms (as in Stevenson and Wolfers 2008; Easterlin et al. 2010; Diener et al. 2013). We test whether the coefficients on $OwnIncome_{isjt}$ and $RefIncome_{isjt}$ are of equal and opposite signs, in which case the Easterlin Paradox holds within countries. We also test if the coefficient on $RelGNDI_{jt}$ is positive; if it is positive, an increase in a country's GNDI relative to those of its international comparators, *ceteris paribus*, raises the life satisfaction of its residents.

We differentiate our estimates based on whether the individual resides within (i) a founding OECD member country versus a transitional economy (indexed by $k = 1$, 2 respectively); and (ii) whether the individual lives in one of four types of settlement: rural, town, small city or large city (indexed by $s = 1, 2, 3, 4$ respectively). Thus we estimate 8 parameters (2 country-types by 4 settlement-types) for each of our main variables of interest. This enables us to test hypotheses not only about the Easterlin Paradox and international comparisons, but also whether responses of life satisfaction to the income variables are identical across country- and settlement-type. We include settlement size intercept dummies (δ_{sk}) for each country type (large cities ($s = 4$) are the base category). These dummy variables enable us to test whether any settlement type differences in life satisfaction (across each country type) remain once all other factors in the equation are accounted for. We do not (and cannot) include separate intercept dummies for transitional versus developed countries since we already include country fixed effects which, *inter alia*, account for this distinction in country-type.

Our base equation is therefore of the form:

$$
\begin{aligned}
LS_{isjt} = \boldsymbol{\alpha}X_{isjt} + \beta_j + \tau_t + \sum_{s\neq4}\sum_k \delta_{sk} + \sum_s\sum_k \varepsilon_{sk}OwnIncome_{isjt} \\
+ \sum_s\sum_k \theta_{sk}RefIncome_{isjt} + \sum_s\sum_k \gamma_{sk}RelGNDI_{jt} + \mu_{isjt}
\end{aligned}
\tag{4.2}
$$

where μ_{isjt} is the residual term that, inter alia, includes the v_{it} random additive term.

---

[2]We control for a quartic polynomial in age (Clark et al. 1996), marital status (married, divorced, widowed, cohabiting, separated), employment status (unemployed, full-time worker, part-time worker, retired, house-spouse, self-employed, student), gender, and gender interacted with the other controls. Education controls (relating to eight different education levels) are included in all but one regression.

Life satisfaction (the dependent variable) is measured on an ordinal (1–10) scale. While this would normally suggest the use of a limited dependent variable estimation technique such as ordered logit, prior studies (e.g. Ferrer-i-Carbonell and Frijters 2004; Luttmer 2005) show that OLS estimation produces similar results in terms of signs and significance of variables to ordered logit results. We test the robustness of this common finding by estimating the equation both by ordered logit and by OLS, producing consistent results across the two estimation methods. Given this finding, and the simpler interpretations enabled by OLS estimation, we concentrate principally on the OLS results, but also include our fullest specification estimated using ordered logit. We also subject the estimation of (4.2) to a range of other robustness tests, discussed in Sect. 4.4. The OLS estimation approach may result in heteroskedastic errors, while the inclusion of *RelGNDI* in the regression introduces observations that are common to all respondents within a country. In addition, error terms within a country may be correlated given cultural similarities within countries. All estimates therefore use robust, country clustered standard errors.

4.3 Data

We utilise life satisfaction, income and personal characteristics data from four waves of the European Values Survey (EVS), supplemented with compatible World Values Survey (WVS) data for 1990–2009.[3] Data for life satisfaction comes from the question: *"All things considered, how satisfied are you with your life as a whole these days?"* Respondents are asked to respond on a 1–10 integer scale with 1 denoted "dissatisfied" and 10 "satisfied".

For household income data, we drop all country-wave survey responses in which interpretation of responses is unclear or where necessary information is not available. In all other cases, we code country and wave specific income observations as the midpoint of the corresponding income category.[4] We source CPI indices from the IMF World Economic Outlook Database and real GNDI per capita (at purchasing power parity) from the AMECO (European Commission) database.

Our country sample is chosen to include established developed countries, for which our definition is that the country had to be a founder member of the OECD. Given the literature on the wellbeing versus income relationship in transitional countries, we include a group of transitional middle-income countries, six of which have joined the OECD since 1994; the remaining five are middle-income

---

[3]The EVS data are publicly available from *http://www.europeanvaluesstudy.eu*; see EVS (2011). Wave 1 is not considered due to a lack of data. Grimes and Reinhardt (2015) provide more detail on data cleaning procedures, especially with respect to income.

[4]Reflecting the approach of Donnelly and Pol-Eleches (2012), we code income in the (unlimited) top band as the lower bound plus half the band-width of the second highest band. Use of other imputation techniques for this income category result in very little change to any of our findings.

Table 4.1 Countries and waves

	2	3	4	5	Total
OECD Founding Countries					
Australia	1414	1214	0	1246	3874
Belgium	1705	1532	0	1354	4591
Canada	1461	1714	1735	0	4910
Denmark	0	902	0	1038	1940
France	0	1292	882	1359	3533
Germany	0	1553	0	1796	3349
Great Britain	1101	0	803	691	2595
Greece	0	910	0	1276	2186
Ireland	893	802	0	389	2084
Italy	1422	1513	672	956	4563
Netherlands	779	910	0	1307	2996
Portugal	1124	676	0	807	2607
Spain	2262	805	0	946	4013
Sweden	0	654	952	1098	2704
Turkey	0	1185	0	1440	2625
United States	1644	1127	1180	0	3951
Sub-Total	13,805	16,789	6224	15,703	52,521
Other Transitional Countries					
Bulgaria	0	942	0	1327	2269
Croatia	0	971	0	1293	2264
Czech Rep.	0	1719	0	1414	3133
Estonia	0	884	0	1326	2210
Latvia	0	954	0	1295	2249
Lithuania	0	848	0	1267	2115
Macedonia	0	1022	0	1439	2461
Malta	0	715	0	420	1135
Mexico	1443	999	1418	0	3860
Slovakia	0	1232	0	1143	2375
Slovenia	0	648	0	818	1466
Sub-Total	1443	10,934	1418	11,742	25,537
Total	15,248	27,723	7642	27,445	78,058

Wave 2 dates: 1990–1991
Wave 3 dates: 1998–2003
Wave 4 dates: 2004–2007
Wave 5 dates: 2008–2009

European countries. We drop any country that has only one wave of data to enable inclusion of country fixed effects. This process results in inclusion of 27 countries across 4 waves with 68 cross-sections that include 78,058 individual observations. Of the 27 countries, 16 are OECD founder members and 11 are classed as transitional (other) countries.

Table 4.1 lists the countries, waves and number of observations in each country-wave. Wave 2 includes 10 OECD founders but only one transitional country. This

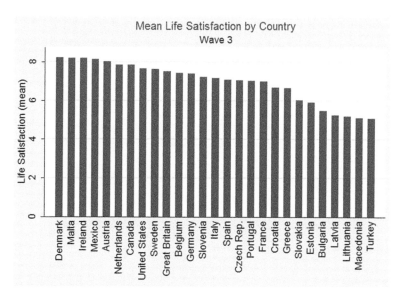

Fig. 4.1   Mean Life Satisfaction by Country (Wave 3)

wave is also problematic in its omission of education data for individuals. Education is significant in equations that include just waves 3–5; for this reason, wave 2 is included in only one of our regressions which we use to test the robustness of our main results.The above table should have an extra line above the line starting 'Australia' which reads: OECD Founding Countries   [This should appear in an equivalent fashion to the line half-way through the table which reads: Other Transitional Countries]

Figure 4.1 graphs mean life satisfaction by country for wave 3 (which includes data for all our countries other than Great Britain) plus mean life satisfaction for Great Britain averaged over waves 2 and 4. Life satisfaction in most transitional countries is below that of most founder OECD countries with the exception of three outliers: high life satisfaction for both Malta and Mexico, and low life satisfaction for Turkey and, to a lesser extent, Greece. (In our estimates, country fixed effects account for systematically high or low life satisfaction in particular countries). Figure 4.2 shows a strong relationship between (wave 3) life satisfaction and the logarithm of GNDI per capita (at PPP).

We construct $OwnIncome_{isjt}$ as the log of (CPI-adjusted) income of individual respondent i. $RefIncome_{isjt}$ is the log of the mean income of similar individuals within a country for each wave, where a similar individual is defined as one of the same gender, age (divided into age bands: <25, 26–35, 36–45, 46–55, 56–65, 65+) and employment status.

The relative national income variable ($RelGNDI_{jt}$) is defined as the log GNDI per capita (at PPP) of the individual's country (country j) for a given year minus the log of the EU15 mean GNDI for that year. Use of the exact year is important both to

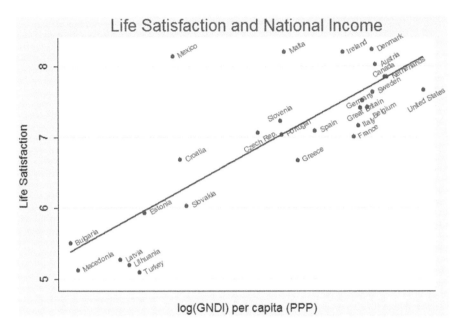

Fig. 4.2 Life Satisfaction and log(GNDI per capita at PPP) (Wave 3)

include the appropriate GNDI for each individual and to ensure year to year fluctuations in the comparator country GNDI data within waves so allowing for inclusion of wave dummies that are not perfectly collinear with comparator country GNDI. As well as using EU15 GNDI as our international comparator, we test robustness by variously using US GNDI and the mean of EU15 and US GNDI as the international comparator with very similar results. Figures 4.3 and 4.4 graph *RelGNDI* for each of the country sub-sets for the period 1990–2009 showing considerable cross-country variation in *RelGNDI* for both country sub-sets.

The EVS/WVS offers 8 categories for settlement size. We undertook a series of pairwise comparison tests of life satisfaction in each settlement type (without controls) and could not reject a grouping that collapses each successive pair into a single category. Thus the four settlement size groupings that we use in this study are defined as:

1. Rural: population under 5000 people
2. Town: population between 5000 and 20,000 people
3. Small City: population between 20,000 and 100,000 people
4. Large City: population over 100,000 people.

Figure 4.5 graphs mean life satisfaction by settlement size for each of the founder OECD sample and the transitional (other) country sample. The graphs cover all four waves for all eligible samples. Consistent with prior literature, the raw data (without controls) indicate that mean life satisfaction in OECD founder large cities is lower

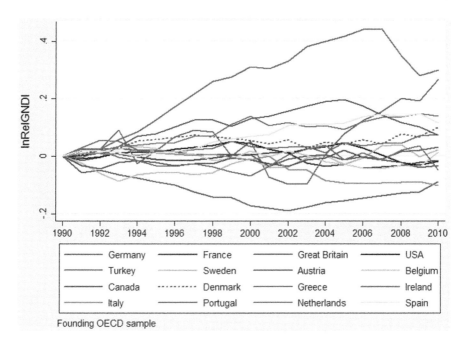

Fig. 4.3 RelGNDI for OECD Founder Countries

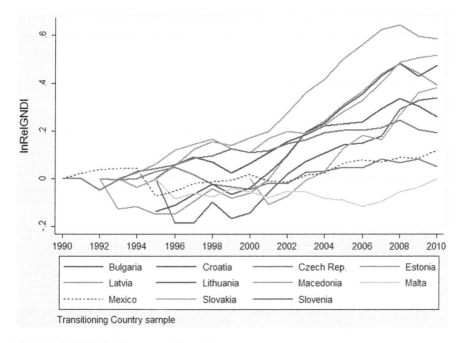

Fig. 4.4 RelGNDI for Transitional Countries

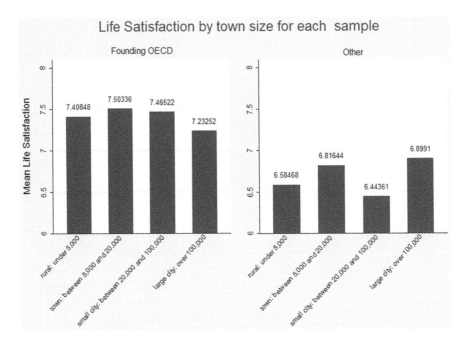

Fig. 4.5 Mean Life Satisfaction by Settlement-Type

than in all other settlement-types, while life satisfaction in transitional country large cities is higher than in all other settlement-types.

4.4   Results

Our prime focus is to estimate Eq. (4.2), testing hypotheses about intra-national and inter-national comparative income effects across country- and settlement-type. We begin, however, with a simpler set of (OLS) equations (presented in Table 4.2) that ignore the settlement size dimension so providing a baseline for the subsequent results that differentiate by settlement-type.

In all equations presented in Tables 4.2 and 4.3, we allow the income coefficients to differ between the OECD founders and the transitional countries. Any variable with a "Trans" suffix is the interaction of the prefixed variable with a dummy variable for transitional country status; thus the total effect of the prefixed variable on life satisfaction for a transitional country is the sum of the two variables with the same prefix.

Column [1] in Table 4.2, estimated over waves 3 to 5, is our simplest equation that relates each individual's life satisfaction just to their own income, with no reference group effects included. Personal characteristics (including education) are,

Table 4.2 Life satisfaction equations by country-type (excluding settlement-type)

Dependent variable: Life satisfaction	[1]	[2]	[3]
OwnIncome	0.126**	0.356***	0.349***
	(0.047)	(0.045)	(0.043)
OwnIncome-Trans	0.113	0.0868	0.0882
	(0.0829	(0.084)	(0.083)
RefIncome		−0.270***	−0.354***
		(0.043)	(0.049)
RefIncome-Trans		0.0043	0.0724
		(0.095)	(0.092)
RelGNDI			4.161***
			(1.184)
RelGNDI-Trans			−2.131*
			(1.157)
Constant		9.257***	9.844***
		(0.884)	−0.922)
Observations	62,383	62,383	62,383
No. of Countries	27	27	27
Waves included	3–5	3–5	3–5
Wave fixed effects	Y	Y	Y
Country fixed effects	Y	Y	Y
Education controls	Y	Y	Y
Other personal controls	Y	Y	Y
Estimation method	OLS	OLS	OLS
R^2	0.176	0.18	0.187

Life satisfaction is measured on a 1–10 scale
"*Trans*" interaction variables provide estimates for transitional countries relative to founder OECD countries
Robust standard errors clustered by country in parentheses; *** $p < 0.01$, ** $p < 0.05$, * $p < 0.1$
Other personal controls comprise a quartic polynomial in age, marital status (4 categories plus 1 omitted), employment status (5 categories plus 1 omitted), education (7 categories plus 1 omitted), gender, and gender interacted with the other controls

however, controlled for. The equation indicates that an individual's life satisfaction is enhanced by an increase in *OwnIncome*, with a 10% increase in income resulting in a 0.012 increase in life satisfaction points (within the 1–10 life satisfaction scale). Individuals in transitional countries have a higher estimated life satisfaction return to an increase in their *OwnIncome* of 0.023 life satisfaction points (consistent with decreasing marginal utility of income) but the difference relative to OECD founders is not statistically significant.

Column [2] adds each individual's intra-national reference income. Again, we find no significant differences between transitional countries and OECD founders for either variable. The coefficient on *RefIncome* is negative (and almost identical for both sets of countries) while the coefficient on *OwnIncome* is positive and greater in absolute value than that for *RefIncome* (more so in transitional countries). For each

Table 4.3 Life satisfaction equations by country-type including settlement-type

Dependent variable: Life satisfaction	[4]	[5]	[6]	[7]
Rural (<5K)	0.113	−0.867	−0.0485	0.636
Town (5-20K)	0.115	0.859	0.844	2.68
SmallCity (20-100K)	0.0568	−0.229	0.963	0.62
Rural-Trans	−0.342**	0.643	0.0354	1.57
Town-Trans	−0.284*	0.0596	−0.488	0.931
SmallCity-Trans	−0.284**	−0.0103	−0.740**	1.029
*OwnIncome*Rural*		0.379***	0.356***	1.383***
*OwnIncome*Town*		0.327***	0.357***	1.309***
*OwnIncome*SmallCity*		0.327***	0.315***	1.301***
*OwnIncome*LargeCity*		0.364***	0.380***	1.352***
*OwnIncome*Rural-Trans*		0.0725	0.12	1.029
*OwnIncome*Town-Trans*		0.0631	0.0721	1.052
*OwnIncome*SmallCity-Trans*		0.159**	0.191**	1.125*
*OwnIncome*LargeCity-Trans*		−0.0203	−0.0497	0.956
*RefIncome*Rural*		−0.376***	−0.318***	0.723***
*RefIncome*Town*		−0.354***	−0.357***	0.745***
*RefIncome*SmallCity*		−0.335***	−0.306***	0.764***
*RefIncome*LargeCity*		−0.362***	−0.363***	0.742***
*RefIncome*Rural-Trans*		0.0393	−0.131	1.074
*RefIncome*Town-Trans*		0.119	−0.0309	1.118
*RefIncome*SmallCity-Trans*		0.0302	−0.110**	1.036
*RefIncome*LargeCity-Trans*		0.186	−0.0119	1.201*
*RelGNDI*Rural*		4.160***	2.154*	27.86***
*RelGNDI*Town*		4.300***	2.217*	30.68***
*RelGNDI*SmallCity*		3.926***	2.041*	21.91***
*RelGNDI*LargeCity*		4.235***	2.258**	28.55***
*RelGNDI*Rural-Trans*		−1.853	0.0436	0.237
*RelGNDI*Town-Trans*		−2.188*	−0.229	0.175
*RelGNDI*SmallCity-Trans*		−1.947	−0.123	0.233
*RelGNDI*LargeCity-Trans*		−2.555**	−0.665	0.140*
Constant	7.523***	10.07***	8.992***	n/a
Observations	62,383	62,383	77,630	62,383
No. of countries	27	27	27	27
Waves included	3–5	3–5	2–5	3–5
Wave fixed effects	Y	Y	Y	Y
Country fixed effects	Y	Y	Y	Y
Education controls	N	Y	N	Y
Other personal controls	N	Y	Y	Y
Estimation method	OLS	OLS	OLS	OLogit
R^2	0.117	0.188	0.168	n/a

Life satisfaction is measured on a 1–10 scale

"*Trans*" interaction variables provide estimates for transitional countries relative to founder OECD countries

"*Rural, Town, SmallCity, LargeCity*" variables provide estimates by settlement-type, defined by population size

LargeCity is the omitted category for the settlement-type intercept variables

*** $p < 0.01$, ** $p < 0.05$, * $p < 0.1$ using robust standard errors clustered by country

Odds ratios presented for ordered logit (OLogit) in column [7]

Other personal controls are as listed below Table 4.2

country sub-set, a Wald test rejects the Easterlin Paradox (at $p < 0.05$), so that an equi-proportionate rise in all incomes results in an estimated rise in life satisfaction (albeit considerably tempered by the impact of reference incomes).

Column [3] is the counterpart of Eq. (4.2) excluding settlement type, with international income comparisons now included. Again we find that the coefficients on *OwnIncome* and *RefIncome* are positive and negative respectively. Considering just these terms, a Wald test shows that we cannot reject the Easterlin Paradox (at $p < 0.05$) for OECD founder countries, but we again reject it for the transitional countries. The latter is consistent with an (attenuated) tunnel effect in lower income nations.

A rise in a country's real GNDI relative to other countries has a substantial effect on individual life satisfaction. A 10% increase in an OECD founder country's *RelGNDI* increases life satisfaction for individuals in that country by 0.40 points. The effect is smaller in transitional countries (with the difference being statistically significant at the 10% level); in these countries the effect of a 10% increase in *RelGNDI* is for an increase in life satisfaction of 0.19 points. The smaller effect in transitional countries is again consistent with a tunnel effect.

For developed countries, column [3] indicates that the Easterlin Paradox holds within countries but not across countries. If a country becomes richer (poorer) relative to its international counterparts, the life satisfaction of its residents rises (falls). Furthermore, this inter-national reference income effect has a much greater impact on life satisfaction than would the same percentage rise in an individual's own income (ceteris paribus). This result is consistent with that of Becchetti et al. (2013). We extend these results to the case of transitional countries. Here we find that the reference group effects are attenuated relative to those for developed countries. In particular, the intra-national Easterlin Paradox result no longer holds, while the inter-national reference income effect is less marked – though still present – compared with developed countries.

In Table 4.3 (which retains the standard star system for significance, but drops standard errors to keep the table manageable), we add the settlement dimension. Equation [4] in Table 4.3 is the simplest regression (that includes wave and country fixed effects) to test the hypotheses that: (a) within a particular country-type, individuals have different life satisfaction according to their settlement-type, and (b) that within a particular settlement-type, individuals have different life satisfaction according to their country-type. Large city is the base category so coefficients should be interpreted relative to life satisfaction in large cities. In keeping with prior literature, the estimates indicate that life satisfaction is (significantly) higher in large cities than in other settlement types within transitional countries. In developed countries, the typical pattern is shown whereby rural/town satisfaction is higher than in small cities with a further decline to large cities, albeit with none of the developed country settlement-type effects being statistically significant.

Column [5] is our main equation as specified in Eq. (4.2). It regresses life satisfaction on wave and country fixed effects, personal characteristics (including education), own income, (within country) reference income for like individuals, and GNDI of the country relative to that of the EU15. Each of the income coefficients is differentiated according to country-settlement type. Wave 5 (2008–2009) includes the immediate post Global Financial Crisis period which provides considerable cross-country and cross-time variation. Column [6] includes wave 2 at the expense of omitting education controls. Results are qualitatively similar to those from waves 3 to 5. We prefer to include controls for education given their significance in column [5] and their differing effects across settlement types, and so we do not discuss the results from column [6] further here. Column [7] re-estimates [5] using ordered logit; results are presented as odds ratios, so a coefficient that is greater (less) than unity corresponds to an OLS coefficient that is greater (less) than zero. The results are very similar to the OLS results. All coefficients that are significant at 5% in [5] are significant and of the same sign in [7] (albeit with two coefficients significant at 10% in the latter) and there is no coefficient that is significant at the 5% level in [7] that is not significant and of the same sign in [5].

We have also estimated [5] using other comparators within the *RelGNDI* variable. First, we used USA GNDI as the comparator and second, we used the mean of USA and EU15 GNDI as the comparator. Results are very similar to those in column [5]. This should be expected mathematically; countries are surveyed in different years within each wave (e.g. Wave 3 covers 1998 to 2003) and we express each country's GNDI relative to the comparator's GNDI in the country's specific survey year. Thus we do have variation within each wave for *RelGNDI*. Nevertheless, this differentiation may be overshadowed by the across-wave variability of comparator group GNDI, the latter being picked up by the wave fixed effects. We return to the interpretation of our *RelGNDI* results in the concluding section.

Given the similarity of results across the specifications, we confine our discussion to the findings from column [5], with reference also to the naïve results from column [4]. The discussion exploits the results of Wald tests of joint coefficient significance using $p < 0.05$ significance level unless otherwise specified. Our findings can be summarised as follows.

First, no settlement-type intercept dummy is positive either for OECD founders or for transitional countries in the full equation; thus there are no (statistically significant) differences in life satisfaction by settlement-type in either country-type once other factors are controlled for.

Second, *OwnIncome* has a positive relationship with life satisfaction in all country- and settlement-types. Furthermore, the coefficients on *OwnIncome* are very similar across country- and settlement-types apart from one case (*OwnIncome* has a higher impact on life satisfaction in transition country small cities).

Third, *RefIncome* has a negative relationship with life satisfaction in all country- and settlement-types. The (within country) Easterlin Paradox holds for all settlement-types in OECD founders and in rural areas in transitional countries. However, it does not hold in non-rural settlements in transitional countries. Thus, relative to founder OECD settlements and relative to transition country rural settlements, there is a form of tunnel effect in non-rural transition country settlements.

Fourth, an increase in *RelGNDI* raises life satisfaction in all country- and settlement-types. The effect of *RelGNDI* on life satisfaction in transitional country large cities is smaller than for founding OECD large cities. In addition, transitional country large cities place a lower weight on *RelGNDI* than do transitional country rural and town areas. These results are again consistent with a form of tunnel effect for transitional countries that is most prominent in vibrant areas (cities) so that an increase in foreign incomes relative to home incomes is not viewed as negatively in these more mobile areas compared with more stagnant areas.

The third and fourth sets of findings are crucial. Prior literature finds that the Easterlin Paradox holds in immobile areas but not in faster developing, mobile areas (which are characterised by tunnel effects). We conjecture that rural transitional economy areas are immobile (relative to urban centres in transitional economies) and hence share the OECD founder Easterlin Paradox result, while the larger population areas in transitional economies are more vibrant and so do not share the full Easterlin Paradox result. Not only are there intra-country tunnel effects in more mobile transition country settlements, but these tunnel effects operate also at the inter-country level. Thus, residents in transition country cities are less negatively affected by income increases elsewhere whether these increases are within the country or in comparator countries.

The first set of results is also important. Unlike column [4] which has no income variables or controls (other than wave and country fixed effects), settlement dummies are not significant for either country type in column [5]. Thus, if personal characteristics and preferences are fixed, we cannot reject the notion of spatial equilibrium since (on average) residents from one settlement-type do not increase their life satisfaction by shifting to a differing settlement-type.

Taken overall, our results provide strong support for the hypothesis that the impact of reference and relative incomes depends on whether the individual is located in a country and/or settlement type that is mobile versus one that is stagnant. Our findings show that this is not simply a developed versus transitional country dichotomy or rural versus urban dichotomy. Rural transition country residents are akin to their founder OECD counterparts in their attitudes to others' success, while large city transition country residents are less likely to experience others' success negatively.

4.5 Conclusions

Research into the Easterlin Paradox has cast a long shadow over the proposition that raising incomes across a country raises subjective wellbeing for individuals in that country. The paradox calls into question the widespread quest to raise incomes within countries (though see Stevenson and Wolfers (2008, 2013) and Becchetti et al. (2013) for contrary views). A separate body of research has analysed whether life satisfaction is higher or lower in urban relative to rural areas, but findings in this literature have been inconclusive.

We bridge these two areas of study by testing whether life satisfaction differences between rural and urban areas and across countries reflect differing emphases placed on income relativities in different area types. As well as differentiating by four settlement-types, we differentiate by country-type. We therefore bring inter-personal relativity effects face-to-face with the rural-urban wellbeing literature.

We find that an individual's own income has a positive relationship with life satisfaction that is similar across all country- and settlement-types. We find also that the income of like individuals in the same country has a negative relationship with life satisfaction in all country- and settlement-types. The within country Easterlin Paradox holds for all settlement-types in OECD founders and for rural settlements in transitional countries. However, the pure Easterlin Paradox does not hold in non-rural settlements in transitional countries. Thus, relative to founder OECD settlements and relative to transition country rural settlements, there is a form of tunnel effect in non-rural transition country settlements.

An increase in own country Gross National Disposable Income, relative to that in other countries, raises life satisfaction in all country- and settlement-types. We find, however, that this effect is smaller in transitional country large cities than for founding OECD large cities. In addition, the effect is smaller in transitional country large cities than in smaller transitional country settlements. These results are again consistent with a form of tunnel effect that is more prominent in vibrant areas.

Together, our intra-national and inter-national results help to bridge the gap between Easterlin's (intra-country) findings and Stevenson and Wolfers' findings that residents increase their subjective wellbeing as their countries become richer. Our results also provide a bridge between the Easterlin Paradox and the rural-urban wellbeing literatures, and between two contrary sets of results within the Easterlin Paradox literature.

One additional finding of our study is that once all variables in the model are controlled for, there are no differences in life satisfaction by settlement-type in either OECD founders or transitional countries. Thus we cannot reject the hypothesis that a spatial equilibrium holds across settlement-types in both country-types.

Two potential extensions to this research could be considered. First, our interpretation of the inter-national comparison result as a relative rather than as an absolute income effect relies on identification from the within wave movements in national income. This may provide only weak identification of the relative effect. It is possible that our relative inter-national income finding may in part reflect an absolute life satisfaction effect. For instance, higher national income may enable provision of better health or education services that increase life satisfaction across the country. The relative income interpretation of the inter-national effect is consistent with the standard cross-country Easterlin Paradox result that (developed) country residents do not experience increases in life satisfaction over time, whereas the absolute income interpretation is consistent with the Stevenson and Wolfers result that rising income does raise national levels of life satisfaction. At the policy level for an individual country, either interpretation yields the same imperative: since governments must take other countries' national incomes as given, both interpretations imply that a government (ceteris paribus) can aim to increase its own citizens' wellbeing through an increase in its own country's GNDI.

Second, while we cannot reject a spatial equilibrium under the assumption of fixed preferences, we may not be able to do so (especially for transitional countries) if preferences change as a result of migration. For instance, if a transitional country rural resident moves to a large city – and if their preferences regarding relative incomes then change to the norm for transitional country large cities – they will view higher relative incomes elsewhere less negatively. This will raise their wellbeing according to the estimates here, whereas their wellbeing due to relative incomes would not change if their preferences were fixed. The question of whether personal preferences (and also personal characteristics, such as education) change upon migration – and whether these changes then affect an individual's life satisfaction – is an open question that merits further research.

Acknowledgements We thank Robert MacCulloch, Tim Hazledine, Philip Morrison, John Helliwell, Motu colleagues and participants at the Regional Studies Association conference (Piacenza) and the New Zealand Association of Economists conference (Wellington) for comments on earlier drafts. We are grateful for funding from the Marsden Fund of the Royal Society of New Zealand (MEP1201) and from the Resilient Urban Futures programme (Ministry of Business, Innovation and Employment). The authors are solely responsible for the views expressed.

References

Becchetti, L., Castriota, S., Corrado, L., & Ricca, E. G. (2013). Beyond the Joneses: Inter-country income comparisons and happiness. *The Journal of Socio-Economics, 45*, 187–195.

Berry, B., & Okulicz-Kozaryn, A. (2009). Dissatisfaction with city life: A new look at some old questions. *Cities, 26*(3), 117–124.

Brickman, P., & Campbell, D. (1971). Hedonic relativism and planning the good society. In M. H. Appley (Ed.), *Adaptation – level theory: A symposium* (pp. 287–302). New York: Academic.

Cantril, H. (1965). *The pattern of human concerns.* New Brunswick: Rutgers University Press.

Clark, A., Oswald, A., & Warr, P. (1996). Is job satisfaction U-shaped in age? *Journal of Occupational and Organizational Psychology, 69*(1), 57–81.

Clark, A., Frijters, P., & Shields, M. (2008). Relative income, happiness, and utility: An explanation for the Easterlin paradox and other puzzles. *Journal of Economic Literature, 46*(1), 95–144.

Deaton, A. (2008). Income, health, and well-being around the world: Evidence from the Gallup world poll. *Journal of Economic Perspectives, 22*(2), 53–72.

Di Tella R. And Macculloch R. (2006). Some uses of happiness data in economics. Journal of Economic Perspectives, 20(1), 25–46.

Di Tella, R., Macculloch, R. J., & Oswald, A. J. (2003). The macroeconomics of happiness. *Review of Economics and Statistics, 85*(4), 809–827.

Di Tella, R., Haisken-De New, J., & MacCulloch, R. (2010). Happiness adaptation to income and to status in an individual panel. *Journal of Economic Behavior & Organization, 76*(3), 834–852.

Diener, E., Suh, E., Lucas, R., Smith, H., & Eisenberg, N. (1999). Subjective well-being: Three decades of progress. *Psychological Bulletin, 125*(2), 276–302.

Diener, E., Tay, L., & Oishi, S. (2013). Rising income and the subjective well-being of nations. *Journal of Personality and Social Psychology, 104*(2), 267–276.

Dolan, P., Peasgood, T., & White, M. (2008). Do we really know what makes us happy? A review of the economic literature on the factors associated with subjective well-being. *Journal of Economic Psychology, 29*(1), 94–122.

Donnelly M., & Pol-Eleches G. (2012). *The questionable validity of income measures in the World Values Survey.* Princeton University Political Methodology Seminar, mimeo.

Drichoutis, A., Nayga, R., & Laziridis, P. (2010). Do reference values matter? Some notes and extensions on "income and happiness across Europe". *Journal of Economic Psychology, 31*(4), 479–486.

Duesenberry, J. (1949). *Income, saving and the theory of consumer behavior.* Cambridge, MA: Harvard University Press.

Easterlin, R. A. (1974). Does economic growth improve the human lot? Some empirical evidence. In P. A. David & M. W. Reder (Eds.), *Nations and households in economic growth: Essays in honour of Moses Abramovitz* (pp. 89–125). New York: Academic.

Easterlin, R. A. (2010). Well-being, front and center: A note on the Sarkozy report. *Population and Development Review, 36*(1), 119–124.

Easterlin R. A., Mcvey L., Switek M., Sawangfa O. And Zweig, J. (2010). The happiness-income paradox revisited. Proceedings of the National Academy of Sciences of the United States of America, 107(52), 22463–22468.

Easterlin, R. A., Angelescu, L., & Zweig, J. (2011). The impact of modern economic growth on urban–rural differences in subjective wellbeing. *World Development, 39*(12), 2187–2198.

Ekman, P., Davidson, R., & Friesen, W. (1990). The duchenne smile: Emotional expression and brain physiology: II. *Journal of Personality and Social Psychology, 58*(2), 342–353.

EVS. (2011). European values study longitudinal data file 1981–2008 (EVS 1981–2008). GESIS Data Archive, Cologne. *ZA4804 Data file Version 2.0.*

Ferrer-I-Carbonell, A., & Frijters, P. (2004). How important is methodology for the estimates of the determinants of happiness? *The Economic Journal, 114*(491), 641–659.

Festinger, L. (1954). A theory of social comparison processes. *Human Relations, 7*(2), 117–140.

Frey, B., & Stutzer, A. (2002). What can economists learn from happiness research? *Journal of Economic Literature, 40*(2), 402–435.

Glaeser E., Gottlieb J., & Ziv O. (2014). Unhappy cities. NBER Working Paper 20291; forthcoming in *Journal of Labor Economics.*

Grimes, A., & Reinhardt, M. (2015). *Relative income and subjective wellbeing: Intra-national and inter-national comparisons by settlement and country type* (Motu Working Paper 15–10). Wellington: Motu.

Grimes, A., Oxley, L., & Tarrant, N. (2014). Does money buy me love? Testing alternative measures of national wellbeing. In D. McDaid & C. Cooper (Eds.), *Economics of wellbeing* (Wellbeing: A complete reference guide) (Vol. 5). Oxford: Wiley-Blackwell.

Helliwell, J., Layard, R., & Sachs, J. (2013). *World happiness report.* New York: UN Sustainable Development Solutions Network.

Kahneman, D., & Krueger, A. (2006). Developments in the measurement of subjective well-being. *Journal of Economic Perspectives, 20*(1), 3–24.

Kapteyn, A., Van Praag, B., & Van Herwaarden, F. (1978). Individual welfare functions and social reference spaces. *Economics Letters, 1*(2), 173–177.

Kettlewell, N. (2010). The impact of rural to urban migration on wellbeing in Australia. *Australasian Journal of Regional Studies, 16*(3), 187–213.

Krueger, A., & Schkade, D. (2008). The reliability of subjective well-being measures. *Journal of Public Economics, 92*(8–9), 1833–1845.

Layard, R. (2011). *Happiness: Lessons from a new science* (2nd ed.). London: Penguin.

Layard, R., Mayraz, G., & Nickell, S. (2008). The marginal utility of income. *Journal of Public Economics, 92*(8–9), 1846–1857.

Layard, R., Mayraz, G., & Nickell, S. (2009). *Does relative income matter? Are the critics right?* London: Centre for Economic Performance, London School of Economics and Political Science.

Luttmer, E. (2005). Neighbors as negatives: Relative earnings and well-being. *The Quarterly Journal of Economics, 120*(3), 963–1002.

Morrison, P. (2011). Local expressions of subjective well-being: The New Zealand experience. *Regional Studies, 45*(8), 1039–1058.

Morrison, P. (2014). The measurement of regional growth and wellbeing. In M. Fischer & P. Nijkamp (Eds.), *Handbook of regional science*. Berlin: Springer.

Okulicz-Kozaryn, A. (2011). Geography of European life satisfaction. *Social Indicators Research, 101*(3), 435–445.

Oswald, A., & Wu, S. (2010). Objective confirmation of subjective measures of human well-being: Evidence from the U.S.A. *Science, 327*(5965), 576–579.

Senik, C. (2008). Ambition and jealousy: Income interactions in the 'old' Europe versus the 'new' Europe and the United States. *Economica, 75*(299), 495–513.

Stevenson, B., & Wolfers, J. (2008). Economic growth and subjective well-being: Reassessing the Easterlin paradox. *Brookings Papers on Economic Activity, 2008*, 1–87.

Stevenson, B., & Wolfers, J. (2013). *Subjective well-being and income: Is there any evidence of satiation?* Rochester: Social Science Research Network.

Stiglitz, J. E., Sen, A., & Fitoussi, J. P. (2009). Report of the Commission on the Measurement of Economic Performance and Social Progress (CMEPSP). Paris.

Van Praag, B., & Kapteyn, A. (1973). Further evidence on the individual welfare function of income: An empirical investigation in the Netherlands. *European Economic Review, 4*(1), 33–62.

Veblen, T. (1899). *The theory of the leisure class: An economic study of institutions* ([Reprinted] ed.). London: Allen and Unwin.

Veenhoven, R. (1994). Is happiness a trait? Tests of the theory that a better society does not make people any happier. *Social Indicators Research, 32*, 101–160.

Veenhoven, R. (2009). Well-being in nations and well-being of nations: is there a conflict between individual and society? *Social Indicators Research, 91*(1), 5–21.

Chapter 5
Relative Income and Happiness in Latin America: Implications for Inequality Debates

Mariano Rojas

'No man is an island, entire of itself.'
John Donne

Abstract This chapter studies the importance of absolute-income and relative-income effects in explaining people's well-being in Latin America. A happiness approach is followed. The empirical research uses the Latin American Gallup Survey 2007, with more than 14,000 observations covering all countries in the region and which contains information on household income and on life satisfaction. Reference-groups are constructed on the basis of country-gender-age criteria. It is found that Latin American's well-being strongly depends on their relative income, while the absolute-income effect is of lesser importance. The relative-income effect is important and significant for all segments of the income distribution. These findings are consistent with Easterlin (1974) and have important implications for the implementation and design of economic policies and development strategies.

5.1 Introduction

The most unequal region in the world; this is a common assertion when talking about income inequality in Latin America; it is also a well-deserved qualification because country-level Gini coefficients above 0.50 are frequent in the region. Even though income inequality is high, most Latin American countries have expressed a clear preference for economic growth rather than for income-redistribution strategies. This preference is justified in the belief that economic growth has a large impact on people's well-being and, in special, in the well-being of those with low income. The

M. Rojas (✉)
FLACSO-México & UPAEP, Tlalpan, Ciudad de México, Mexico

© Springer Nature Switzerland AG 2019
M. Rojas (ed.), *The Economics of Happiness*,
https://doi.org/10.1007/978-3-030-15835-4_5

preference is also well-grounded on traditional economic theory, which stresses an absolute-income view; this is: it is assumed that well-being is a matter between the person and her consumption bundle and that contextual factors -such as what other people consume- are of little importance.

The absolute-income view fosters the implementation of development strategies that favor rapid economic growth even at the cost of raising inequality. It is argued that economic growth trickles down from the top to the bottom-income deciles and that what really matters are to get those at the bottom out of poverty. It is also assumed that greater income automatically translates into greater well-being, in special when income is low. Hence, the absolute-income view justifies some disregard for redistributive policies; it is believed that growth will benefit the income poor, while redistributive policies may deter economic growth and may end up hurting those at the bottom of the income distribution. Thus, when an apparent trade-off between pro-economic growth policies and pro-egalitarian policies exists policy makers opt for promoting growth rather than pursuing a more egalitarian distribution of income.

The absolute-income view has been predominant in economic theory. Reflecting this predominance, most countries in Latin America focused on promoting economic growth through the implementation of pro-market reforms during the last decades. With a few exceptions, income redistribution policies have been marginalized from the economic-policy discussion, and social policies have shown a preference for reducing (absolute) poverty rates rather than for reducing income inequality in the region. This focus on reducing (absolute) poverty and on promoting growth rather than egalitarianism is justified on the idea that raising the income of all increases the well-being of all. Along the twentieth century there was some distrust on this view, but it is with Easterlin (1974) that empirical research provides evidence corroborating the skepticism on the presumed strong relationship between income and well-being. Further research has shown that social comparisons, endogenous aspirations, habituation to income and non-materialistic values undermine the role of income in explaining people's well-being. Easterlin's work shows that relative effects in the relationship between income and well-being may be substantial.

If absolute income is crucial in explaining people's well-being then the interest in reducing (absolute) poverty rates and the preference for economic growth as an instrument for raising people's well-being could be justified: those at the bottom of the income distribution would see their well-being increasing when their income rises, independently of what happens with the distribution of income. However, if there are substantial relative effects then the gap between the top and the bottom income deciles matters, and strategies for economic growth which do not contemplate the income gap may be futile in raising people's well-being, even when absolute income at the bottom deciles is increasing. In this case redistributive policies should be considered as constitutive of any strategy that aims at increasing people's well-being and, in particular, the well-being of those in the bottom of the income distribution.

This paper follows a happiness approach to study the relevance of absolute and relative income in explaining well-being in Latin America. The paper uses the

Gallup 2007 survey which contains happiness and income information for about 14,000 people in 19 Latin American countries. The investigation constructs reference groups on the basis of age brackets and gender.[1] Relative income is constructed from a comparison of people's income to their reference group's mean income.

It is found that relative income plays a large role in explaining people's experience of being well. Thus, generalized income increases have a small -almost negligible- impact on people's well-being.

The paper is structured as follows: Section 5.2 makes a revision of the relevant literature. Section 5.3 explains the database as well as the criteria used to construct reference groups; it also presents some descriptive statistics. Section 5.4 studies the relationship between happiness and relative income under different specifications. Section 5.5 discusses the main findings from the investigation as well as their policy implications.

5.2 Literature Review

5.2.1 Absolute Income in Economic Theory

Economic theory states that a person's utility[2] depends on her absolute income and only on her absolute income; no direct role is played by other people's income (Frank 2005). Thus, most economic models assume that well-being is affected by changes in own income but not by changes in other people's income. In the happiness literature this view is called the absolute-income hypothesis, and it is inspired in an individualistic approach where out-of-context individuals constitute the building blocks of economic models. The individualistic approach stresses the view that the social context emerges as a result from the aggregation of out-of-context individualistic decisions, rather than being a circumstance that frames people's decisions and which is an inherent constituent of what a person is. It is also within this individualistic perspective that income-distribution indicators end up playing the unique role of qualifying mean indicators, such a per-capita income. In consequence, the distribution of income does not have an independent impact on a person's well-being -or on her behavior- beyond that produced by its influence in the determination of a person's absolute income.

Many economists have postulated that a person's utility, either in its ordinal-behavioral interpretation or in its well-being interpretation, depends on this person's

---

[1]Other criteria such as age brackets, gender and education or age brackets, gender and area of living provide results that are, in essence, similar. However, these criteria imply a pulverization of the data and lead to greater standard errors.

[2]Utility is understood either in its ordinal conception -which is useful for explaining and predicting behavior- or in its latent well-being conception -which is useful for public policy and for the design and evaluation of social-programs.

relative standing in society.[3] In the happiness literature this view is called the relative-income hypothesis. The assumption that utility does depend on absolute income alone may not only be incorrect, but it may also lead to wrong public-policy recommendations, as well as to the emergence of apparent paradoxes in our understanding of human actions and reactions. For example, policies that generate high economic growth rates with increasing inequality may be considered as more beneficial than egalitarian-oriented policies that generate low growth rates. These high-growth-with-inequality policies are even assumed to be beneficial for the poor if their absolute income rises. These public-policy recommendations assume that people's relative income is not important for their well-being and also assume that people's aspirations and goals remain constant even when income disparities are rising.

During the past decades there has been a surge in research about the relevance of relative standings in well-being. It is a recurrent finding in the emerging happiness literature that well-being does depend not only on people's absolute income but also on their relative income. However, research on the importance of relative income has been carried out mostly in high-income countries, but not in low and mid-income countries, where absolute poverty is larger and where high income inequality is common.

5.2.2 Relative Income in Economic Theory

The emphasis economic theory places on absolute income is surprising when it is recognized that classical economists emphasized the role played by a person's relative position in her well-being and in her decisions. Smith (1776) and Keynes (1931) stressed the role of relative needs, while Marx (1849 (1977)) emphasized human comparisons. The view that most needs are relative rather than absolute has led to understanding well-being deprivation as a situation where people are not living a decent life according to the consumption standards of their society (Townsend 1962).

At the brink of the twentieth century Veblen (1899) argued for the importance of conspicuous consumption, stating that some consumption patterns have a positional foundation; and Duesenberry (1949) noticed that savings patterns could be better explained if relative income was taken into consideration. The recent literature on economic behavior and relative income is large and supports the view that people's relative standing matters (Schor 1998, 2002; Robson 1992; Samuelson 2004; Corneo and Jeanne 1997; Knell 1999; and Pham 2005). There is also research on the interdependence of preferences (Kapteyn and van Herwaarden 1980; Kapteyn et.

---

[3]This paper makes a semantic distinction between a person, who is defined as such in society, and an individual, who is out of any social context and whose role in functionalist models is to be the kernel for the construction of societies.

al. 1997; Postlewaite 1998). The importance of relative concerns is also recognized by other disciplines. Marmot (2004) shows that health and life expectancy are related to a person's relative standing in society; Gidron and Hall (2017) show its relevance in explaining political movements. Bio-science has shown that status is related to specific biological activity in human males (Mazur and Lamb 1980); while Brosnan and De Waal (2003) shows that even primates react to relative rewards. Thus, it is possible for relative concerns to be entrenched in human evolution.

Furthermore, Parducci (1968, 1995) argues that human beings are not designed to make absolute judgments and that relative judgments are necessary for human decisions and evaluations. This is an argument that is closely linked to the social-norms literature (van Praag and Ferrer-i-Carbonell 2004). Hirsch (1976) introduced the concept of a positional society, placing greater importance on the status a person holds within her society rather than on her absolute situation. The importance of status has been popularized by de Botton (2004) in his *Status Anxiety* book.

5.2.3 Reference Groups: Sociological Theories

Sociologists have long accepted that people's behavior, evaluations, and aspirations are not individualistically determined but that they do depend on people's immersion in society and, thus, are affected by comparisons and social positions (Weber 1922; Suls and Wills 1991). The literature on reference groups studies whom people do compare themselves with and what kind of comparisons they do make (Merton and Kitt 1950; Hyman 1960; Runciman 1966). Sociologists distinguish among different kinds of comparison groups: there are groups of competition so that comparisons are made in order to evaluate if one is doing better than others; there are groups of aspiration so that comparisons are made to define evaluation norms and to form aspirations; there are groups of membership so than comparisons are made to form expectations; and there are groups of social distance so that comparisons are made to define what a worst performance means.

The nature of the information which is provided by comparisons has been widely studied in the literature (Senik 2004; Kingdon and Knight 2007; and Hirschman 1973). Similarly, the object of comparison, whether it is income or any other observable variable, has received attention from some researchers (Michalos 1985; Frank 1985, 1989; and van Praag et al. 1979)

5.2.4 Relative Income and Happiness

Easterlin (1974) shows that a raise in a person's income increases her happiness as long as the income of other people does not change; however, if everybody's income also rises then there is little impact on this person's happiness. Thus, Easterlin shows that there is a positive relationship between income and happiness in cross-section studies, but the relation is practically nil in longitudinal studies. Easterlin concludes that the existence of a large relative income effect constitutes one potential explanation for this finding. Many subsequent studies (Ferrer-i-Carbonell, 2005; Clark and Oswald 1996; Luttmer 2005; Binswanger 2006) find out that relative income does have a significant influence on a person's assessment of her well-being and, probably, on her behavior.

Van Praag (1977, 1993) shows that both relative income and aspiration gaps (difference between current income and that income considered as sufficient to satisfy all material needs) are important variables in the assessment of income satisfaction and in human decisions. Van Praag finds out that a person's satisfaction with her income does depend on her relative income; thus, a rise in satisfaction takes place when absolute income increases, but a drift occurs if everybody else's income also increases. van Praag also shows that aspirations are endogenous to absolute income and that they tend to rise as income increases; thus, a person's aspiration gap does not necessarily decline when her absolute income rises. Subsequent studies (Stutzer 2004; McBride 2010; Senik 2007) have arrived to similar findings. van Praag (1971) and collaborators (van Praag and Ferrer-i-Carbonell 2004) show that income-evaluation norms are based on aspirations and comparisons; which are not independent of their absolute income.

Clark and Oswald (1996) find that relative wages are also important for workers' reported satisfaction; thus, job satisfaction does depend on relative wages as well as on absolute wages. Similar results are found by Sloane and Williams (2000) using Canadian and British data, respectively.

5.2.5   Methodological Issues in the Study of Relative Income

There are many methodological considerations when studying a relative-income concept (Clark 2007; Clark et.al. 2008). Three issues emerge when dealing with relative income: The definition of a person's reference group, the definition of a reference income, and the construction of a person's relative income.

The definition of the reference group does play a crucial role in relative-income studies. It has been argued that people may compare themselves to different groups and that they may use different comparison criteria. Stutzer (2004) assumes that persons do compare their income to that of people in their Swiss region. Similar regional criteria are used by Luttmer (2005) and Persky and Tam (1990). Ball and Chernova (2005) assume that this comparison takes place with respect to everybody in the country. Senik (2004) assumes that the comparison takes place with respect to a person's professional/occupational groups. McBride (2001) uses age-cohorts' criteria. Kingdon and Knight (2007) emphasize the role played by ethnicity; they do distinguish between a comparison made by a person with respect to her own ethnic group (membership comparison) and that made with respect to other ethnic groups (competition comparison). Ferrer-i-Carbonell (2005) works with comparisons within a person's socio-demographic group.

The construction of a relative-income variable is handled in diverse ways in the literature; for example, as the ratio of a person's income to the mean income of her reference group, or even to the mean income in some income deciles of her reference group (Ferrer-i-Carbonell 2005). It is also possible to define relative income as the distance (in monetary units or in standard-deviation units) between a person's income and her reference income. Comparison do not have to be symmetric, upward and downward comparisons may differ and, in consequence, the impact of a person's relative income position on her well-being may depend on whether she is above or below her reference income.

5.2.6 Relative Income and Economic Policy

The Importance of Relative Income May Have Many Economic-Policy Implications

First, generalized income rises have smaller impacts on people's well-being than person-specific income rises. Economic growth faces treadmills that are not contemplated by individualistic-based models (Easterlin 1974; Biswanger 2006; Frijters et al. 2004; Clark et al. 2008). A person's raise in income may emerge from systemic factors that also raise the income of most people in her reference group; thus, absolute income could rise with little impact on relative income. In addition, a person's raise in income may lead her to change her group of comparison; if this person begins comparing her income to that of a wealthier group then her relative income may even decline (Falk and Knell 2004). Schor (1999, 2002) and Frank (2000) have shown that social trends may alter the focus of comparison, leading to changes in relative income (as well as in aspirations) even when a person's absolute income does not change.

Second, it is important to distinguish between absolute income changes and relative (to reference group) income changes. It may be possible for absolute income to rise while relative income declines; people's well-being could decline in this case. Graham and Pettinato (2002) argue that people may have significant absolute achievements, but that they may become frustrated as a consequence of comparison effects. Economic reforms and social-program design and evaluations should take into consideration both the absolute and the relative impact of income rises. It may be possible for people to reject policies that raise their absolute income because of relative-income implications (Graham and Sukhtankar 2004)

Third, the sense of exclusion and deprivation may be reference-group based rather than country-level based. If people's well-being does depend on within-reference-group comparisons, then deprivation measures based on country-level indicators are of little relevance for understanding their well-being and their sense of deprivation (Bossert and D'Ambrosio 2006; D'Ambrosio and Frick 2004; and Bossert et al. 2007)

5.3   The Database

5.3.1   The Gallup Survey

The Gallup survey is applied yearly in many countries in the world. It is a representative survey at country level. In the year 2007 the Latin American and Caribbean survey incorporated a happiness module as well as a question regarding household income. The following countries are considered in this investigation: Argentina, Bolivia, Brazil, Chile, Colombia, Costa Rica, Dominican Republic, Ecuador, El Salvador, Guatemala, Honduras, Mexico, Nicaragua, Panama, Paraguay, Peru, Uruguay and Venezuela. About 14,000 observations are available for the empirical analyses.

5.3.2   The Information

a) **Happiness variable:** The Gallup 2007 survey includes two commonly used happiness questions. The first one is the life-satisfaction question and it is phrased as *"Taking everything in your life into consideration, how satisfied are you with your life?"*; the response scale goes from 0 to 10 and for practical purposes it can be treated as a cardinal scale. The second question in the Gallup survey is the so called best-worst life question (life evaluation); the specific phrasing of the question is: *"Please imagine a ladder/mountain with steps numbered from zero at the bottom to ten at the top. Suppose we say that the top of the ladder/mountain represents the best possible life for you and the bottom of the ladder/mountain represents the worst possible life for you. On which step of the ladder would you say you personally feel you stand at this time assuming that the higher the step the better you feel about your life and the lower the step the worse you feel about it? Which step comes closest to the way you feel?"*. The response scale goes from of 0 to 10 where 0 is the least possible and 10 the highest possible life evaluation. In principle, this life-evaluation variable is categorical; however, for practical purposes it can be treated as a cardinal variable.[4]

Happiness information is used only for those people for whom there is also income information. Table 5.1 presents descriptive information on happiness variables. It is observed that on average Costa Ricans report the highest well-being in the region, with a mean life satisfaction of 8.48 and a mean life evaluation (best-worst question) of value of 7.41.

---

[4]The assumption of cardinality allows for simplifying the presentation of descriptive statistics as well as the implementation of simple econometric techniques, such as ordinary least squared regressions. It is important to state that the treatment of these variables as ordinal –such as using ordered-probit econometric techniques- does not imply any significant change in the main results from this investigation.

Table 5.1 Happiness in Latin America, 0–10 scale, Descriptive Statistics

| | | | Life Satisfaction | |
Country	Mean	Std. Dev	Mean	Std. Dev
Argentina	7.09	1.85	5.92	2.11
Bolivia	6.27	1.9	5.33	1.93
Brazil	7.53	2.04	6.11	2.4
Chile	6.45	2.11	5.69	2.16
Colombia	7.35	2.13	6.19	2.52
Costa Rica	8.48	1.74	7.41	2.2
Dominican Rep	7.42	2.36	4.94	2.79
Ecuador	6.35	2.04	4.88	2.12
El Salvador	6.68	2.03	5.21	2.22
Guatemala	7.85	1.77	6.11	2.06
Honduras	7.04	2.46	5.21	2.72
Mexico	7.76	1.63	6.5	2.04
Nicaragua	7.07	2.5	4.88	2.83
Panama	7.76	2.02	6.9	2.22
Paraguay	6.77	2.04	5.2	2.02
Peru	5.98	1.91	5.27	2.2
Uruguay	6.72	2.01	5.62	2.08
Venezuela	*na*	*na*	6.57	2.16

Source: Latin American Gallup 2007 Survey

b) **Income variable.** The Gallup survey includes one question about household monthly income. The information is captured in income brackets expressed in local currency units; thus, brackets are not homogeneous across countries when expressed in U.S. dollars adjusted for purchasing power parity. Gasparini et al. (2008) use the Gallup survey to calculate household per capita income figures which are comparable across countries; they make assumptions on household demographic composition and on the within-income-bracket distribution of household incomes. Their income figures perform well when contrasted with other income figures gathered by official country sources. Thus, they are confident about the quality of their income figures. This investigation uses Gasparini et al. (2008) computed figures on household per capita income expressed in U.S. dollars adjusted by purchasing power parity.

c) **Other relevant variables.** The survey also has information regarding people's age (in years), marital status (dummies for marital status were constructed; *single* is used as the category of reference), area where a person lives (categorical variables with the following options: rural, small town, urban, and suburb. Dummies for area where the person lives were constructed taking *rural area* as category of reference), and education in categories.[5]

---

[5]Information regarding education in categories was calculated and provided by Cárdenas et al. (2008)

5.3.3 Reference-Group Construction: Country, Age and Gender

Based on the relevant literature and contingent on the availability of information, different group-formation criteria were explored. The survey had information regarding country, gender, age, and place of living of person (urban, semi-urban, small town, rural); and education. A country-age-gender criterion was followed in the construction of the reference groups.

People were first classified in different groups according to their age group, their gender, and their country of residence. Seven age-groups were formed (less than 20 years old, from 20 to 29, from 30 to 39, from 40 to 49, from 50 to 59, from 60 to 69, and 70 years old and more)[6]. A reference-group formation based on age groups and gender renders 14 reference groups within each country. Because there are 19 countries in the survey, this implies 266 groups, with an average of about 50 observations by group.[7] There are substantial differences in average income across the reference groups (See Table 5.5 in the Appendix); for example, the highest average monthly income is US$ 929 dollars for men with ages in between 60 and 69 in Colombia; while the lowest average monthly income is US$ 107 dollars for women with ages in between 30 and 39 in Peru. Because mean income for each age-gender-country group will be used as a proxy for reference income, it is important to have substantial variability in reference-group income across groups.

5.4 Relative Income and Well-being

5.4.1 Estimating the Impact of Reference Income

The following general specification is used to study whether reference income does play a role in happiness:

---

[6]This is an arbitrary classification; McBride (2001) used a variation that assumes people compare with those who are in a range of $(-5, +5)$ years their age.

[7]If an additional criterion were considered, e.g.: a rural-urban criterion, then the number of groups would increase to 560; reducing the average number of observations in each group to about 25. Different criteria for group formation were followed: country-age-gender; country-age- gender-location; country-age-gender-education; and so on. It was found that the country-age-gender criterion provides clear results; while the country-age-gender-location criterion leads to similar results but with weaker significance tests, probably due to the reduced number of observations in each group.

$$swb_{igk} = \alpha_0 ly_{igk} + \alpha_1 ly_{gk}^{ref} + \beta edu_{igk} + \delta area_{igk} + \gamma mst_{igk} + \theta country_k$$
$$+ \mu_{igk} \tag{5.1}$$

Where:

swb_{igk} refers to either life satisfaction or to life evaluation (best-worst life) of person i who belongs to gender-age group g in country k.

ly_{igk} refers to the natural logarithm of household per capita income for person i who belongs to gender-age group g in country k. The use of the natural logarithm of income rather than raw income obeys to the well-established finding of the relationship between income and happiness variables being concave.

ly_{gk}^{ref} refers to the natural logarithm of the mean income for people in gender-age group g in country k. Mean income is assumed to be the income of reference for everybody in the group.

$country_k$ refers to country fixed effects, it is a vector of dichotomous variables, with a value of 1 for the country of residence of person i and 0 otherwise.

edu_{igk} is a vector of dichotomous variables, with a value of 1 for the education category of person i and 0 otherwise. *No schooling* is the category of reference.

$area_{igk}$ is a vector of dichotomous variables, with a value of 1 for the area of residence of person i and 0 otherwise. *Rural* is the category of reference.

mst_{igk} is a vector of dichotomous variables, with a value of 1 for the area marital status category of person i and 0 otherwise. *Single* is the category of reference.

It is important to remark that the specification allows for the existence of country fixed effects; in other words, it contemplates the existence of country-level specificities that do imply differences in happiness across countries.

According to the literature, it is expected in Eq. (5.1) for $\alpha_0 > 0$ and for $\alpha_1 < 0$. It is also of interest to test whether $\alpha_0 + \alpha_1 = 0$. If this last hypothesis cannot be rejected, then it would imply that a generalized increase in income (person i's income raises in same percentage as her reference group's income) would have little impact in people's well-being. In other words, income raises do have an impact in well-being as long as they allow for a change in a person's relative position.

Table 5.2 shows the results from the econometric exercise when using ordinary-least squares regressions; the main results are mostly similar when treating the variables as ordinal and using ordered-probit techniques.

It is observed in Table 5.2 that reference income does play a significant and large role in explaining happiness. A person's satisfaction with life raises with own income and declines with the income of her group of reference. An increase in income of 100 percent would increase life satisfaction in about 0.40 while an increase of 100 percent in the average income of her reference group would reduce life satisfaction in about 0.23. The same trend is observed with respect to the life evaluation question; life moves closer to the best possible one when income rises; however, it moves farther away from the best possible life when the income of the reference group increases.

Table 5.2 Relative income and happiness, Latin America, ordinary least squares

	Life satisfaction	Life evaluation
ly	0.401***	0.443***
lyref	−0.228***	−0.304***
Incomplete primary	0.46***	0.30**
Complete primary	0.50***	0.51***
Incomplete secondary	0.76***	0.72***
Complete secondary	0.81***	0.91***
Incomplete technical	0.53***	1.03***
Complete technical	0.90***	1.12***
Incomplete university	0.69***	0.87***
Complete university	0.801***	1.11***
Post-graduate	0.84***	1.27***
Small town	−0.08	−0.11
Large city	−0.04	−0.04
Suburb	0.06	−0.1
Married	−0.09**	−0.25***
Separated	−0.45***	−0.48***
Divorced	−0.26**	−0.34***
Widowed	−0.31***	−0.31***
Stable partner	−0.20***	−0.30***
Observations	12,859	13,491
R_sq	0.149	0.161
Test	F-value	F-value
$\alpha_0 + \alpha_1 = 0$	4.11	2.21

Significance levels: 0.01 (***), 0.05 (**)
Estimated coefficients for country variables are not presented
Source: Gallup 2007 Latin America Survey

5.4.2 The Importance of Absolute and Relative Income

Equation 5.1 can also be expressed as:

$$swb_{igk} = (\alpha_0 + \alpha_1)ly_{igk} + \alpha_1\left(ly_{igk}^{ref} - ly_{igk}\right) + \beta edu_{igk} + \delta area_{igk} + \gamma mst_{igk}$$
$$+ \theta country_k + \mu_{igk} \tag{5.2}$$

This equation separates the absolute from the relative effect of an increase in income. In other words, there are two effects when a person's income rises:

First, there is an absolute effect which emerges income allowing people to have access to goods and services that provide comfort and needs satisfaction, independently of the context these people are located in. This absolute effect reflects the

Table 5.3 Happiness and Absolute and Relative Income Effects Latin America

	Life satisfaction	Life evaluation
Absolute income effect	0.173**	0.139
Relative income effect	0.228***	0.304***

Significance levels: 0.01 (***), 0.05 (**)
Based on estimated coefficients from Eq. (5.1); see Table 5.4.
Source: Gallup 2007 Latin America Survey

commonly accepted view in economic theory that well-being is a matter of a relation between a person and her objects; in Eq. (5.2) the absolute effect is captured by $\alpha_0 + \alpha_1$.

Second, there is a relative effect which holds because the increase in income implies an upward movement in a person's relative standing - as long as the reference income remains constant -. This relative effect emerges because people's well-being depends on their status in society and, in most societies, it is income - and the objects it can purchase - which mark people's status. The relative effect is captured by the absolute value of the parameter α_1, and it shows how a person's relative standing affects her well-being.

The absolute effect (as measured by $\alpha_0 + \alpha_1$) holds even when there is a generalized increase in income, because it reflects the happiness impact of income which does not depend on the social context; however, the relative effect (as measured by $|\alpha_1|$) holds only when the raise in income is exclusive to the person rather than generalized. In a completely egalitarian society the value of the parameter α_1 would become irrelevant; however, in very unequal societies α_1 becomes a relevant parameter in understanding people's well-being.

Table 5.3 presents the estimated coefficients for absolute and relative income effect on the basis of the estimated parameters presented in Table 5.2.

The $\alpha_0 + \alpha_1 = 0$ hypothesis (significance of the absolute-income effect) is rejected at 5 percent for the life-satisfaction variable and it cannot be rejected for the life-evaluation variable. This means that absolute income does play a positive and significant role in life satisfaction, and a positive –but smaller and not statistically significant- role in life evaluation (a more cognitive-oriented variable which is highly influenced by social comparisons and aspirations). The relative-income effect is statistically significant and of greater magnitude for both the life satisfaction and the life evaluation variables. This finding shows that income inequality has intrinsic well-being relevance in Latin America.

5.4.3 Asymmetric Comparisons

It has been postulated that comparisons may be asymmetric. Ferrer-i-Carbonell (2005) finds that Western Germans show asymmetric comparison; she concludes that "*the coefficient for richer is non-significant and smaller than the coefficient for poorer. The coefficient of the variable poorer is significant for both subsamples. This yields the conclusion that for West Germans comparisons are, as postulated by Duesenberry (1949), asymmetric and upwards."* (p. 20) In other words, people who are beneath their group's reference income are strongly influenced by their relative position, while people who are above their group's reference income are not. New variables are constructed in order to test this hypothesis; let's define:

$$D^{below} = \begin{cases} \left(ly_{igk}^{ref} - ly_{igk}\right) & if \ y_{igk} < y_{igk}^{ref} \\ 0 & if \ y_{igk} < y_{igk}^{ref} \end{cases} \qquad (5.3)$$

$$D^{above} = \begin{cases} \left(ly_{igk} - ly_{igk}^{ref}\right) & if \ y_{igk} > y_{igk}^{ref} \\ 0 & if \ y_{igk} \leq y_{igk}^{ref} \end{cases} \qquad (5.4)$$

On the basis of Eq. (5.2), the following regression specification is used to estimate the asymmetric impact of relative income on people's well-being; it distinguishes between people who are above their reference income and people who are beneath it.

$$swb_{igk} = \varphi ly_{igk} + \lambda_1 D^{below} + \lambda_2 D^{above} + \beta edu_{igk} + \beta area_{igk} + \gamma mst_{igk}$$
$$+ \theta country_k + \mu_{igk} \qquad (5.5)$$

In principle, based on the results from Ferrer-i-Carbonell (2005) it is expected for $|\lambda_1| > \lambda_2$, indicating that the relative-income effect is larger for people who are in the bottom half of their reference-group's income distribution. This would imply for upward income comparisons to have a larger well-being impact than downward income comparisons.

Table 5.4 presents the results from the econometric exercises.

Table 5.4 Happiness and relative income asymmetric comparison specification Latin America

	Life satisfaction	Life evaluation
ly	0.172**	0.141
Dbelow	−0.225***	−0.316***
Dabove	0.241***	0.263***
R-squared	0.15	0.16
Test	F value	F value
$\|\lambda_1\| > \lambda_2$	0.07	0.59

Significance levels: 0.01 (***), 0.05 (**)
Estimated coefficients from Eq. (5.5)
Estimated coefficients for control variables are not shown
Source: Gallup 2007 Latin America Survey

It is observed that the general hypothesis of $|\lambda_1| > \lambda_2$ cannot be rejected, neither for life satisfaction nor for life evaluation. The relative effect of income is similar whether people are beneath or above their reference income. In other words, there are both upward and downward income comparisons which impact people's well-being in a similar way. This is an important result which suggests that income distribution may have both positive and negative effects in well-being depending on whether people end up in the top section of the distribution (making downward comparisons) or in the bottom section of the distribution (making upward comparisons).

These findings contradict Duesenberry's argument about people looking upward but not downward when assessing their situation.

5.5   Final Considerations

5.5.1   Main Findings

This paper has found that relative income matters for people's well-being; that relative-income effects are larger than absolute-income effects; and that this happens at all income levels and in all points of the income distribution. Absolute income does also play a significant, although minor, role.

The specific findings from this research are:

First, comparisons within a person's group of reference are important for her well-being. The mean income of a person's reference group significantly matters for her happiness.

A raise in a person's income has two effects in her well-being (life satisfaction and life evaluation): First, an absolute effect which emerges from this person having access to comforts and satisfaction of needs that income allows for; second, a relative effect which emerges from this person attaining a better relative standing in his or her group of reference. This investigation shows that in Latin America the absolute effect is smaller than the relative effect, and that in the case of life evaluation (a cognitive-oriented variable highly influenced by social comparisons) the absolute effect is nil.

Both upward and downward comparisons within reference groups are relevant. People with a relative high income do benefit from their better status while people with a relative low income are harmed by their worse status.

5.5.2 Findings' Implications

The main findings from this research imply that:

Generalized increases in income do have a much smaller impact in people's well-being than person-specific increases in income. This happens because a large portion of the impact of income on well-being is due to its role as status marker. Hence, economic growth may not be as important as it seems from cross-section regressions of the relationship between happiness and income. Generalized income raises do not necessarily ensure generalized well-being increases. This finding is clearly in coherence with Easterlin (1974).

In situations where inequality is high it would even be possible for economic growth to imply for some people to end up being absolutely better off but relatively worse off; the relevance of the relative effect could imply for these people's well-being to decline even when their income is increasing. This is particularly important in the Latin American region due to the high income-inequality situation.

The relationship between the distribution of income and people's well-being deserves greater attention in economic theory. Development economists usually express concern regarding the unequal distribution of income in some regions of the world; however, their concern is still based on an absolute-income view. In other words, they approach the distribution of income as qualifying per capita income figures; this is, the distribution of income informs economists on how reliable per capita figures are in portraying the situation of the country's population. Egalitarian concerns have usually been justified on the basis of normative theories of justice. However, the importance of the relative-income effect at all income levels implies for a new justification for holding egalitarian concerns: a very unequal distribution of income hurts those at the bottom of the distribution, independently of their absolute-income situation. Development economists should be concerned about the distribution of income not because it qualifies per capita income, but because it has a direct impact on people's happiness.

It is also important to distinguish between country-level income distribution indicators and group-specific income-distribution indicators. It is common to focus on country-level indicators of the distribution of income; however, it seems that people's well-being depends on intra-group rather than on intra-country inequality.

The importance of relative income shows that human beings are not *out-of-context individuals* but *fully-immersed-in-society persons*. It also shows that some relevant factors for understanding people's well-being and their behavior are neglected when agents are considered and modelled out of their social context.

Appendix

Table 5.5 Mean income values. Monthly household per capita income in PPP US dollars. By reference group[1] in each count

	W 15–19	W 20–29	W 30–39	W 40–49	W 50–59	W 60–69	W 70+	M 15–19	M 20–29	M 30–39	M 40–49	M 50–59	M 60–69	M 70+	Std. dev. across ref. groups[4]
Argentina	255	352	352	429	428	425	425	349	424	407	526	543	574	320	88
Bolivia	158	155	132	177	162	201	237	154	219	175	191	167	155	292	42
Brazil	234	283	229	275	305	258	239	276	404	282	323	461	348	316	66
Chile	234	300	313	290	475	242	225	369	444	431	386	430	372	318	82
Colombia	303	442	270	371	361	265	265	419	509	379	549	457	929	602	177
Costa Rica	441	315	303	361	370	343	330	454	605	411	480	549	511	285	99
Dominican Rep	247	238	233	431	295	190	155	388	305	297	245	355	414	319	82
Ecuador	133	155	144	174	194	129	152	208	190	187	206	232	162	121	34
El Salvador	201	133	120	123	170	135	113	182	193	186	142	200	193	437	81
Guatemala	174	134	158	170	150	123	122	168	183	203	183	306	226	112	50
Honduras	226	192	151	257	180	125	244	196	290	214	189	282	183	200	47
Mexico	192	231	191	249	217	156	140	221	237	219	223	257	206	490	81
Nicaragua	217	221	199	163	143	123	364	282	258	208	294	216	214	185	63
Panama	206	227	177	249	259	221	153	235	269	210	246	304	195	328	47
Paraguay	211	235	183	189	205	237	165	282	267	201	202	235	347	262	48
Peru	130	131	107	156	228	208	182	150	174	153	217	210	162	127	38
Uruguay	366	289	267	456	353	401	434	395	369	297	496	492	569	451	87
Venezuela	188	193	176	195	215	204	189	135	179	208	223	213	158	145	26
Mean income[2]	229	235	206	262	262	221	230	270	307	259	296	328	329	295	137
Std. dev. along countries[3]	78	84	71	106	100	92	100	103	126	90	132	127	208	137	

[1]Reference groups are defined in terms of Country, Gender, and Age Range. W stands for women and M for male, age is presented in ranges
[2]Refers to average value of mean income values across countries
[3]Refers to standard deviation of mean income values across countries
[4]Refers to standard deviation of mean income values across gender-age groups for each country
Source: Gallup 2007 Survey

References

Ball, R. & Chernova, K. (2005). *Absolute Income, Relative Income, and Happiness*. Manuscript
Binswanger, M. (2006). Why does income growth fail to make us happier? Searching for the treadmills behind the paradox of happiness. *The Journal of Socio-Economics, 35*(2), 366–381.
Bossert, W., & D'Ambrosio, C. (2006). Reference groups and individual deprivation. *Economic Letters, 90*(3), 421–426.
Bossert, W., D'Ambrosio, C., & Peragine, V. (2007). Deprivation and social exclusion. *Economica, 74*(296), 777–803.
Brosnan, S. F., & de Waal, F. B. (2003). Monkeys reject unequal pay. *Nature, 425*(6955), 297–299.
Cárdenas, M., di Maro, V., & Mejía, C. (2008). *Understanding the role of educational perceptions and victimization on wellbeing*. Colombia: Fedesarrollo.
Clark, A. (2007). *Happiness, habits and high rank: Comparisons in economic and social life*. Working Paper, Paris School of Economics, March.
Clark, A., & Oswald, A. (1996). Satisfaction and comparison income. *Journal of Public Economics, 61*(3), 359–381.
Clark, A., Frijters, P., & Shields, M. (2008). Relative income, happiness and utility: An explanation for the easterlin paradox and other puzzles. *Journal of Economic Literature, 46*(1), 95–144.
Corneo, G., & Jeanne, O. (1997). On relative wealth effects and the optimality of growth. *Economics Letters, 54*(1), 87–92.
D'Ambrosio C. & Frick, J. (2004). *Subjective well-being and relative deprivation: An empirical link*. Discussion Paper 449, DIW Berlin.
De Botton, A. (2004). *Status anxiety*. Mishawaka, IN: Hamish Hamilton Ltd.
Duesenberry, J. (1949). *Income, saving and the theory of consumer behavior*. Cambridge, MA: Harvard University Press.
Easterlin, R. A. (1974). Does economic growth improve the human lot? Some empirical evidence. In P. A. David & M. Reder (Eds.), *Nations and households in economic growth* (pp. 89–125). Palo Alto: Stanford University Press.
Falk, A., & Knell, M. (2004). Choosing the Joneses: Endogenous goals and reference standards. *Scandinavian Journal of Economics, 106*(3), 417–435.
Ferrer-i-Carbonell, A. (2005). Income and well-being: An empirical analysis of the comparison income effect. *Journal of Public Economics, 89*(5–6), 997–1019.
Frank, R. (1985). *Choosing the right pond. Human behavior and the quest for status*. New York/Oxford: Oxford University Press.
Frank, R. (1989). Frames of Reference and the Quality of Life. *American Economic Review, 79*(2), 80–85.
Frank, R. (2000). *Luxury fever: Money and happiness in an era of excess*. Princeton/Oxford: Princeton University Press.
Frank, R. (2005). Does absolute income matter? In L. Bruni & P. L. Porta (Eds.), *Economics & happiness: Framing the analysis* (pp. 65–90). Oxford: Oxford University Press.
Frijters, P., Haisken-DeNew, J. P., & Shields, M. A. (2004). Money does matter! evidence from increasing real income and life satisfaction in East Germany following reunification. *American Economic Review, 94*(3), 730–740.
Kingdon, G., & Knight, J. (2007). Community, comparisons and subjective well-being in a divided society. *Journal of Economic Behavior & Organization, 64*(1), 69–90.
Gasparini, L., Sosa Escudero, W., Marchionni, M. & Olivieri, S. (2008). *Income, deprivation, and perceptions in Latin America and the Caribbean: New evidence from the Gallup World Poll*. CEDLAS, Universidad Nacional de La Plata.
Gidron, N., & Hall, P. A. (2017). The politics of social status: Economic and cultural roots of the populist right. *The British Journal of Sociology, 68*(S1), S57–S84.
Graham, C., & Pettinato, S. (2002). *Happiness & hardship: Opportunity and insecurity in new market economies*. Washington, DC: Brookings.

Graham, C., & Sukhtankar, S. (2004). Is economic crisis reducing support for markets and democracy in Latin America? Some evidence from the economics of happiness. *Journal of Latin American Studies, 36*, 349–377.

Hirsch, F. (1976). *Social limits to growth*. Cambridge: Harvard University Press.

Hirschman, A. (1973). The changing tolerance for income inequality in the course of economic development. *Quarterly Journal of Economics, 87*(4), 544–566.

Hyman, H. H. (1960). Reflections on reference groups. *The Public Opinion Quarterly, 24*(3), 383–396.

Kapteyn, A., & van Herwaarden, F. G. (1980). Interdependent welfare functions and optimal income distribution. *Journal of Public Economics, 14*(3), 375–397.

Kapteyn, A., van de Geer, S., van de Stadt, H., & Wansbeek, T. (1997). Interdependent preferences: An econometric analysis. *Journal of Applied Econometrics, 12*(6), 665–686.

Keynes, J. M. (1931). *Economic possibilities of our grandchildren, essays in persuasion*. London: MacMillan.

Knell, M. (1999). Social comparisons, inequality, and growth. *Journal of Institutional and Theoretical Economics, 112*(4), 664–695.

Luttmer, E. (2005). Neighbors as Negatives: Relative Earnings and Well-Being. *The Quarterly Journal of Economics, 120*(3), 963–1002.

Marmot, M. (2004). *Status Syndrome*. London: Bloomsbury.

Marx, K. (1977). Wage Labour and Capital. In D. McLellan (Ed.), *Karl Marx: Selected Writings*. Oxford: Oxford University Press.

Mazur, A., & Lamb, T. A. (1980). Testosterone, status, and mood in human males. *Hormones and Behavior, 14*(3), 236–246.

McBride, M. (2001). Relative-income effects on subjective well-being in the cross-section. *Journal of Economic Behavior and Organization, 45*(3), 251–278.

McBride, M. (2010). Money, happiness, and aspirations: An experimental study. *Journal of Economic Behavior & Organization, 74*(3), 262–276.

Merton, R., & Kitt, A. (1950). Contribution to the theory of reference group behavior. In R. Merton & P. Lazarsfeld (Eds.), *Continuities in social research: Studies in the scope and method of 'The American Soldier'*. Glencoe: Free Press.

Michalos, A. (1985). Multiple Discrepancy Theory. *Social Indicators Research, 16*(4), 347–414.

Parducci, A. (1968). The relativism of absolute judgments. *Scientific American, 219*(6), 84–90.

Parducci, A. (1995). *Happiness, pleasure, and judgment: The contextual theory and its applications*. Hillsdale: Lawrence Erlbaum.

Persky, J., & Tam, M. Y. (1990). Local status and national social welfare. *Journal of Regional Science, 30*(2), 229–238.

Pham, T. K. C. (2005). Economic growth and status-seeking through personal wealth. *European Journal of Political Economy, 21*(2), 407–427.

Postlewaite, A. (1998). The social basis of interdependent preferences. *European Economic Review, 42*(3–5), 779–800.

Robson, A. (1992). Status, the distribution of wealth, private and social attitudes to risk. *Econometrica, 60*(4), 837–857.

Runciman, W. G. (1966). *Relative deprivation and social justice: A study of attitudes to social inequality in Twentieth-Century England*. London: Routledge.

Samuelson, L. (2004). Information-based relative consumption effects. *Econometrica, 72*(1), 93–118.

Schor, J. (1998). *The overspent American: Upscaling, downshifting and the new consumer*. New York: Basic Books.

Schor, J. (1999). The new politics of consumption: Why Americans want so much more than they need. *Boston Review, 24*(3–4), 4–9.

Schor, J. (2002). Understanding the new consumerism: Inequality, emulation and the erosion of well being. *Tijdschrift voor Sociologie, 23*(1).

Senik, C. (2004). *Relativizing relative income*. Working Paper 2004–17. DELTA.

Senik, C. (2007). *Income comparisons. Which income gaps matter most to people?* Working Paper 2007–19. Paris School of Economics.

Sloane, P. J., & Williams, H. (2000). Job satisfaction, comparison earnings, and gender. *Labour, 14* (3), 473–501.

Smith, A. (1776). *An inquiry into the nature and causes of the wealth of nations.* New York: Modern Library. Edition 1937.

Stutzer, A. (2004). The role of income aspirations in individual happiness. *Journal of Economic Behavior & Organization, 54*(1), 89–109.

Suls, J., & Wills, T. A. (1991). *Social comparison: Contemporary theory and research* (pp. 237–260). New Jersey: Lawrence Erlbaum Associates, Inc..

Townsend, P. (1962). The meaning of poverty. *British Journal of Sociology, 13*(3), 221–223.

Van Praag, B. (1971). The welfare function of income in Belgium: An empirical investigation. *European Economic Review, 2*(3), 337–369.

Van Praag, B. (1977). The perception of welfare inequality. *European Economic Review, 10*(2), 189–207.

Van Praag, B. (1993). The relativity of welfare. In M. Nussbaum & A. Sen (Eds.), *The quality of life* (pp. 362–385). Oxford: Clarendon Press.

Van Praag, B., Kapteyn, A., & van Herwaarden, F. G. (1979). The definition and measurement of social reference spaces. *The Netherlands' Journal of Sociology, 15*(1), 13–25.

Van Praag, B., & Ferrer-i-Carbonell, A. (2004). *Happiness quantified: A satisfaction calculus approach.* Oxford: Oxford University Press.

Veblen, T. (1899). *The Theory of the Leisure Class.* Reprint 1934. New York: Modern Library.

Weber, M. (1922). *Wirtschaft und Gesellschaft*, 1978 English edition as *Economy and Society*. Berkeley: University of California Press.

Part III
Happiness in Welfare Economics

Chapter 6
Does Happiness Improve Welfare Economics a Lot?

Gabriel Leite Mota

Abstract The vision that Richard Easterlin had back in the 1970s with its "Does economic growth improve the human lot? Some empirical evidence", that subjective well-being might be the variable economics should look at to assess the welfare gains from economic growth was a "Columbus' egg": no matter how obvious could it be, mainstream economics completely neglected that line of research throughout the twentieth century. This chapter tries to analyse how important is the usage of happiness for the betterment of welfare analysis in economics, contrasting it with both the tools and theoretical apparatus form orthodox welfare economics and the capabilities approach.

6.1 Introduction

The essay "Does economic growth improve the human lot? Some empirical evidence" that Richard Easterlin wrote for a book in memory of Moses Abramovitz, back in 1974,[1] is now a classic on the economics of happiness.

Although that work went mostly unnoticed for almost 20 years, it earned the well-deserved recognition at the end of the twentieth century, when the economics of happiness grew as a hot topic in economics.

In that essay, Easterlin was interested in evaluating if economic growth was actually capable of improving human well-being, by observing the effect such growth had on the happiness of individuals.

Knowing that data on the subjective well-being was available since the 1950s, Richard Easterlin was able to do the unnoticed obvious – empirically assess the relationship between economic growth and the perception of well-being.

---

[1] Easterlin (1974).

G. Leite Mota (✉)
Independent researcher, Porto, Portugal

© Springer Nature Switzerland AG 2019
M. Rojas (ed.), *The Economics of Happiness*,
https://doi.org/10.1007/978-3-030-15835-4_6

For him, that was the best way to empirically analyse an old-time assumption in economics: economic growth is good for humans.

Despite the inattention that such pioneer move had, what Easterlin did was a "Columbus' egg" discovery: using happiness data to assess the welfare gains from economic growth was probably the best way available for economists to test their trademark argument in defence of economic growth, that more growth is always better.

Easterlin's discovery disproved that assumption. In fact, the relationship between economic growth and happiness is non-linear, sometimes not present at all.

Such result defied orthodoxy, which was not ready to accept that economic growth could be anything else than good, despite the absence of empirical evidence to support such claim.

Nowadays, the credibility the literature on the economics of happiness has gained is forcing the mainstream to revisit the assumption that economic growth is always a good thing for humans. That is, Easterlin eventually won the game: one must always ask how and why does economic growth improve well-being. And that question is empirically answerable.

But not only that, happiness literature is producing empirical evidence demonstrating that many traditional welfare conclusions were wrong, and that economics needs a paradigm change regarding its assumption about human behaviour and human welfare.[2]

As a paradigm change that is, it will not happen suddenly.

The purpose of this chapter is to analyse if, and how, the incorporation of the concept of happiness, and the use of the respective data, is being capable of changing welfare economics analysis for better.

To do that, we first illuminate some incongruences mainstream economics exhibit regarding the separation between normative and positive economics.

Secondly, we detail the theoretical apparatus, and applied work, of three different approaches to the welfare analysis in economics: the mainstream, the capabilities approach (CA) and the happiness literature (HL).

Finally, contrasting those approaches, we show that there is a room for happiness in welfare economics, because both the data on subjective well-being and the concept of happiness bring unique and original contributions that promote a better comprehension of welfare in economics.

6.2 Exposing a Hidden Truth: Incongruences of Orthodox Welfare Analysis in Economics

In orthodox economics, the separation between positive and normative analysis isn't clear, despite all the rhetoric economists use claiming such problem has been solved during the transition from the nineteenth to the twentieth century, when economics became a "pure" science.

---

[2]See, for instance, Frey and Stutzer (2002), Layard (2005), Layard (2006), Frey (2008).

Such rhetoric proclaims that normative analysis is a subject only for welfare economics or, even worse, that it is beyond the scope of the economic science.[3]

Nevertheless, whenever a researcher defines a utility function, for theoretical or empirical analysis, and draws policy implications, he or she is introducing a normative dimension on a, supposedly, positive analysis.

The fact that researchers operating that way do not acknowledge such problems only aggravates this issue. Recognizing such incongruences is the first step to find alternative ways to deal with the normative/welfare dimensions of the discipline.

In fact, welfare analysis in economics is messy. For one side, orthodoxy developed a branched called Welfare Economics (WE), totally devoted to the analysis of the welfare consequences of different economic states and policies. For some, that is a respectable branch of economic inquiry. Relying on assumptions from orthodox microeconomics it would produce some value neutral (economic efficiency) analysis used to inform policy. At the same time, others disregard it, considering it is polluted with normative and ideological biases that destroy its scientific credibility. Complicating things even more, many of those who look down on WE engage in welfare considerations or policy recommendations derived from the models and empirical research they produce. In those papers, there is a section devoted to policy/welfare implications, presented as being value neutral, scientific policy advice. In reality, such conclusions are undermined by hidden value assumptions and are inconsistent with the theoretical framework of ordinal preferences. Those who proceed this way slip into the messy world of incoherent welfare analysis, masked with the complex mathematical apparatus employed.[4]

It is known that the main purpose of WE is to assess the welfare consequences of different policy proposals (market vs. central planning, different tax systems, subsidy policies, laws on international trade). And WE is the branch of economic analysis where the normative problems are more salient: starting with positive analysis from economic models, ends with policy advice.[5] This step from positive to normative reasoning is not always easy: even if one accepts the validity of the underlying "positive" model, there are always conceptual and value issues to be solved before some normative consensus can appear.[6]

According to Robbins (1981) this is a critical issue, one that could even discredit WE as a science. He believes WE should be relabelled as Political Economy; at the same time, it would become clear that it is a subjective domain of analysis. For him,

---

[3]See the classical argument from Robbins (1932).

[4]These recent papers published in top ranked economics journals can be used as good examples of the mentioned incongruences: Bhattacharya (2015), Handel and Kolstad (2015), Colombo et al. (2014).

[5]See Johansson (1991) for a standard textbook definition.

[6]Note that it can be argued that a normative consensus will never appear (which is Lionel Robins' position on WE, shown next): dealing with normative and axiomatic issues (such as the definition of welfare or of the "good") one might be forced to accept the impossibility of an unanimously supported definition. In fact, the very aim of the political process is to try to solve disagreements regarding normative options.

it becomes imperative to make the choice about "what good is" transparent. Welfare economists must first reveal their conception of good (which is mostly a subjective and philosophical issue), and only then use economic models to perform welfare analysis. In his own words:

> As regards the subject matter of Economic Science, I adhere to its description in terms of behaviour conditioned by scarcity. As regards its status as a science, I see no reason to deny its susceptibility to the usual logical requirements of a science, though I have emphasized the peculiar nature of its subject as concerned with conscious beings capable of choice and learning. I see no reason why we should be terrified into thinking that such analysis necessarily involves ideological bias. But beyond that, in the application of Economic Science to problems of policy, I urge that we must acknowledge the introduction of assumptions of value essentially incapable of scientific proof. For this reason, while not denying the value of some thought going under that name, I have urged that the claims of Welfare Economics to be scientific are highly dubious; and I go on to argue the lack of realism which is involved by some of the inferences which may be drawn from its assumptions. Instead I recommend what I call Political Economy which, at each relevant point, declares all relevant non-scientific assumptions; and I furnish some indications of the leading criteria and fields of speculation which should underlie this branch of intellectual activity. Robbins (1981, p. 9).

Even if one disagrees with Robbins on the need for WE relabelling, it is clear that the definition of welfare is critical to building an approach to WE: is it material progress, psychological well-being, freedom (political, economic or social) or enlargement of consumption options? The answer to this question will not only determine one's approach to WE, but also the type of policy advice.

The concept of welfare within the discipline of economics has a long history and has been subject to various paradigm changes over time. Classical utilitarianism held that the welfare of the society was conceived as the sum of the welfare of all the individuals, and the welfare of individuals as the utility they obtained from the goods they had at their disposal. Later, its welfarist version asserted that utility could only be inferred from the choice behaviour of rational agents and was assumed to be ordinal, interpersonally incomparable and the sole valid informational base for WE.[7] Meanwhile there was the max-min principle, a neoclassical interpretation of the work of Rawls (1971), where the welfare of society was to be determined through the utility of the most disadvantaged. Furthermore, there are alternatives proposed by Amartya Sen and others (capabilities and primary goods as competing informational

---

[7]This is the dominant rhetoric about utility amongst economists and is considered the standard for mainstream WE. Nevertheless, it is easy to find discrepancies between the rhetoric and practice: in many papers, where welfare analysis is done, an additive social welfare function (as objective function of maximization) is used (see Laffont and Tirole (1986) as an example). That implies a cardinal conception of utility even if it is not explicitly admitted. Furthermore, the Arrow Impossibility Theorem, Arrow (1951), has shown all ordinal interpretations of utility as unable to generate a solid social decision rule (and hence, any Social Welfare Function). Even so, many mainstream welfare economists try to avoid SWF and use other tools of WE which they believe to be valid within the ordinal utility framework (see Just et al. (2005) where this line of reasoning is supported within the public policy context) or claim that ordinalism does not destroy SWF (see Fleurbaey and Mongin (2005)).

bases for welfare assessments, opposing utility) and the contemporary analysis of subjective assessments of utility (Happiness, Subjective Well-Being (SWB), Life Satisfaction). All this demonstrates how WE has been struggling, without ever reaching a "stable equilibrium".[8]

In practice, welfare has been alternatively associated with material things (wealth, GDP, income, consumption bundles, basic goods), with psychological phenomena (happiness, good emotions or, more broadly, utility as a subjective concept), with utility as an abstract concept, inferred from preference orderings from rational choice behaviour, or with freedom and capabilities. Each alternative has brought a specific framework of analysis and domain of application (not always compatible or complementary with each other).[9]

Eventually, out of the myriad of alternatives, some get more credit than others, some are more widely used than others, some are labelled orthodox, others heterodox.

It is this sea of complexity and alternatives that one must navigate when dealing with the problem of welfare and policy analysis in economics.

The fact that many orthodox economists do not recognize even the mainstream WE (MWE) as a relevant field of analysis is an alarming reality. Who can give coherent and honest policy advice without first sorting out all the complexities above mentioned?

It is not by accident that so many economic policy advices have produced disastrous consequences for humankind. Without a philosophically sound welfare concept and a way to empirically test the actual welfare consequences of economic policies, chances are that bad things will happen.

Despite the reputation economists have gained within the political sphere – both in national and international political organizations – many mainstream economics welfare analyses are fundamentally wrong.

The critique Amartya Sen and others are putting forward since the 1970's, with the capabilities approach, and the literature on happiness that emerged during the 1990's, both are being capable of two very important endeavours: unveiling the fragilities, inconsistencies and intellectual deceit of some mainstream economic policy advice; producing sound alternatives that can be used as guides for economic policy design and welfare assessment.

---

[8]For a more detailed analysis on the evolution of welfare concepts throughout the history of economics see Bruni (2004a, b), Chipman and Moore (1978), Cooter and Rappoport (1984), Viner (1925), Wolfe (1931), Bharadwaj (1972) and Stigler (1950).

[9]Note that classifying WE evolution as scientific progress might not be correct. Frequently, changes in WE are such that only new and different questions can be answered, not the old ones. Such changes are not scientific progress, but rather evidence of interests refocusing. See Cooter and Rappoport (1984) on the ordinalist revolution as an example.

6.3 Happiness Forcing Its Way Amidst the Mainstream and the Capabilities Approach

While MWE is the dominant view in economics, and so are its respective methods and conceptions, Sen's capabilities approach (CA) and the happiness literature (HL) are two of the strongest contemporary alternatives. Each have different conceptions of welfare, methods and philosophical backgrounds, and most of the time, different policy conclusions.

We are particularly focused on trying to understand how HL challenges MWE and implies revisions on the standard policy advice. We will also contrast HL with CA, as this is an established alternative to MWE that shares several concerns and results with HL (namely policy advice, conclusions and criticisms of MWE). The final goal is to show that HL has established a place within WE.

6.3.1 Mainstream Welfare Analysis

There are numerous forms of welfare analysis in economics, not all compatible or even complementary to each other. Nevertheless, it is possible to find a core analysis which is sufficiently integrated and standardized that we may call it mainstream WE.

MWE can be characterized by the use of certain tools of analysis, two theorems and the acceptance of some traditional assumptions of mainstream economics. Specifically, we argue that MWE uses the first and second welfare theorems (1st and 2nd WT), consumer/producer surplus (CS/PS), compensating and equivalent variations (CV/EV), the Pareto criterion (PC), the compensation principle (CP), cost-benefit analysis (CBA), other tools for applied WE, like survey data, the Clarke-Groves mechanism, travel costs and hedonic prices and social welfare functions (SWF) as the main tools.[10] Furthermore, it subscribes to methodological individualism, consequentialism, rationality principle, modelization and mathematical formalization as fundamentals for these tools. The majority of these tools also rely on the validity of the price system as a mechanism for value assessment (in a competitive framework) and on the idea of utility as a directly non-measurable and interpersonally incomparable entity.[11]

It is possible to group those tools into four different classes: theorems (1st and 2nd WT), tools for applied WE (CBA and the others), social decision rules (SWF) and tools based on the rhetoric of ordinal utility (PC, CP, CV/EV and CS/PS). Secondly, although these four classes refer to mainstream techniques, some incompatibilities might be found between them, particularly between SWF and the other tools of analysis in MWE. A

---

[10]This list is not exhaustive but it is representative of MWE's main tools of analysis, as a quick look at contemporary WE textbooks will confirm.

[11]Again, remember the usual disparities between the rhetoric and the practice of many economists on their welfare analysis (ordinal rhetoric with cardinal practice).

description of each tool mentioned above follows. We start with a description of the tools based on the rhetoric of ordinal utility and finish with SWF.

6.3.1.1   Tools Based on the Rhetoric of Ordinal Utility[12]

PC: this concept is credited to the Italian nineteenth century economist Vilfredo Pareto who proposed that in evaluating different social states we could only say that one state is preferred to another if in the latter all individuals (or at least one) are better (without anyone being worse off) than in the former.

This concept has great potential for acceptance because it is very restricting in making value comparisons and has the potential to be deemed obvious and intuitively correct.[13]

This concept entered the core of WE in the form of Paretian Efficiency, according to which a state is only considered efficient when there is no possible resources reallocation that can improve the welfare of some without harming the welfare of others. Appealing as this may be, this can be a very restrictive and limited criterion. It has no power whatsoever to help WE in analysing situations in which we deal with welfare gains for some and welfare losses for others (which is frequently the case).

CS/PS: the concept of surplus, that can be traced back to A. Marshal, tries to capture the utility gain that individuals obtain from acquiring (selling) the goods they want in the market at a lower (higher) price than that they were willing to pay (accept).

Using this device as a tool for analysing the welfare impacts of some economic change, all we have to do is to calculate these surpluses before and after the change and see what the sign of its variation is. If it is positive, we have a welfare gain, if it is negative, we have a welfare loss. According to CS/PS, social welfare is maximized when the sum of consumer and producer surplus is maximized.[14]

CV/EV: These two concepts were first introduced by J. Hicks (1940, 1943), and can be defined as follows: in the face of a possible economic change we can calculate the amount that is necessary to transfer from or to the consumer in order to make him stay at the same level of utility as before the change – this is the CV; we can also calculate the amount that is necessary to transfer from or to the consumer in order to let her enjoy the new utility level (post-change) if the change does not occur – this is the EV.

---

[12]The tools analyzed here are usually conceived of as operational under ordinal utility. Nevertheless, it can be argued that is not the case for some of those tools, as some form of cardinality is often implicit (even if not recognized by those who use the tools). If that is the case, these tools might be biased towards some conceptions of welfare that many might deem unfair or unreasonable. For that not to happen an explicit assumption of cardinality is required. Also note that the same problem happens with the tools for applied WE. For more on this see Sen (2000).

[13]Although, see Sen (1970), for surprising results.

[14]In the framework of mainstream economics (perfect rationality, perfect information and inexistence of public goods and externalities), this happens in a perfectly competitive market economy.

CP: this device was first proposed by Kaldor (1939) and Hicks (1939). Their idea was to allow potential income transfers amongst individuals in a way that gainers from some economic changes could compensate the losers, so that all agents will gain from the change.

For Kaldor, if after some change there is some hypothetically appropriate income redistribution so that all individuals of society are better off, then that change is supported, even if the compensation is not actually carried out.

Hicks proposed a somewhat different approach. Using his criterion, the change is only desirable if there is no potential income redistribution in the pre-change state that can leave individuals as well-off as they become after the change. That is, a change is desirable only if doing the reverse change does not respect the Kaldor CP.

The most interesting point about these CPs is that they have deepened the focus of analysis towards efficiency issues.[15] In trying to enlarge the scope of the Pareto criterion to situations where someone would lose from change and not demand compensation, these CPs made the focus on efficiency spread to a situation where previously nothing could have been said. Hicks and Kaldor state their advice using only potential compensations. The step of actually compensating the losers is understood as a separate thing. If the change can respect the CP it should be supported, even if the compensation is never done. So, CP can support a change that actually violates the PC.

6.3.1.2   Theorems

From the combination of various tools and principles described above and basic assumptions of mainstream economics (perfect rationality, non-convexities in production and utility functions, competitive markets, perfect and symmetric information and non-existence of externalities and public goods) two theorems appear as benchmarks of MWE.

They can be described as:

1st WT: any competitive market allocation is Pareto efficient. That is, if we have rational consumers and producers left alone in a perfectly competitive market environment, the final allocation will be such that no possible trade among the agents could improve the welfare of some without harming the welfare of others. In brief, all competitive market allocations are Pareto efficient.

2nd WT: under some reasonable hypotheses, all the Pareto efficient allocations can be attained through competitive markets given appropriate initial endowment redistribution. That is, all Pareto efficient allocations are competitive equilibriums for some endowment distribution. Any feasible and optimal resource allocation can be obtained via market mechanism, after appropriate initial endowment redistribution.

---

[15]Nevertheless, see Sen (2000) to understand how that can be reinterpreted (CPs are not purely efficient measures as they imply some form of cardinality and interpersonal comparison of utility).

These theorems show that market allocations can be superior (in terms of efficiency) to other alternative resource allocations (such as dictatorships, social plans, etc.).[16] Nevertheless, these theorems are silent when a decision is needed between two different resource allocations that are both Pareto efficient. That is why tools such as SWF are needed to "close" the analysis.

6.3.1.3   Social Decision Rules

Within MWE, the Social Welfare Function (SWF) is a device used to create a social decision rule over any set of relevant alternative social states. It was first created by A. Bergson (1938), and has been used with the intent of producing a complete social ordering over all the possible social states a society might face.

The basis for an SWF is a Social Welfare Ordering (SWO) that can be represented by a function if it is continuous. This function aggregates the utility of individuals in such a way that higher values of this function indicate a social preference for the social state to which that higher value is imputed.

MWE assumes that SWFs obey some basic characteristics that prompt their usefulness: welfarism (SWF depends only on the individual utility valuations of social states), a positive derivative[17] in each individual utility level (assumes the strong PC criterion[18]) and convex to the origin indifference curves (assumption of diminishing marginal utility).

With this theoretical device, the definition of the social state that maximizes the social welfare becomes possible: it will be the tangency point between the social welfare indifference curve and the utility possibilities frontier. Given that, the main problem that remains is the definition of a specific SWF.

According to the ideology each welfare economist chooses, it is possible to create a SWF that reflects such option. So, welfare economists are forced to define their assumptions on the type of Moral Philosophy that should be used to carry out the welfare analysis.

Using a utilitarian ordinal conception of SWF, the problem of finding a consistent way of ranking social states becomes a puzzle. Arrow's Impossibility Theorem, Arrow (1951), shows that there is no SWF that can fulfil some very basic desirable properties. That is, in this ordinal utilitarian framework, we cannot get a consistent

---

[16]Note, however, that this is different to saying that the market mechanism is the only mechanism that should exist to perform the production and distribution of resources. The 2nd WT clearly opens space for State intervention in determining which final state is desirable after an initial endowment redistribution operation. Only after that redistribution, markets will operate and bring the system to the desired and efficient final state.

[17]Allowing for null derivate is necessary if one wants to include Rawlsian SWF. Nevertheless, that kind of SWF might be considered beyond MWE.

[18]The notion that sate A is only preferable to state B if in B at least one person is better off than in A and no one is worse off.

ranking of social states[19] (even if we use any democratic rule such as majority voting), unless we use some individual ordering as society's representative ordering. But that would not be correct because it would correspond to a social dictatorship.[20] If, on the other hand, we allow SWF to be cardinal and fully measurable (which implies some form of interpersonal comparison of utilities) we will face the reverse problem: there will be a large number of possible SWFs that we can construct based on individual utilities. It will be then crucial to specify the ethical assumption we want to use in order to be able to choose from that wide range of possible SWFs.[21] From that position we can use SWF to rank different social states, but those rankings will always be dependent on moral values and so, in some way, subjective.

6.3.1.4 Tools for Applied WE

Applied WE is the branch of WE that uses its theoretical apparatus to proceed with analysis of actual policy issues (like deciding the amount of a tax, the construction of a new road or bridge). It is by using the tools of applied WE that economists can advise policy makers in devising their strategy.

Not surprisingly, problems of public goods are what decision-makers most usually deal with. Consequently, most tools developed by applied WE intend to assess the welfare consequences of decisions over public goods. A brief description of CBA and other practical approaches to applied WE follows.

The *CBA* is widely-used as an instrument for assessing the social welfare consequences of medium and small public projects. It is an attempt to know what the social benefits and social costs of the implementation of some public project will be.

When a government decides to implement some project it must be aware of the welfare consequences that project will have on society. It has to analyse the impacts of the project on consumer social welfare (the aggregate consumers' willingness to pay for the changes that will occur), on the social cost (namely the consumers' valuation of the production losses due to the move of some inputs from private to the public project), their own governmental gains from that project and the impact of alternative distributions of the gains on households. The CBA is and endeavour to provide some practical rules that can allow governments to control these areas of impact of a public project by trying to accurately predict and measure its consequences on social welfare.

The other most often used practical methods are: Survey data, Clarke-Groves Mechanism, Travel costs and Hedonic Prices.

---

[19]However, see Fleurbaey and Mongin (2005), Little (1952), Bergson (1954), Samuelson (1977).

[20]The hypothesis of an elected benevolent dictator could diminish the undesirability of such social dictatorship but is, nevertheless, of very little practical interest (due to the implausibility of a benevolent dictator due to incentive problems).

[21]There are typically two types of ethical assumptions: Utilitarianism – which generates convex social indifference curves; Rawlsianism – which implies Leontieff-type social welfare indifference curves.

The Survey method is simply the use of survey information to gauge the agents' willingness to pay for or accept some economic change. In a very direct way, agents are asked how much they are willing to pay for change to take place (CV) or how much they would require to be paid (how much they accept) for change not to happen (EV). If those amounts compensate the costs of implementation, then the project should be approved.

The *Clarke-Groves mechanism* is a device devised by Clarke (1971) and Groves (1973) that induces individuals to reveal their actual preferences over a public good. This scheme is thought to be incentive-compatible and works in the following way: for a project to be approved we impose a share of its cost on all individuals. Then we ask about their willingness to pay and tell them that the project will only be undertaken if the total willingness to pay exceeds the total cost. Finally, every pivotal individual (i.e., every individual that might change the decision of implementing the project or not according to his willingness to pay) is required to pay a tax equal to the absolute value of the sum of each of the remaining individuals' willingness to pay less their total cost share of supplying the good. With this we hope to obtain the true welfare values of the economic change but we impose a non-Pareto efficient allocation: the collected tax must disappear from the economy (in order for agents not to behave strategically and corrupt this scheme) so we face a resource waste. Besides, some agents will lose and others gain with the changes supported by this scheme.

The *Travel Costs*[22] method uses the idea that even for a free-of-charge service or public good, agents who actually use it will face some costs. One of them is the travel cost. Therefore, in trying to evaluate a public good of this kind we can add the travel costs that agents accept in order to utilize it, and calculate an approximated welfare value of that good (again using the idea of surplus).

The last method we mention here is *Hedonic Prices*.[23] The idea behind this method is to try to capture the value of some public goods through the prices of some private goods. Using econometric techniques, it is possible to isolate the contribution of the different characteristics of some goods to their price. If some of those characteristics are a public good, we can assess the value of that public good by finding the difference between the prices of two private goods (similar in all but the public good characteristic).

The preceding analysis allows us to draw some conclusion: MWE is a vast discipline, encompassing the utilization of different applied techniques and relatively different theoretical models; it shows a good level of coherence between the tools for applied WE and the theoretical analysis based on ordinal utility[24] (coherent

---

[22]See, for instance, Timmins and Murdock (2007), Shrestha et al. (2002), Hailu et al. (2005), Clarke (1998).

[23]See, for instance, Sengupta and Osgood (2003), Wang (2003), Dickie et al. (1997), Arimah (1992), Tse (2002), Hamilton (2007), Pope (2008).

[24]Not forgetting the difficulties that might arise once we start to deepen the methodological analysis and find that there is a tension between the rhetoric of economists (advocating ordinalism) and the reality of their practices (such as using additive SWF which implies cardinality).

with mainstream economics assumptions); PC is structural to MWE, making it biased towards efficiency issues and away from equity ones[25]; MWE determines the supremacy of market outcomes (market efficiency in terms of Pareto), that is, the best social welfare can be achieved through free markets, free agent interactions[26]; SWF is the most controversial part of MWE because the ordinal utility paradigm does not fit (due to AIT) and there is no consensus over the alternatives (which is why it is also disregarded in most applied works[27]).

In conclusion we can state that there is a core of well-defined techniques that characterize MWE but there are still some disputes and unsolved issues within it. Furthermore, those disputes are more visible at the theoretical level (choosing between different SWFs[28] and discerning the role of cardinality and ordinality) than at the applied one (where CP dominates).

Nevertheless, many applied and theoretical welfare economists are aware of those difficulties and find MWE too narrow to encompass the real problems of social welfare. It is mostly amongst economists who are more interested in social welfare issues such as unemployment, poverty, discrimination, freedom or development, that we readily find support for alternative theories of welfare, precisely because it is on those issues that the major weakness and flaws of MWE techniques show up.[29]

That is why, in wanting to enrich the scope and power of WE many economists criticize the WE state of the art and propose alternatives. From myriad authors and alternatives, two deserve our special attention: Sen's Capabilities approach and the Happiness Literature.

For Sen, MWE is limited, primarily because it uses a very incomplete source of information when conducting welfare analysis: utility derived from rational

---

[25]Nevertheless, remember that PC is of very little use when it comes to practical issues (someone is always worsened as a consequence of policy implementation).

[26]Even when markets face some difficulties (like externalities, natural monopoly or asymmetry of information) the best way to overcome those problems (so that the market interaction recovers its "natural" efficiency) is through interventions on agents' incentive schemes, not through state planning. Nevertheless, this does not imply the abolishment of the State. The State might still have a role in determining the social optimum.

[27]See, for instance, Just et al. (2005). Even so, SWF is a central issue for social choice theorists (most of them explicitly assuming cardinal SWF). Many economists also use SWF as arguments of maximization problems (even though no explicit reasoning is made about which conception of utility is being used).

[28]It is worth noticing that it is in the context of SWF discussions that most criticism to MWE appears. For the critics, MWE cannot neglect SWF just because it doesn't fit the revealed preferences/ordinalism framework. Quite the opposite, that incapacity of ordinalism to define a reasonable SWF is a good reason why the ordinalist paradigm should be abandoned, because not explicitly defining the ethical background hidden behind ordinalism doesn't eliminate the fact that some choices have been made implicitly.

[29]When facing real-life facts, those economists realize there is a huge discrepancy between the expected welfare consequences of MWE policies and their actual consequences on the populations.

choice behaviour. Instead, information about capabilities (the actual possibilities humans have to lead the life they want or have reason to value) should be the answer.[30]

For the HL, the main problem with MWE lays in its incapacity to accept cardinal and subjective assessments of utility and to admit that not all is revealed through choice behaviour (as when there is imperfect rationality).

Another possible weakness of MWE is the already-cited reliance on methodological individualism and rationality principle: criticism might focus on the need to escape the "homo economicus" paradigm reverting to more empirical versions of economic agents (with reasoning influenced by emotions, habits or myopia); embrace a more realistic conception of welfare as a psychological phenomenon; or accept relational notions of welfare (escaping the individualistic paradigm where all kinds of welfare can be reduced to individual experience[31]). The methodological individualism is by itself a long and complex line of criticism to MWE, but one that we will not be paying special attention to here, unless related to CA's or HL's main criticisms. On the other hand, the reliance on the perfect rationality principle is a major criticism that both CA and HL direct against MWE.

6.4   The Capabilities Critique

If one wants to understand the role HL is having on WE it is important to examine what the CA is, and its role in WE. There is only room for HL in WE if it adds something to MWE that CA has not already been able to put forward.[32]

Nowadays, the CA is a well-established form of dealing with welfare problems within Economics.[33]

Amartya Sen is the founder of the CA.[34] Sen was not content with the answers MWE gave: for him, there was a vast list of important issues that orthodoxy could not deal with. So he proposed other methods, and mainly that the capability set should be the informational base welfare economists ought to use in their analyses. For Sen, MWE basically relies on an especially restricted idea of utilitarianism, one that accepts only ordinal utility inferred from choice behaviour as a reliable source of

---

[30]This is also a big difference (and, at the same time, a linking point between HL and MWE) between CA and HL: CA is a non-welfarist approach to WE whereas HL remains within the welfarist tradition. That is, CA stresses the need to use extra-utility information to proceed with welfare analysis while HL only demands new forms of measuring and new conceptions of utility. See Duclos and Araar (2006) for a distinction between welfarist and non-welfarist approaches.

[31]See Zamagni (2005) for a detailed analysis.

[32]On the similarities and differences between CA and HL see Comim (2005).

[33]This can be witnessed by the penetration this approach has on both economic journals and international institutions (such as the World Bank and United Nations).

[34]A detailed analysis of this theory can be found on Sen (1999).

information for welfare analysis. Even considering the most powerful version of utilitarianism (the cardinal one), Sen argues for its demerits: the persistency of some extension of the AIT and incompatibilities between Pareto criterion and liberal values (which imply that even the most-used and supposedly uncontroversial welfare criterion of MWE is useless when one imposes private spheres of freedom[35]) are just two examples of the weaknesses utilitarianism suffers from Sen's viewpoint.[36] Consequently, Sen believes it is crucial to employ extra-utility information in order to produce more solid welfare analysis.[37] Using extra-utility information (capabilities deprivation, for instance), Sen believes one can escape the impossibility results and analyse distributional issues of welfare.

Sen is very concerned with the subjective nature of utility (even when inferred from choice behaviour) because he finds agents too prone to adaptation in order for utility to stand as a good welfare criterion (not to mention as the only one).[38] He identifies the capability set as the true objective information that welfare analysts should look at. From this, one could objectively assess where agents stand in welfare: whether they are undernourished, ill, under-educated, relatively poor, isolated from social life, have a chance for long fife, have access to health care, have a chance to actively participate in social life and flourish. All these questions can be answered objectively without the need of utility assessments (that is, independently of what people think or feel about it). For him, the possibility of feeling well (having high levels of subjective well-being and reported happiness) is just one capability that should be taken into account. Yet, there are also different capabilities which are just as valuable that cannot be reduced to their consequences on psychological well-being: life-expectancy at birth, equality of opportunities amongst gender, race and social class or political and economic freedoms. These are just few examples of capabilities that Sen deems to be crucial for every human society and which cannot be reduced (or judged by their importance) to their impact on happiness.

Furthermore, Sen is also concerned with the procedural facet of welfare: not only are the consequences and results valuable, but also the number of options and the very process by which one obtains certain results.[39]

---

[35]See Sen (1979a, b).

[36]See Sen (1983) for a closer analysis.

[37]And to reconcile welfare analysis with some notions of justice and values such as freedom: Sen claims that on utilitarian grounds all sorts of barbarities (like slavery, hunger or genocide) can be theoretically justified.

[38]Sen is very concerned with the possibility of a person acquiescing (because the person was raised that way or has an acquiescent personality) to very bad and degrading situations, see Sen (1999). Note that this very process of adaptation also undermines perfect rationality. So, not only is the concept of utility poor, the perfectly rational agent used by MWE in its models is unrealistic. As a result, MWE conclusions and policy advice can be misleading.

[39]This departure from a pure consequentialist framework contrasts with MWE (and with the standard versions of Utilitarianism).

By introducing CA one can enlarge the power of analysis of WE and rank situations which could not be ranked before. Processes, relational problems and absolute and relative deprivations can be judge. Yet, there is a new problem: if neither agents' behaviour nor their subjective assessments are crucial to welfare judgments, what is the criterion to define welfare?

Some uncertainty is inherent in Sen's definition of capabilities: capabilities are everything humans value or have reasons to value. From there he makes a list of things that people normally tend to value (like health, income, subjective well-being, freedom). Nevertheless, he gives us no definite criterion to classify something as a capability or not, opening the way to discussion, confusion, ambiguity and, interestingly enough, subjectivity (each person can determine what is, or is not a capability[40]). At the end of the day, the desired objectivity remains unattainable.

In this respect it is worth noting that CA cannot be fully understood without a reference to the Rawlsian Theory of Justice as Fairness expressed on "A Theory of Justice", Rawls (1971). The ideas developed by Rawls, namely his concept of primary goods, can be regarded as the inspiration for Sen's Capabilities.

Interesting enough, Rawls has also served as an inspiration for some mainstream welfare economists who tried to incorporate his ideas within the welfarist framework (with the max-min principle and the Leontieff-type social indifference curves already mentioned). Nevertheless, that incorporation has to be seen as misleading: Rawls clearly departs from both welfarism and utilitarianism (cornerstones of MWE that Sen also rejects). He builds his theory within the *social contract theory* (where Locke, Rousseau and Kant are prominent authors, all disagreeing with utilitarianism) and defines primary goods as the informational base one should look at when evaluating the welfare of individuals, not utility. So, Rawls is clearly closer to Sen (or Sen is closer to Rawls) and his work has opened the way to the CA within WE.

One last remark serves the purpose of highlighting a difference between Rawls' and Sen's ideas. As a welfare economist who is very concerned with poverty and underdevelopment issues, Sen has a pragmatic inclination which is reflected in his conception of capabilities where the word *actual* is essential: capabilities are the *actual* possibilities an individual possesses to lead the life he/she wants. Formal, constitutional possibilities alone are not enough to be counted as capabilities. Contrarily, Rawls (as a philosopher) was more concerned with the design of a fair society and gave primary goods a more formal/constitutional flavour, stressing the importance of constitutional fair rules that generate fair expectations about primary goods, and not so much to the actual fair opportunities in accessing those primary goods (as he was dealing with the construction of the basic structure of a society, not with any particular real society).

---

[40]One mild restriction Sen imposes is the necessity of an ideally long period of open, public and democratic discussion so the concept of capability might emerge. See Sen (1999).

6.5   Happiness: Accepting Subjectivity in Welfare Economic Analysis

Happiness is a vast concept: one of the main concerns of philosophers and of great dispute about its content. It is also one of the most important values for humankind.

It is reasonable to argue that economics, a social science which studies the society and the individual, should give a relevant place to happiness, at least in its welfare analysis. In fact, we know that is not the case (or at least not in a straight-forward narrative).

MWE uses a very abstract notion of utility, one that clearly does not need to have any connection with a notion of happiness. In MWE, utility is empty of psychological meaning as it is assumed that all one needs is the observation of rational choice behaviour (and the consequent revealed preferences).

Nevertheless, this has not always been the case in economics[41] and the research with subjective indicators of welfare has put happiness back on the track of many economists' research agenda. In particular, data on Subjective Well-Being (SWB) has given rise to some interesting and puzzling findings for the economic profession: Easterlin's Paradox, Easterlin (1974), is probably the most widely used finding to demonstrate that something is wrong with MWE.

MWE seems to look at income growth as an objective way of increasing welfare: if mean income rises and no one's falls, then welfare ought to rise (as the Pareto criterion would corroborate). Easterlin's Paradox clearly shows such a correlation is not always present, and that the reason why MWE fails to see it lays in its utility conceptions and rationality assumptions.

For HL there are new stylized facts that are incompatible with MWE assumptions. In HL, agents are systematically myopic. For instance, agents fail to perceive that consumption[42] only produces happiness if one's consumption is greater than the reference group's average (comparison effect), greater than what it was in the past (adaptation effect), and close to one's expectations. As a consequence, agents over-invest in consumption (and in work) gaining less happiness than what they had thought. Furthermore, subjective assessments of welfare are counted as reliable, comparable and scientifically rigorous.[43] Utility is understood as a psychological reality that might have a cardinal nature (comparable interpersonally and across countries) and that can be grasped, namely through questionnaires.

HL can be understood as a return to the early days of neoclassicism, and to the ideas of J. Bentham (who conceived of agents as pleasures seekers and pain evaders) of cardinal and measurable utility.[44] But HL uses new findings and techniques (from

---

[41] See Bruni (2004a, b).

[42] Mainly conspicuous consumption, see Frank (2005).

[43] See Veenhoven (2002) for a detailed analysis why subjective measures are important in welfare assessments.

[44] Although not necessarily endorsing the Benthamite moral theory (which states that "good" is everything that prompts human pleasure and "bad" is all that dooms it).

economics, and also from psychology, neuroscience and sociology), empowering its analysis such that the old criticisms early neoclassicism faced are overcome.[45]

HL also challenges MWE in several ways: not only with respect to the techniques employed but also on the basic assumptions about rationality and utility. As already stated, HL disputes perfect rationality, revealed ordinal utility, classical preference axioms, surplus analysis, the role of GDP in orthodox welfare policy, but offers, amongst others, comparison and adaptation effects analysis, hedonic treadmills, SWB and survey data.

Nevertheless, many authors within HL still retain the utilitarian and individual-istic paradigms, typical of MWE.[46] And that is what stands HL apart from CA, as this last approach is clearly non-utilitarian and anti methodological individualism. In a way, HL could be understood as standing between MWE and CA (or as the closest version of utilitarianism to CA): both HL and CA reject restrict utilitarianism, ordinalism, perfect rationality, and choice behaviour paradigm (fundamentals of MWE) but where CA places demands for capabilities (non-utility information, a radical cut with utilitarianism), HL stands for happiness (new interpretation and measures of utility, new versions of utilitarianism). The supporters of CA consider happiness as just one capability amongst others of equal or higher importance (such as freedom) while HL regards capabilities as explanatory variables on happiness equations (well-nourished, free and rich persons will be happier).[47] Thus, HL is not equivalent to MWE as it uses types of information and methods that were rejected by the latter (although sharing utilitarian philosophy) and is not equivalent to CA since it accepts utilitarianism while CA proposes capabilities (although sharing some techniques, data and policy conclusions). More, HL might be closer to CA from an applied/political point of view, but from a philosophical point of view HL is closer to MWE.[48] Ultimately, there is justification for HL to stand out as an alternative approach to WE, from both MWE and CA.[49]

Although HL deals with some internal incoherencies and disputes it is gaining prominence and credibility, attracting more and more economists to its milieu, which

---

[45]More and more evidence, see Layard (2005), from psychology and neurology shows that the sensation of well-being can be assessed (via brain scans and electroencephalographs) and that it has a physical and chemical nature. That strengthens the idea that utility is something real and objective (also strengthening the hypotheses that it can be grasped objectively via questionnaires). See also Oswald and Wu (2010) for an objective confirmation of subjective perceptions.

[46]Of course some reject utilitarianism (most of those being closer to CA than to HL) and others the methodological individualism. See Zamagni (2005), Sugden (2005) and Bruni and Stanca (2006), claiming the need for relational views on economics if happiness is to be properly incorporated.

[47]See Hojman and Miranda (2018).

[48]Which proximity is more important might be subject to discussion. Nevertheless, from a funda-mental point of view, the distinction between utilitarian (MWE and HL) and non-utilitarian (CA) analysis appears as the most relevant.

[49]Even if there is the temptation of MWE to incorporate HL main findings and assumptions (as HL remains utilitarian and as the imperialism of economics would predict) that is not a problem to HL's relevance: quite the contrary, that would mean that MWE has recognized validity and robustness in this new line of work.

can be witnessed by the increasing number of papers published on this topic in top-rated journals.[50]

At the end of the day HL proves it cannot be neglected when making an economic analysis of welfare.

6.6   The Policy Issue: Happiness is Different from Capabilities and the Mainstream

After all that has been said in the previous sections, some fundamental questions remain to be clarified: do these theoretical and conceptual disputes have practical consequences? Does the chosen theoretical framework give rise to different policy advice? The answer is yes, and for three main reasons: first, different conceptual frameworks allow economists to analyse different problems; second, even for the same problems, the different theoretical setups may imply different policy conclusions; third, even if for the same problems different theories imply similar policies the justification for such policies will be different, grounded in different concepts and values.[51]

Over the previous sections we have analysed the main characteristics of three approaches to WE: CA, HL and MWE. We have noted that each has its specific set of assumptions and tools. Now we need to clarify which policy consequences each brings about.

MWE, CA and HL differ in many ways: theoretical, philosophical and methodologically. Therefore, it is not surprising that each approach advocates different kinds of policies for welfare enhancement.

Using methodological individualism, consequentialism and behaviourism (the revealed preference and ordinal utility framework), most MWE models end up with liberal policy advice: free individual interaction through markets is the best way for society to reach welfare (once the basic rules of law and justice are guaranteed). The welfare analyst can support market liberalization policies since those same policies generally promote Pareto movements (in the Kaldor-Hicks sense). Besides that, he or she has very little space of action: cannot judge non-Pareto movements, cannot judge distributional issues of welfare between two Pareto efficient states and, extremely important, cannot judge welfare variations not grasped through choice behaviour.[52] All these are lacunas that can be overcome with a paradigm change.

That's exactly what CA and HL try to do, even if using different strategies.

---

[50]Di Tella et al. (2001), Clark and Oswald (1994), Blanchflower and Oswald (2004), Stevenson and Wolfers (2009), Deaton and Stone (2013), Benjamin et al. (2014) are just a few examples.

[51]Important as this philosophical issue might be, the relevance of new approaches in WE springs mostly from the different policy conclusions and enlarged domain of analysis.

[52]For instance, cannot qualify between different situations in terms of the actual range of choices, processes and freedoms.

CA marks a clear change in most assumptions and structures of welfare analysis: it departs from consequentialism (as it puts great emphasis on the processes through which every final state might be achieved, ranking those states accordingly), from ordinal utility (as it deems all forms of utilitarianism poor in terms of the used informational base, using capabilities instead), from hedonism (advocating a more eudaemonistic conception of welfare where happiness can only emerge through human flourishing and relinquishing happiness as the ultimate goal of human existence), from methodological individualism (as it considers that many welfare phenomena can only be understood when using a relational approach[53]) and from perfect rationality (agents are conceived as complex psychological entities). With all this it is not surprising that its welfare analysis and policy conclusions differ from those of MWE.

Using CA, the core of welfare lays in the actual possibilities individuals have to lead the life they want or have reasons to value. For that end, issues like access to food, healthcare, education, political activity, income, work and protection from abuse, tyranny and discrimination figure high on the list of welfare essentials.

In terms of policy, the promotion of healthcare, education, democracy, markets and the rule of law are top priorities.

CA as a framework of analysis is used more and more to ground and conduct welfare analysis and policy[54] and marks a clear departure from MWE ideals.

HL is a different research track. Using econometrics to estimate happiness equations (discovering its determinants or unveiling happiness shadow prices),[55] utilizing experiments to assess the impact of life events on happiness,[56] constructing new indexes of welfare or engaging in interdisciplinary theoretical conversations, it is plural, uses different methods, models and techniques, reaches different results and policy conclusions.[57] Nevertheless, it is now possible to identify a set of core assumptions, ideas and main conclusions that almost all researchers agree with. Within that core we can put forward the *comparison effect*, the *adaptation effect*, the *expectation effect*, the *diminishing marginal utility of money*, the difference between

---

[53]Considering that some aspects of human welfare are intrinsically relational.

[54]When the United Nations' Human Development Index was created it was embodied with CA ideas: the introduction of life expectancy at birth and literacy in combination with GDPpc in a development index is a concession to the idea that not everything can be translated into money (each capability is autonomous and cannot be transformed/translated into another).

[55]See Powdthavee (2008) or van Praag and Baarsma (2005).

[56]See Loewenstein et al. (2015) or Proto et al. (2012).

[57]Some prefer to use subjective notions of happiness (with underlying utilitarianism, hedonism and methodological individualism), adopt an empirical route and believe that life events (demographic, economic, social, etc.) can have a large and permanent impact over happiness (see Blanchflower and Oswald (2004), Clark and Oswald (1994), Frey and Stutzer (2002), amongst others) while others prefer to rely on objective happiness (see Kahneman and Tversky (2000)), proceed with theoretical analysis, use relational approaches, adopt procedural views and support eudaemonism (see Zamagni (2005), Bruni and Stanca (2006)), or even support (mostly psychologists) the set point theory where SWB appears as stable over time for every individual, like a personality trait that can only be temporarily affected by life events (see Diener and Diener (1996)).

decision and experienced utility,[58] and the different impact each *life domain* has on happiness.

All these facts have strong policy implications in directions that clearly diverge from those of MWE.

Once we accept that agents compare what they have in the present with what they had in the past and adapt, more or less quickly, to the new standard, compare what others (from one's reference group) have, compare this with their expectations of what they should have (again, these expectations depend on the society and group culture, norms and values) and do all this differently for each life domain (like work, family, leisure or income), we are forced to regard MWE as unreliable. After all, in this context, agents are not perfectly rational (they make repeated mistakes and show signs of addictive behaviour), information doesn't flow easely, and markets become imperfect.

One stylized fact of HL is the diminishing marginal utility of GDP per capita: after a certain level, continuous increases in GDP cannot push happiness any further. That is, despite agents moving in line with increasing income, that becomes unproductive in terms of welfare augmentation. The so-called Pareto movements are, after all, not efficient in terms of welfare (they might be "Pareto efficient in income", not in welfare). If what WE tries to analyse and promote is real welfare, then HL shows that it has to do much more than stick to agent's behaviour, income and monetary evaluations.

We have seen that both CA and HL criticize the purity of markets and agents and consequently the validity of MWE. They try to build new evidence, tools and theories. In the end, they advocate different policies for welfare. Those differences can be exemplified.

Freedom and income are basic goods[59] that are generally considered crucial to human welfare. In WE that is also the case (although more the case for income than for freedom).

Income is the most well-studied issue within economics (and consequently, in MWE) and is normally regarded as a benchmark of economic well-being and as an objective scale through which most types of welfare can by analysed.[60]

Freedom is a more controversial issue since it is a vaguer concept. It can assume a political nature (democracy versus dictatorship), an economic nature (free entrepreneurship versus planned economy), a societal nature (closed versus open societies), an individual nature (individuals with private spheres of freedom versus totally controlled individuals). In WE, freedom is usually analysed as economic freedom (also as

---

[58]See Kahneman et al. (1997).

[59]Or primary goods as in Rawls (1971).

[60]This is a consequence of the admitted objectivity of income in comparison with other proxies of welfare and the conviction that most relevant economic welfare issues can be translated into monetary figures. Nevertheless, economists have long realized that these income measures of welfare have several problems. See, for instance, Samuelson (1974).

freedom of choice over consumption goods) and is integrated into policy advice by the idea that more freedom leads to more competition and enhanced market efficiency.

Given their significance, we should analyse both of these issues more carefully.

6.6.1 Freedom

Being a vast concept, freedom is prone to confusion and disagreement. Nevertheless, it is normally regarded as highly important for human welfare.

Within MWE analysis freedom usually enters as freedom of choice over various options: more choices mean greater opportunity for maximization and hence, higher levels of welfare. More fundamentally, freedom is only regarded as a precondition for maximization: agents must be free to maximize their utility. Freedom also means the liberty to participate in markets through buying, selling and producing goods.

For the CA this is a clearly poor way of dealing with freedom when performing welfare analysis. Here, freedom deserves the highest position when thinking about welfare. After all, the freedom to live the life one wants or has reason to value is at the core of the concept of capability. Hence, freedom deserves close scrutiny if one wants to proceed with a reliable welfare analysis.

Freedom can be thought of as the concept CA most approximates with the ultimate goal of human existence[61]: life expectancy at birth, school education, access to food and health, civil and political rights, are all conceived of as important to welfare, since all contribute to enhancing the freedom individuals have to choose a path for their lives. The CA goes as far as to state that what really matters is the *actual* freedoms individuals enjoy, not the potential or legal ones. Freedom is conceived of as valuable per se, even if the results are not affected by its presence or absence, let those results be measured in terms of wealth, health or happiness.

So, Enhancing freedoms is the major political concern of CA, a prominence not granted by the policies of MWE.

As we have already mentioned, HL might be thought of as an intermediate position between MWE and CA. Here, it considers freedom a very important welfare issue, not because it thinks of it as the objective value but rather because freedom usually enhances SWB. Political freedoms and civil rights, freedom to participate in economic and social life, and so on, usually show high levels of positive correlation with reported happiness.[62] That is why there is room for policy intervention in the direction of increasing freedoms even in situations where MWE would recommend no action (because agents were supposedly maximizing their welfare and the lack of freedom was not grasped through their behaviour).

Nevertheless, HL's stance on freedom only as instrumental and not as a fundamental of welfare marks a sharp difference with CA. For instance, Schwartz et al.

---

[61]See Sen (1999).

[62]See, for instance, Frey and Stutzer (2002) and Hojman and Miranda (2018).

(2002) show that more options are not always on par with more satisfaction.[63] Instead, the gains of having more options to choose from might be annulled by the increased cost of selecting the right option. The increased opportunity cost, the anguish of not knowing if we've made the best choice and the very cost of processing the information might lead us to a worse situation after an option enlargement. Within CA such a conflict would be given little relevance.

From all we have said so far, it becomes clear that the choice of framework will impinge on the policy conclusions. Whether we consider freedom as a precondition for market operation, as instrumental for happiness or as a fundamental of welfare, different policies will emerge as to what is best for welfare enhancement.

6.6.2 Income

Income might be seen as the core of WE. Income has been the main concern of economics since the early ages of Political Economics. Trying to understand what could promote the enlargement of national wealth was probably the first research and political question in the history of economics.

From those early days until today different paths have been followed concerning assumptions, models and tools of analysis. Nonetheless, income has remained at the core of what economic welfare should be/was.[64]

As a result, welfare policy has long been biased towards income enlargement, neglecting all sorts of other possibly relevant dimensions (like environment, family life or freedom).

MWE is on a par with these ideals as it sees income as the main source of welfare and the benchmark against which all can be compared (the same as saying that almsot everything can be translated into a price). Forgetting the old lessons of early Neoclassicicsm on the diminishing marginal utility of money, most modern welfare policies regard GDP per capita enhancement as the sole objective and uncontroversial means of increasing welfare. As might be intuitively perceived, this analysis neglects countless effects that income growth policies might have on various domains of social and individual life. Those effects might be detrimental to welfare. If so, then a global effect of an income raising policy might be diminished

---

[63]See also Evrensel (2015) explaining how the relationship between happiness and economic freedom might be mediate by religious beliefs.

[64]Interestingly, during the classical period income was regarded as very important to welfare, not the welfare itself. So, understanding the way through which income increases was important, as long as income could be transformed into welfare. Later, this "transformation problem" was forgotten as the non-monetary part of welfare (*ophelimity*) was deemed unscientific and behind the scope of WE, see Robbins (1945). With that it became implicitly assumed that income would go hand-in-hand with welfare, since rational agents (who always maximize utility) with higher incomes would have the opportunity to increase their utility. So, the "transformation problem" disappeared. See Bruni (2004a, b).

welfare. Exactly because some economists think that is the case, new approaches have appeared.

The advocates of HL point out four main reasons why an income raise might not be always good: *comparison effect, adaptation effect, expectations effect* and *life domains specificities.*

Comparison effect refers to the fact that people tend to compare their income with that of others (relevant others) so that their welfare level will mostly depend on their position relative to others, and not on an absolute level. With that, there cannot be an increase in welfare (happiness) through an increase in average income: if my income rises by the same proportion as that of others, then my satisfaction level will remain constant.

Adaptation effect refers to the fact that people tend to adapt to their current level of income, reverting to some baseline level of welfare after a while. Again people compare themselves, now with their past, and tend to gain happiness right after an increase on their income but quickly adapt and return to their previous level of satisfaction.[65] That is, an income augmenting policy might be extremely short-lived in terms of welfare gains.

Expectations also play a crucial role in SWB. The *expectation effect* states that our satisfaction with any income level will be a function of the difference between our expectation and the actual level of income. So, we can only increase our welfare if our actual income approaches our expectations. The problem is that, normally, our expectations will move along with our income level: for a rising income, rising expectations. If that's the case, our income oriented policy fails again.[66]

Finally, *life domains specificities* are crucial to complete the picture of HL in respect to income: the above-cited effects are not equally present in diferent life domains. Specifically, satisfaction with income is the life domain which is the most prone to adaptation and comparison: we adapt much quicker to a bigger salary than to an extended period of vacations; we compare the size of our house with those of the neighbours much more than the time we have for leisure; we adapt our expectations in term of income as it grows while our expectations of what a good number of children is doesn't change with the actual number of children we have.[67]

Knowing this, it becomes simple to understand that left to themselves (via market interactions), agents will over-invest in work, production and consumption (as they fail to anticipate adaptation and comparison effects[68] and behave as addict s to

---

[65]There is evidence of this effect even from a sample of lottery winners who quickly lost their initial euphoria and remained as happy as (or little more than) before their lucky day (see Brickman et al. (1978)).

[66]See Stutzer (2004) for empirical evidence.

[67]See Frank (2005).

[68]Note that comparison effect might be anticipated but, nevertheless, agents might be forced to act accordingly: in some situations, what others have affects us directly even if one wants to stop comparing oneself with others. For instance, a student without a computer is thrown into such a deprived situation that he/she is forced to keep on the road of continuous technology adaptation, which implies continuous consumption.

consumption[69]) in a way that markets become inefficient in producing welfare: there are externalities (like the income of others affecting me) and imperfect rationality that destroy market efficiency.

Furthermore, there are "standard" market imperfections (like environmental issues and monopolies) that further condemn the market to be inefficient in welfare production. Nevertheless, these four effects are key contributions of HL.

In HL, income is important as long as it is instrumental for happiness. The policies for income must be those that promote the greater enhancement over SWB, not those that maximize income.

For CA, income is also a very relevant issue.[70] Welfare is impossible without income and its augmentation and distribution are deep concerns of this line of work. However, we find in CA sharp criticism to the dogmatic importance MWE gives to income and a repositioning of income within the framework of capabilities: income is important because it is instrumental to the development of capabilities. In order to survive, to participate in society and to flourish, every human being needs some sort of income. If he or she does not have that endowment, any welfare achievement becomes impossible. Income is a sine qua non for welfare, but it is not welfare itself. In fact, what is important is the power income brings to people so that they can transform it into capabilities.[71]

As in the HL case, for CA the relationship between income and welfare is not linear: more income might not generate more capabilities and so more income might not always be the best outcome there is.

Policies that enhance GDP per capita but do nothing (or do harm) to capabilities must be discarded and replaced by others which are more effective in enhancing capabilities. In this context, a poor but democratic country might be preferable to a wealthy dictatorship.

From all that has been said, it becomes clear why HL stands as an alternative for a welfare analysis that cannot be reduced to either MWE nor CA. HL can even be seen as a "third way" of complementing capabilities and the mainstream: it shares and rejects some principles of both capabilities and mainstream approaches but stands as an autonomous alternative. It postulates a specific set of policies and is an operational approach to WE.

6.7 Conclusion

Since the seminal work of Richard Easterlin in 1974 using happiness data as a measure of welfare, a lot has been happening in welfare analysis in economics.

---

[69]That is why decision and experienced utility diverge, and a total reliance on the former causes policy mistakes.

[70]Sen has always been very concerned with poverty and deprivation, and therefore, with access to income.

[71]That is why poverty, for instance, is seen as capability deprivation, not as income deprivation.

But only the turn of the twentieth to the twentieth-first century was able to advance on Easterlin's insight. The continuous growth that can be witnessed on the HL since the 1990s is a well-deserved reward to those who have first notice the obvious – if economics wants to produce welfare judgments, and perceive the impact of economic policies and different economic states on the well-being of humankind, it has to measure and study happiness.

The aim of this chapter was to make clear that this set of publications that we call the HL might be seen as a plural but congruent bunch of welfare analysis where happiness, the subjective well-being of individuals and societies, is the central measure of welfare. Furthermore, we wanted to demonstrate that this literature is producing autonomous knowledge that cannot be encompassed by the existing mainstream welfare analysis neither by the competing approach of Sen's capabilities.

Beginning by pointing out the complexities that any serious welfare analysis requires and stressing out that many mainstream economists produce incoherent work when jumping from their positive models to policy conclusions, we then addressed separately different ways to engage in an economic analysis of welfare.

We have analysed three forms of looking at WE and have endeavoured to examine and compare main postulates, assumptions and policy conclusions of each. We have been able to determine that MWE, CA and HL are all different and stand as alternative and autonomous ways of performing WE analysis. In fact, although we might find some similarities between them (MWE and HL share a utilitarian, hedonistic, individualistic and consequentialist background, CA and HL share concern with freedoms and processes and are critical of MWE's support of ordinal utility), their core of assumptions differs and many policy conclusions vary (mostly from MWE to CA and HL).

We have also made clear that all three approaches have different conceptions of what welfare is (due to different philosophical backgrounds). Consequently, the policy differences among them are not just a product of disagreements over which techniques are more suitable for reaching a certain and common goal, but a result of different conceptions on which goal is to be achieved: that is, the paths (policies) are different because the final destination (welfare conception) is not the same.

Retaining the ideas of Robbins (1981), any approach might be considered scientifically valid only after one first decides, making a moral, non-scientific choice, which conception of welfare is to be used.

References

Arimah, B. C. (1992). Hedonic prices and the demand for housing attributes in a third-world city – The case of Ibadan, Nigeria. *Urban Studies, 29*(5), 639–651.

Arrow, K. J. (1951). *Social choices and individual values*. New York: Wiley.

Benjamin, D. J., Heffetz, O., Kimball, M. S., & Rees-Jones, A. (2014). Can marginal rates of substitution be inferred from happiness data? Evidence from residency choices. *American Economic Review, 104*(11), 3498–3528.

Bergson, A. (1938). A reformulation of certain aspects of welfare economics. *The Quarterly Journal of Economics, 52*(2), 310–334.

Bergson, A. (1954). On the concept of social welfare. *The Quarterly Journal of Economics, 68*(2), 233–252.

Bharadwaj, K. (1972). Marshall on Pigou's wealth and welfare. *Economica, 39*(153), 32–46.

Bhattacharya, D. (2015). Nonparametric welfare analysis for discrete choice. *Econometrica, 83*(2), 617–649.

Blanchflower, D. G., & Oswald, A. J. (2004). Money, sex and happiness: An empirical study. *Scandinavian Journal of Economics, 106*(3), 393–415.

Brickman, P., Coates, D., & Janoff-Bulman, R. (1978). Lottery winners and accident victims: Is happiness relative? *Journal of Personality and Social Psychology, 36*(8), 917–927.

Bruni, L. (2004a). The 'Happiness transformation problem'in the Cambridge tradition. *The European Journal of the History of Economic Thought, 11*(3), 433–451.

Bruni, L. (2004b). The "technology of happiness" and the tradition of economic science. *Journal of the History of Economic Thought, 26*(1), 19–44.

Bruni, L., & Stanca, L. (2006). Income aspirations, television and happiness: Evidence from the world values survey. *Kyklos, 59*(2), 209–225.

Chipman, J. S., & Moore, J. C. (1978). The new welfare economics 1939–1974. *International Economic Review, 19*(3), 547–584.

Clark, A. E., & Oswald, A. J. (1994). Unhappiness and unemployment. *The Economic Journal, 104*(424), 648–659.

Clarke, E. H. (1971). Multipart pricing of public goods. *Public Choice, 11*(1), 17–33.

Clarke, P. M. (1998). Cost–benefit analysis and mammographic screening: A travel cost approach. *Journal of Health Economics, 17*(6), 767–787.

Colombo, L., Femminis, G., & Pavan, A. (2014). Information acquisition and welfare. *The Review of Economic Studies, 81*(4), 1438–1483.

Comim, F. (2005). Capabilities and happiness: Potential synergies. *Review of Social Economy, 63*(2), 161–176.

Cooter, R., & Rappoport, P. (1984). Were the ordinalists wrong about welfare economics? *Journal of Economic Literature, 22*(2), 507–530.

Deaton, A., & Stone, A. A. (2013). Two happiness puzzles. *American Economic Review, 103*(3), 591–597.

Di Tella, R., MacCulloch, R. J., & Oswald, A. J. (2001). Preferences over inflation and unemployment: Evidence from surveys of happiness. *American Economic Review, 91*(1), 335–341.

Dickie, M., Delorme, C. D., Jr., & Humphreys, J. M. (1997). Hedonic prices, goods-specific effects and functional form: Inferences from cross-section time series data. *Applied Economics, 29*(2), 239–249.

Diener, E., & Diener, C. (1996). Most people are happy. *Psychological Science, 7*(3), 181–185.

Duclos, J. Y., & Araar, A. (2006). *Poverty and equity: Measurement, policy and estimation with DAD* (Vol. 2). New York: Springer.

Easterlin, R. A. (1974). Does economic growth improve the human lot? Some empirical evidence. In P. A. David & M. W. Reder (Eds.), *Nations and households in economic growth: Essays in honour of Moses Abramovitz* (pp. 89–125). New York: Academic Press.

Evrensel, A. Y. (2015). Happiness, economic freedom and culture. *Applied Economics Letters, 22*(9), 683–687.

Fleurbaey, M., & Mongin, P. (2005). The news of the death of welfare economics is greatly exaggerated. *Social Choice and Welfare, 25*(2-3), 381–418.

Frank, R. H. (2005). Does absolute income matter? In L. Bruni & P. L. Porta (Eds.), *Economics and happiness: Framing the analysis*. Oxford: Oxford University Press.

Frey, B. S. (2008). *Happiness: A revolution in economics*. Cambridge: MIT press.

Frey, B. S., & Stutzer, A. (2002). What can economists learn from happiness research? *Journal of Economic Literature, 40*(2), 402–435.

Groves, T. (1973). Incentives in teams. *Econometrica: Journal of the Econometric Society, 41*, 617–631.

Hailu, G., Boxall, P. C., & McFarlane, B. L. (2005). The influence of place attachment on recreation demand. *Journal of Economic Psychology, 26*(4), 581–598.

Hamilton, J. M. (2007). Coastal landscape and the hedonic price of accommodation. *Ecological Economics, 62*(3–4), 594–602.

Handel, B. R., & Kolstad, J. T. (2015). Health insurance for "humans": Information frictions, plan choice, and consumer welfare. *American Economic Review, 105*(8), 2449–2500.

Hicks, J. R. (1939). The foundations of welfare economics. *The Economic Journal, 49*(196), 696–712.

Hicks, J. R. (1940). The valuation of the social income. *Economica, 7*(26), 105–124.

Hicks, J. R. (1943). The four consumer's surpluses. *The Review of Economic Studies, 11*(1), 31–41.

Hojman, D. A., & Miranda, A. (2018). Agency, human dignity, and subjective well-being. *World Development, 101*, 1–15.

Johansson, P. O. (1991). *An introduction to modern welfare economics*. Cambridge/New York/Melbourne: Cambridge University Press.

Just, R. E., Hueth, D. L., & Schmitz, A. (2005). *The welfare economics of public policy: A practical approach to project and policy evaluation*. Cheltenham/Northampton: Edward Elgar Publishing.

Kahneman, D., & Tversky, A. (2000). Experienced utility and objective happiness: A moment-based approach. In *Choices, values, and frames*. Cambridge/New York/Melbourne: Cambridge University Press/Russell Sage Foundation.

Kahneman, D., Wakker, P. P., & Sarin, R. (1997). Back to Bentham? Explorations of experienced utility. *The Quarterly Journal of Economics, 112*(2), 375–406.

Kaldor, N. (1939). Welfare propositions of economics and interpersonal comparisons of utility. *The Economic Journal, 49*, 549–552.

Laffont, J. J., & Tirole, J. (1986). Using cost observation to regulate firms. *Journal of Political Economy, 94*(3, Part 1), 614–641.

Layard, R. (2005). *Happiness: Lessons from a new science*. New York: The Penguim Press.

Layard, R. (2006). Happiness and public policy: A challenge to the profession. *The Economic Journal, 116*(510), C24–C33.

Little, I. M. (1952). Social choice and individual values. *Journal of Political Economy, 60*(5), 422–432.

Loewenstein, G., Krishnamurti, T., Kopsic, J., & McDonald, D. (2015). Does increased sexual frequency enhance happiness? *Journal of Economic Behavior & Organization, 116*, 206–218.

Oswald, A. J., & Wu, S. (2010). Objective confirmation of subjective measures of human well-being: Evidence from the USA. *Science, 327*(5965), 576–579.

Pope, J. C. (2008). Buyer information and the Hedonic: The impact of a seller disclosure on the implicit price for airport noise. *Journal of Urban Economics, 63*, 498–516.

Powdthavee, N. (2008). Putting a price tag on friends, relatives, and neighbours: Using surveys of life satisfaction to value social relationships. *The Journal of Socio-Economics, 37*(4), 1459–1480.

Proto, E., Sgroi, D., & Oswald, A. J. (2012). Are happiness and productivity lower among young people with newly-divorced parents? An experimental and econometric approach. *Experimental Economics, 15*(1), 1–23.

Rawls, J. (1971). *A theory of justice*. Cambridge, MA: Belknap Press.

Robbins, L. (1932). *An essay on the nature and significance of economic science*. London: Macmillan and Co., Limited.

Robbins, L. (1945). *An essay on the nature and significance of economic science*. London: Macmillan and Co., Limited.

Robbins, L. (1981). Economics and political economy. *American Economic Review, 71*(2), 1–10.

Samuelson, P. A. (1974). Analytical notes on international real-income measures. *The Economic Journal, 84*, 595–608.

Samuelson, P. A. (1977). Reaffirming the existence of "Reasonable" Bergson-Samuelson social welfare functions. *Economica, 44*, 81–88.

Schwartz, B., Ward, A., Monterosso, J., Lyubomirsky, S., White, K., & Lehman, D. R. (2002). Maximizing versus satisficing: Happiness is a matter of choice. *Journal of Personality and Social Psychology, 83*(5), 1178–1197.

Sen, A. (1970). The impossibility of a Paretian liberal. *Journal of Political Economy, 78*(1), 152–157.

Sen, A. (1979a). Personal utilities and public judgements – Or what's wrong with welfare economics. *Economic Journal, 89*, 537–558.

Sen, A. (1979b). Utilitarianism and welfarism. *The Journal of Philosophy, 76*(9), 463–489.

Sen, A. (1983). Liberty and social choice. *The Journal of Philosophy, 80*(1), 5–28.

Sen, A. (1999). *Development as freedom*. Oxford: Oxford University Press.

Sen, A. (2000). The discipline of cost-benefit analysis. *The Journal of Legal Studies, 29*(S2), 931–952.

Sengupta, S., & Osgood, D. E. (2003). The value of remoteness: A hedonic estimation of ranchette prices. *Ecological Economics, 44*(1), 91–103.

Shrestha, R. K., Seidl, A. F., & Moraes, A. S. (2002). Value of recreational fishing in the Brazilian Pantanal: a travel cost analysis using count data models. *Ecological Economics, 42*(1–2), 289–299.

Stevenson, B., & Wolfers, J. (2009). The paradox of declining female happiness. *American Economic Journal: Economic Policy, 1*(2), 190–225.

Stigler, G. J. (1950). The development of utility theory. I. *Journal of Political Economy, 58*(4), 307–327.

Stutzer, A. (2004). The role of income aspirations in individual happiness. *Journal of Economic Behavior & Organization, 54*(1), 89–109.

Sugden, R. (2005). Correspondence of sentiments: An explanation of the pleasure of social interaction. In L. Bruni & P. L. Porta (Eds.), *Economics and happiness: Framing the analysis*. Oxford: Oxford University Press.

Timmins, C., & Murdock, J. (2007). A revealed preference approach to the measurement of congestion in travel cost models. *Journal of Environmental Economics and Management, 53*(2), 230–249.

Tse, R. Y. (2002). Estimating neighbourhood effects in house prices: Towards a new hedonic model approach. *Urban Studies, 39*(7), 1165–1180.

Van Praag, B. M., & Baarsma, B. E. (2005). Using happiness surveys to value intangibles: The case of airport noise. *The Economic Journal, 115*(500), 224–246.

Veenhoven, R. (2002). Why social policy needs subjective indicators. *Social Indicators Research, 58*(1–3), 33–46.

Viner, J. (1925). The utility concept in value theory and its critics. *Journal of Political Economy, 33*(6), 638–659.

Wang, Z. (2003). Hedonic prices for crude oil. *Applied Economics Letters, 10*(13), 857–861.

Wolfe, A. B. (1931). On the content of welfare. *The American Economic Review*, 207–221.

Zamagni, S. (2005). Happiness and individualism: A very difficult union. In L. Bruni & P. L. Porta (Eds.), *Economics and happiness: Framing the analysis*. Oxford: Oxford University Press.

Chapter 7
Why the Easterlin Paradox? The Scitovsky Hypothesis

Maurizio Pugno

Abstract Starting from the mid-1970s and the mid-1990s, Richard Easterlin has provided three key contributions to the development of Happiness Economics. These regard: the existence of the paradox that takes his name, its explanation, and the use of psychological concepts in economics, like happiness and aspirations. Each of these issues is still unresolved. Tibor Scitovsky, working in the same years on the same issues, advanced an explanation of the paradox that endogenizes what are today the most widespread explanations, i.e. those based on adaptation and relative income. Confirmation of his hypothesis can be found in psychology and in economics that now use psychological concepts, like motivations and non-cognitive skills.

7.1 Introduction

With the article of 1974, then re-elaborated in 1995, Richard Easterlin gave momentum to the stream of research now called Happiness Economics. He proposed three issues at the same time: about facts, by showing a paradox, i.e., that subjective well-being tends to be constant over time despite economic growth; about theory, by explaining this paradox with a psychological mechanism whereby people's aspirations persistently grow with income, thus counterbalancing the welfare-improving effect of income; about methodology, by thus introducing some psychology into economics.

The first issue – the existence of the paradox – has spurred a great deal of interesting empirical research, but without a shared conclusion being reached on whether the paradox tends to apply to all countries. The second issue – explanation of the paradox – has mainly become a test of Easterlin's argument, with the finding that the negative effect of people's aspirations on their subjective well-being is important, but it varies across life domains. It thus remains to be explained why

M. Pugno (✉)
Department of Economics and Law, University of Cassino, Cassino, Italy
e-mail: m.pugno@unicas.it; http://mauriziopugno.com/en/

© Springer Nature Switzerland AG 2019
M. Rojas (ed.), *The Economics of Happiness*,
https://doi.org/10.1007/978-3-030-15835-4_7

157

people do not learn to form their aspirations so as to improve their subjective well-being permanently. To this end, more psychology would be needed, so that the third issue remains unresolved as well.

Tibor Scitovsky worked during the same span of time as Easterlin on the same issues, but he was so original in each of the three issues that his contributions are not yet fully explored. In regard to the empirical issue, he relaxed the paradox by recognizing that the tendency towards a joyless economy may be true for the United States but not necessarily for other countries, like some European countries. In regard to the theoretical issue, he proposed an explanation of the paradox which endogenizes people's aspirations. In regard to the methodological issue, he paved the way to substantially introduce psychology into economics as required by the study of how people change preferences (Scitovsky 1976, 1986, 1995, 1996; Pugno 2013, 2014a, 2016, 2017).

The paper is organised as follows: Sect. 7.2 introduces the paradox as stated by Easterlin, and then it highlights the open issues; Sect. 7.3 shows how Scitovsky contributed to these and other issues; and Sect. 7.4 concludes by re-stating Scitovsky's hypothesis.

7.2   The Easterlin Paradox and the Open Issues

7.2.1   The Two Versions of the 'Easterlin Paradox'

The Paradox states that at a point in time happiness varies directly with income both among and within nations, but over time happiness does not trend upward as income continues to grow (Easterlin 2016, p. 2).

This is the paradox that Easterlin has stated in a recent paper, adding that '"happiness" is used here interchangeably with subjective well-being as a proxy for all evaluative measures of self-reported feelings of well-being' and that '"income" is a proxy for real GDP per capita' (Easterlin 2016, p. 2).

In the same 2016 paper, Easterlin updates the empirical evidence on the paradox, in line with Easterlin (2015) and Easterlin et al. (2010). He first shows that the paradox applies to the United States for the recent period 1972–2014 even better with respect to the 1946–1970 period of his original evidence (Easterlin 1974). In fact, the period is now longer, the data points are many, and the trend of happiness is even declining, while GDP per capita has more than tripled.[1]

Other authors show that the Easterlin paradox applies to other growing economies as well. In the United Kingdom the trend of life satisfaction is approximately flat in the period 1973–1998, when controlled for socio-demographic variables (Blanchflower and Oswald 2004), and similarly in the period 1996–2007 (Clark et al. 2014). In West

---

[1]This puzzling result for the United States is even recognized by Stevenson and Wolfers (2008), and then confirmed on the basis of a different dataset by Herbst (2011).

Germany the trend of life satisfaction has an insignificant slope for the period 1984–2009 (Clark et al. 2014; see also Pfaff and Hirata 2013), and the same applies in Australia although for the shorter period 2001–2008 (Clark et al. 2014; see also Paul and Guilbert 2013). Even China exhibits a declining trend, although the data points are rather few (Easterlin et al. 2012; Bartolini and Sarracino 2015).

In the same 2016 paper, Easterlin then states a second version of the paradox, according to which:

> ... countries with a higher rate of growth of GDP have no significantly greater change in happiness than countries with a lower rate of economic growth. This lack of relationship holds for the developed, less developed, and transition countries, both pooled and separately... (Easterlin 2016, p. 7).

In this case, the paradox does not apply to single countries, but to a sample of countries as a general law; it does not require a non-downward trend of happiness, but an insignificant (bivariate)[2] correlation between the trends of GDP per capita and of happiness. Indeed, several countries of the sample used in the paper exhibit an upward trend of happiness, so that they do not appear to conform with the first version of the paradox.

Easterlin shows that this second version is confirmed by the available data by stressing the importance of considering happiness and GDP in their long run trends, rather than in their short term fluctuations. He thus dismisses Stevenson and Wolfers' (2008) finding that the bivariate correlation is positive and significant by observing that they do not properly compute the trends, so that they rather capture cyclical movements.

The second version of the paradox is important because it enables Easterlin to reply to the criticisms and evidence conflicting with the paradox, such as those in Stevenson and Wolfers (2008), Veenhoven and Vergunst (2014), and Diener et al. (2013). Nevertheless, the debate on this second version remains open (see Beja 2014), because the tests are not powerful enough to be conclusive, being based on too small samples of countries and on too short time series (Powdthavee and Stutzer 2014). Indeed, with the available data, Krueger (2008) shows that cross-country heterogeneity cannot be ignored, thus suggesting that what accounts for it should be sought.[3]

Therefore, the empirical issue remains more open for the second version of the Easterlin paradox than for the first one, while the theoretical issue is open for both of them. Specifically, why do at least four major countries with a growing trend of GDP per capita, such as the United States, the United Kingdom, West Germany and Australia, exhibit a non-upward trend of happiness, thus failing to conform with the prediction of the general law as stated in the second version?

---

[2]Easterlin (2001, p. 468) defends bivariate correlation in that it captures all the channels through which GDP can affect subjective well-being.

[3]More precisely, on using the same data as Stevenson and Wolfers (2008), Krueger (2008) shows that if the coefficient of (the logarithm of) GDP per capita on life satisfaction is not restricted to being the same across countries, but country-distinct coefficients are estimated, then the coefficient for the average country is negative and non-significant.

7.2.2 Easterlin's Explanation of the Paradox

Easterlin has provided a clear explanation of the paradox through his writings, starting from the seminal one, thus tracing a major research line for Happiness Economics (see, e.g., Clark et al. 2008). He has argued, and supported with some evidence and references, that income growth increases people's happiness but also their material aspirations, so that the direct positive effect on happiness of the former and the indirect negative effect of the latter roughly cancel each other out, and some aspirations remain constantly unrealized. Aspirations are formed on the basis of both habit formation (or hedonic adaptation for psychologists), especially when people are aged, and Duesenberry's relative income effect (or social comparison), especially when people are young (Easterlin 1974, 1995, 2001, 2005).

A question thus naturally arises: why do people not learn to form aspirations that can be realized so as to avoid committing systematic errors? Easterlin answers by referring to a result found in behavioral economics: people take wrong decisions because their memory is imperfect in recalling past experience. Specifically, they evaluate the past with the standard of the present, thus perceiving an improvement that they project into the future and aspire to realize (Easterlin 2001).

This does not imply that Easterlin agrees with the psychological 'set-point theory', according to which people's happiness is fixed by their genes and personality, so that the flow of events has only temporary effects on happiness. In fact, he argues with supporting evidence that people do not only hold material aspirations, but they are also concerned about other domains, i.e. health, family, work, and personal characteristics, in which hedonic adaptation is incomplete (Easterlin 2005). Other authors further show that comparison of one's income with that of others does not have a fixed negative effect on life satisfaction. For example, this negative effect seems more important for people who watch more television, meet socially more rarely, set more value on success and wealth, are not self-employed, and have achieved tertiary education (Clark and Senik 2010). Therefore, people seem to have the possibility to achieve permanent changes of happiness in both the downward and the upward direction.

A second similar question thus arises: why do people not learn to shift their aspirations towards the most rewarding domains and behaviors? This is not an innocuous question for economic theory, because it asks why people do not maximize their welfare by changing their preferences. Easterlin remarks that in fact there is no social learning, and people persist in a self-defeating behavior but he does not answer this question, and cites the need for further research in psychology and other related disciplines. However, he recognizes that people might learn, by observing that 'serious policy attention is needed to education as a vehicle for shaping more informed preferences'. In so doing, he addresses Scitovsky's book *The Joyless Economy* (1976) (Easterlin 2005, p. 57).

To recapitulate: arguments and evidence show that habit formation and the relative income effect can explain why the trend of happiness in some important countries is not upward sloping despite economic growth. Easterlin thus introduces psychology into economics not only by using happiness as an indicator of utility, but also by using psychological mechanisms in order to explain why people fail to maintain the trend of happiness in line with economic growth, i.e. why they may fail to maximize happiness over time.

However, Easterlin's address to education and to Scitovsky suggests the possibility that people could learn to form more realistic aspirations, so that the trend of happiness could become upward. In order to better understand this case better, Scitovsky's work should be examined.

7.3   Scitovsky's Hypothesis

7.3.1   Scitovsky's Own Discovery of the Paradox

Scitovsky may have discovered the paradox, which later took Easterlin's name, when he moved to Paris for 2 years, in 1966–1968, as a fellow of the Organization for Economic Co-operation and Development. Although he found himself at the age of 58 living on half the disposable income that he had received as professor at Stanford, he especially enjoyed the new lifestyle, and started to make changes to his research which would induce him to write *The Joyless Economy*. The book was published in 1976 after several years of intense reading of psychology, but it received cool response. This neglect was vindicated by the success of the revised edition of the book, published in 1992, because it was discussed in a Symposium organized by the *Critical Review* 4 years later, and it had the honour of being classified as one of "The hundred most influential books since World War II" by the *Times Literary Supplement* (6 October 1996). Scitovsky thus paralleled Easterlin in both discovering the paradox and receiving consideration (Bianchi 2012; Pugno 2014a).

Scitovsky was fascinated by psychology when he learned about 'stimulation' and 'adaptation.' He first used these two concepts to define 'novelty' and 'comfort', and then argued that over-indulging in 'comfort,' rather than pursuing 'novelty,' brings people to dissatisfaction in the long run. The book reports Easterlin's 1974 finding, thus recognizing the puzzle for the United States. It reports a large body of other descriptive evidence by showing people's inability to pursue a healthy lifestyle, to enjoy products during leisure time, to avoid over-education when entering the labor market, although people also exhibit examples of enjoyable work, such as when it is voluntary. The focus was originally on the United States, as the example where comfort is 'excessive;' but in his following writings, Scitovsky de-emphasized the difference with respect to the European countries, without, however, providing further evidence. He instead extended his theoretical interpretation to the poor unemployed, who may in fact be more likely to lapse into addiction as a form of habit (Scitovsky 1976, 1995, 1996; Pugno 2016).

Overall, on considering both the book and the companion papers, it can be said that Scitovsky contributed together with Easterlin to discovering the paradox, but he devoted much more effort to understanding the reasons that might explain it, rather than to proving its existence.

7.3.2   Scitovsky's Explanation of the Paradox

Scitovsky is often cited by studies of Happiness Economics, and his explanation of the paradox has been sometimes reported; but his most important and original contribution has not yet been properly recognized (Pugno 2014a, 2016). Scitovsky is known for hedonic adaptation (Easterlin 2005), for the social comparison effect on happiness (Oswald 1997; Layard 1980), for his criticism of consumer's perfect information (Frey and Stutzer 2005), and for his distinction between 'novelty' and 'comfort'. In this last case, the reported explanation of the paradox is that mass consumption induces people to prefer comfort, which turns out to be boring, whereas novelty gives pleasure (Bruni and Porta 2005; Layard 2005; Frey and Stutzer 2002). It thus emerges that Scitovsky's contribution to the explanation of the paradox is limited to the hedonic adaptation and the social comparison effect, which is the same explanation given by Easterlin and many other authors, and to the mass consumption effect, which seems a rather out-of-date argument.[4] Unfortunately, an original and key piece of analysis by Scitovsky remains unrecognized: this concerns the role of 'consumption skill', alias 'leisure skill', eventually called 'life skill' (Scitovsky 1976).

Recognizing the role of 'life skill' helps to understand why education can inform people's preferences, as Easterlin suggests by drawing on Scitovsky (1976). Easterlin refers to the possibility to induce people to devote more time to the domains of health, family, work, and personal characteristics, rather than to the economic domain, whereas Scitovsky refers to people's changing preference for novelty rather than comfort. More precisely, Scitovsky argued that preference for novelty can be learned through adequate education, starting from childhood by satisfying children's spontaneous curiosity, and during adulthood by drawing from "culture [...as] society's accumulated stock of past novelty" (Scitovsky 1976, p. 235). In so doing, a sufficient life skill can be developed so that novelty can be preferred to comfort.

Life skill can thus be defined as the set of skills which provide the proper motivation to identify, appreciate, and pursue novelty, so that people can "get [...]" the most out of life" (Scitovsky 1986, p. 40), and "make life meaningful and worth living" (Scitovsky 1976, p. 301). Life skill overlaps with education achieved at school, but it is not the same because it is more extended over types of skills and over people's life cycle. In particular, Scitovsky stressed that life skill is generalist, because it helps to choose among very different options, as in the case of life choices, while formal education ends up by being specialized, as required by producers (Scitovsky 1976).

Scitovsky's concept of 'life skill' clarifies the distinction between novelty and comfort as well, because this is not necessarily based on products, but rather on

---

[4]The argument that people's mass consumption moulds their preferences refers to the old American Institutionalists, like John K. Galbraith, but Scitovsky soon emphasised another argument: that people's preferences may be moulded by market pressure if they have not sufficiently learned consumption skill (see the discussion in Pugno 2016).

"forms of satisfaction," because "most products [...] yield both stimulus and comfort" (Scitovsky 1976, p. 109). The stimulus of novelty gives the pleasure and excitement to learn and realise something new, thus developing the life skill further and renewing the pursuit of novelty.[5] By contrast, comfort gives temporary satisfaction because of habituation and relative income effect. The distinction between novelty and comfort was observed by Scitovsky also from the input perspective, beyond this output perspective. While the pursuit of novelty is intrinsically motivated, i.e. pursued for its own sake, comfort is achieved because of an economic motivation to do something in exchange for it (Scitovsky 1986, p. 197).

7.3.3 What Scitovsky Added to Easterlin's Explanation of the Paradox

Scitovsky's explanation of the paradox is rich because it contributes to the issues left open by Easterlin's and most popular explanations, because it adds further contributions to related issues, such as those on limited information about happiness pursuits, and on the two types of happiness.

According to Scitovsky, people can learn to form aspirations in the most rewarding life domains and behaviors, thus tending to improve their happiness permanently. To this end, people should have developed sufficient life skill, i.e. they should have experienced satisfaction in the past from pursuing novelty, especially in their early years. People are thus not necessarily subject to fixed negative effects on happiness due to habituation and social comparison. Both of these psychological mechanisms are endogenous. Social comparison may be even used as a further stimulus for novelty. Therefore, the simple relationship between social comparison and happiness may be a reduced form that hides people's different motivations.

If people are able to form aspirations that they can realize, then the trend of happiness is not necessarily flat or declining, and people can fruitfully exploit the opportunities offered by economic growth. The first version of the Easterlin paradox is thus not a necessary outcome, but remains a real possibility (see Sect. 7.2.1). Furthermore, looking at economic growth does not enable any safe prediction about the trend of happiness, as the second version of the Easterlin paradox suggests (see Sect. 7.2.1).

The fact that people maintain limited information on their happiness pursuits becomes clear if Scitovsky's analysis is again considered. In the case of novelty, limited information is obvious, and the uncertainty about people's skill in meeting the challenge of novelty should be added. If novelty is not appreciated and pursued, then people may be induced to prefer comfort even if its temporary impact on

---

[5]"[I]n man's striving for his various goals in life, being on the way to those goals and struggling to achieve them are more satisfying than is the actual attainment of the goals" (Scitovsky 1976, p. 62).

happiness is perfectly known.[6] This latter case can be also applied to addictive products. People with deteriorated life skill may be induced to undertake behaviours with a risk of becoming addicted even if they are perfectly informed about such risk (Pugno 2014b).

Scitovsky further hints at distinguishing between two types of happiness. Rather than delving into the question on how people conceive happiness,[7] he considers the underlying motivations and the consequences. The pursuit of novelty clearly points to people's personal growth, but not in isolation from others. In fact, the pursuit of novelty originally arises thanks to secure relationship with caregivers, then it draws on others achievements as a 'stock of past novelty', and finally it lays the bases for creating something new, which can be useful to others.[8] Therefore, the pursuit of novelty yields a type of happiness that is characterized by the realization of one's skill, and by synergies with others, i.e. by positive internalities and by positive social externalities.[9] By contrast, comfort involves the negative internality of habituation, and the negative externality due to social comparison.

One might see the contrast between these two types of happiness as the modern version of the contrast drawn in ancient Greek philosophy between *eudaimonia* and *hedonism* (Pugno 2016), as suggested by the recent stream of research in Positive Psychology (see below).

Therefore, although Scitovsky began to introduce psychology into economics by looking at the physiology of stimulation with the aim of going beyond the method of 'revealed preferences' (Scitovsky 1976), his explanation of the paradox as based on 'life skill', 'novelty', 'comfort', addiction, and two types of happiness brought his research forwards. In fact, this suggests opening to interdisciplinary research with different fields of psychology, in order to understand how people's choices interact with their change of preferences.

7.4   Some Supporting Evidence from the Literature

Scitovsky's concept of 'life skill' is comprehensive because it includes imagination and social skills, besides more cognitive skills, and because it concerns children as well as adults. Recently, James Heckman (and co-authors) has followed a similar

---

[6]"It is also possible [. . .] that [. . .people] were gradually lured into a new way of life by their love of comfort, unaware at first of the costs involved and finding themselves fully accustomed to their new ways by time they realize the extent of the loss of pleasure suffered" (Scitovsky 1976, p. 73).

[7]See, for example, Rojas (2007).

[8]Scitovsky further adds that human relationships give opportunities to "exchange [. . .] information and ideas" (Scitovsky 1976, p. 236), so that they are "probably the main sources of human satisfaction" (Scitovsky 1986, p. 19) in the form of stimulation and challenge (Scitovsky 1976, p. 83).

[9]It should be recalled that Scitovsky is also well-known for his seminal article on externalities (Scitovsky 1954).

route by extending the concept of 'human capital', traditionally used only for production, to include cognitive and non-cognitive skills acquired from infancy onwards. Heckman recognizes that these skills are closely linked with preferences and personality traits, which can change over the entire life cycle, and which are important for both work and other life outcomes (Heckman 2008; Almlund et al. 2011; Heckman and Corbin 2016). In Happiness Economics studies, the importance of children's emotional health and of experience with parents for life satisfaction when they are adults is also recognized (Clark et al. 2017; Clark and Lee 2017). Even the variability of personality traits during adulthood has been detected as more important than income for life satisfaction (Boyce et al. 2013).

Developmental psychology helps to identify children's skill in exploring novelty and new relationships when they have experienced a 'secure' attachment with their parents (Bowlby 1969). For example, several studies show that children who are more securely attached to their parents tend to report a higher exploration of career alternatives when they grow older in order to find their own career-related skills (Mikulincer and Shaver 2007).

Positive Psychology helps to understand the links going from intrinsic motivations[10] for novelty exploration to personal growth and positive social relations, and then to well-being in the form of *eudaimonia* (Csikszentmihalyi 1990; Ryff and Singer 1998; Ryff 2014). A number of interesting results emerge from this research. For example, if the eudaimonic motive is captured by questions like "are you seeking to pursue a personal ideal/ to develop a skill, learn, or gain insight into something?", and the hedonic motive is captured by the questions like "are you seeking pleasure/ to take it easy", then the two types of questions load to two distinct factors, and both factors are positively correlated with life satisfaction (Huta and Ryan 2010).[11] According to another study, on capturing eudaimonia with high scores in personal growth, positive relationships, purpose in life, autonomy, environmental mastery, and self-acceptance, and on capturing hedonism with life satisfaction and positive affect, then the two types of well-being seem neither orthogonal nor closely correlated. Indeed, people high in eudaimonia and low in hedonism significantly exhibit the personality trait called 'openness to experience,' which is in stark contrast to people high in hedonism and low in eudaimonia (Ryff and Singer 1998). On considering health, eudaimonic people are observed to be in a better position than hedonic people, because they exhibit worse biomarker assessments (Ryff 2014; Fredrickson et al. 2015).

Interesting evidence on these aspects also emerges from the economic literature. According to a study using an international sample of countries, people with intrinsic motivations on the job, as captured by answers that definitely give priority to

---

[10]Edward Deci and Richard Ryan define "intrinsically motivated activities as those that individuals find interesting and would do in the absence of operationally separable consequences" (Deci and Ryan 2000, p. 233). Scitovsky referred to Deci and intrinsic motivations in Scitovsky (1986, ch. 14).

[11]In a survey, Huta (2015) observes that the links of life satisfaction with eudaimonia and with hedonism are rather sensitive to the measures used.

'working with people you like' and doing a job that gives you a 'feeling of accomplishment,' enjoy more life satisfaction, while people with extrinsic motivations, as captured by answers definitely addressing a 'good income' and a 'safe job,' enjoy less life satisfaction. On considering the age pattern, an interesting contrast emerges: people with intrinsic motivations exhibit an almost constant life satisfaction if aged 16–30, and a rising life satisfaction if older, while people with extrinsic motivations exhibit the standard U-shaped pattern with a slowly rising arm (Salinas-Jiménez et al. 2010).[12] Scitovsky's interpretation would be that people with intrinsic motivations on the job draw rising enjoyment because they improve their life skill, while people with extrinsic motivations are disappointed by over-aspirations when they are relatively young, and then they recover by downwardly adjusting the aspirations, as also Schwandt (2014) suggests. The fact that eudaimonic people are especially healthy is confirmed by an economic study which shows that the simple eudaimonic measure of 'meaning in life' is able to predict some years ahead less diagnosed disease events even when controlling for life satisfaction in a sample of population aged 50 and over (Bachelet et al. 2016).

Other pieces of evidence concern some direct tests of the Easterlin paradox. These confirm Scitovsky's arguments by focusing on the social aspect of people's life skill and openness to novelty. The first version of the paradox has been tested for the United States by Bartolini et al. (2013) who first confirm the paradox by showing that the trend of happiness from 1975 to 2004 is slightly declining. They then show that while this trend is predicted to grow by household income, it is predicted to decline by both the relative income and the deterioration of social relationships, as captured, in particular, by trust in strangers.

The second version of the paradox has been tested for an international sample of countries by Bartolini and Sarracino (2014), who first confirm the paradox by showing that there is no bivariate correlation between the trend of GDP per capita and the trend of subjective well-being. They then show, in a trivariate correlation, that the trend of GDP per capita predicts a growing trend of subjective well-being, while trust in strangers predicts a declining trend of subjective well-being. The second version of the paradox has also been tested by Böckerman et al. (2016). They use the novel variable 'attachment security,' which captures both social skill and autonomy from social comparison,[13] and then they find evidence that economic growth increases subjective well-being more in those countries where 'attachment security' is higher.

---

[12]Similar patterns have been identified by Nikolaev (2016). An even more surprising result is found by estimating the probability of enjoying both high eudemonia and low life satisfaction in a European sample. The age related pattern becomes *inverted* U-shaped, with the peak at 45 (Clark and Senik 2012, Tab. 6).

[13]The statement used in the survey to measure 'attachment' is as follows: "It is easy for me to become emotionally close to others. I am comfortable depending on others and having others depend on me. I don't worry about being alone or having others not accept me."

7.5 Conclusions

The hypothesis of Scitovsky's book *The Joyless Economy* and related writings makes little explored contributions to the issues left unresolved by the discussion on the Easterlin paradox. The current explanation of the paradox takes up Easterlin's suggestion that people's economic aspirations tend to rise in proportion to their income, because these aspirations are based on comparison with others' income, and with people's own past income. The Easterlin paradox, according to which subjective well-being does not tend to rise despite economic growth and despite the positive correlation with income at a point of time, can thus be explained, because the effects of economic growth and of the rise of aspirations tend to cancel each other out. What remains unclear is why people do not learn to form aspirations that can be realized, given that people draw subjective well-being also from domains and behaviours other than the economic ones.

By proposing an answer to this latter question, Scitovsky's hypothesis qualifies the Easterlin paradox and endogenizes its current explanation. Scitovsky argued that people can pursue satisfaction with their lives both through seeking comfort as economic satisfaction, and through stimulating and even creative activities, where novelty is the key ingredient which provides pleasure and excitement. While comfort is especially subject to social comparison and habituation, thus yielding temporary satisfaction, novelty activities, such as exploration, challenge, exchange of ideas with others, and scientific research, contribute to the formation of life skill in individuals, and of culture in society, which, in their turn, provide further stimulation and motivation. People could thus choose between comfort and novelty activities, but inadequate education, from parenting during infancy to excessive focus on specialization, weakens people's life skill, and induces them to prefer comfort.

Therefore, people's apparent insistence on a self-defeating behaviour is due to their lack of ability in exploring alternatives and learning, so that the prevalence of social comparison and habituation may be explained, rather than taken as given. In this case, subjective well-being at country level may fail to increase despite economic growth, as stated by the first version of the Easterlin paradox. However, this outcome is not inescapable, because education for life skill is a possible remedy, so that people may become open to exploration and to others. Indeed, even if the trend of subjective well-being may not be correlated with economic growth in a sample of countries, as stated by the second version of the Easterlin paradox, some countries may exhibit a rising trend. Scitovsky's hypothesis may thus account for such country heterogeneity.

References

Almlund, M., Duckworth, A. L., Heckman, J., & Kautz, T. (2011). Personality psychology and economics. In E. A. Hanushek, S. Machin, & L. Woessmann (Eds.), *Handbook of economics of education* (pp. 1–181). Amsterdam: Elsevier.

Bachelet, M., Becchetti, L., & Pisani, F. (2016). Eudaimonic happiness as a leading health indicator (No. 150–2016). Associazione Italiana per la Cultura della Cooperazione e del Non Profit.

Bartolini, S., & Sarracino, F. (2014). Happy for how long? How social capital and economic growth relate to happiness over time. *Ecological Economics, 108*, 242–256.

Bartolini, S., & Sarracino, F. (2015). The dark side of Chinese growth. *World Development, 74*, 333–351.

Bartolini, S., Bilancini, E., & Pugno, M. (2013). Did the decline in social connections depress Americans' happiness? *Social Indicators Research, 110*(3), 1033–1059.

Beja, E. L. (2014). Income growth and happiness: Reassessment of the Easterlin Paradox. *International Review of Economics, 61*(4), 329–346.

Bianchi, M. (2012). A joyful economist. Scitovsky's memoirs. *History of Economic Thought and Policy, 2*, 57–73.

Blanchflower, D. G., & Oswald, A. J. (2004). Well-being over time in Britain and the USA. *Journal of Public Economics, 88*(7–8), 1359–1386.

Böckerman, P., Laamanen, J. P., & Palosaari, E. (2016). The role of social ties in explaining heterogeneity in the association between economic growth and subjective well-being. *Journal of Happiness Studies, 17*(6), 2457–2479.

Bowlby, J. (1969). *Attachment and loss*. New York: Basic Books.

Boyce, C. J., Wood, A. M., & Powdthavee, N. (2013). Is personality fixed? Personality changes as much as "variable" economic factors and more strongly predicts changes to life satisfaction. *Social Indicators Research, 111*(1), 287–305.

Bruni, L., & Porta, P. L. (2005). Introduction. In L. Bruni & P. L. Porta (Eds.), *Economics and happiness* (pp. 1–28). Oxford: Oxford University Press.

Clark, A. E., & Senik, C. (2012). Is happiness di different from flourishing? *Revue d'économie politique, 121*, 17–34.

Clark, A. E., & Lee, T. (2017). *Early-life correlates of later-life well-being: Evidence from the Wisconsin longitudinal study* (PSE Working Papers No. 2017-32). London: Centre for Economic Performance.

Clark, A. E., & Senik, C. (2010). Who compares to whom? The anatomy of income comparisons in Europe. *The Economic Journal, 120*(544), 573–594.

Clark, A. E., Frijters, P., & Shields, M. A. (2008). Relative income, happiness, and utility: An explanation for the Easterlin paradox and other puzzles. *Journal of Economic Literature, 46*(1), 95–144.

Clark, A. E., Flèche, S., & Senik, C. (2014). The great happiness moderation. In A. E. Clark & C. Senik (Eds.), *Happiness and economic growth* (pp. 32–138). Oxford: Oxford University Press.

Clark, A. E., Flèche, S., & Lefkuangfu, W. N. (2017). *The long-lasting effects of family and childhood on adult wellbeing: evidence from British cohort data* (CEP Discussion Paper No 1493). London: Centre for Economic Performance.

Csikszentmihalyi, M. (1990). *Flow*. London: Rider.

Deci, E. L., & Ryan, R. M. (2000). The 'what' and 'why' of goal pursuits. *Psychological Inquiry, 11*, 227–268.

Del Mar Salinas-Jiménez, M., Artés, J., & Salinas-Jiménez, J. (2010). Income, motivation, and satisfaction with life: An empirical analysis. *Journal of Happiness Studies, 11*(6), 779–793.

Diener, E., Tay, L., & Oishi, S. (2013). Rising income and the subjective well-being of nations. *Journal of Personality and Social Psychology, 104*(2), 267–276.

Easterlin, R. A. (1974). Does economic growth improve the human lot? Some empirical evidence. In P. A. David & M. W. Reder (Eds.), *Nations and households in economic growth: Essays in honour of Moses Abramovitz* (pp. 89–125). New York: Academic.

Easterlin, R. A. (1995). Will raising the incomes of all increase the happiness of all? *Journal of Economic Behavior & Organization, 27*(1), 35–47.

Easterlin, R. A. (2001). Income and happiness. *Economic Journal, 111*(473), 465–484.

Easterlin, R. A. (2005). Building a better theory of well-being. In L. Bruni & P. L. Porta (Eds.), *Economics and happiness* (pp. 29–64). Oxford: Oxford University Press.

Easterlin, R. A. (2015). Happiness and economic growth: The evidence. In W. Glatzer, L. Camfield, V. Møller, & M. Rojas (Eds.), *Global handbook of quality of life* (pp. 283–299). Dordrecht: Springer.

Easterlin, R. A. (2016). *Paradox lost?* (IZA DP. No. 9676).

Easterlin, R. A., McVey, L. A., Switek, M., Sawangfa, O., & Zweig, J. S. (2010). The happiness–income paradox revisited. *Proceedings of the National Academy of Sciences, 107*, 22463–22468. 201015962.

Easterlin, R. A., Morgan, R., Switek, M., & Wang, F. (2012). China's life satisfaction, 1990–2010. *Proceedings of the National Academy of Sciences, 109*(25), 9775–9780.

Fredrickson, B. L., Grewen, K. M., Algoe, S. B., Firestine, A. M., Arevalo, J. M., Ma, J., & Cole, S. W. (2015). Psychological well-being and the human conserved transcriptional response to adversity. *PLoS One, 10*(3), e0121839.

Frey, B. S., & Stutzer, A. (2002). What can economists learn from happiness research? *Journal of Economic Literature, 40*(2), 402–435.

Frey, B., & Stutzer, A. (2005). Testing theories of happiness. In L. Bruni & P. L. Porta (Eds.), *Economics and happiness* (pp. 116–146). Oxford: Oxford University Press.

Heckman, J. (2008). School, skills, and synapses. *Economic Inquiry, 46*(3), 289–324.

Heckman, J. J., & Corbin, C. O. (2016). Capabilities and skills. *Journal of human development and Capabilities, 17*(3), 342–359.

Herbst, C. M. (2011). 'Paradoxical'decline? Another look at the relative reduction in female happiness. *Journal of Economic Psychology, 32*(5), 773–788.

Huta, V. (2015). An overview of hedonic and eudaimonic well-being concepts. In L. Reinecke & M. B. Oliver (Eds.), *Handbook of media use and well-being* (pp. 14–33).. Chapter 2). New York: Routledge.

Huta, V., & Ryan, R. M. (2010). Pursuing pleasure or virtue: The differential and overlapping well-being benefits of hedonic and eudaimonic motives. *Journal of Happiness Studies, 11*(6), 735–762.

Krueger, A. B. (2008, May). Comment to B. Stevenson & J. Wolfers *Economic growth and happiness* (Brookings Papers on Economic Activity, pp 95–100).

Layard, R. (1980). Human satisfactions and public policy. *The Economic Journal, 90*(360), 737–750.

Layard, R. (2005). *Happiness: Lessons from a new science*. New York: Penguin.

Mikulincer, M., & Shaver, P. R. (2007). *Attachment in adulthood*. New York: Guilford.

Nikolaev, B. (2016). *Does higher education increase hedonic and eudaimonic happiness?* (MPRA WP 78438).

Oswald, A. J. (1997). Happiness and economic performance. *The Economic Journal, 107*(445), 1815–1831.

Paul, S., & Guilbert, D. (2013). Income–happiness paradox in Australia: Testing the theories of adaptation and social comparison. *Economic Modelling, 30*, 900–910.

Pfaff, T., & Hirata, J. (2013). *Testing the Easterlin hypothesis with panel data* (SOEP papers 554).

Powdthavee, N., & Stutzer, A. (2014). Economic approaches to understanding change in happiness. In K. M. Sheldon & R. E. Lucas (Eds.), *Stability of happiness* (pp. 219–244). New York: Academic.

Pugno, M. (2013). Scitovsky and the income-happiness paradox. *The Journal of Socio-Economics, 43*, 1–10.

Pugno, M. (2014a). Scitovsky's 'The Joyless Economy' and the economics of happiness. *The European Journal of the History of Economic Thought, 21*(2), 278–303.

Pugno, M. (2014b). Scitovsky, behavioural economics, and beyond. *Economics: The Open-Access, Open-Assessment E-Journal, 8*(2014–24), 1–29.

Pugno, M. (2016). *On the foundations of happiness in economics*. London: Routledge.

Pugno, M. (2017). Scitovsky meets Sen: Endogenising the dynamics of capability. *Cambridge Journal of Economics, 41*(4), 1177–1196.

Rojas, M. (2007). Heterogeneity in the relationship between income and happiness: A conceptual-referent-theory explanation. *Journal of Economic Psychology, 28*(1), 1–14.

Ryff, C. D. (2014). Psychological well-being revisited: Advances in the science and practice of eudaimonia. *Psychotherapy and Psychosomatics, 83*(1), 10–28.

Ryff, C. D., & Singer, B. (1998). The contours of positive human health. *Psychological Inquiry, 9* (1), 1–28.

Schwandt, H. (2014). *Unmet aspirations as an explanation for the age U-shape in wellbeing* (CEP dp 1229). Bonn: IZA.

Scitovsky, T. (1954). Two concepts of external economies. *Journal of Political Economy, 62*(2), 143–151.

Scitovsky, T. (1976). *The joyless economy: The psychology of human satisfaction* (Revised Edition 1992 ed.). Oxford: Oxford University Press.

Scitovsky, T. (1986). *Human desires and economic satisfaction*. New York: New York University Press.

Scitovsky, T. (1995). *Economic theory and reality*. Aldershot: Elgar.

Scitovsky, T. (1996). My own criticism of 'The Joyless Economy'. *Critical Review, 10*(4), 595–606.

Stevenson, B., & Wolfers, J. (2008, May). *Economic growth and happiness* (Brookings Papers on Economic Activity, pp 1–87).

Veenhoven, R., & Vergunst, F. (2014). The Easterlin illusion: Economic growth does go with greater happiness. *International Journal of Happiness and Development, 1*(4), 311–343.

Chapter 8
Homo Economicus and Happiness: Towards More Sustainable Development

Martin Binder

Abstract Sustainable development is often seen through the lens of the standard income-based welfare framework which neglects insights from the "Beyond GDP" debate. This chapter suggests ways in which a subjective well-being framework can enrich sustainability economics. Drawing on Richard Easterlin's insights and replacing homo economicus with *homo felix* in theories of sustainable behaviour does not prompt excessive consumerism but rather fosters concerns for altruism and justice in regard to future generations and nature. On the micro-level, individuals derive lasting well-being from doing good and leading responsible, sustainable lifestyles. On the societal level, policy-makers can use a subjective well-being framework to more coherently incorporate ideas of sustainable development, civic consumerism and well-being.

8.1 Introduction

"The Easterlin theory is all the more valuable for its scarcity among economic theories, standing out in welcome relief from the rather sterile verbalizations by which economists have tended to describe [. . .] decisions in terms of the jargon of indifference curves, thereby tending to intimidate non-economists who have not mis-spent their youth in mastering the intricacies of modern utility theory" (Samuelson 1976, p. 244)

The above quotation from eminent economist Paul Samuelson refers to Richard Easterlin's theory of fertility decisions, but it can also be cited in tribute to Easterlin's ground-breaking contribution to subjective well-being research (1974), which inspired, if it did not found, the development of a whole field, and which may yet replace the rather sterile utility theory as central building block in economics and beyond. The Easterlin Paradox has proven to be a powerful reminder that rising

M. Binder (✉)
Bard College Berlin, Berlin, Germany

Levy Economics Institute of Bard College, Blithewood, Bard College, Annandale-on-Hudson, NY, USA
e-mail: m.binder@berlin.bard.edu

© Springer Nature Switzerland AG 2019
M. Rojas (ed.), *The Economics of Happiness*,
https://doi.org/10.1007/978-3-030-15835-4_8

incomes and rising well-being may not go hand in hand, that they are two different things, supporting and reinforcing criticisms made in the Beyond GDP debate (Stiglitz et al. 2009). In the present chapter, I will argue that Easterlin's work prompts an overdue revision of the concept of homo economicus and has broad implications for the sustainable development of societies (i.e. whether the human lot improves, Easterlin 1974). Such considerations of sustainability (the idea of meeting society's present needs, yet at the same time accounting for the needs of nature and future generations) have come to play an increasingly important role in policy-making (OECD 2013) and economic thought (e.g., Baumgaertner and Quaas 2010) since the Brundtland Commission's report (World Commission on Environment and Development 1987). While this constitutes a clear improvement over present-based approaches that see nature as a resource that can be arbitrarily exploited without concern for nature itself or for the consequences for future generations, much of the debate about sustainability in economics is still couched in terms of income and GDP and hence operates within the standard economic framework, neglecting important aspects about societal progress and human well-being (Gowdy 2005; Stiglitz et al. 2009; Spash 2012).

Showing how we can follow Easterlin's lead, I will discuss how using insights from the debate "Beyond GDP" can enrich debates about sustainability, viz. by focusing on "subjective well-being".[1] The chapter argues that a subjective well-being view offers a fruitful framework for thinking about sustainability that gives systematic place to determinants of well-being beside income (the chapter is thus related to work by Welsch 2002; Gowdy 2005; Common 2007; Engelbrecht 2009; Binder 2013, 2014). While one might imagine that consumption brings happiness and consequentially a subjective well-being view is at odds with the idea of sustainability, quite the opposite is true: on the level of the person, individuals derive more lasting satisfaction not from excessive consumption but from social activities (Prouteau and Wolff 2008), from caring for others (e.g., through voluntary work, Binder 2016), from bringing about social change (through other-regarding "social entrepreneurship", Yunus 2010) and from caring for nature (through actions benefiting the environment, see Binder and Blankenberg 2016). On a societal level, high levels of well-being are likely to be realized by changing patterns of consumption towards happiness-increasing activities that do not heavily tax the environment and future generations (Kasser 2017).

The present chapter thus aims to contribute to sustainability economics by spelling out how insights from subjective well-being research, pioneered by

---

[1]The measurement of subjective well-being has made tremendous progress in recent years and consensus has emerged that deceptively simple measures ("Taking all things together, how satisfied are you with your life as a whole?") can validly and reliably capture individuals' evaluations of their lives (Krueger and Schkade 2008). In the present chapter, I will use the term "subjective well-being" as umbrella term encompassing more specific notions such as "life satisfaction" measures (cognitively centered notions of SWB) or "happiness" measures (mood, affect or emotion-centered). There seems to be a consensus in the literature that life satisfaction measures are the most informative for policy-making.

Richard Easterlin, are relevant on the individual and societal level and allow the integration of different streams of research. I will begin in Sect. 8.2 by sketching how the traditional focus on growth and income in (sustainability) economics is related to the view of homo economicus as rational maximizer of utility (most often conveniently measured through income) and how this has shaped not only our view of human activity (in consumption and production) but also of societal progress. I will then sketch how a revision of the traditional view of homo economicus fuelled by subjective well-being research will lead to a strong, systematic embodiment of sustainability concerns into our picture of human behaviour not only on the individual level (Sect. 8.3), but also on the societal level (Sect. 8.4). I will close with implications for a future research agenda of the view sketched in this chapter (Sect. 8.5).

8.2 Growth: Homo Economicus and the Focus on Income

The standard view of economic rationality equates increasing individual welfare with increasing income. There are two different formulations of the approach, which are equivalent under certain conditions (Mas-Colell et al. 1995). The choice-based formulation starts with the individual's choices as basic building block and imposes a consistency axiom such as the "weak axiom of revealed preference" (WARP): if x is chosen (always) in the presence of y, then x is revealed preferred to y. No reasons need to be given, all types of behaviour are compatible with this, so long as choice is consistent. Economists were drawn to this approach because no introspection or reasoning about the content of individuals' motivations is necessary, the economist can observe actions and infer rational behaviour from them (or rather can "rationalize" behaviour). The second approach is preference-based[2]: a preference-ordering of the individual is assumed and taken as given and stable. That preferences are assumed exogenous (given) is taken as a sign of "ethical neutrality" (Gintis 1974, p. 415); that they are assumed stable is a technical necessity without which much of the normative content of the theory would break down (Bergh et al. 2000; Binder 2010). The equivalent rationality (consistency) assumptions in the preference-based approach are the completeness (the individual has preferences over all potential bundles) and transitivity conditions (there are no cycles in preferences such that if a is preferred to b and b preferred to c, a must be preferred to c).[3] By assuming continuity (a technical condition), the preference ordering can be expressed as a continuous utility function. If both approaches are equivalent, consistent choices are rationalized by a preference ordering or a rational preference ordering always will

---

[2]It is equivalent to the choice-based formulation if the "strong" (SARP) or "generalized" (GARP) axioms of revealed preference are fulfilled (Burnham et al. 2016; Mas-Colell et al. 1995).

[3]These axioms themselves have been found wanting in many respects (Sen 1973, 1977; Witt 1991).

give rise to consistent choices. It seems that most economists favour the preference-based formulation of the above theory (Mas-Colell et al. 1995, p. 5).[4]

The individual is assumed to act rationally when it maximizes its utility function based on given and unchanging preferences. However, in a world of scarcity, this maximization exercise is always subject to constraints: it is the given income of the consumer that constrains individual choice. Note that income is purely a means to an end and only a restriction condition (constraint) on choice.[5]

The rational choice model has been extremely successful in economics based on its pretense of being able to explain (read: rationalize) all human behaviour. Under the above conditions, any behaviour can be treated as a result of a rational utility-maximization calculus. It is important to note that while in classical economics, utility has had connotations of pleasure (e.g., Bentham 1789), these have been purged in the wake of the marginalist revolution to increase utility theory's "mathematical fitness" (Warke 2000). The notion of utility hence has become an empty place-holder, an index-number that represents individual preferences. It is one of the hallmarks of utility theory that under further technical assumptions (especially quasi-homothetic preferences), increasing incomes can be shown to be equivalent to increasing utility (on an ordinal level). The charm of this model is that, given the mix of the mentioned psychological and technical assumptions, economists can use an objective and (allegedly) easy-to-measure quantity such as income to make inferences about a subjective, non-measurable phenomenon such as utility. Instead of having to measure psychological correlates (subjective well-being, pleasure or happiness), economists can measure incomes and point out that they have proven that increases in the former translate (ordinally) into increases of the latter. The basic unit in economics, the individual, is thus rationally maximizing their income (and hence utility).

Unfortunately, the preference and constraint side of the model are often conflated, mostly due to economists' reluctance to deal with psychological concepts (i.e. give utility a psychological or neurobiological meaning, see Witt and Binder 2013): while we started out with individual choices (be they based on preferences or not) as the main building block of rational choice, the constraint (income) stands centre-stage as proxy for what is ultimately more important: by maximizing income, we maximize utility (preference). But through the disregard for utility as a psychological concept what is emphasized is the maximization of income.[6] And since economic thought is firmly rooted in the principle of methodological individualism, i.e. it is the individual

---

[4]Much has been criticized about this, especially the fact that this breaks down in the face of menu-dependent preferences (Sen 1993). Subjective well-being research can also help make sense of these violations of the axioms of rational choice theory (Koeszegi and Rabin 2008) but I will not go into this issue here.

[5]Note also that implicit in this calculus is an additional choice-rule: the consumer will choose the best bundle from the affordable set (see on this "choice determination", Hausman 2011).

[6]A similar rationale holds for the individual building block of economics on the production side, the firm: a firm's main goal is not assumed to be survival, social change or anything else, but the maximization of the firm's income, i. e. profits.

that forms the building block of all models, societal progress consists of the total of individual increases in income. With these assumptions, economics consistently argues that rising societal incomes translate into rising societal welfare and hence it is rational for society to strive to maximize GDP.

The above view simplifies the idea of utility maximization. Rational choice theory is ambiguous in many ways (Vanberg 2004): the economic "rationality principle" is empirically empty, "metaphysical" (Boland 1981), unless given more precise (and potentially falsifiable) meaning. And utility-maximization does not necessarily imply narrow egoism: one can be utility maximizer, hence rational, but strive for altruistic or other goals (this distinction refers to the present-aim view vs. self-interest view of utility maximization, see Parfit 1984). But most often, rational choice theory is conceived of as utility-maximization plus the assumption of narrow self-interest ("rational egoism") and hence equivalent to the idea of "homo economicus" as the rational, lightning-quick and egotistical utility-maximizer.

Do economists take this model at face-value? Even in this version, "homo economicus" does not have to be meant as an empirically accurate description of human behaviour, but rather a heuristic for model building, where the assumption of rational narrow self-interest is an abstraction that was chosen because it fits in many contexts. Yet, even if economists know and agree that this model does not accurately depict human behaviour but is a mere modelling device and heuristic, it is important to realize how contentious such a view is.

For one, there are methodological problems associated with using such a model based on Friedman's instrumentalist justification (F-twist) that good models are good at prediction and their assumptions may be empirically inaccurate (Friedman 1953). One could reasonably argue that economic models fail when it comes to prediction (Blaug 1992), but Friedman's view is also problematic because it essentially treats human behaviour as black box. If predictions fail, we cannot improve the model as it is not based on empirical accuracy. It would thus be better to use an empirically (more) accurate model of human behaviour because the explanatory power of models that incorporate it will likely be much higher and thus more useful for economics as a science.

Secondly, there is a danger associated with "homo economicus" and its use in economics: even though it may be used (at times) fruitfully as a modelling device, homo economicus is often understood to represent also a picture of a person by those who draw on economic research (for example in policy contexts). Homo economicus as narrow caricature of human behaviour is then emulated by students of business and economics, who are being taught that rational behaviour will always consist in the calculation of benefits and costs for oneself and in ignorance of external costs or other-regarding motivations in favour of one's own utility: research shows that being subjected to economics can make students act more selfish and in accordance with the above model (Frank et al. 1993). Homo economicus thus becomes a world view, where people maximize their income and companies their profits at the detriment of other motivations. Economic (instrumental) rationality then is not only seen as description of human behaviour but it also has normative force as the benchmark for all human behaviour. In this normative view, it is postulated that individuals should act like *homines economici*, and if they do not do so, they are "irrational". The normative application of rational choice theory thus creates "rational fools" (Sen 1977), or a society of "knaves", and purely self-interested economic behaviour may crowd out intrinsic motivations (Frey 1997). Such an economics has been aptly likened to a "black hole" by Amartya Sen (Sen 1987, p. 29): no ethical considerations can have an impact on given, self-interested behaviour and all moral motivations are swallowed up by the overarching assumption of self-interest. In its most crunched down formulation, the self-interested "rational fool" even forgets that income is an instrument (merely a constraint) but seeks income for itself, which ultimately turns the theory on its head.[7]

Focussing on the person through the lens of subjective well-being research offers empirically well-founded insights that may prompt a revision of the above picture of human behaviour. Where homo economicus has been criticized by welfare economists and philosophers from a normative point of view (Sen 1973, 1977), behavioural economics and subjective well-being research offer an empirical critique and prompt for a constructive alternative. This empirically founded revision turns out to be not only psychologically richer but also ethically so. Like homo economicus, the individual in that modified view strives for utility, but understood properly with respect to the psychological concept of subjective well-being. As a modelling device, we may assume that the individual will strive (and maybe should strive) to achieve a most favourable life-time balance of their subjective well-being. Subjective well-being research then provides empirical knowledge about the sources of subjective well-being and these challenge conventional economic wisdom and modelling assumptions: when looking at an individual seeking to achieve subjective well-being, Richard Easterlin pioneered research that has shown that increasing income will play a more limited, indirect role in achieving this, somewhat shifting focus to other sources of subjective well-being (Easterlin 1974; Kahneman and Deaton 2010, find that over 75,000 USD p.a., increases in income no longer yield positive effects on affective measures of well-being). There is still debate about the extent to which income translates into subjective well-being (even above the threshold mentioned, income gains impact positively on life satisfaction, but here, too, the extent is somewhat contested, see Easterlin 2013, Sacks et al. 2012). This is an important first qualification to any misapplication of the above-mentioned theory of rational choice. Income as a constraint is a means to an end and its limited efficacy in achieving that end highlights

---

[7]Even behavioral economics, that seeks to improve the descriptive model of human behavior, mostly takes rational choice as normative benchmark, as the ideal of how behavior should be, and in many cases, this normative benchmark is equated with self-interested utility maximization. By this, all 'normal' human behavior becomes irrational and pathological, ignoring that non-rational (in the economic sense) behavior can be very well adaptive and successful for individuals and society (Gigerenzer et al. 1999), whereas much rational behavior can be, on aggregate, quite unsuccessful for society (e.g., Schelling 1978).

what the homo economicus caricature world-view often neglects, viz. the idea of a decreasing marginal utility of income (Layard et al. 2008).

While these findings should not be construed as income having no relevance for subjective well-being at all, many other things also bring subjective well-being more reliably (see on this also Layard et al. 2012, p. 64), e.g. health, a meaningful job, personal freedom (Dolan et al. 2008; Helliwell et al. 2013, p. 9) and some of these sources such as friends and social networks are only very remotely related to one's income or consumption. Income expectations and comparisons are even negatively related to subjective well-being (Stutzer 2004). Even more, there is much evidence that one strong source of subjective well-being lies in ethical behaviour and altruistic motivations (such as charitable giving, volunteering, caring for others, see, e.g., Benz 2005) and in concerns for fairness (inequality negatively impacts on well-being, see, e.g., Graham and Felton 2006).

"*Homo felix*" here differs from homo economicus in that models being built on this picture of human behaviour will more accurately reflect how individuals decide and what their motivations are (a mixture, it turns out, of selfish and selfless preferences) and if interpreted as a description of the individual and normative guiding principle ("Leitbild", leitmotif, see Binder 2013) will no longer produce caricatures and policies that focus only on one source of well-being such as income. In this sense, empirically informed SWB research will help to open the black box of the utility function and materially specify human preferences (Witt and Binder 2013). Building models that capture this empirical content will likely yield better descriptions and explanations of human behaviour and may improve predictive accuracy of economic models. I will now discuss how this model of "*homo felix*" can inform sustainability economics on both individual and societal level.

8.3 Individual Level: Individual and Corporate Sustainability

Homo economicus has no systematic reason to incorporate considerations of sustainability into its utility maximization calculus (Spash 2012, p. 45). If we conceive of sustainable development in the form of the definition of the Brundtland commission, as "development that meets the needs of the present without compromising the ability of future generations to meet their own needs" (World Commission on Environment and Development 1987, chapter 2), then self-interested behaviour seems easily put at odds with the incorporation of the needs of future generations and the preservation of nature (hence a different framework than the standard economic one seems necessary to address this question fruitfully, see also Gowdy 2005; Spash 2012). Even when only focusing on weak sustainability, non-decreasing incomes over time (which would be compatible with weak sustainability) might paint too narrow a picture and ignore non-market welfare gains/losses within a broader subjective well-being framework.[8] But how does *homo felix* fare regarding the preservation of nature and the incorporation of other-regarding aims?

Research shows links between the quality of the environment, individuals' attitudes about the environment and their subjective well-being: we know that the objective quality of the environment has an impact on subjective well-being (Welsch 2007; Brereton et al. 2008; Engelbrecht 2009; White et al. 2013; MacKerron and Mourato 2013), a fact that has been shown relevant for environmental policy (e.g., environmental regulation and policy, see Welsch and Kuehling 2009). Climate change, pollution and environmental disasters were shown to negatively impact on individuals' subjective well-being (Welsch 2002; Van Praag and Baarsma 2005; Rehdanz and Maddison 2005; Rehdanz et al. 2013; Goebel et al. 2014), whereas well-functioning aspects of the environment such as parks are associated with higher subjective well-being (White et al. 2013). These findings extend to subjective attitudes about the environment as well: individual concerns about the environment can impact on subjective well-being (Ferrer-i-Carbonell and Gowdy 2007) and are associated with higher well-being for those individuals who are engaging in pro-environmental behaviour, such as volunteering in environmental organizations (Binder and Blankenberg 2016). Conservation efforts that are often seen in the literature and in public policy discourse as sacrifices that need to be made for the sake of sustainability become, through the lens of the present research on subjective well-being, rather activities that constitute much less of a sacrifice than one would expect (Kasser 2017). Such knowledge can be harnessed to inform citizens and is likely to decrease resistance to environmentally-friendly behaviour. Even if the present generation might need to sacrifice some economic growth and material wealth, the ultimate sacrifice in the currency of subjective well-being will be much smaller if one takes the view seriously that income is only instrumental and that what matters is well-being (see also below). In a subjective well-being view, the income loss (small negative impact on SWB) could likely be balanced by the well-being gain of environmentally-friendly behaviour (positive impact of altruistic volunteering, etc.). Whether these impacts fully cancel out is an empirical question to be asked in future work, but the point here is that this question only systematically arises in a view of welfare that is broader than that of the standard economic framework.

An intact environment can thus have important beneficial effects on individual well-being and to the extent that individuals know about this, their appreciation for the environment can trigger systematic environment-preserving behaviour. While one certainly could criticize that the environment in this sense is nothing but a resource for individual consumption, it is important to note that this differs in that a compromised environment already today impacts negatively on individuals' well-

---

[8]The precise meaning of "sustainability" is debated (Vallance et al. 2011) and it is probably not necessary to go beyond a rather general notion in the present context. An empirical analysis of how the term is used shows, however, that considerations of well-being (apart from material well-being) seem to be not central to the concept so far (White 2013).

being, thus triggering (maybe partly selfish) action to preserve it, which will directly benefit nature and future generations. The environment is more than an exploitable resource for increasing material consumption but rather a direct resource that can be only consumed if sufficiently preserved.[9] The presence of a "value-action gap" (e.g., Kollmuss and Agyeman 2002) makes clear that such individual attitudes do not map one to one into pro-environmental behaviour (due to all types of biases in human action and decision-making) but it would be mistaken to conceive of the individual as not having these systematic pro-environmental attitudes and motivations. The question then becomes not so much one of how to move selfish individuals to sacrifice their own well-being for the sake of nature and future generations, but rather how to translate already existing altruistic motivations into actual behaviour despite individuals' inertia and institutional barriers.

Less directly related to the environment, more eco-friendly and sustainable life-styles (those that downplay material consumption) will not lead to substantive losses in subjective well-being (Kasser 2017). On the contrary, empirical evidence so far shows that homo economicus seems less happy than *homo felix*, who does not mindlessly spend income on material goods but also uses income for other-regarding aims (Konow and Earley 2008). While it is true that money can buy happiness if one knows how to spend it right (Dunn et al. 2011), many of the "right" ways of spending money involve altruistic motivations such as gift-giving, charitable dona-tions, volunteering and so on (Meier and Stutzer 2008; Aknin et al. 2011). In the same vein, materialistic lifestyles are associated with lower well-being than more wholistic and less consumerist lifestyles (Inglehart et al. 2008; Delhey 2010; Konow and Earley 2008). This is likely to carry through to greener lifestyles (Binder and Blankenberg 2017) as it can be conjectured that the increase in subjective well-being resulting from these less materialistic life-styles comes from the fact that such lifestyles convey meaning to individuals' lives. Finding meaning in one's activities is an important driver of subjective well-being (as shown, for example, when it comes to one's job life and finding meaningful work, see Binder 2016) and may well satisfy a deep-seated psychological need. Connected to leading meaningful lives is obviously also the need for autonomy more directly (Deci and Ryan 2000) and the positive well-being impact of leading non-materialistic and eco-friendly lifestyles might be due to individuals consciously and autonomously deciding on a lifestyle more in sync with human nature (a nature that also includes altruistic motivations).

Apart from these considerations, the last, and potentially best researched area relevant for a systematic link between sustainability and subjective well-being is the relationship between altruistic behaviour in general and subjective well-being. Individuals have been shown to systematically derive well-being from thinking about and caring for others through either donating money (Aknin et al. 2011) or donating their time in volunteering activities (Meier and Stutzer 2008).[10] This goes

---

[9]This abstracts from the presence of tragedy of the commons properties relating to individuals' enjoyment of nature.

[10]Positive effects here extend to health and mental well-being (e.g., Post 2005).

so far that individuals work in organizations (e.g. in the third sector) that might pay systematically lower wages (Benz 2005) and yet are consistently more satisfied with their jobs in these organizations. Positive benefits of voluntary work also extend to life satisfaction and these effects can be rather uniform over the well-being distribution, i.e. irrespective of one's initial level of well-being (Binder 2016): the causal link here also seems to run from finding meaning in one's activities and this has a much more powerful impact on well-being than wages.

These findings potentially also extend to social entrepreneurship (Bornstein and Davis 2010) and social business (one the guiding principles of Yunus' social business is to "Do it with joy", see Yunus 2010). The recent rise in social entrepreneurship (also in environmental protection), i.e. harnessing market organizations to affect social change, can be explained more fruitfully within a subjective well-being framework: why should individuals found businesses which aim to do good instead of maximizing profits? Understanding that other-regarding behaviour is not necessarily a sacrifice but positively impacts happiness explains why social entrepreneurship has the potential to become a major force of change in capitalist societies. The payoff for running such firms, however, is psychological, not monetary because one has found something one can "do with joy". Research also shows that many self-employed individuals are much more satisfied with their work and life due to higher autonomy of their business enterprises (Benz and Frey 2008) and this positive effect is likely to be bigger if the enterprise also serves one's altruistic motivations. In this regard, taking a subjective well-being view can explain why some firms do maximize not only profits but the well-being of their owners (and employees) and in the wake of this affect social change. Again, one could criticize that social change is instrumental to achieving well-being but this criticism might be misplaced: is doing good only valuable if one does it only for the sake of it? Is it only good if it is a sacrifice? From an outcome-centred (and pragmatic) perspective, I think one should be agnostic whether the environment is preserved based on non-selfish or selfish motivations.

Social entrepreneurship is probably the most direct form of firm behaviour that can enable and foster sustainable development, but we also observe other, more mixed forms of firm behaviour that are more compatible with *homo felix* than homo economicus. In the same way in which *homo felix* cares about themselves and others, we could extend this argument to firms and argue that firms, like individuals, can also care about profits and have other motivations. This is reflected in recent notions of "corporate sustainability" (sustainability here in a loser definition than the one above, see Lozano et al. 2015) and what has been called "corporate social responsibility" (Carroll 1991) and is operationalized for example in the "triple bottom line" (Elkington 1997). In a more realistic picture of human economic activity, not only the individual has more complicated motivations than self-interest that drive their actions, but also the firms that consist of these motivationally more complicated individuals. Even though most firms will be limited by a constraint that they need to recoup at least their investment (or avoid losses to remain in business), corporate sustainability would attribute a broader set of responsibilities and interests to firms than the sole maximization of profits. Beside the economic bottom line (which is necessary for the firm to survive), social and environmental bottom lines are added and complement the purely selfish perspective. In such a view, the firm is supposed to act like a good "corporate citizen" (akin to the person that is not purely selfish and should not act solely in that way), behaving responsibly towards society (social cohesion bottom line) and towards nature (environmental bottom line). Contrary to the (normative) view of homo economicus, which suggests that it would be irrational for firms to have motives apart from the maximization of profit, our subjective well-being view is compatible with the idea that there might exist such a systematic triple bottom line for companies (and that working in companies that only exhibit selfish motives will make their employees, managers and holders unhappy).

We here see another example where homo economicus as metaphor and normative guiding principle narrows down the scope of goals a firm could rationally pursue: if the idea of human rational action is narrowed down to purely egotistical maximization of self-interest, it is straightforward to argue for a similar view on the firm-level through maximization of firm profits (Friedman 1970). But given that such descriptive models of human behaviour also develop normative force, such a narrow view reinforces the (false) understanding that the business of business is *only* business. Research shows that selfish individuals self-select into economics programs at university and that economics teaching increases these self-interested tendencies (Frank et al. 1993). Teaching models of homo economicus thus plays a role in creating guiding principles, where people imitate apparently successful behaviour of paragons of business (imitational learning is an important mechanism to transmit behaviours, Bandura 1986). Replacing the model of homo economicus in sustainability economics with a more empirically descriptive model of *homo felix* and the equivalent profit-oriented firm with the model of a firm as "good corporate citizen" that has a similar set of motivations as *homo felix* is likely to develop the same sort of normative force and will be necessary to lead to a sustainable implementation of different types firms (social business) and business practices (corporate social responsibility). The (often somewhat forced) justification that good corporate citizenship is beneficial to a firm's (single) financial bottom line becomes obsolete within a broader framework that also accounts for individuals' more altruistic and socially or environmentally minded motivations.[11] A subjective well-being view

---

[11] Arguments for a "business case" of CSR (on empirical evidence for such a business case, see, e.g., Orlitzky et al. 2003), i.e. the idea that socially responsible behavior will pay-off for a firm's financial bottom-line (at least in the long-run) seem Panglossian especially for publicly traded firms whose financial bottom line might be negatively impacted on in the short run by socially responsible behavior. This might drive the firm out of business (or the firm will be bought up) long before CSR might pay-off. The threat of this happening will likely act as strong barrier to implementing effective CSR. If we shift, however, our view to systematically incorporate other goals that are not subsidiary to financial performance, the afore-mentioned pressures vis-à-vis stockholders will be alleviated. The demand for ethically-responsible investment opportunities, even if they do not pay as high a financial return as other investments, reflects the fact that individuals, even investors, can act more like *homo felix* than homo economicus. Institutional setups that reinforce individuals' other-regarding motivations instead of crowding them out in favor of their selfish motivation can help to more systematically anchor these behaviors in society.

treats such behaviour not as an irrational anomaly but relevant force and promoting awareness of the better descriptive adequacy of such a view as model of human behaviour will aid in promoting the goals of sustainability economics. Corporate sustainability along a triple bottom line becomes a much more natural extension of a subjective well-being framework than within the prevailing standard economic framework.

8.4 Societal Level: Global Sustainable Development

The considerations made in the previous section extend quite straightforwardly from individuals and firms to the societal and global level. Sustainable development on these levels will then have to address macro-level phenomena related to "happy nations" (Ng 2008; Abdallah et al. 2008; Engelbrecht 2009; Fritz and Koch 2014; Hall 2013) or even a "happy planet" (NEF 2013). A subjective well-being view can inform public discourse and public policies in various ways (Graham 2011; Veenhoven 2010; Frey and Stutzer 2012; Binder 2013). Money (as measured by GDP) as indicator of societal progress has been chosen because it was easier to measure than well-being itself, but this has come at the cost of forgetting that money is a means to an end, viz. well-being (Diener and Seligman 2004, p. 2). With the possibility to directly measure subjective well-being, a broader-based framework for welfare assessments has become feasible. As argued in Binder (2013), these measures are better amenable to reflect a much broader assessment of societal and economic change as many welfare-relevant factors do not influence income but well-being (Hall 2013).

Through empirical happiness regression equations, it is possible to measure shadow prices for activities and institutional arrangements for which individuals can reveal no preferences directly (Frey et al. 2010). While this pertains to the valuation of democratic institutions, crime, corruption, freedom, or macroeconomics variables such as inflation, unemployment rates or inequality, in the present case, the hedonic evaluation of public goods such as the level of pollution or environmental quality are of paramount importance. When accounting for the usual known influences on subjective well-being, adding variables for the above-mentioned factors allows to assess their effects on subjective well-being directly. If e.g. new forms of work organization (self-employment, increases in flexibility of working arrangements, decreased job security) increase incomes but at the same time also negatively impact on individuals' sense of autonomy, security or meaning in life, a subjective well-being view offers the potential to measure the summary welfare assessment, while an income-based welfare framework would neglect this. Empirical knowledge about the relevant life domains that have reliable influence on subjective well-being (Helliwell et al. 2013) will thus allow a more nuanced assessment of societal progress as well as inform citizens about options of improving their lives and policy-makers about welfare-improving policies. Regarding the former, it is well known that individuals often mispredict the resulting happiness from different consumption activities and life choices (Wilson and Gilbert 2005). In the present context, this would pertain to welfare effects of curbing down consumption or living in ecologically sustainable ways. Knowing better about these effects can help citizens consume in more "civically engaged" ways. With respect to policies, such a broader framework can be used to better justify policies before implementation and it can help to figure out trade-offs between different policies that have positive and negative impact on different life domains. Subjective well-being here would offer the ultimate summary judgement (the common currency) to decide on the benefits or costs of a policy. Other metrics are useful, too, and should not be discarded, but subjective well-being in this view would provide a "*Leitbild*" (a leitmotiv, or guiding principle) that offers a coherent framework for public policy (obviously public policy has other goals, but it is difficult to argue against the importance of well-being as basic value for society, Layard 2005). With the measurement of SWB and the effects different life domains (among them the environment) will have on it, these concerns will have a more systematic place on policy-makers' agendas (what is measured is becoming a target for policy).

The empirical findings from subjective well-being research will provide useful input in discussions about the sustainable development of societies in a variety of more concrete ways (Gowdy 2005; Costanza et al. 2007; Fritz and Koch 2014; Giannetti et al. 2015; Frugoli et al. 2015). Within such a framework, sustainable development would centre around the improvement of societal well-being as indicated by the summary judgement on the subjective well-being of the populace (Hall 2013). This does not mean that all other indicators of progress should be neglected but rather that they be systematized along the life domains which empirically have shown to impact on individuals' well-being ("happiness-relevant functionings", see Binder 2014). Subjective well-being as the overall summary judgement on how people are doing aggregated over all these life domains remains the overarching guidance principle and offers an empirically-informed measure of how individuals trade-off life domains vis-à-vis each other. Income, jobs, the social domain, inequality, the environment (etc.) all are domains with a set of indicators that gain their systematic relevance through their impact on subjective well-being. To account for individual heterogeneity and individual agency, and to deal with the objection that happiness-based policies conceive of the individual as mere "metric stations" (Frey and Stutzer 2010), policy-makers should focus centrally on improving individuals' subjective well-being capabilities, i.e. creating institutions and opportunities for individuals to attain happiness through the various life domains and channels within the framework. Concerns of sustainability and the environment here gain their systematic place through a direct SWB impact (channels here being pollution or vice versa an intact environment as well through behaving altruistic towards future generations and nature). Existing multidimensional frameworks such as the OECD's "How's life" initiative are related to this proposal (OECD 2013), but lack one unifying principle to trade-off the different dimensions of societal progress (it is left open in these approaches how to assess improvement in one dimension when other dimensions show deterioration. Is society then on a path of improvement or not?). Within such a framework, notions of "*degrowth*" (Ayres 1996) and civic consumerism could hold a systematic place through the impact they create on various life domains and hence subjective well-being.

One may criticize that such a subjective well-being view of sustainable development might make sense for developed societies who have attained a level of wealth that allows them to proceed to considerations "Beyond GDP" but that it is irrelevant for the poorest countries that find themselves in poverty traps and rather need increases in their material standard of living. The above view, however, is fully compatible with this idea and research supports this by finding that at low levels of income, countries experience strong improvements in subjective well-being through raising GDP (Inglehart et al. 2008; Helliwell et al. 2013). Only at higher levels of GDP, the relationship between income and subjective well-being becomes less pronounced, with the marginal utility of income decreasing (Layard et al. 2008) and many (positional) consumption activities becoming self-defeating from a subjective well-being point of view (compare also the above-mentioned threshold of 75,000 USD above which individuals seem to gain no more benefits at least in terms of emotional well-being, see Kahneman and Deaton 2010). For poor countries, successful development, even within a subjective well-being framework, will coincide with rising levels of income. A subjective well-being framework will, however, even in the case of the bottom billion, stress that income is a means to an end and that sustainable increases of subjective well-being can only be reached by fostering the right uses of income. Some determinants of SWB might also be favourably influenced by policies in the absence of high incomes (e.g. strengthening communities and social networks). Sustainable development here will take into account the various other factors that influence well-being and help in establishing institutions that will positively impact on these domains. Increasing GDP at massive expense to the environment, to social solidarity and community, at the expense of creating inequality, increases in corruption or decreases in political freedom (and associated institutions) will all lead to offsetting well-being losses that would find no systematic place in a standard-income-based development framework, but which find systematic assessment and consideration within the larger subjective well-being view.

China provides a good case study for this argument as it has seen massive increases in income in the last decades as a result of a deep transformation of its society towards market-based organization: while per-capita income and consumption expenditures have risen four-fold from 1990 to 2010 (Easterlin et al. 2012) and absolute poverty levels have decreased from 80% to 13% from 1978 to 2009 (Brockmann et al. 2009), levels of subjective well-being have not increased (they have exhibited somewhat of a u-shape over these years and life satisfaction as measured by WVS data has decreased by −0.53 points; Easterlin et al. 2012, p. 2).[12] What would be labelled a success-story in purely income-based terms, gives a much less positive impression in the framework proposed here and would lead

---

[12]A similar development can be seen for other developing countries (e.g., Graham and Pettinato 2002).

policy-makers to try to understand why the Chinese development has not improved subjective well-being. It would then lead to an analysis of different life domains that impact on subjective well-being and in which China has seen marked deteriorations during this time: rising incomes in China have been accompanied with strong increases in uncertainty and both rapid growth and societal change seem to impact negatively on SWB ("paradox of unhappy growth", Graham and Lora 2009). At the same time, rising incomes have led to rising aspirations and where aspirations rise quicker than incomes, frustration ensues ("paradox of frustrated achievers", Graham and Pettinato 2002). Similarly, material inequality negatively impacts on SWB and China may have experienced a raise in absolute incomes, but large parts of society are worse off in relative terms (much of the gains have gone to a small elite; Brockmann et al. 2009, p. 393). Finally, the rising incomes were also accompanied by a worsening of the social safety nets and rising rates of (urban) unemployment, both of which are important (non-)income drivers of subjective well-being (Easterlin et al. 2012, p. 3). Other factors such as increased corruption and criminality might also play a role in explaining why China's development over the past decades has been disappointing for many in the Chinese populace. Applying a broader subjective well-being view with subjective well-being as summary indicator and a range of subsidiary life domain indicators will provide societies with a better focus on what is important for a life going well and would have allowed to avoid such a development path earlier on. Such a view does not mean that development will always proceed along lines, where all dimensions that impact on SWB improve simultaneously, yet it does allow a society to pay more attention to trade-offs involved in fostering sustainable well-being development and allows citizens to lead a debate (in the face of scarce resources) where to put the emphasis on (Binder 2014).

A final point of overlap between notions of sustainability and a subjective well-being framework on the macro-level lies in the systematic exploration of inefficiencies in the attainment of given levels of subjective well-being (Common 2007). A well-publicized example of this has been the "Happy Planet Index" (NEF 2013), which sets a country's average happy life years in relation to its ecological footprint. It is thus a measure of the sustainability of subjective well-being attained (countries rank low if their well-being is attained at high expense of the environment, so the measure is both about the happiness of the planet and its populace). This idea generalizes and allows to add a complementary welfare measure for societies, namely that of "happiness efficiency" (Binder and Broekel 2012). Such a measure would allow to track how efficiently individuals reach given levels of subjective well-being in different societies and with different means and helps to avoid waste in the inputs that generate SWB (inputs might be natural resources but also any other resource). While in the sustainable well-being context, the well-being generated per natural resource expenditure is of paramount importance because it focusses on reaching well-being at the lowest cost to the environment, such measures are also important when it comes to different life domains and hedonic adaptation patterns within them: research has shown that the well-being gain of income increases level off very quickly, while this is less so the case for pleasures of giving or in the social domain (see Frederick and Loewenstein 1999). Shifting one's lifestyle towards things that promise more lasting subjective well-being increases efficiency (for any given absolute level of well-being) and leads to a more efficient use of one's resources in general. Here again, an approach that comes from production theory and has been used otherwise in promoting sustainability in production and conservation of resources can be fruitfully applied within the subjective well-being framework spelled-out above.

8.5 Summary and Outlook

Decades ago, Richard Easterlin made social scientists aware that improvements in the human lot cannot easily be equated with economic growth. Yet even today, sustainable development is too often seen through the lens of the standard income-based welfare framework. The present chapter offered a subjective well-being framework to incorporate into the field of sustainability research. Subjective well-being was argued to enrich the present debates about sustainability and offers fruitful ways of how to conceive of and operationalize sustainable development. *Homo felix* has been argued to present a better view of human economic behaviour and the normative force that such conceptions of individual behaviour play in shaping future consumers and leaders should not be underestimated (Frank et al. 1993).

While one would prima facie have thought that a subjective well-being view is at odds with the idea of sustainability (with consumerism as means to achieve happiness and materialistic life-styles leading to resource exploitation), it turns out that quite the opposite is true: such a view does not prompt excessive consumerism but rather prompts concerns that are embedded in the Brundtland Commission's definition of sustainability (compare also Sachs 2013). Individuals derive more lasting satisfaction from social activities, from caring for others, from bringing about social change and from caring for nature. On a societal level, higher levels of subjective well-being are likely to be realized by changing patterns of consumption towards activities that do not heavily tax the environment and future generations. Living green does not necessarily imply sacrifice in the currency of subjective well-being. Policy-makers can use a subjective well-being framework to more coherently incorporate ideas of sustainable development and well-being, de-growth, corporate social responsibility and civic consumerism.

One could object to the argument above that such a proposal replaces one view of self-interested behaviour with another, that individuals now chase happiness instead of money to the detriment of the environment. This criticism concerns the question whether just and virtuous behaviour can never be in parts associated with well-being and should impart a cost on the individual. Is altruism devalued if it is done (partly) for one's own sake? I do not want to deny that some behaviours might be necessary to ensure sustainable development that will impact negatively on SWB. These behaviours should be pursued nevertheless because we are morally obligated to be stewards to our planet and future generations, one could hold. But these latter concerns per se do not invalidate the above argument. Especially when considering that individuals might hold moral views about the environment but often lack the motivation to follow through on these (moral obligations per se often seem to have no motivating force, compare the value-action gap), harnessing knowledge that moral behaviour can often lead to a "warm glow" of happiness can offer a powerful motivating force to close the value-action-gap and help ingrain behaviours that are sustainable. And although my argument has been predominantly prudential, a view of *homo felix* is also at least in parts moral (through our altruistic and fairness concerns) and more naturally integrates the two perspectives (Sachs 2013). Furthering subjective well-being in this way can be seen akin to the idea of enlightened self-interest, but going beyond this by allowing for both selfish and altruistic behaviour being entangled within the individual as human being.

A second concern could be that a subjective well-being framework (not unlike its alternatives) would systematically neglect long-term concerns by focussing attention to present measurements. Short-term policy focus on GDP or any other indicators such as subjective well-being would then still systematically neglect long-term sustainability considerations. One way to deal with such an objection within the framework discussed above would be to complement a focus on subjective well-being measures with a set of objective indicators ordered along well-being-relevant dimensions (see more extensively Binder 2014). In that way, a dimension "environment" could consist of indicators relating to conservation of the environment and natural resources, being justified by their above-mentioned relevance to improving individuals' subjective well-being. The above framework thus provides an orientation of how to select a set of multidimensional indicators (and a systematic rationale for selecting them), some of which can be very well long-term oriented.

Sustainability and subjective well-being are thus not at odds but rather could reinforce each other. Further research should more fully explore the extent to which individuals and society alike can simultaneously live sustainably and happily.

Acknowledgement The author is grateful for helpful comments and suggestions to Ann-Kathrin Blankenberg and seminar participants at the universities of Vechta and Marburg. All errors are mine.

References

Abdallah, S., Thompson, S., & Marks, N. (2008). Estimating worldwide life satisfaction. *Ecological Economics, 65*(1), 35–47.

Aknin, L., Dunn, E., & Norton, M. (2011). Happiness runs in a circular motion: Evidence for a positive feedback loop between prosocial spending and happiness. *Journal of Happiness Studies, 13*(2), 347–355.

Ayres, R. U. (1996). Limits to the growth paradigm. *Ecological Economics, 19*(2), 117–134.

Bandura, A. (1986). *Social foundations of thought and action – A social cognitive theory*. Upper Saddle River/New Jersey: Prentice Hall.

Baumgaertner, S., & Quaas, M. (2010). What is sustainability economics? *Ecological Economics, 69*, 445–450.

Bentham, J. (1789). *An introduction to the principles of morals and legislation (Reprint 1948)*. New York: Hafner.

Benz, M. (2005). Not for the profit, but for the satisfaction? – Evidence on worker well-being in non-profit firms. *Kyklos, 58*(2), 155–176.

Benz, M., & Frey, B. S. (2008). Being independent is a great thing: Subjective evaluations of self-employment and hierarchy. *Economica, 75*, 362–383.

Binder, M. (2010). *Elements of an evolutionary theory of welfare*. London: Routledge.

Binder, M. (2013). Innovativeness and subjective well-being. *Social Indicators Research, 111*(2), 561–578.

Binder, M. (2014). Subjective well-being capabilities: Bridging the gap between the capability approach and subjective well-being research. *Journal of Happiness Studies, 15*(5), 1197–1217.

Binder, M. (2016). '...Do it with joy!' – subjective well-being outcomes of working in non-profit organizations. *Journal of Economic Psychology, 54*, 64–84.

Binder, M., & Blankenberg, A. K. (2016). Environmental concerns, volunteering and subjective well-being: Antecedents and outcomes of environmental activism in Germany. *Ecological Economics, 124*, 1–16.

Binder, M., & Blankenberg, A. K. (2017). Green lifestyles and subjective well-being: It's more about self-image than actual behaviour. *Journal of Economic Behavior & Organization, 137*, 304–323.

Binder, M., & Broekel, T. (2012). Happiness no matter the cost? An examination on how efficiently individuals reach their happiness levels. *Journal of Happiness Studies, 13*(4), 621–645.

Blaug, M. (1992). *The methodology of economics* (2nd ed.). Cambridge: Cambridge University Press.

Boland, L. A. (1981). On the futility of criticizing the neoclassical maximization hypothesis. *The American Economic Review, 71*(5), 1031–1036.

Bornstein, D., & Davis, S. (2010). *Social entrepreneurship: What everyone needs to know*. Oxford/New York: Oxford University Press.

Brereton, F., Clinch, J. P., & Ferreira, S. (2008). Happiness, geography and the environment. *Ecological Economics, 65*(2), 386–396.

Brockmann, H., Delhey, J., Welzel, C., & Yuan, H. (2009). The china puzzle: Falling happiness in a rising economy. *Journal of Happiness Studies, 10*, 387–405.

Burnham, T. C., Lea, S. E. G., Bell, A. V., Gintis, H., Glimcher, P. W., Kurzban, R., Lades, L., McCabe, K., Panchanathan, K., Teschl, M., & Witt, U. (2016). Evolutionary behavioral economics. In D. S. Wilson & A. Kirman (Eds.), *Complexity and evolution: Toward a new synthesis for economics*. Cambridge, MA: MIT Press.

Carroll, A. B. (1991). The pyramid of corporate social responsibility: Toward the moral management of organizational stakeholders. *Business Horizons, 34*(4), 39–48.

Common, M. (2007). Measuring national economic performance without using prices. *Ecological Economics, 64*(1), 92–102.

Costanza, R., Fisher, B., Ali, S., Beer, C., Bond, L., Boumans, Nicholas, L., Dickinson, J., Elliott, C., Farley, J., Gayer, D., MacDonald, L., Hudspeth, T., Mahoney, D., McCahill, L., McIntosh, B., Reed, B., Turab Rizvi, A., Rizzo, D. M., Simpatico, T., & Snapp, R. (2007). Quality of life: An approach integrating opportunities, human needs, and subjective well-being. *Ecological Economics, 61*(2–3), 267–276.

Deci, E. L., & Ryan, R. M. (2000). The "what" and "why" of goal pursuits: Human needs and the self-determination of behaviour. *Psychological Inquiry, 11*(4), 227–268.

Delhey, J. (2010). From materialist to post-materialist happiness? National affluence and determinants of life satisfaction in cross-national perspective. *Social Indicators Research, 97*, 65–84.

Diener, E., & Seligman, M. E. P. (2004). Beyond money – Toward an economy of well-being. *Psychological Science in the Public Interest, 5*(1), 1–31.

Dolan, P., Peasgood, T., & White, M. (2008). Do we really know what makes us happy? A review of the economic literature on the factors associated with subjective well-being. *Journal of Economic Psychology, 29*, 94–122.

Dunn, E. W., Gilbert, D. T., & Wilson, T. D. (2011). If money doesn't make you happy, then you probably aren't spending it right. *Journal of Consumer Psychology, 21*, 115–125.

Easterlin, R. A. (1974). Does economic growth improve the human lot? Some empirical evidence. In P. A. David & M. W. Reder (Eds.), *Nations and households in economic growth: Essays in honour of Moses Abramovitz* (pp. 89–125). New York: Academic Press.

Easterlin, R. A. (2013). *Happiness and economic growth: The evidence*. IZA Discussion Paper No. 7187.

Easterlin, R. A., Morgan, R., Switek, M., & Wang, F. (2012). China's life satisfaction, 1990–2010. *Proceedings of the National Academy of Sciences, 109*(25), 9775–9780.

Elkington, J. (1997). *Cannibals with forks: The triple bottom line of 21st century business*. Oxford: Capstone.

Engelbrecht, H.-J. (2009). Natural capital, subjective well-being, and the new welfare economics of sustainability: Some evidence from cross-country regressions. *Ecological Economics, 69*(2), 380–388.

Ferrer-i-Carbonell, A., & Gowdy, J. M. (2007). Environmental degradation and happiness. *Ecological Economics, 60*(3), 509–516.

Frank, R. H., Gilovich, T., & Regan, D. T. (1993). Does studying economics inhibit cooperation? *The Journal of Economic Perspectives, 7*(2), 159–171.

Frederick, S., & Loewenstein, G. F. (1999). Hedonic adaptation. In D. Kahneman, E. Diener, & N. Schwarz (Eds.), *Well-being: The Foundations of hedonic psychology* (pp. 302–329). New York: Russell Sage Foundation.

Frey, B. S. (1997). A constitution for knaves crowds out civic virtues. *The Economic Journal, 107*(443), 1043–1053.

Frey, B., & Stutzer, A. (2010). Happiness and public choice. *Public Choice, 144*(3), 557–573.

Frey, B., & Stutzer, A. (2012). The use of happiness research for public policy. *Social Choice and Welfare, 38*(4), 659–674.

Frey, B. S., Luechinger, S., & Stutzer, A. (2010). The life satisfaction approach to environmental valuation. *Annual Review of Resource Economics, 2*, 139–160.

Friedman, M. (1953). The methodology of positive economics. In M. Friedman (Ed.), *Essays in positive economics* (pp. 1–42). Chicago/London: The University of Chicago Press.

Friedman, M. (1970, September 13). The social responsibility of business is to increase its profits. *New York Times*.

Fritz, M., & Koch, M. (2014). Potentials for prosperity without growth: Ecological sustainability, social inclusion and the quality of life in 38 countries. *Ecological Economics, 108*, 191–199.

Frugoli, P., Almeida, C., Agostinho, F., Giannetti, B., & Huisingh, D. (2015). Can measures of well-being and progress help societies to achieve sustainable development? *Journal of Cleaner Production, 90*, 370–380.

Giannetti, B., Agostinho, F., Almeida, C., & Huisingh, D. (2015). A review of limitations of GDP and alternative indices to monitor human wellbeing and to manage eco-system functionality. *Journal of Cleaner Production, 87*, 11–25.

Gigerenzer, G., Todd, P. M., & the ABC Research Group. (1999). *Simple heuristics that make us smart*. New York/Oxford: Oxford University Press.

Gintis, H. (1974). Welfare criteria with endogenous preferences: The economics of education. *International Economic Review, 15*(2), 415–430.

Goebel, J., Krekel, C., Tiefenbach, T., & Ziebarth, N. R. (2014). *Natural disaster, environ- mental concerns, well-being and policy action. Technical report*. Duisburg: Universitaet Duisburg-Essen, CINCH.

Gowdy, J. (2005). Toward a new welfare economics for sustainability. *Ecological Economics, 53*(2), 211–222.

Graham, C. (2011). *The pursuit of happiness*. Washington, DC: The Brookings Institution Press.

Graham, C., & Felton, A. (2006). Inequality and happiness: Insights from Latin America. *Journal of Economic Inequality, 4*, 107–122.

Graham, C., & Lora, E. (2009). *Paradox and perception: Measuring quality of life in Latin America*. Washington, DC: The Brookings Institution Press.

Graham, C., & Pettinato, S. (2002). Frustrated achievers: Winners, losers and subjective well-being in new market economies. *Journal of Development Studies, 38*(4), 100–140.

Hall, J. (2013). From capabilities to contentment: Testing the links between human development and life satisfaction. In J. F. Helliwell, R. Layard, & J. Sachs (Eds.), *World happiness report* (pp. 138–153). New York: UN Sustainable Development Solutions Network.

Hausman, D. M. (2011). *Preference, Value, Choice, and Welfare*. Cambridge/New York: Cambridge University Press.

Helliwell, J. F., Layard, R., & Sachs, J. (2013). *World happiness report*. New York: UN Sustainable Development Solutions Network.

Inglehart, R., Foa, R., Peterson, C., & Welzel, C. (2008). Development, freedom, and rising happiness: A global perspective (1981–2007). *Perspectives on Psychological Science, 3*(4), 264–285.

Kahneman, D., & Deaton, A. (2010). High income improves evaluation of life but not emotional well-being. *Proceedings of the National Academy of Sciences, 107*(38), 16489–16493.

Kasser, T. (2017). Living both well and sustainably. A review of the literature, with some reflections on future research, interventions, and policy. *Philosophical Transactions of the Royal Society A, 375*(20160369), 1–13.

Koeszegi, B., & Rabin, M. (2008). Choices, situations, and happiness. *Journal of Public Economics, 92*(8–9), 1821–1832.

Kollmuss, A., & Agyeman, J. (2002). Mind the gap: Why do people act environmentally and what are the barriers to pro-environmental behaviour? *Environmental Education Research, 8*(3), 239–260.

Konow, J., & Earley, J. (2008). The hedonistic paradox: Is homo economicus happier. *Journal of Public Economics, 92*, 1–33.

Krueger, A. B., & Schkade, D. (2008). The reliability of subjective well-being measures. *Journal of Public Economics, 92*, 1833–1845.

Layard, R. (2005). *Happiness – Lessons from a new science*. London: Allen Lane.

Layard, R., Mayraz, G., & Nickell, S. (2008). The marginal utility of income. *Journal of Public Economics, 92*, 1846–1857.

Layard, R., Clark, A. E., & Senik, C. (2012). The causes of happiness and misery. In J. Helliwell, R. Layard, & J. Sachs (Eds.), *World happiness report* (pp. 58–90). New York: The Earth Institute.

Lozano, R., Carpenter, A., & Huisingh, D. (2015). A review of 'theories of the firm' and their contributions to corporate sustainability. *Journal of Cleaner Production, 106*, 430–442.

MacKerron, G., & Mourato, S. (2013). Happiness is greater in natural environments. *Global Environmental Change, 23*(5), 992–1000.

Mas-Colell, A., Whinston, M. D., & Green, J. R. (1995). *Microeconomic theory*. New York/ Oxford: Oxford University Press.

Meier, S., & Stutzer, A. (2008). Is volunteering rewarding in itself? *Economica, 75*, 39–59.

NEF. (2013). *New Economics Foundation*. https://www.happyplanetindex.org.

Ng, Y. K. (2008). Environmentally responsible happy nation index: Towards an internationally acceptable national success indicator. *Social Indicators Research, 85*, 425–446.

OECD. (2013). *How's life? 2013 – Measuring well-being*. Paris: OECD Publishing. https://doi.org/10.1787/9789264201392-en.

Orlitzky, M., Schmidt, F. L., & Rynes, S. L. (2003). Corporate social and financial performance: A meta-analysis. *Organization Studies, 24*(3), 403–441.

Parfit, D. (1984). *Reasons and persons*. Oxford: Oxford University Press.

Post, S. G. (2005). Altruism, happiness, and health: It's good to be good. *International Journal of Behavioral Medicine, 12*(2), 66–77.

Prouteau, L., & Wolff, F.-C. (2008). On the relational motive for volunteer work. *Journal of Economic Psychology, 29*(3), 314–335.

Rehdanz, K., & Maddison, D. (2005). Climate and happiness. *Ecological Economics, 52*(1), 111–125.

Rehdanz, K., Welsch, H., Narita, D., & Okubo, T. (2013). *Well-being effects of a major negative externality: The case of Fukushima*. Kiel Working Paper No. 1855.

Sachs, J. (2013). Restoring virtue ethics in the quest for happiness. In J. F. Helliwell, R. Layard, & J. Sachs (Eds.), *World happiness report* (pp. 80–97). New York: UN Sustainable Development Solutions Network.

Sacks, D. W., Stevenson, B., & Wolfers, J. (2012). The new stylized facts about income and subjective well-being. *Emotion, 12*(6), 1181.

Samuelson, P. A. (1976). An economist's non-linear model of self-generated fertility waves. *Population Studies: A Journal of Demography, 30*(2), 243–247.

Schelling, T. C. (1978). *Micromotives and macrobehavior*. New York: W.W. Norton.

Sen, A. (1973). Behaviour and the concept of preference. *Economica, 40*(159), 41–259.

Sen, A. (1977). Rational fools: A critique of the behavioural foundations of economic theory. *Philosophy and Public Affairs, 6*(4), 317–344.

Sen, A. (1987). *On ethics & economics*. Oxford: Basil Blackwell.

Sen, A. (1993). Internal consistency of choice. *Econometrica: Journal of the Econometric Society, 61*(3), 495–521.

Spash, C. L. (2012). New foundations for ecological economics. *Ecological Economics, 77*, 36–47.

Stiglitz, J. E., Sen, A., & Fitoussi, J. P. (2009). *Report of the Commission on the Measurement of Economic Performance and Social Progress (CMEPSP)*. http://www.stiglitz-sen-fitoussi.fr

Stutzer, A. (2004). The role of income aspirations in individual happiness. *Journal of Economic Behavior & Organization, 54*, 89–109.

Vallance, S., Perkins, H. C., & Dixon, J. E. (2011). What is social sustainability? a clarification of concepts. *Geoforum, 42*(3), 342–348.

Van de Bergh, J. C., Ferrer-i-Carbonell, A., & Munda, G. (2000). Alternative models of individual behaviour and implications for environmental policy. *Ecological Economics, 32*(1), 43–61.

Van Praag, B., & Baarsma, B. (2005). Using happiness surveys to value intangibles: The case of airport noise. *Economic Journal, 115*, 224–246.

Vanberg, V. J. (2004). The rationality postulate in economics: Its ambiguity, its deficiency and its evolutionary alternative. *Journal of Economic Methodology, 11*(1), 1–29.

Veenhoven, R. (2010). Greater happiness for a greater number. *Journal of Happiness Studies, 11*, 605–629.

Warke, T. (2000). Mathematical fitness in the evolution of the utility concept from Bentham to Jevons to Marshall. *Journal of the History of Economic Thought, 22*(1), 5–27.

WCED, S. W. S. (1987). World Commission on Environment and Development. *Our common future*: Oxford/UK: Our Common Future. Oxford University Press.

Welsch, H. (2002). Preferences over prosperity and pollution: Environmental valuation based on happiness studies. *Kyklos, 16*(11), 1227–1244.

Welsch, H. (2007). Environmental welfare analysis: A life satisfaction approach. *Ecological Economics, 62*(3), 544–551.

Welsch, H., & Kuehling, J. (2009). Using happiness data for environmental valuation: issues and applications. *Journal of Economic Surveys, 23*(2), 385–406.

White, M. A. (2013). Sustainability: I know it when i see it. *Ecological Economics, 86*, 213–217.

White, M. P., Alcock, I., Wheeler, B. W., & Depledge, M. H. (2013). Would you be happier living in a greener urban area? A fixed-effects analysis of panel data. *Psychological Science, 24*(6), 920–928.

Wilson, T. D., & Gilbert, D. T. (2005). Affective forecasting – Knowing what to want. *Current Directions in Psychological Science, 14*(3), 131–134.

Witt, U. (1991). Economics, sociobiology, and behavioural psychology on preferences. *Journal of Economic Psychology, 12*, 557–573.

Witt, U., & Binder, M. (2013). Disentangling motivational and experiential aspects of "utility" – A neuroeconomics perspective. *Journal of Economic Psychology, 36*(1), 27–40.

Yunus, M. (2010). *Building social business: The new kind of capitalism that serves humanity's most pressing needs*. New York: Public Affairs.

Part IV
Applications of Happiness in Economics

Chapter 9
Distaste for Inequality? The Role of Risk Aversion

Ada Ferrer-i-Carbonell and Xavier Ramos

Abstract Risk aversion is an important argument to explain why individuals may dislike inequality. However, this relationship has not been empirically tested for large representative samples. Using a representative panel for Germany, we estimate this relationship by linking subjective well-being (a proxy for utility), inequality, and self-reported risk attitudes. The results confirm that risk aversion has a positive effect on dislike for inequality: more risk averse individuals are also more inequality averse. This relationship however is partly driven by other individual characteristics (gender, education, and income) that are correlated with risk attitudes.

9.1 Introduction and Background

In recent years there has been an accumulation of empirical evidence suggesting that individuals dislike inequality (Alesina and Giuliano 2011; Dawes et al. 2007). Individuals' preference for inequality are shaped by several factors, including: (i) their own characteristics, such as endowments and abilities; current income, for instance, is a good predictor of preferences for redistribution (Romer 1975; Meltzer and Richard 1981), (ii) their individual history, which in turn shapes subjective expectations on own economic position (Piketty 1995; Bénabou and Ok 2001; Ravallion and Lokshin 2000; Alesina and La Ferrara 2005), and (iii) social norms and fairness perceptions; e.g. in societies where individual effort, and not luck, is

A. Ferrer-i-Carbonell (✉)
Institute for Economic Analysis (CSIC), Barcelona, Spain
e-mail: ada.ferrer@iae.csic.es

X. Ramos
Departament d'Economia Aplicada, Universitat Autònoma de Barcelona, Barcelona, Spain
e-mail: xavi.ramos@uab.cat

© Springer Nature Switzerland AG 2019
M. Rojas (ed.), *The Economics of Happiness*,
https://doi.org/10.1007/978-3-030-15835-4_9

thought to determine economic success, individuals are likely to be less concerned about inequality (Alesina and Glaeser 2004; Alesina and Angeletos 2005).[1]

Within the group of individual characteristics, risk attitude is an important factor that shapes individuals' taste for inequality directly, but also in indirect ways. The direct effect operates mainly through the information that the current income distribution may reveal about individual's future position. If indeed the current income distribution is informative about the income distribution in the near future, as risk attitudes influence the weight that individuals assign to different points of the income distribution (Vickerey 1945; Harsanyi 1955), more risk averse individuals will assign a higher utility value to worse outcomes and therefore have a strongest dislike for inequality. For instance, the notion that good prospects of upward mobility may explain distaste for inequality-reducing policies even amongst poor individuals only holds if individuals are not too risk averse, for otherwise (risk averse) individuals will "realize that redistribution provides valuable insurance against the fact that their income may go down as well as up" (Bénabou and Ok 2001, p. 448). Likewise, more risk averse individuals are more in favor of welfare policies that socially insure against income-risk and reduce income disparities, such as unemployment or disability benefits.

Indirectly, risk attitudes also exert influence on inequality tolerance, as they also shape or condition some of the factors that in turn have a direct effect on individuals' taste for inequality. For example, individuals' risk attitudes are correlated with gender, education, and wages, which in turn correlate with inequality aversion. In addition, risk attitude is also the channel through which other factors affect inequality preferences. As outlined above, individual history is related to their taste for inequality. Now, the effect of individual history, and especially of negative life experiences, such as unemployment spells or negative income shocks is (partly) captured by risk attitudes, as such negative life experiences makes individuals more risk averse—which in turn increases their inequality dislike (Alesina and Giuliano 2011). In Sect. 9.2.2 we discuss the endogeneity issue.

Despite the theoretically appealing importance of risk attitudes on shaping individuals' dislike for inequality, the empirical literature on individual dislike for inequality, however, has not paid much attention to the role of risk attitudes. The relationship between risk attitudes and distaste for inequality has only been tested in the lab, and not for general population samples. Using experimental data, Carlsson et al. (2005) find that more risk averse people tend also to be more inequality averse. Kroll and Davidovitz (2003) as well as Brennan et al. (2008) report evidence in support of the positive relationship between risk aversion and inequality intolerance.[2]

---

[1]See Alesina and Giuliano (2011) for a recent comprehensive survey of the many determinants of individual preference for redistribution.

[2]A related strand of the literature examines the relationship between social welfare judgments and choice under uncertainty from a normative standpoint, using questionnaire experiments (Amiel et al. 2009; Bosmans and Schokkaert 2004; Bernasconi 2002). Ours is a positive and not a normative study.

This paper fills this gap by characterizing dislike for inequality according to individuals risk aversion. To this end, we use for first time a large representative panel data set with about 25,000 individuals living in Germany to estimate this relationship. In particular, we study whether the correlation between inequality and utility depends on individuals' risk attitudes by using a self-reported measure of satisfaction as a proxy for utility. Our findings corroborate that more risk averse individuals show a stronger dislike for inequality. These results are robust to different specifications, econometric methods, and to the inclusion of variables that correlate with individual risk attitudes and individual economic vulnerability. In this paper we use a self-reported measure of satisfaction as a proxy for utility, one of the empirical strategies used to understand individuals' dislike for inequality. Subjective measures of satisfaction have been increasingly used in economics since the pioneer work of Easterlin in 1974. Since then, subjective measured have empirically shown its validity as a measure of individuals' well-being and utility and have been therefore used in various applications. The existing empirical evidence has shown that inequality, usually measured as the Gini coefficient in the region or country where the individual lives, has a negative effect on self-reported well-being or life satisfaction (see Ferrer-i-Carbonell and Ramos 2014, for a recent survey). This means that other things being equal individuals in more unequal societies report on average a lower score in the satisfaction scale.

The rest of the paper is organized as follows. Section 9.2 explains our empirical strategy and describes the data and key variables, notably our direct measures of utility and risk as well as the measure of inequality. Section 9.3 presents our main findings, robustness checks, and heterogeneous effects, while the last section provides concluding comments.

9.2 Empirical Strategy

9.2.1 The Model and Its Estimation

We start from the premise that, *ceteris paribus*, individual utility U (or satisfaction) depends on the inequality I existing in the region and year where the individual lives. In other words

$$U = f(X, I) \qquad (9.1)$$

where X is a set of variables that describe the situation of the individual. Assume a linear functional form, we can rewrite (9.1) as

$$U = \alpha + \beta I + \gamma X \qquad (9.2)$$

where, in accordance with previous literature, we expect β to be negative. The objective of this paper is to try to disentangle whether the relationship between inequality dislike (β) and life satisfaction (U) can be partly explained by individuals' risk attitudes. To test for this, we estimate β for individuals with different risk attitudes, using the following augmented specification:

$$U_{it} = \alpha + \beta_r I_{gt} + \gamma_r X_{it} + \delta_r T + \zeta_r G + \eta_{i+} \varepsilon_{it} \qquad (9.3)$$

where i indicates the individual, t the time, g the region where the respondent lives, and $r = (L, H)$ represents the individual risk attitude. Since we use a measure of willingness to take risk (as opposed to aversion to risk), H denotes high willingness to take risk, while L denotes low willingness to take risk—we explain below in Sect. 9.2.2 how high and low willingness to take risk are defined and measured. Different β_r estimates for individuals with different risk attitudes would indicate that the effect of inequality on individuals' satisfaction or utility is partly explained by their risk attitude. If, as explained above, inequality dislike is positively related to risk aversion (i.e. negatively related to willingness to take risk) we should find $\beta_H > \beta > \beta_L$. If $\beta < 0$, this means that $\beta_L < 0$. However, β_H, may take any sign, and if negative needs to be larger than β_L. It will be also negative if risk lovers are also worse-off with higher inequality levels, or alternatively positive if regional inequality increases risk lover's life satisfaction.

Equation (9.3) includes a set of time dummy variables (T), which capture all those unobservable variables that are time specific, and a set of regional dummy variables (G), which indicate in which of the 39 Government Regions (*Regierungsbezirke*, corresponding to NUTS2) the respondent lives. The inclusion of time and region variables will allow us to distinguish the inequality effect from that of other regional and time characteristics, such as inflation or tax systems, which we do not specifically control for. Although the regional and time dummy variables collapse characteristics that can be correlated with both, inequality and life satisfaction, we do control in Eq. (9.3) for regional unemployment (unemployment shapes inequality over the business cycle), GDP growth, median income in the region, and poverty separately. While the first two variables are obtained from official sources, the other two are calculated from the data.

The empirical analysis uses longitudinal data and we can thus include an individual fixed effect (η_i) that captures individual traits that are unobservable and time persistent (e.g. cognitive and non-cognitive abilities). Finally, the equation includes the usual error term (ε_{it}). Since observations are clustered at the regional level, we use two methods to address the possible correlation of errors within the cluster. To start with, we report standard errors clustered at the region level. Now, since the number of clusters (39) is too small (Angrist and Pischke 2008; Cameron and Miller 2010; Wooldrige 2006), we also report bootstrapped standard errors that result from estimating the fixed effect regression with clustered standard errors at regional level

500 times. Since we cannot include the regional dummies in the specification of the bootstrapped regressions, point estimates of the two methods will be different. Since there is virtually no difference in terms of trade-offs between variables and statistical significance between estimating equation by means of a linear or an ordered categorical estimator (Ferrer-i-Carbonell and Frijters 2004), we estimate the equation using a linear estimator (OLS extensions), as it is usually done in the literature.

9.2.2 Measuring Strategy

9.2.2.1 Life Satisfaction

The empirical strategy uses a measure of subjective life satisfaction, as in Easterlin's pioneering work in 1974, as a proxy for well-being or utility. Since Easterlin's first work, there is accumulating evidence that individuals are able and willing to provide a meaningful answer when asked to value their satisfaction with their live. Over the last years, economists have used this self-reported satisfaction measure as a proxy for utility so as to contribute to a better understanding of individuals' preferences and behavior by empirically testing existing theoretical assumptions and concepts, and socially and politically relevant ideas. One such application is the measurement of inequality dislike or inequality aversion by examining the correlation between inequality in the region and individuals' reported life satisfaction (Alesina et al. 2004; Morawetz et al. 1977; Schwarze and Harpfer 2007). This evidence points to a negative relationship between inequality and life satisfaction, i.e., individuals are inequality averse. In this paper we extend this current work by looking at heterogeneity defined through individual risk aversion. This indirect way of measuring inequality dislike avoids some important shortcomings of the alternative experimental methods used for the same purpose, which are based either on Okun's (1975) leaky bucket experiment (Pirttilä and Uusitalo 2010; Amiel et al. 1999) or on directly letting respondents choose between different income distributions in a hypothetical society (Carlsson et al. 2005). The increasing availability of self-reported satisfaction questions in large representative datasets allows estimate inequality aversion parameters that are representative of the population of a country. In addition, evidence from the lab is prone to biases, such as the social desirability bias, which are not present when estimating inequality attitudes indirectly with life satisfaction.

In the data set used in this paper individuals are asked *How satisfied they are with their life, all things considered*, where the answers are reported on a 0 (completely dissatisfied) to 10 (completely satisfied) scale. The three basic assumptions underlying subjective satisfaction measures (Ferrer-i-Carbonell and Frijters 2004) are: (i) individuals are able to evaluate their life satisfaction, (ii) there is a positive monotonic relationship between the answer to such questions and the theoretical concept we are interested in, and (iii) the answer to such questions are interpersonal comparable. A good account of such measures, the underlying assumptions, its applications, and its (empirical) validity can be found in Clark et al. (2008), Ferrer-i-Carbonell and Frijters (2004), Senik (2005), and Van Praag and Ferrer-i-Carbonell (2004).

9.2.2.2 Risk Attitudes

The German Socio-Economic Panel (SOEP) questionnaire asked respondents to report their willingness to take risk in 8 years: 2004, 2006, and every year from 2008 to 2013. Our sample is confined to these 8 years. The question runs as follows: "How do you see yourself: Are you generally a person who is fully prepared to take risks or do you try to avoid taking risks?" Respondents can answer on a 0 (risk averse) to 10 (fully prepared to take risks) scale. The answer to this question provides a direct measure of risk on an 11 point scale. Such measure contrasts with indirect approaches in which measures of risk attitudes are derived from observed behavior, such as playing the lottery or investing in risky assets. Direct measures of risk can be easily introduced in general large household panel questionnaires, as the present case proofs. This allows the researcher to test for new ideas in general large population surveys, which contrasts with the most experimental studies done with small groups of individuals, which may suffer from external validity as they are often difficult to generalize to the whole population. In other words, the use of general measures of risk attitudes (or attitudes in general) opens up new lines of research in the same way that subjective satisfaction measures did. It remains very important to validate this direct measure of risk, which has been done by a group of economists (Dohmen et al. 2005) involved in the introduction of this survey measure in the German SOEP. Their main result is that there is a relationship between the answer to the risk question used in this paper and individual behavior. To come to this conclusion, the authors perform a complementary experiment with a group of individuals that are comparable to the ones answering the German SOEP questionnaire. In addition, the authors show that there is a correlation between the reported willingness to take risk and self-reported behavior in the questionnaire, such as holding stocks, smoking, and occupational choice. We have also examined the relationship between this measure of risk attitude and a set of individual characteristics that are known to correlate with risk attitudes and came to very consistent results, e.g. women are more risk averse, and years of education and income correlate negatively with risk aversion.

As outlined in Sect. 9.2.1, to explore the role of risk attitudes on inequality dislike, we will compare the effect of inequality on life satisfaction for risk lovers (β_H), i.e. respondents who report being very much prepared to take risks (corresponding to answers 9 and 10), and no risk lovers (β_L). Risk lovers comprise a small proportion, 2.6%, of the sample. This divide between the two groups allows identifying risk lovers as those individuals who show different behavior from the rest of the population.

9.2.2.3   Are Risk Changes Endogenous to Life Events and Individual Characteristics?

A relevant question is whether risk attitude is a persistent trait (e.g., Cooper et al. 2000; Zuckerman and Kuhlman 2000) or instead it changes over time or, most importantly, it depends on individuals' changing circumstances that at the same time are related to characteristics correlated with life satisfaction. We check our data for yearly changes on risk attitudes (or 2 years for 2006 and 2008) on the 0–10 original scale. The average yearly change for all observations (over 115,000) is -0.026 (sd. 2.24), 25% of which do not report any change, 31% report a one-point change, and 11% report a two points change on the 0–10 scale. If we look at the longer term difference from 2004 to 2013, we have over 7900 respondents who participated in both years. The average difference between those two nineteen-years-apart reported risk is -0.23 (sd 2.51). While only 20% of the respondents do not change their risk attitude, 30% change it with by one point, 21% by two points, and the remaining 30% change it by 3 (half of them) or more points. Most important, changes in risk attitudes from one wave to the other do not correlate with most individual characteristics. Regression analysis shows that the only statistically significant coefficient between risk attitudes and individual characteristics is being disabled (1.6% significance). The remaining coefficients are non-significant and are very small in size. The complete table is in the appendix (Table 9.10).

9.2.2.4   Inequality: The Gini Coefficient

To examine the impact of inequality on life satisfaction or utility we need to estimate a measure of inequality that is able to reflect individual's perceptions. To this end, we will measure inequality at Government region level (*Regierungsbezirke*, corresponding to NUTS2), which is an area closer to the individual than the country and, at the same time, is large enough not to be picking up relative income effects.[3] In order to capture changes over time, the inequality measure will be allowed to change for every sample year. This means that we distinguish among 39 different government regions in 8 different time periods. In line with the literature, we use the Gini coefficient to measure inequality in the distribution of equivalized income of the region, that is, income deflated by the modified OECD scale, which weights the first adult by 1, the second and subsequent adults by 0.5, and each child by 0.3. The Gini coefficient is known to give more importance to income disparities in the middle of the distribution than the tails, when aggregating income differences. To check the robustness of our findings we will use the Mean Log Deviation (MLD) and the Theil

---

[3]Measuring individual's perceptions about (income) inequality is far from trivial. Individuals may have incorrect perceptions about the 'true' level of inequality depending on the relative position they have in their reference group (Cruces et al. 2013). As the SOEP does not report information about this source of bias, we cannot correct for it and rely on the standard estimate that results from reported income levels.

index, two measures of the Generalized Entropy Family that give more weight to
differences in the lower tail of the distribution (Cowell 2011).

9.2.3 The Data

The empirical analysis uses the German Socio-Economic Panel (SOEP) (Wagner
et al. 2007), a representative German household panel that started in 1984 in West
Germany, which includes East German respondents since 1990. As outline above,
we use data for the 8 years for which there is available information on individual risk
attitudes, that is, 2004, 2006, and every year from 2008 to 2013. Table 9.1 shows
descriptive statistics for the main variables used in the empirical analysis.

Table 9.1 shows that on average individuals are rather satisfied with their life,
which is a usual finding in Western societies. Although the Gini coefficient is
calculated by using equivalent income, in explaining life satisfaction we use

Table 9.1 Sample descriptive statistics, German SOEP 2004, 2006, 2008–2013

Variable	Mean	Std. Dev.
Life satisfaction (0–10)	6.99	1.77
Prepared to take risks (0–10)	4.42	2.31
NUTS 2 Gini coefficient	0.27	0.04
Ln (age)2	15.13	2.79
Individual has a partner [0,1]	0.62	0.49
Household income (per month, after taxes)	2864.64	2140.93
Individual is unemployed [0,1]	0.05	0.22
Individual does not work [0,1]	0.43	0.49
Savings (in €)	330.32	869.71
Individual is disabled [0,1]	0.14	0.34
Ln (number of adults in the household)	1.12	0.26
Ln (number children in the household)	0.24	0.42
Ln (years education)	2.48	0.21
Federal GDP	99.11	7.12
Federal unemployment rate	7.92	3.96
Federal Poverty	0.13	0.02
Federal Median income	1457.65	152.10
Year		
2006	0.14	0.35
2008	0.12	0.33
2009	0.13	0.33
2010	0.12	0.32
2011	0.12	0.32
2012	0.12	0.33
2013	0.12	0.33

household income. The reason behind this decision is that if we were to use equivalent income we would be imposing the same transformation to all individuals and we would therefore ignore the different consumption patterns and preferences that households may have. In order to control for differences in household size, however, the regression equation for life satisfaction introduces the number of adults and children as explanatory variables. The regression analysis also includes other individual characteristics that are typically found important determinants of life satisfaction: amount of savings in Euro, age of the individual (introduced in squared logarithms), whether the individual has a partner, is unemployed, does not work, or suffers from some disability, and years of education.

The average willingness to take risk is 4.42 (sd. 2.31) with most individuals (21%) concentrated at 5 and 47% of them reporting a 4 or less. In other words, 68% of individuals report a 5 or below. Individuals classified as risk lovers (categories 9 and 10) represent 2.6% of the sample. The average unemployment rate over the sample period is about 7.9%, ranging from 3% (in Bavaria in 2013) to 22.4% (Saxony-Anhalt in 2004). The regional unemployment trends reflect the business cycle of the German economy as well as the regional disparities that tend to persist over time. The GDP growth also shows large regional and time variations.

The average Gini coefficient across the 39 Government regions over the sample period is 0.265. Within state (over time) variation of the Gini coefficient is key to our empirical strategy. As Fig. 9.1 shows, such variation is not driven by few states or certain episodes. Gini differences between Government regions are time persistent and range from an average Gini over the years of 0.218 (nuts Middle Hesse) to 0.342 (nuts Muenster). As Fig. 9.1 clearly shows, the largest Gini estimate for region

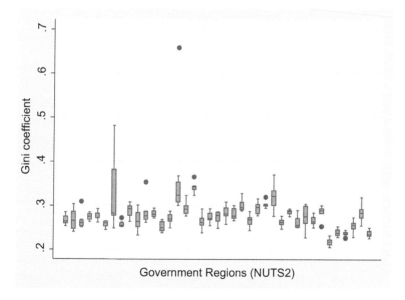

Fig. 9.1 Distribution (Box-Cox) of Gini coefficient by Government regions

Brunswick is implausibly larger than any other estimate. However, our main results are robust to dropping this possible outlier from the analysis. Variation over time is smaller than between region variation, and ranges from 0.281 in 2004 to 0.271 in 2013.

9.3   Results

9.3.1   The Effect of Inequality on Satisfaction

Table 9.2 shows the results of estimating Eq. (9.3) with individual fixed effects. As outlined above, we present estimates and its standard errors, when the latter are clustered at regional level (in the upper panel), and when the standard errors are obtained by bootstrapping Eq. (9.3) with 50 replications (lower panel). Recall that point estimates are different because we cannot include regional fixed effects in the lower panel.

In the first specification we do not allow risk attitudes to play any role on life satisfaction, and find the expected negative relationship between inequality (measured by the Gini coefficient at NUTS 2 level) and life satisfaction. This means that on average individuals dislike inequality. This finding is in line with the previous literature that has also used subjective measures to empirically test inequality aversion in Western European countries (Alesina et al. 2004; Schwarze and Harpfer 2007).

In order to assess the importance of individuals' dislike for inequality, we can compare its effect on life satisfaction with that of other variables of interest (e.g. income). For example, we can compute the equivalent income of a change in inequality, using the results of the upper panel of Table 9.2. This is the income change equivalent, in terms of life satisfaction, to a percentage change in inequality. A 0.05 drop in the Gini coefficient (which represents about an 18.9% reduction from the current level) would be equivalent to a 10.94% income increase, which is equivalent to 314 Euro a month at the sample mean. Similarly, a 10% reduction in the average Gini is equivalent to a 5.77% household income increase, at sample mean this is 165 Euro per month.

As outlined above, our inequality aversion estimates are in line with previous empirical evidence. Using the same data for Germany (SOEP) for a time period previous to ours (1985–1998), a similar regression-based approach and estimation method, Schwarze and Haerpfer (2007) find a similar estimate of inequality aversion: a 5.5% income increase offsets the negative effect on life satisfaction of a 10% increase in average inequality. The effect of the Gini coefficient and of log household income on life satisfaction is estimated to be −0.362 and 0.319 respectively.

The coefficient estimates for the control variables shown in Appendix Tables 9.8 and 9.9 offer no surprises: we find the usual positive relationship between life satisfaction and household income, having a partner, amount of savings, and the logarithm of age squared, and the also common negative relationship between

Table 9.2 Life satisfaction, by risk attitudes. German SOEP, 2004, 2006, 2008–2013, fixed effects estimators

	-1	-2	-3
	Total sample	Risk taking	No risk taking
Clustered standard errors			
Gini	-0.536^{***}	0.919	-0.558^{***}
	-0.195	-2.242	-0.198
Bootstrapped standard errors			
Gini	-0.482^{*}	1.336	-0.511^{**}
	-0.25	-2.517	-0.251
N	137,851	3548	134,303

Individual FE regression with year (and NUTS 2 in the upper panel) FE. Standard errors clustered at NUTS 2 level. Botstrapped standard errors obtained after 500 replications
Controls include: ln2(age), partner, ln (household income), unemployed, not employed, savings, disability, ln(number of adults), ln (number of children), ln(years of education), unemployment rate, GDP, poverty rate, and median income at the federal level
Standard errors in parentheses; $* p < 0.1$, $** p < 0.05$, $*** p < 0.01$

satisfaction and being unemployed, being disabled, the number of adults and children in the household, and years of education. In order to control for time and region characteristics and to distinguish them from the inequality in the region and year, we included a set of dummy variables indicating the region and year where the respondent lives. In addition, and as we have pointed out above, since regional unemployment, economic growth, poverty, and median income affect life satisfaction and may correlate with inequality, we have singled out these two macro variables from the regional and time characteristics and have separately controlled for it. The results in Appendix Tables 9.8 and 9.9 show that GDP growth, poverty, and median income do not have an independent effect beyond the effects already captured by the regional and time dummies. Regional unemployment, like the Gini, however does have a statistically significant negative coefficient.

9.3.2 The Role of Risk on Shaping Inequality Dislike

This section focuses on the main empirical test of this paper, namely to examine the role that individual's risk attitudes have on determining inequality dislike. To this end we estimate Eq. (9.3) for two groups that differ in their risk attitudes, and test whether the β_r coefficient, which measures dislike for inequality, is the same or differs across the two groups, i.e. we test whether $\beta_L = \beta_H$. In particular, the expected positive relationship between inequality dislike and risk aversion implies $\beta_H > \beta > \beta_L$.

Columns (2) and (3) of Table 9.2 report β_H and β_L, respectively. The estimate of β_L in column (3) indicates that inequality reduces life satisfaction of individuals who are not prepared to take risks. This result is statistically significant regardless of the estimation method used to compute standard errors. The effect of inequality on life satisfaction, however, is the opposite for individuals who are prepared to take risks, although the point estimate is very imprecisely estimated, with a standard error larger than the coefficient. Now $\beta_H > 0$, implying that risk lovers like inequality. Thus, we conclude that inequality does not seem to affect risk takers, and if it does, the effect would be positive. Finally, a simple test of means indicates that $\beta_H > \beta_L$, as expected (p-value <0.000 in both panels).

In order to assess the importance of risk attitudes in shaping individuals' inequality dislike, we calculate the equivalent income of a 0.05 decrease in the Gini for individuals who are not prepared to take risks, using the estimates of the upper panel, where standard errors are clustered at regional level. A 0.05 decrease in the Gini coefficient increases the life satisfaction of non-risk-takers by 0.028 ((-0.558) * (-0.05)), which is equivalent to an 11.7% income increase or, at sample average 334 Euro per month. At sample averages, this implies an elasticity of 0.002 (0.4%/18.9%).

In sum, the results using self-reported life satisfaction as a proxy for utility indicate that risk attitudes are one of the reasons why individuals might dislike inequality, to the extent that risk lovers do not show inequality aversion.

9.3.3 Robustness Analysis

For the sake of comparability with previous findings in the literature, our baseline analysis relies on the Gini coefficient. This index, however, has two salient features which bear on the inequality estimates and orderings across regions and years: First, the Gini coefficient is mostly sensitive to differences in income shares in the middle part of the distribution, which implies that it is less sensitive to such differences in either tail of the distribution, where outliers may lie. Because of this, the Gini coefficient is more robust to outliers than other indices. Second, the distance concept of the Gini coefficient is rank dependent. That is, the relative position of individuals in the income distribution matters for the inequality assessment.

In this section we check whether our main findings are robust to using indices of inequality that are sensitive to different parts of the income distribution and whose distance concept does not depend on rank. Tables 9.3 and 9.4 show the effect of inequality on life satisfaction by risk attitudes, when inequality is measured by the Mean Logarithmic Deviation (MDL) and Theil's entropy index, respectively. Both the MLD and the Theil index are members of the Generalized Entropy Family of inequality indices, which satisfy basic properties such as the principle of transfers, anonymity, scale invariance and population invariance, like the Gini coefficient. Both indices however use a distance concept which is rank independent and are more sensitive to differences in income shares in the bottom part of the distribution, especially so the MLD (Cowell 2011).

Table 9.3 Effect of inequality (MLD) on life satisfaction, by risk attitudes. German SOEP, 2004, 2006, 2008–2013, fixed effects estimators

	−1	−2	−3
	Total sample	Risk taking	No risk taking
Clustered standard errors			
Theil	−0.325***	0.826	−0.350***
	−0.103	−1.381	−0.107
Bootstrapped standard errors			
Theil	−0.307	0.898	−0.334*
	−0.19	−1.735	−0.19
N	137,851	3548	134,303

Individual FE regression with year (and NUTS 2 in the upper panel) FE. Standard errors clustered at NUTS 2 level. Botstrapped standard errors obtained after 500 replications. Same controls as in Table 9.2

Standard errors in parentheses; $*p < 0.1$, $**p < 0.05$, $***p < 0.01$

Table 9.4 Effect of inequality (Theil) on life satisfaction, by risk attitudes. German SOEP, 2004, 2006, 2008–2013, fixed effects estimators

	−1	−2	−3
	Total sample	Risk taking	No risk taking
Clustered standard errors			
Theil	−0.151***	0.305	−0.165***
	−0.043	−0.651	−0.045
Bootstrapped standard errors			
Theil	−0.144	0.322	−0.158
	−0.13	−0.948	−0.131
N	137,851	3548	134,303

Individual FE regression with year (and NUTS 2 in the upper panel) FE. Standard errors clustered at NUTS 2 level. Botstrapped standard errors obtained after 500 replications. Same controls as in Table 9.2

Standard errors in parentheses; $*p < 0.1$, $**p < 0.05$, $***p < 0.01$

The estimates displayed in Tables 9.3 and 9.4 suggest that our main finding (i.e. risk aversion shapes individual's dislike for inequality) is robust to how inequality is measured. Inequality dislike is larger amongst individuals who are not very prepared to take risks than amongst risk takers. The negative estimate of inequality dislike is statistically significant when standard errors are clustered by NUTS2, but are more imprecisely estimated when standard errors are bootstrapped, regardless of the inequality index employed. In particular, the effect of both the MLD and the Theil on life satisfaction is more imprecisely estimated than that of the Gini coefficient, when standard errors are bootstrapped. This may be due to the larger robustness of the Gini coefficient to extreme or outlier observations, pointed out above.

9.3.4   Heterogeneous Effects

This section explores heterogeneous effects of risk attitudes on inequality dislike, across the individual characteristics that are found to correlate with risk attitudes, namely gender, education, and income (Hartog et al. 2002). As argued in the introduction, risk attitudes correlate with other individual characteristics that, at the same time, correlate with inequality aversion. In particular, women, lower educated and also poorer individuals tend to be more risk averse and, at the same time, more inequality averse, as they face larger risks of falling down in the income distribution. To this we estimate β_r in Eq. (9.3) for four population subgroups, defined by the interaction of risk attitude, on the one hand, and gender (men and women), education attainment (high education (tertiary education) and lower education); or poverty status (when the poverty line is set at 60% of the median equivalent household income, at the year and federal level). Tables 9.5, 9.6 and 9.7 show the estimates by risk attitudes and gender, poverty status, and education, respectively.

Given the smaller sample sizes, point estimates for risk takers have large standard deviations, which render the interpretation of heterogeneous effects for risk takers meaningless. We shall thus discuss heterogeneous effect amongst no risk takers. The upper panel of Table 9.5 shows that the inequality dislike for non-risk-taker women is -0696, while that for non-risk-taker men is -0.405 (and imprecisely estimated). Therefore, women show a stronger inequality dislike than men (the difference between the two point estimates being significant with a p-value<0.000, regardless of the estimation method). Non-risk-taker poor individuals also show a stronger distaste for inequality than non-risk-taker non-poor individuals (see Table 9.6). Although the point estimate for non-poor individuals is not precisely estimated, the difference between the two coefficients is statistically significant (p-value<0.000, regardless of the estimation method). Table 9.7 shows that by

Table 9.5 Effect of inequality on life satisfaction, by risk attitudes and gender. German SOEP, 2004, 2006, 2008–2013, fixed effects estimators

	−1	−2	−3	−4	−5
	Total sample	Female no risk taker	Male no risk taker	Female risk taker	Male risk taker
Clustered standard errors					
Gini	−0.536***	−0.696***	−0.405	−2.931	3.054*
	−0.195	−0.211	−0.386	−4.059	−1.762
Bootstrapped standard errors					
Gini	−0.482*	−0.636**	−0.361	−3.149	3.627
	−0.25	−0.287	−0.49	−7.27	−2.275
N	137,851	71,043	63,260	1227	2321

Individual FE regression with year (and NUTS 2 in the upper panel) FE. Standard errors clustered at NUTS 2 level. Botstrapped standard errors obtained after 500 replications. Same controls as in Table 9.2
Standard errors in parentheses; *$p < 0.1$, **$p < 0.05$, ***$p < 0.01$

Table 9.6 Effect of inequality on life satisfaction, by risk attitudes and poverty status. German SOEP, 2004, 2006, 2008–2013, fixed effects estimators

	−1	−2	−3	−4	−5
	Total sample	Not poor no risk taker	Poor no risk taker	Not poor risk taker	Poor risk taker
Clustered standard errors					
Gini	−0.536***	−0.457**	−1.211	1.729	−6.048
	−0.195	−0.175	−0.786	−1.725	−4.855
Bootstrapped standard errors					
Gini	−0.482*	−0.466**	−1.017	2.617	−4.538
	−0.25	−0.224	−0.941	−2.139	−16.973
N	137,851	117,226	17,077	2925	623

Individual FE regression with year (and NUTS 2 in the upper panel) FE. Standard errors clustered at NUTS 2 level. Botstrapped standard errors obtained after 500 replications. Same controls as in Table 9.2
Standard errors in parentheses; *$p < 0.1$, **$p < 0.05$, ***$p < 0.01$

Table 9.7 Effect of inequality on life satisfaction, by risk attitudes and education level. German SOEP, 2004, 2006, 2008–2013, fixed effects estimators

	−1	−2	−3	−4	−5
	Total sample	Not high educated no risk taker	High educated no risk taker	Not high educated risk taker	High educated risk taker
Clustered standard errors					
Gini	−0.536***	−0.653**	−0.315	2.957	−2.528
	−0.195	−0.255	−0.256	−2.985	−1.557
Bootstrapped standard errors					
Gini	−0.482*	−0.603*	−0.273	2.864	−1.472
	−0.25	−0.327	−0.339	−3.379	−3.153
N	137,851	97,303	37,000	2682	866

Individual FE regression with year (and NUTS 2 in the upper panel) FE. Standard errors clustered at NUTS 2 level. Botstrapped standard errors obtained after 500 replications. Same controls as in Table 9.2
Standard errors in parentheses; *$p < 0.1$, **$p < 0.05$, ***$p < 0.01$

education level, non-risk-taker lower educated individuals also display lower tolerance for inequality than their higher educated counterpart, who displays a lower and imprecisely estimated point estimate. Again, the difference between the two coefficients is statistically significant (p-value<0.000, regardless of the estimation method).

In sum, conditional on not being very prepared to take risks, women, poorer and lower educated individuals show larger distaste for inequality. These population subgroups are also found to be more risk averse. Although poorly estimated, we can argue that the role that risk attitudes play on shaping inequality aversion is partly

driven by individual characteristics (gender, education, and income) that are correlated with risk attitudes. In fact, our sample sizes already show that there are more
males, poor individuals, and low educated not willing to take risk, while the opposite
is true for risk takers.

9.4   Conclusions

Individual preference parameters are central to the modelling and understanding of
individual behavior. Risk aversion has been said to help explain why individuals
may dislike inequality, since it influences the weight that individuals give to the risk
of having a worse social or income position in the future. Only recently, researchers
have started to elicit individual preferences for equality separately from individuals'
attitudes towards risk and have explored the relationship between the two. So far,
this has been only done by means of experiments and not for large representative
samples. This paper employs a self-reported happiness question as in Easterlin
(1974) and a measure of risk attitudes from a large and representative panel data
set for Germany (SOEP) to empirically identify the link between the two. To the best
of our knowledge these are the first estimates ever obtained from representative
survey data. We empirically explore the relationship between inequality and risk
aversion and find that risk attitudes is and individual characteristic that explains
dislike for inequality. These findings are in line with patterns found in experimental
setups. The role of risk attitudes in shaping inequality aversion can be assessed by
examining the income equivalent of a change in current inequality. Our results show
that while most individuals would be indifferent between a 0.05 Gini reduction (18%
of the average Gini across years and regions) and an about 11% household income
increase, this number is negative although very imprecisely estimated for risk lover
individuals (2.6% of the sample). In other words, most individuals in our sample
would be willing to give up 11% of their income to see the Gini coefficient in their
region reduced by 18%. Our results are rather robust to other measures of inequality.
In the paper however we also show that the importance of risk attitudes on shaping
individuals own inequality aversion is partly driven by other individual characteristics (gender, education, and income) that are correlated with risk attitudes. In other
words, inequality aversion is not only driven by risk attitudes per se, but also by
individual characteristics that strongly correlate with them. Disentangling the independent effect of both is a difficult task that falls outside the realm of this paper.

Acknowledgements Ada Ferrer-i-Carbonell acknowledges financial support from the Spanish
Ministry of Economy and Competitiveness, through the Severo Ochoa Programme for Centres of
Excellence in R&D (SEV-2015-0563), from the Spanish Ministry of Science and Innovation
(ECO2014-59302-P), and the Catalan Government (01414-SGR). Xavier Ramos acknowledges
financial support from the Spanish Ministry of Economy and Competitiveness' project ECO2016-
76506-C4-4-R), and the Catalan Government (SGR2014-1279).

Appendix

Table 9.8 Effect of inequality on life satisfaction, by risk attitudes. German SOEP, 2004, 2006, 2008–2013, fixed effects estimators. Clustered standard errors

Variable	(1) Total sample Coeff.	Std. Error	(2) Risk taking Coeff.	Std. Error	(3) No risk taking Coeff.	Std. Error
giniEQInuts	−0.536	0.195	0.919	2.242	−0.558	0.198
Individual characteristics						
Ln (age)^2	0.065	0.053	−0.062	0.39	0.075	0.054
Individual has a partner [0,1]	0.122	0.032	0.393	0.219	0.121	0.032
Ln (Household income (net, monthly))	0.258	0.025	0.517	0.238	0.253	0.024
Individual is unemployed [0,1]	−0.559	0.037	−0.28	0.252	−0.554	0.04
Individual does not work [0,1]	0.007	0.023	−0.084	0.233	0.009	0.023
Savings (in €)	0	0	0	0	0	0
Individual is disabled [0,1]	−0.228	0.03	−0.727	0.388	−0.23	0.029
Ln (# of adults in the household)	−0.108	0.051	−0.281	0.399	−0.117	0.051
Ln (# children in the household)	−0.018	0.035	−0.241	0.234	−0.022	0.035
Ln (years education)	−0.405	0.155	−0.416	1.148	−0.426	0.163
Federal State variables						
Federal GDP	−0.006	0.003	−0.027	0.029	−0.005	0.003
Federal unemployment rate	−0.036	0.005	−0.028	0.051	−0.036	0.005
Federal Poverty	−0.034	0.351	−3.347	3.355	−0.118	0.339
Federal Median income	0	0	−0.004	0.002	0	0
Constant	6.436	0.88	15.427	5.424	6.128	0.886
Nuts 2 dummies	Yes		Yes		Yes	
Year dummies	Yes		Yes		Yes	
Std. dev. Individual fixed effect	1.55		2.797		1.556	
Std. dev. Error term	1.184		1.43		1.176	
R2: Within	0.016		0.078		0.015	
R2: Between	0.031		0.004		0.025	
R2: Overall	0.032		0.004		0.027	
Corr(regresors, ind. fixed eff.)	−0.072		−0.74		−0.098	
Number of observations	137,851		3548		134,303	
Number of individuals	34,345		2476		33,950	

Individual FE regression with year and NUTS 2 fixed effects. Standard errors clustered at NUTS 2 level

Controls include: ln2(age), partner, ln(household income), unemployed, not employed, savings, disability, ln(number of adults), ln (number of children), ln(years of education), unemployment rate, GDP, poverty rate, and median income at the federal level

Standard errors in parentheses; $*p < 0.1$, $**p < 0.05$, $***p < 0.01$

Table 9.9 Effect of inequality on life satisfaction, by risk attitudes. German SOEP, 2004, 2006, 2008–2013, fixed effects estimators. Bootstrapped standard errors

	(1) Total sample		(2) Risk taking		(3) No risk taking	
Variable	Coeff.	Std. Error	Coeff.	Std. Error	Coeff.	Std. Error
giniEQInuts	−0.482	0.25	1.336	2.517	−0.511	0.251
Individual characteristics						
Ln (age)^2	0.065	0.051	−0.047	0.4	0.074	0.052
Individual has a partner [0,1]	0.122	0.03	0.352	0.24	0.121	0.03
Ln (Household income (net, monthly))	0.259	0.026	0.459	0.244	0.254	0.025
Individual is unemployed [0,1]	−0.558	0.038	−0.175	0.263	−0.554	0.041
Individual does not work [0,1]	0.006	0.023	−0.181	0.227	0.009	0.023
Savings (in €)	0	0	0	0	0	0
Individual is disabled [0,1]	−0.228	0.029	−0.764	0.382	−0.23	0.028
Ln (# of adults in the household)	−0.11	0.052	−0.191	0.396	−0.119	0.052
Ln (# children in the household)	−0.02	0.035	−0.161	0.244	−0.022	0.035
Ln (years education)	−0.397	0.141	−0.339	1.177	−0.417	0.147
Federal State variables						
gdpfederal	−0.006	0.003	−0.038	0.031	−0.005	0.003
urfederal	−0.037	0.005	−0.06	0.055	−0.037	0.005
poverty	−0.165	0.375	−3.842	3.793	−0.247	0.364
medianincome	0	0	−0.002	0.002	0	0
Constant	6.146	0.828	13.197	5.327	5.982	0.841
Nuts 2 dummies	No		No		No	
Year dummies	Yes		Yes		Yes	
Std. dev. Individual fixed effect	1.54		1.883		1.544	
Std. dev. Error term	1.184		1.443		1.176	
R2: Within	0.015		0.046		0.015	
R2: Between	0.037		0.053		0.031	
R2: Overall	0.038		0.058		0.033	
Corr(regresors, ind. fixed eff.)	−0.004		−0.059		−0.032	
Number of observations	137,851		3548		134,303	
Number of individuals	34,345		2476		33,950	

Individual FE regression with year fixed effects. Botstrapped standard errors obtained after 500 replications

Controls include: ln2(age), partner, ln(household income), unemployed, not employed, savings, disability, ln(number of adults), ln (number of children), ln(years of education), unemployment rate, GDP, poverty rate, and median income at the federal level

Standard errors in parentheses; *$p < 0.1$, **$p < 0.05$, ***$p < 0.01$

Table 9.10 Changes in risk attitudes across waves German SOEP, 2004, 2006, 2008–2013

Variable	Coeff.	Std. Err.
Constant	0.212	−0.161
Ln (age)^2	0.001	−0.004
Individual has a partner [0,1]	0.034	−0.021
Ln (Household income (net, monthly))	−0.015	−0.02
Individual is unemployed [0,1]	0.033	−0.041
Individual does not work [0,1]	0.026	−0.02
Savings (in €)	0	0
Individual is disabled [0,1]	−0.056**	−0.024
Ln (# of adults in the household)	−0.02	−0.041
Ln (# children in the household)	−0.011	−0.022
Ln (years education)	−0.052	−0.043
Number of observations	77,733	77,733

Standard errors in parentheses. Statistical significance: * 0.1 ** 0.05 *** 0.01

References

Alesina, A., & Angeletos, G. M. (2005). Fairness and redistribution: US vs. Europe. *American Economic Review, 95*, 913–935.

Alesina, A., & Giuliano, P. (2011). Preferences for redistribution. In A. Bisin & J. Benhabib (Eds.), *Handbook of social economics* (pp. 93–132). Amsterdam: North Holland.

Alesina, A., & Glaeser, E. (2004). *Fighting poverty in the US and Europe: A world of difference.* Oxford: Oxford University Press.

Alesina, A., & La Ferrara, E. (2005). Preferences for redistribution in the land of opportunities. *Journal of Public Economics, 89*(5–6), 897–931.

Alesina, A., Di Tella, R., & MacCulloch, R. (2004). Inequality and happiness: Are Europeans and Americans different? *Journal of Public Economics, 88*(9–10), 2009–2042.

Amiel, Y., Creedy, J., & Hurn, S. (1999). Measuring attitudes towards inequality. *Scandinavian Journal of Economics, 101*(1), 83–96.

Amiel, Y., Cowell, F. A., & Gaertner, W. (2009). To be or not to be involved: A questionnaire-experimental view on Harsanyi's utilitarian ethics. *Social Choice and Welfare, 32*(2), 299–316.

Angrist, J. D., & Pischke, J. S. (2008). *Mostly harmless econometrics: An empiricist's companion.* Princeton: Princeton university press.

Benabou, R., & Ok, E. A. (2001). Social mobility and the demand for redistribution: The POUM hypothesis. *The Quarterly Journal of Economics, 116*(2), 447–487.

Bernasconi, M. (2002). How should income be divided? Questionnaire evidence from the theory of "impartial preferences". *Journal of Economics, 77*(1), 163–195.

Bosmans, K., & Schokkaert, E. (2004). Social welfare, the veil of ignorance and purely individual risk: An empirical examination. In F. Cowell (Ed.), *Inequality, welfare and income distribution: Experimental approaches* (pp. 85–114). Bingley: Emerald Group Publishing Limited.

Brennan, G., González, L. G., Güth, W., & Levati, M. V. (2008). Attitudes toward private and collective risk in individual and strategic choice situations. *Journal of Economic Behavior & Organization, 67*(1), 253–262.

Cameron, A. C., & Miller, D. L. (2010). Robust inference with clustered data. In A. Ullah & D. E. Giles (Eds.), *Handbook of empirical economics and finance* (pp. 1–28). Boca Raton: Chapman and Hall/CRC Press.

Carlsson, F., Daruvala, D., & Johansson-Stenman, O. (2005). Are people inequality-averse, or just risk-averse? *Economica, 72*(287), 375–396.

Clark, A. E., Frijters, P., & Shields, M. A. (2008). Relative income, happiness, and utility: An explanation for the Easterlin paradox and other puzzles. *Journal of Economic Literature, 46*(1), 95–144.

Cooper, M. L., Agocha, V. B., & Sheldon, M. S. (2000). A motivational perspective on risky behaviors: The role of personality and affect regulatory processes. *Journal of Personality, 68*(6), 1059–1088.

Cowell, F. A. (2011). *Measuring inequality*. Oxford: Oxford University Press.

Cruces, G., Perez-Truglia, R., & Tetaz, M. (2013). Biased perceptions of income distribution and preferences for redistribution: Evidence from a survey experiment. *Journal of Public Economics, 98*, 100–112.

Dawes, C. T., Fowler, J. H., Johnson, T., McElreath, R., & Smirnov, O. (2007). Egalitarian motives in humans. *Nature, 446*(7137), 794.

Dohmen, T. J., Falk, A., Huffman, D., Sunde, U., Schupp, J., & Wagner, G. G. (2005). *Individual risk attitudes: New evidence from a large, representative, experimentally-validated survey* (IZA working paper n.1730). London: Centre for Economic Policy Research.

Easterlin, R. A. (1974). Does economic growth improve the human lot? Some empirical evidence. In P. A. David & M. W. Reder (Eds.), *Nations and households in economic growth: Essays in honour of Moses Abramovitz* (pp. 89–125). New York: Academic.

Ferrer-i-Carbonell, A., & Frijters, P. (2004). How important is methodology for the estimates of the determinants of happiness? *The Economic Journal, 114*(497), 641–659.

Ferrer-i-Carbonell, A., & Ramos, X. (2014). Inequality and happiness. *Journal of Economic Surveys, 28*(5), 1016–1027.

Harsanyi, J. C. (1955). Cardinal welfare, individualistic ethics, and interpersonal comparisons of utility. *Journal of Political Economy, 63*(4), 309–321.

Hartog, J., Ferrer-i-Carbonell, A., & Jonker, N. (2002). Linking measured risk aversion to individual characteristics. *Kyklos, 55*(1), 3–26.

Kroll, Y., & Davidovitz, L. (2003). Inequality aversion versus risk aversion. *Economica, 70*(277), 19–29.

Meltzer, A. H., & Richard, S. F. (1981). A rational theory of the size of government. *Journal of Political Economy, 89*(5), 914–927.

Morawetz, D., Atia, E., Bin-Nun, G., Felous, L., Gariplerden, Y., Harris, E., … & Zarfaty, Y. (1977). Income distribution and self-rated happiness: Some empirical evidence. *The Economic Journal, 87*(347), 511–522.

Okun, A. (1975). *Equality and efficiency: The big trade-off*. Washington, DC: Brookings Institution.

Piketty, T. (1995). Social mobility and redistributive politics. *The Quarterly Journal of Economics, 110*(3), 551–584.

Pirttilä, J., & Uusitalo, R. (2010). A 'leaky bucket' in the real world: Estimating inequality aversion using survey data. *Economica, 77*(305), 60–76.

Ravallion, M., & Lokshin, M. (2000). Who wants to redistribute? The tunnel effect in 1990s Russia. *Journal of Public Economics, 76*(1), 87–104.

Romer, T. (1975). Individual welfare, majority voting, and the properties of a linear income tax. *Journal of Public Economics, 4*(2), 163–185.

Schwarze, J., & Härpfer, M. (2007). Are people inequality averse, and do they prefer redistribution by the state?: Evidence from german longitudinal data on life satisfaction. *The Journal of Socio-Economics, 36*(2), 233–249.

Senik, C. (2005). What can we learn from subjective data? The case of income and well-being. *Journal of Economic Surveys, 19*, 43–63.

Van Praag, B. & Ferrer-i-Carbonell, A. (2004). *Happiness quantified, a satisfaction calculus approach* (Reprint 2008). Oxford: Oxford University Press.

Vickerey, W. (1945). Measuring marginal utility by reactions to risk. *Econometrica, 13*, 215–236.

Wagner, G. G., Frick, J. R., & Schupp, J. (2007). The German Socio-Economic Panel study (SOEP) – scope, evolution and enhancements. *Schmollers Jahrbuch, 127*, 139–169.

Wooldrige, J. M., (2006). *Cluster-sample methods in applied econometrics: An extended analysis.* Unpublished paper. University of Michigan.

Zuckerman, M., & Kuhlman, D. M. (2000). Personality and risk-taking: Common biosocial factors. *Journal of Personality, 68*(6), 999–1029.

Chapter 10
Advertising as a Major Source of Human Dissatisfaction: Cross-National Evidence on One Million Europeans

Chloe Michel, Michelle Sovinsky, Eugenio Proto, and Andrew J. Oswald

Abstract Advertising is ubiquitous in modern life. Yet might it be harmful to the happiness of nations? This paper blends longitudinal data on advertising with large-scale surveys on citizens' well-being. The analysis uses information on approximately 1 million randomly sampled European citizens across 27 nations over 3 decades. We show that increases in national advertising expenditure are followed by significant declines in levels of life satisfaction. This finding is robust to adjustments for a range of potential confounders -- including the personal and economic characteristics of individuals, country fixed-effects, year dummies, and business-cycle influences. Further research remains desirable. Nevertheless, our empirical results are some of the first to be consistent with the hypothesis that, perhaps by fostering unending desires, high levels of advertising may depress societal well-being.

C. Michel (✉)
University of Zurich, Zurich, Switzerland

M. Sovinsky
University of Mannheim, Mannheim, Germany

Centre for Economic Policy Research, London, UK

E. Proto
Centre for Economic Policy Research, London, UK

University of Bristol, Bristol, UK

IZA Institute for the Study of Labor, Bonn, Germany

A. J. Oswald
University of Warwick, Warwick, UK

IZA Institute for the Study of Labor, Bonn, Germany
e-mail: Andrew.Oswald@warwick.ac.uk

© Springer Nature Switzerland AG 2019
M. Rojas (ed.), *The Economics of Happiness*,
https://doi.org/10.1007/978-3-030-15835-4_10

10.1 Introduction

In a classic article, Richard Easterlin (1974) documented some of the first evidence for the striking idea that society does not seem to become happier as it grows richer. He suggested that one mechanism at work might be an intrinsic tendency of human beings to compare themselves with their neighbors. Easterlin's thesis drew, in part, on Thorstein Veblen's (1899, 1904) arguments about people's desires for conspicuous consumption. If humans have 'relativistic' preferences, so that they constantly look over their shoulders before deciding how contented they feel, then as those individuals consume more and more goods they might fail to become happier because they see others around them also consuming more and more. The pleasure of my new car might be nullified by the fact that Ms. Jones, in the parking spot next to mine, has also just bought one.

As Thorstein Veblen anticipated, there is today a global industrial sector -- known as the advertising industry – that is devoted to the unceasing encouragement of consumption. Advertising plays a prominent role in all countries of which we are knowledgeable. Might that industry, by fostering discontent with what people already own, be harmful to human happiness, perhaps because of the relativistic kinds of utility functions alluded to by scholars such as Richard Easterlin?

It is not known for certain how much advertising the typical citizen witnesses. However, one modern study, Speers et al. (2011), concluded for the United States that on prime-time television the brand names of food, beverages and restaurants appeared approximately 35,000 times in 1 year. Coca Cola products, for example, were seen 198 times by the average child and 269 times by the average adolescent. These influences appear to be gradually strengthening through time. Other research, by Cowling and Poolsombat (2007), documented a four-fold increase in real advertising per-capita in the US over 5 decades.

Links between advertising and human well-being are imperfectly understood. Effects might operate along two broad channels. First, one way to conceive of advertising is as *a force for good*. Advertising informs. It may therefore promote human welfare by allowing people to make better choices about the right products for them. Second, an alternative way to conceive of advertising is as *a force that creates dissatisfaction* and stimulates potentially infeasible desires. If correct, that would imply that advertising might reduce net human welfare by unduly raising the consumption aspirations of human beings. Since Veblen, many writers have worried about the possibility of, and in some cases found small-scale evidence for, negative effects of advertising upon people's well-being (see e.g. Richins 1995; Easterlin and Crimmins 1991; Bagwell and Bernheim 1996; Sirgy et al. 1998; Dittmar et al. 2014; Frey et al. 2007; Harris et al. 2009). A moderately large literature exists, primarily on the likely detrimental effects upon children (Andreyeva et al. 2011; Borzekowski and Robinson 2001; Buijzen and Valkenburg 2003a; Opree et al. 2012; Buijzen and Valkenburg 2003b), although the most recent work, by Opree et al. (2016), produced mixed results. More broadly, Clark (2018) reviews recent evidence consistent with important 'comparison effects' in adult humans, and Mujcic and Oswald (2018) document longitudinal evidence consistent with negative wellbeing consequences from envy.

At the national level, it is not known which of the two forces -- one beneficial and one detrimental -- is dominant. There are apparently no cross-country econometric studies on representative samples of adults. The now-large modern literature on the social science of well-being, described in sources such as Easterlin (2003), Oswald (1997), Layard (2011) and Clark (2018), has so far paid little attention to the role of advertising. A number of national variables have been shown to influence well-being in country fixed-effects equations (in particular, the generosity of the welfare state and various macroeconomic variables such as unemployment, in sources such as Di Tella et al. 2001, Di Tella et al. 2003, and Radcliff 2013).

In this study we examine -- and provide evidence of -- links between national advertising and national well-being. Using longitudinal information on countries (built up from pooled cross-sectional surveys), this study finds that rises and falls in advertising are followed, a small number of years later, by falls and rises in national life-satisfaction. The results thus reveal an inverse connection between advertising levels and the later well-being levels of nations.

To perform the statistical analysis, we take a sample of slightly over 900,000 randomly sampled European citizens, who report information on their life-satisfaction levels and on many other aspects of themselves and their lives. The data are from repeated surveys, collected annually, for 27 countries from 1980 to 2011. For each nation, and each year, total advertising expenditure levels are also gathered (details are given later in the appendix on Data and Methods). We then match one set of data with the other. To adjust in the analysis for possible confounding factors, we use regression analysis, and estimate fixed-effects equations in which the unobservable characteristics of nations can be held constant. Although strict causal interpretations are not possible, none of the paper's results depend on elementary cross-sectional regression equations.

10.2   Results

Figure 10.1 illustrates the study's key idea. The figure divides the data into tertiles and then plots the (uncorrected) relationship between the change in advertising and the change in life satisfaction. The three vertical bars separate the data into countries that over our period of study had particularly large increases in advertising expenditure, moderate increases, and small increases. Fig. 10.1 demonstrates that the greater is the rise in advertising within a nation, the smaller is any later improvement in life satisfaction.

Regression equations in Table 10.1 provide evidence of a more formal kind. They demonstrate the same type of pattern as in Fig. 10.1. The variable "Adv Expenditure" measures the level of advertising expenditure in that particular country in that particular year.

In column 1 of Table 10.1, the now-standard statistical specification for national happiness equations (as in Di Tella et al. 2001, for example) fits the data in the conventional way. A variable for the person's age enters with the quadratic form that

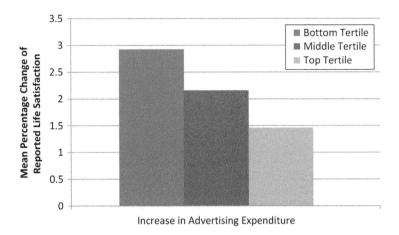

Fig. 10.1 An illustration of the inverse longitudinal relationship between changes in advertising and changes in the life satisfaction of countries. This is based on a sample of approximately 1 million individuals over the years 1980–2011 (or for shorter periods where full data are not available for a particular country). Here are the details about the three groups: Bottom Tertile: Mean Change: 2.925241. Countries: Czech Republic, Germany after 1989, Estonia, Finland, Lithuania, Hungary, Latvia, Poland, Romania, Slovakia. Middle Tertile: Mean Change: 2.154662. Countries: Bulgaria, Western Germany (before 1989), Denmark, UK, Sweden, Slovenia, Netherlands, Turkey, Spain. Top Tertile. Mean Change: 1.457801. Countries: Austria, Belgium, France, Greece, Croatia, Ireland, Italy, Norway, Portugal

is commonly found in the well-being literature; being married and highly educated are both associated with greater satisfaction with life; being unemployed is associated with low levels of life satisfaction; the unemployment rate in the country enters negatively. Interestingly, the coefficient on GDP is positive but, consistent with Easterlin's famous 'paradox', statistically weak.

Columns 2–9 of Table 10.1 reveal a correlation between life-satisfaction scores in the current period with past advertising levels. Table 10.1 shows what happens when advertising variables are included within the regression equation, where columns 4 and 7 give the base results without advertising included. In each case, the advertising variables enter negatively, with small standard errors (this is after adjustment for potential biases from clustering). In column 2, for example, the coefficient on the logarithm of advertising expenditure is -0.069 with a standard error of 0.028. This variable is for advertising lagged one period. In column 3, the coefficient on the stock of advertising (measured as the sum of advertising expenditures over three previous years, again in logarithms) is -0.097 with a standard error of 0.036.

There is a natural potential criticism of the regression equations in the second and third columns of Table 10.1. It is that an advertising variable might in some way be erroneously standing in for earlier business-cycle movements. The later columns of Table 10.1 probe that possibility. In each case, however, the study's key result

Table 10.1 Life satisfaction equations for 27 countries from year 1980 to year 2011, OLS. [GDP Dynamics Included]

Explanatory variables	(1)	(2)	(3)	(4)	(5)	(6)	(7)	(8)	(9)
Demographics									
Age	−0.022***	−0.022***	−0.022***	−0.022***	−0.022***	−0.022***	−0.022***	−0.022***	−0.022***
	(0.001)	(0.001)	(0.001)	(0.001)	(0.001)	(0.001)	(0.001)	(0.001)	(0.001)
Age squared	0.000***	0.000***	0.000***	0.000***	0.000***	0.000***	0.000***	0.000***	0.000***
	(0.000)	(0.000)	(0.000)	(0.000)	(0.000)	(0.000)	(0.000)	(0.000)	(0.000)
Unemployed	−0.382***	−0.385***	−0.385***	−0.385***	−0.385***	−0.385***	−0.386***	−0.386***	−0.385***
	(0.027)	(0.027)	(0.025)	(0.027)	(0.027)	(0.025)	(0.027)	(0.027)	(0.025)
Married	0.170***	0.170***	0.171***	0.170***	0.170***	0.171***	0.170***	0.170***	0.172***
	(0.008)	(0.008)	(0.008)	(0.008)	(0.008)	(0.008)	(0.008)	(0.008)	(0.008)
Male	−0.017**	−0.018**	−0.017**	−0.017**	−0.018**	−0.017**	−0.017**	−0.017**	−0.017**
	(0.007)	(0.007)	(0.007)	(0.007)	(0.007)	(0.007)	(0.007)	(0.007)	(0.007)
Size of the household	0.005	0.005	0.005	0.005	0.005	0.005	0.005*	0.005	0.005
	(0.003)	(0.003)	(0.003)	(0.003)	(0.003)	(0.003)	(0.003)	(0.003)	(0.003)
Age when completed education									
Up to 14	−0.227***	−0.227***	−0.229***	−0.227***	−0.227***	−0.229***	−0.226***	−0.226***	−0.229***
	(0.022)	(0.022)	(0.022)	(0.022)	(0.022)	(0.022)	(0.022)	(0.022)	(0.022)
Between 15 and 19	−0.156***	−0.156***	−0.157***	−0.157***	−0.156***	−0.157***	−0.155***	−0.155***	−0.157***
	(0.019)	(0.019)	(0.019)	(0.019)	(0.019)	(0.019)	(0.019)	(0.019)	(0.019)
Older than 20	−0.030**	−0.030**	−0.030**	−0.029**	−0.030**	−0.030**	−0.028**	−0.028**	−0.030**
	(0.013)	(0.013)	(0.013)	(0.013)	(0.013)	(0.013)	(0.013)	(0.013)	(0.013)
Macroeconomic variables									
Unemployment rate in the country	−0.010**	−0.008*	−0.006	−0.010**	−0.008*	−0.006	−0.009*	−0.006	−0.005
	(0.004)	(0.004)	(0.005)	(0.005)	(0.004)	(0.005)	(0.005)	(0.005)	(0.005)
Log GDP per capita	0.134	0.234*	0.297**	0.398*	0.415*	0.517**	0.432**	0.388*	0.454**
	(0.105)	(0.121)	(0.138)	(0.216)	(0.231)	(0.228)	(0.178)	(0.190)	(0.191)
Log 1st Lag GDP per Capita				−0.278	−0.182	−0.229	−0.087	0.313	0.209
				(0.184)	(0.198)	(0.203)	(0.200)	(0.208)	(0.186)
Log 2nd Lag GDP per Capita							−0.225	−0.431*	−0.360*
							(0.218)	(0.213)	(0.209)

(continued)

Table 10.1 (continued)

First lag of adv expenditure									
Log total adv expenditure	−0.069** (0.028)			−0.066** (0.028)			−0.085** (0.036)		
Stock of adv expenditure (1st to 3rd lags)									
Sum of log adv expenditure			−0.097** (0.036)			−0.092** (0.036)			−0.094** (0.037)
Country FE	Yes	Yes	Yes	Yes	Yes	Yes	Yes	Yes	Yes
Year FE	Yes	Yes	Yes	Yes	Yes	Yes	Yes	Yes	Yes
Constant	2.177* (1.066)	1.608 (1.142)	1.286 (1.249)	2.327** (1.094)	1.628 (1.126)	1.372 (1.224)	2.384** (1.150)	1.422 (1.242)	1.232 (1.227)
Observations	760,252	742,497	683,551	742,497	683,551	683,551	717,441	717,441	683,551
R-sqared	0.214	0.213	0.215	0.213	0.213	0.215	0.213	0.214	0.216

Significance ***p < 0.01, **p < 0.05, *p < 0.1. Clustered (by country) robust standard errors in parentheses. Number of clusters: 27. All regressions include year and country dummies (base line country is Austria). Dependent variable: reported life satisfaction. The exact question is: "On the whole, are you very satisfied, fairly satisfied, not very satisfied or not at all satisfied with the life you lead". The overall mean of the dependent variable is 2.98. Natural logarithm of GDP per capita and lagged advertising expenditures is used. Advertising expenditures are in constant 2005 million USD and GDP per capita in constant 2005 USD

appears to be robust. The most general specifications are in columns 8 and 9 of Table 10.1, but even with three GDP per-capita terms included (that is, current GDP and two variables for lagged GDP in each of the two prior years) the advertising variables continue to be negative, statistically significantly different from zero, and of similar size to that in earlier columns. Hence the advertising variables seem not to be creating a spurious association that is attributable merely to the state of the business cycle in any particular year or country.

One noticeable feature of Table 10.1 is that the estimated GDP coefficients tend to become somewhat larger after the inclusion of the advertising variables (for example, in column 2 compared to column 1). This is consistent with the hypothesis that, although rises in GDP may *ceteris paribus* be beneficial, the benefits of economic growth are somewhat offset by a rise in advertising expenditure. Following the tradition in much of the literature on the economics of advertising (Bain 1956; Bagwell 2001), Table 10.1 also checks a specification that uses a variable for the 'stock of advertising'. This is designed to capture the idea that commercial organizations spend money on advertising to build up a lasting brand in the minds of their consumers.

The results reported here allow for the following covariates: age, whether unemployed, whether married, whether male, size of family, level of education, the unemployment rate in the country, and GDP-per-capita in the country (for a detailed specification of these variables, see the appendix). Throughout the paper's tables, variables for country dummies and year dummies are included. Unlike previous longitudinal studies of national well-being, the data set has the advantage that it makes it possible to incorporate measures of advertising expenditure for each country and year.

It may take time for advertising to have its effects upon human beings. Table 10.2 therefore explores a range of lag lengths. The approximate robustness of the original result is evident: rises in advertising are precursors to declines in well-being. The size of the predictive power of advertising on later life-satisfaction depends on the time lag between the two variables. Longer lags, as in the right-hand columns of Table 10.2, are associated with more-negative estimates.

In these tables the estimated advertising effect-size is substantial. For column 3 of Table 10.1, for example, the coefficient on the stock of advertising is -0.097. Because this variable is in logarithms, the percentage change of life satisfaction with respect to the percentage change in (the stock of) advertising is approximately -0.03 (this calculation uses the fact that the mean of life satisfaction is 2.98, which has to be used to divide the number -0.097), and -0.03 can thus be thought of approximately as the long-run elasticity of national well-being with respect to advertising spending. This implies, given the assumed cardinalization, that a hypothetical doubling of advertising expenditure would result in a 3% drop in life satisfaction. Around the mean of 2.98, therefore, that 3% figure would translate into a fall of 0.09 life satisfaction points when measured on the one to four scale used in the Eurobarometer Surveys. That is not minor in size. It is approximately one half

Table 10.2 Life satisfaction equations for 27 countries from year 1980 to year 2011, OLS. [Long Lags Included]

Explanatory variables	(1)	(2)	(3)	(4)
Demographics				
Age	−0.022***	−0.022***	−0.022***	−0.022***
	(0.001)	(0.001)	(0.001)	(0.001)
Age squared	0.000***	0.000***	0.000***	0.000***
	(0.000)	(0.000)	(0.000)	(0.000)
Unemployed	−0.382***	−0.385***	−0.386***	−0.385***
	(0.027)	(0.027)	(0.027)	(0.025)
Married	0.170***	0.170***	0.170***	0.171***
	(0.008)	(0.008)	(0.008)	(0.008)
Male	−0.017**	−0.018**	−0.017**	−0.017**
	(0.007)	(0.007)	(0.007)	(0.007)
Size of the household	0.005	0.005	0.005	0.005
	(0.003)	(0.003)	(0.003)	(0.003)
Age when completed education				
Up to 14	−0.227***	−0.227***	−0.226***	−0.229***
	(0.022)	(0.022)	(0.022)	(0.022)
Between 15 and 19	−0.156***	−0.156***	−0.155***	−0.157***
	(0.019)	(0.019)	(0.019)	(0.019)
Older than 20	−0.030**	−0.030**	−0.028**	−0.030**
	(0.013)	(0.013)	(0.013)	(0.013)
Macroeconomic variables				
Log GDP per Capita	0.213*	0.234*	0.264**	0.296**
	(0.115)	(0.121)	(0.127)	(0.132)
Unemployment rate in the country	−0.009**	−0.008*	−0.006	−0.005
	(0.004)	(0.004)	(0.004)	(0.005)
Log of adv expenditure (Natural Logarithm)				
Log total adv expenditure	−0.051*			
	(0.029)			
Log 1st Lag Total Adv Expenditure		−0.069**		
		(0.028)		
Log 2nd Lag Total Adv Expenditure			−0.085***	
			(0.029)	
Log 3rd Lag Total Adv Expenditure				−0.094***
				(0.031)
Country FE	Yes	Yes	Yes	Yes
Year FE	Yes	Yes	Yes	Yes
Constant	1.738 (1.095)	1.638 (1.138)	1.485 (1.201)	1.195 (1.226)
Observations	760,252	742,497	717,441	683,551
R-squared	0.214	0.213	0.214	0.215

Significance ***$p < 0.01$, **$p < 0.05$, *$p < 0.1$. Clustered (by country) robust standard errors in parentheses. Number of clusters: 27. All regressions include year and country dummies (base line country is Austria). Dependent variable: reported life satisfaction. The exact question is: *"On the whole, are you very satisfied, fairly satisfied, not very satisfied or not at all satisfied with the life you lead"*. The overall mean of the dependent variable is 2.98. Natural logarithm of GDP per capita and lagged advertising expenditures is used. Advertising expenditures are in constant 2005 million USD and GDP per capita in constant 2005 USD

Table 10.3 Advertising expenditure by country: as percent of GDP and per capita

Country	Adv exp as % of GDP	Adv exp per capita
Austria	0.822	297.682
Belgium	0.590	191.633
Bulgaria	1.425	63.014
Czech Republic	0.549	79.078
Western Germany before 1989	.	228.417
Germany after 1989	0.852	277.089
Denmark	0.804	331.678
Estonia	0.037	4.025
Spain	0.828	178.838
Finland	0.750	253.400
France	0.591	177.633
UK	0.911	288.355
Greece	0.802	147.355
Croatia	2.087	224.648
Hungary	0.746	83.254
Ireland	0.374	126.301
Italy	0.426	120.146
Lithuania	0.446	38.557
Latvia	0.496	38.553
Netherlands	0.737	257.164
Norway	0.454	226.266
Poland	0.585	53.950
Portugal	0.473	80.912
Romania	0.119	6.617
Sweden	0.677	260.986
Slovenia	0.006	1.194
Slovakia	0.849	114.504
Turkey	0.314	23.551
Total	0.683	195.003

the absolute size of the marriage effect on life satisfaction, or approximately one quarter of the absolute size of the effect of being unemployed (the coefficient on marriage is 0.17 and that on unemployment is -0.38).

As background, Table 10.3 summarizes the levels of advertising expenditure for the different nations. On average, countries spend just under 1% of GDP in this way. Table 10.4 presents results for fixed-effects models in which the kind of advertising expenditure is disaggregated into five different categories (newspapers, magazines, TV, radio, cinema). It is the first two kinds that exhibit large and significant negatives. Tables 10.5 and 10.6 show that, dividing the data period into two halves for the non-transition countries, the coefficient on advertising is fairly stable across time. This is a check on robustness. Importantly, all twelve of the coefficients, across

Table 10.4 Life satisfaction equation for 27 countries from year 1980 to year 2011, OLS. [Disaggregated Measures]

Explanatory variables	(1)	(2)	(3)	(4)
Demographics				
Age	−0.022*** (0.001)	−0.022*** (0.001)	−0.021*** (0.001)	−0.021*** (0.001)
Age squared	0.000*** (0.000)	0.000*** (0.000)	0.000*** (0.000)	0.000*** (0.000)
Unemployed	−0.387*** (0.025)	−0.385*** (0.025)	−0.382*** (0.024)	−0.381*** (0.024)
Married	0.171*** (0.008)	0.171*** (0.008)	0.178*** (0.008)	0.178*** (0.008)
Male	−0.017** (0.007)	−0.017** (0.007)	−0.017** (0.007)	−0.017** (0.007)
Size of the household	0.005 (0.003)	0.005 (0.003)	0.005* (0.003)	0.005* (0.003)
Age when completed education				
Up to 14	−0.229*** (0.022)	−0.229*** (0.022)	−0.228*** (0.024)	−0.228*** (0.024)
Between 15 and 19	−0.157*** (0.020)	−0.157*** (0.019)	−0.159*** (0.022)	−0.159*** (0.022)
Older than 20	−0.030** (0.013)	−0.030** (0.013)	−0.035** (0.015)	−0.034** (0.014)
Macroeconomic variables				
Log GDP per capita	0.413*** (0.080)	0.297** (0.138)	0.409*** (0.123)	0.408* (0.210)
Country in transition	0.389** (0.148)	0.233 (0.219)	0.212 (0.250)	0.214 (0.361)
Unemployment rate in the country		−0.006 (0.005)		0 (0.005)
Stock of adv expenditure (1st to 3rd lags)				
Sum of log total adv expenditure	−0.118*** (0.031)	−0.097** (0.036)		
Sum of log newspaper adv expenditure			−0.080** (0.033)	−0.079** (0.035)
Sum of log magazines adv expenditure			−0.053* (0.029)	−0.053* (0.030)
Sum of log TV adv expenditure			0.051 (0.033)	0.05 (0.035)
Sum of log radio adv expenditure			0.003 (0.020)	0.003 (0.019)
Sum of log cinema adv expenditure			0 (0.023)	0 (0.024)
Constant	0.24 (0.717)	1.286 (1.249)	−0.051 (1.18)	−0.043 (2.005)

(continued)

Table 10.4 (continued)

Explanatory variables	(1)	(2)	(3)	(4)
Country FE	Yes	Yes	Yes	Yes
Year FE	Yes	Yes	Yes	Yes
Observations	686,139	683,551	572,226	569,638
R-squared	0.215	0.215	0.207	0.208

Significance ***$p < 0.01$, **$p < 0.05$, *$p < 0.1$. Clustered (by country) robust standard errors in parentheses. Number of clusters: 27. All regressions include year and country dummies (base line country is Austria). Dependent variable: reported life satisfaction. The exact question is: "On the whole, are you very satisfied, fairly satisfied, not very satisfied or not at all satisfied with the life you lead". The overall mean of the dependent variable is 2.98. Natural logarithm of GDP per capita and lagged advertising expenditures is used. Advertising expenditures are in constant 2005 million USD and GDP per capita in constant 2005 USD

the two tables, are negative. In Table 10.5 the advertising coefficient is approximately −0.06, and in Table 10.6 it averages to a similar size (though is somewhat smaller for lagged advertising and bigger for the stock of advertising). Standard errors, of course, are inevitably larger than for the full sample of 30 years taken as a whole; the appropriate test is instead for stability in coefficient sizes.

We also check, in the spirit of a Granger-causality test, for possible reverse linkages. Encouragingly, Table 10.7 reveals no evidence that lagged values of life satisfaction have predictive power in an advertising equation.

10.3   Conclusions

This study explores a potentially important question in social science: how is the well-being of a nation affected by large-scale advertising? We believe this is the first empirical study of its kind.

Our results are consistent with societal concerns raised more than a century ago by authors such as Thorstein Veblen (1904) and Joan Robinson (1933); they are consistent with arguments discussed by Easterlin (1974, 2003) and in Layard (1980); they may also be consistent with ideas about the deleterious consequences of materialism (Sirgy et al. 2012; Burroughs and Rindfleisch 2002; Speck and Roy 2008; Snyder and Debono 1985). Rises and falls in advertising expenditure in Europe's nations have been found here to be followed by -- respectively -- falls and rises in life-satisfaction levels.

Although much remains to be discovered about genuinely causal mechanisms, there is evidence of an inverse longitudinal relationship between national advertising and national dissatisfaction. The estimated effect-size here seems substantial and not merely statistically well-determined. These issues demand further scrutiny.

Table 10.5 Life satisfaction equations for 12 non-transition countries from year 1980 to year 1995, OLS. [First Half of Sample Period]

Explanatory variables	(1)	(2)	(3)	(4)	(5)	(6)	(7)	(8)	(9)
Demographics									
Age	-0.021***	-0.021***	-0.021***	-0.021***	-0.021***	-0.021***	-0.021***	-0.021***	-0.021***
	(0.002)	(0.002)	(0.002)	(0.002)	(0.002)	(0.002)	(0.002)	(0.002)	(0.002)
Age squared	0.000***	0.000***	0.000***	0.000***	0.000***	0.000***	0.000***	0.000***	0.000***
	(0.000)	(0.000)	(0.000)	(0.000)	(0.000)	(0.000)	(0.000)	(0.000)	(0.000)
Unemployed	-0.400***	-0.402***	-0.393***	-0.402***	-0.402***	-0.393***	-0.401***	-0.401***	-0.393***
	(0.042)	(0.042)	(0.042)	(0.042)	(0.042)	(0.042)	(0.042)	(0.042)	(0.042)
Married	0.159***	0.160***	0.161***	0.160***	0.160***	0.161***	0.159***	0.159***	0.161***
	(0.012)	(0.012)	(0.011)	(0.012)	(0.012)	(0.011)	(0.012)	(0.011)	(0.012)
Male	-0.026**	-0.026**	-0.024*	-0.026**	-0.026**	-0.024*	-0.025**	-0.025**	-0.024*
	(0.010)	(0.010)	(0.011)	(0.010)	(0.010)	(0.011)	(0.011)	(0.011)	(0.011)
Size of the household	0.001	0.001	0.001	0.001	0.001	0.001	0.002	0.002	0.001
	(0.003)	(0.003)	(0.003)	(0.003)	(0.003)	(0.003)	(0.003)	(0.004)	(0.003)
Age when completed education									
Up to 14	-0.190***	-0.190***	-0.199***	-0.191***	-0.191***	-0.199***	-0.191***	-0.191***	-0.199***
	(0.031)	(0.030)	(0.029)	(0.030)	(0.030)	(0.029)	(0.030)	(0.030)	(0.029)
Between 15 and 19	-0.114***	-0.115***	-0.122***	-0.116***	-0.115***	-0.122***	-0.116***	-0.116***	-0.123***
	(0.025)	(0.024)	(0.025)	(0.024)	(0.024)	(0.026)	(0.025)	(0.025)	(0.025)
Older than 20	-0.026*	-0.027*	-0.029*	-0.026*	-0.027*	-0.029*	-0.025*	-0.026*	-0.029*
	(0.014)	(0.013)	(0.013)	(0.014)	(0.013)	(0.014)	(0.014)	(0.013)	(0.014)
Macroeconomic variables									
Unemployment rate in the country	-0.005	-0.005	-0.004	-0.005	-0.005	-0.005	-0.005	-0.005	-0.004
	(0.006)	(0.007)	(0.006)	(0.006)	(0.007)	(0.006)	(0.006)	(0.007)	(0.006)
Log GDP per capita	0.770***	0.745***	0.946***	1.096***	1.001***	1.112*	1.159**	0.972*	0.899*
	(0.226)	(0.205)	(0.282)	(0.368)	(0.437)	(0.554)	(0.416)	(0.446)	(0.455)
Log 1st lag GDP per capita				-0.423	-0.281	-0.189	-0.131	0.194	0.475
				(0.497)	(0.536)	(0.667)	(0.537)	(0.590)	(0.508)
Log 2nd lag GDP per capita							-0.298	-0.433**	-0.495**
							(0.184)	(0.201)	(0.169)

	C1	C2	C3	C4	C5	C6	C7	C8	C9
First lag of adv expenditure									
Log total adv expenditure		−0.072 (0.043)			−0.067 (0.049)			−0.086 (0.066)	
Stock of adv expenditure (1st to 3rd Lags)									
Sum of log adv expenditure			−0.059 (0.076)			−0.055 (0.084)			−0.058 (0.088)
Country FE									
Germany after 1989	−0.193*** (0.012)	0.001 (0.118)	0.001 (0.214)	−0.191*** (0.011)	−0.013 (0.136)	−0.008 (0.233)	−0.179*** (0.010)	0.053 (0.179)	0.003 (0.244)
Denmark	0.225*** (0.063)	0.250*** (0.050)	0.190** (0.071)	0.253*** (0.081)	0.255*** (0.059)	0.196** (0.082)	0.237** (0.098)	0.257*** (0.069)	0.212** (0.091)
Spain	0.240** (0.087)	0.355** (0.138)	0.388* (0.203)	0.194 (0.115)	0.335* (0.170)	0.372 (0.243)	0.203 (0.139)	0.361* (0.200)	0.347 (0.263)
France	−0.244*** (0.005)	−0.091 (0.095)	−0.115 (0.165)	−0.244*** (0.005)	−0.101 (0.109)	−0.123 (0.182)	−0.242*** (0.005)	−0.059 (0.142)	−0.118 (0.191)
UK	0.090*** (0.004)	0.272** (0.109)	0.244 (0.198)	0.091*** (0.004)	0.260* (0.125)	0.234 (0.218)	0.090*** (0.004)	0.308* (0.167)	0.240 (0.228)
Greece	−0.031 (0.133)	−0.090 (0.113)	0.035 (0.149)	−0.079 (0.160)	−0.096 (0.122)	0.027 (0.164)	−0.042 (0.190)	−0.093 (0.142)	0.004 (0.179)
Ireland	0.270*** (0.047)	0.158*** (0.038)	0.222** (0.098)	0.240*** (0.066)	0.156*** (0.038)	0.221** (0.100)	0.248*** (0.080)	0.123 (0.071)	0.197* (0.108)
Italy	−0.187*** (0.023)	−0.071 (0.085)	−0.071 (0.138)	−0.195*** (0.028)	−0.081 (0.100)	−0.080 (0.156)	−0.192*** (0.031)	−0.051 (0.124)	−0.080 (0.165)
Netherlands	0.217*** (0.018)	0.290*** (0.040)	0.254*** (0.072)	0.221*** (0.023)	0.287*** (0.042)	0.251*** (0.077)	0.214*** (0.028)	0.302*** (0.059)	0.259*** (0.080)
Norway	−0.148 (0.099)	−0.157 (0.106)	−0.243 (0.156)	−0.084 (0.122)	−0.149 (0.123)	−0.233 (0.180)	−0.114 (0.151)	−0.168 (0.143)	−0.218 (0.198)
Portugal	0.152 (0.178)	0.044 (0.148)	0.182 (0.186)	0.080 (0.222)	0.028 (0.164)	0.168 (0.209)	0.109 (0.258)	0.005 (0.189)	0.127 (0.229)

(continued)

Table 10.5 (continued)

Explanatory variables	(1)	(2)	(3)	(4)	(5)	(6)	(7)	(8)	(9)
Year FE									
1981	-0.006 (0.039)								
1982	0.056 (0.035)	0.066 (0.037)		0.061* (0.033)	0.065 (0.036)				
1983	0.038 (0.043)	0.052 (0.058)		0.039 (0.049)	0.049 (0.060)		-0.025 (0.029)	-0.019 (0.036)	
1984	0.048 (0.041)	0.067 (0.058)	0.008 (0.016)	0.042 (0.048)	0.058 (0.062)	0.005 (0.019)	-0.024 (0.033)	-0.010 (0.043)	0.006 (0.017)
1985	0.009 (0.050)	0.037 (0.064)	-0.028 (0.018)	0.010 (0.047)	0.029 (0.065)	-0.031* (0.015)	-0.062* (0.029)	-0.044 (0.044)	-0.035* (0.016)
1986	0.020 (0.051)	0.041 (0.064)	-0.036 (0.020)	0.019 (0.049)	0.034 (0.067)	-0.038 (0.023)	-0.067* (0.032)	-0.045 (0.052)	-0.041* (0.022)
1987	-0.006 (0.059)	0.025 (0.066)	-0.071*** (0.022)	-0.006 (0.048)	0.017 (0.067)	-0.073*** (0.020)	-0.076** (0.032)	-0.053 (0.046)	-0.072*** (0.020)
1988	0.007 (0.052)	0.048 (0.062)	-0.033* (0.018)	0.005 (0.038)	0.037 (0.065)	-0.038** (0.017)	-0.070** (0.023)	-0.032 (0.047)	-0.035* (0.017)
1989	-0.001 (0.050)	0.050 (0.063)	-0.039** (0.018)	0.003 (0.033)	0.041 (0.067)	-0.043* (0.020)	-0.077*** (0.025)	-0.032 (0.049)	-0.045** (0.020)
1990	-0.028 (0.059)	0.034 (0.065)	-0.060** (0.023)	-0.013 (0.041)	0.027 (0.066)	-0.062** (0.023)	-0.093** (0.041)	-0.042 (0.051)	-0.060* (0.029)
1991	-0.039 (0.070)	0.020 (0.058)	-0.064* (0.029)	-0.025 (0.052)	0.016 (0.057)	-0.063* (0.033)	-0.090 (0.064)	-0.035 (0.047)	-0.058 (0.041)
1992	-0.069 (0.067)	-0.008 (0.060)	-0.104** (0.035)	-0.050 (0.057)	-0.010 (0.059)	-0.103** (0.040)	-0.129* (0.066)	-0.074 (0.048)	-0.092* (0.051)
1993	-0.087 (0.072)	-0.024 (0.063)	-0.128*** (0.036)	-0.062 (0.064)	-0.021 (0.063)	-0.123** (0.047)	-0.139* (0.075)	-0.083 (0.054)	-0.115* (0.057)

1994	−0.091	−0.026	−0.135***	−0.077	−0.032	−0.136***	−0.151*	−0.086	−0.114*
	(0.073)	(0.072)	(0.042)	(0.061)	(0.071)	(0.042)	(0.071)	(0.065)	(0.052)
Constant	−4.248*	−3.534*	−5.531*	−3.267	−3.317	−5.319	−3.787	−3.263	−4.861
	(2.288)	(1.967)	(2.687)	(2.890)	(2.272)	(3.071)	(3.460)	(2.618)	(3.374)
Observations	304,355	298,544	263,153	298,544	298,544	263,153	285,268	285,268	263,153
R-squared	0.163	0.162	0.165	0.162	0.162	0.165	0.163	0.163	0.165

Significance ***p < 0.01, **p < 0.05, *p < 0.1. Clustered (by country) robust standard errors in parentheses. Number of clusters: 12. All regressions include year and country dummies (base line country is Belgium). Dependent variable: reported life satisfaction. The exact question is: *"On the whole, are you very satisfied, fairly satisfied, not very satisfied or not at all satisfied with the life you lead"*. The overall mean of the dependent variable is 3.04. Natural logarithm of GDP per capita and lagged advertising expenditures is used. Advertising expenditures are in constant 2005 million USD and GDP per capita in constant 2005 USD

Table 10.6 Life satisfaction equations for 14 non-transition countries from year 1996 to year 2011, OLS. [Second Half of Sample Period]

Explanatory variables	(1)	(2)	(3)	(4)	(5)	(6)	(7)	(8)	(9)
Demographics									
Age	-0.019***	-0.019***	-0.019***	-0.019***	-0.019***	-0.019***	-0.019***	-0.019***	-0.019***
	(0.001)	(0.001)	(0.001)	(0.001)	(0.001)	(0.001)	(0.001)	(0.001)	(0.001)
Age squared	0.000***	0.000***	0.000***	0.000***	0.000***	0.000***	0.000***	0.000***	0.000***
	(0.000)	(0.000)	(0.000)	(0.000)	(0.000)	(0.000)	(0.000)	(0.000)	(0.000)
Unemployed	-0.391***	-0.391***	-0.391***	-0.391***	-0.391***	-0.391***	-0.391***	-0.391***	-0.391***
	(0.041)	(0.041)	(0.041)	(0.041)	(0.041)	(0.041)	(0.041)	(0.041)	(0.041)
Married	0.181***	0.181***	0.182***	0.181***	0.181***	0.182***	0.181***	0.181***	0.182***
	(0.012)	(0.012)	(0.012)	(0.012)	(0.012)	(0.012)	(0.012)	(0.012)	(0.012)
Male	-0.010	-0.010	-0.010	-0.010	-0.010	-0.010	-0.010	-0.010	-0.010
	(0.008)	(0.008)	(0.008)	(0.008)	(0.008)	(0.008)	(0.008)	(0.008)	(0.008)
Size of the household	0.010**	0.010**	0.010**	0.010**	0.010**	0.010**	0.010**	0.010**	0.010**
	(0.004)	(0.004)	(0.004)	(0.004)	(0.004)	(0.004)	(0.004)	(0.004)	(0.004)
Age when completed education									
Up to 14	-0.252***	-0.252***	-0.251***	-0.251***	-0.251***	-0.251***	-0.251***	-0.251***	-0.251***
	(0.029)	(0.029)	(0.029)	(0.029)	(0.029)	(0.029)	(0.029)	(0.029)	(0.029)
Between 15 and 19	-0.142***	-0.142***	-0.142***	-0.142***	-0.142***	-0.142***	-0.142***	-0.142***	-0.142***
	(0.023)	(0.023)	(0.022)	(0.022)	(0.022)	(0.022)	(0.022)	(0.022)	(0.022)
Older than 20	-0.028*	-0.028*	-0.028*	-0.027*	-0.028*	-0.028*	-0.027*	-0.027*	-0.028*
	(0.015)	(0.015)	(0.015)	(0.015)	(0.014)	(0.014)	(0.015)	(0.014)	(0.014)
Macroeconomic variables									
Unemployment rate in the country	-0.010	-0.009	-0.008	-0.007	-0.007	-0.007	-0.006	-0.007	-0.007
	(0.006)	(0.006)	(0.007)	(0.007)	(0.007)	(0.007)	(0.007)	(0.007)	(0.007)
Log GDP per capita	0.104	0.267	0.320	0.879	0.865	0.787	0.739	0.750	0.734
	(0.444)	(0.515)	(0.485)	(0.599)	(0.593)	(0.578)	(0.514)	(0.518)	(0.504)
Log 1st Lag GDP per capita				-0.763	-0.667	-0.520	-0.253	-0.259	-0.321
				(0.628)	(0.720)	(0.763)	(0.664)	(0.655)	(0.643)
Log 2nd Lag GDP per capita							-0.359	-0.303	-0.153
							(0.408)	(0.431)	(0.526)

	(1)	(2)	(3)	(4)	(5)	(6)	(7)	(8)	(9)
First lag of adv expenditure									
Log total adv expenditure		−0.077 (0.118)			−0.039 (0.124)			−0.030 (0.126)	
Stock of adv expenditure (1st to 3rd Lags)									
Sum of log adv expenditure			−0.118 (0.122)			−0.085 (0.137)			−0.078 (0.147)
Country FE									
Belgium	0.093*** (0.018)	0.112*** (0.033)	0.115*** (0.030)	0.088*** (0.023)	0.098** (0.042)	0.105** (0.039)	0.086*** (0.024)	0.094* (0.044)	0.103** (0.043)
Germany after 1989	−0.059** (0.025)	0.117 (0.271)	0.211 (0.283)	−0.065** (0.030)	0.025 (0.295)	0.131 (0.324)	−0.066** (0.030)	0.003 (0.300)	0.115 (0.351)
Denmark	0.495*** (0.096)	0.442*** (0.132)	0.426*** (0.121)	0.497*** (0.098)	0.470*** (0.146)	0.447*** (0.139)	0.497*** (0.098)	0.476*** (0.146)	0.451*** (0.143)
Spain	0.091 (0.137)	0.233 (0.264)	0.289 (0.255)	0.074 (0.151)	0.148 (0.311)	0.222 (0.313)	0.069 (0.151)	0.127 (0.315)	0.208 (0.335)
Finland	0.186*** (0.024)	0.141* (0.077)	0.114 (0.080)	0.177*** (0.028)	0.156* (0.075)	0.129 (0.083)	0.172*** (0.031)	0.156* (0.074)	0.131 (0.085)
France	−0.075** (0.034)	0.053 (0.199)	0.117 (0.204)	−0.083* (0.042)	−0.017 (0.222)	0.057 (0.240)	−0.085* (0.043)	−0.034 (0.226)	0.046 (0.260)
UK	0.192*** (0.013)	0.348 (0.237)	0.435 (0.251)	0.193*** (0.013)	0.272 (0.251)	0.367 (0.280)	0.193*** (0.014)	0.253 (0.255)	0.353 (0.304)
Greece	−0.373 (0.236)	−0.285 (0.273)	−0.258 (0.257)	−0.367 (0.238)	−0.323 (0.301)	−0.286 (0.290)	−0.367 (0.237)	−0.333 (0.302)	−0.293 (0.297)
Ireland	0.211* (0.101)	0.087 (0.224)	0.027 (0.223)	0.198* (0.098)	0.137 (0.238)	0.070 (0.248)	0.194* (0.099)	0.147 (0.237)	0.078 (0.258)
Italy	−0.206** (0.076)	−0.086 (0.204)	−0.028 (0.206)	−0.203** (0.077)	−0.143 (0.225)	−0.076 (0.238)	−0.201** (0.078)	−0.155 (0.226)	−0.085 (0.251)
Netherlands	0.300*** (0.036)	0.333*** (0.055)	0.358*** (0.063)	0.299*** (0.036)	0.316*** (0.054)	0.341*** (0.066)	0.298*** (0.037)	0.311*** (0.057)	0.337*** (0.072)

(continued)

Table 10.6 (continued)

Explanatory variables	(1)	(2)	(3)	(4)	(5)	(6)	(7)	(8)	(9)
Portugal	-0.385 (0.303)	-0.339 (0.303)	-0.339 (0.283)	-0.381 (0.305)	-0.358 (0.324)	-0.349 (0.304)	-0.377 (0.305)	-0.360 (0.324)	-0.350 (0.305)
Sweden	0.326*** (0.054)	0.308*** (0.062)	0.300*** (0.060)	0.316*** (0.052)	0.308*** (0.063)	0.301*** (0.061)	0.313*** (0.054)	0.307*** (0.062)	0.301*** (0.061)
Year FE									
1998	-0.032 (0.020)	-0.032 (0.020)	-0.033 (0.019)	-0.031 (0.020)	-0.031 (0.019)	-0.032 (0.019)	-0.034* (0.019)	-0.034* (0.019)	-0.033* (0.019)
1999	0.075* (0.041)	0.076* (0.040)	0.074* (0.039)	0.077* (0.043)	0.077* (0.042)	0.076* (0.041)	0.074* (0.042)	0.075* (0.041)	0.075* (0.040)
2000	-0.035 (0.042)	-0.035 (0.039)	-0.034 (0.037)	-0.035 (0.043)	-0.035 (0.042)	-0.034 (0.039)	-0.037 (0.043)	-0.037 (0.041)	-0.035 (0.039)
2004	0.033 (0.077)	0.022 (0.077)	0.029 (0.070)	0.044 (0.082)	0.037 (0.089)	0.037 (0.081)	0.047 (0.082)	0.041 (0.090)	0.039 (0.083)
2005	0.022 (0.085)	0.012 (0.084)	0.014 (0.078)	0.038 (0.093)	0.031 (0.099)	0.027 (0.094)	0.035 (0.092)	0.030 (0.098)	0.027 (0.093)
2006	0.042 (0.090)	0.030 (0.089)	0.032 (0.083)	0.048 (0.093)	0.041 (0.100)	0.039 (0.093)	0.050 (0.093)	0.045 (0.101)	0.041 (0.095)
2007	0.020 (0.102)	0.008 (0.101)	0.011 (0.093)	0.031 (0.108)	0.023 (0.113)	0.021 (0.106)	0.027 (0.106)	0.022 (0.112)	0.020 (0.105)
2008	-0.033 (0.103)	-0.041 (0.100)	-0.036 (0.093)	-0.000 (0.118)	-0.008 (0.124)	-0.013 (0.118)	-0.006 (0.117)	-0.011 (0.123)	-0.014 (0.117)
2009	0.019 (0.089)	0.015 (0.085)	0.025 (0.078)	0.083 (0.115)	0.073 (0.123)	0.068 (0.118)	0.080 (0.114)	0.073 (0.122)	0.067 (0.118)
2010	0.024 (0.095)	0.009 (0.097)	0.022 (0.085)	0.038 (0.099)	0.029 (0.107)	0.032 (0.095)	0.061 (0.101)	0.050 (0.117)	0.042 (0.111)
2011	0.069 (0.096)	0.055 (0.096)	0.059 (0.088)	0.087 (0.102)	0.078 (0.111)	0.075 (0.103)	0.085 (0.101)	0.078 (0.110)	0.075 (0.103)

Constant	2.426	1.316	1.195	2.251	1.710	1.424	2.142	1.742	1.442
	(4.647)	(4.906)	(4.552)	(4.641)	(5.253)	(4.898)	(4.648)	(5.239)	(4.916)
Observations	295,803	295,803	295,803	295,803	295,803	295,803	295,803	295,803	295,803
R-squared	0.219	0.219	0.219	0.219	0.219	0.219	0.219	0.219	0.219

Significance ***p < 0.01, **p < 0.05, *p < 0.1. Clustered (by country) robust standard errors in parentheses. Number of clusters: 14. All regressions include year and country dummies (base line country is Austria). Dependent variable: reported life satisfaction. The exact question is: "On the whole, are you very satisfied, fairly satisfied, not very satisfied or not at all satisfied with the life you lead". The overall mean of the dependent variable is 3.07. Natural logarithm of GDP per capita and lagged advertising expenditures is used. Advertising expenditures are in constant 2005 million USD and GDP per capita in constant 2005 USD

Table 10.7 Log total advertising expenditure equations for 27 countries from year 1981 to year 2011, OLS

Explanatory variable	(9)	(10)	(11)	(12)	(13)	(14)	(15)	(16)	(17)
Advertising last period									
Log of total adv expenditures last period	0.940*** (0.016)	0.941*** (0.013)	0.837*** (0.084)	0.820*** (0.078)	0.945*** (0.027)	0.943*** (0.023)	0.822*** (0.082)	0.969*** (0.022)	0.967*** (0.021)
Macroeconomic variables									
Unemployment rate in the country	−0.008*** (0.002)	−0.007*** (0.002)	−0.012** (0.005)	−0.012** (0.005)	−0.015*** (0.003)	−0.014*** (0.003)	−0.006 (0.004)	−0.010** (0.004)	−0.009** (0.004)
Log GDP per capita	1.771*** (0.280)	1.766*** (0.292)					1.872*** (0.238)	1.752*** (0.242)	1.730*** (0.257)
Log 1st lag GDP per capita	−1.550*** (0.377)	−1.497*** (0.374)	−0.030 (0.235)	0.024 (0.212)	−0.194 (0.177)	−0.164 (0.161)	−1.640*** (0.297)	−1.821*** (0.232)	−1.705*** (0.355)
Log 2nd lag GDP per capita	−0.202 (0.196)	−0.242 (0.218)							−0.090 (0.188)
Mean satisfaction									
Current mean satisfaction			0.068 (0.100)				0.004 (0.128)	0.132 (0.087)	0.128 (0.087)
1st lag mean satisfaction				0.002 (0.085)			−0.010 (0.084)	−0.051 (0.063)	−0.053 (0.063)
2nd lag mean satisfaction	−0.037 (0.056)				−0.104 (0.084)			−0.094 (0.067)	−0.088 (0.069)
3rd lag mean satisfaction		0.054 (0.052)				0.000 (0.083)			
Country FE	Yes	Yes	Yes	Yes	Yes	Yes	Yes	Yes	Yes
Year FE	Yes	Yes	Yes	Yes	Yes	Yes	Yes	Yes	Yes
Constant	0.459 (0.877)	0.103 (0.767)	1.325 (1.986)	1.105 (1.733)	2.835* (1.654)	2.247 (1.478)	−1.014 (1.609)	1.088 (1.493)	1.057 (1.508)
Observations	412	389	438	435	412	389	420	386	386
R-squared	0.999	0.999	0.997	0.997	0.998	0.998	0.997	0.999	0.999

Significance ***$p < 0.01$, **$p < 0.05$, *$p < 0.1$. Clustered (by country) robust standard errors in parentheses. Number of clusters: 27. All regressions include year and country dummies (base line country is Austria). Dependent variable: log of total advertising expenditure (in constant 2005 million USD). Mean satisfaction variable is the average of reported life satisfaction by year and country. GDP is per capita in constant 2005 USD

Acknowledgement Sovinsky acknowledges support from European Research Council Grant #725081 FORENSICS and from the Collaborative Research Center Transregion 224 grant. Oswald acknowledges support from the CAGE center at the University of Warwick. Information on how to obtain the Eurobarometer data is available on the European Commission website http://ec.europa.eu/public_opinion/index_en.htm.

Appendix on Data and Methods

For this paper, data are taken from three different sources: The Eurobarometer Survey, Zenith-Optimedia, and the World Bank. The Eurobarometer survey, which began in 1972, is a set of public opinion surveys conducted on behalf of the European Commission. Each spring and autumn, face-to-face interviews are conducted for a new sample of residents of European Union (EU) Member States (around 1000 per country). The questions that respondents are asked are varied and include items intended to assess life satisfaction, to elicit opinions about the state of politics in Europe, to gain insight into perceptions of political institutions, etc. The data recorded in the Eurobarometer are used by the European Commission to monitor the evolution of public opinion and ultimately to aid in decision making.

For this study, data are gathered from individuals from 27 countries over the years 1980–2011. Specifically, data are available on the following transition European countries: Bulgaria, Czech Republic, Estonia, Croatia, Hungary, Latvia, Lithuania, Poland, Romania, Slovenia, Slovakia, and Turkey, and on the following non-transition countries: Austria, Belgium, Germany, Denmark, Spain, Finland, France, UK, Greece, Ireland, Italy, Netherlands, Norway, Portugal, and Sweden. The survey contains information on individual demographics, such as age, gender, education, marital status, employment status, and household size, as well as life satisfaction indicators. In particular, the survey asks "On the whole, are you very satisfied, fairly satisfied, not very satisfied or not at all satisfied with the life you lead?" Answers to this question are available for every year except 1996.

Annual country total advertising expenditure data are available from Zenith-Optimedia, which is a global media services company. They publish a quarterly report (the "Advertising Expenditure Forecasts") that covers advertising from a large number of markets around the world. This record contains the total amount spent on advertising in the country historically as well as forecasts for the future. Here historical data are used from 1980 to 2011, as reported in the issue "Advertising Expenditure Forecasts of December 2013." Further details are available in Austin A, Barnard J, Hutcheon N, Advertising Expenditure Forecasts. *Zenith-Optimedia*, December 2013.

Macroeconomic indicators are taken from the World Bank. In particular, data are available by country for the years 1980–2011 on GDP, GDP per capita, and the national unemployment rate. These are published in World Development Indicators. Information is combined from all three data sources for the same 27 countries and time periods (1980–2011). The final sample-size for the current study consists of a little over 900,000 observations on randomly sampled European citizens.

The data are used to estimate coefficients from linear regression models, where robust clustered standard errors are computed to account for the fact that the errors may be correlated within countries. Life satisfaction scores are regressed on a variety of control variables as detailed below. Specifically, the main Eq. (10.1) that is estimated is

$$LS_{ijt} = \alpha + \beta AdvExp_{jt} + \Phi Demo_{ijt} + \Gamma Macro_{jt} + \nu_j + \eta_t + \epsilon_{ijt} \qquad (10.1)$$

where i denotes an individual, j a country, and t a year. The variable LS_{ijt} is reported life satisfaction, $AdvExp_{jt}$ represents advertising expenditures (measured, in turn, as the lag of natural logarithm of total advertising expenditure and as the sum of three previous lags of natural logarithm of total advertising expenditures), the vector $Demo_{ijt}$ contains individual demographic characteristics (age, education, gender, etc.), and $Macro_{jt}$ is a vector of macroeconomic variables that may impact life satisfaction, such as the lag of GDP per capita and the unemployment rate. To control for common country and year attributes, the statistical analysis allows for country (ν_j) and time (η_t) fixed effects. The ϵ_{ijt} term captures an individual, country, year specific error. A number of different specifications are estimated as robustness checks.

References

Andreyeva, T., Kelly, I. R., & Harris, J. L. (2011). Exposure to food advertising on television: associations with children's fast food and soft drink consumption and obesity. *Economics & Human Biology, 9*(3), 221–233.

Bagwell, K. (2001). *The economics of advertising*. Cheltenham: Edward Elgar Publishing.

Bagwell, L. S., & Bernheim, B. D. (1996). Veblen effects in a theory of conspicuous consumption. *The American Economic Review, 86*, 349–373.

Bain, J. S. (1956). *Barriers to new competition* (Vol. 3, p. 55). Cambridge, MA: Harvard University Press.

Borzekowski, D. L., & Robinson, T. N. (2001). The 30-second effect: an experiment revealing the impact of television commercials on food preferences of preschoolers. *Journal of the American Dietetic Association, 101*(1), 42–46.

Buijzen, M., & Valkenburg, P. M. (2003a). The unintended effects of television advertising: A parent-child survey. *Communication Research, 30*(5), 483–503.

Buijzen, M., & Valkenburg, P. M. (2003b). The effects of television advertising on materialism, parent–child conflict, and unhappiness: A review of research. *Journal of Applied Developmental Psychology, 24*(4), 437–456.

Burroughs, J. E., & Rindfleisch, A. (2002). Materialism and well-being: A conflicting values perspective. *Journal of Consumer Research, 29*(3), 348–370.

Clark, A. E. (2018). Four decades of the economics of happiness: Where next? *Review of Income and Wealth, 64*(2), 245–269.

Cowling, K., & Poolsombat, R. (2007). *Adverising and labour supply: Why do Americans work such long hours?* Coventry: Department of Economics, University of Warwick.

Di Tella, R., MacCulloch, R. J., & Oswald, A. J. (2001). Preferences over inflation and unemployment: Evidence from surveys of happiness. *American Economic Review, 91*(1), 335–341.

Dittmar, H., Bond, R., Hurst, M., & Kasser, T. (2014). The relationship between materialism and personal well-being: A meta-analysis. *Journal of personality and social psychology, 107*(5), 879.

Easterlin, R. A. (1974). Does economic growth improve the human lot? Some empirical evidence. In *Nations and households in economic growth* (pp. 89–125). New York: Academic Press.

Easterlin, R. A. (2003). Explaining happiness. *Proceedings of the National Academy of Sciences, 100*(19), 11176–11183.

Easterlin, R. A., & Crimmins, E. M. (1991). Private materialism, personal self-fulfillment, family life, and public interest THE nature, effects, and causes of recent changes in the values of American youth. *Public Opinion Quarterly, 55*(4), 499–533.

Frey, B. S., Benesch, C., & Stutzer, A. (2007). Does watching TV make us happy? *Journal of Economic Psychology, 28*(3), 283–313.

Harris, J. L., Bargh, J. A., & Brownell, K. D. (2009). Priming effects of television food advertising on eating behavior. *Health Psychology, 28*(4), 404.

Layard, R. (1980). Human satisfactions and public policy. *The Economic Journal, 90*(360), 737–750.

Layard, R. (2011). *Happiness: Lessons from a new science*. London: Penguin.

Mujcic, R., & Oswald, A. J. (2018). Is envy harmful to a society's psychological health and wellbeing? A longitudinal study of 18,000 adults. *Social Science & Medicine, 198*, 103–111.

Opree, S. J., Buijzen, M., & Valkenburg, P. M. (2012). Lower life satisfaction related to materialism in children frequently exposed to advertising. *Pediatrics*, peds-2011.

Opree, S. J., Buijzen, M., & van Reijmersdal, E. A. (2016). The impact of advertising on children's psychological wellbeing and life satisfaction. *European Journal of Marketing, 50*(11), 1975–1992.

Oswald, A. J. (1997). Happiness and economic performance. *The Economic Journal, 107*(445), 1815–1831.

Radcliff, B. (2013). *The political economy of human happiness: How voters' choices determine the quality of life*. New York: Cambridge University Press.

Richins, M. L. (1995). Social comparison, advertising, and consumer discontent. *American Behavioral Scientist, 38*(4), 593–607.

Robinson, J. (1933). *Economics of imperfect competition*. London: Macmillan.

Sirgy, M. J., Lee, D. J., Kosenko, R., Lee Meadow, H., Rahtz, D., Cicic, M., et al. (1998). Does television viewership play a role in the perception of quality of life? *Journal of Advertising, 27*(1), 125–142.

Sirgy, M. J., Gurel-Atay, E., Webb, D., Cicic, M., Husic, M., Ekici, A., et al. (2012). Linking advertising, materialism, and life satisfaction. *Social Indicators Research, 107*(1), 79–101.

Snyder, M., & DeBono, K. G. (1985). Appeals to image and claims about quality: Understanding the psychology of advertising. *Journal of personality and Social Psychology, 49*(3), 586.

Speck, S. K. S., & Roy, A. (2008). The interrelationships between television viewing, values and perceived well-being: A global perspective. *Journal of International Business Studies, 39*(7), 1197–1219.

Speers, S. E., Harris, J. L., & Schwartz, M. B. (2011). Child and adolescent exposure to food and beverage brand appearances during prime-time television programming. *American Journal of Preventive Medicine, 41*(3), 291–296.

Tella, R. D., MacCulloch, R. J., & Oswald, A. J. (2003). The macroeconomics of happiness. *Review of Economics and Statistics, 85*(4), 809–827.

Veblen, T. (1899). *The theory of the leisure class*. New York: Macmillan.

Veblen, T. (1904). *The theory of business enterprise*. New York: Charles Scribner's Sons.

Chapter 11
What Makes for a Good Job? Evidence Using Subjective Wellbeing Data

Christian Krekel, George Ward, and Jan-Emmanuel De Neve

Abstract We study what makes for a good job, by looking at which workplace characteristics are conducive or detrimental to job satisfaction. Using data from 37 countries around the world in the 2015 Work Orientations module of the International Social Survey Programme, we find that having an interesting job and good relationships at work, especially with management, are the strongest positive predictors of how satisfied employees are with their jobs, along with wages. Stressful or dangerous jobs, as well as those that interfere with family life, have the strongest negative correlation with job satisfaction. We discuss implications for firms and other organisations as well as for public policy-makers, and point toward future avenues for research in the area.

An extended version of this chapter was published as Krekel, C., G. Ward, and J.-E. De Neve, "Work and Wellbeing: A Global Perspective," in: Sachs, J. (ed), Global Happiness Policy Report, 2018. An online appendix with additional tables and figures (as well as full replication materials) can be found at https://doi.org/10.7910/DVN/0EEOTM. For helpful advice and comments, we are very grateful to Amy Blankson, Andrew Clark, Cary Cooper, Ed Diener, Jim Harter, John Helliwell, Jenn Lim, Richard Layard, Paul Litchfield, Ewan McKinnon, Jennifer Moss, Mike Norton, Mariano Rojas, Jeffrey Sachs, Martin Seligman, and Ashley Whillans.

C. Krekel
London School of Economics, London, UK
e-mail: c.krekel@lse.ac.uk

G. Ward
Massachusetts Institute of Technology, Cambridge, MA, USA
e-mail: wardg@mit.edu

J.-E. De Neve (✉)
University of Oxford, Oxford, UK
e-mail: jan-emmanuel.deneve@sbs.ox.ac.uk

11.1 Introduction

Work plays a central role in most people's lives. In OECD countries, for example, people spend around a third of their waking hours in paid work.[1] Not only do we spend considerable amounts of our time at work, but work and employment also frequently rank among the most important drivers of how happy we are in our lives overall.[2] Yet, what exactly is it about work – and the characteristics of different jobs and workplaces – that makes some jobs more enjoyable and others less so? In this chapter, we shed light on this question by examining the ways in and extent to which workplace and job characteristics are associated with subjective wellbeing.

The question of what makes for a satisfying work life is not only important because work plays such a significant role for people's overall wellbeing, but also because people's wellbeing is a significant predictor of important labour market outcomes themselves (De Neve and Oswald 2012). Such outcomes include job-finding and future job prospects when people are out of work (Krause 2013; Gielen and van Ours 2014), productivity while they are in work, and, ultimately, their firms' performance (Harter et al. 2002; Edmans 2011, 2012; Bockerman and Ilmakunnas 2012; Tay and Harter 2013; Oswald et al. 2015; Krekel et al. 2019).[3] Being happier also brings with it objective benefits such as increased health and longevity, which themselves can contribute positively to work outcomes (De Neve et al. 2013; Graham 2017). Likewise, wellbeing has been shown to be positively associated with intrinsic motivation and creativity (Amabile 1996; Amabile and Kramer 2011; Yuan 2015). For policy-making, which often boils down to prioritising attention and resources, it is important to know which characteristics of work, and workplace quality, most strongly drive people's wellbeing. This can help point the way towards what should be focused upon in any efforts to improve overall wellbeing, which is an important good in itself, and in doing so potentially unlock any subsequent performance gains.

This chapter looks at these characteristics in a systematic way. We employ data from the International Social Survey Programme, a dataset that comprises nationally representative samples of 37 countries around the world, and includes information on a wide array of working conditions and job characteristics, as well as subjective wellbeing. We study the extent to which each of these characteristics is associated with job satisfaction – an important domain of people's overall subjective wellbeing (Easterlin 2006) – and then complement these analyses with findings from the academic literature. The chapter concludes with a discussion of the implications for firms and policy-makers, as well as of important areas for future research.

---

[1] See OECD (2017a) for data on daily time use in OECD countries.

[2] See Web Appendix Table W1, adapted from van Praag et al. (2003).

[3] See Tenney et al. (2016) for a review on the relationship between people's wellbeing and labour market outcomes, as well as Judge et al. (2001) and Harrison et al. (2006) for recent meta-analyses. See Whitman et al. (2010) for a recent meta-analysis on people's wellbeing and firm performance.

11.2   Data and Methods

Our principal data source is the Work Orientations module of the 2015 International Social Survey Programme. Our outcome of interest is job satisfaction. Respondents are asked: "How satisfied are you in your main job?" The question offers six answer possibilities, including "completely satisfied", "very satisfied", "fairly satisfied", "neither satisfied nor dissatisfied", "fairly dissatisfied", and "very dissatisfied". We assign numerical values to these categories, and use the indicator as a cardinal measure. We then standardise it such that it has mean zero and standard deviation one.

Not only does this measure offer a distinctively democratic way of asking people what exactly makes a good job, but it is also strongly correlated with employee retention, an outcome that is itself highly important to firm performance. In fact, if we correlate job satisfaction with the willingness of employees to turn down a competing job offer, which is also reported in this survey, we obtain a sizeable correlation coefficient of about 0.4, suggesting that employees who are more satisfied with their jobs are also, to a large extent, more likely to remain in their jobs.

Our goal is to find out which elements of workplace quality explain job satisfaction, our outcome of interest. Within a multivariate linear regression framework, we regress job satisfaction on various domains of workplace quality as well as a rich set of control variables. Building on Clark (2009), we define twelve domains:

- Pay
- Working Hours
- Working Hours Mismatch
- Work-Life Balance
- Skills Match
- Job Security
- Difficulty, Stress, Danger
- Opportunities for Advancement
- Independence
- Interesting Job
- Interpersonal Relationships
- Usefulness

In some cases, a domain includes a single element, as in case of working hours (it simply includes the actual working hours of the respondent). In other cases, a domain includes several elements. For example, *Pay* includes both the actual income of the respondent and her subjective assessment of whether that income is high. In such cases, we conduct a principle component analysis to extract a single, latent explanatory factor from these elements, and then relate job satisfaction to this factor. In other words, we first establish which broad domains of workplace quality are relatively more important for job satisfaction than others, and then go on to look at the different elements within these domains in order to measure their specific contribution to job satisfaction.

244 C. Krekel et al.

As with our outcome, we standardise our explanatory variables such that they have mean zero and standard deviation one. This makes interpretation easier: the coefficient estimate of an explanatory variable is the partial correlation coefficient and, when squared, indicates the variation in job satisfaction that this variable explains.

To account for potentially confounding individual characteristics of respondents that may drive both working conditions and wellbeing, we control for a rich set of demographic variables by holding them constant in our regression. These include a wide array of individual demographic characteristics, including age, gender, and education. In the appendix, we provide full definitions as well as summary statistics of job satisfaction, the different elements of workplace quality, and the control variables.

In our main specification, we also include industry and occupation fixed effects. It is quite imaginable that there are significant differences in job satisfaction between different occupations and industries. We are not principally interested in explaining level differences in job satisfaction between, for example, a manager in the pharmaceutical industry and a farmer. Instead, we are interested in answering the more fundamental question of which broad domains of workplace quality are relatively more important for job satisfaction than others in more directly comparable occupations and industries.[4] Finally, we control for the respective country in which the respondent lives, for the same reason, and restrict the sample to private households with individuals who report to be working (regardless of age or how many hours).

11.3 Results

We now turn to our regression results, and look more deeply into which of these domains of workplace quality are relatively more important for job satisfaction than others. Figure 11.1 plots the coefficient estimates obtained from our regression of job satisfaction on the different domains. The corresponding, more detailed regression results are available in Table 11.1. Table 11.2 employs, instead of the broad domains of workplace quality, the different constituent elements within these domains.[5]

In what follows, we discuss, in turn, the relative importance of the different domains of workplace quality, including, where appropriate, the different elements within these domains, for job satisfaction. We look mostly at their association with job satisfaction for the average employee, but, where interesting, point towards

---

[4]Of course, some of these domains are more prevalent in certain occupations and industries than in others.

[5]For a comprehensive summary of a systematic review on the relationship between job quality and wellbeing, see also What Works Centre for Wellbeing (2017a).

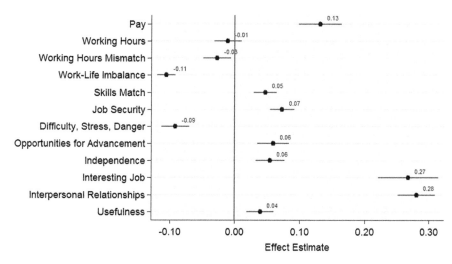

Fig. 11.1 Workplace quality and job satisfaction (International Social Survey Programme, Module on Work Orientations, Year 2015; 95% Confidence Intervals). (*Notes:* The figure plots effect estimates obtained from regressing job satisfaction on different domains of workplace quality. All variables (both left and right-hand side) are standardised with mean zero and standard deviation one. Squaring a regressor yields the respective share in the variation of job satisfaction that this regressor explains. *Pay, Working Hours Mismatch, Work-Life Imbalance, Skills Match, Difficulty, Stress, Danger, Independence, Interpersonal Relationships,* and *Usefulness* are principle components obtained from separate principle component analyses that condense various variables in the respective domain of workplace quality into a single indicator; see Section 2 for a description of the procedure and Table W8 in the Web Appendix for summary statistics of the variables. The sample is restricted to all individuals who state that they are working and who report working hours greater than zero. See Table 11.1 for the corresponding table)

effect heterogeneities between the employed and the self-employed (Fig. 11.2a), full-time and part-time (Fig. 11.2b), and between basic demographic characteristics such as gender (Fig. 11.2c) and different levels of education (Fig. 11.2d).

11.3.1   Pay

It may come as little surprise that we find pay to be an important determinant of job satisfaction. In classic economic theory, labour enters the utility function negatively, and theory predicts that individuals are compensated by wages that equal the marginal product of labour. That said, pay is not only an important compensation for the hardship that individuals incur when working but also an important signal of their productivity. We thus expect job satisfaction to be higher the greater the wedge between compensation and hardship incurred, and the more social-status relevant pay is.

The importance of pay for job satisfaction seems universal, with no statistically significant differences between respondents who are employed or self-employed and

Table 11.1 Workplace quality and job satisfaction, aggregated domains

Workplace quality	Coefficient	S. E.	Ranking of importance for job satisfaction
Pay	0.131***	0.016	3
Working hours	−0.011	0.010	12
Working hours mismatch	−0.027**	0.011	11
Work-life imbalance	−0.106***	0.007	4
Skills match	0.047***	0.009	9
Job security	0.073***	0.009	6
Difficulty, stress, danger	−0.092***	0.011	5
Opportunities for advancement	0.060***	0.012	7
Independence	0.055***	0.011	8
Interesting job	0.267***	0.023	2
Interpersonal relationships	0.281***	0.015	1
Usefulness	0.040***	0.010	10
Constant	Yes		
Controls	Yes		
Occupation fixed effects	Yes		
Industry fixed effects	Yes		
Country fixed effects	Yes		
Observations	16,326		
Adjusted R-squared	0.422		

Robust standard errors clustered at country level in parentheses
***p < 0.01, **p < 0.05, *p < 0.1
Notes: All variables (both left- and right-hand side) are standardised with mean zero and standard deviation one. *Pay, Working Hours Mismatch, Work-Life Imbalance, Skills Match, Difficulty, Stress, Danger, Independence, Interpersonal Relationships*, and *Usefulness* are principle components obtained from separate principle component analyses that condense various variables in the respective domain of workplace quality into a single indicator; see Section 2 for a description of the procedure and Table W8 in the Web Appendix for summary statistics of the variables. The sample is restricted to all individuals who state that they are working and who report working hours greater than zero. See Table W2 in the Web Appendix for the full set of controls
Source: International Social Survey Programme, Module on Work Orientations, Year 2015

working full-time or part-time, or between gender and different levels of education. In our analysis, the domain *Pay* consists of two elements: the actual income of respondents and their subjective assessment of whether that income is high. Both elements are almost equally important, but objective income a little more.

Perhaps more surprising is the finding that, although pay is an important determinants of job satisfaction, it is not the most important one. In fact, it only ranks third, behind interpersonal relationships at work and having an interesting job. We discuss these determinants in detail below.

Most people, when being asked why they are working, respond that they are working to earn money. This is, of course, true, but once they are working, other

Table 11.2 Workplace quality and job satisfaction, disaggregated domains

Workplace quality	Coefficient	S. E.
Pay		
High income	0.087***	0.012
Individual income (natural log)	0.105**	0.051
Working hours		
Working hours (natural log)	−0.011	0.010
Working hours mismatch		
Wants to work same hours	Reference category	
Wants to work more hours	−0.010	0.007
Wants to work less hours	−0.030***	0.010
Work-life imbalance		
Working on weekends	0.017**	0.007
Work interfering with family	−0.109***	0.009
Difficulty of taking time off	−0.039***	0.009
Skills match		
Skills match	0.048***	0.009
Skills training	0.019**	0.009
Job security		
Job security	0.070***	0.008
Difficulty, stress, danger		
Hard physical work	−0.007	0.012
Stressful work	−0.085***	0.011
Opportunities for advancement		
Opportunities for advancement	0.054***	0.011
Independence		
Independent work	0.028**	0.011
Working from home	−0.010	0.011
Daily work flexible	Reference category	
Daily work fixed	−0.011	0.008
Daily work free	0.039***	0.010
Working hours flexible	Reference category	
Working hours fixed	−0.002	0.007
Working hours free	−0.003	0.008
Working schedule flexible	Reference category	
Working schedule fixed	−0.021**	0.008
Working schedule free	−0.017**	0.008
Interesting job		
Interesting job	0.265***	0.022
Interpersonal relationships		
Contact with other people	0.006	0.009
Relationship with management	0.222***	0.011
Relationship with co-workers	0.091***	0.012

(continued)

Table 11.2 (continued)

Workplace quality	Coefficient	S. E.
Usefulness		
Helping other people	0.026***	0.009
Being useful to society	0.036***	0.009
Constant	Yes	
Controls	Yes	
Occupation fixed effects	Yes	
Industry fixed effects	Yes	
Country fixed effects	Yes	
Observations	16,326	
Adjusted R-squared	0.438	

Robust standard errors clustered at country level in parentheses
***p < 0.01, **p < 0.05, *p < 0.1
Notes: All variables (both left- and right-hand side) are standardised with mean zero and standard deviation one. See Table W8 in the Web Appendix for summary statistics of the variables. The sample is restricted to all individuals who state that they are working and who report working hours greater than zero. See Table W3 in the Web Appendix for the full set of controls

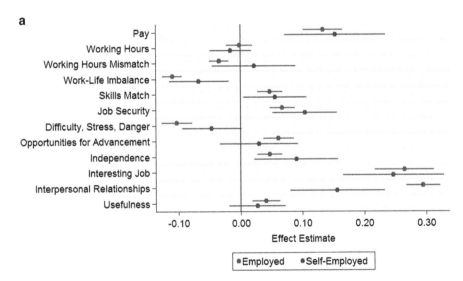

Fig. 11.2a Workplace quality and job satisfaction, by employment status (International Social Survey Programme, Module on Work Orientations, Year 2015; 95% Confidence Intervals). (Notes: See Figure 2. See Table W4 in the Web Appendix for the corresponding table)

workplace characteristics become more salient, and thus potentially more important than previously thought. Experimental research, for example, has shown that intrinsic motivations gain in importance relative to extrinsic ones (such as income) once individuals are engaged in an activity (Woolley and Fishbach 2015). Purpose, in particular, may be such a characteristic: Ariely et al. (2008) show, in a laboratory

b

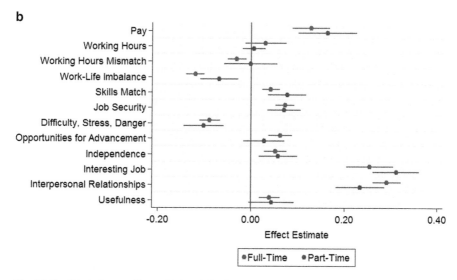

Fig. 11.2b Workplace quality and job satisfaction, by working time (International Social Survey Programme, Module on Work Orientations, Year 2015; 95% Confidence Intervals). (*Notes:* See Figure 2. See Table W5 in the Web Appendix for the corresponding table)

c

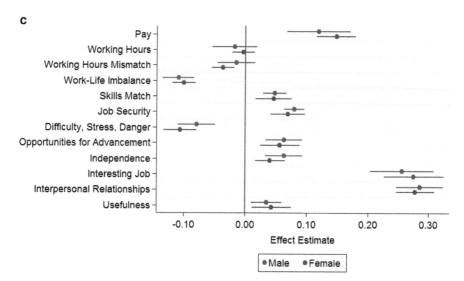

Fig. 11.2c Workplace quality and job satisfaction, by gender (International Social Survey Programme, Module on Work Orientations, Year 2015; 95% Confidence Intervals). (*Notes:* See Figure 2. See Table W6 in the Web Appendix for the corresponding table)

d

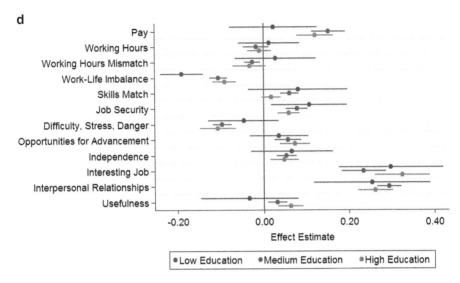

Fig. 11.2d Workplace quality and job satisfaction, by education level (International Social Survey Programme, Module on Work Orientations Year 2015; 95% Confidence Intervals). (*Notes:* See Figure 2. See Table W7 in the Web Appendix for the corresponding table)

setting, that people who see a purpose in what they do perform relatively better at work, even in the context of simple, repetitive effort tasks.[6] Using both experimental and observational data, Hu and Hirsh (2017) find that employees report minimum acceptable salaries that are 32% lower for personally meaningful jobs compared to jobs that are perceived as personally meaningless. The important role of purpose may be even more pronounced when in interplay with good management practices (Gartenberg et al. 2016), including employee recognition (Bradler et al. 2016).

11.3.2   Working Hours

As labour enters the utility function negatively, classic economic theory predicts a negative relationship between the number of working hours and wellbeing. This is precisely what we find for job satisfaction.

Interestingly, however, when controlling for all other domains of workplace quality, the relationship between working hours and job satisfaction is not only tiny (it ranks as the least important domain of workplace quality) but turns out to be statistically insignificant altogether. This finding is again universal: there are no

---

[6]The important role of purpose for performance has also been studied in educational contexts: Yeager et al. (2014) show that promoting a pro-social, self-transcendent purpose improves academic self-regulation in students.

statistically significant differences between respondents who are employed or self-employed and working full-time or part-time, or between gender and different levels of education.

This seems odd at first, but as we shall see below, is in line with a growing evidence base that documents the negative impact of working hours mismatch and work-life imbalance on people's wellbeing.

11.3.3   Working Hours Mismatch

Rather than the total number of working hours, what seems to matter more for job satisfaction is working hours mismatch, defined as the difference between the actual and the desired number of working hours.

Individuals differ in their preferences for how much they want to work, and classic economic theory assumes that they can freely choose their desired bundle of labour and leisure hours. Empirical evidence, however, suggests that this is often not the case: work contracts, labour market conditions, and social norms, amongst others, may affect their choices, and may lead to a realised bundle that is different from the desired one. In Britain, for example, more than 40% of employees who work full-time report to prefer working fewer hours (Boeheim and Taylor 2004). In such situations, theory predicts that individuals end up on a lower utility level.

Working hours mismatch has a significant negative association with how satisfied employees are, on average, with their jobs. It is still unsettled in the literature, however, whether underemployment is more detrimental to people's wellbeing, as has been found for Germany (Wunder and Heineck 2013), or overemployment, as has been found for Australia (Wooden et al. 2009) or Britain (Angrave and Charlwood 2015). In our analysis, the domain *Working Hours Mismatch* consists of two elements: the desire to work more hours (for more pay) and the desire to work less hours (for less pay). We find that the latter drives the tempirical linkage of working hours mismatch to job satisfaction, suggesting that overemployment is more of an issue than underemployment. Diverging results in the literature may point towards the importance of accounting for differences in institutional settings between countries, including, for example, differences in labour market regulations (especially regarding job security), social policy, social norms, and lifestyles. Note that working hours mismatch has also been found to have negative spillovers on other household members (Wunder and Heineck 2013).

It turns out that the negative association between working hours mismatch and job satisfaction is driven primarily by the employed as opposed to the self-employed (who probably have more control over their working hours) and, in line with our finding for overemployment, by employees working full-time as opposed to part-time.

Importantly, there is a gender dimension to working hours mismatch: its negative association with job satisfaction is driven primarily by women. Evidence shows that women spend considerably larger amounts of time caring for other household members (for example, they spend more than twice as much time on childcare) and doing routine household work than men, even in the case that actual working hours are equal between women and men (OECD 2014). For women, achieving a better balance between the actual and the desired number of working hours would therefore be an effective means of reducing time crunches. The fact that working fewer hours may be detrimental to their long-term career prospects presents a dilemma, and may – at least in part – explain the declining life satisfaction of mothers over the past decades (Stevenson and Wolfers 2009).

In sum, we find that working hours mismatch, in particular overemployment, has a significant negative impact on job satisfaction. The size of this association, however, is rather small: in fact, working hours mismatch is only ranked eleventh out of twelve domains of workplace quality in terms of their importance for job satisfaction. If working hours mismatch is not so bad after all, then what is? The answer is work-life imbalance.

11.3.4   *Work-Life Balance*

Working hours mismatch may not be so bad as long as it does not seriously interfere with other important domains of life, especially the family. If, however, work and private life threaten to get out of balance, negative consequences for people's wellbeing are large.

Although work-life (im)balance ranks only fourth out of twelve domains of workplace quality in terms of power to explain variation in job satisfaction, it is the domain that has the strongest negative impact on job satisfaction amongst all negative workplace characteristics. It is highly significant, and statistically indistinguishable from having a job that is difficult, stressful, or even dangerous. The negative association between work-life imbalance and job satisfaction job satisfaction seems to be almost universal: there are no statistically significant differences between respondents who are employed or self-employed and between gender. Perhaps not surprisingly, employees working full-time are more heavily affected than those working part-time, and there is some evidence that the negative consequences of work-life imbalance are stronger for workers with low levels of education.

In our analysis, the domain *Work-Life Balance* consists of three elements, which have a clear ranking in terms of importance: work interfering with the family exerts, by far, the strongest negative impact on job satisfaction, followed by the difficulty of taking time off on short notice when needed. The coefficient for working on weekends actually suggests a positive relationship, but is negligible in terms of effect size.

From our findings on working hours mismatch and work-life balance, we can derive some important policy implications: policies that target more supportive and flexible working time regulations have the potential to considerably increase people's wellbeing. This is especially true for people who experience disproportionally more time crunches, including, amongst others, women, parents (especially single parents), and caretakers of other household members such as elderly. The public policy mix that enables people to strike a better balance between their work and private lives can be quite diverse, ranging from specific labour market regulations on flexible working times to the provision of infrastructure such as public transportation in order to reduce commuting times or early childcare facilities in sufficient quantity and quality. At the same time, for firms, offering more flexible working times may be a promising strategy to effectively attract and retain skilled workers.

Is there a trade-off between flexible work practices and performance? To answer this question, Bloom et al. (2014) conducted an experiment at Ctrip, a NASDAQ-listed Chinese travel agency with more than 16,000 employees. The authors randomly allocated call centre agents who volunteered to participate in the experiment to work either from home or in the office for 9 months. They found that working from home led to a 13% performance increase, due to fewer breaks and sick days as well as a quieter and more convenient working environment. At the same time, job satisfaction rose and attrition halved. Conditional on their performance, however, participants in the experiment were less likely to get promoted.[7]

For employees, of course, this raises the question of whether flexible work practices are associated with a career penalty. This does not necessarily have to be the case: Leslie et al. (2012) show, in both a field study at a Fortune 500 company and a laboratory experiment, that flexible work practices result in a career penalty only in case that managers attribute their use as being motivated primarily by reasons related to personal lives. To the extent that mangers attribute their use to reasons related to organisational needs, however, their use can actually result in a career premium. The latter category includes reasons related to, for example, work performance and efficiency. Part of this attribution is communication, and training supervisors on the value of demonstrating support for employees' personal lives while prompting employees to reconsider when and where to work can help reduce work-family conflict (Kelly et al. 2014).

Finally, Moen et al. (2011) studied the turnover effects of switching from standard time practices to a results-only working environment at Best Buy, a large US retailer that implemented the scheme sequentially in its corporate headquarters: eight months after implementation, turnover amongst employees exposed to the scheme fell by 45.5%. Evidence therefore suggests that carefully designed, implemented, and communicated flexible work schemes can actually have positive impacts on organisational performance.

---

[7]The company later offered the option to work from home to the whole firm, allowing formerly treated employees to re-select between working from home or working in the office: about half of them switched back, which almost doubled performance gains to 22%. This highlights the importance of accounting for self-selection and learning. In fact, in a recent discrete choice experiment, Mas and Pallais (2017) demonstrate that employee preferences for flexible work practices are quite heterogeneous: while most employees prefer a little extra income over flexibility, to a small number of employees, flexible work practices are very important.

11.3.5 Skills Match

A job that is asking too much from the skills of an employee can lead to frustration, and so can a job that is asking too little. Matching the demand for and the supply of skills in a particular job, and enabling employees to effectively apply the skills they have or, if necessary, to acquire new skills, should thus be reflected in higher job satisfaction.

This is precisely what we find. Achieving a skills match in a particular job has a significant positive association with how satisfied employees are with that job. This is again an almost universal finding: there are no statistically significant differences between respondents who are employed or self-employed, between respondents who are working full-time or part-time, and between gender. Differences between levels of education are minor. The domain *Skills Match* includes two elements: whether respondents have participated in a skills training in the previous year and their subjective assessment of whether their skills generally match those required in their job. Both elements matter, but their subjective assessment a little more.[8] Importantly, skills match is not only directed towards the self but also towards others in the workplace. In fact, Artz et al. (2017) find that supervisor technical competence is amongst the strongest predictors of workers' job satisfaction. Willis Towers Watson, a leading human resources consultancy, estimates that in companies where leaders and managers are perceived as effective, 72% of employees are highly engaged (Willis Tower Watson 2014). On a more abstract level, the concept of skills match may also be applied to matching individual character strengths, although there is yet little evidence on the causality of this relationship in organisational settings.

Although skills match ranks only ninth out of twelve domains of workplace quality in terms of power to explain variation in job satisfaction, places five to nine are close to each other, and thus constitute a category of medium importance for wellbeing at work.

What are the wellbeing returns to essential skills training in practice? UPSKILL was a workplace literacy and essential skills training pilot in Canada (Social Research and Demonstration Corporation, 2014a). It was implemented as a randomised controlled trial, involving 88 firms (primarily in the accommodation and food services sector) and more than 800 workers who were randomly allocated to receiving 40 hours of literacy and skills training on site during working hours. The pilot was not only effective in increasing basic literacy scores and thus job performance and retention, but, importantly, also in increasing mental health: at follow-up, participants in the treatment group were 25% points more likely than those in the control group to have reported a significant reduction in stress levels. Effects were particularly pronounced amongst participants with low baseline skills at the outset. These positive impacts at the worker level also translated into positive impacts at the firm level: even though firms bore the full costs of training and release time for workers, they incurred a 23% return on investment, primarily though gains in

---

[8]On the importance of learning on the job for wellbeing, see also What Works Centre for Wellbeing (2017b).

revenue (customer satisfaction increased by 30% points), cost savings from increased productivity (wastage and errors in both core tasks and administrative activities were significantly reduced), and reductions in hiring costs. Besides firms' commitment to learning and training, organisations that offered work environments with high levels of trust gained relatively more from the programme (Social Research and Demonstration Corporation, 2014b). This is in line with a growing evidence base on the importance of trust in the workplace (Helliwell et al. 2009; Helliwell and Huang 2011; Helliwell and Wang 2015).

11.3.6   Job Security

Slightly more important than skills match is job security: it ranks sixth out of twelve domains of workplace quality, and is thus also part of the category of medium importance for wellbeing at work.

Job security is universally important: we find no evidence of effect heterogeneities between respondents who are employed or self-employed and working full-time or part-time, or between gender and different levels of education. The literature shows that the unemployment rate in a particular region has a significant negative effect on the life satisfaction of the employed in that region (Luechinger et al. 2010). This is often interpreted as a signal of general job insecurity, which is detrimental to happiness.

11.3.7   Difficulty, Stress, Danger

Not surprisingly, we find that jobs which are associated with difficulty, stress, or even danger are also associated with lower levels of job satisfaction. This holds true even when controlling for all other domains of workplace quality, including pay, working hours, and job security. This is an interesting finding in itself, as classic economic theory predicts that workers should be compensated, either monetarily or non-monetarily, for any job disamenities such that the net wellbeing effect is zero. Empirical evidence on so-called *compensating differentials*, however, is rather mixed. In our data, which are clearly limited (for example, we are not fully able to account for ability differences), we find little evidence of them.

In our analysis, the domain *Difficulty, Stress, Danger* consists of two elements: hard physical and stressful work. It turns out that the latter drives the negative empirical linkage of this domain to job satisfaction; the former, on the contrary, turns out statistically insignificant. The fact that stress at work is detrimental to health is well-established in the literature: for example, Chandola et al. (2006), in a large-scale prospective cohort study involving more than 10,000 men and women aged 35 to 55 who were employed in 20 London civil service departments, study the relationship between exposure to stressors at work and the risk of developing the metabolic syndrome, a cluster of at least three of five medical conditions including, amongst others, obesity, high blood pressure, and high blood sugar. They find that employees with chronic work stress were more than twice as likely to develop the syndrome 14 years into the study than those without.

Having a job that is difficult, stressful, or even dangerous ranks fifth out of twelve domains of workplace quality in terms of power to explain variation in job satisfaction. It is the domain that has the second strongest negative association with job satisfaction amongst all negative workplace characteristics, and comes right after work-life imbalance from which it is – at least in terms of effect size – statistically not distinguishable. We find little evidence that its negative impact varies for different people.

11.3.8   Opportunities for Advancement

We know from the literature that being in a stable employment relationship, be it full-time or part-time, has a positive relationship with how people evaluate their lives globally, as well as how they feel on a daily basis. Part of why this is the case is that jobs provide opportunities for advancement, be it steps to climb up the career ladder, new challenges that give room for personal development, and many others.

Our data do not discriminate between different types of opportunities for advancement, but simply ask respondents whether their current job provides them. This gives respondents the freedom to interpret the question in whatever way they themselves find most important.

We find that opportunities for advancement have a significant positive impact on the job satisfaction of the average respondent. There is quite some effect heterogeneity, though: the association is primarily driven by respondents who are employed as opposed to self-employed (probably because the self-employed are themselves more in control of which opportunities for advancement to create or not) and by respondents who work full-time as opposed to part-time. There also seems to be a gradient in education: opportunities for advancement become more important for job satisfaction the higher the level of education. They are equally important to men and women.

Opportunities for advancement rank seventh out of twelve domains of workplace quality in terms of power to explain variation in job satisfaction. Perceived progress through well-defined goal-setting and planning as well as measurable evaluations – based on clearly defined expectations and performance – and employee recognition may increase agency and make the way towards career advancement more transparent, thereby contributing positively to wellbeing at work.

11.3.9   Independence

Independence at work can have many facets. Our survey asks respondents to what extent they can work independently, whether they often work at home, and whether they have agency about the organisation of their daily work, their working hours, and their usual working schedule.

We find that independence at work occupies the middle ground of importance for wellbeing: it has a significant positive relationship with job satisfaction, with an effect size similar to skills match, job security, opportunities for advancement, and usefulness. It is ranked eighth out of twelve domains of workplace quality in terms of power to explain variation in job satisfaction. Independence at work seems to be important to everybody: there are no statistically significant differences between respondents who are employed or self-employed and working full-time or part-time, or between gender and different levels of education.

In our analysis, the domain *Independence* includes eight elements: the subjective assessment of respondents as to what extent they can work independently, how often they work at home during their usual working hours, and whether the organisation of their daily work, their working hours, and their usual working schedule is entirely free for them to decide as opposed to fixed. Some of these elements are important, others are not. There also seems to be a ranking of importance: we find that the positive impact of independence at work on job satisfaction is driven primarily by whether respondents report that they can freely organise their daily work, followed by their subjective assessment as to what extent they can work independently. The nature of having discretion about the usual working schedule is more complex: we find that both full discretion and no discretion at all have a negative impact on job satisfaction. Here, it seems that the reference category – having limited discretion – yields a higher job satisfaction than both ends of the spectrum.

Independence at work is related to the concept of job crafting (Wrzesniewski and Dutton 2001), and the question of whether organisations should give their employees, to a certain extent, the freedom to design their jobs based on personal needs and resources. Studies have shown that enabling employees to craft their jobs in this way can have positive benefits in terms of increased employee engagement and job satisfaction as well as decreased likelihood of burnout (Tims et al. 2013). More generally, the concept of individual job crafting may be transferred to the level of the entire organisation, in the sense of organisational design. It can also be applied to the physical environment: Knight and Haslam (2010) studied, in an experiment involving different office spaces, the effect of giving employees the opportunity to design their physical working environment. In line with the notion of social identity, they found that employees who were randomly allocated to the crafting condition showed higher organisational identification, job satisfaction, and productivity, measured in terms of task performance. Independence at work has also been identified as a contributing factor to creativity (Amabile et al. 1996). Evidence is thus rather positive about independence at work, but its precise impact is probably highly context-specific.

Does autonomy over working schedules raise employee wellbeing? STAR ("Support. Transform. Achieve. Results") was a flexible working practices pilot developed by the interdisciplinary Work Family and Health Network (King et al. 2012). It aimed at *(i)* increasing employees' control over their working schedule, *(ii)* raise employee perceptions of supervisor support for their personal and family lives, and *(iii)* reorient the working culture from face time to results only. Eight hours of preparatory sessions encouraged managers and their teams to identify new, flexible work practices, for example, by communicating via instant messenger or by planning ahead periods of peak-demand more effectively. The pilot was implemented as a group-randomised controlled trial in a Fortune 500 company, involving 867 IT workers who were, including their entire team, allocated to either the intervention or business-as-usual and followed for over a year. Moen et al. (2016) find that the intervention significantly reduced burnout by about 44% of a standard deviation while raising job satisfaction by about 30%. These large effect sizes were partially mediated by decreases in family-to-work conflict and, perhaps less surprisingly, increases in schedule control. There is also some evidence that the intervention decreased perceived stress and psychological distress. Although it has not been evaluated with respect to employee performance (possibly because it is difficult to measure performance in the given context), recent experimental evidence (see Bloom et al. (2014), for example) suggests that, in a very similar context, giving employees more autonomy over where and when to work can have strong, positive performance impacts.

11.3.10   Interesting Job

It should not come as a big surprise that having an interesting job is positively associated with being more satisfied with it.

But it is astonishing just how important interestingness is. Amongst all positive workplace characteristics, it has the second strongest impact on job satisfaction, right after interpersonal relationships at work (from which it is, in terms of effect size, not statistically distinguishable), and thus ranks second out of twelve domains of workplace quality in terms of power to explain variation in job satisfaction. There is little evidence that the impact of interestingness varies for different people: having an interesting job is important to everybody.

Note that interestingness is not the same as purposefulness. A job can score both high on being interesting and low on being purposeful. In contrast to interestingness, purposefulness is best described in terms of a long-term alignment between a job and an individual's own evolutionary purpose in the sense of doing something greater than self.

11.3.11   Interpersonal Relationships

In most jobs, employees interact, in one way or another, with supervisors, co-workers, or clients.[9] The way in which these interactions occur, and interpersonal

---

[9]On the importance of team work more generally for wellbeing, see What Works Centre for Wellbeing (2017c).

relationships are maintained, shows up as the most important determinant of how satisfied employees are with their jobs.

Interpersonal relationships have a sizeable, significant positive association with the job satisfaction of the average employee. They rank first out of our twelve domains of workplace quality in terms of power to explain variation in job satisfaction. The size of the relationship, however, is statistically not different from that of having an interesting job, which ranks second. Interpersonal relationships are particularly important for the employed as opposed to the self-employed (probably because the self-employed can, if necessary, avoid interactions) and employees who are working full-time as opposed to part-time (probably because people become relatively more important the more time is spent with them). There is no gender dimension to interpersonal relationships: they are equally important to men and women. Their importance for job satisfaction does not vary by educational level either.

In our analysis, the domain *Interpersonal Relationships* consists of three elements: contact with other people in general, the respondents' subjective assessment of their relationship with the management, and the equivalent subjective assessment of their relationship with co-workers. The driver behind the positive impact of interpersonal relationships on job satisfaction is, by far, the relationship with the management. The relationship with co-workers is, although important, only half as important. This is in line with evidence showing that about 50% of US adults who have left their job did so in order to get away from their manager (Gallup News 2015). Contact with other people seems to matter less for job satisfaction.

How does the relationship between managers and employees affect wellbeing at work? Managers can have many functions: for employees, they may provide training, advice, and motivation (Lazear et al. 2015). To effectively fulfil these functions, managers should be competent. Artz et al. (2017) study the relationship between managers' technical competence and employees' job satisfaction, using the Working in Britain Survey in the UK and the National Longitudinal Study of Youth in the US. They find that a manager's technical competence – measured in terms of whether the manager worked herself up the ranks, knows her job, or could even do the employee's job – is the single strongest predictor of an employee's job satisfaction. In terms of effect size, having a competent boss is even more important for job satisfaction than having friendly colleagues.

In a study on the National Health Service in England, Ogbonnaya and Daniels (2017) find that Trusts (the organisational entities the National Health Service is comprised of) which make the most use of people management practices are over twice as likely to have staff with the highest levels of job satisfaction as compared to those which make the least use of these practices. People management practices refer here to training, performance appraisals, team working, clear definition of roles and responsibilities, provision of autonomy in own decision-making, and supportive management that involves staff in organisational decisions. Importantly, they are also three times more likely to have the lowest levels of sickness absence, and four times more likely to have the most satisfied patients. White and Bryson (2013) confirm this finding for a wider range of organisations in Britain, using an index constructed from various domains of human resource management – participation, team working, development, selection, and incentives – and nationally representative, linked employee-employee data: firms with more human resource practices in place tend to score higher in terms of employees' job satisfaction and organisational commitment (although the relationship seems to be non-linear).

Fairness and transparency in managerial decision-making seems to be an important factor as well: Heinz et al. (2017) conduct a field experiment in which the authors set up a call centre to study the impact of treating some employees unfairly on the productivity of the others. They set up two work shifts, and randomly lay off 20% of employees between shift one and two due to stated cost reductions (which, as confirmed by interviews with actual HR managers, is perceived as unfair). The productivity of the remaining, unaffected workers, which are notified by this decision at the beginning of the second shift, drops by about twelve percent. The effect size of the productivity decline is close to the upper bound of the direct effects of wage cuts.

11.3.12   Usefulness

How important is pro-sociality – doing something that is beneficial for other people or for society at large – when it comes to job satisfaction?

Pro-social behaviour is behaviour intended to benefit one or more individuals other than oneself (Eisenberg et al. 2013). This type of behaviour can cover a broad range of actions such as helping, sharing, and other forms of cooperation (Batson and Powell 2003).[10] It has been shown to have positive wellbeing benefits at the individual level (Meier and Stutzer 2008). At the societal level, it can help build social capital through fostering cooperation and trust, and social capital is linked to higher levels of wellbeing in societies (Helliwell et al. 2016, 2017). Pro-sociality is not the same as purpose (although they probably overlap to a very large extent): whereas pro-sociality is always directed towards others, purpose could, in the narrower sense, only be directed towards the self. That said, a job can score both high on individual purpose and low on pro-sociality. In reality, however, most jobs probably score either high or low on both constructs.

We can replicate this finding for wellbeing at work: doing something that is beneficial for other people or for society at large is associated with higher levels of job satisfaction, on average. However, in line with the notion of humans as *conditional* co-operators (Fehr and Fischbacher 2003), the size of this relationship is rather small. Usefulness ranks only tenth out of our twelve domains of workplace quality in terms of power to explain variation in job satisfaction. There is also quite some effect

---

[10]Note that pro-social behaviour is distinct from altruism in that it is not purely motivated by increasing another individual's welfare, but can be motivated by, for example, empathy, reciprocity, or self-image (Evren and Minardi 2017).

heterogeneity: doing something useful is more important for the job satisfaction of the employed as opposed to the self-employed (probably because the self-employed have, in the first place, more choice over which activities to engage in or not) and employees who are working full-time as opposed to part-time. Pro-sociality also becomes more important the higher the level of education. There are no significant differences between gender.

In our analysis, the domain *Usefulness* consists of two elements: helping other people and being useful to society. Both are important, but being useful to society a little more.

There is a growing literature on pro-sociality in the workplace. Anik et al. (2013) studied the impact of pro-social bonuses – a novel type of bonus spent on others rather than oneself – on wellbeing and performance. In a field experiment at a large Australian bank, the authors found that employees who were randomly allocated to receive bonuses in form of (relatively small) financial donations to be made to local charities showed significant, immediate improvements in job satisfaction and happiness compared to employees not given these bonuses. In two follow-up experiments, one involving sports teams in Canada and another one involving a sales team at a large pharmaceutical company in Belgium, they found that spending bonuses on team members rather than oneself led to better team performance in the longer term. The finding that spending money on others can buy you happiness has also been shown by Dunn et al. (2008): the authors find that pro-social spending in form of gifts to others or financial donations to charities is positively correlated with general happiness. Longitudinally, they show that (arguably otherwise comparable) employees who received – unexpectedly – a profit-sharing bonus and spent more of it pro-socially experienced an increase in general happiness, even after controlling for income and the amount of the bonus.

Two other intervention studies stand out: Gilchrist et al. (2016) studied the impact of pay rises – masked as gifts – on performance in a setting where there were no future employment possibilities. The authors hired one-time data entry assistants on an online platform for freelancers, and then randomly allocated them into different experimental conditions, one involving an unexpected, benevolent pay rise. They found that freelancers allocated to this condition entered 20% more data than those who were either initially offered the same pay or initially offered a lower pay, both of which performed equally. In other words, simply paying more at the outset did not elicit higher task performance, but an unexpected pay rise masked as a benevolent gift did. Grant (2008), in a randomised field experiment involving fund raisers at a university, found that bringing together fund raisers and beneficiaries to show the former the purpose of their work significantly increased their subsequent task performance.

How organisations can organise work to make it more fulfilling, and connect people with the pro-social impact they may have, for example, by providing incentives to elicit behaviours that help accumulating altruistic capital (Ashraf and Bandiera 2017), is a promising area of research.

11.4 Discussion

Despite the importance of work for people's happiness, unfortunately, most people do not perceive work as a particularly enjoyable activity. A recent study that asked respondents to record their wellbeing via a smartphone at random points in time on a given day found that paid work is ranked lower than any other of the 39 activities sampled, with the exception of being sick in bed (Bryson and MacKerron 2016). In fact, the worst time of all seems to be when people are with their boss (Kahneman et al. 2004). Not surprisingly then, costs of absenteeism and presentism are high: in a recent report for the UK, it was estimated that absenteeism costs UK businesses about GBP 29 billion per year, with the average worker taking 6.6 days off due to sickness (PwC Research 2013). Costs of presentism due to, for example, mental health problems are estimated to be almost twice as high as those of absenteeism (The Sainsbury Centre for Mental Health 2007). It is imperative, therefore, that we know which elements of work are least and most conducive to wellbeing, and how these might be changed in order to make work more satisfying.

This is not only important because work plays such a significant role for individuals' overall wellbeing, but also because people's wellbeing is an important predictor of outcomes related to worker productivity and firm performance. Harter et al. (2010), exploiting a large longitudinal dataset that includes 141,900 respondents within 2178 business units of ten large organisations across industries, study the relationship between perceived working conditions of employees and firm-level outcomes. They find that working conditions – including overall satisfaction within the organisation – are predictive of key outcomes such as employee retention and customer loyalty. Krekel et al. (2019) confirm a strong, positive relationship between employee satisfaction and customer loyalty, employee productivity, and firm profitability as well as a strong, negative relationship with staff turnover in a meta-analysis of 339 independent studies that include observations on the wellbeing of 1,882,131 employees and performance of 82,248 business units. Importantly, Harter et al. (2010) are able to show that the effect tends to run from working conditions to firm-level outcomes rather than the other way around – this is suggestive of a causal impact. The strength of the relationship is not trivial: in a previous meta-analysis, Harter et al. (2002) estimate that business units in the top quartile on employee engagement conditions realise between one and four percentage points higher profits and between 25% to 50% lower turnover than those in the bottom quartile.

These findings have direct implications for managerial practice. Frey (2017) argues that managers should create workplaces that are conducive to wellbeing, for example, by supporting workers' independence and creativity or by fostering interpersonal relationships at work. At the same time, work should not be so demanding and burdensome that workers are unable to enjoy their leisure time. Providing more flexible working hours may be a means to strike a better balance between work and life. Income provided should be sufficient to lead a good life with respect to material standards. All of these factors have been found to be conducive to wellbeing at work, although to varying degrees. At the same time, however, Frey (2017) argues that managers should not engage in directly trying to maximising the happiness of stakeholders (which can be subject to manipulation). Rather, they should lay the foundations within organisations for stakeholders to achieve happiness in the way they choose themselves. The importance of autonomy, therefore, applies to the question of how to achieve happiness itself.

The importance of work, and workplace quality, in influencing wellbeing (as well as the impact of wellbeing on key firm-level outcomes) suggests there is a case for active policy intervention. Independent staff wellbeing audits may be one means to raise awareness for wellbeing at work. Awards for work environments that are conducive to wellbeing may also be bestowed on single managers or entire organisations (Gallus and Frey 2016; Frey and Gallus 2017). Systematic measurement of wellbeing within organisations may serve as a diagnostic tool, for example, to uncover wellbeing inequalities within organisations, which have been found to be a powerful driver of behaviour at the community level and may be relevant to organisations just as well. It may also serve as a vehicle to pave the way towards interventions, directed at one or more domains of workplace quality. The evidence presented here and reviewed elsewhere (see Arends et al. (2017) or OECD (2017b), for example) suggests that workplace quality has positive impacts on productivity and performance, in line with recent experimental evidence in various contexts (Bloom et al. 2014; Oswald et al. 2015). Ultimately, however, more experimental evidence from the field is needed in order to be able to make strong causal claims about the relationship between individual elements of workplace quality, wellbeing, and its objective benefits for both individuals and firms.

This chapter can only offer a cautious exploration into the nexus between work and wellbeing. Clearly, there are methodological issues: first, and foremost, the evidence presented here is mostly descriptive, and from descriptive evidence alone we cannot make causal statements. There may be characteristics of respondents that explain both workplace quality and their wellbeing at the same time. We need longitudinal data – repeated observations of the same individuals over time – to get closer to causal effects, and ideally, some sort of randomised experimental intervention or policy change as an exogenous variation in order to reduce concerns about self-selection and omitted variables. We bypassed this issue by presenting, where available, supporting evidence from causal-design studies in the literature.

Our tools are also limited in other dimensions – for example, in that our dataset is limited in terms of the outcome variable we employ. The latest module on Work Orientations of the International Social Survey Programme includes only job satisfaction as a domain-specific, evaluative measure of wellbeing. It is quite possible, however, that some workplace qualities are more likely to have a stronger impact either on eudemonic measures of wellbeing such as purpose or on hedonic measures of workplace mood. We cannot verify this with our data, and importantly, cannot check which construct is relatively more important for which domain of workplace quality. Ultimately, firms and policy-makers will likely be interested in tracking a set of evaluative, experiential, and eudemonic measures to give a more complete picture of wellbeing at work.[11]

---

[11]For example, at the national level, following recommendations by Dolan and Metcalfe (2012), the Office for National Statistics (ONS) in the UK now routinely asks people how they think and feel

Concerning variables on workplace characteristics, most datasets today focus on rather standard items and ignore some of the more modern elements of labour markets related to technology and the future of work such as aspects pertaining to the so-called "gig economy" or (fear of) automation and artificial intelligence. Items sampled in different surveys are also quite heterogeneous. The OECD *Guidelines on Measuring the Quality of the Working Environment*, are therefore, a right step into the direction of establishing a unified framework for measuring workplace quality, focusing on objective job attributes and outcomes measured at the individual level (OECD 2017b). These guidelines divide job characteristics into six broad categories, including the physical and social environment of work, job tasks, organisational characteristics, working-time arrangements, job prospects, and intrinsic job aspects.

Finally, questions remain regarding external validity: while there are few datasets that are as comprehensive as the International Social Survey Programme, it is known from country-score comparisons with other datasets that some of its items have low convergent validity. Note, however, that similar findings on the relationship between workplace quality and job satisfaction have been identified by De Neve and Ward (2017) using the European Social Survey. Future research should be directed towards identifying similar patterns in other datasets. Importantly, this research should be seen as an ongoing endeavour: the composition of the labour supply changes continuously, for example, as more and more millennials with preferences different from previous generations enter the labour force.

In view of these limitations, we end this chapter by looking ahead, and appealing for more experimentation in the workplace: academics and businesses could and should cooperate to test how modifications to work processes and practices affect worker wellbeing, and ultimately, performance. Candidates for such modifications should be guided by theory, and tested in such a way as to be subject to rigorous impact evaluation through randomised controlled experiments. This way, we can avoid issues of omitted characteristics and self-selection, and identify causal effects of work and workplace quality on wellbeing and performance. It will be important to establish and agree on a common set of measures, covering evaluative, experiential, and eudemonic measures of wellbeing, to be used across impact evaluations. And it will be important to record and report the costs of these trials (less the costs of impact-evaluating them). This will allow for benchmarking interventions in terms of cost-effectiveness, and rank them according to which buy more worker wellbeing and performance per dollar invested. Evidence from behavioural science suggests that seemingly small, low-cost (or even costless) changes in daily work routines could produce large gains in wellbeing and performance.

Partly, this vision is already reflected in academic practice. Throughout the world, experimental methods are making their way onto curricula in the social sciences. Knowledge generated by way of field experiments should be shared openly as best practices, and doing so should be incentivised. Governments can also become active

---

about their lives, including four items, on evaluative (life satisfaction), experiential (happiness, anxiousness), and eudemonic (worthwhileness) measures of subjective wellbeing in its surveys.

players themselves by introducing wellbeing interventions within the civil service, which could also help to promote happiness more widely in society. After all, a happy and engaged civil service is an obvious starting point for being able to deliver on policies that aim to put wellbeing at the heart of policy-making.

References

Amabile, T. M. (1996). *Creativity in context: Update to the social psychology of creativity*. London: Hachette UK.

Amabile, T., & Kramer, S. (2011). *The progress principle: Using small wins to ignite joy, engagement, and creativity at work*. Boston: Harvard Business Press.

Amabile, T. M., Conti, R., Coon, H., Lazenby, J., & Herron, M. (1996). Assessing the work environment for creativity. *Academy of Management Journal, 39*(5), 1154–1184.

Angrave, D., & Charlwood, A. (2015). What is the relationship between long working hours, over-employment, under-employment and the subjective well-being of workers? Longitudinal evidence from the UK. *Human Relations, 68*(9), 1491–1515.

Anik, L., Aknin, L. B., Norton, M. I., Dunn, E. W., & Quoidbach, J. (2013). Prosocial bonuses increase employee satisfaction and team performance. *PloS One, 8*(9), e75509.

Arends, I., Prinz, C., & Abma, F. (2017). *Job quality, health and at-work productivity*. OECD Social, Employment and Migration Working Papers.

Ariely, D., Kamenica, E., & Prelec, D. (2008). Man's search for meaning: The case of Legos. *Journal of Economic Behavior & Organization, 67*(3–4), 671–677.

Artz, B. M., Goodall, A. H., & Oswald, A. J. (2017). Boss competence and worker well-being. *ILR Review, 70*(2), 419–450.

Ashraf, N., & Bandiera, O. (2017). Altruistic capital. *American Economic Review, 107*(5), 70–75.

Batson, C. D., & Powell, A. A. (2003). Altruism and prosocial behavior. In I. B. Weiner (Ed.), *Handbook of psychology* (Vol. 5). London: Wiley.

Bloom, N., Liang, J., Roberts, J., & Ying, Z. J. (2014). Does working from home work? Evidence from a Chinese experiment. *The Quarterly Journal of Economics, 130*(1), 165–218.

Böckerman, P., & Ilmakunnas, P. (2012). The job satisfaction-productivity nexus: A study using matched survey and register data. *ILR Review, 65*(2), 244–262.

Böheim, R., & Taylor, M. P. (2004). Actual and preferred working hours. *British Journal of Industrial Relations, 42*(1), 149–166.

Bradler, C., Dur, R., Neckermann, S., & Non, A. (2016). Employee recognition and performance: A field experiment. *Management Science, 62*(11), 3085–3099.

Bryson, A., & MacKerron, G. (2016). Are you happy while you work? *The Economic Journal, 127* (599), 106–125.

Chandola, T., Brunner, E., & Marmot, M. (2006). Chronic stress at work and the metabolic syndrome: prospective study. *BMJ, 332*(7540), 521–525.

Clark, A. (2009) *Work, Jobs and Well-Being across the Millennium*. IZA Discussion Paper, 3940.

De Neve, J. E., & Oswald, A. J. (2012). Estimating the influence of life satisfaction and positive affect on later income using sibling fixed effects. *Proceedings of the National Academy of Sciences, 109*(49), 19953–19958.

De Neve, J. E., & Ward, G. (2017). *Happiness at work*. CEP Discussion Paper no. 1474.

De Neve, J. -E., Diener, E., & Tay, L., & Xuereb, C. (2013). The objective benefits of subjective well-being. In J. Helliwell, R. Layard, & J. Sachs (Eds.), *World happiness report 2013*. New York: UN Sustainable Development Solutions Network.

Dolan, P., & Metcalfe, R. (2012). Measuring subjective wellbeing: Recommendations on measures for use by national governments. *Journal of Social Policy, 41*(2), 409–427.

Dunn, E. W., Aknin, L. B., & Norton, M. I. (2008). Spending money on others promotes happiness. *Science, 319*(5870), 1687–1688.

Easterlin, R. A. (2006). Life cycle happiness and its sources: Intersections of psychology, economics, and demography. *Journal of Economic Psychology, 27*(4), 463–482.

Edmans, A. (2011). Does the stock market fully value intangibles? Employee satisfaction and equity prices. *Journal of Financial Economics, 101*(3), 621–640.

Edmans, A. (2012). The link between job satisfaction and firm value, with implications for corporate social responsibility. *Academy of Management Perspectives, 26*(4), 1–19.

Eisenberg, N., Spinrad, T. L., & Morris, A. S. (2013). Prosocial development. In P. D. Zelazo (Ed.), *Oxford handbook of developmental psychology* (Vol. 2). Oxford: Oxford University Press.

Evren, Ö., & Minardi, S. (2017). Warm-glow giving and freedom to be selfish. *The Economic Journal, 127*(603), 1381–1409.

Fehr, E., & Fischbacher, U. (2003). The nature of human altruism. *Nature, 425*(6960), 785.

Frey, B. S. (2017). *Research on well-being: Determinants, effects, and its relevance for management*. CREMA Working Paper, 2017–11.

Frey, B. S., & Gallus, J. (2017). *Honour versus money. The economics of awards*. Oxford: Oxford University Press.

Gallup News. (2015). *Employees want a lot more from their managers*, Online: http://news.gallup.com/businessjournal/182321/employees-lot-managers.aspx, Accessed 01 Dec 2017.

Gallus, J., & Frey, B. S. (2016). Awards: A strategic management perspective. *Strategic Management Journal, 37*(8), 1699–1714.

Gartenberg, C., Prat, A., & Serafeim, G. (2016). *Corporate purpose and financial performance*. Harvard Business School Working Paper, 17-023.

Gielen, A. C., & van Ours, J. C. (2014). Unhappiness and job finding. *Economica, 81*(323), 544–565.

Gilchrist, D. S., Luca, M., & Malhotra, D. (2016). When 3+ 1> 4: Gift structure and reciprocity in the field. *Management Science, 62*(9), 2639–2650.

Graham, C. (2017). Happiness and economics: insights for policy from the new 'science' of well-being. *Journal of Behavioral Economics for Policy, 1*(1), 69–72.

Grant, A. M. (2008). Employees without a cause: The motivational effects of prosocial impact in public service. *International Public Management Journal, 11*(1), 48–66.

Harrison, D. A., Newman, D. A., & Roth, P. L. (2006). How important are job attitudes? Meta-analytic comparisons of integrative behavioral outcomes and time sequences. *Academy of Management Journal, 49*(2), 305–325.

Harter, J. K., Schmidt, F. L., & Hayes, T. L. (2002). Business-unit-level relationship between employee satisfaction, employee engagement, and business outcomes: a meta-analysis. *Journal of Applied Psychology, 87*(2), 268.

Harter, J. K., Schmidt, F. L., Asplund, J. W., Killham, E. A., & Agrawal, S. (2010). Causal impact of employee work perceptions on the bottom line of organizations. *Perspectives on Psychological Science, 5*(4), 378–389.

Heinz, M., Jeworrek, S., Mertins, V., Schumacher, H., & Sutter, M. (2017). Measuring indirect effects of unfair employer behavior on worker productivity – a field experiment. *CEPR Discussion Paper*, 12429.

Helliwell, J. F., & Huang, H. (2011). Well-being and trust in the workplace. *Journal of Happiness Studies, 12*(5), 747–767.

Helliwell, J. F., & Wang, S. (2015). How was the weekend? How the social context underlies weekend effects in happiness and other emotions for US workers. *PloS one, 10*(12), e0145123.

Helliwell, J. F., Huang, H., & Putnam, R. D. (2009). How's the Job? Are trust and social capital neglected workplace investments? In V. O. Bartkus & J. H. Davis (Eds.), *Social capital: Reaching out, reaching in*. London: Edward Elgar.

Helliwell, J. F., Huang, H., & Wang, S. (2016). *New evidence on trust and wellbeing*. NBER Working Paper, 22450.

Helliwell, J. F., Aknin, L. B. Shiplett, H., Huang, H., & Wang, S. (2017). *Social capital and prosocial behaviour as sources of well-being*. NBER Working Paper, 23761.

Hu, J., & Hirsh, J. B. (2017). Accepting lower salaries for meaningful work. *Frontiers in Psychology, 8,* 1649.

Judge, T. A., Thoresen, C. J., Bono, J. E., & Patton, G. K. (2001). The job satisfaction–job performance relationship: A qualitative and quantitative review. *Psychological Bulletin, 127* (3), 376.

Kahneman, D., Krueger, A. B., Schkade, D. A., Schwarz, N., & Stone, A. A. (2004). A survey method for characterizing daily life experience: The day reconstruction method. *Science, 306* (5702), 1776–1780.

Kelly, E. L., Moen, P., Oakes, J. M., Fan, W., Okechukwu, C., Davis, K. D., et al. (2014). Changing work and work-family conflict: Evidence from the work, family, and health network. *American Sociological Review, 79*(3), 485–516.

King, R. B., Karuntzos, G., Casper, L. M., Moen, P. E., Davis, K. D., Berkman, L. F., Durham, M., & Kossek, E. E. (2012). Work-family balance issues and work-leave policies. In R. J. Gatchel & I. Z. Schultz (Eds.), *Handbook of occupational health and wellness.* New York: Springer.

Knight, C., & Haslam, S. A. (2010). The relative merits of lean, enriched, and empowered offices: An experimental examination of the impact of workspace management strategies on well-being and productivity. *Journal of Experimental Psychology: Applied, 16*(2), 158.

Krause, A. (2013). Don't worry, be happy? Happiness and reemployment. *Journal of Economic Behavior & Organization, 96,* 1–20.

Krekel, C., G. Ward, & De Neve, J.-E. (2019). Employee wellbeing, productivity and firm performance. *CEP Discussion Paper,* 1605.

Lazear, E. P., Shaw, K. L., & Stanton, C. T. (2015). The value of bosses. *Journal of Labor Economics, 33*(4), 823–861.

Leslie, L. M., Manchester, C. F., Park, T. Y., & Mehng, S. A. (2012). Flexible work practices: A source of career premiums or penalties? *Academy of Management Journal, 55*(6), 1407–1428.

Luechinger, S., Meier, S., & Stutzer, A. (2010). Why does unemployment hurt the employed? Evidence from the life satisfaction gap between the public and the private sector. *Journal of Human Resources, 45*(4), 998–1045.

Mas, A., & Pallais, A. (2017). Valuing alternative work arrangements. *American Economic Review, 107*(12), 3722–3759.

Meier, S., & Stutzer, A. (2008). Is volunteering rewarding in itself? *Economica, 75*(297), 39–59.

Moen, P., Kelly, E. L., & Hill, R. (2011). Does enhancing work-time control and flexibility reduce turnover? A naturally occurring experiment. *Social Problems, 58*(1), 69–98.

Moen, P., Kelly, E. L., Fan, W., Lee, S. R., Almeida, D., Kossek, E. E., & Buxton, O. M. (2016). Does a flexibility/support organizational initiative improve high-tech employees' well-being? Evidence from the work, family, and health network. *American Sociological Review, 81*(1), 134–164.

OECD. (2014). *Balancing paid work, unpaid work and leisure,* Online: http://www.oecd.org/gender/data/balancingpaidworkunpaidworkandleisure.htm. Accessed 08 Oct 2017.

OECD. (2017a). *Employment: Time spent in paid and unpaid work, by sex,* Online: http://stats.oecd.org/index.aspx?queryid=54757. Accessed 19 Oct 2017.

OECD. (2017b). *OECD guidelines on measuring the quality of the working environment,* Online: http://www1.oecd.org/publications/oecd-guidelines-on-measuring-the-quality-of-the-working-environment-9789264278240-en.htm. Accessed 24 Nov 2017.

Ogbonnaya, C., & Daniels, K. (2017). *Good work, wellbeing and changes in performance outcomes: Illustrating the effects of good people management practices with an analysis of the National Health Service.* London: What Works Wellbeing.

Oswald, A. J., Proto, E., & Sgroi, D. (2015). Happiness and productivity. *Journal of Labor Economics, 33*(4), 789–822.

PwC Research. (2013). *Rising sick bill is costing UK business £29bn a year,* Online: http://pwc.blogs.com/press_room/2013/07/rising-sick-bill-is-costing-uk-business-29bn-a-year-pwcresearch.html. Accessed on 17 Apr 2019.

Social Research and Demonstration Corporation. (2014a). *UPSKILL: A credible test of workplace literacy and essential skills training – Summary report,* Online: http://www.srdc.org/media/199770/upskill-final-results-es-en.pdf. Accessed 29 Nov 2017.

Social Research and Demonstration Corporation. (2014b). *UPSKILL: A credible test of workplace literacy and essential skills training – Technical report*, Online: http://www.srdc.org/media/199774/upskill-technical-report-en.pdf. Accessed 29 Nov 2017.

Stevenson, B., & Wolfers, J. (2009). The paradox of declining female happiness. *American Economic Journal: Economic Policy, 1*(2), 190–225.

Tay, L., & Harter, J. K. (2013). Economic and labor market forces matter for worker well-being. *Applied Psychology: Health and Well-Being, 5*(2), 193–208.

The Sainsbury Centre for Mental Health. (2007). Mental health at work: Developing the business case. *Policy Paper*, 8.

Tenney, E. R., Poole, J. M., & Diener, E. (2016). Does positivity enhance work performance?: Why, when, and what we don't know. *Research in Organizational Behavior, 36*, 27–46.

Tims, M., Bakker, A. B., & Derks, D. (2013). The impact of job crafting on job demands, job resources, and well-being. *Journal of Occupational Health Psychology, 18*(2), 230.

Van Praag, B. M., Frijters, P., & Ferrer-i-Carbonell, A. (2003). The anatomy of subjective well-being. *Journal of Economic Behavior & Organization, 51*(1), 29–49.

What Works Centre for Wellbeing. (2017a). *Briefing: Job quality and wellbeing*, Online: https://www.whatworkswellbeing.org/product/job-quality-and-wellbeing/. Accessed 27 Nov 2017.

What Works Centre for Wellbeing. (2017b). *Briefing: Learning at work and wellbeing*, Online: https://www.whatworkswellbeing.org/product/learning-at-work/. Accessed 27 Nov 2017.

What Works Centre for Wellbeing. (2017c). *Briefing: Team working*, Online: https://www.whatworkswellbeing.org/product/team-working/. Accessed 27 Nov 2017.

White, M., & Bryson, A. (2013). Positive employee relations: How much human resource management do you need? *Human Relations, 66*(3), 385–406.

Whitman, D. S., Van Rooy, D. L., & Viswesvaran, C. (2010). Satisfaction, citizenship behaviors, and performance in work units: A meta-analysis of collective construct relations. *Personnel Psychology, 63*(1), 41–81.

Willis Towers Watson. (2014). *Balancing employer and employee priorities: Insights From the 2014 global workforce and global talent management and rewards studies*, Online: https://www.towerswatson.com/en/Insights/IC-Types/Survey-Research-Results/2014/07/balancing-employer-and-employee-priorities. Accessed 01 Dec 2017.

Wooden, M., Warren, D., & Drago, R. (2009). Working time mismatch and subjective well-being. *British Journal of Industrial Relations, 47*(1), 147–179.

Woolley, K., & Fishbach, A. (2015). The experience matters more than you think: weighting intrinsic incentives more inside than outside of an activity. *Journal of Personality and Social Psychology, 109*(6), 968–982.

Wrzesniewski, A., & Dutton, J. E. (2001). Crafting a job: Revisioning employees as active crafters of their work. *Academy of Management Review, 26*(2), 179–201.

Wunder, C., & Heineck, G. (2013). Working time preferences, hours mismatch and well-being of couples: Are there spillovers? *Labour Economics, 24*, 244–252.

Yeager, D. S., Henderson, M. D., D'Mello, S., Paunesku, D., Walton, G. M., Spitzer, B. J., & Duckworth, A. L. (2014). Boring but important: A self-transcendent purpose for learning fosters academic self-regulation. *Journal of Personality and Social Psychology, 107*(4), 559–580.

Yuan, L. (2015). the happier one is, the more creative one becomes: An investigation on inspirational positive emotions from both subjective well-being and satisfaction at work. *Psychology, 6*, 201–209.

Part V
Happiness in Development

Chapter 12
Unhappiness as an Engine of Economic Growth

Stefano Bartolini

Abstract The citizens of the US, China and India have experienced a significant decline in happiness, social capital and leisure in the past few decades, as well as an epidemic of social comparisons. This deep and long-standing social crisis is puzzling when we consider the sustained economic growth of these countries. Is there a relationship between social crisis and growth? The defensive growth approach argues that they may feed each other. The erosion of environmental and social assets caused by increased market activity limits their accessibility, inducing consumers and producers to search for substitutes in the marketplace. Defensive growth is a process whereby market goods and services progressively replace declining non-market sources of well-being and compensate for the negative externalities generated by the increased marketization of society. This process is a self-reinforcing loop: the externalities generated by the expansion of market activities induce households and producers to compensate by buying more goods, further expanding market activity. Because the flip side of increasing economic affluence is rising social and environmental poverty, the impact of defensive growth on happiness is disappointing. I conclude that declining social capital has boosted GDP, working hours and the decline in happiness in the US, China and India.

12.1 Introduction

The US, China and India account for almost 40% of the world population. In the last few decades, these countries have been celebrated examples of economic growth among developed and developing nations. American growth rates of GDP are envied by most industrial countries, while China and India are experiencing the economic miracle that every developing country aspires to. However, economic success coexists with social failure in these countries. Disquieting trends shared by the US, China and India show a mounting social crisis paralleling the dynamism of their

S. Bartolini (✉)
University of Siena, Siena, Italy
e-mail: stefano.bartolini@unisi.it

© Springer Nature Switzerland AG 2019
M. Rojas (ed.), *The Economics of Happiness*,
https://doi.org/10.1007/978-3-030-15835-4_12

economies in the last few decades. Firstly, these countries share a decline in subjective (and objective) measures of well-being. Secondly, working hours have increased to the point of making overwork a routine experience for a substantial share of the working population. Thirdly, social capital has shown a significant decline. Finally, materialism is on the rise, epitomized by an epidemic of social comparisons.

These trends shape a pattern of social change, meaning that they are related and require a joint explanation. Indeed, cross-country comparisons show that economies that grow relatively quickly are characterized by a deeper social crisis than slower-growing economies. Why do downward trends of well-being and social capital tend to accompany upward trends of social comparisons, working hours and GDP? Why does rising social distress coexist with fast economic growth?

The concurrence of some of these trends is difficult to explain in the light of the existing literature. The long-term coexistence of fast growth and declining social capital challenges the widely-held view that social capital fosters growth, in particular by reducing transaction costs and improving the performance of local and national governments (Knack and Keefer 1997; Helliwell and Putnam 1995; Guiso et al. 2006; Algan and Cahuc 2013; Alesina and Giuliano 2015).

More research has concerned the income-happiness relationship. Adaptation and social comparisons have been proposed as explanations for the Easterlin paradox, i.e. the lack of a long-term relationship between the trends of average GDP and happiness (Easterlin 1974). Adaptation theory posits that positive or negative events can only alter a person's well-being in the short term (Lykken and Tellegen 1996; Lucas et al. 2003; Headey 2008). Evidence of satiation of the impact of income on happiness has been explained as an effect of adaptation, beyond the level of income at which basic needs are largely met (Jebb et al. 2018). Social comparisons are a powerful engine of dissatisfaction (Clark and Senik 2010; Luttmer 2005). In an economy where income comparisons are what matters for well-being, GDP does not measure the relevant output. Economic growth is a statistical illusion, because winners and losers are the output that actually affects well-being. The positional race is a zero sum game, because one person's gain implies another's loss.

Adaptation and social comparisons are solidly grounded in psychological research and are supported by robust empirical evidence. However, they do not explain why the most economically successful countries of the last few decades are precisely the ones where happiness has declined most sharply. Moreover, the tendency to view adaptation and social comparisons as intrinsic human characteristics, with roots in the biology of the brain (Schmitt et al. 2016; Hopper et al. 2014), weakens their potential of explaining the differences in happiness across space and time. In many countries, subjective well-being is trended and trends differ across countries. Social comparisons also show trends, such as their upsurge in the US, China and India. Any explanation of these spatial and temporal changes cannot be centred in human nature.

Happiness trends are more accurately predictable if also social capital is considered, in addition to adaptation and social comparisons. Social capital is a powerful predictor of individual happiness and its trends largely predict the trends of average happiness across and within countries (Helliwell and Aknin 2018; Bartolini and Sarracino 2014).

The increasing trend of working hours in the US and the decreasing trend in Europe have been the subject of heated debate (Schor 1992; Aguiar and Hurst 2007) Most studies have focused on increased taxation of wages and salaries in Europe as an explanation for this divergence (Ohanian et al. 2008). Moreover, some evidence from micro data also shows that overwork is positively associated with social comparisons (Neumark and Postlewaite 1998; Bowles and Park 2005) and negatively associated with subjective well-being (Angrave and Charlwood 2015). This is consistent with the trends observed in American, Chinese and Indian societies.

Little is known about the drivers of materialistic values, beyond the roles of the media and advertising. Materialism and social comparisons are promoted by advertising and their spread has presumably been supported by the soaring media and advertising pressure of recent decades (Schor 2004; Nairn et al. 2007).

In conclusion, the literature on the trends discussed here is fragmented and a joint explanation is still in its early stages. In this chapter, I argue that these trends are all intertwined aspects of *defensive growth*: an undesirable type of economic growth generated by the ways in which individuals defend themselves from declining happiness.

The chapter is organized as follows. Section 12.2 reviews the evidence on long-term trends of happiness, social capital, working hours, social comparisons and materialism in the US, China and India. Section 12.3 presents the defensive growth approach. Section 12.4 provides empirical evidence supporting the defensive growth viewpoint. Section 12.5 focuses on the role played by the crisis of several forms of social capital in boosting sectors of the economy that have driven American growth in the last few decades. Section 12.6 discusses policy recommendations aimed at preventing defensive growth. Section 12.7 concludes.

12.2   Disquieting Trends

12.2.1   Declining Subjective Well-being

The US, China and India are paradigmatic examples of the Easterlin paradox, illustrated in Fig. 12.1 in the case of India. The figure shows that average life satisfaction per income decile shifted downward in 2014 compared to 1990. In both years, income bought some happiness, but despite much higher incomes in 2014, each income decile was less happy than in 1990. The richest decile in 2014 was only slightly more satisfied than the poorest in 1990. Average life satisfaction fell by 25% (Bartolini and Sarracino 2019).

In China, average life satisfaction dropped by 7% between 1990 and 2007, the golden years of the economic boom. In the US, subjective well-being has declined significantly since the 1970s according to GSS data (Blanchflower and Oswald 2004) and Virginia Slim Polls (Stevenson and Wolfers 2008). Shorter time series

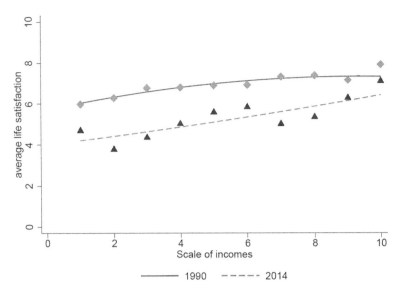

Fig. 12.1 India: relationship between income deciles and life satisfaction in 1990 and 2014. World Values Survey data. (Source: Bartolini and Sarracino (2019))

(since 2006), retrieved by Gallup World Polls, also indicate declining happiness (Sachs 2017).

The declines in subjective well-being of China and India are even more astounding than that of America. Between 1990 and 2005 in China GDP per capita increased fourfold, more than half a billion people in China were lifted out of absolute poverty and life expectancy increased from 67 to 73.5 years (World Bank 2014). Indian figures tell a similar story, just slightly less thriving. China and India are definitely two countries where growth should have increased well-being.

Declining happiness is not a general phenomenon. In other economically successful areas, such as western Europe (which grew less than the US), happiness increased slightly in the last few decades (Stevenson and Wolfers 2008).

12.2.2 Declining Objective Well-being

Data on the spread of psychiatric drugs, mental illness, suicides and addictions provides objective information on a population's (un)happiness. In the US, the picture emerging from objective data is even worse than that depicted by subjective well-being time series. The use of psychiatric drugs has risen so much that the US has become a "sedated society" (Davies 2017). Prescriptions for antidepressants, stimulants, antipsychotics, mood stabilizers and anxiolytics have soared, bringing the share of the psychiatrically medicated adult population to 20%.

This flood of psychiatric drugs in the US is a result of an upsurge in mental illnesses. Twenge et al. (2010) assessed their evolution over many decades using a survey, administered to high school and college students since the 1930s, including many questions regarding symptoms of depression and anxiety. The authors found that depression and anxiety rose significantly in the period 1938–2007 in the US. Another survey showed that between 1982 and 2013, symptoms of depression and anxiety rose significantly in a nationally representative sample of US 12th graders (Twenge 2015). Using measures of anxiety dating back to (and unchanged since) the 1950s, Twenge (2000) showed that normal American kids and teens in the 1980s scored as high on the anxiety scale as children in psychiatric care in the 1950s.

As for addictions, American society has been struck by an epidemic, in particular abuse of opioids. Of the 20.5 million Americans aged 12 or older who had a substance use disorder in 2015, the substance was prescription opioids in 2 million cases and heroin in 591,000 cases (ASAM 2016). Deaths from overdose tripled since the start of the millennium, exceeding 60,000 in 2016, more than the total number of soldiers killed in the war in Vietnam (Huang 2018). Arguably, such a mass addiction has its roots in mass unhappiness.

In the period 1999–2014, the age-adjusted suicide rate in the United States increased by 24%. Suicide rates increased for males and females and for all ages from 10 to 74 years. A total of 42,773 people died from suicide in 2014, compared to 29,199 in 1999. The rise was particularly steep for women. The suicide rate tripled among girls 10–14 years of age (Curtin et al. 2016).

While long time series on objective well-being are abundant for the US, such data is scarce and fragmentary for China and India. However, available evidence suggests that objective indicators are on the rise in both countries, with the possible exception of a recent downturn of suicides in China. There are many reports of increasing drug and internet addiction.[1] Eli Lilly, the leading provider of mental health drugs in China, increased its sales of antidepressant and antipsychotic drugs more than tenfold in the 2000s (Cyranoski 2010). In India, sales of psychiatric drugs are on the rise as well (Poduri 2016). India is also seeing a rising trend in addiction to illegal drugs. The latest available data, from 2004, estimates that 10.7 million Indians are illegal drug users (Singh and Gupta 2017).

About 17.5% of Chinese have some form of mental illness, one of the highest rates in the world (Phillips et al. 2009). According to data from the World Health Organization, 7.5% of Indians suffer from depression or anxiety disorders (Malathy 2017).

In 1967, the suicide rate in India was 7.8 ($\times$ 100,000) but showed a steady increase to about 11.0 in 2013 (Ponnudurai 2015). Estimates from the 1990s showed that China, with 21.5% of the world's population, accounted for a staggering 43.6%

---

[1]https://www.bbc.com/news/world-asia-india-38824478, (last accessed Jun 15 2018)

http://www.scmp.com/news/china/policies-politics/article/2082474/chinas-synthetic-drug-problem-growing-government-says, (last accessed Jun 15 2018)

of the 786,000 suicides worldwide (Murray et al. 1996). Suicides reached their climax in the 1990s and 2000s and then declined (Sha et al. 2018). However, suicide is a politically sensitive issue in China and doubts have been raised on the reliability of recent Chinese statistics (Koetse 2014).

In conclusion, both subjective and objective data concur to paint a gloomy picture of the trend of happiness in the US, China and India in recent decades.

12.2.3 Declining Social Capital

The concept of social capital refers to the quality and quantity of an individual's connections to other individuals and the community (Putnam 2000). The decline of American social capital in recent decades was made a popular argument by Putnam (2000) and was confirmed in the ensuing debate (Paxton 1999; Robinson and Jackson 2001; Costa and Kahn 2003; Bartolini et al. 2013).

Loneliness has become a mass problem in the US. In 2004, a quarter of Americans reported that they had no one with whom they could discuss important matters. This share was 10% in 1985. If family members are not counted, this share amounted to more than half of Americans in 2004 (36% in 1985). The number of persons the average American shares confidences with dropped by one third (from nearly 3 persons in 1985 to about 2 in 2004) (McPherson et al. 2006). One out of three Americans are lonely, up from one out of five in 1980 (Knowledge Networks 2010). For as many as 15–30% of the general population, loneliness has become a chronic state (Heinrich and Gullone 2006; Theeke 2009). According to data from the Census Bureau, "unrelated individuals" (those who do not live in a family group) increased from 6% in 1960 to 16% in 2000 (Shaw 2001).

From the early 1970s to the 2010s the share of the working age population responding that most people can be trusted fell from 50% to nearly 30% (Gould and Hijzen 2016). Solidarity, honesty and associational activity have sharply declined since the 1970s (Putnam 2000; Bartolini et al. 2013). Families have become increasingly unstable. Americans marry less, divorce more, live together less and separate more frequently than in the 1970s (Bartolini et al. 2013).

China has paralleled the American decline in relationships. Trust fell by 11% in the period 1990–2007. The China Daily lamented that trust has become "a scarce commodity".[2] Associational activity dropped (-20%), as did civic behavior and the married population (-16%) (Bartolini and Sarracino 2015). Loneliness spread: between 2000 and 2010 the number of one-person households doubled in China (Zang and Zhao 2017). India shows similar patterns of increasing relational poverty.

However, declining social capital is not an ineluctable consequence of economic growth. There are counter-examples in both the developing and developed worlds.

---

[2]https://www.economist.com/special-report/2016/07/07/a-nation-of-individuals

Social capital has grown in western continental Europe since the 1980s (Sarracino 2012) and in Brazil since the 1990s.[3] Interestingly, Brazil and Europe share trends of income inequality very different from the upsurges experienced in India, China and the US. In Europe, income inequality has increased much more slowly than in the US, while in Brazil it has decreased.[4] An explanation can be found in the literature emphasizing the negative impact of high inequality on social capital (Alesina and La Ferrara 2006; Bjørnskov 2006; Costa and Kahn 2003; Knack and Keefer 1997).

12.2.4   Soaring Materialism and Social Comparisons

A cross-country survey conducted by Ipsos in 2013 documented that nearly 70% of Chinese people and 50% of Americans "feel under a lot of pressure to be successful and make money". China ranks top among developing countries in the international comparison of materialism, and the US ranks top among developed nations. This record is the result of a decades-long rise in materialism in both countries (Luo 2015; Twenge and Kasser 2013).

The upsurge in social comparisons that Chinese people have shared with Americans in the past few decades has mirrored soaring materialism (Brockmann et al. 2009). A high concern for social comparisons is a definitional component of materialism. More materialistic individuals are those who give a high priority to life goals such as money, image and status (Kasser 2002). The collapse of financial satisfaction for the majority of Chinese and Indian people in the 1990s and 2000s – the roaring years of the economic miracle – is only apparently paradoxical (Bartolini and Sarracino 2015, 2019). Financial satisfaction, in fact, is affected by one's relative rather than absolute position (D'Ambrosio and Frick 2007).

The spread of materialism is bad news because more materialistic individuals are less happy and have poorer social capital than people with less materialistic values (Kasser 2016). Interestingly, rising materialism is not a general phenomenon. Bartolini and Sarracino (2017) compared the trends of materialism in western Europe and the US, finding that materialism increased in the USA and decreased in western Europe in the period 1980–2005.

---

[3]In Brazil trust increased by 50% in the period 1991–2006 (own calculation on World Values Survey data). Life satisfaction increased as well.

[4]According to World Bank data, in Brazil the Gini index of income was 60.5 in 1990 and 55.6 in 2006. This is a substantial decline, although levels of inequality remain very high. https://data.worldbank.org/indicator/SI.POV.GINI?locations=BR

Table 12.1 Average hours
worked per year by workers
15–64 years of age

	1970	1980[a]	1990	2004
France	1295	1156	979	905
Germany[b]	–	1127	1004	934
Italy	1122	996	871	910
United States	1169	1213	1344	1299

Source: OECD, Employment Outlook Database and OECD
Employment Outlook, 2005
[a]The 1980 data refers to 1979
[b]The data for Germany refers to West Germany

12.2.5   Overwork

Working hours have increased in the US in recent decades, whereas they have
diminished in Western Europe. In the mid-1970s, German and French citizens
worked an average of 5–10% longer hours than American citizens. Thirty years
later, their working hours were only 70–75% those worked by the average American
(Prescott 2004, see also Alesina et al. 2005 and Stiglitz 2008). Table 12.1 shows the
evolution of working hours in France, Germany, Italy and the US in the period
1970–2004.

The current situation is that Americans work longer hours and have shorter
vacations than Europeans. The initial situation, when Americans worked less than
Europeans, was reversed as a result of opposite trends in hours worked (Burda et al.
2007).

The difference in the working hour trends between Europe and the US is
mitigated by the different trends for housework, i.e. unpaid work in the home,
which dropped more sharply in the US. Indeed, Europeans self-produced part of
the services that Americans had to buy (Davis and Henrekson 2004; Olovsson 2009;
Freeman and Schettkat 2005; Burda et al. 2007; Aguiar and Hurst 2007; Rogerson
2008). However, the stereotype that European mothers cook more at home than their
American counterparts – who eat out at restaurants more frequently – is not sufficient
to belie the evidence that Europeans do indeed have more free time (Bonatti 2008).

Moreover, one should not attach "much weight to those studies emphasizing that
because the number of hours of homework has been reduced, true leisure has
increased" in the US (Stiglitz 2008, p. 46). The reason is that housework is often
not a cost. "For a farmer to toil in his field is work but for a middle-class American or
European to toil in his garden is pleasure. Cooking may be toil but for many
individuals (...) on occasion cooking is a pleasure" (Stiglitz 2008, p. 46). Lastly,
"unpaid domestic work is especially important for the quality of life of families with
young children", since "most of the time spent caring for children is usually
delivered while performing other tasks" (Stiglitz et al. 2009, p. 175).

For China and India, reliable long time series on working hours are lacking.
However, reports of increasingly long work hours and extensive over-work are no
surprise since all industrial revolutions are based on an upsurge in the labour supply
(Lewis 1954; Todaro 1969). Industry intensively employs labour that was previously

underemployed in agriculture. Rates of activity and dependent employment often doubled in the space of 10 years during industrial revolutions, as in the case of the Asian Tigers in the 1990s (Krugman 1995).

12.3 Defensive Growth

Rising social comparisons combined with a poverty of relationships, free time and well-being among American, Chinese and Indian people point to a deep and long-standing social crisis. This evidence is puzzling when compared with the dynamic economies of these nations: is there a relationship between economic growth and social crisis? The defensive growth approach provides an affirmative answer. Defensive growth models not only emphasize the importance of the negative externalities that the growth process – and the related expansion of market activity – brings about, but also the important role played by negative externalities in fuelling GDP growth (Bartolini and Bonatti 2003, 2008a; Antoci and Bartolini 2004). In fact, the erosion of environmental and social assets caused by increased market activity limits their accessibility, inducing consumers and producers to search for substitutes in the marketplace. This creates a self-reinforcing loop: the externalities generated by the expansion of market activities induce households and producers to defend their well-being by buying more goods and services, further expanding market activity. During this growth process, market goods and services progressively replace declining non-market sources of well-being, as a consequence of people's attempts to compensate for the negative externalities generated by the increased marketization of society. Under these conditions, GDP growth "goes too far", in the sense that its harmful effects on well-being outweigh its benefits.

Defensive growth is based on the idea that money is a defense – real or illusory – against poverty of social capital. If an old person is alone and ill, the solution is a care-giver. If our children are alone, the answer is a baby-sitter. If we have few friends and the city has become dangerous, we can spend our evenings at home with home entertainment. If our cities are too hectic, we can lift our spirits with a holiday in some tropical paradise. If we quarrel with someone, we can hire a lawyer to defend us. If we do not trust someone, we can pay to have him monitored. If we are afraid, we can protect our possessions with security systems. While in these examples money offers real protection from poor relationships, advertising spreads illusions of protection. Its message is that if we lack fulfilling relationships, we can be reassured by consumption, status or success. Advertising reminds us that if we feel like losers, we can seek identity and compensation through consumption: "I buy, therefore I am". In advertising goods requite our love, although in our daily life they are lifeless.

Private goods promise to protect us from the decay of resources that were once common and free: a liveable city relatively free of crime, trust and communication among neighbours, a social fabric of neighbourhoods and companionship for children and the elderly. The resulting expenditures drive us to increased workload and production, generating economic growth. When social ties break down, the economy of solitude and fear becomes a driving force of the economy. The same holds for the quality of our environment. Vacations in unspoiled places offer us the clean air, seas and rivers that we can no longer find in our unliveable cities.[5]

These are all examples of defensive expenditures (Hirsch 1976). They occur when private goods substitute declining common goods. In order to finance these defensive expenditures individuals must work more. The increasing expenditure needed to defend oneself against the decline in relational and environmental conditions stimulates a passionate hunt for money even in affluent societies. By amplifying spending needs, the decay of commons stimulates growth, which results in increasing negative externalities. Such growth is fuelled by its own destructive power. This self-feeding loop results in growing economic affluence and increasing environmental and social poverty. Degradation of commons becomes the flip side of private prosperity, giving rise to the contrasts typical of the "affluent society" (Galbraith 1958).

Various public policies can be applied to protect social and environmental assets. Such policies have been adopted to very different degrees in the history and geography of capitalism. For instance, in the decades considered in this study, socially and environmentally protective policies were more often applied in Europe than in the US. Where these policies are lacking or ineffective, defensive growth takes off.

When growth is defensive, the negative impact on well-being of the declining quality of the environment and relationships, as well as high workload, offsets the positive effects of higher income. In this context, haste and unhappiness are two sides of the same coin. People work more when money becomes the private solution to the decay of what they have in common. This decay explains why greater economic prosperity may not lead to greater well-being.

The traditional view of growth only tells a partial story, namely that luxury goods for one generation become standard goods for the next generation and basic needs for the following one. The history of economic growth is obviously full of such examples (appliances, cars, trips, medicine, cultural consumption, etc.). The dark side of this story is that goods that were free for one generation become scarce and costly for the next generation and luxury goods for the generation after that. Silence, clean air, a dip in a clean ocean or lake, pleasant walks in flowering meadows or lush forests, crime-free neighbourhoods, low-cost meeting places or simply human curiosity are examples of goods that previous generations had for free but that are now scarce.

---

[5]Other environmental examples include double glazing to defend against noise, mineral water as a substitute for tap water and private swimming pools as a response to the deterioration of local beaches. Expenditure for pollution abatement/prevention, treatment of illnesses caused by pollution, soil restoration, global warming mitigation (such as investment in energy saving, green transport and conservative agriculture) and emergencies/reconstruction after extreme climate events is a direct response to environmental degradation.

12.3.1 Defensive Growth in Developing Countries

The rapid transitions from an agricultural to an industrial economy, called industrial revolutions, probably offer the clearest examples of the link between economic growth and social and environmental disruption. Although industrial revolutions have taken many forms, they all share certain features of the Industrial Revolution in Britain: erosion of traditional institutions and communities, environmental devastation, reduced access to land for farmers, rapid urbanization, massively increased labour market participation, increasing income inequality, replacement of traditional values with materialistic values.

A long-standing tradition in development studies has identified the decay of traditional institutions and values, environmental disruption and reduced access to land as 'push' factors. Push factors force farmers to feed the ranks of the cheap urban labour force indispensable for industrial take-off. According to Polanyi (1968), economic development is the effect and cause of the erosion of rural communities, cultures and environmental resources. Their decline releases the labour supply that fuel industrialization. Rapid industrialization is thus the cause and consequence of shifts in patterns of production and consumption, from commons-based to market-based.

Although the Chinese industrial revolution was the first transition to capitalism managed by a communist party, it is no exception. Reduced water flow and pollution in the Yellow River basin, heartland of Chinese agriculture, are a contemporary version of the environmental wreckage that accompanied Britain's Industrial Revolution. The expropriation of agricultural land for industrial or residential purposes, provoking thousands of riots every year in China, boosted urban migration much in the same way as enclosures had done in Britain.

China and India replicate – on Chinese and Indian scales – features typical of all industrial revolutions, where growth nourishes and is nourished by massive destruction of environmental and social assets and by cultural change. Current reports of a sharp decline in social capital and an upsurge in social comparisons paralleling the Chinese and Indian take-off seem to mirror similar phenomena in the industrial revolutions of the past, with urbanization linked to the erosion of social capital in rural areas. Urban immigrants (between 100 and 200 million in China depending on the estimates) lose the safety nets offered by community relationships. These phenomena can be described in terms of defensive growth: negative externalities affecting social and environmental resources drive people to increasingly rely on the labour and goods market, thus feeding economic development.

Evidence of pervasive negative externalities connected to current industrial take-offs echoes the arguments of nineteenth century critics of the Industrial Revolution, who generally saw the new social order as devastating for social ties. Market relations were considered responsible for the decline of traditional institutions and of family and social ties. Romantic, conservative and socialist critics of the Industrial Revolution saw the world shaped by the new economic order as destructive of social bonds. The metaphors they used to describe the effects on traditional societies ranged from "dissolution", "erosion", "corrosion" and "contamination" to "penetration" and "intrusion" by the "juggernaut market" (Hirschman 1982). Sociology arose as a result of concerns about the potential decline of communities due to industrialization and the advent of modernity.

Loss of life satisfaction has been particularly sharp for the Chinese and Indian working classes, due to a relatively strong decline in social capital and upsurge of social comparisons (Bartolini and Sarracino 2015, 2019). In these countries the rise in wages did not compensate for the tremendous social and cultural shock experienced by the working class. These findings seem to replicate previous observations on working class conditions during industrial revolutions, including those by Marx and Polanyi. One does not need to agree that "proletarians have nothing to lose but their chains" to suspect that the transition to a market industrial economy may not be an easy walk for many members of the working class.

12.3.2 The Key Equations of Defensive Growth

Defensive growth is obtained by inserting some key equations in traditional exogenous or endogenous growth models. The first equation is the period (or instantaneous) utility function of the representative household, which is increasing in its three arguments:

$$U_t = U(C_{1t}, L_t, X_t), \ U_C > 0, \ U_{CC} < 0, \ U_L > 0, \ U_{LL}, \ U_X > 0, \ U_{XX<0}, \ L_H \leq H \tag{12.1}$$

where C_{1t} is a consumer good that can be purchased on the market, L_t is leisure time and X_t is a service that is provided by combining a good can be purchased on the market, C_{2t}, and a renewable resource, R_t, to which everybody has free access (a "common").

The second equation captures the modality through which C_{2t} can substitute for R_t in the provision of X_t:

$$X_t = S(C_{2t}, \ R_t), \qquad S_{C2} > 0, \quad S_R > 0 \tag{12.2}$$

The third equation gives us Y_t, that is the amount of market output in period t, as a function of leisure time and—possibly—of a bunch of additional variables (such as productive assets):

$$Y_t = F(H - L_t, \ldots) \ F_L < 0 \tag{12.3}$$

where H is the total time endowment of the representative household.

The fourth equation governs the motion of the renewable resource:

$$R_{t+1} = G(Y_t, R_t), \ G_Y < 0, \ G_R > 0 \tag{12.4}$$

Notice that the amount of market production affects negatively the future endowment of R_t.

Finally, we have the economy's resource constraint:

$$C_{1t} + C_{2t} \leq Y_t \qquad\qquad (12.5)$$

Equations (12.1), (12.2) and (12.4) characterize defensive growth and contain the three critical hypotheses on which such models are based: (i) individuals well-being is affected by a common resource; (ii) such common can be substituted by a market good; (iii) the common resource is affected by negative externalities increasing in the level of market output. As for Eqs. (12.3) and (12.5), they can assume one of the standard forms employed in endogenous or exogenous growth models.

Equations (12.1), (12.2) and (12.4), if inserted in traditional growth models generate defensive growth, meaning that aggregate output grows more than in the corresponding traditional growth model.[6] In exogenous growth models, where the steady-state level of economic activity is flat, defensive growth generates a higher steady-state aggregate output. In endogenous growth models, where growth is perpetual in the steady-state, defensive growth generates a higher steady-state rate of output growth.

The engine of defensive growth are negative externalities. The greater they are, the more output grows. Individuals protect their well-being from negative externalities by increasing defensive consumption (C_{2t}). The ensuing growth in production feeds back into negative externalities, leading to a self-fuelling mechanism in which negative externalities generate growth and growth generates negative externalities.

This growth however, is undesirable. Growth goes too far in the sense that, as a result of the internalization of the negative externalities, a benevolent planner would lead the economy towards a steady-state characterized by a lower level of output (or of growth) and a higher well-being of the representative household.

Defensive growth differs from the endogenous growth paradigm, with its insistence that individuals unintentionally generate increasing returns through positive externalities. This gives rise to a self-reinforcing mechanism whereby growth causes externalities and externalities cause growth. Defensive growth offers a complementary explanation, this too based on the unintended effects of individual actions, but with the difference that in our case the externalities under consideration are negative.

12.4   Evidence of Defensive Growth

12.4.1   Envying Alone

In this section I summarize an empirical test on micro data of the hypothesis, implied by Eq. (12.2), that private consumption and the common resource are substitutes in

---

[6]More precisely, to obtain defensive growth Eqs. (12.1) and (12.2) should substitute for the utility function used in standard growth models, while Eq. (12.4) should be added to standard models.

Table 12.2 Moderation effects: absolute and relative income matter less for the life satisfaction of people with rich social lives, German data from SOEP 1985–2011

	SC index=1	SC index=2	SC index=3	SC index=4
Absolute income	−19%	−28%	−42%	−48%
Reference income	−38%	−60%	−78%	−105%

the utility functions (Bartolini et al. 2019). This hypothesis is critical for defensive growth, which is a process of substitution of commons with private consumption. Defensive growth crucially hinges on the assumption that the search for money is stimulated by the decline of common resources to a substantial extent. In this test, the common is measured by social capital and utility by subjective well-being, while consumption is proxied by income.

The hypothesis of substitution between income and social capital implies that income should be more important for the well-being of individuals with poor social capital, than for individuals with a rich social life. Conversely, if social capital and income were complements, the well-being of individuals with more social capital should be more dependent on their income, compared to individuals with less social capital.

Bartolini et al. (2019) test these predictions by focusing on the way social capital interacts with both absolute and relative income in generating subjective well-being. Table 12.2 shows an example of their findings. It documents the results of a life satisfaction regression with interaction terms between an index of social connections, and reference and absolute income. Reference income is the average income of the reference group, defined by gender, age and geographical area. Social capital has a strong moderating effect on the income-life satisfaction relationship. The correlation between both income variables and life satisfaction is weaker for people with thriving social lives than for others. On average, the life satisfaction of a socially isolated person (index = 0) depends twice as much on his absolute income than the life satisfaction of a socially active person (index = 4). With regard to reference income, socially engaged individuals are not concerned about it: their well-being is unrelated to whether the Joneses are more or less well-off.

> Moderation effects indicate by how much each level of the social capital index reduces the income coefficients of the life satisfaction regression. The reference category is social capital index = 0. The social capital index reaches a maximum score of four if a person is involved in the following four activities at least once a month: social gatherings, helping friends, volunteering, participation in local politics. The index has a minimum score of zero for persons who are involved in such activities less often than once per month. Method: OLS regression with individual fixed effects and interaction effects. Effects are significant at 10% or more. Source: Bartolini et al. 2019

We also examined whether the importance of money changes when people's social capital changes throughout their lives. We found that absolute income becomes 13% less important for people's life satisfaction if their social activities increased over the previous year, while reference income loses one third of its importance. In other words, past increases in social capital reduce the importance of absolute and reference income for life satisfaction. This lagged impact suggests that relational poverty is a cause of money concerns.

We checked the robustness of these findings using more than 350,000 interviews from the European Union Statistics on Income and Living Conditions (EU-SILC) and the European Social Survey (ESS). We used various measures of subjective well-being, absolute and reference income, social capital (including trust and socializing with friends), and we obtained the same result: the dependence of people's wellbeing on money is strongly promoted by relational poverty. Roughly 50% of absolute income has a defensive nature. Indeed, the impact of personal income on well-being halves when individuals are socially engaged, compared to socially isolated individuals. This moderating effect of social capital is stronger for social comparisons, which are entirely defensive. In fact, their importance completely cancels out for individuals with a rich social life. Isolated people are the most concerned about how much more or less they earn than other people.

12.4.2   Socially Rich Countries have Low Well-being Inequality

To what extent are the rich happier than the poor? In other words, to what extent does the distribution of income affect the distribution of well-being among income groups? According to the following scatterplot, the answer depends on a country's trust (Bartolini et al. 2019). Figure 12.2 shows the relationship between trust and a measure of the distribution of well-being among income groups, across 32 European countries. The distribution of well-being is measured by the difference in average life satisfaction between the richest and poorest income quintiles, while trust is measured by the share of a country's population who are highly trusting.

In countries rich in trust, there is less difference between the well-being of the rich and poor. The lower a country's trust, the more money matters for well-being. In Serbia or Bulgaria, where trust is very low, the difference in life satisfaction between the rich and poor is more than 25%, whereas in high trust countries – such as Switzerland or Netherlands – it is around 7%. One may think that these differences in well-being are due to income inequality, which is greater in Serbia or Bulgaria than in Switzerland or Netherlands. However, income inequality only partially affects differences in well-being between income groups. Holding constant the Gini index of income inequality, countries where trust is higher exhibit substantially lower subjective wellbeing inequality between income groups. A similar analysis on 99 European countries provide the same results.

These findings, confirmed by other data sources, are the cross-country mirror of the results based on micro data summarized in the preceding section. In fact, the greater the importance of income for well-being, the more income disparities translate into well-being disparities between income groups. Since good relationships make money less important for individuals, in socially richer countries the

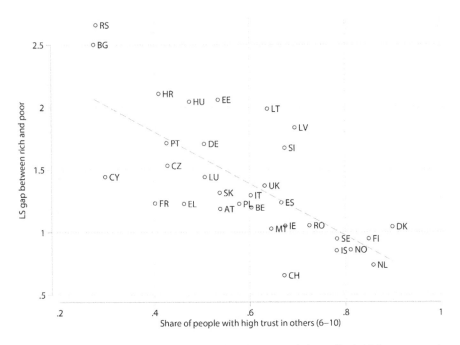

Fig. 12.2 The life satisfaction gap between rich and poor people is smaller in high-trust countries than elsewhere. EU-SILC data (2012) from 32 European countries. (Source: Bartolini et al. 2019)

difference in well-being between income groups shrinks. Relational affluence reduces the impact of income inequality on the distribution of well-being. In conclusion, social capital strongly moderates the extent to which money buys happiness. This is consistent with substitution between income and social capital in the utility functions and it is inconsistent with complementarity. This evidence supports the defensive growth viewpoint that money concerns prosper amidst poor social contexts.

12.4.3 Work Hours and US-Europe Differences

Consistent with a defensive growth hypothesis, "individual differences in happiness appear to be solidly anchored in the invisible threads of connection to others" (Cacioppo et al. 2008). In China, India and the USA, the decline in average reported well-being is largely predicted by the decline in social capital and growing social comparisons, exacerbated by a context of rapidly increasing income inequality (Bartolini et al. 2013; Brockmann et al. 2009; Bartolini and Sarracino 2015, 2019; Lane 2000).

The defensive growth view that the decline of social capital and the increase in working hours are connected by bi-directional causality is supported by empirical evidence. Bartolini and Bilancini (2011), using US survey data for 1972–2004 in a structural equation model, have shown that individuals with poorer social capital tend to work more. People seem to find, in money and work, compensation for the poverty of their social capital. At the same time, those individuals who work more tend to have poorer social capital, because work takes away time and energy that could instead be allocated to relationships. The US may be the paradigmatic example of this mechanism in the light of three decades of declining social capital and increased working hours. US society may be trapped in a vicious circle, in which the poverty of social capital causes an increase in hours worked, which in turn causes a greater poverty of social capital.

Defensive growth can also shed light on some well-known US–Europe differences. Slower growth, shorter work hours and (weakly) increasing happiness in Western Europe from the 1980s to the mid-2000s are connected to a more positive evolution of social capital than in the US. Lower inequality and a less socially aggressive economic model may be at the root of the evidence suggesting that defensive growth is less at work in Europe than in the US. The inability of US economy to promote happiness and leisure time, as well as its capacity to grow, may be a symptom of the disease of social capital.

12.5   US: Loneliness, Fear and Ill-Being as Drivers of Growth

American economic growth in the past few decades has been largely boosted by expenses for defence against the decline of social capital. Examples go well-beyond the impressive boom of the home entertainment sector, fuelled by the loss of social character of leisure. Several sectors of the American economy that are enhanced by rising loneliness, conflict, fear and malaise grew more quickly than the rest of the economy, becoming driving forces of economic growth.

12.5.1   The Industry of Fear: Security and Social Control

The substitution between free and costly goods operates not only in our consumption patterns but in our production patterns as well (Bartolini and Bonatti 2008a, 2008b). The loss of trust, shared social norms, honesty fairness, integrity, business and work ethics, makes market transactions more complicated and therefore costlier. Wallis and North (1986) documented the long-term expansion of the (private plus public) transaction cost sector: 26.1% of US GDP in 1870 and 54% in 1970.

The paradigmatic example of expenditures engendered by declining trust is spending on security and social control, which rocketed since the late 1970s (Putnam 2000). Police and guards increased by 40% and lawyers and judges by 150% over

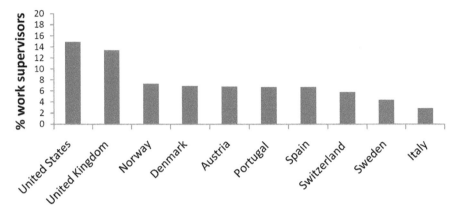

Fig. 12.3 Work supervisors as a share of the workforce: international comparisons in 2002. Source: my calculation on Jayadev and Bowles (2006) data

the levels that had been projected in 1970 (Putnam 2000, p. 146). According to Jayadev and Bowles (2006), the US workforce share employed as work supervisors and guards (police, correctional officers and security personnel) remained stable from 1948 to 1966 (about 10.8%) and then grew to 13.4% in 1979 and shot up to 17.9% in 2002.

This is an astonishing figure: in 2002, the job of almost one out of five American workers consisted in controlling someone else. One out of six American workers monitors other workers. In the US the share of work supervisors as a percentage of the total workforce outnumbers any other country except the UK, as shown in Fig. 12.3.

The flip side of the coin of the upsurge of the security sector is the astounding increase in the US prison population, which skyrocketed from 200,000 inmates in 1973 to 2.2 million in 2009, resulting in a historically unprecedented and internationally unique incarceration rate of nearly 1%" (National Research Council 2014). Expenditures related to the prison and criminal justice system can also be regarded as defensive. Imprisonment, in fact is a deterrent to would-be criminals.

Notice that spending on "guard labour" measured by Jayadev and Bowles is only a fraction of the total spending on security and control. People protect themselves against declining trust not only by buying labour, but also goods (monitoring technologies, property protection systems). The American widespread obsession for weapons must be framed within this context. The extraordinary dimension of American society's disciplinary apparatus gives a concrete idea of the high costs engendered by the erosion of trust. This thriving industry of fear fed American economic growth.

12.5.2   The Industry of Economic Segregation: Urban Sprawl

Urban sprawl was the backbone of the construction boom that contributed vigorously to American growth until the recession of 2008. Not less importantly, urban sprawl was the engine of soaring residential income segregation. This term designates the tendency of families with different incomes to cluster in different neighbourhoods. Since the 1980s, as a consequence of suburbanization, neighbourhoods in which families with different incomes mixed have gradually disappeared from American cities. Indeed, urban sprawl is a pattern of income segregation. The similarity of houses in suburban neighbourhoods shows that they are conceived for people with similar incomes. Segregation increased at both ends of the income distribution: high- and low-income families alike became increasingly residentially isolated, exacerbating the polarization of neighbourhoods by income (Reardon and Bischoff 2011).

At the root of suburbanization there is a collapse of mutual trust between persons with different incomes, and this is closely linked to the astronomical increase in income inequality. Fear and insecurity have played a critical role in boosting American urban sprawl. Income segregation was the goal of middle-class households who sought refuge from unsafe inner-city areas by moving out to the suburbs. They wanted to live among people with similar middle-class incomes.

Urban sprawl is a consequence of the crisis of relationships between different income classes. In turn, it feeds this crisis because in cities segregated by income, people with different incomes meet and become acquainted less. Residential segregation by income also causes segregation by income of major amenities that benefit large shares of the population, such as schools, parks and public services. Different income groups end up having nothing in common. The growing lack of social connections feeds mistrust between different income groups. Defensive growth well describes a pattern of urban expansion that responds to a crisis of social capital and results in even less social connection.

12.5.3   The Industry of Malaise: Healthcare

Healthcare is probably the sector that most fed American economic growth in the past few decades. Figure 12.4 shows that in only 12 years, the weight of healthcare spending on the American GDP increased by almost 30%.

The size reached by the US healthcare sector is unequalled in any other country. In European countries the ratio of healthcare spending to GDP is around 10%, with far better results in all health outcome indicators.

There are supply-side reasons for the disproportionate cost of American healthcare, such as the higher rate of inflation for health-related goods and services as compared to other goods and services, which is largely connected to routine use of expensive high-tech devices (Callahan 2008). However, soaring demand plays a

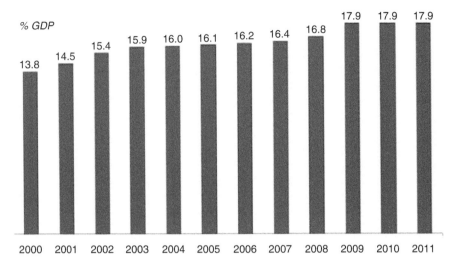

Fig. 12.4 Healthcare spending as a percentage of GDP in the United States, 2000–2011. (Source: OECD Health Data 2013)

crucial role. Spending on healthcare is boosted by the worsening health of Americans shown in the next section.

Such evidence comes as no surprise to epidemiologists in the light of the trend of American social capital and happiness. Indeed, in the past 50 years, epidemiology documented that psycho-social factors such as unhappiness, poor relationships and social comparisons are major risk factors for psychological as well as physical health. Studies conducted in many countries, adopting different methods and measures of happiness, following samples of hundreds, thousands, sometimes tens of thousands of persons over many years, sometimes decades, find that malaise translate into increased morbidity. Initial well-being predicts the development of cardiovascular disease (Hemingway and Marmot 1999), incidence of cancer and survival of cancer patients (Williams and Schneiderman 2002), speed of recovery after coronary by-pass surgery and speed of return to normal activities after discharge from hospital (Scheier et al. 1989), probability of survival after stem-cell transplant (Loberiza et al. 2002), hypertension (Raikkonen et al. 1999), female fertility (Buck et al. 2011), mortality among the chronically ill (Guven and Saloumidis 2009), HIV seropositivity (Moskowitz 2003), diabetes (Moskowitz et al. 2008), immune competence, cardiovascular reactivity (Lyubomirsky et al. 2005) and wound healing speed (Kiecolt-Glaser et al. 2005).

Similarly, citizens of highly unequal countries experience poorer health and shorter lives than citizens of more equal countries (Wilkinson and Pickett 2009). Inequality boosts social comparisons and since they play a critical role in generating distress, their impact on health is likely to be mediated by happiness. The same holds for relational poverty, which is a source of poor health probably because it is a powerful source of ill-being. Since the seventies, a flood of research has documented that having friends, identity and loving relationships, participating in groups and associations, and enjoying social support are effective ways to protect our health (Berkman and Glass 2000; Stanfeld 2006). A meta-analysis of 148 longitudinal studies, observing more than 300,000 individuals for an average of 7.5 years, found that individuals who have poor social connections have double the mortality risk of individuals with strong social ties (Holt-Lunstad et al. 2010). This effect is greater than that of other well-established risk factors for mortality, such as physical inactivity and obesity, and comparable with cigarette smoking.

The negative impact of poor relationship on health is even stronger for the older population, the major burden of healthcare. Isolated older adults are at greater risk for all-cause mortality (Valtorta and Hanratty 2012). Similarly, older individuals who are lonely are at greater risk of increased morbidity related to the major causes of disease burden in the elderly. Social isolation has been associated with increased risk of development and progression of cardiovascular disease (Hawkley and Cacioppo 2010; Knox and Uvnäs-Moberg 1998), dementia (Fratiglioni et al. 2000), memory losses (Ertel et al. 2008), Alzheimer's disease. The longest study of adult life ever conducted tracked the lives of 724 males for 75 years. Those who were more connected were happier, physically healthier, and lived longer than those who were less well connected. On the other hand, loneliness killed. People who were more isolated were less happy, their health declined earlier in midlife, their brain function declined sooner and they lived shorter lives than people who were not lonely.[7]

Psycho-social risk factors increase the risk of mental as well as physical disease because they induce people to lead less healthy lifestyles and, above all, weaken the immune and cardiovascular system (Wilkinson and Pickett 2009; Hawkley et al. 2003). This implies that part of healthcare spending is aimed at repairing or mitigating the unhealthy consequences of unhappiness, relational poverty and social comparisons. This part of healthcare spending is defensive in nature. The booming healthcare industry is one more example of the disproportionate size in the American economy of the sectors that are fueled by declining relationships and happiness.

12.5.4   Troubled Lives, Troubled Health

Ill-being is costly for the healthcare system. In 2003, the United States spent around $100 billion to treat its citizens' mental illnesses (Wilkinson and Pickett 2009). The crisis of opioids in the US generated 1.3 million hospitalizations in 2016. The profile of the American citizen most affected by addiction provides much information about the causes of the distress that underlies such a mass vulnerability to addiction. Young or middle aged, poorly educated, non-Hispanic white males who live in the Rust Belt (previously known as the industrial heartland of America), were more frequent

---

[7]http://www.adultdevelopmentstudy.org/

victims of the opioids epidemic (Huang 2018). This is the profile of the losers of globalization. Deindustrialization eroded the community and social connections, beyond the jobs and the self-esteem of white males. The decline in marriages and fertility, and the rise in the share of children born to unmarried mothers or living in single-parent households, were particularly sharp in the Rust Belt (Autor et al. 2017).

Increasing distress boosted morbidity and healthcare spending. Case and Deaton (2015) recently provided large scale evidence of the health problems caused by malaise. In one population group, middle-aged white non-Hispanics, distress was so sharp as to lead to increased morbidity and mortality since 1998. The list of causes for the increase in mortality (alcohol poisoning, suicide, chronic liver disease and cirrhosis) speaks volumes about the underlying epidemic of dissatisfaction. Concurrent declines in self-reported health, mental health and ability to work, increased reports of pain and deteriorating measures of liver function – particularly among middle-aged whites – all point to increasing midlife distress. This data aroused much attention because it shows an exception to the worldwide increasing trend in longevity. What strikes in Case and Deaton's findings is the extent to which mass dissatisfaction and frustration can turn into health deterioration. And of course, into health spending.

Graham and Pinto (2018) show that data on subjective well-being and mortality has a very similar geographical, racial and generational distribution in the US. Both mortality and various subjective measures of well-being, such as optimism, life satisfaction and stress, depict a sharp crisis in a population group: low-income, middle aged, rural whites. This is the America that mobilized to support Trump. The crisis of happiness and hope in the traditional white middle class of America, worst hit by deindustrialisation and increasing inequality, is not only an excellent predictor of the crisis of its health; it predicts Trump's election as well.

12.6 Policies for Social Capital

In defensive growth models, negative shocks affecting common resources increase the steady-state growth rate (or level of activity) of the economy. This growth-enhancing effect of exogenous reductions of common goods is not surprising in a context in which the expansion of the economy is fed by their decline. Such shocks can be provoked by institutional changes. A reduction in the quality or in access to public schooling, the privatization of a common, the Tudor enclosures (that caused access to land to collapse for the poorest segments of the rural population), are all examples of institutional shocks that reduce access to a common resource. The same can be said of the firing of millions of workers in state-owned companies in China – with the loss of job-related safety nets, such as healthcare. In this light, the diverging evolution of the US and Europe underlined in this chapter may be linked to the greater abundance of universal entitlements and collective infrastructure in Europe and to the "starve the beast" therapy imposed on the US welfare state since the 1980s. This defensive growth viewpoint is consistent with the notion that privatizations and the shrinking welfare state enhance growth but not for the reasons set out in neo-liberal theories. Neo-liberal reforms work for growth because they worsen quality of life, not because they improve it. Defensive reactions of individuals to declining commons boost growth and are the key to growth's undesirable impact on happiness.

In particular, the evidence I summarized suggests that the crises of one common asset – social capital – is critical in promoting defensive growth. Policies that prevent defensive growth therefore crucially rely on policies that promote social capital. Quantitative evidence and successful implementations suggest that public policies promoting social capital are possible in three domains: urban planning, schooling and regulation of advertising.

Urban planning plays a major role in the formation of social capital. High residential density, walkability, pedestrian areas, parks, car restrictions, public transport and cycling can relieve the urban pressure of cars, which is essential for enhancing social capital. Indeed, in a city the social fabric is created in common spaces – such as squares and streets – where citizens meet and get to know each other. Cities were created 5000 years ago to aggregate people and the quality of common spaces have always been critical for aggregation. Recently however (in historical terms), cars invaded streets and their relational function collapsed. Car-oriented urban development after WW2 especially damaged the relational opportunities of individuals with reduced mobility, such as the elderly and children, whose connections largely depend on access to the social fabric within walking distance. Contemporary cities are largely responsible for transforming children and old people into the population groups most at risk of solitude (Pinquart and Sorensen 2001). Until a few generations ago, old people and children maintained dense social connections. These ideas are at the centre of New Urbanism, an urban design movement that emphasizes pedestrian-oriented, mixed-use, high-density neighbourhoods as a means for building relationships among residents. According to New Urbanists, residents are more likely to walk about in such neighbourhoods and therefore have more chance of casual interactions (encounters, conversations, exchange of favours). This enhances the neighbourhood's social fabric, engagement of residents in neighbourhood-related activities, and sense of community. Urban planning aimed at social capital is well-established in many northern European cities and is being taken up across the world (Montgomery 2013).

Education is a stressing experience for most students (OECD 2017). Traditional (or vertical) teaching – based on lecturing, memorization and repetition – overlooks the role of positive emotions and intrinsic motivations in promoting learning. However, in recent decades many northern European countries have increasingly integrated participatory teaching into mainstream education (Brulé and Veenhoven 2014). Participatory teaching, aimed at promoting the engagement of students in their own learning, was first developed in the context of Montessori education (Montessori 1964). This century-old schooling system (Biswas-Diener 2011) has been found to fosters social and academic skills more than traditional education

(Lillard and Else-Quest 2006). Participatory teaching emphasizes students working in groups on common projects, in student-centred classrooms, where the central relationship is between students. Participatory practices have been shown to be supportive of several dimensions of students' social capital, including cooperation with other students and teachers, membership in associations, trust in institutions, and participation in civil society (Algan et al. 2011). These results support the notion that beliefs and skills underlying social capital are acquired through the practice of cooperation. Predictably, schooling practices that are more cooperative form individuals that are more cooperative.

Advertising has a negative impact on people's happiness and relationships. The reason is that advertising fosters materialistic values and in particular social comparisons, by triggering feelings of exclusion in those who do not buy the advertised products (Schor 2004). This effects are amplified in kids and teens compared to adults (Goldberg and Gorn 1978; Pollay 1986; Greenberg and Brand 1993; Buijzen and Valkenburg 2003; Schor 2004; Nairn et al. 2007). For this reason, young people have become the primary target of advertising. In the United States, total spending on advertising targeting children in the early 2000s was 150 times the amount spent in 1983 (Schor 2004). Various western countries have regulated advertising as a consequence of an increasing awareness of the harm associated with mounting commercial pressure on children and teenagers. Sweden, Norway and Greece banned television advertising to children, New Zealand prohibits advertising of junk food, Austria and Flanders (Belgium) do not allow ads targeting children before, during or after children's TV programs. Australia, Canada, and the UK have powerful advertising regulating authorities, who are at the forefront in regulating children's media (Lisosky 2001; Caron and Hwang 2014). As advertising fosters social comparisons among adults as well, regulating advertising would benefit them too.

Importantly, these policies are relatively inexpensive to implement and may ultimately improve public budgets because they are expected to decrease morbidity and thus spending on healthcare. The healthcare system appears to be the end station of distress, because ill-being translates into greater morbidity.

12.7 Conclusion

The coexistence over the long-term of high growth, decline in happiness, loss of social capital, longer working hours and soaring social comparisons is difficult to explain in the light of the existing economic literature. In the framework presented here, these trends emerge as interconnected aspects of defensive growth. The evidence provided in this paper highlights the role played by defensive growth in giving rise to the Easterlin paradox. Defensive growth emphasizes the contribution of declining social capital, increasing overwork and soaring social comparisons to the happiness decline. At the same time, it underlines that these factors enhance economic growth. In particular, the crisis of social capital feeds social comparisons and ambitious consumption goals, which can only be afforded under a high work-load. In this way defensive growth is a key to why high-growth countries show substantial and persistent negative trends of happiness. The reason is linked to their substantial and persistent declines in social capital, which feed GDP and unhappiness.

The coexistence of fast growth and declining social capital is especially puzzling for the dominant view that considers social capital an ingredient of economic growth. The explanation provided by defensive growth theory is that declining social capital and rapid growth may coexist because they feed each other. This explanation is not incompatible with the plausible idea that social capital contributed to trigger the path to economic prosperity in the West many decades ago. However, in recent decades, and especially in the US, this type of growth has been replaced by defensive growth, which is fuelled by the erosion of social capital.

The issue of the social quality of growth is critical for developing countries, although their need for *any* kind of economic growth may appear more compelling than for developed countries. China and India are striking examples of the Easterlin paradox. These countries warn us that social sustainability is not a luxury that can only be afforded when primary needs are reasonably met. The signs of defensive growth are clearly visible in the Chinese and Indian take-offs.

References

Aguiar, M., & Hurst, E. (2007). Measuring trends in leisure: The allocation of time over five decades. *The Quarterly Journal of Economics, 122*(3), 969–1006.

Alesina, A., & Giuliano, P. (2015). Culture and institutions. *Journal of Economic Literature, 53*(4), 898–944.

Alesina, A., & La Ferrara, E. (2006). Who trusts others? *Journal of Public Economics, 85*, 207–234.

Alesina, A., Glaeser, E. L., & Sacerdote, B. (2005). *Work and leisure in the US and Europe: Why so different?* (CEPR Discussion Paper No. 5140). London: Centre for Economic Policy Research.

Algan, Y., Cahuc, P., & Shleifer, A. (2011). Teaching practices and social capital. *American Economic Journal: Applied Economics, 5*, 189–210.

Algan, Y., & Cahuc, P. (2013). Trust, growth, and Well-being: New evidence and policy implications. In P. Aghion & S. Durlauf (Eds.), *Handbook of economic growth*. Elsevier: North-Holland.

Angrave, D., & Charlwood, A. (2015). What is the relationship between long working hours, over-employment, under-employment and the subjective well-being of workers? Longitudinal evidence from the UK. *Human Relations, 68*(9), 1491–1515.

Antoci, A., & Bartolini, S. (2004). Negative externalities, defensive expenditures and labour supply in an evolutionary context. *Environment and Development Economics, 9*(5), 591–612.

ASAM (American Association of Addiction Medicine). (2016). *Opioid addiction 2016 facts & figures.* https://www.asam.org/docs/default-source/advocacy/opioid-addiction-disease-facts-figures.pdf

Autor, D., Dorn, D., & Hanson, G. (2017). *When work disappears: Manufacturing decline and the falling marriage-market value of men* (NBER Working Paper No. 23173). Stanford: National Bureau of Economic Research.

Bartolini, S., & Bilancini, E. (2011). *Social participation and hours worked* (No. 620). Siena: Department of Economics, University of Siena.

Bartolini, S., & Bonatti, L. (2003). Endogenous growth and negative externalities. *Journal of Economics, 79*(2), 123–144.

Bartolini, S., & Bonatti, L. (2008a). Endogenous growth, decline in social capital and expansion of market activities. *Journal of Economic Behavior & Organization, 67*(3–4), 917–926.

Bartolini, S., & Bonatti, L. (2008b). The role of social capital in enhancing factor productivity: Does its erosion depress per capita GDP? *The Journal of Socio-Economics, 37*(4), 1539–1553.

Bartolini, S., & Sarracino, F. (2014). Happy for how long? How social capital and economic growth relate to happiness over time. *Ecological Economics, 108*, 242–256.

Bartolini, S., & Sarracino, F. (2015). The dark side of Chinese growth: Declining social capital and well-being in times of economic boom. *World Development, 74*, 333–351.

Bartolini, S., & Sarracino, F. (2017). Twenty-five years of materialism: Do the US and Europe diverge? *Social Indicators Research, 133*(2), 787–817.

Bartolini, S., & Sarracino, F. (2019). *Happiness during industrial revolutions. The broken promise of Indian economic growth*. Siena: Mimeo.

Bartolini, S., Bilancini, E., & Pugno, M. (2013). Did the decline in social capital depress Americans' happiness? *Social Indicators Research, 110*(3), 1033–1059.

Bartolini, S., Piekalkiewicz, M., & Sarracino, F. (2019). *A social cure for social comparisons* (No. 797). Department of Economics and Statistics: University of Siena.

Berkman, L. F., & Glass, T. (2000). Social integration, social networks, social support, and health. In L. F. Berkman & I. Kawachi (Eds.), *Social epidemiology*. New York: Oxford University Press.

Biswas-Diener, R. (2011). Manipulating happiness: Maria Montessori. *International Journal of Wellbeing, 1*(2).

Bjørnskov, C. (2006). Determinants of generalized trust: A cross-country comparison. *Public Choice, 130*(1), 1–21.

Blanchflower, D. G., & Oswald, A. J. (2004). Well-being over time in Britain and the USA. *Journal of Public Economics, 88*(7–8), 1359–1386.

Bonatti, L. (2008). Evolution of preferences and cross-country differences in time devoted to market work. *Labour Economics, 15*(6), 1341–1365.

Bowles, S., & Park, Y. (2005). Emulation, inequality, and work hours: Was Thorsten Veblen right? *The Economic Journal, 115*(507), F397–F412.

Brockmann, H., Delhey, J., Welzel, C., & Yuan, H. (2009). The China puzzle: Falling happiness in a rising economy. *Journal of Happiness Studies, 10*(4), 387–405.

Brulé, G., & Veenhoven, R. (2014). Participatory teaching and happiness in developed nations. *Advances in Applied Sociology, 4*, 235–245.

Bruni, L., & Stanca, L. (2008). Watching alone. Happiness, relational goods and television. *Journal of Economic Behavoir and Organization, 65*(3–4), 506–528.

Buck, L. G. M., et al. (2011). Stress reduces conception probabilities across the fertile window: Evidence in support of relaxation. *Fertility and Sterility, 95*(7), 2184–2189.

Buijzen, M., & Valkenburg, P. M. (2003). The unintended effects of television advertising: A parent-child survey. *Communication Research, 30*(5), 483–503.

Burda, M., Hamermesh, D. S., & Weil, P. (2007). *Total work, gender and social norms* (IZA Discussion Papers 2705). Bonn: Institute for the Study of Labor (IZA).

Cacioppo, J. T., Hawkley, L. C., Kalil, A., Hughes, M. E., Waite, L., & Thisted, R. A. (2008). Happiness and the invisible threads of social connection. In *The science of subjective well-being* (pp. 195–219).

Callahan, D. (2008). Health Care Costs and Medical Technology. In M. Crowley (Ed.), *From birth to death and bench to clinic: The hastings center bioethics briefing book for journalists, policymakers, and campaigns* (pp. 79–82). Garrison, NY: The Hastings Center.

Caron, A. H., & Hwang, J. M. (2014). Analysis of children's television characters and media policies. In A. Ben-Arieh, F. Casas, I. Frønes, & J. Korbin (Eds.), *Handbook of child well-being* (pp. 1957–1977). Dordrecht: Springer.

Case, A., & Deaton, A. (2015). Rising morbidity and mortality in midlife among white non-Hispanic Americans in the 21st century. *Proceedings of the National Academy of Sciences, 112*(49), 15078–15083.

Clark, A. E., & Senik, C. (2010). Who compares to whom? The anatomy of income comparisons in Europe. *The Economic Journal, 120*(544), 573–594.

Costa, D. L., & Kahn, M. E. (2003). Understanding the decline in social capital, 1952–1998. *Kyklos, 56*, 17–46.

Curtin S. C., Warner M., & Hedegaard H. (2016, April) *Increase in suicide in the United States, 1999–2014, NCHS Data Brief No. 241.* https://www.cdc.gov/nchs/products/databriefs/db241.htm

Cyranoski, D. (2010). China tackles surge in mental illness. *Nature, 468*, 145. https://www.nature.com/news/2010/101110/full/468145a.html.

D'Ambrosio, C., & Frick, J. R. (2007). Income satisfaction and relative deprivation: An empirical link. *Social Indicators Research, 81*(3), 497–519.

Davies, J. (2017). *The sedated society: The causes and harms of our psychiatric prescribing epidemic.* Cham, Switzerland: Palgrave Macmillan.

Davis, S. J., & Henrekson, M. (2004). *Tax effects on work activity, industry mix and shadow economy size: Evidence from rich-country comparisons* (Working Paper no. 10509). Cambridge: National Bureau of Economic Research.

Easterlin, R. (1974). Does economic growth improve the human lot? Some empirical evidence. In P. A. David & M. W. Reder (Eds.), *Nations and households in economic growth* (pp. 89–125). New York: Academic Press.

Eisenberger, N. I., & Lieberman, M. D. (2004). Why rejection hurts: A common neural alarm system for physical and social pain. *Trends in Cognitive Sciences, 8*(7), 294–300.

Ertel, K. A., Glymour, M. M., & Berkman, L. F. (2008). Effects of social integration on preserving memory function in a nationally representative us elderly population. *American Journal of Public Health, 98*(7), 1215–1220.

Fratiglioni, L., Wang, H. X., Ericsson, K., Maytan, M., & Winblad, B. (2000). Influence of social network on occurrence of dementia: A community-based longitudinal study. *The Lancet, 355*(9212), 1315–1319.

Freeman, R. B., & Schettkat, R. (2005). Marketization of household production and the EU–US gap in work. *Economic Policy, 20*(41), 6–50.

Galbraith, J. K. (1958). *The affluent society.* Harmondsworth: Penguin Books.

Goldberg, M. E., & Gorn, G. J. (1978). Some unintended consequences of TV advertising to children. *Journal of Consumer Research, 5*(1), 22–29.

Gould, E. D., & Hijzen, A. (2016). *Growing apart, losing trust? The impact of inequality on social capital.* Washington, DC: International Monetary Fund.

Graham, C., & Pinto, S. (2018). Unequal hopes and lives in the USA: Optimism, race, place, and premature mortality. *Journal of Population Economics, 687*, 1–69.

Greenberg, B. S., & Brand, J. E. (1993). Television news and advertising in schools: The "Channel One" controversy. *Journal of Communication, 43*(1), 143–151.

Guiso, L., Sapienza, P., & Zingales, L. (2006). Does culture affect economic outcomes? *Journal of Economic Perspectives, 20*, 23–48.

Guven, C., & Saloumidis, R. (2009). *Why is the world getting older? The influence of happiness on mortality* (SOEPpapers, 198). Berlin: DIW Berlin, The German Socio-Economic Panel (SOEP).

Hawkley, L. C., & Cacioppo, J. T. (2010). Loneliness matters: a theoretical and empirical review of consequences and mechanisms. *Annals of Behavioral Medicine, 40*(2), 218–227.

Hawkley, L. C., Burleson, M. H., Berntson, G. G., & Cacioppo, J. T. (2003). Loneliness in everyday life: cardiovascular activity, psychosocial context, and health behaviors. *Journal of Personality and Social Psychology, 85*(1), 105.

Headey, B. (2008). The set-point theory of well-being: Negative results and consequent revisions. *Social Indicators Research, 85*(3), 389–403.

Heinrich, L. M., & Gullone, E. (2006). The clinical significance of loneliness: A literature review. *Clinical Psychology Review, 26*(6), 695–718.

Helliwell, J. (2006). Well-being, social capital and public policy: What's new? *The Economic Journal, 116*, 34–45.

Helliwell, J. F., & Aknin, L. B. (2018). Expanding the social science of happiness. *Nature Human Behaviour, 2*, 1.

Helliwell, J. F., & Putnam, R. D. (1995). Economic growth and social capital in Italy. *Eastern Economic Journal, 21*(3), 295–307.

Hemingway, H., & Marmot, M. (1999). Psychosocial factors in the aetiology and prognosis of coronary heart disease: Systematic review of prospective cohort studies. *British Medical Journal, 318*(7196), 1460–1467.

Hirsch, F. (1976). *Social limits to growth*. Cambridge: Harvard University Press.

Hirschman, A. O. (1982). Rival interpretations of market society: Civilizing, destructive, or feeble? *Journal of Economic Literature, 20*(4), 1463–1484.

Holt-Lunstad, J., Smith, T. B., & Layton, J. B. (2010). Social relationships and mortality risk: a meta-analytic review. *PLoS Medicine, 7*(7), e1000316.

Hopper, L. M., et al. (2014). Social comparison mediates chimpanzees' responses to loss, not frustration. *Animal cognition 17*(6), 1303–1311.

Huang, L. C. (2018). Opioid overdoses: A webliography. *Journal of Consumer Health on the Internet, 22*(1), 42–52.

Jayadev, A., & Bowles, S. (2006). Guard labor. *Journal of Development Economics, 79*(2), 328–348.

Jebb, A. T., Tay, L., Diener, E., & Oishi, S. (2018). Happiness, income satiation and turning points around the world. *Nature Human Behaviour, 2*(1), 33.

Kasser, T. (2002). *The high price of materialism*. Cambridge: MIT Press.

Kasser T. (2016). Materialistic values and well-being: Problems and policy. S. Bartolini, E. Bilancini, L. Bruni, & P. Porta (red.), *Policies for happiness* (129–148).

Kiecolt-Glaser, J. K., Loving, T. J., Stowell, J. R., Malarkey, W. B., Lemeshow, S., Dickinson, S. L., & Glaser, R. (2005). Hostile marital interactions, proinflammatory cytokine production, and wound healing. *Archives of General Psychiatry, 62*(12), 1377–1384.

Knack, S., & Keefer, P. (1997). Does social capital have an economic payoff? A cross-country investigation. *The Quarterly Journal of Economics, 112*(4), 1251–1288.

Knowledge networks and insight policy research. (2010). *Loneliness among older adults*. Washington, DC: ARRP. https://assets.aarp.org/rgcenter/general/loneliness_2010.pdf.

Knox, S. S., & Uvnäs-Moberg, K. (1998). Social isolation and cardiovascular disease: An athero-sclerotic pathway? *Psychoneuroendocrinology, 23*(8), 877–890.

Koetse M. (2014, August 14). Suicide in China: The story behind the declining numbers. *Whatsonweibo*. https://www.whatsonweibo.com/suicide-in-china-the-story-behind-the-declining-numbers/

Krugman, F. (1995). *Pop internationalism*. Cambridge: MIT Press.

Lane, R. (2000). *The loss of happiness in market democracies*. New Haven/London: Yale University Press.

Lewis, W. A. (1954). Economic development with unlimited supplies of labour. *The Manchester School, 22*(2), 139–191.

Lillard, A., & Else-Quest, N. (2006). The early years: Evaluating Montessori education. *Science, 313*(5795), 1893–1894.

Lisosky, J. M. (2001). For all kids' sakes: Comparing children's television policy-making in Australia, Canada and the United States. *Media, Culture and Society, 23*(6), 821–842.

Loberiza, F. R., Rizzo, J. D., Bredeson, C. N., Antin, J. H., Horowitz, M. M., Weeks, J. C., et al. (2002). Association of depressive syndrome and early deaths among patients after stem-cell transplantation for malignant diseases. *Journal of Clinical Oncology, 20*, 2118–2126.

Lucas, R. E., Clark, A. E., Georgellis, Y., & Diener, E. (2003). Reexamining adaptation and the set point model of happiness: Reactions to changes in marital status. *Journal of Personality and Social Psychology, 84*(3), 527.

Luo, Z. (2015). 10 the rise of materialism: A trend in twentieth-century Chinese culture. In *Inheritance within rupture* (pp. 353–387). Boston: BRILL.

Luttmer, E. F. (2005). Neighbors as negatives: Relative earnings and well-being. *The Quarterly Journal of Economics, 120*(3), 963–1002.

Lykken, D., & Tellegen, A. (1996). Happiness is a stochastic phenomenon. *Psychological Science, 7*(3), 186–189.

Lyubomirsky, S., King, L., & Diener, E. (2005). The benefits of frequent positive affect: Does happiness lead to success? *Psychological Bulletin, 131*, 803–855.

Malathy L. (2017, February 25). 7.5% Indians suffer from mental disorders: WHO report. *The Times of India*. (https://timesofindia.indiatimes.com/india/7-5-indians-suffer-from-mental-disorders-who-report/articleshow/57344807.cms)

McPherson, M., Smith-Lovin, L., & Brashears, M. E. (2006). Social isolation in America: Changes in core discussion networks over two decades. *American Sociological Review, 71*(3), 353–375.

Montgomery, C. (2013). *The happy city*. New York: Farrar, Straus and Giroux.

Moskowitz, J. T. (2003). Positive affect predicts lower risk of AIDS mortality. *Psychosomatic Medicine, 65*, 620–626.

Moskowitz, J. T., Epel, E. S., & Acree, M. (2008). Positive affect uniquely predicts lower risk of mortality in people with diabetes. *Health Psychology, 27*, S73–S82.

Montessori, M. (1964). *The Montessori method*. New York: Schocken.

Murray, C. J., Lopez, A. D., & World Health Organization. (1996). *The global burden of disease: A comprehensive assessment of mortality and disability from diseases, injuries, and risk factors in 1990 and projected to 2020: Summary*. Geneve: World Health Organization.

Nairn, A., Ormrod, J., & Bottomley, P. (2007). *Watching, wanting and well-being. Exploring the links*. London: National Consumer Council.

National Research Council (NRC). (2014). In J. Travis, B. Western, S. Redburn, & Committee on Law and Justice, Division of Behavioral and Social Sciences and Education (Eds.), *The growth of incarceration in the United States:Exploring causes and consequences*. Washington, DC: The National Academies Press.

Neumark, D., & Postlewaite. (1998). A. Relative income concerns and the rise in married women's employment. *Journal of Public Economics, 70*(1), 157–183.

OECD. (2017). *PISA 2015 results: Students well-being (Volume III)*. http://www.keepeek.com/Digital-Asset-Management/oecd/education/pisa-2015-results-volume-iii_9789264273856-en#page1

Ohanian, L., Raffo, A., & Rogerson, R. (2008). Long-term changes in labor supply and taxes: Evidence from OECD countries, 1956–2004. *Journal of Monetary Economics, 55*(8), 1353–1362.

Olovsson, C. (2009). Why do Europeans work so little? *International Economic Review, 59*(1), 39–61.

Paxton, P. (1999). Is social capital declining in the United States? A multiple indicator assessment. *American Journal of Sociology, 105*(1), 88–127.

Phillips, M. R., Zhang, J., Shi, Q., Song, Z., Ding, Z., Pang, S., et al. (2009). Prevalence, treatment, and associated disability of mental disorders in four provinces in China during 2001–05: An epidemiological survey. *The Lancet, 373*(9680), 2041–2053.

Pinquart, M., & Sorensen, S. (2001). Influences on loneliness in older adults: A meta-analysis. *Basic and Applied Social Psychology, 23*(4), 245–266.

Poduri, G. S. (2016). Analysis of psychotropic drug sales in India. *Acta Medica International, 3*(1), 122–125.

Polanyi, K. (1968). *The great transformation*. Boston: Beacon Press.

Pollay, R. W. (1986). The distorted mirror: Reflections on the unintended consequences of advertising. *Journal of Marketing, 50*(2), 18–36.

Ponnudurai, R. (2015). Suicide in India–changing trends and challenges ahead. *Indian Journal of Psychiatry, 57*(4), 348–354. https://www.ncbi.nlm.nih.gov/pmc/articles/PMC4711233/.

Prescott, E. C. (2004). *Why do Americans work so much more than Europeans?* (No. w10316). Cambridge: National Bureau of Economic Research.

Putnam, R. (2000). *Bowling alone: The collapse and revival of American community.* New York, London, Toronto, Sidney: Simon and Schuster.

Raikkonen, K., Matthews, K. A., Flory, J. D., Owens, J. F., & Gump, B. B. (1999). Effects of optimism, pessimism, and trait anxiety on ambulatory blood pressure and mood during everyday life. *Journal of Personality and Social Psychology, 76*, 104–113.

Reardon, S. F., & Bischoff, K. (2011). Growth in the residential segregation of families by income, 1970–2009. *US 2010 project.* Brown University.

Rilling, J. K., Gutman, D. A., Zeh, T. R., Pagnoni, G., Berns, G. S., & Kilts, C. D. (2002). A neural basis for social cooperation. *Neuron, 35*(2), 395–405.

Robinson, R. V., & Jackson, E. F. (2001). Is trust in others declining in America? An age—period—cohort analysis. *Social Science Research, 30*, 117–145.

Rogerson, R. (2008). Structural transformation and the deterioration of European labor market outcomes. *Journal of Political Economy, 116*(2), 235–259.

Sachs J., (2017). Restoring American happiness, in *World Happiness Report 2017, 178.* http://worldhappiness.report/ed/2017/

Sarracino, F. (2012). Money, sociability and happiness: are developed countries doomed to social erosion and unhappiness? *Social Indicators Research, 109*(2), 135–188.

Scheier, M. F., Matthews, K. A., Owens, J. F., Magovern, G. J., Lefebvre, R. C., Abbott, R. A., & Carver, C. S. (1989). Dispositional optimism and recovery from coronary artery bypass surgery: The beneficial effects on physical and psychological well-being. *Journal of Personality and Social Psychology, 57*(6), 1024.

Schmitt, V., et al. (2016). Do monkeys compare themselves to others? *Animal Cognition, 19*(2), 417–428.

Schor, J. (2004). *Born to buy.* New York: Scribner.

Schor, J. (1992). *The overworked American. The unexpected decline of leisure in America.* New York: Basic Books.

Sha, F., Chang, Q., Law, Y. W., Hong, Q., & Yip, P. S. (2018). Suicide rates in China, 2004–2014: Comparing data from two sample-based mortality surveillance systems. *BMC Public Health, 18* (1), 239.

Shaw Crouse J., (2001). *A profile of American women in the twentieth century.* Beverly LaHaye Institute. http://concernedwomen.org/wp-content/uploads/2013/11/gg1-72.pdf

Singh, J., & Gupta, P. K. (2017). Drug addiction: Current trends and management. *The International Journal of Indian Psychology, 5*(1), 186–201.

Stanfeld, S. A. (2006). Social support and social cohesion. In M. Marmot & R. G. Wilkinson (Eds.), *Social determinants of health.* Oxford: Oxford University Press.

Stevenson, B., & Wolfers, J. (2008). *Economic growth and subjective well-being: Reassessing the Easterlin paradox* (No. w14282). Cambridge: National Bureau of Economic Research.

Stiglitz, J. E. (2008). Toward a general theory of consumerism: Reflections on Keynes's Economic possibilities for our grandchildren. L. Pecchi, & G. Piga (red.), *Revisiting Keynes: Economic possibilities for our grandchildren* (pp. 41–86).

Stiglitz, J. E., Sen, A., & Fitoussi, J. P. (2009). *Measurement of economic performance and social progress.* Online document http://bit. ly/JTwmG

Theeke, L. A. (2009). Predictors of loneliness in US adults over age sixty-five. *Archives of Psychiatric Nursing, 23*(5), 387–396.

Todaro, M. P. (1969). A model of labor migration and urban unemployment in less developed countries. *The American Economic Review, 59*(1), 138–148.

Twenge, J. M. (2000). The age of anxiety? The birth cohort changes in anxiety and neuroticism, 1952–1993. *Journal of Personality and Social Psychology, 79*(6), 1007.

Twenge, J. M. (2015). Time period and birth cohort differences in depressive symptoms in the US, 1982–2013. *Social Indicators Research, 121*(2), 437–454.

Twenge, J. M., & Kasser, T. (2013). Generational changes in materialism and work centrality, 1976–2007: Associations with temporal changes in societal insecurity and materialistic role modeling. *Personality and Social Psychology Bulletin, 39*(7), 883–897.

Twenge, J. M., Gentile, B., DeWall, C. N., Ma, D., Lacefield, K., & Schurtz, D. R. (2010). Birth cohort increases in psychopathology among young Americans, 1938–2007: A cross-temporal meta-analysis of the MMPI. *Clinical Psychology Review, 30*(2), 145–154.

Valtorta, N., & Hanratty, B. (2012). Loneliness, isolation and the health of older adults: Do we need a new research agenda? *Journal of the Royal Society of Medicine, 105*(12), 518–522.

Wallis, J. J., & North, D. (1986). Measuring the transaction sector in the American economy, 1870-1970. In *Long-term factors in American economic growth* (pp. 95–162). Chicago: University of Chicago Press.

Wilkinson, R., & Pickett, K. (2009). *The spirit level: Why more equal societies almost always do better.* London: Allen Lane.

Williams, R. B., & Schneiderman, N. (2002). Resolved: Psychosocial interventions can improve clinical outcomes in organic disease (pro). *Psychosomatic Medicine, 64,* 552–557.

World Bank. (2014). *Poverty and equity. Country dashboard: China.* Available at. http://povertydata.worldbank.org/poverty/country/CHN. Accessed 24 Sep2014.

Zang, X., & Zhao, L. X. (2017). The state of the field: The family and marriage in China. In X. Zang & L. X. Zhao (Eds.), *Handbook on the family and marriage in China* (pp. 1–19). Chaltenham: Elgar.

Chapter 13
Keynes' Grandchildren and Easterlin's Paradox: What Is Keeping Us from Reducing Our Working Hours?

Johannes Hirata

Abstract In1930 Keynes famously predicted that 100 years later—i.e. in 2030—the "economic problem" would be solved and we would be living in an "age of leisure and of abundance" working only 3 h a day. In the same text, Keynes stated that there are absolute and relative needs ("in the sense that we feel them only if their satisfaction lifts us above, makes us feel superior to, our fellows"), but he thought that relative needs are of minor importance. Richard Easterlin's work, on the other hand, suggests that relative needs are pervasive and that wellbeing depends much more on one's relative income than Keynes once thought.

It will be argued in this text that Richard Easterlin's findings, in spite of proving Keynes off the mark in his understatement of relative needs, strengthens the case for working time reductions: the larger the proportion of goods subject to the relative-income effect, the greater are the benefits of working fewer hours. Perhaps the main explanation for why we are still sticking to the 40-h work-week is that the Easterlin paradox has not been widely understood yet.

13.1 Introduction

In 1930, John Maynard Keynes famously predicted that 100 years later—i.e. in 2030—"the economic problem" (Keynes 1978, 326) would be solved and we would be living in an "age of leisure and of abundance" (p. 328), working only 3 h a day. Keynes guessed that "the standard of life in progressive countries" would grow between four and eightfold (p. 325–26) until the year 2030 and that this would satisfy our needs "in the sense that we prefer to devote our further energies to non-economic purposes." (p. 326).

Keynes prediction of economic growth is turning out to be astonishingly correct: if we take per capita real GDP—a concept yet to be invented at the time Keynes wrote his essay—as an indicator for the "standard of life", a little more than a decade

J. Hirata (✉)

Hochschule Osnabrück, University of Applied Sciences, Osnabrück, Germany
e-mail: j.hirata@hs-osnabrueck.de

© Springer Nature Switzerland AG 2019
M. Rojas (ed.), *The Economics of Happiness*,
https://doi.org/10.1007/978-3-030-15835-4_13

before his target year the standard of life in the United Kingdom has grown more than fourfold and that in the USA fivefold since 1930 (The Maddison Project 2013; Bolt and van Zanden 2014). However, his prediction of our working time is far off the mark: despite substantial reductions of working hours in many countries since 1930, the typical employed person in the high-income countries still works about 40 h per week rather than only 15 h per week or 3 h per day. How could Keynes get it so wrong?

Satisfaction was not being measured in Keynes' times, so he must have relied for his prediction on the extrapolation of observation and introspection and, perhaps, on the fundamental assumption of economic theory that consumption has diminishing marginal utility. Given that leisure time competes with consumption in the classical utility function, a world in which utility maximizing individuals use real wage increases to buy both more consumption and more leisure time is perfectly consistent with standard economic theory, even though the result depends on the relative magnitudes of the substitution effect and of the income effect (see below for a further discussion of these two effects).

Shortly after Keynes died in 1946, the systematic collection of life satisfaction data began in a few countries and then gradually expanded across the world. Richard Easterlin was the first economist to seize the opportunity that these new data offered: one could finally test the fundamental assumption of economic theory that happiness depends positively on the material standard of living. His famous 1974 paper and the subsequent research that gained momentum in the 1990s seem to be key to understanding Keynes' mistake and to developing reasonably realistic scenarios for a happiness-augmenting reduction of working hours.

In addition to Keynes' prudential case for working-hour reductions, more recently a strong moral case for reducing working hours in high-income countries has been added: since rising consumption contributes to environmental damages, ceteris paribus,[1] limiting consumption can be seen as a moral obligation towards the victims of environmental deterioration, including future generations. While working time reductions are probably not the most directly targeted instrument for reducing the environmental impact—people could theoretically make more ecologically sustainable consumption choices or they could reduce consumption without earning less—, reducing working hours can be seen as a particularly effective way of lowering environmental damages, and one that does not risk leading to rising unemployment as would a one-sided reduction of aggregate demand that is not accompanied by a reduction in aggregate supply. What makes it particularly attractive, however, is precisely the prudential case made by Keynes: working fewer hours may make us happier and more responsible at the same time.

---

[1]This ceteris paribus clause is meant to take continuous technological progress for granted, including innovations that improve resource efficiency. Even if technological progress leads to absolute decoupling (cf. UNEP 2011) between consumption growth and total environmental costs, rising consumption will entail more environmental costs than stationary consumption levels *for any given technology*. Absolute decoupling as such does not settle the moral debate around consumption restraint.

In the following, I will contrast Keynes' prediction regarding working hours with the data. I will then take a closer look at the explanations he offered (or implied), discussing some potential sources for his misprediction. Next I will turn to Richard Easterlin's work and show how his more than four decades old interpretation of the early data covered almost all plausible explanations of Keynes' misprediction. Easterlin's later writings and those of some other authors will also be explored in order to arrive at a better understanding of the role of aspirations and how they are shaped—one of the central themes in Easterlin's argument.

13.2 Secular Trends in Working Hours: Evidence and Explanations

Keynes' piece was a short essay that was first presented in 1928 and which he then expanded into a lecture,[2] but it was not an elaborate piece of meticulous research. We therefore are not told what his prediction of a 3-h workday exactly meant in terms of annual or lifetime work hours because he said nothing about vacation days or retirement age. It is important to be rather specific because there is a world of difference between 3 h of work from Monday to Friday for each fully employed person and 3 h on average across the entire adult population and across 365 days of the year. One might even argue, as Jeffrey Sachs (2017, 6) does, that Keynes was almost exactly right if he had the latter interpretation in mind. Based on rough estimates, Sachs arrives at 3.2 working hours per day on average on each of the 365 days of the year averaging across all American adults, which compares to an average of 7.8 h in 1900. However, Keynes clearly did not have such a gross average number in mind since he himself talked about "[t]hree-hour shifts or a fifteen-hour week": he was not averaging across a wide population and 365 days, but was rather talking about actual workdays of working adults.

How did the actual number of working hours develop and what is the trend for Keynes' target year 2030? Anyone who has ever tried to analyze working time data will know that there is a large variety of specifications and quite some methodological difficulties. What can be said, using UK figures as an example, is the following: since 1930 the number of years that men work during their lifetime has declined by about 5 years to around 47 years, which was also roughly the duration of the working life in the middle of the nineteenth century. Yet, the average number of hours per week and the number of weeks per year at work have decreased substantially. In sum, the total number of hours that British men work over their lifetime is estimated to have decreased from 123,000 h in 1931 to 88,000 h in 1981, or by about 28% (Ausubel and Grübler 1995, 198). However, the duration of the work week for the full-time employed has stayed at around 40 h since the 1990s in most European

---

[2]See the editors' note introducing Keynes' essay in the "Collected Writings, Vol. 9" edited by Elizabeth Johnson and Donald Moggridge.

countries (Messenger 2011, 298), and data for the US even show a 12% increase from 1973 to 2000 in total hours worked per year per employed person (Schor 2003, p. 7) and a 20% increase for joint hours of paid work per week for married couples from 1970 to 1997 (Jacobs and Gerson 2001, 51).

The big picture therefore shows that it is safe to say that Keynes' prediction will not come true until 2030 in any country, and not even close. Rather than 15 h per week, full-time workers typically work more than twice as much. The increase in part-time work has started to reduce average hours per employed person in a few countries, but nowhere to less than 30 h (as of 2006; Messenger 2011), and this trend also reflects an increase in female labor force participation, implying a simultaneous increase in joint working hours for couples.

Through the lens of microeconomic theory, one can speculate that Keynes was misled in his prediction by the erroneous inference that continuous labor productivity growth combined with the diminishing marginal utility of consumption must make leisure more attractive. In fact, however, economic theory predicts that increasing labor productivity (assuming it translates into higher real wages) has two contrary effects: on the one hand the income effect raising demand for leisure, consistent with Keynes' conclusion. On the other hand, however, increasing hourly wages also mean that the opportunity cost of leisure goes up, implying a substitution effect in the opposite direction, and it is not a priori clear which of the two effects will prevail (Stiglitz 2010).

Another explanation for Keynes' mistake might be that he did not anticipate how much people would intrinsically like spending time on the job in the twenty-first century. Maybe he did not sufficiently envision the improvement of working conditions and the positive role of mechanization and automation in making paid work less of a burden and, at least for some workers, even enjoyable. This argument is not easy to verify because there seem to be no data on work satisfaction from the early twentieth century, and it is certainly not consistent with the neoclassical economics assumption that work is a source of disutility. Still, just going by historical accounts, it does not seem implausible to assume that for many people work is less arduous and more often even gratifying today than at the time Keynes wrote his essay (cf. Sachs 2017).

Any effect of an improvement in working conditions on people's leisure preference should be expected to be gradual: it would make people less eager to take more leisure time, but of course not unwilling to spend any time away from work.

We thus have a couple of possible effects working in both directions that are difficult or impossible to ascertain individually. If we could trust that actual working hours reflect a labor market equilibrium in which every worker works exactly the desired number of hours, then we could at least say that the joint effect of these forces is the rather stable pattern we have been observing over the last decades. However, labor markets are inherently inflexible and unlikely to come close to an ideal welfare maximizing equilibrium (cf. Golden and Gebreselassie 2007, p. 19), so a revealed preference approach would be misleading.

A more promising way to find out if people preferred to work fewer hours as incomes go up even if they do not actually have that choice is to ask them directly. Fortunately, various surveys ask such a question, all of them asking respondents in one or another way to take the effect of changes in working hours on income into account. Unfortunately, however, the results vary widely, apparently because the wording of the question and context make a decisive difference (Golden 2014), even though the exact pattern is still poorly understood (Holst and Bringmann 2017).

For example, in the 2004 wave of the German Socio-Economic Panel (GSOEP), 54% of employed people said they wanted to work fewer hours than they actually worked while 18% said they wanted to work more (cf. also Bell and Freeman 2001, p. 184; Grözinger et al. 2008, p. 10). Similarly, an EU-wide survey of 1998 asking a similar question confirmed this picture: on average across all countries surveyed, employed workers would prefer to work almost 10% fewer hours per week, namely 34 instead of 37.7 h (Bielenski et al. 2002, p. 67; quoted in Grözinger et al. 2008, p. 11).

On the other hand, according to data from the International Social Survey Programme reported by Bell and Freeman (2001, p. 185), in 1997 21% of German workers said they would rather work more hours than currently and only 10.3% said they would rather work fewer hours (the difference was even larger in the US). The German Micro Census data produce a similar picture, even though with lower percentages (Holst and Bringmann 2017, p. 1).

While the evidence does not settle the question if people would work fewer hours if they could choose freely, even those surveys suggesting people would prefer to work less come up with a value more than twice as high than what Keynes predicted. Yet, this does not necessarily mean that he was fundamentally wrong about the welfare maximizing consumption-leisure tradeoff before the backdrop of further increases in labor productivity. Perhaps he simply underestimated an important aspect that became apparent when Richard Easterlin studied the relationship between happiness and income.

13.3 Easterlin's Paradox

In his essay, Keynes noted in passing that there are two different kinds of needs, one of which is insatiable. It is worthwhile to quote this paragraph in full:

> Now it is true that the needs of human beings may seem to be insatiable. But they fall into two classes—those needs which are absolute in the sense that we feel them whatever the situation of our fellow human beings may be, and those which are relative in the sense that we feel them only if their satisfaction lifts us above, makes us feel superior to, our fellows. Needs of the second class, those which satisfy the desire for superiority, may indeed be insatiable; for the higher the general level, the higher still are they. But this is not so true of the absolute needs—a point may soon be reached, much sooner perhaps than we all of us are aware of, when these needs are satisfied in the sense that we prefer to devote our further energies to non-economic purposes (Keynes 1978, p. 326).

Here Keynes is clearly up to something, but he does not pursue the role of relative needs any further in his essay. One reason for this neglect is probably that he sees "relative needs" as limited to situations where people want to feel superior to others, even though the scope of relative needs is much wider than that (cf. Frank 2010).

Another reason is probably that Keynes did not have the benefit of happiness data that allowed Richard Easterlin and others to empirically estimate the role of relative needs.

The first such study was of course Easterlin's famous 1974 paper in which he found no positive happiness trend in a time series for the US from 1946 to 1970 despite real per capita GDP growth of 63% over that period (The Maddison Project 2013). He was well aware of the limitations of a single short time series and concluded carefully that "it seems safe to say that if income and happiness go together, it is not as obvious as in the within-country cross-sectional comparisons" (Easterlin 1974, p. 111). This prima facie contradiction—a positive within-country cross-section correlation between income and happiness but no correlation between average income and average happiness over time—is now known as the Easterlin paradox.

What is remarkable, though, is that in his original study, Easterlin already provided an interpretation of the paradox that included the two general effects that summarize almost all subsequent theoretical explanations: relative-income effects and hedonic adaptation.

Making reference to James Duesenberry (1949) and citing several lines of sociological and economic research as evidence, including two of his own earlier papers (Easterlin 1969, 1973), Easterlin argued that the satisfaction value of individual consumption depends negatively on other people's consumption. The consumption of others within one's society constituted a "frame of reference" or "consumption norms" (p. 112), and a person's happiness would depend on own consumption relative to this consumption norm. This interpretation was not entirely novel—Adam Smith already clearly saw this when he wrote in his *Wealth of Nations* that "[b]y necessaries I understand . . . whatever the custom of the country renders it indecent for creditable people, even of the lowest order, to be without" (Smith 1776, 869–870). In fact, the idea can be traced all the way back to Roman and Greek ancient philosophy (Schneider 2007).

Easterlin, just as Adam Smith, did not commit Keynes' mistake of believing that the only reason for which relative income mattered is people's desire to feel superior. Instead, Easterlin's interpretation allowed for any number of unspecific mechanisms mediating between rising consumption standards and subjective (as well as objective) well-being, notably those highlighted by Robert Frank (1989, 1997, 2010, 2012) that do not necessarily have to do with a desire to feel superior, with envy or even with social comparison in a wider sense. In other words, relative-income may matter even when people are not at all concerned about favorable comparisons but merely about their objective quality of life because that happens to also depend on relative consumption. Moreover, even where comparison plays a role, one need not assume a desire for superiority—a desire to merely "keep up with the Joneses", rather than to "surpass the Joneses", is all it takes for SWB to depend on relative income (Lichtenberg 1996).

Easterlin's second point was that people get used to improved living conditions. As economic growth raises the material standard of living, people come to take historical improvements for granted and derive less and less satisfaction from a given standard of living. This effect later came to be called hedonic adaptation (cf. Frederick and Loewenstein 1999) and, in contrast to the relative-income effect, does not depend on comparisons with others but rather on one's own past experience.

In any specific setting or in empirical studies, it is often difficult to separate both effects. For some purposes this distinction is also not very important because their effects are similar: the higher the consumption standard in a given society, the more people consumption it takes for people to be satisfied with their lives.

13.4   Relative Income, Hedonic Adaptation and Working Time

A key concept that Easterlin used to describe and analyze both effects, the relative-income effect and hedonic adaptation, is aspirations (e.g. Easterlin 1974, p. 90, 2001). A given person's aspirations can be expected to increase when others around her consume more or when she experienced an increase in consumption in the past. An increase in aspirations would mean that satisfaction for any given level of consumption would decrease.

To back up his hypothesis, Easterlin's 1974 paper cited from qualitative research—something few economists do and many regard with skepticism. Re-reading the quotations (which he took from Cantril 1965), however, makes one wish that qualitative research were more accepted in economics because the statements by Indian and American survey respondents are uniquely compelling and provide more explanatory depth to the rather sterile econometric evidence that is now abundantly available. Easterlin (1974, p. 114–15) quoted Indian respondents describing as their aspirations to "have a cow for milk and ghee", "to own a fan and maybe a radio", and one of them states that "[i]f the food and clothing problems were solved, then I would [...] be satisfied." American respondents, in contrast, often mentioned a new car as one central aspiration and also "better furniture [...] and more vacations", "a boat", to have "all my bills [...] paid, [...] play more golf and to hunt more than I do." Clearly, the satisfaction obtained from a particular standard of living by a given person is not independent of context as economic theory would have one believe.

An instructive way to look at this picture is to take seriously another axiom of the economic theory of consumer behavior: the axiom of the stability of preferences over time. This is just another way of reconciling the utility-maximization view of the homo economicus with the evidence of more or less stagnant life satisfaction over time. While the first way assumes that preferences (and therefore aspirations) change over time (which may be called the endogenous-preferences approach, cf. e.g. Pollak 1978), the second assumes that preferences and aspirations remain fundamentally stable over time because they are defined on a different conceptual level. What changes over time in this view is the amount or the quality of goods required to satisfy those preferences, meaning that preferences are not defined over goods but over inner states or relevant outcomes. To take a straightforward example (and one unrelated to the relative-income effect or to adaptation), when the sale of air conditioning appliances increases over the years because summers get hotter, this would be interpreted not as a change in preferences for air conditioning appliances but as a change in the amount of goods required to achieve a constant relevant outcome, such as a tolerable room temperature. This interpretation is sometimes framed in terms of (stable) meta-preferences (Jonsson 1996) and has been put forward most prominently by Gary Becker (1976, p. 99–103). A methodological benefit of this approach is that changes in observed preferences would have to be non-arbitrary, i.e. a preference change itself can be explained as an exercise in utility maximization along stable meta-preferences.[3]

In the case of the relative-income effect and of hedonic adaptation, the increase in the amount of goods required to achieve a constant relevant outcome (i.e., utility) is triggered by an increase in consumption itself, either that of others or that of oneself in the past. A classic example is that of increasing car ownership leading to deteriorating public transport, fewer neighborhood shops and changing social norms (cf. Frank 1989, p. 82). As a consequence of these changes, people will have to get a car just to avoid a deterioration of their life in terms of relevant outcomes and life satisfaction. Their new car may end up simply restoring the original level of life satisfaction rather than lifting it above the situation in which nobody owned a car.[4]

As Easterlin noted, this process works in essentially the same way as inflation: just as rising prices mean that people need more nominal income to afford a given consumption basket, "real income is being deflated by rising material aspirations, in this case to yield essentially constant subjective economic well-being" (Easterlin 1996, p. 153). To highlight the close analogy between the relative-income effect and hedonic adaptation on the one hand and monetary inflation on the other, this effect can be labeled "secondary inflation" (Hirata 2011, p. 46): whereas monetary inflation stands for the increase in the monetary units required to purchase a given basket of goods and service, secondary inflation stands for the increase in goods and services required to attain a given level of satisfaction or utility, be it due to the relative-income effect or to hedonic adaptation.

---

[3]I am not endorsing this approach for the purposes Becker had in mind—I rather agree with Amartya Sen (1978) that the utility maximization paradigm is deeply flawed. Nevertheless, Becker's method can be illuminating for better understanding the relative-income effect and hedonic adaptation.

[4]Of course, a given individual may derive additional benefits from car ownership that end up raising her utility above the original situation. Determining the size of these two effects—restoring lost satisfaction or gaining additional satisfaction—will be difficult or impossible in any practical setting, but for conceptual clarity I will assume that these two effects can be observed and analyzed separately.

13.5 Explaining Labor Supply in Terms of Income and Substitution Effects

Secondary inflation may help explain Keynes' misprediction in the following way: As mentioned earlier, according to standard microeconomic theory, rising hourly wages will only make people choose fewer working hours if the positive income effect outweighs the negative substitution effect ("positive" and "negative" referring to the effect of wage increases on the desired amount of leisure time). The dominant interpretation of the empirical evidence, however, seems to be that both effects are of about the same absolute size (Kimball and Shapiro 2008, p. 1–4). While it is inherently difficult to infer "pure" labor supply preferences from labor market data (because the observed data reflect the interaction of supply with demand at going wages and also of institutional influences), this interpretation would be consistent with the relatively small observed correlation over time between wage levels and hours worked as reported above (see also Kimball and Shapiro 2008). In this view, starting from a short-term optimum of, say 40 h of work per week where the marginal utility of one extra hour of work equals that of one extra hour of leisure, the additional utility of that amount of consumption to be had from working one extra hour would be unaffected by changes in hourly wage rate (and therefore remain equal to the additional utility of one more hour of leisure time). Thus, as one's hourly wage increases, the reduced benefit from an additional unit of consumption (because of diminishing marginal utility per unit of consumption) is exactly offset by the additional "consumption reward" per hour of labor (or, equivalently, by the increased opportunity cost of leisure). As a result, people do not find it worthwhile to forgo even a part of the additional income to "buy" more leisure time.

Figure 13.1 sketches this interpretation: the length of the horizontal axis represents total available time (such as 8760 h per year) where time spent working (L) is measured from left to right and leisure time (H, defined as time not spent working for pay) from right to left, and any point along that axis represents a certain division of that time budget between paid work and leisure. The downward-sloping curve A shows the marginal utility of consumption with respect to changes in the number of hours worked, L, where consumption is given by the number of hours worked times the hourly wage rate (assuming no savings). The right-hand curve J, to be read

Fig. 13.1 Dominant interpretation of evidence

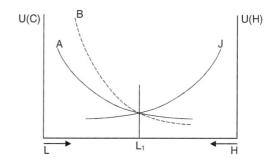

from right to left, shows the marginal utility of leisure. (This graphical representation is based on the simplifying assumption that utility from consumption and utility from leisure are additively separable in order to isolate the effects under consideration.) The individual maximizes utility at that allocation of hours where marginal utilities of consumption (with respect to hours of work) and of leisure are equal, i.e. L_1. If the hourly wage goes up but the observed labor supply remains at the same number of hours because the substitution effect offsets the income effect, this must mean that curve A became steeper in such a way that it still intersects curve J at L_1, such as curve B.

In this conceptual framework, the relative-income effect and hedonic adaptation could mean that an increase in consumption standards (of others and of one's past self) has the same effect as a decrease in one's real hourly wage, once again exactly as monetary inflation. If the effect of secondary inflation is sufficiently large, a gradual increase in wages may be offset entirely by secondary inflation, leaving people treading in the same place as far as the utility-value of leisure and consumption is concerned.[5] Graphically, this would mean that an increase in consumption standards tilts a person's marginal utility of consumption curve to make it flatter.

In this interpretation, the failure of labor supply to go down over time as much as Keynes predicted would not reflect an offsetting substitution effect. Instead, the explanation for the continually large labor supply choices would lie in the devaluation of the utility-value of goods and services through rising consumption standards due to the relative-income effect and hedonic adaptation. We do not know how a person's labor supply would change in the absence of secondary inflation—perhaps Keynes was right in believing that the income effect of rising wages outweighs the substitution effect, but he drew the wrong conclusions because he underestimated the relevance of secondary inflation. Graphically speaking, in the absence of secondary inflation, a wage increase may shift the marginal utility of consumption curve from A to D in Fig. 13.2, resulting in a reduced labor supply L_2. However, secondary inflation induced by rising consumption standards would have the effect of tilting curve D back to A. Curve D would stay in place if other people's wages remained constant, or, importantly, if they cut their working hours as their wages go up, leaving consumption levels stationary.

The relative-income effect implies a straightforward game-theoretical explanation for our failure to further reduce our working hours: we are trapped in the Nash-equilibrium of a prisoners' dilemma because even though we would all collectively be better off working fewer hours, everyone individually would be worse off

[5] I am making the simplifying assumption here that secondary inflation simply downscales the utility-value of consumption in a proportionate manner, even though this is not necessarily the case. For example, cutting back on public transport because of increasing car ownership may affect low-income earners more than high-income earners, thus having an asymmetric effect on the marginal utility of consumption of different groups of people. Bowles and Park (2005) argue that an asymmetric Veblen effect where utility depends on upward comparison only is a more plausible model than a symmetric relative-income effect that depends on average earnings.

Fig. 13.2 Possible
interpretation of evidence
controlling for secondary
inflation

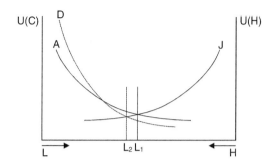

working fewer hours if others do not cut their working hours at the same time.[6] The
obvious welfare-maximizing solution to this prisoners' dilemma is to have a collective agreement enforcing a reduced number of working hours, or some kind of
disincentive or Pigou tax. Indeed, working time laws, labor union agreements and
mandatory retirement saving schemes can be interpreted as (partial) solutions to this
prisoners' dilemma (Frank 1999, p. 159–170). However, as discussed above, progress in this direction has stalled a few decades ago and has not covered all high-
income countries equally, and if my reading of the news is any guide, this is not so
much due to resistance by employers or lawmakers to demands for working time
reductions, but primarily reflects a low priority of working time reductions on the
wish list of workers and labor unions.

A particularly interesting case study provides at least some anecdotal evidence for
explaining the limited interest on the side of unions in working time reductions. In the
wake of the financial crisis, Amador County in California responded to a shrinking
budget in 2009 by cutting salaries and working hours of county employees by 10%,
thus avoiding layoffs and having employees come in from Monday to Thursday for
9 h each day, giving them Fridays off. Workers and the union protested because the
pay cut was deemed unacceptable, but the union eventually agreed to the scheme for a
limited period of two years in order to prevent immediate layoffs. In 2011, the 40 h
work week was restored, but union members insisted on a vote on sticking with the
4-day (36 h) week which won with a clear margin of 71–29%, and the four-day week
was restored, also saving 16 jobs that would otherwise have been lost. One county
employee explained that "I was at first very concerned about losing the 10%, but I
found that I could make it work without a huge hardship. And I found that what I
gained in time actually outweighed what I lost in money" (Graaf et al. 2014, p. 206).

This case study suggests that people either overestimate the benefits of consumption or underestimate the benefits of increased leisure time or both. The problem is
that, if people mispredict the satisfaction they get from different leisure-consumption

---

[6]Since the simple prisoners' dilemma is a perfectly symmetric game, this is only true if all players
have the same preferences for more leisure. In reality, of course, there will always be some workers
who would prefer to work longer hours. This means that the suggested "solution" is of course no
Pareto improvement. Rather, any solution will be a political arbitration between conflicting
interests, as in all real-world collective choice exercises.

Fig. 13.3 Possible
interpretation of evidence
controlling for secondary
inflation and reflecting
positive external effects of
joint leisure time

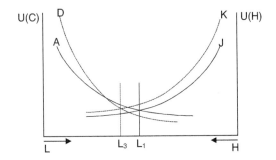

bundles, we can no longer rely on their observed choices to be utility maximizing even from an individual's own perspective. This also implies that it is not hedonic adaptation as such that poses a problem, but the fact that hedonic adaptation to consumption is not correctly anticipated (Loewenstein and Schkade 1999). We would expect fully rational utility maximizers to learn from past hedonic adaptation and to factor that experience into forward looking choices, but that may not be an accurate description of how people think about work and consumption choices.

People may underestimate the value of additional collective leisure time for another reason. An individual pondering whether to cut his work week down to 4 days may see limited benefit in having Fridays off if none of his friends are available for leisure activities on Fridays. The benefit of having Fridays off would be larger if many others also don't have to work on Fridays. A collective move to a 4-day week will likely have Friday or Monday as a focal point, and empirical evidence supports the notion that the utility of "synchronous leisure" (Hallberg 2003) may be larger than that of asynchronous leisure due to a social multiplier effect (Hamermesh 1999; Glaeser et al. 2003; Jenkins and Osberg 2004; cf. also Alesina et al. 2006). In other words, an individual's decision to take more leisure time may have a positive externality on the value of other people's leisure time or, equivalently, a person's decision to spend more hours on the job may have a negative externality, giving rise to multiple working time equilibria, not all of which are welfare maximizing (Jenkins and Osberg 2004, 114). If all workers take Fridays off at the same time, the positive externality might shift each worker's marginal utility of leisure curve upward, such as from J to K in Fig. 13.3. Thus, in the presence of positive leisure externalities and secondary inflation effects, a collective move to more leisure will lead to an even lower equilibrium number of working hours such as L_3. If people fail to anticipate the shift in the marginal utility of consumption associated with the shift from A to D (reflecting stationary consumption standards) and the shift in the marginal utility of leisure associated with the shift from J to K, they may be locked in the equilibrium L_1 even though a collective transition to L_3 would increase welfare.

The Amador County experience does not shed much light on the impact of the relative-income effect because the scheme did not affect the consumption patterns of the entire socio-economic environment of the county employees concerned. In fact, since the relative-income effect predicts that an individual's utility from consumption will depend on the consumption standards of thousands or even millions of people, it is difficult to think of any case study, let alone a controlled experiment, to test for the effect of relative income on work-leisure preferences. However, econometric approaches are suggestive of a positive relationship between income inequality on labor supply, which is exactly what the relative-income effect would predict (Bowles and Park 2005, F405). Another piece of suggestive evidence comes from an analysis of US data of the 1980s showing that a woman is more likely (by about 20%) to take on a job when her husband earns less than her sister's husband (Neumark and Postlewaite 1998, p. 180).

13.6 Conclusion

It is safe to say that Keynes prediction will not come true: 15 h will not be the typical work week in any country a decade hence. While the trend in many European countries seemed to be almost on track to validate Keynes until the 1980s, working times have not decreased much since then.

A temptingly simple explanation for this pattern would be to conclude that people simply value additional consumption sufficiently to prefer using wage increases for additional consumption rather than for additional leisure and that therefore current working time patterns express individual and social preferences and maximize welfare. Yet this view assumes that there is no interaction between work-leisure choices and consumption standards, and there is quite some evidence to suggest that this view needs to be discarded.

A more plausible view would take advantage of the long tradition of theories that explain why the value of one's own consumption also depends on others people's consumption and on one's own past consumption. These theories boil down, as Richard Easterlin recognized, to relative-income effects and hedonic adaptation, and their combined effect is very similar to that of monetary inflation, which should make it rather easy for economists to incorporate these effects into standard theory.

Since it is difficult to estimate the size of the effects in question, it is not possible to determine the welfare maximizing number of working hours per person. There is some anecdotal evidence that people might benefit from working fewer hours even if they do not expect that ex ante, but that is of course too weak a basis for substantive predictions.

To end on a positive note, the preceding considerations suggest that a collective reduction of working hours is a much less costly way of reducing our environmental impact than standard theory would have it (taking the future benefits of less environmental damage into account, one should expect a substantial welfare gain). Maybe selfish utility maximization would make people prefer a 40 h work week, but working only 30, 20 or, at some point, even 15 h may turn out not to be so bad if working hours are reduced collectively. Even if Keynes prediction is off the mark, there are good reasons to welcome further progress towards the 15 h work week.

References

Alesina, A., Glaeser, E., & Sacerdote, B. (2006). Work and leisure in the United States and Europe: Why so different? *NBER Macroeconomics Annual 2005, 20*, 1–64.

Ausubel, J. H., & Grübler, A. (1995). Working less and living longer: Long-term trends in working time and time budgets. *Technological Forecasting and Social Change, 50*(3), 195–213.

Becker, G. S. (1976). *The economic approach to human behavior (EPUB-edition)* (Reprint 2013). Chicago: University of Chicago Press.

Bell, L. A., & Freeman, R. B. (2001). The incentive for working hard: Explaining hours worked differences in the US and Germany. *Labour Economics, 8*(2), 181–202.

Bielenski, H., Bosch, G., & Wagner, A. (2002). *Wie die Europäer arbeiten wollen: Erwerbs- und Arbeitszeitwünsche in 16 Ländern*. Frankfurt: Campus Verlag.

Bolt, J., & Van Zanden, J. L. (2014). The Maddison Project: Collaborative research on historical national accounts. *The Economic History Review, 67*(3), 627–651.

Bowles, S., & Park, Y. (2005). Emulation, inequality, and work hours: Was Thorsten Veblen right? *The Economic Journal, 115*(507), F397–F412.

Cantril, H. (1965). *The pattern of human concerns*. New Brunswick: Rutgers University Press.

De Graaf, J., Wann, D., & Naylor, T. H. (2014). *Affluenza: How overconsumption is killing us—and how to fight back*. San Francisco: Berrett-Koehler Publishers.

Duesenberry, J. S. (1949). *Income, saving and the theory of consumer behavior*. Cambridge: Harvard University Press.

Easterlin, R. A. (1969). Towards a socio-economic theory of fertility. In S. J. Behrman, L. Corsa, & R. Freedman (Eds.), *Fertility and family planning: A world view* (pp. 127–156). Ann Arbor: University of Michigan Press.

Easterlin, R. A. (1973). Relative economic status and the American fertility swing. In E. B. Sheldon (Ed.), *Family economic behavior: Problems and prospects* (pp. 170–227). New York: Lippincott.

Easterlin, R. A. (1974). Does economic growth improve the human lot? Some empirical evidence. In P. A. David & M. W. Reder (Eds.), *Nations and households in economic growth: Essays in honour of Moses Abramovitz* (pp. 89–125). New York: Academic Press.

Easterlin, R. A. (1996). *Growth triumphant* (Reprint 2009). Ann Arbor: University of Michigan Press.

Easterlin, R. A. (2001). Income and happiness: Towards a unified theory. *The Economic Journal, 111*(473), 465–484.

Frank, R. H. (1989). Frames of reference and the quality of life. *The American Economic Review, 79*(2), 80–85.

Frank, R. H. (1997). The frame of reference as a public good. *The Economic Journal, 107*(445), 1832–1847.

Frank, R. H. (1999). *Luxury fever: Why money fails to satisfy in an era of excess*. Princeton: Princeton University Press.

Frank, R. H. (2010). Context is more important than Keynes realized. In L. Pecchi & G. Piga (Eds.), *Revisiting Keynes. Economic possibilities for our grandchildren* (pp. 143–150). Cambridge, MA: The MIT Press.

Frank, R. H. (2012). The Easterlin paradox revisited. *Emotion, 12*(6), 1188–1191.

Frederick, S., & Loewenstein, G. (1999). Hedonic adaptation. In D. Kahneman, E. Diener, & N. Schwarz (Eds.), *Well-being: The foundations of hedonic psychology* (pp. 302–329). New York: Russel Sage Foundation.

Glaeser, E. L., Sacerdote, B. I., & Scheinkman, J. A. (2003). The social multiplier. *Journal of the European Economic Association, 1*(2–3), 345–353.

Golden, L., & Gebreselassie, T. (2007). Overemployment mismatches: The preference for fewer work hours. *Monthly Labor Review, 130*, 18.

Golden, L. (2014). *Measuring Long, Overtime, and Un-Preferred Hours of Work*. Working Paper for the EINet Measurement Group, University of Chicago School of Social Service Administration.

Grözinger, G., Matiaske, W., & Tobsch, V. (2008). *Arbeitszeitwünsche, Arbeitslosigkeit und Arbeitszeitpolitik* (No. 103). SOEP papers on multidisciplinary panel data research.

Hallberg, D. (2003). Synchronous leisure, jointness and household labor supply. *Labour Economics, 10*(2), 185–203.

Hamermesh, D. S. (1999). The timing of work over time. *The Economic Journal, 109*(452), 37–66.

Hirata, J. (2011). *Happiness, ethics, and economics*. London: Routledge.

Holst, E. & Bringmann, J. (2017). *Arbeitszeitwünsche von Beschäftigten: eine Black Box? Zu Unschärfen der Ermittlung von Unter- und Überbeschäftigung*. DIW. DIW Roundup 106.

Jacobs, J. A., & Gerson, K. (2001). Overworked individuals or overworked families? *Work and Occupations, 28*(1), 40–63.

Jenkins, S. P., & Osberg, L. (2004). Nobody to play with? In D. S. Hamermesh & G. A. Pfann (Eds.), *The economics of time use* (pp. 113–145). Bingley: Emerald Group Publishing Limited.

Jonsson, P. O. (1996). On meta-preferences and incomplete preference maps. *International Advances in Economic Research, 2*(2), 112–119.

Keynes, J. M. (1978). Economic possibilities for our grandchildren. In J. M. Keynes (Ed.), *Collected writings vol. 9: Essays in persuasion* (pp. 321–332). London: Royal Economic Society/Macmillan Press.

Kimball, M. S., & Shapiro, M. D. (2008). *Labor supply: Are the income and substitution effects both large or both small?* (No. w14208). National Bureau of Economic Research.

Lichtenberg, J. (1996). Consuming because others consume. *Social Theory & Practice, 22*(3), 273–297.

Loewenstein, G., & Schkade, D. (1999). Wouldn't it be nice? Predicting future feelings. In D. Kahneman, E. Diener, & N. Schwarz (Eds.), *Well-being: The foundations of hedonic psychology* (pp. 85–105). New York: Russel Sage Foundation.

Messenger, J. C. (2011). Working time trends and developments in Europe. *Cambridge Journal of Economics, 35*(2), 295–316.

Neumark, D., & Postlewaite, A. (1998). Relative income concerns and the rise in married women's employment. *Journal of Public Economics, 70*(1), 157–183.

Pollak, R. A. (1978). Endogenous tastes in demand and welfare analysis. *The American Economic Review, 68*(2), 374–379.

Sachs, J. D. (2017). *Man and machine: The macroeconomics of the digital revolution*. Mimeo from a conference organized by the Centre for Economic Performance and the International Growth Centre.

Schneider, M. (2007). The nature, history and significance of the concept of positional goods. *History of Economics Review, 45*, 60–81.

Schor, J. (2003). The (even more) overworked American. In J. de Graaf (Ed.), *Take back your time. Fighting overwork and time poverty in America* (pp. 6–11). San Francisco: Berrett-Koehler Publishers.

Smith, A. (1776). *An inquiry into the nature and causes of the wealth of nations* (Reprint 1979). Oxford: Oxford University Press.

Stiglitz, J. E. (2010). Toward a general theory of consumerism: Reflections on Keynes's economic possibilities for our grandchildren. In L. Pecchi & G. Piga (Eds.), *Revisiting Keynes. Economic possibilities for our grandchildren* (pp. 41–85). Cambridge, MA: The MIT Press.

The Maddison Project. (2013). The Maddison project database, version 2013. (cf. Bolt & van Zanden 2014). Groningen Growth and Development Centre. http://www.ggdc.net/maddison/maddison-project/home.htm

UNEP. (2011). *Decoupling natural resource use and environmental impacts from economic growth. A report of the working group on decoupling to the international resource panel*. In M. Fischer-Kowalski, M. Swilling, E.U. von Weizsäcker & Y. Ren. Nairobi: UNEP.

Chapter 14
Using Well-Being Metrics to Assess Social Well-Being and Ill-Being: Lessons from Rising Mortality Rates in the United States

Carol Graham and Sergio Pinto

Abstract Richard Easterlin inspired the use of well-being metrics in economics. This chapter highlights their potential to help us identify and understand social ill-being. The 2016 election in the United States exposed unhappiness and frustration among poor and uneducated whites. The starkest marker is the rise in preventable deaths and suicides among the middle aged of this cohort. In contrast, minorities have higher levels of optimism, and their life expectancies continue to rise. Low-income respondents display the largest differences, with poor blacks by far the most optimistic, and poor whites the least. African Americans and Hispanics also report higher life satisfaction and lower stress than poor whites, with the gaps peaking in middle age. We explored the association between our well-being data and mortality trends. The absence of hope among less than college-educated whites matches the trends in premature mortality among 35–64 year olds. Reported pain, reliance on disability insurance, low labor force participation, and differential levels of resilience across races all have mediating effects in the desperation-mortality associations. We explore the role of place, which is also associated with the well-being trends for different cohorts. The matches between indicators of well-being and mortality suggest that the former could serve as warning indicators in the future, rather than waiting for rising mortality to sound the alarms.

A slightly different version of this chapter was originally published in the *Journal of Population Economics* as "Unequal Hopes and Lives in the U.S.: Optimism, Race, Place, and Premature Mortality" (https://doi.org/10.1007/s00148-018-0687-y), and is published here with the permission of Springer Nature.[1]

The authors are, respectively, Leo Pasvolsky Senior Fellow at the Brookings Institution and College Park Professor, University of Maryland (CGRAHAM@brookings.edu), and PhD student, University of Maryland (sergio_tiago_pinto@yahoo.com).

C. Graham (✉)
Brookings Institution, Washington DC, USA

University of Maryland, College Park, MD, USA
e-mail: CGRAHAM@brookings.edu

S. Pinto
University of Maryland, College Park, MD, USA

14.1   Introduction

Over the past several years, stark disparities in well-being have emerged across the U.S. population, revealing pockets of desperation and despair. Most notably, minorities, who have traditionally faced discrimination, are more optimistic and less frustrated than are poor and uneducated whites, who live primarily in suburban and rural areas in the heartland. Rising mortality among uneducated whites – driven by preventable deaths such as suicides and opioid poisoning – is the starkest marker of this desperation.

These trends reflect a social crisis with multiple and complex causes, not all of which we fully understand. An important first step is to seek better understanding of its reach and causes. We hope that the results of our research, based on metrics of well-being, such as life satisfaction and optimism about the future on the one hand, and stress, worry, and anger on the other, contribute to that effort. The usage of these metrics in economic analysis, meanwhile, was inspired by Richard Easterlin, the first modern economist to study happiness and a distinguished demographer.

We found marked differences in life satisfaction, optimism, and stress across poor blacks, Hispanics, and whites. The latter cohort demonstrates signs of deep desperation and the former two are happier, more optimistic, and less stressed (our measure of optimism is a question that asks respondents where on a 0–10 scale ladder they think their life satisfaction will be in 5 years). The gaps between African Americans and whites peak in the middle age years. We also find that individuals who exercise more and smoke less are happier and less stressed. Poor rural whites, meanwhile, are the least hopeful among the poor groups. Additionally, we find important differences across *places* after controlling for respondents' traits and map the states associated with higher and lower indicators of well-being. Finally, we explore the associations between the patterns in premature mortality and in well-being by matching our individual well-being data with CDC mortality statistics.

Our metrics highlight the high costs of being poor in the U.S. and uncover costs that are less in the form of the material deprivation more typical of poverty in poor countries, and more in the form of stress, insecurity, poor health, and lack of hope.[1] These costs manifest themselves differently across race and place, and show up among poor and uneducated whites in the form of deep desperation.

14.1.1   Existing Studies

What explains these surprising trends, which are, at least among wealthy countries, unique to the U.S.? A number of studies have focused on differential trends in

---

[1] For example, the high material costs of being poor in Latin America in the 1970s, which included paying as much as 18 times more per unit of water and electricity, with inferior health outcomes (Adrianzen and Graham 1974).

mobility (and fear of downward mobility, Cherlin 2016); differential health behaviors (Chetty et al. 2016); inequality of opportunity (Chetty et al. 2014); and structural economic trends. The latter include the bottoming out of manufacturing in many regions and a related increase in dropouts from the labor market (Krueger 2017).

Numerous studies provide evidence of particular policies or shocks that result in changes in the happiness and/or hope of particular cohorts (Herbst 2013; Angelini et al. 2015). In the U.S. in recent decades, it is likely that employment trends in manufacturing regions, followed by the 2008–2009 financial crisis, had a strong negative effect in the same places. At the same time, the causality likely runs in the other direction as well, and the unhappiness and lack of hope related to these trends has broader implications for health and longevity. Happier people tend to be healthier and more productive (Graham 2008; Graham et al. 2004; deNeve et al. 2013). And individuals with a greater sense of purpose—described as eudemonic well-being by some economists and psychologists, and as "flourishing" by others—also tend to live longer (Steptoe et al. 2015; Keyes and Simoes 2012).

In November 2015, Case and Deaton (2015a) published a study showing a marked increase in the all-cause mortality of high school (and below) educated white middle-aged non-Hispanic men and women between 1999 and 2013.[2] The change reversed decades of progress in mortality and is most prevalent among uneducated non-Hispanic whites. Drug and alcohol poisoning, suicide, chronic liver diseases, and cirrhosis were the major factors in the mortality rate increase. Self-reported health, mental health, and ability to conduct activities of daily living in this group also saw a marked decrease.

The authors' follow-up (Case and Deaton 2017) suggests that the trends in mortality encompass a broader range of ages and that these cohorts experienced a stalling of progress against other major conditions (e.g., heart disease and cancer), with obesity and smoking as possible contributors. They also found that the trends pertained not only to rural areas but also to smaller cities and suburban areas, with the exception of the largest coastal cities.

Dwyer-Lindgren et al. (2016) found that cardiovascular disease mortality tended to be highest along the Mississippi River, while self-harm and interpersonal violence were elevated in southwestern counties, and chronic respiratory disease was highest in Kentucky and West Virginia. Deaths from self-harm declined in the past decade in California, Texas, and other coastal areas, but increased in the Midwest and in parts of New England. Our primary focus was on the increase in premature deaths due to these so-called "deaths of despair" and the extent to which reflect the patterns in desperation that we found in our data.

Neither blacks nor Hispanics experienced an increase in death rates during the same period. Assari and Lankarani (2016) found that while black Americans have worse health indicators than white Americans on average, they are better off in terms

---

[2]Gelman and Auerbach (2016) posit that these trends are driven in part by aggregation bias at the older ages of the 45–54 cohort.

of mental health: depression, anxiety, and suicide are all more common among whites.

Shiels et al. (2017) show the preventable death increases occurring at an earlier age (25–30) for white men and women, as well as for Native Indian men and women, in addition to the increases in the 30–49 age group for these same cohorts. The increase in suicides and accidental deaths underlying these increases stand in sharp contrast to the flat or decreasing trends for these kinds of deaths for the same age groups of blacks and Hispanics.

Pierce and Schott (2016) found that U.S. counties with more exposure to exogenous trade liberalization had an increase in suicide deaths. Despite the geographic variation, these were concentrated among whites, a group with disproportionately high employment in manufacturing.

14.2 Data and Empirical Specification

The main data source of our paper is the Gallup Healthways (GH) survey, collected daily for adult individuals all across the U.S. It covers a wide range of demographic details and economic and self-reported health conditions of the respondents, as well as a series of subjective well-being questions. In some specifications, we complement the GH with data from the American Community Survey (ACS), the Centers for Disease Control and Prevention (CDC), and the Survey of Epidemiology and End Results (SEER).[3] These three data sources allow us to compute several variables at the Metropolitan Statistical Area (MSA) level: household income, income inequality, mortality rates, and population race shares.

In our main specification, we use only GH data and we focus on the 2010–2015 period. While our interest is the entire U.S. adult population, data availability imposes some constraints. Firstly, we only consider those living in MSAs. As of 2015, according to United States Census Bureau (USCB) estimates,[4] the 381 MSAs in U.S. territory accounted for 85.6% of the population.[5] Secondly, GH only computes MSA-level sampling weights for MSAs with more 300 respondents.[6] As a result, between 188 and 190 of the 381 MSAs can be used for 2010–12 (representing about 89% of the population living in MSAs), and between 105 and 108 can be used for the 2013–15 period (approximately 79% of the population living in MSAs). Because the number and definition of MSAs changed in 2013, a total of 196 MSAs appear in at least 1 year, and 103 are present in every year between 2010

---

[3]Obtained through NBER at http://www.nber.org/data/seer_u.s._county_population_data.html

[4]Source: http://factfinder.census.gov/faces/tableservices/jsf/pages/productview.xhtml?pid=PEP_2015_PEPANNRES

[5]This proportion has increased very slightly over time: from 85% to 85.5% from 2010–2014.

[6]In additional specifications, we use national-level weights (doubling the number of MSAs), with no meaningful changes.

and 2015 (approximately 78% of the population living in MSA). In broad terms, the 196 MSAs tend to correspond to those above 300,000 people and the more restricted group of 103 to those above 500,000 people.[7]

For the 2010–15 period, GH provides us with a repeated cross section of approximately 1.6 million U.S. adults, of which 1.3 million live in MSAs, with the remaining in micropolitan statistical areas or even smaller counties. Over 1 million have MSA-level survey weights. From these, approximately 0.8 million have data for both the dependent variables under analysis and the controls. This group will be the focus of our analysis, although we also have some analyses that include the smaller areas.

In some instances, we had to make additional adjustments to the individual level data. The income variable collected in GH assigns respondents to a 0–10 scale for the household's pretax income, with 0 being the lowest value (below \$720/year) and 10 the highest (above \$120,000/year). That prevents us from directly applying the Census bureau poverty thresholds based on exact values.[8] We divided respondents into three categories: poor, middle-income, and rich. Respondents in the top income bracket defined by GH, those with a pretax household income of over \$120,000/year identified as "rich" (roughly 18% of total respondents). We assigned those in the bottom five categories, whose pretax income is below \$22,000 per household to the "poor" category (approximately 17% of the respondents).[9] We classified those in the remaining five income categories as middle income. For race, GH assigns respondents to one of five categories (Asian, Black, Hispanic, Other Race, and White).

Equation (14.1) below describes the empirical specification for our race-income exploration:

$$
\begin{aligned}
WB_{ijt} = \beta_0 &+ \beta_1{}^*\left(poorhh_{ijt}\right) + \beta_2{}^*\left(richhh_{ijt}\right) + \beta_3{}^*\left(black_{ijt}\right) \\
&+ \beta_4{}^*\left(hispanic_{ijt}\right) + \beta_5{}^*\left(asian_{ijt}\right) + \beta_6{}^*\left(other\ race_{ijt}\right) \\
&+ \beta_7{}^*\left(poorhh_{ijt}\right) * \left(black_{ijt}\right) + \beta_8{}^*\left(poorhh_{ijt}\right) * \left(hispanic_{ijt}\right) \\
&+ \beta_9{}^*\left(poorhh_{ijt}\right) * \left(asian_{ijt}\right) + \beta_{10}{}^*\left(poorhh_{ijt}\right) * \left(other\ race_{ijt}\right) \quad (14.1) \\
&+ \beta_{11}{}^*\left(richhh_{ijt}\right) * \left(black_{ijt}\right) + \beta_{12}{}^*\left(richhh_{ijt}\right) * \left(hispanic_{ijt}\right) \\
&+ \beta_{13}{}^*\left(richhh_{ijt}\right) * \left(asian_{ijt}\right) + \beta_{14}{}^*\left(richhh_{ijt}\right) * \left(other\ race_{ijt}\right) \\
&+ \beta_{15}{}^*\left(Z_{ijt}\right) + \varnothing_j + \gamma_t + \varepsilon_{ijt}
\end{aligned}
$$

WB represents one of the well- or ill-being markers under consideration for individual i, in MSA j, for time t. We consider: (i) reported life satisfaction today, (ii) expected life satisfaction in 5 years (i.e., optimism), (iii) experienced stress

---

[7]GH halved the number of daily interviews to 500 in 2013, decreasing the number of weighted MSAs.

[8]We employed alternative definitions for poor, middle-income, and rich individuals, including that from the Census Bureau. The results we obtained are quantitatively similar to those in our main specification.

[9]This percentage and the previous one do not use Gallup's survey weights. The corresponding shares of weighted respondents are 15% and 24%.

yesterday, (iv) worry yesterday, (v) satisfied with place of residence, (vi) experienced anger yesterday, and (vii) has a social support network that can be relied on in times of need. The first two questions are on a 0–10 scale, while the remaining ones are binary (0–1 scale). We estimate all specifications using linear OLS models for ease of interpretation (we also provide the estimation results under ordered logistic and logistic regression models – see Sect. 14.3 for additional details).

Poorhh and *richhh* are dummy variables identifying if the respondent belongs to a poor or a rich household, respectively. *Black, Asian, Hispanic,* and *Other race* are dummy variables identifying the respondent's race. They are interacted with those for income level (*poorhh* and *richhh*) to explore race-income heterogeneities. The omitted category for income corresponds to middle-income respondents, while that for race corresponds to whites.

Z is a vector of individual socio-demographic controls. These include the following dummy variables:

- age groups[10] (18–24, 25–34, 35–44, 45–54, 55–64, 65+);
- gender (male and female);
- marital status (single, married or in a domestic partnership, divorced or separated, and widowed);
- educational level (high school dropout, high school graduate, technical/vocational school, college dropout, college graduate, post-graduate);
- employment status (employed full-time, employed part-time, self-employed, employed part-time but wanting full-time, unemployed, and not in the workforce);
- religious preference (preference, no preference, or atheist);

We also included binary variables for several health-related characteristics: experiencing pain the previous day; having (self-reported) health problems that prevent "normal" activities for someone of the respondent's age; body mass index (BMI)-based categories (underweight, normal range, overweight, obese); smoking; and having exercised at least once over the previous week. We controlled for reporting lack of money for food or for healthcare over the previous 12 months. $\varnothing_j$ represents MSA dummies and γ_t represents year dummies. All regressions use MSA-level survey weights unless otherwise specified.[11]

As an additional control within our baseline framework, we use two specifications where the dependent variable is the expected future life satisfaction. In the first, we follow Eq. (14.1) precisely, while in the second one we include current life satisfaction as an additional control. The reason is that individuals may anchor their

---

[10]The age dummies have ranges that contain a similar number of observations and generally match the age brackets present in the other databases that we used, such as the CDC's Compressed Mortality File.

[11]The inclusion of (MSA)*(Year) interactions, month of interview dummies, other types of survey weights, and no survey weights at all, does not meaningfully change in the coefficients.

beliefs about future life satisfaction on their own answer about their current life satisfaction. As a result, if a certain group (e.g., low-income respondents) reports low life satisfaction, they may also report low future expected life satisfaction, although that might only be a reflex of their low starting point, rather than an indication of unusually low optimism.

We estimate all specifications using linear OLS models for ease of interpretation. The use of nonlinear models makes direct interpretations of the estimated coefficients difficult, as they express log odds rather than linear effects. Additionally, our main parameters of interest include the coefficients for race and income variables, as well as the corresponding interactions. The latter type of variables makes the computation of odds ratios more complex, as they depend on the value of the components of the interaction term. The results we obtain under OLS are fairly similar to those under ordered logit (for current and expected life satisfaction) and logit (for the remaining dependent variables) specifications and our findings are robust to the choice of model.[12] In addition, with either specification, as all the independent variables are binary, the coefficients reflect relative magnitudes that we can compare to the omitted category.

14.3 Baseline Results and Interpretation

14.3.1 Results

We first used a simple specification exploring the race-income interactions without other individual sociodemographic controls.[13] Yet our results here are remarkably similar to the specification including the full battery of controls (Table 14.1). The main result (in both specifications) is that poor blacks are significantly more optimistic about their future life satisfaction and both less stressed and less worried than poor whites (Table 14.1). The black-white optimism difference holds across income levels, although it diminishes as incomes increase. Hispanics demonstrate a similar trend, with poor Hispanics also more optimistic than poor whites, but the gap is less stark than between blacks and whites, and there is no trend across income categories. Heterogeneities across races are also visible in life satisfaction and in incidence of

---

[12]While the logit and ordered logit models are technically the appropriate specification, it has become accepted practice to use OLS in happiness regressions, for ease of interpretation, as long as the results are very close. In our case, the OLS specifications yield slightly more significant coefficients for some variables of interest, but the patterns are otherwise identical and the choice of model does not affect our conclusions.

[13]However, we include both year and MSA dummies in every specification.

C. Graham and S. Pinto

Table 14.1 Race-income heterogeneities, with individual-level controls (2010–2015)

Variables	(1) OLS: bpl	(2) OLS: bpla	(3) OLS: bpla	(4) OLS: worry	(5) OLS: stress	(6) OLS: citysat	(7) OLS: anger	(8) OLS: Social support
	Full set of controls (196 MSAs)	Full set of controls (196 MSAs)	Full set of controls + bpl control (196 MSAs)	Full set of controls (196 MSAs)	Full set of controls (196 MSAs)	Full set of controls (196 MSAs)	Full set of controls (196 MSAs)	Full set of controls (200 MSAs)
Reported life satisfaction today (0–10)			0.556***					
			(0.0042)					
Poor household	−0.334***	−0.225***	−0.040***	0.029***	0.016***	−0.019***	−0.001	−0.025***
	(0.0107)	(0.0113)	(0.0100)	(0.0025)	(0.0026)	(0.0023)	(0.0023)	(0.0028)
Rich household	0.398***	0.275***	0.054***	−0.007***	0.015***	0.017***	0.002	0.008***
	(0.0072)	(0.0079)	(0.0069)	(0.0020)	(0.0024)	(0.0018)	(0.0017)	(0.0019)
Black	0.171***	0.643***	0.548***	−0.083***	−0.131***	−0.053***	−0.006**	−0.029***
	(0.0133)	(0.0146)	(0.0127)	(0.0035)	(0.0040)	(0.0069)	(0.0029)	(0.0040)
Hispanic	0.244***	0.279***	0.143***	−0.021***	−0.085***	0.004	−0.005	−0.019***
	(0.0139)	(0.0169)	(0.0166)	(0.0048)	(0.0044)	(0.0040)	(0.0029)	(0.0044)
Asian	−0.079***	−0.166***	−0.122***	−0.002	−0.056***	0.013***	−0.007	−0.042***
	(0.0204)	(0.0277)	(0.0204)	(0.0063)	(0.0055)	(0.0043)	(0.0045)	(0.0071)
Other race	0.094***	0.163***	0.111***	−0.020***	−0.060***	−0.026***	0.008	−0.038***
	(0.0232)	(0.0238)	(0.0232)	(0.0053)	(0.0063)	(0.0057)	(0.0050)	(0.0064)
(Rich household) *(Black)	−0.216***	−0.216***	−0.096***	0.006	−0.002	0.019***	−0.001	−0.007
	(0.0258)	(0.0236)	(0.0222)	(0.0067)	(0.0066)	(0.0045)	(0.0055)	(0.0088)
(Rich household) *(Hispanic)	−0.175***	−0.149***	−0.051**	0.026***	0.043***	0.003	0.018**	0.006
	(0.0258)	(0.0282)	(0.0236)	(0.0077)	(0.0073)	(0.0052)	(0.0073)	(0.0072)

	(1)	(2)	(3)	(4)	(5)	(6)	(7)	(8)
(Rich household) *(Asian)	−0.112***	−0.036	0.026	−0.003	0.010	0.003	0.003	−0.018**
	(0.0326)	(0.0350)	(0.0258)	(0.0089)	(0.0102)	(0.0049)	(0.0069)	(0.0091)
(Rich household) *(Other race)	−0.075*	−0.181***	−0.139***	0.009	0.011	−0.001	0.012	−0.015
	(0.0445)	(0.0505)	(0.0474)	(0.0136)	(0.0140)	(0.0109)	(0.0106)	(0.0138)
(Poor household) *(Black)	0.381***	0.261***	0.049**	−0.014***	−0.007*	−0.023***	0.008*	−0.015**
	(0.0227)	(0.0214)	(0.0219)	(0.0051)	(0.0040)	(0.0051)	(0.0045)	(0.0067)
(Poor household) *(Hispanic)	0.285***	−0.137***	−0.296***	0.000	−0.020***	0.019***	0.025***	−0.035***
	(0.0184)	(0.0281)	(0.0266)	(0.0049)	(0.0056)	(0.0045)	(0.0049)	(0.0079)
(Poor household) *(Asian)	0.212***	0.149***	0.031	0.008	0.017	−0.014	0.008	0.001
	(0.0389)	(0.0413)	(0.0363)	(0.0120)	(0.0127)	(0.0092)	(0.0103)	(0.0130)
(Poor household) *(Other race)	0.154***	0.100*	0.014	−0.000	0.009	−0.022**	0.025**	−0.031**
	(0.0501)	(0.0541)	(0.0460)	(0.0105)	(0.0110)	(0.0106)	(0.0102)	(0.0132)
Lacked money for food (past 12 m)	−0.715***	−0.255***	0.142***	0.152***	0.136***	−0.074***	0.073***	−0.122***
	(0.0126)	(0.0120)	(0.0096)	(0.0029)	(0.0026)	(0.0024)	(0.0026)	(0.0032)
Lacked money for healthcare (past 12 m)	−0.534***	−0.309***	−0.012	0.125***	0.111***	−0.050***	0.050***	−0.118***
	(0.0097)	(0.0100)	(0.0096)	(0.0028)	(0.0022)	(0.0018)	(0.0021)	(0.0028)
Age 25–34	−0.204***	−0.190***	−0.076***	0.009***	−0.029***	−0.012***	−0.005*	−0.036***
	(0.0132)	(0.0111)	(0.0117)	(0.0032)	(0.0035)	(0.0026)	(0.0027)	(0.0033)
Age 35–44	−0.305***	−0.542***	−0.373***	0.021***	−0.056***	0.005	−0.005*	−0.076***

(continued)

Table 14.1 (continued)

	(1)	(2)	(3)	(4)	(5)	(6)	(7)	(8)
Age 45–54	−0.362***	−0.852***	−0.651***	0.018***	−0.099***	0.022***	−0.027***	−0.111***
	(0.0146)	(0.0134)	(0.0133)	(0.0036)	(0.0033)	(0.0033)	(0.0028)	(0.0038)
Age 55–64	−0.295***	−1.276***	−1.112***	−0.021***	−0.166***	0.036***	−0.050***	−0.117***
	(0.0154)	(0.0142)	(0.0138)	(0.0039)	(0.0035)	(0.0031)	(0.0030)	(0.0039)
Age 65+	−0.030**	−1.745***	−1.728***	−0.100***	−0.273***	0.063***	−0.073***	−0.080***
	(0.0150)	(0.0165)	(0.0171)	(0.0034)	(0.0036)	(0.0034)	(0.0031)	(0.0036)
Male	−0.286***	−0.339***	−0.180***	−0.028***	−0.047***	−0.008***	0.013***	−0.011***
	(0.0146)	(0.0203)	(0.0184)	(0.0037)	(0.0042)	(0.0031)	(0.0034)	(0.0037)
Single	−0.215***	−0.050***	0.069***	−0.001	−0.003*	−0.011***	0.001	0.026***
	(0.0084)	(0.0083)	(0.0052)	(0.0018)	(0.0016)	(0.0017)	(0.0011)	(0.0016)
Divorced/separated	−0.314***	−0.016	0.159***	0.021***	0.019***	−0.018***	0.004**	0.012***
	(0.0085)	(0.0078)	(0.0066)	(0.0021)	(0.0019)	(0.0018)	(0.0018)	(0.0023)
Widowed	−0.185***	−0.236***	−0.133***	−0.006*	−0.017***	0.017***	−0.021***	0.057***
	(0.0083)	(0.0126)	(0.0117)	(0.0020)	(0.0020)	(0.0020)	(0.0020)	(0.0024)
Underweight	−0.137***	−0.146***	−0.070***	0.018***	0.003	−0.011**	−0.003	−0.010*
	(0.0129)	(0.0156)	(0.0134)	(0.0031)	(0.0025)	(0.0023)	(0.0022)	(0.0033)
Overweight	−0.057***	−0.005	0.027***	−0.009***	−0.001	−0.004***	0.002	−0.007***
	(0.0267)	(0.0242)	(0.0211)	(0.0050)	(0.0052)	(0.0046)	(0.0051)	(0.0059)
Obese	−0.139***	−0.038***	0.039***	−0.021***	−0.005***	−0.005***	0.003*	−0.016***
	(0.0062)	(0.0062)	(0.0054)	(0.0015)	(0.0016)	(0.0013)	(0.0013)	(0.0017)
Health problems	−0.375***	−0.414***	−0.205***	0.079***	0.083***	−0.027***	0.018***	−0.030***
	(0.0075)	(0.0074)	(0.0065)	(0.0016)	(0.0018)	(0.0019)	(0.0017)	(0.0023)
Experienced physical pain	−0.350***	−0.327***	−0.132***	0.181***	0.183***	−0.040***	0.113***	−0.044***
	(0.0095)	(0.0096)	(0.0087)	(0.0019)	(0.0021)	(0.0017)	(0.0017)	(0.0024)

	(1)	(2)	(3)	(4)	(5)	(6)	(7)	(8)
Smokes	−0.283*** (0.0082)	−0.010 (0.0089)	0.147*** (0.0065)	0.030*** (0.0026)	0.043*** (0.0019)	−0.040*** (0.0016)	0.036*** (0.0022)	−0.026*** (0.0024)
Exercises at least once over last 7 days	0.245*** (0.0078)	0.246*** (0.0089)	0.110*** (0.0075)	−0.037*** (0.0018)	−0.035*** (0.0019)	0.008*** (0.0018)	−0.015*** (0.0019)	0.007*** (0.0024)
Religious preference (vs. atheist)	0.101*** (0.0057)	0.117*** (0.0092)	0.061*** (0.0079)	0.001 (0.0015)	−0.004** (0.0015)	0.016*** (0.0012)	−0.006*** (0.0015)	0.019*** (0.0016)
Less than HS	−0.028 (0.0066)	−0.359*** (0.0074)	−0.344*** (0.0071)	−0.035*** (0.0018)	−0.070*** (0.0018)	−0.006** (0.0020)	0.014*** (0.0018)	−0.062*** (0.0022)
HS graduate	−0.068*** (0.0174)	−0.158*** (0.0245)	−0.120*** (0.0216)	−0.045*** (0.0036)	−0.076*** (0.0046)	−0.006*** (0.0029)	−0.000 (0.0031)	−0.020*** (0.0048)
Technical/vocational school	−0.154*** (0.0080)	−0.108*** (0.0087)	−0.023** (0.0077)	−0.030*** (0.0025)	−0.051*** (0.0026)	−0.018*** (0.0021)	0.003 (0.0016)	−0.025*** (0.0024)
Some college	−0.111*** (0.0116)	−0.053*** (0.0136)	0.009* (0.0109)	−0.018*** (0.0030)	−0.026*** (0.0032)	−0.017*** (0.0026)	0.001 (0.0025)	−0.015*** (0.0032)
Post-graduate	0.135*** (0.0062)	0.113*** (0.0062)	0.038*** (0.0050)	0.011*** (0.0025)	0.023*** (0.0021)	0.001 (0.0016)	−0.001 (0.0014)	0.004** (0.0020)
Self employed	0.007 (0.0062)	0.220*** (0.0066)	0.216*** (0.0054)	0.049*** (0.0019)	0.026*** (0.0019)	−0.008*** (0.0012)	0.015*** (0.0016)	(0.0018)
Employed PT	0.238*** (0.0122)	0.122*** (0.0126)	−0.011 (0.0117)	−0.014*** (0.0038)	−0.057*** (0.0037)	0.008*** (0.0027)	−0.008*** (0.0030)	
Underemployed	−0.280*** (0.0101)	−0.017* (0.0108)	0.139*** (0.0089)	0.056*** (0.0039)	0.007** (0.0035)	−0.025*** (0.0025)	0.016*** (0.0024)	
Unemployed	−0.513*** (0.0123)	0.052*** (0.0100)	0.337*** (0.0100)	0.095*** (0.0031)	0.024*** (0.0033)	−0.039*** (0.0027)	0.026*** (0.0028)	

(continued)

Table 14.1 (continued)

	(1)	(2)	(3)	(4)	(5)	(6)	(7)	(8)
	(0.0150)	(0.0150)	(0.0151)	(0.0034)	(0.0040)	(0.0033)	(0.0028)	
Not in workforce	0.112***	−0.076***	−0.138***	0.000	−0.056***	−0.001	0.001	
	(0.0071)	(0.0080)	(0.0071)	(0.0018)	(0.0021)	(0.0014)	(0.0018)	
Constant	7.668***	8.838***	4.577***	0.264***	0.536***	0.891***	0.148***	1.026***
	(0.0185)	(0.0162)	(0.0338)	(0.0051)	(0.0042)	(0.0043)	(0.0035)	(0.0049)
Observations	770,899	770,899	770,899	770,899	770,899	770,899	608,787	347,080
R-squared	0.175	0.165	0.367	0.129	0.130	0.064	0.062	0.109
MSA dummies	Yes	Yes	Yes	Yes	Yes	Yes	Yes	Yes
Year dummies	Yes	Yes	Yes	Yes	Yes	Yes	Yes	Yes

Clustered standard errors (at the MSA level) in parentheses

Note: These regressions include the 196 MSAs for which sampling weights were available at least in 1 year, except for Social support, where 200 MSAs were available. All specifications use the 2010–2015 period, except for anger (2010–2013) and social support (2008–2012)

***$p < 0.01$; **$p < 0.05$; *$p < 0.1$

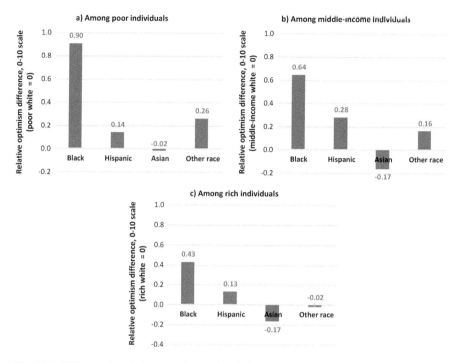

Fig. 14.1 Differential optimism associated with different race groups (relative to white), within each income group

stress and worry, in particular among the poor, where whites fare clearly worse than other race groups.[14]

When we control for socio-demographic factors blacks are again *by far* the most optimistic cohort. This is particularly so *within* poor respondents, where they are almost an entire point (0.90) higher on the 0–10 scale than are poor whites (Table 14.1; Fig. 14.1).[15] Again, the gap decreased as one moves from lower to higher income classes. Among rich individuals, African Americans are only half a point (0.43) higher than whites on the optimism scale.[16] There are modest

[14]We also explored reported depression and found that it was also highest among low-income whites. A more comprehensive account, however, would require a separate study. Depression and happiness are distinct emotional states. While positive emotional states, such as happiness and smiling, tend to track closely, negative states – stress, anger, and depression – track differently, with depression the most distinct. See Stone and Mackie (2013).

[15]We computed Fig. 14.1 using the coefficients from column (2), the BPLA regression without BPL as a control. When we use current BPL as a control (column (3)), we get slightly lower gaps between poor blacks and poor whites and they decrease less as income increases.

[16]These race-income heterogeneities are also very strong when generating separate regressions by year.

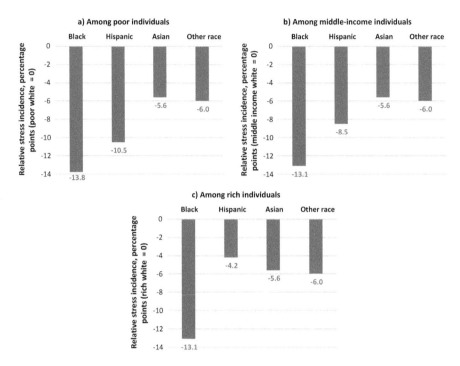

Fig. 14.2 Differential stress incidence, by race group (relative to white), within each income group

differences in the results based on the specification that controls for current life satisfaction, but they do not alter our main findings.

The inclusion of individual socio-economic controls accentuates the heterogeneities across race groups for life satisfaction, worry, and stress, particularly between black and white respondents. Nevertheless, blacks in general reported lower levels of satisfaction with their place of residence and lower levels of social support.[17] This discrepancy suggests that the findings are not simply a "polyanna" effect, but rather that blacks are distinguishing between their circumstances and challenges today and where their future is going. Along these same lines, our results on anger are noteworthy. Poor blacks and poor Hispanics are more likely to experience anger the previous day than are poor whites, even though they are more optimistic about the future at the same time. Reported pain, meanwhile, had a higher positive correlation with stress, worry, and anger than any other control variable, and a negative (although not the most negative) correlation with current and future life satisfaction.

Stress is an important marker of ill-being and the differences between poor blacks and their white counter-parts are large, even after accounting for all the controls in

---

[17]The social support and anger questions were asked in 2008–2012 and 2010–2013 respectively. Therefore, the time period under consideration differs for those two cases.

Table 14.1. Poor blacks are 14 percentage points less likely than are poor whites to report experiencing stress in the previous day. Unlike optimism, these differences between blacks and whites remain constant across income groups (Fig. 14.2).

For an alternative and perhaps simpler interpretation of these baseline results, we also standardized the dependent variables of interest, so that we can measure each coefficient in terms of standard deviations. For example, when controlling for socio-demographic factors as in Table 14.1, among the poor and holding everything else constant, being black is associated with an optimism increase of 0.43 standard deviations (the standard deviation for the optimism variable is approximately 2.122). Regarding worry and stress (with standard deviations of 0.47 and 0.49, respectively), among the poor being black decreases stress by 0.21 and 0.28 standard deviations.

Table 14.1 also displays the coefficients for the socio-economic controls. After controlling for other individual-level factors, males have lower levels of life satisfaction and optimism, lower likelihood of being satisfied with the place of living and of having social support, and higher likelihood of reporting anger. They also report lower incidence of stress and worry. Reporting pain or health problems is associated with lower life satisfaction and more stress, worry, and anger. Exercising the previous week has the opposite associations. Smoking is associated with lower life satisfaction and likelihood of stress, worry, and anger, but also with higher optimism. Unemployment has the usual large negative association with life satisfaction and increases worry.

Additionally, we attempted to address some potential concerns regarding the robustness of our race-income heterogeneity results. We re-estimated Eq. (14.1) using several household size adjustments to the income variable. We built on these and incorporated the Census Bureau poverty measure. We checked the possibility that MSAs with a small number of African American respondents drove the results. We also assessed the robustness of our results to the inclusion of both month and (MSA) x (Year) dummies. Finally, we checked the sensitivity of our estimates to the inclusion and type of survey weights used. The results are robust to all these measures. Finally, as referenced in the previous section, there may be a concern regarding the use of OLS in the estimation of potentially nonlinear relationships. We replicated the exercises using ordered logit and logit models instead of OLS, and those estimates show that our conclusions are robust to the choice of estimation framework.

The coefficients for the age categories are of particular interest. Column (1) in Table 4.1 displays the previously established age-life satisfaction U curve (Graham and Ruiz-Pozuelo 2017; Blanchflower and Oswald 2008). Social support (Column (8)) seems to display a similar, though less pronounced, trend. Optimism (columns (2)–(3)) displays a different pattern, however, as it decreases with age, with particularly large negative effects in middle and old age. Stress and anger (columns (5) and (7), respectively) also decrease with age, worry tends to display an inverted U shape, peaking in middle age, and satisfaction with place of living (column (6)) increases with age.

Table 14.2 Race-age heterogeneities (2010–2015)

Variables	(1) OLS: bpl — Full set of controls (196 MSAs)	(2) OLS: bpla — Full set of controls (196 MSAs)	(3) OLS: bpla — Full set of controls + bpl control (196 MSAs)	(4) OLS: worry — Full set of controls (196 MSAs)	(5) OLS: stress — Full set of controls (196 MSAs)	(6) OLS: citysat — Full set of controls (196 MSAs)	(7) OLS: anger — Full set of controls (196 MSAs)	(8) OLS: Social support — Full set of controls (200 MSAs)
Black	−0.023	0.440***	0.452***	−0.067***	−0.149***	−0.080***	0.037***	−0.045***
	(0.0268)	(0.0197)	(0.0206)	(0.0058)	(0.0071)	(0.0075)	(0.0060)	(0.0072)
Age 25–34	−0.260***	−0.211***	−0.066***	0.011***	−0.023***	−0.016***	0.001	−0.027***
	(0.0126)	(0.0140)	(0.0139)	(0.0041)	(0.0046)	(0.0031)	(0.0031)	(0.0032)
Age 35–44	−0.392***	−0.585***	−0.367***	0.026***	−0.050***	0.001	0.005	−0.068***
	(0.0128)	(0.0157)	(0.0154)	(0.0043)	(0.0040)	(0.0037)	(0.0030)	(0.0038)
Age 45–54	−0.474***	−0.912***	−0.649***	0.026***	−0.098***	0.012***	−0.016***	−0.108***
	(0.0151)	(0.0155)	(0.0163)	(0.0045)	(0.0043)	(0.0036)	(0.0031)	(0.0040)
Age 55–64	−0.390***	−1.330***	−1.114***	−0.015***	−0.172***	0.025***	−0.040***	−0.118***
	(0.0147)	(0.0194)	(0.0201)	(0.0040)	(0.0041)	(0.0039)	(0.0033)	(0.0037)
Age 65+	−0.106***	−1.794***	−1.735***	−0.100***	−0.283***	0.054***	−0.062***	−0.077***
	(0.0149)	(0.0221)	(0.0207)	(0.0042)	(0.0043)	(0.0036)	(0.0032)	(0.0041)
(Black)* (Age 25–34)	0.117***	0.095***	0.030	0.005	−0.000	−0.004	−0.026***	−0.015
	(0.0302)	(0.0263)	(0.0249)	(0.0073)	(0.0075)	(0.0067)	(0.0068)	(0.0102)
(Black)* (Age 35–44)	0.236***	0.270***	0.140***	−0.015**	0.009	0.007	−0.044***	0.000
	(0.0344)	(0.0300)	(0.0265)	(0.0072)	(0.0072)	(0.0073)	(0.0070)	(0.0095)
(Black)* (Age 45–54)	0.520***	0.446***	0.158***	−0.051***	0.006	0.035***	−0.057***	0.026***
	(0.0313)	(0.0310)	(0.0292)	(0.0068)	(0.0071)	(0.0075)	(0.0070)	(0.0092)

(Black)* (Age 55–64)	0.478***	0.467***	0.201***	−0.044***	0.031***	0.054***	−0.061***	0.053***
	(0.0335)	(0.0313)	(0.0310)	(0.0068)	(0.0075)	(0.0071)	(0.0075)	(0.0104)
(Black)* (Age 65+)	0.376***	0.350***	0.142***	−0.014*	0.074***	0.056***	−0.065***	0.009
	(0.0392)	(0.0355)	(0.0343)	(0.0070)	(0.0081)	(0.0074)	(0.0072)	(0.0112)
Observations	770,899	770,899	770,899	770,899	770,899	770,899	608,787	347,080
R-squared	0.175	0.165	0.367	0.129	0.130	0.064	0.062	0.109
MSA dummies	Yes	Yes	Yes	Yes	Yes	Yes	Yes	Yes
Year dummies	Yes	Yes	Yes	Yes	Yes	Yes	Yes	Yes

Clustered standard errors (at the MSA level) in parentheses

Note: These regressions include the 196 MSAs for which sampling weights were available at least in 1 year, except for Social support, where 200 MSAs were available. All specifications use the 2010–2015 period, except for anger (2010–2013) and social support (2008–2012). The remaining race-age interactions, as well as the individual-level controls from Table 14.1 with the exception of race-income interactions, were included but are not displayed

***p < 0.01; **p < 0.05; *p < 0.1

We assessed if the heterogeneities across races change with age. We estimated an analogous specification to that outlined in Eq. (14.1), but interacting race with age groups, instead of income (Table 14.2). Because we find the largest optimism gap between African Americans and whites and due to space considerations, we display only the coefficients for black, age groups, and black-age interactions.

The black-white gaps in life satisfaction and optimism are larger for those between 45 and 64. The gap in worry incidence is also highest for that group. Younger blacks are more likely to report anger and less likely to have social support (relative to young whites). This trend reverses for anger after age 35, as older whites are increasingly more likely to report feelings of anger than their black counterparts. The gap on social support also decreases with age up to the 55–64 group, as whites become less likely to report social support.[18]

14.3.2 Discussion

There are many potential explanations for these findings. Poor whites have fallen in status in relative terms, as competition for low-skilled jobs has intensified. In contrast, minorities have made gradual, hard-fought progress, although many challenges remain. Black-white wage and education gaps have narrowed. Black males earned 69% of the median wage for white males in 1970 and 75% by 2013. While the gaps in educational achievement and proficiency have widened across *income* groups, they have narrowed between blacks (and Hispanics) and whites, with the former becoming larger than the latter (Porter 2015).

Gaps in life expectancy between blacks and whites have also narrowed, from 7.0 years in 1990 to 3.4 in 2014 (Tavernise 2016; Case and Deaton 2017). Blanchflower and Oswald (2004) showed a closing in the historical black-white happiness gap. Oswald and Wu (2011) use mid-2000s data and find that blacks reported fewer bad mental health days than whites.

Assari and Lankarani (2016, cited above) highlight higher levels of resilience among blacks and other minorities. Resilience — defined as maintaining health in spite of a range of psychosocial risk factors — may be higher among blacks and minorities as they have had more experience with adversity. Community and religious factors may also be at play; in our data, blacks are the most likely group to report that religion is important in their lives. Other accounts of the role of religion and community in African Americans' lives (Jackson 2015; Ryff 2015) corroborate this. While we control for religion in our analysis, it is plausible that it also affects optimism in ways that we cannot observe.

---

[18]We also collapsed the data at the MSA level, using MSA fixed effects to control for non-time-varying MSA-specific unobservables. This reduces the significance of some variables, but the main ones hold.

Another sign of differential resilience is the higher level of optimism of older blacks, among older respondents (cited above). In general, older respondents are less optimistic about their future life satisfaction, which makes objective sense if respondents are predicting health and other troubles to increase with age (Graham 2017). Schwandt (2016) found that younger respondents tend to overestimate their future life satisfaction, while older ones underestimate it, but in our data that is less the case for older blacks.

There are two other plausible explanations for the higher levels of black optimism compared to whites, neither of which appear to be supported by the data. One is that black optimism levels are a result of the raised hope associated with the election and two-term tenure of the first African American president. Yet the time trends – including from other data sets – do not support this. Black life satisfaction began to increase steadily in the 1970s, decades before President Obama's time. In addition, black life satisfaction *and* optimism for the future remained steady throughout his tenure, including through ups and downs, and the conclusion of his tenure.[19]

Another potential explanation is that poor black optimism is simply a "polyanna" or "happy peasant and frustrated achiever" effect, associated with low expectations and/or adaptation to adversity.[20] Yet the available evidence – including the psychological and sociological studies cited above and recent historical work (Isenberg 2016) – suggests otherwise, highlighting resilience and determination rather than low expectations. A review of our work by Blanchflower and Oswald (2018), meanwhile, contrasts rising black happiness levels with a flat trend in blacks' financial satisfaction. Similarly, in the regressions reported in Table 14.3, we find that the same poor optimistic black respondents are far less satisfied with their place of living than are poor whites. These results do not support the "polyanna" interpretation nor suggest that poor blacks have a different conception of happiness than do their Hispanic or white counter-parts.

These trends contrast sharply with the experiences of working class whites. Krugman (2015) noted that the economic setbacks of this group have been particularly bad because they expected better: "We're looking at people who were raised to believe in the American Dream, and are coping badly with its failure to come true." A recent study by Cherlin (2016) found that poor and middle-class blacks are more likely to compare themselves to parents who were worse off than they are, while blue-collar whites have more precarious lives and employment than their parents did. Not coincidentally, this latter group formed the base of support for Donald Trump's populist, anti-establishment electoral campaign.

---

[19]While we find a sharp drop in the life satisfaction and optimism of Democrats and Independents in weeks following the 2016 election, a partial recovery seems to be underway by the end of the year (https://www.brookings.edu/blog/up-front/2017/02/02/the-trump-unhappiness-effect-nears-the-great-recession-for-many/). We do not yet have the data to test if there is a longer-term negative effect of trends since then – and plan to do so going forward. The evidence above, though, suggests that this is not a finding that is explained by short-term events.

[20]Graham and Pettinato (2002) coined the term "happy peasants and frustrated achievers" to describe such optimistic poor individuals in many poor countries over a decade ago.

Table 14.3 Race and urban-rural heterogeneities (2010–2015)

Variables	(1) OLS: bpl — Full set of controls	(2) OLS: bpla — Full set of controls	(3) OLS: bpla — Full set of controls + bpl control	(4) OLS: worry — Full set of controls	(5) OLS: stress — Full set of controls	(6) OLS: citysat — Full set of controls	(7) OLS: anger — Full set of controls	(8) OLS: Social support — Full set of controls
Rural	−0.008	−0.146***	−0.142***	−0.010***	−0.017***	−0.012***	−0.011***	0.009**
	(0.0166)	(0.0158)	(0.0146)	(0.0034)	(0.0040)	(0.0043)	(0.0025)	(0.0042)
Black	0.458***	0.801***	0.569***	−0.088***	−0.129***	−0.078***	0.007*	−0.046***
	(0.0254)	(0.0239)	(0.0228)	(0.0054)	(0.0046)	(0.0065)	(0.0034)	(0.0064)
Hispanic	0.478***	0.054	−0.188***	−0.001	−0.084***	0.018***	0.019***	−0.059***
	(0.0173)	(0.0368)	(0.0370)	(0.0058)	(0.0040)	(0.0053)	(0.0046)	(0.0090)
Asian	0.133***	−0.128***	−0.195***	0.014	−0.022**	0.005	−0.006	−0.039***
	(0.0328)	(0.0441)	(0.0401)	(0.0122)	(0.0097)	(0.0081)	(0.0081)	(0.0103)
Other race	0.240***	0.157***	0.036	−0.013	−0.054***	−0.039***	0.020**	−0.070***
	(0.0449)	(0.0374)	(0.0346)	(0.0077)	(0.0065)	(0.0127)	(0.0080)	(0.0129)
(rural)*(Black)	0.132***	0.000	−0.067*	0.000	0.011	−0.006	−0.001	−0.002
	(0.0401)	(0.0435)	(0.0381)	(0.0092)	(0.0110)	(0.0071)	(0.0092)	(0.0125)
(rural)*(Hispanic)	−0.101*	0.134***	0.186***	−0.004	0.004	0.007	0.001	0.026
	(0.0584)	(0.0459)	(0.0581)	(0.0100)	(0.0113)	(0.0089)	(0.0081)	(0.0163)
(rural)*(Asian)	0.246	0.439***	0.315***	−0.045	−0.010	−0.026	0.030	0.002
	(0.1848)	(0.1530)	(0.1149)	(0.0368)	(0.0328)	(0.0361)	(0.0348)	(0.0455)
(rural)*(other race)	−0.087	0.030	0.073	0.001	0.002	−0.017	0.002	0.045**
	(0.0941)	(0.0749)	(0.0576)	(0.0197)	(0.0152)	(0.0143)	(0.0130)	(0.0194)

Constant	7.219***	8.665***	5.017***	0.271***	0.494***	0.888***	0.121***	1.026***
	(0.0436)	(0.0388)	(0.0465)	(0.0067)	(0.0077)	(0.0083)	(0.0068)	(0.0091)
Observations	225,576	225,576	225,576	225,576	225,576	225,576	177,294	104,326
R-squared	0.155	0.194	0.363	0.186	0.200	0.076	0.085	0.128
State dummies	Yes	Yes	Yes	Yes	Yes	Yes	Yes	Yes
Year dummies	Yes	Yes	Yes	Yes	Yes	Yes	Yes	Yes

Clustered standard errors (at the State level) in parentheses

Note: These regressions include only poor individuals. The remaining individual-level controls that were used for Table 14.1 were also used, but are not displayed

***$p < 0.01$; **$p < 0.05$; *$p < 0.1$

Chetty et al. (2016) found that, beyond income, there are also strong geographic markers associated with these trends. Mortality rates and the associated behaviors are particularly prevalent in rural areas in the Midwest and much less in cities. This could be due to healthier behaviors associated with living in cities (e.g., more walking) and to the combination of social isolation and economic stagnation in rural areas. Krugman (2015) also noted the regional dimension to these trends: life expectancy is high and rising in the Northeast and California, where social benefits are highest and traditional values weakest, while low and stagnant life expectancy is concentrated in the Bible belt.

14.3.3 Alternative Specifications Across Race and Rural Areas

We explored whether there were differences in our race and optimism findings among poor individuals in rural versus urban areas. To do this, we used only poor respondents but no longer restricted our sample to respondents living in MSAs, instead including both those living in counties belonging to micropolitan areas and those living in smaller counties.[21] We again modify Eq. (14.1) and now use race by urban/rural status interactions. Table 14.3 shows that poor rural blacks are modestly less optimistic than their urban counterparts. Similarly, poor rural whites are also less optimistic than their poor urban counterparts.

We then focused only on whites and explored income by urban/rural status. Table 14.4 shows the income gradient that might be expected, with richer individuals generally being more likely to report higher life satisfaction, optimism, satisfaction with place of living (only in urban areas), and social support, and less likely to report worry and anger. However, rural respondents across income groups report higher life satisfaction and lower incidence of worry, stress, and anger than urban ones (although they are still less optimistic about the future and exhibit lower satisfaction with their place of living).

14.4 Do Desperation and Premature Mortality Go Together? An Initial Exploration

The mortality data and our well-being metrics highlight a paradox of higher well-being and improving health among minorities juxtaposed against the opposite trend among uneducated whites. Here we explore the extent to which our markers of well

---

[21]These use national-level, rather than MSA-level, survey weights.

Table 14.4 Income and rural-urban heterogeneities (2010–2015)

Variables	(1) OLS: bpl	(2) OLS: bpla	(3) OLS: bpla	(4) OLS: worry	(5) OLS: stress	(6) OLS: citysat	(7) OLS: anger	(8) OLS: Social support
	Full set of controls	Full set of controls	Full set of controls + bpl control	Full set of controls	Full set of controls	Full set of controls	Full set of controls	Full set of controls
Rural	0.046***	−0.056***	−0.084***	−0.015***	−0.020***	−0.010***	−0.011***	0.005***
	(0.0071)	(0.0087)	(0.0085)	(0.0021)	(0.0022)	(0.0024)	(0.0015)	(0.0016)
Poor household	−0.287***	−0.192***	−0.016	0.028***	0.020***	−0.019***	0.006***	−0.022***
	(0.0131)	(0.0112)	(0.0103)	(0.0022)	(0.0022)	(0.0018)	(0.0018)	(0.0027)
Rich household	0.368***	0.257***	0.031***	−0.003*	0.016***	0.022***	0.001	0.007***
	(0.0056)	(0.0069)	(0.0070)	(0.0015)	(0.0022)	(0.0018)	(0.0016)	(0.0014)
(Rural)*(Poor household)	−0.034**	−0.095***	−0.074***	0.006	0.005	0.001	0.002	0.003
	(0.0168)	(0.0152)	(0.0152)	(0.0039)	(0.0046)	(0.0028)	(0.0029)	(0.0045)
(Rural)*(Rich household)	−0.017	0.038*	0.048**	−0.000	−0.014**	−0.020***	0.007*	−0.011**
	(0.0175)	(0.0214)	(0.0196)	(0.0041)	(0.0054)	(0.0033)	(0.0041)	(0.0041)
Observations	926,901	926,901	926,901	926,901	926,901	926,901	721,240	408,110
R-squared	0.202	0.168	0.390	0.133	0.138	0.053	0.059	0.099
State dummies	Yes	Yes	Yes	Yes	Yes	Yes	Yes	Yes
Year dummies	Yes	Yes	Yes	Yes	Yes	Yes	Yes	Yes

Clustered standard errors (at the State level) in parentheses

Note: These regressions include only white non-hispanic individuals. The remaining individual-level controls that were used for Table 14.1 were also used, but
are not displayed

***p < 0.01; **p < 0.05; *p < 0.1

and ill-being have a statistically robust association with the trends in mortality. We matched our metrics of well-being from the GH – using the same individual level data as in Table 14.1 – with MSA-level mortality data from the CDC, along with some other MSA-level controls.

For mortality rates, we rely on 2010–2015 data from the CDC Compressed Mortality File.[22] We compute a MSA-level composite mortality measure using the causes of death that Case and Deaton (2015a) identified as being key drivers of the change. We use the classifications as defined by the International Statistical Classification of Diseases and Related Health Problems 10th Revision codes (ICD 10):

- intentional self-harm (ICD10 codes X60-X84) and sequelae of intentional self-harm, assault and events of undetermined intent (Y87);
- alcoholic liver disease (K70), chronic hepatitis, not elsewhere classified (K73), and fibrosis and cirrhosis of liver (K74);
- multiple types of accidental poisoning (X40-45);
- multiple types of poisoning with undetermined intent (Y10-15);
- analgesics, antipyretics and anti-inflammatory drugs (Y45), sedatives, hypnotics and antianxiety drugs (Y47), and psychotropic drugs, not elsewhere classified (Y49).

We take into account all individuals aged 35–64 years old, and subsequent references to mortality rates in this section refer to this measure.[23] The mortality rate varies across MSAs from 27 to 151 deaths per 100,000 people (with a mean of 56) and tends to decrease with MSA size.

We use the ACS to obtain MSA-level measures for mean household income and inequality (as measured by the Gini coefficient). These variables allow us to account for possible correlations between income, inequality, and mortality. For instance, if higher mortality MSAs are also those with lowest average incomes and/or higher inequality levels, then our mortality variable might simply be picking up the effects of low income or high inequality. Finally, we use the SEER for MSA-level population statistics, broken down by race groups, and use the share of white non-Hispanics as a proxy for (lack of) racial diversity.

We found that MSA-level mortality rates for 35–64 year olds are significantly and negatively associated with current and future expected life satisfaction, and positively associated with feelings of worry (Table 14.5). For instance, holding all else constant, a 50% increase in a MSA's composite mortality rate –a relatively small change for the range of rates indicated in earlier paragraphs – would be associated with a 0.04 point decrease in expected future life satisfaction, a 0.45% decrease

---

[22]National Center for Health Statistics. Compressed Mortality File, 2008–2015 (CD-ROM Series 20, No. 2 U) Vital Statistics Cooperative Program. Hyattsville, Maryland. 2016.
[23]The three decades considered (35–44, 45–54, 55–64) all had similar "composite" mortality rates.

Table 14.5 Race-income heterogeneities, with MSA-level variables (2010–2015)

Variables	(1) OLS: bpl — Full set of controls (194 MSAs)	(2) OLS: bpla — Full set of controls (194 MSAs)	(3) OLS: bpla — Full set of controls + bpl control (194 MSAs)	(4) OLS: worry — Full set of controls (194 MSAs)	(5) OLS: stress — Full set of controls (194 MSAs)	(6) OLS: citysat — Full set of controls (194 MSAs)	(7) OLS: anger — Full set of controls (194 MSAs)	(8) OLS: Social support — Full set of controls (198 MSAs)
Reported life satisfaction today (0–10)			0.555***					
			(0.0042)					
Log(Gini index)	−0.159	0.152	0.241	0.027	−0.038	−0.101**	−0.050	0.113*
	(0.2248)	(0.2710)	(0.2301)	(0.0592)	(0.0590)	(0.0484)	(0.0587)	(0.0591)
Log(mean MSA household income)	0.030	0.248	0.231	0.085**	0.038	−0.020	−0.003	−0.021
	(0.1688)	(0.1643)	(0.1442)	(0.0411)	(0.0389)	(0.0386)	(0.0439)	(0.0414)
Log(MSA composite death rate per 100,000 people, all races, 35–64)	−0.078*	−0.087**	−0.044	0.025***	0.007	−0.006	−0.001	−0.013
	(0.0404)	(0.0396)	(0.0353)	(0.0094)	(0.0090)	(0.0097)	(0.0101)	(0.0102)
Log(White non-Hispanic share of population (%), MSA-level)	−0.808**	−0.176	0.272	0.010	0.056	−0.126	0.139	0.095
	(0.3793)	(0.2530)	(0.2889)	(0.0966)	(0.0898)	(0.0793)	(0.1351)	(0.1456)
Poor household	−0.334***	−0.225***	−0.040***	0.029***	0.017***	−0.018***	−0.001	−0.025***
	(0.0107)	(0.0113)	(0.0100)	(0.0025)	(0.0026)	(0.0023)	(0.0023)	(0.0028)
Rich household	0.398***	0.275***	0.054***	−0.007***	0.015***	0.017***	0.002	0.008***
	(0.0073)	(0.0079)	(0.0069)	(0.0020)	(0.0024)	(0.0018)	(0.0017)	(0.0019)
Black	0.171***	0.643***	0.548***	−0.083***	−0.131***	−0.052***	−0.006**	−0.029***
	(0.0133)	(0.0146)	(0.0127)	(0.0035)	(0.0040)	(0.0069)	(0.0029)	(0.0040)

(continued)

Table 14.5 (continued)

	(1)	(2)	(3)	(4)	(5)	(6)	(7)	(8)
Hispanic	0.244***	0.278***	0.142***	-0.021***	-0.085***	0.004	-0.005*	-0.019***
	(0.0141)	(0.0170)	(0.0167)	(0.0048)	(0.0045)	(0.0040)	(0.0028)	(0.0044)
Asian	-0.078***	-0.167***	-0.123***	-0.002	-0.056***	0.013***	-0.007	-0.042***
	(0.0204)	(0.0277)	(0.0205)	(0.0063)	(0.0055)	(0.0043)	(0.0045)	(0.0071)
Other race	0.094***	0.163***	0.111***	-0.020***	-0.060***	-0.025***	0.008	-0.038***
	(0.0233)	(0.0238)	(0.0232)	(0.0053)	(0.0063)	(0.0057)	(0.0050)	(0.0064)
(Rich household)*(Black)	-0.217***	-0.217***	-0.096***	0.006	-0.002	0.019***	-0.001	-0.007
	(0.0257)	(0.0237)	(0.0222)	(0.0067)	(0.0066)	(0.0045)	(0.0055)	(0.0088)
(Rich household)*(Hispanic)	-0.174***	-0.149***	-0.052**	0.026***	0.042***	0.002	0.018**	0.007
	(0.0258)	(0.0282)	(0.0236)	(0.0078)	(0.0073)	(0.0052)	(0.0073)	(0.0073)
(Rich household)*(Asian)	-0.113***	-0.035	0.028	-0.003	0.010	0.003	0.004	-0.018**
	(0.0326)	(0.0350)	(0.0258)	(0.0089)	(0.0102)	(0.0049)	(0.0069)	(0.0091)
(Rich household)*(Other race)	-0.077*	-0.177***	-0.134***	0.010	0.011	-0.002	0.013	-0.014
	(0.0445)	(0.0506)	(0.0475)	(0.0136)	(0.0141)	(0.0109)	(0.0106)	(0.0139)
(Poor household)*(Black)	0.382***	0.260***	0.048**	-0.014***	-0.007*	-0.023***	0.008*	-0.015**
	(0.0227)	(0.0214)	(0.0220)	(0.0051)	(0.0040)	(0.0051)	(0.0045)	(0.0067)
(Poor household)*(Hispanic)	0.284***	-0.136***	-0.294***	-0.000	-0.020***	0.019***	0.026***	-0.035***
	(0.0184)	(0.0282)	(0.0267)	(0.0049)	(0.0056)	(0.0046)	(0.0049)	(0.0079)
(Poor household)*(Asian)	0.214***	0.150***	0.031	0.008	0.017	-0.014	0.007	0.001
	(0.0390)	(0.0413)	(0.0363)	(0.0120)	(0.0127)	(0.0092)	(0.0103)	(0.0130)
(Poor household)*(Other race)	0.155***	0.102*	0.016	-0.001	0.009	-0.022**	0.024**	-0.031**
	(0.0502)	(0.0541)	(0.0461)	(0.0105)	(0.0110)	(0.0106)	(0.0102)	(0.0133)

Observations	768,810	768,810	768,810	768,810	768,810	768,810	606,699	345,631
R-squared	0.175	0.165	0.367	0.129	0.130	0.064	0.062	0.109
MSA dummies	Yes	Yes	Yes	Yes	Yes	Yes	Yes	Yes
Year dummies	Yes	Yes	Yes	Yes	Yes	Yes	Yes	Yes

Clustered standard errors (at MSA-level) in parentheses

These regressions include all the MSAs for which sampling weights and death rates were available at least in 1 year. The individual-level controls from Table 14.1 are not displayed (except those related to race and income) but were included

***$p < 0.01$; **$p < 0.05$; *$p < 0.1$

relative to its mean.[24] A similar increase would be associated with a 1 percentage point increase in the incidence of worry, a 3.14% increase relative to its mean.

We also ran the same regression, but omitting all health-related variables, and the coefficient estimates increased their magnitude.[25] This is precisely what we would expect if the mortality level is negatively associated with both subjective well-being and self-reported health.

Individuals who live in more racially homogeneous MSAs are more likely to have lower life satisfaction and lower satisfaction with the place of living.[26] This complements the general pattern of premature mortality rates being higher – and subjective well-being markers being lower – among whites compared to minorities.

These are associations, of course, and we cannot assume causality. Indeed, one can imagine dual directions. Having less hope about the future could increase one's likelihood of premature death (e.g., via under-investment in one's health and/or via simply giving up); at the same time, living with more premature death in one's locale could dampen hope and increase worry and other markers of ill-being. Even without causality, the association between our metrics of ill-being and these "deaths of despair" suggests that they could play a leading role in highlighting desperation among certain cohorts or in certain places rather than waiting for rising death rates to sound the alarm bells.

14.5   Interrelated Trends and Explanations

There are several other trends in the data that suggest a pattern of interrelated explanations. Our baseline regressions include a variable measuring reported pain, which Case and Deaton (2015b) found to correlate with suicide rates. Pain, not surprisingly, positively correlates with stress and worry and is highest in middle-aged years, precisely when life satisfaction is lowest (and when the mortality rate increases among uneducated whites are highest). Individuals who experience pain have a decrease in expected future life satisfaction of 0.33 points (Table 14.1) or .15 standard deviations. The magnitudes on stress, worry, and anger are larger: individuals that experience pain are 18 percentage points more likely to report both worry and stress and 11 percentage points more likely to report anger. Reported pain for poor whites is also higher in rural areas than in MSAs (Fig. 14.3).

In addition to pain – and possibly related to it –, the reliance on disability insurance increased over the past two decades, from under 3% of the working age

---

[24]The calculation is: $\exp(-0.087 * log\,(1.50))$. The log represents a 50% increase and $(log\,(1.50) = 0.40547)$; the product equals approximately -0.04. The mean optimism or expected future life satisfaction is 7.86, so the change above corresponds to approximately 0.5% of this mean value.

[25]Regression results available from the authors.

[26]This is not the case in Table 14.5, but is indeed the case when using a logit estimation framework.

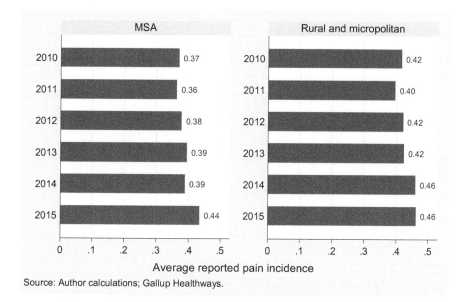

Source: Author calculations; Gallup Healthways.

Fig. 14.3 Pain incidence by rural status, for low income, white individuals

population to almost 5% for men, and from 1.3% to 4.5% for women.[27] While it is concentrated in former coal mining regions, it extends beyond them and roughly patterns the reported pain data in GH. While disability insurance provides an important and often lifelong safety net for many, it also introduces additional barriers to labor force participation. Potential recipients cannot participate in the labor force during the wait time for approval for disability, a period that can last up to 2 years.[28] Long-term unemployment is strongly associated with unhappiness and is a condition that most individuals do not adapt back from (Clark and Oswald 1994; Clark 2006).

Another trend which may help explain the lack of optimism we find is that of prime age (25–54-year-old) males dropping out of the labor force, with projections from 15% today to 25% in 2050 (Eberstadt 2016). Krueger (2017) finds that between 25–35% of prime age males out of the labor force are on SSDI and that another 30% applied in the past and may be awaiting a decision. Yet the rise in SSDI is concentrated among 55–64 year olds, while the post-2000 decrease in participation rates is highest among younger cohorts (Ruffing 2017). Demand-driven factors (e.g., declining labor market opportunities, lack of active job search and training assistance, high incarceration rates) are also important (Black et al. 2016).

Another issue is the difficulty of moving to new places to seek jobs. Moving rates declined in the years surrounding the financial crisis, and a common explanation was

---

[27]Social Security Advisory Board: http://www.ssab.gov/Disability-Chart-Book. These are not age-adjusted numbers.

[28]We thank Henry Aaron for raising this.

the decline in the housing market. The ability of people to move to new jobs hinges on their ability to foreclose on their mortgages and on being in a position to find jobs elsewhere. The common traits of prime age blue-collar workers who have dropped out of the labor force are not associated with a strong possibility of finding employment in another location (Krueger 2017).

A potentially reinforcing factor in this cycle is that these same cohorts, who are disproportionately in remote rural areas, are less likely to have a range of social connections outside their locales or broadband internet. A recent study found that the majority of rural youth live in "Civic Deserts" – places characterized by a dearth of opportunities for civic and political engagement. The limited access to broadband internet limits both social connections and information about jobs outside their immediate area (Kawashima-Ginsburg and Sullivan 2017).[29]

14.5.1 The Role of Place

In addition to the trends discussed above, there are unobservable differences across places that make it more (or less) likely that particular demographic cohorts are happy, optimistic, and healthy. In the maps below, we show patterns across states in life satisfaction, optimism, and worry – the three variables that are most closely associated with premature mortality in our regressions above – for non-Hispanic whites and for minorities,[30] respectively.

To explore the place-specific patterns, we ran a standard regression with the well-being variable of interest as the dependent variable, and again for simplicity of interpretation we use OLS. We control for socio-demographic variables such as age, gender, race, marital status, education, employment status, religiosity, and use month and year of interview dummies.[31] We also include state-specific identifiers. We then rank the states by the estimated coefficients on these identifiers; these values represent the left over differences specific to states that different levels of education, employment status, and so forth, *do not account for*.

For each map, the comparison is relative to the state with the lowest coefficient. For life satisfaction and optimism, we kept the original 0–10 scale. For worry, we rescaled the state coefficients into a 0–100 scale, so that state-level variations can be comparable to percentage point increases. For life satisfaction and optimism, higher values are better, while for worry lower values are better. The colors on the maps reflect what range of values specific states are in for each race group, with dark green being a higher score and light green a lower one, so that dark green states are better for life satisfaction and optimism, but worse for worry. States that are coded gray do

---

[29]For the distribution of broadband, see: https://www.broadbandmap.gov/technology

[30]In this case, minorities comprise only African Americans and Hispanics.

[31]We omitted income variables as otherwise state dummies would disproportionately pick up the disadvantageous state-level aspects, such as higher costs of living (Oswald and Wu 2011).

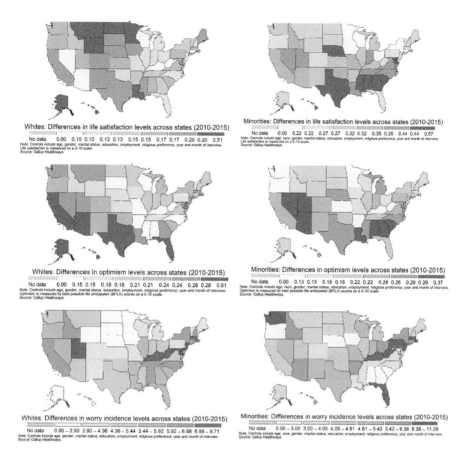

Fig. 14.4 The geography of life satisfaction, optimism, and worry ("Authors' Calculations" based on Gallup Healthways)

not have sufficient observations to allow an estimate for the race group and variable of interest (Fig. 14.4).[32]

Our geographic analysis yields many patterns that are consistent with those reported in other kinds of data – and in our earlier work. As the maps show, the best places in terms of optimism for minorities, except for the District of Columbia, are the Southern states, where there are proportionately more minorities and a well-established African American culture (although at the same time worse objective health and poverty conditions). The patterns are quite different for non-Hispanic whites. The most optimistic states for this group are Hawaii, Alaska, California, Delaware, Texas, Florida, and Arizona. The most desperate states are in Appalachia

---

[32]We excluded states with less than 50 observations/year for the group in question.

and the Midwest, mirroring the patterns in poor health and lack of employment for these same cohorts.

The subtle differences across place are difficult to quantify. There are factors, such as historical levels of segregation, which tend to vary at more disaggregated levels such as counties (Andrews et al. 2017), which we have not explored here, but hope to in future research, as there is much more to understand about these trends – including the specifics of place.

14.6   Conclusions and Potential Policies

Our findings identified linkages between markers of reported ill-being, such as lack of hope, high levels of stress, and reported pain, and the rising rates of mortality among uneducated whites. These markers stand in sharp contrast to much higher levels of life satisfaction and hope for the future and lower levels of stress among poor blacks and Hispanics, who are continuing to make gradual progress in narrowing gaps in life expectancy with whites. Our findings are strong associations, but we cannot claim causality.

Our findings also suggest a role for place. MSAs that are more racially homogeneous (white) and rural, and have more social isolation are more likely to have higher mortality rates. They also tend to have worse health behaviors, such as smoking prevalence and a lack of physical activity. Respondents in these areas are also more likely to report pain, which is a channel to suicide. The combination of fear of downward mobility, weak safety nets, and eroding social cohesion likely contributes to the high levels of desperation that we have found. In contrast, places with more diversity and higher concentrations of minorities – and likely their shared cultures and extensive informal safety nets as well – tend to be the most optimistic.

While our results suggest a need to restore hope and sense of purpose to places characterized by desperation and premature death, it is not obvious how to do so. One component (of many) should include a major effort to introduce healthier behaviors. One part of this will entail taking on the role of prescription practices in generating the excess supply of opioids.[33]

Our safety nets, meanwhile, are notoriously weak compared to other rich countries, and their reach is uneven across states. With the exception of disability insurance, they are also very weak for those out of the labor force (Trisi 2016a, b). While the Earned Income Tax Credit (EITC) is an effective program for working families, it is far less so for those unable to find work or out of the labor force. A related challenge is the strong anti-government sentiment among uneducated whites, which makes designing effective policies difficult. Much of the U.S. political dialogue stigmatizes recipients of welfare assistance and the

---

[33]The U.S. has the world's highest per capita consumption of opioids: http://www.painpolicy.wisc. edu/country/profile/united-states-america

bureaucracies are particularly difficult to navigate. Not by coincidence, the effi cient bureaucracies that administer universal programs like social security and Medicare are distinctly different, and many recipients are not aware they are on government programs.[34]

The same places with hollowed out labor forces and high deaths of despair tend to have low rates of internet access and are more likely to be "civic deserts", at a time that the internet is an increasingly important means for access to safety net programs and other community outreach efforts. Building up communities, meanwhile, is a related challenge. There are many relevant lessons in the rich literature on well-being, which highlight the benefits of volunteering and participating in other community level activities, particularly for those out of the labor force.[35]

There are, no doubt, other possible solutions, many of which are long-term in nature, including improvements in public education, vocational training, and relocation incentives. Importantly, while the starkest trends in terms of lack of hope and mortality incidence are among poor whites, policies directed at improving opportunities and well-being must also focus on poor minorities, who despite higher levels of resilience, continue to face real disadvantages are real.

A first step is to get a better handle on the causes of the problem. This must entail listening to what desperate people themselves have to say, as well as learning from those who have shown more resilience when coping with crisis. Well-being metrics can play a role, for example by undertaking regular polling to gauge life satisfaction, optimism, pain, stress, and worry across people and places, an approach which is in keeping with Easterlin's careful attention to demographic trends in all of his economic analysis. Meanwhile, countries such as the U.K. are already collecting these metrics. Reporting on the patterns and trends regularly in public and policy discussions would be a simple and inexpensive way to monitor the well-being and ill-being of our society. It certainly seems a better path than waiting for mortality rates to sound the alarm bells.

Acknowledgements We thank Andrew Oswald and Eddie Lawlor, as well as Alice Rivlin, Alan Blinder, Belle Sawhill, Bill Galston, Mike O'Hanlon, Bradley Hardy and other participants at a Brookings "restoring the middle class" seminar, for very helpful comments. They also appreciate the suggestions of an anonymous reviewer. Graham acknowledges the generous support from a Robert Wood Johnson Foundation pioneer award, and Pinto from a flagship fellowship at UMD.

---

[34] 40% of Medicare recipients are unaware of being on a government program (Kuziemko et al. 2015).

[35] See, e.g., https://www.whatworkswellbeing.org/

References

Adrianzen, B., & Graham, G. (1974). The high costs of being poor. *Archives of Environmental Health, 28*(6), 312–315.

Andrews, R., Casey, M., Hardy, B. L., & Logan, T. D. (2017). Location matters: Historical racial segregation and intergenerational mobility. *Economics Letters, 158*, 67–72.

Angelini, V., Casi, L., & Corazzini, L. (2015). Life satisfaction of immigrants: Does cultural assimilation matter? *Journal of Population Economics, 28*(3), 817–844.

Assari, S., & Lankarani, M. M. (2016). Depressive symptoms are associated with more hopelessness among white than black older adults. *Frontiers in Public Health, 4*(82), 1–10.

Black, S., Furman, J., Rackstraw, E., & Rao, N. (2016, July 6). The long-term decline in US prime-age male labour force participation, *VoxEU.org*.

Blanchflower, D. G., & Oswald, A. J. (2004). Well-being over time in Britain and the USA. *Journal of Public Economics, 88*(7–8), 1359–1386.

Blanchflower, D., & Oswald, A. (2008). Is Well-being U-shaped over the life cycle? *Social Science and Medicine, 66*(8), 1733–1749.

Blanchflower, D., & Oswald, A. (2018). Unhappiness and pain in modern America: A review essay and further evidence on Carol Graham's happiness for all? *Journal of Economic Literature*, forthcoming.

Case, A., & Deaton, A. (2015a). Rising morbidity and mortality in midlife among white non-hispanic Americans in the 21st century. *Proceedings of the National Academy of Sciences, 112*(49), 15078–15083.

Case, A., & Deaton, A. (2015b). *Suicide, age, and wellbeing: an empirical investigation* (No. w21279). National Bureau of Economic Research. http://www.nber.org/papers/w21279.

Case, A., & Deaton, A. (2017). Mortality and morbidity in the 21st century. *Brookings Papers on Economic Activity, 2017, 48*, 397.

Cherlin, A. (2016, February 22). Why are white death rates rising? *New York Times*.

Chetty, R., Hendren, N., Kline, P., & Saez, E. (2014). Where is the land of opportunity? The geography of intergenerational mobility in the United States. *Quarterly Journal of Economics, 129*(4), 1553–1623.

Chetty, R., Stepner, M., Abraham, S., Lin, S., Scuderi, B., Turner, N., Bergeron, A., & Cutler, D. (2016). The association between income and life expectancy in the United States, 2001–2014. *Journal of the American Medical Association, 315*(16), 1750–1766.

Clark, A. (2006, October). *A note on unhappiness and unemployment duration* (IZA discussion papers, no. 2406).

Clark, A., & Oswald, A. (1994). Unhappiness and unemployment. *The Economic Journal, 104*(424), 648–659.

De Neve, J. E. (2013). The objective benefits of subjective Well-being. In J. Helliwell, R. Layard, & J. Sachs (Eds.), *World happiness report, 2013*. New York: Earth Institute Press.

Dwyer-Lindgren, L., Bertozzi-Villa, A., Stubbs, R. W., Morozoff, C., Kutz, M. J., Huynh, C., Barber, R. M., Shackelford, A., Mackenbach, J. P., Van Lenthe, F. J., Flaxman, A. D., Naghavi, M., Mokdad, A. H., & Murray, C. J. L. (2016). US county-level trends in mortality rates for major causes of death, 1980–2014. *JAMA, 316*(22), 2385–2401.

Eberstadt, N. (2016). *Men without work: America's invisible crisis*. Templeton: W.C. Pennsylvania.

Gelman, A., & Auerbach, J. (2016). Age aggregation bias in mortality trends. *Proceedings of the National Academy of Sciences, 113*(7), E816–E817.

Graham, C. (2008). Happiness and health: Lessons – and questions – for policy. *Health Affairs, 27*(2), 72–87.

Graham, C. (2017). *Happiness for all? Unequal hopes and lives in pursuit of the American dream*. Princeton: Princeton University Press.

Graham, C., & Pettinato, S. (2002). Frustrated achievers: Winners, losers and subjective Well-being in new market economies. *Journal of Development Studies, 38*(4), 100–140.

Graham, C., & Ruiz-Pozuelo, J. (2017). Happiness, stress, and age: How the U-curve varies across people and places. *Journal of Population Economics, 30*(1), 225–264.

Graham, C., Eggers, A., & Sukhtankar, S. (2004). Does happiness pay? An initial exploration based on panel data from Russia. *Journal of Economic Behavior and Organization, 55*, 319–342.

Herbst, C. M. (2013). Welfare reform and the subjective well-being of single mothers. *Journal of Population Economics, 26*(1), 203–238.

Isenberg, N. (2016). *White trash: The 400-year untold history of class in America*. New York: Viking.

Jackson, J. (2015, November 18). *The role of well-being measures in minority aging research*. Presentation to National Institutes of aging conference on well-being and aging, Orlando.

Kawashima-Ginsberg, K., & Sullivan, F. (2017, March 27). Sixty percent of rural millennials lack access to a political life. *The Conversation*.

Keyes, C. L., & Simoes, E. J. (2012). To flourish or not: Positive mental health and all-cause mortality. *American Journal of Public Health, 102*(11), 2164–2172.

Krueger, A. B. (2017). Where have all the workers gone? An inquiry into the decline of the US labor force participation rate. *Brookings Papers on Economic Activity, 2017, 48*(2), 1–87.

Krugman, P. (2015, November 9). Despair, American Style. *New York Times*, A19.

Kuziemko, I., Norton, M., Saez, E., & Stantcheva, S. (2015). How elastic are preferences for redistribution? Evidence from randomized survey experiments. *American Economic Review, 105*(4), 1478–1508.

Oswald, A., & Wu, S. (2011). Well-being across America. *Review of Economics and Statistics, 93*(4), 1118–1134.

Pierce, J. R., & Schott, P. K. (2016). *Trade liberalization and mortality: Evidence from US counties* (No. w22849). National Bureau of Economic Research.

Porter, E. (2015, September 23). Education gap widens between rich and poor. *New York Times*, B1.

Ruffing, K. (2017, August 25). Decline in labor-force participation not due to disability programs. *Center on budget and policy priorities blogs*.

Ryff, C. (2015, November 18). Varieties of well-being and their links to health. Presentation to National Institutes of Aging Conference on well-being and aging, Orlando.

Schwandt, H. (2016). Unmet aspirations and an explanation for the age-U shape in Well-being. *Journal of Economic Behavior and Organization, 122*, 75–87.

Shiels, M. S., Chernyavskiy, P., Anderson, W. F., Best, A. F., Haozous, E. A., Hartge, P., et al. (2017). Trends in premature mortality in the USA by sex, race, and ethnicity from 1999 to 2014: An analysis of death certificate data. *The Lancet, 389*(10073), 1043–1054.

Steptoe, A., Deaton, A., & Stone, A. (2015). Subjective well-being, health, and ageing. *The Lancet, 385*(9968), 640–648.

Stone, A., & Mackie, C. (2013). *Subjective well-being: Measuring happiness, suffering, and other dimensions of human experience*. Washington, DC: National Research Council of the National Academies. http://www.nap.edu/catalog.php?record_id=18548

Tavernise, S. (2016, May 8). Black Americans see gains in life expectancy. *The New York Times*.

Trisi, D. (2016a, September 14). Safety net cut poverty nearly in half last year. *Center on Budget and Policy Priorities Blogs*.

Trisi, D. (2016b). *Three essays on poverty and social welfare policy*. Ph.D. dissertation. University of Maryland, College Park.

Chapter 15
When Does Economic Growth Improve Well-Being?

Francesco Sarracino

Abstract Is economic growth the way to pursue better lives? After the second world war, many industrialized countries experienced an unprecedented economic growth that significantly improved people's living conditions. However, the raising wealth did not result in higher well-being. This conclusion is inconsistent with the well established belief that economic growth is the way to improve the human lot. In this chapter I discuss the evidence on some of the conditions for durable improvements in well-being, namely promoting social capital, and reducing income inequality. I conclude that the quality of growth matters for well-being and that it is possible to adopt policies to make economic growth and well-being compatible.

15.1 Introduction

As governments worldwide seek to promote well-being via economic growth, scholars hold mixed opinions. Thus, governments wishing to improve their citizens' well-being miss clear indications about which policies to adopt. Researchers have been investigating whether economic growth is the way to pursue higher well-being for many years. To date the answer seems to be: "it depends". While the initial literature polarized on two opposite views, the supporters and the opponents of economic growth as a way to improve well-being, some recent evidence suggests that the way to better lives depends on the quality of economic growth. United States and China, for example, are two paradigmatic cases of economic growth that failed to increase well-being. In both countries increasing income inequality and declining social capital are among the causes of such disappointing results.

Whether economic growth increases well-being is a matter of its social, political, economic, cultural and institutional features: if economic growth is compatible with

F. Sarracino (✉)
Institut National de la Statistique et des Etudes Economiques du Grand-Duché du Luxembourg (STATEC), Luxembourg City, Luxembourg

LCSR National Research University Higher School of Economics, Moscow, Russia
e-mail: Francesco.Sarracino@statec.etat.lu

© Springer Nature Switzerland AG 2019
M. Rojas (ed.), *The Economics of Happiness*,
https://doi.org/10.1007/978-3-030-15835-4_15

a cohesive and inclusive society, it is reasonable to expect that well-being will improve. Vice-versa, if economic growth leads to isolation and inequality, well-being may arguably reduce. This chapter briefly reviews the literature on the relationship between economic growth and well-being, and it discusses the empirical evidence supporting the view that policy makers should promote social capital, and reduce income inequalities to pursue durable improvements in well-being.

Just as economic growth, also income inequality and social capital can be object of policies. In particular, recent studies showed that social capital can change over time because of ad-hoc policies, such as those concerning urban environment, educational and work-related organization, healthcare, as well as media and advertisement.

For long time scholars acknowledged that the "quality" of economic growth mattered for well-being. Now we know a bit more about what characterizes such "quality", and how to pursue it to promote durable well-being.

15.2   Easterlin Paradox and Beyond

The measurement and analysis of subjective well-being is rooted in social psychology, and it boomed after the year 2000, when subjective well-being entered the vocabulary and the research agendas of other social sciences, including economics (Bruni and Porta 2007). The information underlying this literature is trivial for it comes from a very simple question: in the course of surveys, people are asked to evaluate their lives as a whole, i.e. their subjective well-being[1].

The availability of a valid and reliable way to observe people's well-being allows answering an important question: after years of almost uninterrupted economic growth, to what extent have modern societies truly benefited? Paraphrasing Easterlin (1974): did economic growth keep its promise of improving the human lot? Contrary to the common belief that a growing economy is the key to better lives, available

---

[1]Subjective well-being is usually observed thanks to questions asking the respondents to state how happy or satisfied with their lives they are. For example, subjective well-being, sometimes also referred to as "happiness" or "life satisfaction", is usually observed through answers to survey questions such as: "Taking all things together, how happy would you say you are?" or "All things considered, how satisfied are you with your life as a whole these days?" (Van Praag et al. 2003). These measures proved to be reliable sources of information about individual's well-being and, in the last decades, have been employed in many fields of applied social research. The reliability of these measures has been corroborated by experimental evidence from several disciplines. For example, subjective well-being correlates with objective measures of well-being such as heart rate, blood pressure, frequency of Duchenne smiles, and neurological tests of brain activity (Blanchflower and Oswald 2004; Van Reekum et al. 2007). Moreover, subjective measures of well-being are strongly correlated with other proxies of subjective well-being (Schwarz and Strack 1999; Wanous and Hudy 2001; Schimmack et al. 2010) and with the judgments about the respondent's happiness provided by friends, relatives or clinical experts (Schneider and Schimmack 2009; Kahneman and Krueger 2006; Layard 2005).

evidence suggests that modern societies shouldn't expect significant improvements in well-being from economic growth (Easterlin et al. 2010).

Two main theories have been proposed to explain the paradox: adaptation and social comparisons (Blanchflower 2009). Both theories rest on the idea that one's income aspirations negatively affect subjective well-being (Frederick and Loewenstein 1999; Truyts 2010). Aspirations may depend either on one's own past income (adaptation) or on the income of one's own reference group (social comparisons). In the first case, the negative effect of higher income depends on people's past achievements. On the basis of what they get, people set their future aspirations. For example, last year's wage is the reference point for the current year's wage: if the actual wage does not meet the aspirations, the result for well-being is negative. The second mechanism works in a similar way, but relies on comparing people's achievements with those of others. In this case, the effect of a higher income for well-being depends on a relative amount: do I earn more, the same, or less than my colleagues, neighbors and friends? These "others" may comprise various groups of people whom we consider a reference point to assess our success. Both theories are well-established in economic and psychological literature, and they are both supported by a large body of empirical evidence (Brickman et al. 1978; Frank 1997; Diener et al. 2009).

The idea that economic growth does not translate in well-being gains – the essence of the so-called "Easterlin paradox" – is not commonly shared. The reasons are twofold. On one hand, some authors criticize the evidence supporting the Easterlin paradox and question its existence (see e.g. Stevenson and Wolfers 2008; Deaton 2008; Sacks et al. 2012; Veenhoven and Vergunst 2013). This discrepancy is due to the fact that these researchers neglected the temporal dimension of the relationship between economic growth and well-being. Easterlin et al. (2010) clarified that economic growth improves people's well-being only over the business cycle (1 or 2 years), but in the long run (more than 10 years) economic growth does not have any significant effect on well-being. In other words, the positive effect of a flourishing economy on well-being lasts for only a few years. This evidence found further support in some recent works (see e.g. Bruni and Stanca 2008; Easterlin and Angelescu 2009; Becchetti et al. 2011; Clark et al. 2012). Moreover, Beja (2014) showed that even if the trends of subjective well-being and economic growth are statistically related, the magnitude is small for growth to have a meaningful impact on well-being. On the other hand, the availability of newer and longer time-series clarified that subjective well-being is not always flat over time: for instance, it declines in United States (Easterlin 1974; Bartolini et al. 2013a) and China (Brockmann et al. 2009; Easterlin et al. 2012; Steele and Lynch 2013; Bartolini and Sarracino 2015), whereas it follows a U-shape trend in many transition countries (Bartolini et al. 2017), including Russia (Easterlin 2009). Vice-versa, there are countries where quality of life improved along with economic growth, such as Denmark and Switzerland. This indicates that economic growth, per se, is not sufficient to warrant better lives: its quality matters too (Helliwell 2008).

Although the literature has often investigated *whether* economic growth improves well-being, the issue is rather *when* – under which conditions – economic growth durably improves well-being. Oishi and Kesebir (2015) and Mikucka et al. (2017) provided evidence indicating that economic growth correlates with well-being when income inequality declines and social capital increases. Although the evidence about the relationship between income inequality and well-being is mixed (see, for instance, Clark and D'Ambrosio 2015), increasing income inequality seems to have negative consequences for well-being. When income inequality increases, the differences among people widen, and the opportunities to establish social comparisons increase, thus undermining the positive effect of income growth for well-being. Raising income inequality can undermine well-being also by reducing feelings of fairness and trust in others (Oishi et al. 2011). Finally, empirical studies suggest that when economic growth is accompanied by increasing income inequality, social linkages and feelings of cooperation weaken, leading to well-being losses (Graham and Felton 2006). A number of recent studies documented that social capital – and, in particular, the quality of the relationships among people – has a predominant impact on well-being (Uhlaner 1989; Helliwell and Putnam 2004; Helliwell 2006, 2008; Bruni and Stanca 2008; Becchetti et al. 2009). Bartolini and Sarracino (2014) showed that social capital is a strong correlate of well-being in the long-run, and that such correlation weakens in the short run, when economic growth exerts a stronger influence on well-being. These studies refer to social capital as "networks together with shared norms, values and understandings that facilitate co-operation within or among groups" (OECD 2001, p. 41). Finally, Easterlin (2013) showed that the disconnect between economic growth and well-being in China and Russia is largely due to the deterioration of the social safety net and to the privatization of social insurance which accompanied the transition. In sum, whether economic growth improves the human lot is a matter of conditions.

15.2.1 Defensive Growth

Why are economic growth and well-being associated in some countries, and not in others? The theories proposed to explain the Easterlin paradox can't answer this question: both adaptation and social comparisons predict flat trends of subjective well-being, but they are not able to explain growing, declining, or curvilinear trends. The possible existence of a trade-off between economic growth and well-being over time is the subject of a long-lasting debate (Polanyi 1968; Hirsch 1976). Bartolini and Bonatti (2008) proposed a theory of defensive growth according to which economic growth is the outcome of a substitution process of free public goods for expensive private ones. Free goods – natural (e.g., air, water, sun, etc.) and social (e.g., trust, honesty, generosity, pro-social behaviors) resources – are renewable and available to everybody, and people benefit from the consumption of such goods (Helliwell and Putnam 2004; Helliwell 2007).

In societies where free goods become scarce, people buy substitute goods which are expensive and private. For example, if cities become polluted, dangerous, and unfriendly, people compensate for the lower quality of the living environment by buying a second home at the seaside or in the countryside. In other words, people engage in a new layer of expenses – so-called *defensive* expenditures – to defend themselves from the degradation of the social and natural environment. Also social relationships – and more in general social capital – normally freely available, can be substituted by private goods, which are provided by the market. This process feeds economic growth because the consumption of private and expensive goods, differently from free goods, is recorded in national accounts. Moreover, to afford greater levels of private consumption, people need to increase their working hours, further feeding economic growth. In this way, the erosion of social capital, and of other free goods, increases the demand for private substitute goods. The result is an economic growth that undermines free goods. Increasing private expenditures and working time result in less time available for other activities, affecting the opportunities to cultivate social relationships. This is a vicious circle in which economic growth and social erosion reinforce each other.

Summarizing, according to the defensive growth theory, economic growth produces negative externalities which, in turn, fuel economic growth: when the quality of their living environment erodes, people are pushed to consume private goods to compensate for their lower levels of well-being. The defensive growth theory predicts that the higher the rate of economic growth, the longer the working time, the more negative the trend of well-being, and the greater the erosion of free goods, social capital in particular. These predictions found empirical support in a number of cross-country and within country studies (Bartolini and Bilancini 2011; Sarracino and Mikucka 2017; Bartolini and Sarracino 2017; Bartolini et al. 2016).

15.3 Conditions for a Happy Growth

Previous literature found that economic growth and well-being are associated when at least one of the following three conditions are met: presence of a welfare state (Easterlin 2013; Ono and Kristen 2016), growing social capital (Uhlaner 1989; Helliwell 2003, 2008; Bartolini et al. 2013a; Clark et al. 2012), and reducing income inequality (Oishi and Kesebir 2015; Mikucka et al. 2017). It goes without saying that these are only some of the possible aspects to safeguard while promoting well-being through economic growth. Other aspects may include environmental quality, health, tolerance, religiosity, in sum all those aspects that matter for well-being and that, under given circumstances, may be eroded by economic growth. From this point of view, the quest for other relevant aspects is just beginning (Table 15.1).

15.3.1 Cross-Country Studies

Bartolini and Sarracino (2014) explored the long-term relationship among economic growth, social capital and well-being at aggregated level using WVS-EVS data. The

Table 15.1 Long-term trends of proxies of subjective well-being over trends of social capital and GDP*

	Happiness	Life satisfaction
Group membership	0.608**	0.330**
	−2.19	−3.58
Log GDP	−0.01	0.0447
	(−0.07)	−0.35
Constant	−0.690***	−0.634***
	(−3.88)	(−6.87)
Observations	27	27
Adjusted R2	0.302	0.087

t-statistics in brackets
Source: Bartolini and Sarracino (2014), WVS-EVS integrated data-set
*All the variables are standardized
$*p < 0.1$; $**p < 0.05$; $***p < 0.01$

authors compared the trends of social capital – as proxied by the participation of people in groups and associations – with the trends of subjective well-being and of GDP per capita. Results support the view that in the long run the trend of group membership is significantly and positively correlated with the trend of subjective well-being (see Fig. 15.1). This is a robust result since it holds after controlling for the trend of GDP per capita (see Table 15.1). Additionally, it confirms Easterlin's evidence that in the long run economic growth is not correlated with the trends of subjective well-being.

This result is confirmed also after adopting another proxy of social capital: social trust, available in the European Social Survey (ESS). Table 15.2 reports the results of the correlations of the trends of subjective well-being with those of social trust and of GDP per capita computed over a period of at least 6 years, a medium rather than a long-term. Also in this case, the coefficients associated with the trends of trust in others are strongly and significantly associated with the trends of well-being, whereas economic growth shows a weak correlation.

However, this result can be driven by more developed countries, where basic needs have been met and people are free to care for something else, such as social relationships. Evidence from poorer countries is scarce, nonetheless two recent works provided some evidence in this regard. Easterlin (2009) and Bartolini et al. (2017) show that even if economic growth does matter for well-being in transition countries, social relationships remain an important correlate of subjective well-being.

Oishi and Kesebir (2015) and Mikucka et al. (2017) applied multilevel regression analysis to a large sample of countries extracted from the integrated World Values Survey – European Values Study data-set. They studied the conditions under which economic growth and subjective well-being correlate in the long run. Oishi and Kesebir (2015) found that economic growth correlates positively with well-being when income inequality decreases. Mikucka et al. (2017) tested the same relationship accounting for social capital and income inequality. The results of the two teams

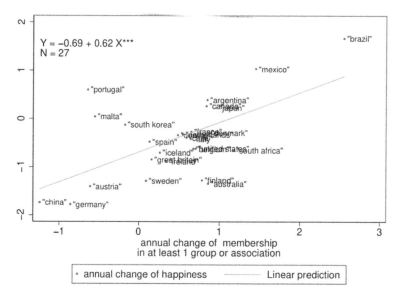

Fig. 15.1   Correlation among long-term trends of subjective well-being and social capital.
Trends are computed regressing the proxies of subjective well-being and the share of people who
are members of at least one group or association over a time variable including all the years when
the dependent variable is observed. The β coefficients thus represent the average yearly change of
the dependent variable as measured over a period of at least 15 years. Trends are computed
separately for each country and then standardized to ease comparisons among variables. (Source:
Bartolini and Sarracino (2014), WVS-EVS integrated data-set)

Table 15.2 Trends of
subjective well-being over
changes of the index of social
trust and trends of GDP

	Happiness	Life satisfaction
Index of social trust	0.797***	0.731***
	−4.03	−8.06
Trend of log GDP	0.268**	0.323*
	−2.41	−2.02
Constant	−7.96e − 10	5.56e − 10
	(−0.00)	0
Observations	24	24
Adjusted R2	0.702	0.63

t-statistics in brackets
[*]The index of social trust is the weighted average of the answers to
questions about whether most people can be trusted or not,
whether other people try to take advantage of others and whether
people try to be helpful or rather looking for themselves. Each of
these three items ranges on a 0–10 scale, where the lowest category corresponds to the worst judgement and the highest to the
best one. Weights are obtained from a factor analysis. All the
trends are standardized. (Source: Bartolini and Sarracino (2014),
ESS data-set)
*$p < 0.1$; **$p < 0.05$; ***$p < 0.01$

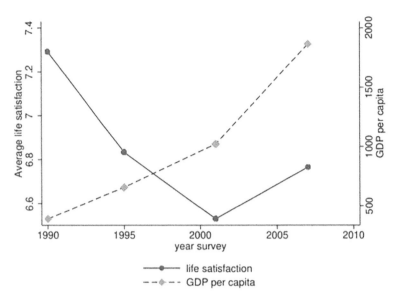

Fig. 15.2 Life satisfaction and GDP across time in China**GDP per capita (2000 US$), World Development Indicators, The World Bank. (Source: Bartolini and Sarracino (2015), WVS data-set)

of researchers are strikingly consistent. To illustrate the results, I will focus on the predictions for China, a country of particular interest in this literature. Until 1990s, China was a substantially poor country. However, since then its economy grew at a pace of about 10% each year, radically transforming Chinese society and significantly improving the living conditions of millions of people. Mainstream economic theory suggests that such a "leap forward" should have significantly improved Chinese well-being. Figure 15.2 illustrates the trends of GDP per capita and of average life satisfaction over time (Bartolini and Sarracino 2015). The dashed line, representing real GDP per capita (expressed in US dollars of 2000), points upward, whereas average life satisfaction – the solid line – declines. Despite the moderate recovery of life satisfaction between 2001 and 2007, the two curves depict an extreme example of Easterlin paradox: in China, life satisfaction declined – it did not stay constant, as the paradox suggests – while the economy took off.

What does explain the discrepancy between economic growth and the trend of life satisfaction? The answer is represented graphically in Fig. 15.3 (Mikucka et al. 2017). The chart is organized on two axes: the y-axis reports inequality changes over time – above the zero, inequality increases; below the zero, inequality decreases. The x-axis reports the changes of social trust over time: on the right of the zero, social trust increases; on the left of the zero, social trust decreases. The area of the diagram is color-coded: red areas indicate a negative association between economic growth and well-being over time, whereas green areas indicate a positive association. More intense colors stand for stronger associations. The dots on the diagram are the countries included in the available sample as predicted by the multilevel model.

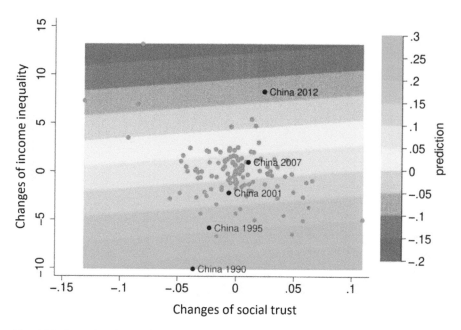

Fig. 15.3 Increasing income inequality and stagnating social trust predict the decoupling of economic growth and life satisfaction in China. The prediction is the result of a multilevel regression analysis to model people's life satisfaction as a function of both individual and country characteristics, including the changes over time of social trust, economic growth and income inequality (Gini index). The model allows average life satisfaction to vary randomly across country-waves and across countries (random intercept model). The macro variable social trust is derived from aggregating the individual-level variable trust in others. Real GDP per capita is derived from the Penn World Table 9.0 (expenditure-side) and is expressed in international dollars of the year 2011 transformed into logarithm. The Gini index (based on individual income) is extracted from the World Income Inequality Database. (Source: Mikucka et al. (2017), WVS data-set)

For ease of interpretation, the dots relative to China have been emphasized. By observing the dots, it is possible to see the evolution of the relationship between economic growth and well-being in China from 1990 to 2012. The fact that the dots move gradually from the green to the red area suggests that over time the relationship between economic growth and well-being turned from positive to negative. This shift, according to the model, is accompanied by two transformations: a negligible change in social trust over time, and a strong increase in income inequality. This conclusion is supported by the descriptive statistics of Fig. 15.4, which reports the evolution of well-being and the Gini index since 1990. The figure shows that the first years of economic take-off were associated to a strong acceleration of income inequality which frustrated Chinese well-being.

Summarizing, the evidence from two different data-sets providing internationally comparable information about social capital and well-being trends across countries

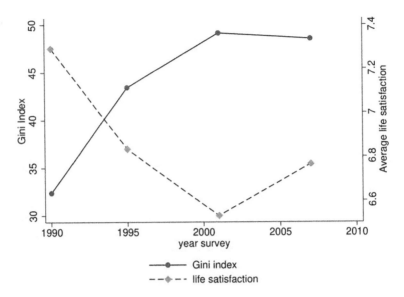

Fig. 15.4 Inequality and life satisfaction in China. The Gini index (based on individual income) is extracted from the World Income Inequality Database. Average life satisfaction is computed using sample weights and it is issued from the WVS. (Source: Author's own elaboration)

confirms that economic growth is only weakly associated with the trend of well-being. The longer the perspective, the less important is the role of GDP and the more social capital matters for well-being.

This conclusion hinges on cross-country studies – analyses run with aggregated data on sample of various countries. This casts the doubt that present results are an artifact due to pulling together countries with different histories, socio-economic backgrounds and political and cultural systems. For this reason, in the next section, I will review the evidence from within-country studies.

15.3.2 Within Country Studies

Using data from the US General Social Survey over the last 30 years, Bartolini et al. (2013a) show that a large portion of the declining American happiness trend is explained by four forces acting in contrasting directions. The first one is the increase in per capita income, which positively affects subjective well-being, while the remaining three have a negative effect. These forces are: first, social comparisons, which erode approximately 2/3 of the positive impact of increasing income; second, the decrease in the confidence in institutions, a component of social capital and, third, the erosion of social capital. Many studies suggest that the American society experienced an increase in solitude, communicative difficulties, anxiety, loneliness, distrust, family instability, generational cleavages, civic engagement, social participation and a reduction in solidarity and honesty (Putnam 2000). The magnitude of the effect of the erosion of social capital for well-being is comparable to the one exerted by social comparisons. Moreover, simulations reveal that, if social capital had stayed constant at its 1975 levels, American subjective well-being would have been higher today.

These relationships have been confirmed more recently also for three other countries: Germany, Luxembourg and China. Using the German Socio-Economic Panel and a wider set of variables, Bartolini et al. (2013b) confirm previous results about the US showing that the variation in the German subjective well-being between 1994 and 2007 is explained by the same forces shaping the American well-being. The only difference, in this case, is that, during the last 15 years, German social capital has been increasing with an overall positive effect on subjective well-being. If social capital had not increased, the net result for subjective well-being would have been the same as the American one.

Looking at data from the European Value Study, Sarracino (2013) focused on the relationship between social capital and subjective well-being in Luxembourg. Despite its small dimensions and its peculiarities (the small population size as well as the high share of migrant workers), Luxembourg is one of the countries with the highest income per capita. Hence, it is an interesting case to study whether people in rich countries are destined to wealthy but unsatisfactory lives. After accounting for the heterogeneous social fabric of the country, the figures between 1999 and 2008 document that in Luxembourg social capital, in the form of trust in others, participation in groups and associations and confidence in various institutions, increased together with subjective well-being. These results are encouraging because they suggest that the erosion of social capital is not a legacy of the richest countries in the world.

In an international perspective, the cases of Germany and Luxembourg indicate that economic performance can be compatible with overall rich social environments and well-being. This evidence has important implications for policy making since it supports the idea that the way economic systems are organized matters for their social and well-being outcomes. In other words, whether economic growth is associated to unhappiness and erosion of social capital is a matter of economic and social organization.

More recently, Easterlin et al. (2012), Brockmann et al. (2009), Steele and Lynch (2013), and Easterlin et al. (2017) have used various datasets to explore the relationship between economic growth and well-being in China. An average yearly economic growth of 9.7% should result in a general improvement of several social, economic and sanitary conditions of people's life and of their well-being more in general. However, Chinese economic growth failed to keep its promise of improving the human lot. What is behind this failure? Since the early 1990s, employment conditions deteriorated and were slow to improve due to restructuring of state-owned companies, and to large rural to urban migration. The loss of jobs was accompanied by the loss of social safety nets which were tied to jobs. Partly as a result of these changes, inequalities – in particular income inequality – increased (see Fig. 15.4). At a micro level increasing income inequality corresponds to increasing social

comparisons, which many studies identify as the main driver of Chinese dissatisfaction. In particular, Bartolini and Sarracino (2015) used WVS data and the Blinder-
Oaxaca decomposition to analyze what happened to Chinese well-being between
1990 and 2007. In line with previous results, the authors find that the increased
importance of social comparisons largely contribute to explain the disappointing
trend of well-being. However, a second force also contributed to shaping the trend of
Chinese well-being: the erosion of social capital. Estimates suggest that about 18.6%
of the well-being loss in China is related to social capital. Moreover, the computa-
tions suggest that if the latter stayed constant at its level of 1990, the loss of well-
being would have been 6% smaller. In sum, the declining life satisfaction in China
can be explained by increasing income inequality, which increased the opportunities
for social comparisons; declining social capital; and increasing unemployment and
the associated loss of social safety nets.

Overall, there seems to be convincing evidence that in the long run what really
matters for people's well-being are inequality and social relationships rather than
money. Shall we conclude that economic growth has no role for well-being? Data
show that economic growth has a clear and strong effect on life satisfaction, but only
in the short run. For instance, when the changes over time are computed over
intervals of 2 years, economic growth is almost two times more strongly correlated
to well-being than social capital (Bartolini and Sarracino 2014; Bartolini et al. 2017).

The evidence coming from both within and cross-country studies, various techniques and different data-set supports the conclusion that, except for transition
economies, in the long run economic growth correlates with well-being if certain
conditions are met. The conditions explored so far include increasing social capital,
decreasing income inequality, and extensive social safety nets. Hence, having happy
lives in countries that grow wealthy is a matter of economic and social organization.

15.4   Conclusion

Available evidence suggests that – a priori – economic growth is neither good nor
bad for well-being: what matters is its quality. Economic growth does not work in
the same way everywhere. It can benefit everybody or only a few; it can create
healthy communities or it can weaken the bonds among people. This evidence stems
from the studies on the Easterlin paradox and it represents one of its evolutions.
Rather than asking whether economic growth is the way to pursue better lives, this
line of research asks "when", under which conditions economic growth can be
compatible with raising life satisfaction in the long-run.

Scholars expected that social capital, and in particular the quality of the relationships among people, should matter: social capital is an important correlate of well-
being, and it is one of the few aspects to which people's happiness does not adjust.
Additionally, societies rich in social capital provide their members with material
help, social support and shared activities. This contributes to well-being, and it
favors longer and healthier lives. Available evidence indicates also that economic

growth correlates with increasing well-being in presence of effective social safety nets and, more in general, of generous welfare states. One of the reasons for this result is that welfare state allows to meet people's needs independently from their income. In other words, the welfare state is an antidote to income inequality: societies with few, very rich people and many poor ones are, on average, less happy because of the decreasing marginal utility of income. Moreover, very high inequality may be associated to violence, crime, and social cleavages which may ultimately undermine well-being. Various cross-country and within country studies, using various sources of data and techniques, supported these expectations: economic growth and well-being are more likely to grow together in presence of increasing social capital, decreasing income inequality, and extensive social safety nets.

This observation suggests that, to pursue durable improvements in well-being, both rich and poor countries should adopt a "promote, protect and reduce" policy agenda: promote social safety nets, protect social capital, and reduce income inequality. The good news is that some governments have already adopted policy agendas that, at least in part, are consistent with this framework. This is why in some countries, such as Denmark, Netherlands, Switzerland, Brazil and Japan, well-being increases along with economic growth. The redistribution of income and the strengthening of the welfare state are basic policies to decouple the ability to meet basic needs from people's income. In other words, policies to reduce income inequality make people less dependent on income to satisfy their needs. Which policies are possible to promote social capital? Some examples – for instance in urban organization, education, or advertising regulations – show that it is possible to adopt specific policies to preserve or enhance social capital and well-being (Rogers et al. 2011; Helliwell 2011; Bartolini 2014). Hence, the way many existing institutions work could be reconsidered in the light of the new role that these studies attribute to social capital.

New scenarios are available for policies aiming at increasing well-being. A growing body of research confirms that well-being asks not only for material needs, but also for further aspects coming from the delicate connection of human relationships with others and the surrounding environment. The quest for which conditions and policies matter to durably improve well-being is only at the beginning. Hopefully, new research on high quality data and the availability of new case studies will shed new light on this issue.

Acknowledgements This article reflects the view of the author and does not engage in any way STATEC Research, ANEC and funding partners. The author gratefully acknowledges the support of the Observatoire de la Compétitivité, Ministère de l'Economie, DG Compétitivité, Luxembourg and STATEC. The author wishes to thank Stefano Bartolini, Andrew Clark, Joshua K. Dubrow, Malgorzata Mikucka, Kelsey O'Connor, Chiara Peroni, and the participants to the "Economics of Happiness" conference in honor of prof. Richard Easterlin (Los Angeles, April 6 2018) and to the "International Conference on Policies for Happiness and Health" (Siena, March 19–21 2018). Possible errors or omissions are entirely the responsibility of the author.

ctu .h

References

Bartolini, S. (2014). *Manifesto for Happiness: Shifting society from money to well-being*. Pennsylvania: Pennsylvania University Press. forthcoming.

Bartolini, S. & Bilancini, E. (2011). *Social participation and hours worked*. Department of Economics University of Siena 620, Department of Economics, University of Siena.

Bartolini, S., & Bonatti, L. (2008). Endogenous growth, decline in social capital and expansion of market activities. *Journal of Economic Behavior & Organization, 67*(3), 917–926.

Bartolini, S., & Sarracino, F. (2014). Happy for how long? How social capital and economic growth relate to happiness over time. *Ecological Economics, 108*, 242–256.

Bartolini, S., & Sarracino, F. (2015). The dark side of Chinese growth: Declining social capital and well-being in times of economic boom. *World Development, 74*, 333–351.

Bartolini, S., & Sarracino, F. (2017). Twenty-five years of materialism: Do the US and Europe diverge? *Social Indicators Research, 133*(2), 787–817.

Bartolini, S., Bilancini, E., & Pugno, M. (2013a). Did the decline in social connections depress Americans' happiness? *Social Indicators Research, 110*(3), 1033–1059.

Bartolini, S., Bilancini, E., & Sarracino, F. (2013b). Predicting the trend of well-being in Germany: How much do comparisons, adaptation and sociability matter? *Social Indicators Research, 3* (114), 169–191.

Bartolini, S., Bilancini, E., & Sarracino, F. (2016). Social capital predicts happiness: World-wide evidence from time series. In S. Bartolini, E. Bilancini, L. Bruni, & P. Porta (Eds.), *Policies for happiness* (pp. 175–198). Oxford: Oxford University Press.

Bartolini, S., Mikucka, M., & Sarracino, F. (2017). Money, trust and happiness in transition countries: Evidence from time series. *Social Indicators Research, 130*(1), 87–106.

Becchetti, L., Giachin Ricca, E., & Pelloni, A. (2009). The 60es turnaround as a test on the causal relationship between sociability and happiness. *Econometica Working Papers wp07*, Econometica.

Becchetti, L., Trovato, G., & Bedoya, D. (2011). Income, relational goods and happiness. *Applied Economics, 43*(3), 273–290.

Beja, E. L. (2014). Income growth and happiness: Reassessment of the Easterlin Paradox. *International Review of Economics, 61*(4), 329–346.

Blanchflower, D. (2009). *International evidence on well-being* in measuring the subjective well-being of nations: National accounts of time use and well-being, Krueger (editor).

Blanchflower, D., & Oswald, A. (2004). Money, sex and happiness: An empirical study. *The Scandinavian Journal of Economics, 106*(3), 393–415.

Brickman, P., Coates, D., & Janoff-Bulman, R. (1978). Lottery winners and accident victims: Is happiness relative? *Journal of Personality and Social Psychology, 36*(8), 917–927.

Brockmann, H., Delhey, J., Welzel, C., & Yuan, H. (2009). The China puzzle: Falling happiness in a rising economy. *Journal of Happiness Studies, 10*, 387–405.

Bruni, L., & Porta, P. (2007). *Handbook on the Economics of Happiness*. Cheltenham/Northampton: Edward Elgar Publishing Ltd.

Bruni, L., & Stanca, L. (2008). Watching alone: Relational goods, television and happiness. *Journal of Economic Behavior & Organization, 65*(3), 506–528.

Clark, A. E., & D'Ambrosio, C. (2015). Attitudes to income inequality: Experimental and survey evidence. In *Handbook of income distribution* (Vol. 2, pp. 1147–1208). Elsevier.

Clark, A. E., Flèche, S., & Senik, C. (2012). *The great happiness moderation* (SOEPpapers on multidisciplinary panel data research 468). Berlin: DIW Berlin, The German Socio-Economic Panel (SOEP).

Deaton, A. (2008). Income, health, and well-being around the world: Evidence from the Gallup World Poll. *The Journal of Economic Perspectives, 22*(2), 53–72.

Diener, E., Lucas, R. E., & Scollon, C. N. (2009). Beyond the Hedonic Treadmill: *Revising the adaptation theory of well-being*. In E. Diener (Ed.), *The science of well-being. Social indicators research series* (Vol. 37, pp. 103–118). Dordrecht: Springer.

Easterlin, R. A. (1974). Does economic growth improve the human lot? Some empirical evidence. In P. A. David & M. W. Reder (Eds.), *Nations and households in economic growth: Essays in honour of moses abramovitz* (pp. 89–125). New York: Academic.

Easterlin, R. A. (2009). Lost in transition: Life satisfaction on the road to capitalism. *Journal of Economic Behavior & Organization, 71*(2), 130–145.

Easterlin, R. A. (2013). Happiness, growth, and public policy. *Economic Inquiry, 51*(1), 1–15.

Easterlin, R. A., & Angelescu, L. (2009). *Happiness and growth the world over: Time series evidence on the happiness-income paradox* (IZA discussion paper, (4060)). Bonn: Institute for the Study of Labor (IZA).

Easterlin, R. A., Angelescu, L., Switek, M., Sawangfa, O., & Zweig, J. S. (2010). The happiness-income paradox revisited. *Proceedings of the National Academy of Sciences, 107*(52), 1–6.

Easterlin, R. A., Morgan, R., Switek, M., & Wang, F. (2012). China's life satisfaction, 1990–2010. *Proceedings of the National Academy of Sciences, 109*(25), 9775–9780.

Easterlin, R. A., Wang, F., & Wang, S. (2017). Growth and happiness in China, 1990–2015. In J. F. Helliwell, R. Layard, & J. D. Sachs (Eds.), *World happiness report 2017* (pp. 48–83). New York: USA Sustainable Development Solutions Network.

Frank, R. H. (1997). The frame of reference as a public good. *The Economic Journal, 107*(445), 1832–1847.

Frederick, S., & Loewenstein, G. (1999). Hedonic adaptation. In D. Kanheman & E. Diener (Eds.), *The foundations of hedonic psychology*. New York: Russell Sage.

Graham, C., & Felton, A. (2006). Inequality and happiness: Insights from Latin America. *Journal of Economic Inequality, 4*(1), 107–122.

Helliwell, J. F. (2003). How's life? Combining individual and national variables to explain subjective well-being. *Economic Modelling, 20*(2), 331–360.

Helliwell, J. (2006). Well-being, social capital and public policy: What's new? *The Economic Journal, 116*(510), 34–45.

Helliwell, J. (2007). Well-being and social capital: Does suicide pose a puzzle? *Social Indicators Research, 81*(3), 455–496.

Helliwell, J. F. (2008). *Life satisfaction and quality of development* (Working paper 14507). Cambridge, MA: National Bureau of Economic Research.

Helliwell, J. (2011). Institutions as enablers of wellbeing: The Singapore prison case study. *International Journal of Well-Being, 1*(2), 255–265. https://doi.org/10.5502/ijw.v1i2.7.

Helliwell, J. F., & Putnam, R. D. (2004). The social context of well-being. *Philosophical Transactions: Royal Society of London Series Biological Sciences, 359*(1449), 1435–1446.

Hirsch, F. (1976). *Social limits to growth*. Cambridge, MA: Harvard University Press.

Kahneman, D., & Krueger, A. (2006). Developments in the measurement of subjective well-being. *Journal of Economic Perspectives, 20*, 3–24.

Layard, R. (2005). *Happiness: Lessons from a new science*. New York: The Penguin Press.

Mikucka, M., Sarracino, F., & Dubrow, J. K. (2017). When does economic growth improve life satisfaction? Multilevel analysis of the roles of social trust and income inequality in 46 countries, 1981–2012. *World Development, 93*, 447–459.

OECD. (2001). The evidence on social capital. In *The well-being of nations: The role of human and social capital* (pp. 39–63). Paris: OECD.

Oishi, S., & Kesebir, S. (2015). Income inequality explains why economic growth does not always translate to an increase in happiness. *Psychological science, 26*(10), 1630–1638.

Oishi, S., Kesebir, S., & Diener, E. (2011). Income inequality and happiness. *Psychological science, 22*(9), 1095–1100.

Ono, H., & Kristen, S. L. (2016). *Redistributing happiness: How social policies shape life satisfaction*. Santa Barbara: Praeger.

Polanyi, K. (1968). *The great transformation*. Boston: Beacon.

Putnam, R. (2000). *Bowling alone: The collapse and revival of American community*. New York/London/Toronto/Sidney: Simon and Schuster.

Rogers, S. H., Halstead, J. M., Gardner, K. H., & Carlson, C. H. (2011). Examining walkability and social capital as indicators of quality of life at the municipal and neighborhood scales. *Applied Research in Quality of Life, 6*(2), 201–213.

Sacks, D. W., Stevenson, B., & Wolfers, J. (2012). Subjective well-being, income, economic development and growth. In P. Booth (Ed.), *The pursuit of happiness* (pp. 59–98). London: The Institute of Economic Affairs.

Sarracino, F. (2013). Richer in money, poorer in relationships and unhappy? Time series comparisons of social capital and well-being in Luxembourg. *Social Indicators Research, 115*(2), 561–622.

Sarracino, F., & Mikucka, M. (2017). Social capital in Europe from 1990 to 2012: Trends and convergence. *Social Indicators Research, 131*(1), 407–432.

Schimmack, U., Krause, P., Wagner, G., & Schupp, J. (2010). Stability and change of well-being: An experimentally enhanced latent state-trait-error analysis. *Social Indicators Research, 95*(1), 19–31.

Schneider, L., & Schimmack, U. (2009). Self-informant agreement in well-being ratings: A meta-analysis. *Social Indicators Research, 94*(3), 363–376.

Schwarz, N., & Strack, F. (1999). Reports of subjective well-being: Judgmental processes and their methodological implications. In E. D. Kahneman & N. Schwarz (Eds.), *Well-being: The foundations of hedonist psychology*. New York: Russell Sage Foundation.

Steele, L. G., & Lynch, S. M. (2013). The pursuit of happiness in China: Individualism, collectivism, and subjective well-being during China's economic and social transformation. *Social Indicators Research, 114*(2), 441–451.

Truyts, T. (2010). Social status in economic theory. *Journal of Economic Surveys, 24*(1), 137–169.

Uhlaner, C. (1989). Relational goods and participation: Incorporating sociability into a theory of rational action. *Public Choice, 62*, 253–285.

Van Praag, B., Frijters, P., & Ferrer-i Carbonell, A. (2003). The anatomy of subjective well-being. *Journal of Economic Behaviour and Organization, 51*(1), 29–49.

Van Reekum, C., Urry, H., Johnstone, T., Thurow, M., Frye, C., Jackson, C., Schaefer, H., Alexander, A., & Davidson, R. (2007). Individual differences in amygdala and ventromedial prefrontal cortex activity are associated with evaluation speed and psychological well-being. *Journal of Cognitive Neuroscience, 19*(2), 237–248.

Veenhoven, R., & Vergunst, F. (2013). The Easterlin illusion: Economic growth does go with greater happiness. *International Journal of Happiness and Development, 1*(4), 311–343.

Wanous, J. P., & Hudy, M. J. (2001). Single-item reliability: A replication and extension. *Organizational Research Methods, 4*(4), 361–375.

Chapter 16
The Subjective Well-Being Political Paradox: Evidence from Latin America

Lucía Macchia and Anke C. Plagnol

Abstract The subjective well-being political paradox describes that individuals are on average more satisfied with their lives under left-leaning (liberal) governments than under right-leaning (conservative) governments; however, at the individual level, people who identify as leaning politically more to the right show higher life satisfaction than those who describe themselves as leaning to the left. The present study investigates whether this paradox, previously found in Europe, can also be found across 18 Latin American countries by using data from 9 waves of the Latinobarómetro survey. In addition to life satisfaction, we consider respondents' self-rated ability to meet their financial needs in a satisfactory manner, which can be seen as a proxy for satisfaction with income. Latin America is an interesting region to study this question because of its political history and the emergence of left-leaning governments during the last 15 years. After controlling for macroeconomic indicators and socio-demographic factors, we find that people report higher life satisfaction and a better ability to meet their financial needs under left-leaning governments compared to centre and right-leaning governments. In contrast, conservative individuals report higher financial and overall well-being than liberal individuals. Our findings confirm the subjective well-being political paradox previously found in Europe.

16.1 Introduction

Richard Easterlin famously asked in 1974 whether economic growth improves the human lot (Easterlin 1974). His analysis suggested that despite a positive income-happiness relationship *at one point in time*, economic growth is not positively associated with well-being, i.e. the income-happiness association is nil *over time* (an observation which other authors later called the *Easterlin paradox*). Nevertheless, policymakers have long focused on increasing the gross domestic product

L. Macchia (✉) · A. C. Plagnol
City, University of London, London, UK
e-mail: lucia.macchia@city.ac.uk; anke.plagnol.1@city.ac.uk

© Springer Nature Switzerland AG 2019
M. Rojas (ed.), *The Economics of Happiness*,
https://doi.org/10.1007/978-3-030-15835-4_16

(GDP) as a good way to improve well-being in a society. The promotion of well-being as the central role of governments was already discussed by Adam Smith and Jeremy Bentham, but how societal well-being can be adequately captured remains a subject of considerable debate. The predominant belief in GDP as an adequate proxy for societal well-being (e.g., Sirgy et al. 2006) is reflected in a number of government policies which emphasise economic growth and incomes. At first, this appears to be a reasonable approach because as other authors apart from Easterlin confirmed GDP is significantly positively associated with subjective well-being (SWB) in the cross-section (e.g., Di Tella et al. 2003; Stevenson and Wolfers 2008). However, the second observation that forms the Easterlin happiness-income paradox – namely the nil relationship between economic growth and well-being – has also been confirmed, both in developed and developing countries (Easterlin et al. 2010).

This observation and other known shortcomings of GDP as a measure of societal progress (e.g., Stiglitz et al. 2009) put into perspective the way in which societal well-being has traditionally been assessed. Increasingly, policymakers are now advocating the use of subjective well-being measures to assess their citizens' well-being (e.g., Adler and Seligman 2016; Dolan and White 2007). However, even if an increased use (or at least proposed use) of subjective well-being measures suggests that subjective well-being is starting to be taken more seriously as a goal of government policies, it needs to be established whether governments can indeed actively improve their citizens' well-being. Is individual well-being significantly associated with government policies and activities, as proxied by governments' political orientation? Do preferences for certain policies, as reflected in individuals' political orientation, matter for subjective well-being?

The present chapter aims to contribute to the answers to these questions. The aims of our analysis are twofold: we first ask whether average subjective well-being varies significantly under governments with different political orientations. Governments that can be found on the left of the political spectrum typically implement and promote policies that are in stark contrast to governments on the right of the political spectrum. Second, we ask to what extent individual political orientation, which is typically related to preferences for certain polices, is associated with individual subjective well-being. We employ data from Latin America for our analysis.

A study that employed European data identified a new kind of subjective well-being paradox, namely the *subjective well-being political paradox*. This pardox describes the observation that individuals are on average more satisfied with their lives when they live in welfare states with higher levels of *decommodification*, welfare spending, and equality than other countries; however, people who identify as leaning politically more to the right show higher levels of life satisfaction than those who describe themselves as leaning to the left (Okulicz-Kozaryn et al. 2014). By simultaneously considering political orientation at the micro (individual) and macro (government) level, our analysis will demonstrate whether the subjective well-being political paradox can also be found in Latin America – a region with a recent turbulent economic and political past, which differs considerably from Europe in many aspects. For this purpose, we look at a typical subjective well-being measure, namely life satisfaction, as well as a proxy for financial satisfaction; and the association of these two measures with political orientation at the government and individual level. In contrast to the study by Okulicz-Kozaryn and colleagues (2014), we employ direct measures of the current government's political orientation, whereas they employed three welfare state indicators and a measure of the aggregate of individual political orientation in a country to look at macro-level political orientation. However, it is possible that some welfare indicators are a legacy of previous, maybe more liberal, governments and we therefore prefer a direct measure of the political orientation of the party in power which will better reflect which policies are promoted in the year of the survey. Due to the strong association between a governments' political orientation and the policies implemented and favoured by that government, our analysis further contributes to the debate on which type of policies might improve well-being in a society.

Right-leaning and left-leaning governments are located at the two extremes of the political spectrum and their opinions on economic and social policies often differ markedly. While conservative governments often avoid interference in economic decisions and favour the free market, left-leaning (liberal) governments typically aim to formulate policies that address the social needs of the population. For instance, liberal governments often focus on policies which reduce unemployment, increased equality, and improve access to quality healthcare, education and social protection, among other things.

Our study focuses on Latin America, a region with considerably less economic, political and democratic stability than Europe during the last decades. For instance, Latin America has long been a volatile region with numerous major episodes of political violence (for an overview see Justino and Martorano 2018). The marked differences between the two regions imply that the existence of the subjective well-being political paradox is not obvious in Latin America. During the 1990s, many Latin American countries implemented conservative policies based on free market principles. After an external debt crisis in 2001, there was a shift from right-leaning to left-leaning governments and by 2003, left-wing (liberal) political parties were in power in most countries in Latin America. Subsequently, the focus of many government policies changed across the region.

16.2 Background

Previous studies have shown that people's quality of life can be affected by the functioning of the government as it provides citizens with many services crucial for individual well-being (Frey and Stutzer 2000; Helliwell and Huang 2008). For instance, at the individual level, health, education and social capital are positively associated with subjective well-being (e.g., Blanchflower and Oswald 2004; Putnam 2000) – these are all domains in which government provision of key services could potentially make a big difference for individual well-being. Indeed, public social spending has previously been found to be an important predictor of different happiness patterns in Latin America (Switek 2012).

Liberal policies often aim to increase equality in a society, for example through access to education. An unequal distribution of income in a society has been found to be negatively associated with subjective well-being (Alesina et al. 2004; Fahey and Smyth 2004; Schwarze and Härpfer 2003). In Latin American countries, income inequality is seen as a sign of unfairness as it provides an advantage for the rich; subsequently, it is negatively associated with the happiness of the poor but not of the rich (Graham and Felton 2006).

Whereas conservative or right-leaning governments typically favour free markets, liberal or left-wing governments tend to play an active role in economic and political decisions in order to promote equality and provide citizens with protection against economic, social and political hardship (Green-Pedersen 2004). Therefore, the political orientation of a government can be seen as a proxy for the type of policies and the level of intervention in the provision of services that are potentially beneficial for people's quality of life. Citizens who live in countries with liberal governments, which typically promote policies that aim to improve people's well-being directly instead of indirectly through economic growth, are more likely to report higher subjective well-being than citizens who live in countries led by conservative governments (Bok 2010; Pacek and Radcliff 2008; Radcliff 2001). This observation has been attributed to livability theory which posits that government policies that create better, more liveable conditions in a country will lead to higher average subjective well-being (e.g., Okulicz-Kozaryn et al. 2014; Veenhoven and Ehrhardt 1995). In contrast, at the individual level, conservative individuals tend to report higher subjective well-being than liberal individuals (Napier and Jost 2008). This fact may be explained by system justification theory which describes a preference for the status quo and the belief that the political system is fair (for a summary see Okulicz-Kozaryn et al. 2014). In this view, individuals that find themselves more on the right of the political spectrum may report, on average, higher subjective well-being because they find (in their mind) good justifications for social inequalities and other societal factors that are often associated with lower SWB (Napier and Jost 2008).

As most studies focus on life satisfaction, it remains to be seen whether a government's political orientation is significantly associated with specific domains of subjective well-being. After all, it is possible that government policies affect some domains of life positively while simultaneously decreasing satisfaction in other domains. Our study will partly fill this gap by looking at a proxy for financial satisfaction (in addition to life satisfaction). Financial satisfaction is of course closely related to income, which was the subject of many of the early studies on subjective well-being conducted by economists. Income has been found to be positively associated with subjective well-being, especially, when income helps to cover basic needs (e.g., Oswald 1997). In some cases, the significant and positive association between subjective well-being and absolute income only exists in the lower part of the income range (Argyle 1999). However, once basic needs are met, the relationship between absolute income and subjective well-being is nil as aspirations rise in lockstep with income (Easterlin 2001). Relative income also matters for subjective well-being (e.g., Blanchflower and Oswald 2004; Ferrer-i-Carbonell 2005; Luttmer 2005; McBride 2001) as people tend to compare their living standard to that of their peers (Easterlin 1995).

In the following, we will investigate the existence of the subjective well-being political paradox in Latin America, and then explore which government policies might contribute to the results found here.

16.3   Methods

16.3.1   Data

We employ data from the Latinobarómetro, an annual opinion survey which includes responses collected in 18 Latin American countries with about 1000 respondents per country in each survey year (Latinobarómetro Corporation 2016). The data are repeated cross-sections representative of the population in the majority of the countries in each survey year.[1] Our final sample of 180,069 observations includes all 18 Latin American countries for the 2004–2007 and 2009–2015 survey periods (9 waves). However, only 137,321 of these respondents answered the question concerning their political orientation. We focus on these waves because the answer categories of the life satisfaction measure – one of our main variables – remain constant across these years. Moreover, the survey question appears at the very beginning of the questionnaire which avoids potential bias resulting from preceding questions.

16.3.2   Measures

16.3.2.1   Dependent Variables

Our analysis employs two dependent variables – one assessing overall life satisfaction and one that can be seen as a proxy for financial satisfaction. The latter variable describes the respondent's subjective evaluation of their ability to cover their financial needs in a satisfactory manner. In particular, the survey question asks respondents: "Does the salary you receive and your total family income allow you to cover your needs in a satisfactory manner? Which of the following statements describes your situation? It is sufficient, can save (1); It is just sufficient, doesn't have major problems (2); It is not sufficient, has problems (3); It is not sufficient, has big problems (4)". The four answer categories were reverse coded for the analysis and treated as ordered categorical such that a higher value denotes a better ability to cover one's financial needs. We denote this variable as *Ability to cover financial needs* in the statistical analysis.

Our second dependent variable assesses the respondent's life satisfaction based on the following question: "In general, would you say you are satisfied with your life? Would you say you are very satisfied (1), quite satisfied (2), not very satisfied (3) or not satisfied at all (4)?" This variable was reverse coded such that a higher value denotes a higher level of life satisfaction.

---

[1]Data are representative for all countries except for Chile, Colombia and Paraguay.

Political Orientation

We employ two measures to assess political orientation both at the government (macro) and individual (micro) level:

- *Respondent's political orientation:* This measure is based on the following question "In politics, people normally speak of 'left' and 'right'. On a scale where 0 is left and 10 is right, where would you place yourself?". We kept the original coding for our study.
- *Government's political orientation:* The Latinobarómetro does not include a measure indicating the present government's political orientation. We therefore created a variable which indicates whether the government in power at the time of the survey in the respondent's country is considered left wing, centre or right wing. This classification was primarily derived from information from the Database of Political Institutions (Cruz et al. 2016). Any remaining gaps were filled with information from the Political Database of the Americas (2015), which lists the political party of the president elected in each country in the years used in this study. We also consulted the relevant literature on the topic to confirm the governments' political orientation classification (e.g., Alcántara Sáez and Freidenberg 2001; Flores-Macías 2012; Middlebrook 2000).

Additional Measures

We further included three macroeconomic indicators for each country which have previously been found to be associated with subjective well-being: the unemployment rate (% of total labour force), the inflation rate (GDP deflator, annual %), and the log of gross domestic product (GPD) per capita (in constant 2010 US$).[2] These measures were obtained from the World Bank (2017). Both the unemployment rate and the inflation rate typically show a negative relationship with subjective well-being (Clark and Oswald 1994; Di Tella and MacCulloch 2001).

We further account for socio-demographic variables, such as age, gender, education, employment and socioeconomic status. As previous research suggests that subjective well-being is U-shaped in age (e.g., Blanchflower and Oswald 2008; Frijters and Beatton 2012; Graham and Pettinato 2001), we model age as non-linear by including both age and age squared. Gender is included as a control variable as women tend to report higher subjective well-being than men (Alesina et al. 2004). We include a number of employment status categories with 'self-employed' as the reference category in the statistical models as it presents the largest share of respondents. The informal employment sector – which is likely captured by the 'self-employed' category – is large in Latin America but recent research has shown that informal labour status is not necessarily associated with political attitudes

---

[2]Inflation rate and GDP per capita data are not available for Venezuela in 2015.

(Baker and Velasco-Guachalla 2018). Previous studies have found unemployment to be negatively associated with subjective well-being (e.g., Clark 2003; Clark and Oswald 1994; Winkelmann and Winkelmann 1998). Education (e.g., Blanchflower and Oswald 2004) and income (e.g., Oswald 1997) are both usually positively associated with subjective well-being. We include the respondent's socioeconomic status as estimated by the interviewer as a proxy for household income as the Latinobarómetro does not provide a direct measure of the respondent's income. Table 16.1 shows summary statistics of the variables included in the analysis.

Table 16.1 Summary statistics

Variable	N	Mean	St. Dev.	Min	Max
Ability to cover financial needs	176,153	2.436	0.842	1	4
Life satisfaction	179,278	2.989	0.839	1	4
Government's political orientation					
Left	180,069	0.55	0.497	0	1
Centre	180,069	0.229	0.42	0	1
Right	180,069	0.221	0.415	0	1
Respondent's political orientation (left = 0; right = 10)	137,321	5.365	2.658	0	10
Unemployment rate	180,069	7.023	3.129	1.8	18.4
Inflation rate	178,869	7.734	7.511	−4.62	45.94
Log of GDP per capita	178,869	8.611	0.662	7.24	9.593
Male	180,069	0.485	0.5	0	1
Age	180,069	39.997	16.359	18	99
Level of education					
Without education	180,069	0.097	0.297	0	1
Between 1 and 6 years	180,069	0.308	0.461	0	1
Between 7 and 12 years	180,069	0.402	0.49	0	1
High school/academies/incomplete technical training	180,069	0.021	0.143	0	1
High school/academies/complete technical training	180,069	0.04	0.196	0	1
Incomplete university	180,069	0.071	0.257	0	1
Complete university	180,069	0.061	0.239	0	1
Employment status					
Self-employed	180,069	0.323	0.467	0	1
Temporarily out of work	180,069	0.06	0.237	0	1
Don't work / responsible for shopping and house work	180,069	0.234	0.406	0	1
Salaried employee in a private company	180,069	0.076	0.265	0	1
Salaried employee in a public company	180,069	0.178	0.383	0	1
Student	180,069	0.061	0.24	0	1
Retired	180,069	0.068	0.251	0	1
Socioeconomic status	180,063	3.279	0.896	1	5

16.3.3 Analytical Strategy

We run ordered logit regressions as our two dependent variables are ordered categorical. Ordinary least squares regressions (OLS) yield the same substantive results, suggesting that our results are robust to methodology. We also include country and year fixed effects to account for unobserved variables related to the year of the survey and the country in which the respondent lives.

16.4 Results

Does the subjective well-being political paradox also exist in Latin America? Our regression analysis suggests that people who live in a country where the ruling political party can be classified as left-leaning report a better ability to cover their financial needs and higher life satisfaction than people who live in a country with a centre or right-leaning government (Table 16.2). However, in the life satisfaction regression, the coefficient for right-leaning governments is small and only significant at the 10% level. A larger difference can be observed between the life satisfaction of individuals in countries with a left-leaning government and the life satisfaction of people who live in countries with a centre government. We test the hypothesis that the coefficients for centre and right-leaning governments are identical and find that they are in fact significantly different from each other; i.e., respondents who live in countries with right-leaning governments report better outcomes for both dependent variables than those living under governments that can be found in the centre of the political spectrum.

We do find evidence for the subjective well-being political paradox in Latin America. At the individual level, right-leaning individuals rate, on average, their ability to cover their financial needs and their life satisfaction higher than left-leaning individuals. At the government level, individuals who live in a country with a left-leaning government rate their ability to cover their financial needs and their life satisfaction higher than people who live in a country with a right-leaning government. In all our regressions, we account for gender, age, education, employment status and socioeconomic status as well as three important economic indicators, namely the log of GDP per capita, the unemployment rate and the inflation rate.

We find that the log of GDP per capita is significantly positively associated with both dependent variables. The unemployment rate is significantly negatively associated with the ability to cover financial needs and significantly positively associated with life satisfaction. In contrast, the inflation rate is significantly positively associated with the ability to cover financial needs but significantly negatively associated with life satisfaction.

Men rate their ability to cover financial needs and life satisfaction higher than women. The negative coefficient of age and the positive coefficient of age-squared in both regressions confirms the U-shape in age that has been found in previous

Table 16.2 Ordered logit regressions for Ability to cover financial needs and Life satisfaction

	Dependent variables	
Government's political leaning (ref: left)	Ability to cover financial needs	Life satisfaction
Centre	−0.326***	−0.146***
	−0.022	−0.021
Right	−0.124***	−0.042*
	−0.022	−0.022
Respondent's political orientation	0.004**	0.024***
(left = 0; right = 10)	−0.002	−0.002
Log of GDP per capita	1.198***	1.352***
	−0.009	−0.021
Unemployment rate (%)	−0.035***	0.011***
	−0.004	−0.004
Inflation rate (%)	0.005***	−0.008***
	−0.001	−0.001
Male	0.157***	0.018
	−0.012	−0.011
Age	−0.043***	−0.029***
	−0.002	−0.002
Age squared/100	0.040***	0.027***
	−0.002	−0.002
Level of education (ref: no education)		
Between 1 and 6 years	0.159***	−0.017
	−0.021	−0.022
Between 7 and 12 years	0.466***	0.025
	−0.022	−0.022
High school/academies/incomplete technical training	0.610***	0.192**
	−0.041	−0.041
High school/academies/complete technical training	0.667***	0.115***
	−0.034	−0.033
Incomplete university	0.749***	0.118***
	−0.029	−0.029
Complete university	1.009***	0.219***
	−0.03	−0.03
Employment status (ref: self-employed)		
Temporarily out of work	−0.515***	−0.216***
	−0.023	−0.023
Don't work/responsible for shopping and house work	−0.142***	0.042***
	−0.016	−0.016
Salaried employee in a private company	0.120***	0.053***
	−0.016	−0.015
Salaried employee in a public company	0.106***	0.168***
	−0.021	−0.02
Student	0.119***	0.084***
	−0.026	−0.026

(continued)

Table 16.2 (continued)

	Dependent variables	
Government's political leaning (ref: left)	Ability to cover financial needs	Life satisfaction
Retired	0.001	0.065**
	−0.026	−0.026
Socioeconomic status	0.654***	0.176***
	−0.006	−0.007
Financial ability to cover one's needs	–	0.355***
		−0.007
Country fixed effects	Included	Included
Year fixed effects	Included	Included
N	133,605	133,163
Pseudo R^2	0.203	0.132

Note: $^*p < 0.1$; $^{**}p < 0.05$; $^{***}p < 0.01$. The regression models show raw ordered logit coefficients with standard errors in parentheses. Observations from 18 Latin American countries were included from 2004 to 2015 (except 2008). Cut points (standard errors) are 3.138 (0.027); 5.534 (0.029); 7.505 (0.031) for life satisfaction; 17.520 (0.028); 19.625 (0.029); 22.224 (0.031) for ability to cover financial needs

studies. People with higher levels of education report a better ability to cover their financial needs and higher satisfaction with their lives than people with no education. Only those who are temporarily out of work struggle more to cover their financial needs and report lower life satisfaction than self-employed individuals in both regressions. All other employment categories (except for 'Don't work/responsible for shopping and house work' in the first regression in Table 16.2) report a better ability to cover their financial needs and higher life satisfaction than self-employed individuals, suggesting that self-employment may be associated with jobs of low quality in Latin America. Socioeconomic status is significantly positively associated with ability to cover financial needs and life satisfaction. The life satisfaction regression further includes the subjective ability to cover one's financial needs as a control due to its close association with people's personal income. The association between our two main variables of interest is significant and positive: people who report a better ability to cover their financial needs report, on average, higher levels of life satisfaction. (Table 16.2, model 2).

16.5   Discussion and Conclusion

We used data from the Latinobarómetro collected between 2004–2007 and 2009–2015 (9 survey years) across 18 Latin American countries to examine whether the subjective well-being political paradox that has previously been observed in Europe can also be found in Latin America. Do political inclinations both at the individual (micro) and at the government (macro) level show different associations with subjective well-being? We employed two measures to assess subjective well-being: life satisfaction and the self-reported ability to cover financial needs in a satisfactory manner, which can be seen as a proxy for financial satisfaction – a domain satisfaction measure.

We find that people who live in a country with a left-leaning government report, on average, a better ability to cover financial needs and higher life satisfaction than people who live in a country with a right-leaning or centre government. In contrast, individuals who describe themselves as more right-leaning tend to report higher levels of life satisfaction and ability to cover their financial needs. These results are obtained after controlling for age, gender, level of education, employment and socioeconomic status and three macroeconomic indicators. The individual-level association between conservative values and subjective well-being should therefore not be driven by the potentially more privileged background of right-leaning respondents. The ability to cover financial needs is significantly positively associated with life satisfaction – a result that is consistent with the subjective well-being literature which usually finds a positive income-subjective well-being association at one point in time (however, not for the same individuals or countries over time, as was famously reported by Richard Easterlin in 1974).

At the macro level, the government's political orientation can be seen as a proxy for the policies that left, centre and right-leaning ruling parties typically favour. Our findings suggest that with respect to financial and overall subjective well-being, individuals tend to fare better under left-leaning governments. It is possible that the policies favoured by left-leaning governments exert a positive influence on various domains of life that are important for subjective well-being; other than simply people's income. Indeed, previous research has shown that attainments in non-pecuniary life domains, such as family life and health, are likely more important for long-term subjective well-being than attainments in the financial domain (e.g., Plagnol and Easterlin 2008). While individuals often adapt rather quickly to changes in income with respect to subjective well-being (Easterlin 2001), this is not the case for changes in relationships, for example through divorce and widowhood (e.g., Lucas 2005; Lucas et al. 2003), changes in health status (e.g., Oswald and Powdthavee 2008), or unemployment (e.g., Winkelmann and Winkelmann 1998).

It is possible that left-leaning governments are more likely to provide the services that are crucial for people's quality of life and that this is in turn reflected in their higher subjective well-being. For example, policies that aim to reduce unemployment, promote domestic production and incentivise people to set up their own businesses likely improve income and steady employment and, thus, exert a positive influence on people's ability to cover their financial needs – the domain satisfaction measure in our analysis. Moreover, left-leaning governments are more likely than other types of ruling parties to address social needs such as access to good quality education, healthcare and social protection; all of which are likely to be positively associated with life satisfaction.

Several limitations of our study should be addressed in future research. The Latinobarómetro data are cross-sectional and thus do not allow us to establish the direction of causality of the relationships observed in the analysis. The use of panel data and experimental research might strengthen the results found in this study. However, to the best of our knowledge, such data are not currently available for Latin America. Moreover, most of our measures are self-reported and thus potentially suffer from social desirability bias and other drawbacks of subjective measures.

Our study thus provides a preliminary picture of the association between political orientations and individual subjective well-being in Latin America, which suggests that individuals fare better with liberal policies. However, those who are least likely to vote for left-leaning political parties – i.e. those who report right-leaning political inclinations – tend to report higher subjective well-being than self-described left-leaning individuals. Maybe these respondents are already living a comfortable life and are therefore not in need of liberal policies. We tried to address this possibility through the inclusion of suitable control variables (i.e., education, socioeconomic status, employment status) but it is possible that the measures we employed do not fully capture socio-economic differences between respondents. Overall, we conclude that the subjective well-being political paradox can also be observed in Latin America.

References

Adler, A., & Seligman, M. E. P. (2016). Using wellbeing for public policy: Theory, measurement, and recommendations. *International Journal of Wellbeing, 6*(1), 1–35. https://doi.org/10.5502/ijw.v6i1.429.

Alcántara Sáez, M., & Freidenberg, F. (2001). *Partidos políticos de América Latina: Centroamérica, México y República Dominicana*. Universidad de Salamanca España.

Alesina, A., Di Tella, R., & MacCulloch, R. (2004). Inequality and happiness: Are Europeans and Americans different? *Journal of Public Economics, 88*(9–10), 2009–2042. https://doi.org/10.1016/j.jpubeco.2003.07.006.

Argyle, M. (1999). Causes and correlates of happiness. In D. Kahneman, E. Diener, & N. Schwarz (Eds.), *Well-being: The foundations of hedonic psychology* (pp. 353–373). New York: Russell Sage Foundation.

Baker, A., & Velasco-Guachalla, V. X. (2018). Is the informal sector politically different? (Null) answers from Latin America. *World Development, 102*, 170–182. https://doi.org/10.1016/J.WORLDDEV.2017.09.014.

Blanchflower, D. G., & Oswald, A. J. (2004). Well-being over time in Britain and the USA. *Journal of Public Economics, 88*(7–8), 1359–1386. https://doi.org/10.1016/S0047-2727(02)00168-8.

Blanchflower, D. G., & Oswald, A. J. (2008). Is well-being U-shaped over the life cycle? *Social Science & Medicine, 66*(8), 1733–1749. https://doi.org/10.1016/J.SOCSCIMED.2008.01.030.

Bok, D. (2010). *The politics of happiness: What governments can learn from the new research on well-being*. Princeton: Princeton University Press.

Clark, A. E. (2003). Unemployment as a social norm: Psychological evidence from panel data. *Journal of Labor Economics, 21*(2), 323–351. https://doi.org/10.1086/345560.

Clark, A. E., & Oswald, A. J. (1994). Unhappiness and unemployment. *The Economic Journal, 104*(424), 648. https://doi.org/10.2307/2234639.

Cruz, C., Keefer, P., & Scartascini, C. (2016). *The Database of Political Institutions 2015 (DPI2015)*. Retrieved from https://publications.iadb.org/handle/11319/7408.

Di Tella, R., & MacCulloch, R. J. A. J. O. (2001). Preferences over inflation and unemployment: Evidence from surveys of happiness. *American Economic Review, 91*(1), 335–341.

Di Tella, R., MacCulloch, R. J., & Oswald, A. J. (2003). The macroeconomics of happiness. *Review of Economics and Statistics, 85*(4), 809–827. https://doi.org/10.1162/003465303772815745.

Dolan, P., & White, M. P. (2007). How can measures of subjective well-being be used to inform public policy? *Perspectives on Psychological Science, 2*(1), 71–85. https://doi.org/10.1111/j.1745-6916.2007.00030.x.

Easterlin, R. A. (1974). Does economic growth improve the human lot? Some empirical evidence. In P. A. David & M. W. Reder (Eds.), *Nations and households in economic growth: Essays in honour of Moses Abramovitz* (pp. 89–125). New York: Academic.

Easterlin, R. A. (1995). Will raising the incomes of all increase the happiness of all? *Journal of Economic Behavior & Organization, 27*(1), 35–47. Retrieved from http://ideas.repec.org/a/eee/jeborg/v27y1995i1p35-47.html

Easterlin, R. A. (2001). Income and happiness: Towards a unified theory. *The Economic Journal, 111*(473), 465–484. https://doi.org/10.1111/1468-0297.00646.

Easterlin, R. A., Angelescu McVey, L., Switek, M., Sawangfa, O., & Smith Zweig, J. (2010). The happiness-income paradox revisited. *Proceedings of the National Academy of Sciences of the United States of America, 107*(52), 22463–22468. https://doi.org/10.1073/pnas.1015962107.

Fahey, T., & Smyth, E. (2004). Do subjective indicators measure welfare? Evidence from 33 European societies. *European Societies, 6*(1), 5–27. https://doi.org/10.1080/1461669032000176297.

Ferrer-i-Carbonell, A. (2005). Income and well-being: An empirical analysis of the comparison income effect. *Journal of Public Economics, 89*(5–6), 997–1019. https://doi.org/10.1016/j.jpubeco.2004.06.003.

Flores-Macías, G. A. (2012). *After neoliberalism? The left and economic reforms in Latin America.* Oxford: Oxford University Press.

Frey, B. S., & Stutzer, A. (2000). Happiness, economy and institutions. *The Economic Journal, 110* (466), 918–938. https://doi.org/10.1111/1468-0297.00570.

Frijters, P., & Beatton, T. (2012). The mystery of the U-shaped relationship between happiness and age. *Journal of Economic Behavior & Organization, 82*(2–3), 525–542. https://doi.org/10.1016/J.JEBO.2012.03.008.

Graham, C., & Felton, A. (2006). Inequality and happiness: Insights from Latin America. *Journal of Economic Inequality, 4*(1), 107–122. https://doi.org/10.1007/s10888-005-9009-1.

Graham, C., & Pettinato, S. (2001). Happiness, markets, and democracy: Latin America in comparative perspective. *Journal of Happiness Studies, 2*(3), 237–268. https://doi.org/10.1023/A:1011860027447.

Green-Pedersen, C. (2004). The dependent variable problem within the study of welfare state retrenchment: Defining the problem and looking for solutions. *Journal of Comparative Policy Analysis: Research and Practice, 6*(1), 3–14. https://doi.org/10.1080/1387698042000222763.

Helliwell, J. F., & Huang, H. (2008). How's your government? International evidence linking good government and well-being. *British Journal of Political Science, 38*(4), 595–619. https://doi.org/10.1017/S0007123408000306.

Justino, P., & Martorano, B. (2018). Welfare spending and political conflict in Latin America, 1970–2010. *World Development, 107*, 98–110. https://doi.org/10.1016/J.WORLDDEV.2018.03.005.

Latinobarómetro Corporation. (2016). Latinobarómetro Database.

Lucas, R. E. (2005). Time does not heal all wounds. A longitudinal study of reaction and adaptation to divorce. *Psychological Science, 16*(12), 945–950. https://doi.org/10.1111/j.1467-9280.2005.01642.x.

Lucas, R. E., Clark, A. E., Georgellis, Y., & Diener, E. (2003). Reexamining adaptation and the set point model of happiness: Reactions to changes in marital status. *Journal of Personality and Social Psychology, 84*(3), 527–539.

Luttmer, E. F. P. (2005). Neighbors as negatives: Relative earnings and well-being. *The Quarterly Journal of Economics, 120*, 963–1002. https://doi.org/10.2307/25098760.

McBride, M. (2001). Relative-income effects on subjective well-being in the cross-section. *Journal of Economic Behavior & Organization, 45*(3), 251–278. https://doi.org/10.1016/S0167-2681 (01)0145-7.

Middlebrook, K. J. (2000). *Conservative parties, the right, and democracy in Latin America.* Baltimore/London: The Johns Hopkins University Press.

Napier, J. L., & Jost, J. T. (2008). Why are conservatives happier than liberals? *Psychological Science, 19*(6), 565–572. https://doi.org/10.1111/j.1467-9280.2008.02124.x.

Okulicz-Kozaryn, A., Holmes, O., & Avery, D. R. (2014). The subjective well-being political paradox: Happy welfare states and unhappy liberals. *Journal of Applied Psychology, 99*(6), 1300–1308. https://doi.org/10.1037/a0037654.

Oswald, A. J. (1997). Happiness and economic performance. *The Economic Journal, 107*(445), 1815–1831. https://doi.org/10.2307/2957911.

Oswald, A. J., & Powdthavee, N. (2008). Does happiness adapt? A longitudinal study of disability with implications for economists and judges. *Journal of Public Economics, 92*(5–6), 1061–1077. https://doi.org/10.1016/j.jpubeco.2008.01.002.

Pacek, A. C., & Radcliff, B. (2008). Welfare policy and subjective well-being across nations: An individual-level assessment. *Social Indicators Research, 89*(1), 179–191. https://doi.org/10.1007/s11205-007-9232-1.

PDBA. (2015). *Political Database of the Americas (PDBA).* Retrieved June 20, 2003, from http://pdba.georgetown.edu/.

Plagnol, A. C., & Easterlin, R. A. (2008). Aspirations, attainments, and satisfaction: Life cycle differences between American women and men. *Journal of Happiness Studies, 9*(4), 601–619. https://doi.org/10.1007/s10902-008-9106-5.

Putnam, R. D. (2000). *Bowling alone: The collapse and revival of American community.* New York: Simon & Schuster.

Radcliff, B. (2001). Politics, markets, and life satisfaction: The political economy of human happiness. *American Political Science Review, 95*(4), 939–952.

Schwarze, J., & Härpfer, M. (2003). Are people inequality averse, and do they prefer redistribution by the state? A revised version. *IZA Discussion Paper No. 974.*

Sirgy, M. J., Michalos, A. C., Ferriss, A. L., Easterlin, R. A., Patrick, D., & Pavot, W. (2006). The Quality-of-Life (QOL) research movement: Past, present, and future. *Social Indicators Research, 76*(3), 343–466.

Stevenson, B., & Wolfers, J. (2008). Economic growth and subjective well-being: Reassessing the Easterlin paradox. *Brookings Papers on Economic Activity, 2008*(1), 1–87. https://doi.org/10.1353/eca.0.0001.

Stiglitz JE, Sen A, Fitoussi JP (2009) *Report of the Commission on the Measurement of Economic Performance and Social Progress (CMEPSP).* Available at http://www.stiglitz-sen-fitoussi.fr/en/documents.htm.

Switek, M. (2012). Life satisfaction in Latin America: A size-of-place analysis. *Journal of Development Studies, 48*(7), 983–999. https://doi.org/10.1080/00220388.2012.658374.

The World Bank. (2017). *World Bank World Development Indicators.* Retrieved February 7, 2017, from http://data.worldbank.org.

Veenhoven, R., & Ehrhardt, J. (1995). The cross-national pattern of happiness: Test of predictions implied in three theories of happiness. *Social Indicators Research, 34*(1), 33–68. https://doi.org/10.1007/BF01078967.

Winkelmann, L., & Winkelmann, R. (1998). Why are the unemployed so unhappy? Evidence from panel data. *Economica, 65*(257), 1–15. https://doi.org/10.1111/1468-0335.00111.

Part VI
Happiness Along the Life Course
and the Social Context

Chapter 17
Born to Be Mild? Cohort Effects Don't (Fully) Explain Why Well-Being Is U-Shaped in Age

Andrew E. Clark

Abstract The statistical analysis of cross-section data very often reveals a U-shaped relationship between subjective well-being and age. This paper uses 18 waves of British panel data to try to distinguish between two potential explanations of this shape: a pure life-cycle or aging effect, and a fixed cohort effect depending on year of birth. Panel analysis controlling for fixed effects continues to produce a U-shaped relationship between well-being and age, although this U-shape is flatter for life satisfaction than for the GHQ measure of mental well-being. The pattern of the estimated cohort effects also differs between the two well-being measures and, to an extent, by demographic group. In particular, those born earlier report more positive GHQ scores, controlling for their current age; this phenomenon is especially prevalent for women.

17.1 Introduction

Interest in subjective well-being across the social sciences has developed in parallel with both the greater availability of panel data, where the same individuals are followed over time, and the wider use of statistical tools to better model individual fixed effects. These statistical techniques consist of the use of panel data, or cross-section analysis with careful controls (for example, twin studies, where the initial distribution of the genetic pack of cards can be controlled for: see Bouchard et al. 1990; Kohler et al. 2005; Tellegen et al. 1988). The application of these techniques allows subjective well-being to be split up into a permanent or fixed part, and a transitory component that depends on life events. Contributions in this spirit include Lucas et al. (2003, 2004), Frijters et al. (2004), Van Praag and Ferrer-i-Carbonell (2004), Zimmerman and Easterlin (2006) and Blanchflower and Oswald (2008).

This interest in the effect of fixed individual characteristics has spilled over into the analysis of the relationship between well-being and age: in an econometric world

A. E. Clark (✉)
Paris School of Economics – CNRS, Paris, France
e-mail: Andrew.Clark@ens.fr

© Springer Nature Switzerland AG 2019
M. Rojas (ed.), *The Economics of Happiness*,
https://doi.org/10.1007/978-3-030-15835-4_17

plagued by accusations of endogeneity, age, sex and ethnicity typically stand out as exogenous variables, and have consequently received a great deal of attention. Early work emphasised that older individuals tended to be happier/more satisfied than younger individuals. More recent analyses have refined this approach by considering non-linear relationships between well-being and age. The results here differ somewhat between economics and psychology.

Mroczek and Kolarz (1998) find that positive affect follows an upwardly curved profile with age, while Mroczek and Spiro (2005) suggest that subjective well-being follows an inverted U-shape, peaking at around retirement age. At the same time, a vigorous literature in Economics has introduced terms in age and age-squared into well-being regressions, producing strong evidence of a U-shaped relationship which typically bottoms out somewhere between the mid-thirties and the mid-forties.[1] Curves of this type have now been identified many times in a wide variety of datasets across different countries.[2]

Two popular competing interpretations of this U-shaped relationship have been proposed. One is that it reflects the passage of individuals through various stylised life events; another is that it reflects a cohort effect, so that individuals born in the 1950s, say, have (and always will have) particularly low levels of subjective well-being (hence producing a U-shape in cross-section analysis of 1990s data).[3] This paper uses two measures of well-being in 18 waves of British panel data to test the hypothesis that the age and well-being U-shape is a pure cohort phenomenon. Two types of test are presented, the first indirect, although intuitive, and the second direct. The tests are carried out on both unbalanced and balanced panel data.

The first intuitive test is based on the estimated minimum point of the U-shape. If this latter is picking up a cohort phenomenon, then the point of lowest well-being should move to the right by 1 year from data wave t to wave $t + 1$. The age of minimum well-being should therefore be 17 years greater in Wave 18 than in Wave 1. This turns out not to be the case. The conclusion is that there is an aging phenomenon in well-being: this is something that we will all (statistically) go through, no matter when we were born.

The second test is direct. Panel well-being regressions are estimated which control for unobserved individual fixed effects. These regressions, which hold all cohort effects constant, continue to produce U-shaped relationships between age and well-being. It is important to underline that the age effect here is obtained by examining the different levels of well-being of the same individual at different

---

[1]The sample in Mroczek and Spiro (2005) actually consists of veterans over the age of 40, so that their finding of an upward-sloping profile is not inconsistent with a U-shape over all ages.

[2]Graham and Ruiz Pozuelo (2017) find a U-shape in 44 out of 46 countries investigated in Gallup World Poll data. This conclusion does not however hold for all well-being measures. In Stone et al. (2010), a U-shape is found for the Cantril ladder and positive emotions in Gallup data, but not for negative emotions.

[3]Putnam (2000), page 141, concludes that the decline in trust in the US is purely a cohort phenomenon, with each cohort's trust not changing over time.

ages. Again, the conclusion is that the U-shaped relationship between age and well being is at least partly driven by aging, rather than being a pure cohort effect.

The remainder of the paper is organised as follows. Section 17.2 describes the two tests of cohort effects, and the data on which they will be carried out. Section 17.3 contains the main results regarding the persistence of the U-shaped relationship between well-being and age. Last, Sect. 17.4 concludes.

17.2   Cohort or Life-Cycle?

Empirical work which introduces age as one of the explanatory variables in the analysis of subjective well-being (such as life satisfaction or happiness) very often finds a U-shaped relationship, minimising somewhere in the mid-thirties to the mid-forties. As highlighted in Frey and Stutzer (2002), there is less agreement over why this U-shape so consistently results. One interpretation is that, loosely speaking, the U-shape reflects the different events that occur to individuals over the life cycle, which have a fairly systematic relationship to their age. This reading is found in Argyle (1989), Hayo and Seifert (2002) and Blanchflower and Oswald (2004). Alternatively, we might argue that, controlling for observables, well-being is broadly flat over the life-cycle, with the U-shape coming from unobserved individual heterogeneity or cohort effects.[4] In this case, with our data from the 1990s and 2000s, the hypothesis is that those in the late 1950s/late 1960s birth cohorts report lower well-being scores than do those born earlier or later.

Cross-section data does not allow us to distinguish between the life-cycle and cohort components of well-being; neither does twin data, as age and year of birth (the cohort effect) are identical across matched subjects. Progress can however be made with repeated cross-section or panel data in which we have repeated observations on individuals of the same birth cohort, over different ages, allowing the two effects to be identified separately. The increasing availability of long-run panel data has been a huge boon for the social sciences. This is particularly the case with respect to research on aging or the life-cycle.

Blanchflower and Oswald (2008) use long-run repeated cross-sectional data from the US and Europe to independently model the effect of age (in five-year blocks) and birth cohort (in 10-year blocks) on measures of subjective well-being. Heuristically, over a long enough time period, they will observe people of the same age (group) but born in different birth cohorts. This allows the separate identification of the two effects.

---

[4]This is the conclusion reached by Easterlin and Schaeffer (1999), using 20 years of cohort data from the US General Social Survey. Kassenböhmer and Haisken-DeNew (2012) suggest that the U-shape in German Socio-Economic Panel (SOEP) data is entirely explained by individual fixed effects and experience in the panel. Cribier (2005) is an evocative account of the differences in life experience between two cohorts of French workers born only 14 years apart.

This paper appeals to the same kind of identification strategy, using 18 waves of British panel data to distinguish between life-cycle and cohort effects. We consider two separate tests of the hypothesis that the U-shape represents a cohort effect.

The first, indirect, test relies on the prediction of the cohort explanation that the whole U-shape should move 1 year to the right per year. In the current paper's BHPS data, the unhappy people who were born in 1955 will be unhappy at age 36 in Wave 1 (in 1991), but equally unhappy at age 37 in Wave 2, and so on. One measure of the position of the U-shaped relationship is its minimum. The first test thus consists in seeing whether the point of minimum well-being shifts to the right by 1 year per wave.

The second, direct, test involves controlling explicitly for fixed effects in panel well-being regressions. These fixed effects will include by definition the individual's year of birth: her cohort. Any effect of age variables in fixed-effect well-being regressions must then reflect life-cycle or aging effects: systematic changes in well-being that happen to all individuals (no matter when they were born) as they age.

17.2.1 Data

The data come from the first 18 waves of the British Household Panel Survey (BHPS), a general survey initially covering a random sample of approximately 10,000 individuals in 5500 British households. The Wave 18 sample consists of around 15,000 individuals in 9000 households.[5] The BHPS includes a wide range of information about individual and household demographics, employment, income and health. More information on this survey is available at https://www.iser.essex.ac.uk/bhps/. There is both entry into and exit from the panel, leading to unbalanced data. The BHPS is a household panel: all adults in the same household are interviewed separately. The wave 1 data were collected in late 1991 – early 1992, the wave 2 data were collected in late 1992 – early 1993, and so on. The analysis in this paper refers to individuals aged between 16 and 64, and will be carried out on both unbalanced and balanced panel data.

The central question addressed here is whether individual well-being changes systematically over the life cycle.[6] Two measures of subjective well-being are considered: the 12-item version of the General Health Questionnaire (GHQ-12), which appears in all waves of the BHPS, and overall life satisfaction, which appears in Waves 6–10, and then 12–18. There are 2161 individuals who provided a GHQ score at every wave of the BHPS, so that the balanced panel analysis can be carried out on a

---

[5]The wave 1 sample was drawn from 250 areas of Great Britain. Additional samples of 1500 households in each of Scotland and Wales were added to the main sample in 1999, and in 2001 a sample of 2000 households was added in Northern Ireland.

[6]More precisely: whether subjective well-being changes systematically in a way that cannot be explained by the standard set of explanatory variables (covering income, employment, health, demographics etc.).

maximum of 38,898 observations. Equally, 3063 individuals provided 12 separate life-satisfaction scores, for a maximum balanced sample consisting of 36,756 life satisfaction observations. In practice, the balanced regression analysis uses slightly fewer observations due to missing values for some of the explanatory variables.

The GHQ-12 (see Goldberg 1972) reflects overall mental well-being. It is constructed from the responses to 12 questions (administered via a self-completion questionnaire) covering feelings of strain, depression, inability to cope, anxiety-based insomnia, and lack of confidence, amongst others (the 12 questions are reproduced in Appendix A). Responses are made on a four-point scale of frequency of a feeling in relation to a person's usual state: *"Not at all"*, *"No more than usual"*, *"Rather more than usual"*, and *"Much more than usual"*.[7] The GHQ is widely used in medical, psychological and sociological research, and is considered to be a robust indicator of the individual's psychological state. The between-item validity of the GHQ-12 is high in this sample of the BHPS, with a Cronbach's alpha score of 0.90.

This paper uses the Caseness GHQ score, which counts the number of questions for which the response is in one of the two 'low well-being' categories. This count is then reversed so that higher scores indicate higher levels of well-being, running from 0 (all 12 responses indicating poor psychological health) to 12 (no responses indicating poor psychological health).[8] The distribution of this well-being index in the BHPS sample is shown in the first panel of Appendix B (Table 17.4). The median and mode of this distribution is 12: no responses indicating poor psychological health. There is however a long tail: one-third of the sample have a score of 10 or less, and 13% have a score of 6 or less.

The second measure is satisfaction with life, which appears in Waves 6–10 and 12–18 of the BHPS. Respondents are asked *"How dissatisfied or satisfied are you with your life overall"*, with responses measured on a scale of one (not satisfied at all) to seven (completely satisfied). The distribution of replies is shown in the second panel of Appendix B (Table 17.5). The median score is five, with a mode of six and a mean of 5.2.

---

[7]One worry is that the GHQ is singularly unsuitable for this kind of analysis, as its constituent parts are explicitly phrased in terms of comparisons to usual. It is worth noting that the empirical literature on GHQ scores treats them unambiguously as indicators of the level of well-being, and it was for this purpose that the instrument was designed. On a practical level, the employed's GHQ is more strongly correlated with job satisfaction levels in the BHPS data than with job satisfaction changes. Last, with 18 years of balanced panel data, a relatively direct test of the usefulness of the GHQ score in this respect can be envisaged. If events become more 'usual' as an individual ages, then the standard deviation of GHQ scores (and of its individual components) will fall with age. There is no evidence of this phenomenon in balanced BHPS panel data.

[8]Alternatively, the responses to the GHQ-12 questions can be used to construct what is known as a Likert measure. This is the simple sum of the responses to the 12 questions, coded so that the response with the lowest well-being value scores 3 and that with the highest well-being value scores 0. This count is then reversed, so that higher scores indicate higher levels of well-being. The measure thus runs from 0 (all 12 responses indicating the worst psychological health) to 36 (all responses indicating the best psychological health). Practically, the results are very similar between the Caseness and Likert measures.

The following section considers how both of these well-being measures are related to age, both with and without controls for cohort effects.

17.3   Well-Being and Age: Pooled and Panel Results

17.3.1   Well-Being and Age in Pooled Data

Table 17.1 sets the scene by presenting the results from what are by now fairly 'standard' well-being equations, here estimated on pooled data. All of the regressions in this paper are estimated using linear techniques. The pooled analysis in Table 17.1 comes from OLS estimation; the panel results below come from 'within' regressions. It can, of course, be objected that the assumption of cardinality required for OLS is unlikely for well-being measures (is someone with a life satisfaction score of six exactly twice as happy as someone with a life satisfaction score of three?). However, Ferrer-i-Carbonell and Frijters (2004) have shown that, practically, the difference between the ordinal and cardinal estimation of subjective well-being is small compared to the difference between pooled and panel results. More pragmatically, all of the results presented in this paper can be reproduced using appropriate ordinal estimation methods (ordered probit for the pooled analysis, and conditional fixed effect logits for the panel regressions).

Column 1 of Table 17.1 shows the results from pooled cross-section regressions of GHQ scores, while column 2 carries out the same analysis for life satisfaction. The regressions include age and age-squared as explanatory variables, as well as a standard set of controls (for the log of monthly income, sex, education, labour-force status, marital status, number of children, renter, and wave and region dummies). The very significant coefficients on age (negative) and age-squared (positive) reveal that, *ceteris paribus*, well-being is U-shaped in age. Some simple algebra shows that the age of minimum well-being is 39 for GHQ and 42 for life satisfaction.

The estimated coefficients on the other right-hand side variables are all by now common in the empirical well-being literature. Unemployment, marital status and health have large impacts on both measures of well-being in the expected direction. There are, however, three notable variables that have opposing effects on GHQ and life satisfaction. Both income[9] and self-employment are associated with higher life-satisfaction scores, but also greater mental stress. On the contrary, men report lower life-satisfaction scores, but also less mental stress.[10] One last point to note in the context of well-being and age is that it is contentious to include health as a right-hand

---

[9]Income is measured in real terms, having been deflated by the CPI.

[10]Nolen-Hoeksema and Rusting (1999) conclude in their survey article that women exhibit higher incidence rates for almost all of the mood and anxiety disorders, but in general report higher levels of happiness.

side variable,[11] although this practice is widespread in the literature. Including health does imply that we are comparing individuals of different (working) ages, but with the same level of health. We will return to this issue below.

17.3.2 Test 1: Does the U-Shape Move to the Right by One Year Per Survey Wave?

If the U-shape in age is a pure cohort phenomenon, then the age distribution of well-being should shift to the right by 1 year per wave. This hypothesis can be tested by re-running Table 17.1's regressions separately for each of the 18 waves of the BHPS, and calculating the estimated age of minimum[12] well-being in each wave. The results are summarised in Fig. 17.1. Under the pure cohort hypothesis, the estimated age of minimum well-being would increase by 1 year per wave, tracing out a 45-degree line. Figure 17.1 shows little evidence of this for either of our well-being measures. Although the estimated minimum of GHQ does rise a little at the very beginning of the sample period, there is no strong trend thereafter.

The BHPS is an unbalanced panel. It is therefore theoretically possible that the pattern of well-being amongst those who enter and exit the data distorts the true relationship between well-being and age. To investigate, the bottom panel of Fig. 17.1 repeats the analysis using balanced panel data (over all 18 waves for the GHQ, and over 12 waves for life satisfaction). The balanced results again provide little support for the hypothesis that the age distribution shifts to the right by 1 year per wave.[13]

There is of course quite severe selection in the bottom panel, as we require individuals to be present in all waves for which subjective well-being is measured. As a halfway house, we can look at the balanced results using only the last 10 years of the BHPS (i.e. waves 9 through 18). This more than doubles the number of individuals in the balanced GHQ analysis (from 2161 to 4727) and increases the number in the life-satisfaction analysis by just over a half (3063 to 4828). The results continue to show only weak evidence of a U-shape that shifts to the right by 10 year per year. The age of minimum GHQ figures does rise from Waves 9–18 here, but only in the last two waves, while the rise in the age of minimum life satisfaction is of 3 years over the 10-year period, again concentrated in the last two waves.

This evidence then points to at least some role for a pure life-cycle effect, whereby well-being for the same individual evolves systematically with age. It

---

[11]Blanchflower and Oswald (2004) explicitly do not control for health in their statistical analysis.

[12]Alternatively, interaction terms between age and wave can be introduced into Table 1's regressions; these give qualitatively very similar results.

[13]Blanchflower and Oswald (2004) carry out a similar test on American General Social Survey data, and conclude that there is only slight evidence that the minimum moves to the right over time. The GSS is not, however, a panel.

Table 17.1 Well-being regressions. BHPS waves 1–18 pooled

	Caseness GHQ	Life satisfaction
Age	−0.077**	−0.071**
	(0.007)	(0.004)
Age-squared/100	0.100**	0.084**
	(0.009)	(0.005)
Log monthly income	−0.065**	−0.010*
	(0.010)	(0.005)
Self-employed	−0.076	0.052*
	(0.040)	(0.021)
Unemployed	−1.045**	−0.458**
	(0.055)	(0.031)
Retired	−0.103	0.099**
	(0.055)	(0.029)
Other labour-force status	−0.783**	−0.242**
	(0.038)	(0.019)
Male	0.474**	−0.070**
	(0.027)	(0.013)
Married	0.046	0.244**
	(0.039)	(0.020)
Separated	−0.912**	−0.243**
	(0.082)	(0.040)
Divorced	−0.311**	−0.097**
	(0.059)	(0.029)
Widowed	−0.571**	−0.118*
	(0.107)	(0.055)
One child	−0.011	−0.029
	(0.033)	(0.016)
Two children	0.106**	−0.027
	(0.036)	(0.018)
Three+ children	0.083	−0.034
	(0.056)	(0.027)
Renter	−0.171**	−0.171**
	(0.030)	(0.015)
Education: high	−0.216**	−0.073**
	(0.036)	(0.019)
Education: medium	−0.079*	−0.065**
	(0.036)	(0.019)
Health: excellent	2.144**	1.028**
	(0.032)	(0.015)
Health: good	1.700**	0.676**
	(0.029)	(0.013)
Wave dummies	Yes	Yes
Region dummies	Yes	Yes
Estimated age of minimum well-being	38.5	42.3
Observations	168,794	119,838

Robust standard errors in parentheses
*Significant at 5%; **Significant at 1%

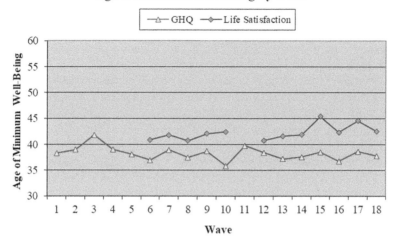

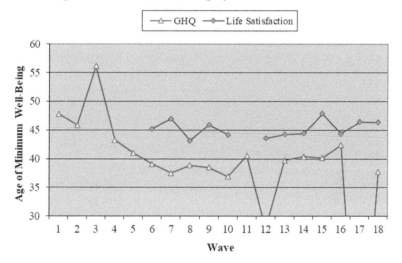

Fig. 17.1 The estimated minimum of the U-shape, by wave

should be borne in mind, however, that the age of minimum well-being, which is the ratio of two estimated coefficients, is likely measured with a certain degree of error; as such we cannot consider Test 1's results to be definitive, but rather suggestive. What follows is a direct test of the importance of cohort effects that escapes this criticism.

17.3.3   Test 2: Introducing Individual Fixed Effects

A perhaps simpler approach to the question is to introduce controls for unobserved heterogeneity, i.e. individual fixed effects. To allow for a flexible relationship between well-being and age, ten age dummies are created. The first refers to age 16–19, then 20–24, 25–29 and so on up to 60–64. The youngest age group is the omitted category, so all of the estimated coefficients in Table 17.2 are to be read as relative to the well-being of the youngest.

This approach is simple, but does fall foul of the Age-Period-Cohort problem. Individuals who are born in year C (this is their cohort) and are currently A years old are interviewed in year P. The issue is that C, A and P are (almost) multicollinear. For example, a 50 year-old BHPS respondent interviewed in 2008 must have been born in either 1957 or 1958. We can only identify age, period and cohort effects separately by (i) Using information on birthdays (as in the example above), and imagining a discrete jump in subjective well-being on the day of the birthday, (ii) Parameterising one of the relationships (for example, imposing a quadratic in age), or (iii) Converting one of the variables into multi-year blocks.

An attractive alternative is to not estimate the cohort effects at all, but rather difference them out. Here the first-difference change in life satisfaction is estimated as a function of age. A first contribution here is Van Landeghem (2012), who shows that this first difference rises somewhat up to age 55 in SOEP data, so that the age to well-being relationship is convex. More recently, Cheng et al. (2017) show that this first difference is positive in four datasets (BHPS, HILDA, SOEP and MABEL), and that it starts negative and then turns positive at around age 30, which is what a U-shaped relationship would predict.

Table 17.2 takes the third approach above, and shows three sets of regression results for both GHQ and life satisfaction.[14] The first two regressions are estimated on pooled data. The first of these includes only the age dummies on the right-hand side, and thus provides a non-parametric unconditional estimate of the relationship between well-being and age. Well-being is U-shaped, with minimum well-being occurring at age 40–44 for both measures. The second column then introduces the other demographic controls used in Table 17.1. These controls make the U-shape more pronounced, if anything,[15] and do not change the age of minimum well-being.

The last column introduces individual fixed effects. The estimated coefficients on the age dummies in column 3 therefore represent the different levels of well-being reported by the same individual as they go through the life cycle. Of course, even

---

[14]This is also the approach is taken in Blanchflower and Oswald (2008), where the cohort appears in 10-year blocks. Wunder et al. (2013) do not introduce cohort effects at all, and estimate the age profile semi-parametrically in BHPS and SOEP data, which produces a U-shape (deeper in the BHPS) up until the age of retirement.

[15]It has often been observed that income is hump-shaped in age, for example, so that holding income constant will deepen the well-being U-shape. Equally, Glaeser et al. (2002) suggest that social capital is hump-shaped in age. Frijters and Beatton (2012) find that introducing controls deepens the U-shape in their analysis of SOEP, Australian HILDA and BHPS panel data.

Table 17.2 Pooled and panel well-being regressions

Dep. Var. GHQ	GHQ		
	No controls	Demographic controls	Demographic controls plus individual fixed effects
Age 20–24	−0.109**	−0.157**	−0.207**
	(0.033)	(0.037)	(0.042)
Age 25–29	−0.043	−0.166**	−0.290**
	(0.036)	(0.043)	(0.056)
Age 30–34	−0.125**	−0.267**	−0.430**
	(0.039)	(0.050)	(0.074)
Age 35–39	−0.232**	−0.342**	−0.521**
	(0.041)	(0.054)	(0.093)
Age 40–44	−0.292**	−0.373**	−0.586**
	(0.043)	(0.056)	(0.111)
Age 45–49	−0.294**	−0.312**	−0.608**
	(0.045)	(0.057)	(0.130)
Age 50–54	−0.228**	−0.195**	−0.538**
	(0.047)	(0.058)	(0.150)
Age 55–59	−0.136**	−0.019	−0.432*
	(0.048)	(0.060)	(0.170)
Age 60–64	0.120*	0.224**	−0.277
	(0.048)	(0.065)	(0.190)
Constant	10.220**	9.532**	9.814**
	(0.027)	(0.090)	(0.147)
Observations	179,582	168,794	168,794
Dep. Var. life satisfaction			
Age 20–24	−0.141**	−0.178**	−0.109**
	(0.018)	(0.020)	(0.020)
Age 25–29	−0.123**	−0.250**	−0.079**
	(0.020)	(0.023)	(0.026)
Age 30–34	−0.129**	−0.314**	−0.066
	(0.021)	(0.026)	(0.034)
Age 35–39	−0.237**	−0.418**	−0.099*
	(0.021)	(0.028)	(0.042)
Age 40–44	−0.294**	−0.477**	−0.116*
	(0.022)	(0.029)	(0.050)
Age 45–49	−0.311**	−0.483**	−0.113
	(0.023)	(0.030)	(0.058)
Age 50–54	−0.213**	−0.396**	−0.065
	(0.024)	(0.030)	(0.066)
Age 55–59	−0.092**	−0.257**	0.019
	(0.025)	(0.032)	(0.074)
Age 60–64	0.092**	−0.118**	0.124
	(0.026)	(0.036)	(0.083)
Constant	5.310**	5.103**	4.947**
	(0.015)	(0.045)	(0.071)
Observations	128,408	119,838	119,838

Robust standard errors in parentheses

The regressions in Columns 2 and 3 include all of Table 1's controls (except for age and age-squared)

*Significant at 5%; **Significant at 1%

with fairly long-run panel data, we do not observe the complete sequence of ages for any respondent. In the BHPS, any one individual can appear in a maximum of five different age categories in the GHQ regressions (over 18 waves) and four different age categories in the life-satisfaction regressions (between waves 6 and 18).

The main result from this panel analysis is that, even controlling for individual fixed effects, well-being continues to show a U-shaped relationship with age. This is true for both GHQ and life satisfaction, although the U-shape is more pronounced for the former than for the latter. The age of minimum well-being, controlling for fixed effects, is in the forties for both measures. The estimated relationships between well-being and age in pooled and panel data are illustrated in Fig. 17.2. It is notable that

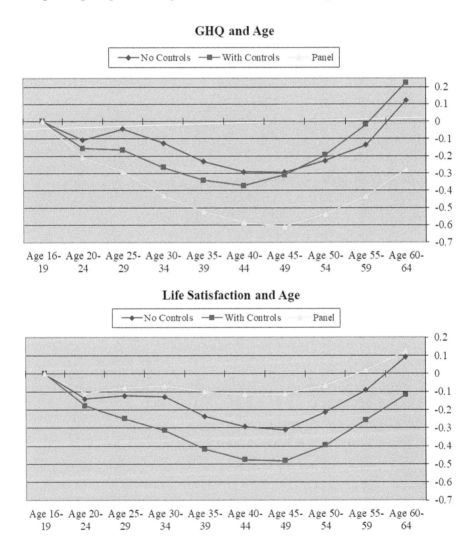

Fig. 17.2 Age and well-being: pooled and panel results

the left-hand side of the 'U' in the life-satisfaction regressions with individual fixed effects depends entirely on the drop in well-being between ages 16–19 and 20–24. Thereafter, life satisfaction stays fairly flat up until the end of the forties.

As with Test 1, which looked at the estimated age of minimum well-being by wave, it is important to take panel exit and entry into account. Table 17.3 therefore repeats the analysis described in Table 17.2, but now estimated only on the balanced sample (a little over 2000 individuals for the GHQ score, and just over 3000 for life satisfaction). Even in this much smaller balanced sample, the top panel of Table 17.3 shows a persistent U-shaped relationship between age and GHQ. In the bottom panel, the relationship between age and life satisfaction is now less evident. Even so, the U-shape persists in the estimated coefficients, which are jointly significant. In addition, the real test of the U-shape is whether the ends are greater than the middle, loosely speaking. This test passes at around the 1% level comparing both the oldest and the youngest age-groups to those in their mid-forties.

17.3.4 Interpreting the Results

Well-being continues to be U-shaped in age even after cohort effects (via individual fixed effects) have been controlled for. As such, the well-being of any one individual, no matter when they were born, will trace out the profile given by the 'panel' lines in Fig. 17.2 as they age. While it is easy to think of some aspects of life which might systematically be more difficult between the ages of 35 and 45, it is worth emphasising that the multivariate analyses controls for a number of these (labour-force and marital status, home ownership, and number of children). One open question is therefore what lies behind the life cycle events that hit hard between the ages of 35 and 45. One possibility might be stress at work (perhaps combined with young or adolescent children), although useful questions measuring such phenomena are not always present in large-scale datasets.

As a by-product of the regression in column 3 of Table 17.2, we can look at the distribution of the estimated fixed effects by birth cohort. Specifically, we calculate the average value of the individual fixed effects by year of birth: these are presented graphically in Appendix C (Figs. 17.3 and 17.4). A small number of birth years for which there were fewer than 20 individuals in the cell have been dropped: this applies particularly to the graphs by level of education. The shape of the cohort effects presented in Appendix C can actually be inferred from Fig. 17.2. In the latter, both of the pooled and panel results GHQ curves are U-shaped, and the distance between the two curves is greater for the older age-groups than for the younger age-groups: in other words, those born earlier report higher levels of well-being on the GHQ scale, independent of their current age.[16] This is indeed what we see in the top left panel of Appendix C: those born earlier have higher levels of SWB (which is

---

[16]Easterlin (2006) reaches a similar conclusion for happiness in US cohorts.

Table 17.3 Pooled and panel balanced well-being regressions

Dep. Var. GHQ	No controls	Demographic controls	Demographic controls plus individual fixed effects
Age 20–24	−0.316**	−0.180	−0.189
	(0.114)	(0.125)	(0.131)
Age 25–29	−0.417**	−0.352*	−0.485**
	(0.121)	(0.137)	(0.146)
Age 30–34	−0.580**	−0.524**	−0.703**
	(0.124)	(0.146)	(0.176)
Age 35–39	−0.581**	−0.547**	−0.735**
	(0.127)	(0.156)	(0.212)
Age 40–44	−0.681**	−0.617**	−0.820**
	(0.130)	(0.161)	(0.249)
Age 45–49	−0.728**	−0.590**	−0.799**
	(0.133)	(0.166)	(0.286)
Age 50–54	−0.470**	−0.294	−0.499
	(0.136)	(0.173)	(0.327)
Age 55–59	−0.417**	−0.211	−0.472
	(0.147)	(0.190)	(0.369)
Age 60–64	−0.251	−0.094	−0.344
	(0.169)	(0.230)	(0.412)
Constant	10.655**	9.833**	9.869**
	(0.116)	(0.244)	(0.258)
Observations	38,898	37,971	37,971
Dep. Var. life satisfaction			
Age 20–24	−0.071	−0.151**	−0.138**
	(0.055)	(0.057)	(0.044)
Age 25–29	−0.078	−0.247**	−0.136**
	(0.054)	(0.060)	(0.049)
Age 30–34	−0.098	−0.310**	−0.145*
	(0.059)	(0.067)	(0.061)
Age 35–39	−0.193**	−0.415**	−0.189**
	(0.059)	(0.070)	(0.073)
Age 40–44	−0.253**	−0.484**	−0.216*
	(0.059)	(0.071)	(0.086)
Age 45–49	−0.292**	−0.502**	−0.215*
	(0.060)	(0.073)	(0.098)
Age 50–54	−0.220**	−0.436**	−0.169
	(0.062)	(0.074)	(0.112)
Age 55–59	−0.144*	−0.353**	−0.089
	(0.065)	(0.080)	(0.126)
Age 60–64	−0.047	−0.310**	−0.013
	(0.077)	(0.095)	(0.140)
Constant	5.323**	5.101**	4.900**
	(0.054)	(0.105)	(0.111)
Observations	36,756	35,462	35,462

Robust standard errors in parentheses

The regressions in Columns 2 and 3 include all of Table 17.1's controls (except for age and age-squared)

*Significant at 5%; **Significant at 1%

what Blanchflower and Oswald, 2004, concluded from their analysis of US General Social Survey data as well). Even so, the size of this estimated cohort effect is not overwhelmingly large: the difference in the cohort effects between those born in the 1930s and those born in the 1970s is about one-eighth of a GHQ point, on the 0–12 scale. By way of comparison, this is the size of the estimated effect of divorce on well-being in the pooled cross-section estimates in Table 17.1, but only about one-third of the size of the effect of separation or unemployment.

The same visual test for the life-satisfaction curves in Fig. 17.2 suggests that the fixed effects are U-shaped. The pooled results are markedly U-shaped, but the panel results are less so. The difference between them is the fixed effect, which must therefore itself have a U-shaped distribution. In this case, it does seem to be true that those born around the late 1950s to early 1960s have (fixed) lower levels of life satisfaction. Again, this is what we see in Appendix C.[17]

Why do the fixed effects have this pattern? Any attempt at explanation will be speculative, as by definition fixed effects reflect unobserved differences between individuals. With respect to the GHQ, one such piece of speculation as to why those born earlier have, *ceteris paribus*, higher levels of mental well-being appeals to social comparisons. Researchers in a number of social-science disciplines have emphasised the importance of comparisons to reference groups (Adams 1965; Frank 1989; Kapteyn et al. 1978; Pollis 1968). One likely type of comparison here is with respect to the past, and perhaps even to a certain defined period (the parents' situation during the individuals' childhood, or the individual's first job, for example). Secularly-rising living standards will then imply that older cohorts compare current outcomes to less well-off reference groups, and will consequently report higher well-being scores.[18] Alternatively, Rodgers (1982) posits that older cohorts might be happier as a result of having survived economic deprivation and other social hardships, whereas younger cohorts could have higher levels of needs once basic survival issues have been resolved. Last, comparisons can themselves change within individual over time, and help to explain the U-shape in age itself (as in Schwandt 2016).

17.3.5 What Should We Control For?

As mentioned above, there are a number of different ways of looking at the relationship between age and well-being. An analysis without any control variables, as in column 1 of Tables 17.2 and 17.3, produces a description of well-being at

---

[17]Blanchflower and Oswald (2008) also find a U-shaped pattern of birth cohort effects in life satisfaction, using 27 years of Eurobarometer data.

[18]Such comparisons to the past imply that, in the long run, the correlation between GDP per capita and individual well-being may well be small. For some recent empirical contributions to this debate, see Diener and Oishi (2000), Easterlin (1995) and Oswald (1997). This literature is surveyed in Clark et al. (2008).

different ages, without taking into account the sex, income, housing etc. composition
of different age groups. The analyses in the other columns of Tables 17.2 and 17.3 do
include some standard right-hand side control variables, so that we are to an extent
comparing like with like. There does remain, however, the question of how sensible
the latter comparisons are. In particular, some of the control variables (income,
marriage, labour-force status) might be thought to be partly determined by well-
being. To check whether reverse causality is behind the findings above, all of the
regressions have been re-run retaining only exogenous explanatory variables (sex,
wave and region). The qualitative results remained unchanged.

17.3.6   Is Everyone the Same?

It is of interest to carry out the above analysis separately for different demographic
groups. Specifically, Table 17.2's regressions were re-run for men and for women,
and for three different educational groups (where high education corresponds to
qualifications obtained in higher education, and medium education to A-Level, O-
Level or Nursing qualifications). The estimated cohort effects are shown in Appendix C.

Both the estimated U-shape and the fixed effects profiles differ by demographic
group. The U-shaped relationship between well-being and age is much more pronounced for men than for women. In addition, the negative trend in the GHQ fixed
effect (so that older cohorts are happier than younger cohorts) is found only for
women. Note that this cannot reflect patterns of employment or number of children,
as these variables are controlled in the regression. The profile is however consistent
with changing work intensity for women, or increasing difficulty in ensuring an
adequate work-life balance. Regarding education, the U-shape is stronger for the
higher-educated than for the other groups, and the negative trend in the GHQ fixed
effect is found only for the higher-educated. However, the U-shaped fixed effect in
life satisfaction is found for all demographic groups.

17.4   Conclusion

This paper has used 18 waves of British panel data to confirm that subjective well-
being is U-shaped in age in pooled data. The application of panel-analysis techniques allows us to distinguish the life-cycle or ageing component of this relationship from the fixed effect or cohort part. The results show that, even controlling for
individual fixed effects, both life satisfaction and GHQ scores remain U-shaped in
age. The analysis of the fixed effect in GHQ scores reveals that individuals from
earlier cohorts (i.e. those who were born earlier) have, *ceteris paribus*, distinctly
higher levels of subjective well-being, as measured by the GHQ-12 score, than those
from later cohorts. This pattern is markedly different by sex, and by level of
education. The fixed effects in life satisfaction exhibit a U-shaped relationship.

The main result of this analysis may be considered as essentially negative: whereas we previously thought that there was only one phenomenon to explain (the U-shape), there would now appear to be two: a U-shaped life-cycle or aging effect, and the cohort profiles. This paper has not explicitly tested any theories of why these data shapes pertain, although the GHQ fixed-effects results are consistent with reference group theory, in that those born earlier may have lower standards of comparison, and with increasing work-life balance stress.

This paper's conclusions are based on British data, although the robust U-shaped relationship is found across two rather different measures of well-being (while weaker for life satisfaction than for the GHQ). It may be that other datasets will produce different results. The simple method used in this paper can be easily applied to any panel data set of sufficiently long duration. The empirical well-being literature should perhaps now pay more attention to the structure of the fixed effect, and in particular to its relationship with year of birth.

Acknowledgements I am grateful to Dick Easterlin, Carol Graham, David Halpern, Mike Hagerty, Laurence Hazelrigg, Felicia Huppert, Hendrik Juerges, Nicolai Kristensen, Ken Land, Orsolya Lelkes, Andrew Oswald, Steve Platt, Claudia Senik, Andrew Sharpe, Peter Warr and Rainer Winkelmann for useful discussions. The BHPS data were made available through the ESRC Data Archive. The data were originally collected by the ESRC Research Centre on Micro-social Change at the University of Essex. Neither the original collectors of the data nor the Archive bear any responsibility for the analyses or interpretations presented here.

Appendices

Appendix A

The 12 questions used to create the GHQ-12 measure appear in the BHPS questionnaire as follows:

1. *Here are some questions regarding the way you have been feeling over the last few weeks. For each question please ring the number next to the answer that best suits the way you have felt.*

    Have you recently....

    a) *been able to concentrate on whatever you're doing?*
        Better than usual   *1*
        Same as usual   *2*
        Less than usual   *3*
        Much less than usual   *4*
    then
    b) *lost much sleep over worry?*
    e) *felt constantly under strain?*
    f) *felt you couldn't overcome your difficulties?*
    i) *been feeling unhappy or depressed?*
    j) *been losing confidence in yourself?*

  k) *been thinking of yourself as a worthless person?*
       with the responses:

             Not at all   *1*
             No more than usual   *2*
             Rather more than usual *3*
             Much more than usual *4*
       then

  c) *felt that you were playing a useful part in things?*
  d) *felt capable of making decisions about things?*
  g) *been able to enjoy your normal day-to-day activities?*
  h) *been able to face up to problems?*
  i) *been feeling reasonably happy, all things considered?*
       with the responses:

             More so than usual   *1*
             About same as usual *2*
             Less so than usual   *3*
             Much less than usual *4*

Appendix B

Table 17.4 The distribution of well-being in the BHPS (Inverted Caseness index of the GHQ-12)

Well-being score	Number of observations	Cumulative percentage
0	3110	1.7
1	2455	3.1
2	2631	4.6
3	2933	6.2
4	3350	8.1
5	4035	10.3
6	4872	13
7	6026	16.4
8	7517	20.6
9	10,078	26.2
10	14,521	34.3
11	24,646	48
12	93,408	100
Total	179,582	100
Mean	10.08	
Median	11	
Mode	12	

Source: BHPS Waves 1–18

Table 17.5 The distribution of well-being in the BHPS (life satisfaction)

Well-being score	Number of observations	Cumulative percentage
1	1839	1.4
2	2952	3.7
3	8190	10.1
4	18,593	24.6
5	39,873	55.6
6	42,801	89
7	14,160	100
Total	128,408	100
Mean	5.16	
Median	5	
Mode	6	

Source: BHPS Waves 6–10 and 12–18

Appendix C

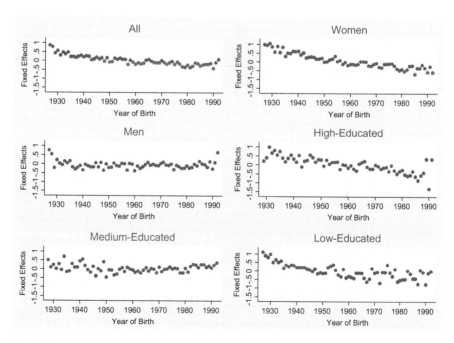

Fig. 17.3 GHQ fixed effects by year of birth

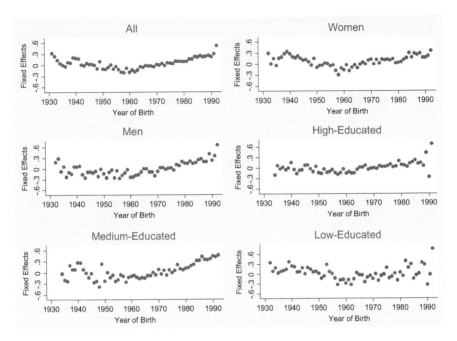

Fig. 17.4 Life satisfaction fixed effects by year of birth

References

Adams, J. S. (1965). Inequity in social exchange. In L. Berkowitz (Ed.), *Advances in experimental social psychology* (Vol. 2). New York/London: Academic.

Argyle, M. (1989). *The psychology of happiness*. London: Routledge.

Blanchflower, D. G., & Oswald, A. J. (2004). Well-being over time in Britain and the USA. *Journal of Public Economics, 88*, 1359–1386.

Blanchflower, D. G., & Oswald, A. J. (2008). Is wellbeing U-shaped over the life cycle? *Social Science and Medicine, 66*, 1733–1749.

Bouchard, T. J., Lykken, D. T., McGue, M., Segal, N. L., & Tellegen, A. (1990). Sources of human psychological differences: The Minnesota Study of twins reared apart. *Science, 250*, 223–228.

Cheng, T., Oswald, A. J., & Powdthavee, N. (2017). Longitudinal evidence for a midlife nadir in human well-being: Results from four data sets. *Economic Journal, 127*, 126–142.

Clark, A. E., Frijters, P., & Shields, M. (2008). Relative income, happiness and utility: An explanation for the Easterlin Paradox and other puzzles. *Journal of Economic Literature, 46*, 95–144.

Cribier, F. (2005). Changes in the experience of life between two cohorts of Parisian pensioners, born in *circa* 1907 and 1921. *Aging & Society, 25*, 1–18.

Diener, E., & Oishi, S. (2000). Money and happiness: Income and subjective well-being across nations. In E. Diener & E. M. Suh (Eds.), *Cross-cultural psychology of subjective well-being*. Boston: MIT Press.

Easterlin, R. A. (1995). Will raising the incomes of all increase the happiness of all? *Journal of Economic Behavior and Organization, 27*, 35–47.

Easterlin, R. A. (2006). Life cycle happiness and its sources. *Journal of Economic Psychology, 27*, 463–482.

Easterlin, R. A., & Schaeffer, C. M. (1999). Income and subjective well-being over the life-cycle. In C. D. Ryff & V. W. Marshall (Eds.), *The self and society in aging processes*. New York: Springer.

Ferrer-i-Carbonell, A., & Frijters, P. (2004). How important is methodology for the estimates of the determinants of happiness? *Economic Journal, 114*, 641–659.

Frank, R. H. (1989). Frames of reference and the quality of life. *American Economic Review, 79*, 80–85.

Frey, B. S. & Stutzer, A. (2002). Happiness and economics. Princeton/Oxford: Princeton University Press.

Frijters, P., & Beatton, T. (2012). The mystery of the U-shaped relationship between happiness and age. *Journal of Economic Behavior & Organization, 82*, 525–542.

Frijters, P., Haisken-DeNew, J., & Shields, M. (2004). Money does matter! Evidence from increasing real incomes and life satisfaction in East Germany following reunification. *American Economic Review, 94*, 730–740.

Glaeser, E., Laibson, D., & Sacerdote, B. (2002). An economic approach to social capital. *Economic Journal, 112*, 437–458.

Goldberg, D. P. (1972). *The detection of psychiatric illness by questionnaire*. Oxford: Oxford University Press.

Graham, C., & Ruiz Pozuelo, J. (2017). Happiness, stress, and age: How the U curve varies across people and places. *Journal of Population Economics, 30*, 225–264.

Hayo, B., & Seifert, W. (2002). Subjective economic well-being in Eastern Europe. *Journal of Economic Psychology, 24*, 329–348.

Kapteyn, A., van Praag, B. M. S., & van Herwaarden, F. G. (1978). Individual welfare functions and social reference spaces. *Economics Letters, 1*, 173–177.

Kassenböhmer, S. C., & Haisken-DeNew, J. (2012). Heresy or enlightenment? The well-being age U-shape effect is flat. *Economics Letters, 117*, 235–238.

Kohler, H.-P., Behrman, J., & Skytthe, A. (2005). Partner + children = happiness? The effects of partnerships and fertility on well-being. *Population and Development Review, 31*, 407–445.

Lucas, R., Clark, A. E., Georgellis, Y., & Diener, E. (2003). Re-examining adaptation and the setpoint model of happiness: Reaction to changes in marital status. *Journal of Personality and Social Psychology, 84*, 527–539.

Lucas, R., Clark, A. E., Georgellis, Y., & Diener, E. (2004). Unemployment alters the set-point for life satisfaction. *Psychological Science, 15*, 8–13.

Mroczek, D. K., & Kolarz, C. M. (1998). The effect of age on positive and negative affect: A developmental perspective on happiness. *Journal of Personality and Social Psychology, 75*, 1333–1349.

Mroczek, D. K., & Spiro, A. (2005). Change in life satisfaction during adulthood: Findings from the veterans affairs normative aging study. *Journal of Personality and Social Psychology, 88*, 189–202.

Nolen-Hoeksema, S., & Rusting, C. L. (1999). Gender differences in well-being. In D. Kahneman, E. Diener, & N. Schwarz (Eds.), *Well-being: The foundations of hedonic psychology*. New York: Russell Sage Foundation.

Oswald, A. J. (1997). Happiness and economic performance. *Economic Journal, 107*, 1815–1831.

Pollis, N. P. (1968). Reference group re-examined. *British Journal of Sociology, 19*, 300–307.

Putnam, R. D. (2000). *Bowling alone*. New York: Simon & Schuster.

Rodgers, W. (1982). Trends in reported happiness within demographically defined subgroups, 1957–78. *Social Forces, 60*, 826–842.

Schwandt, H. (2016). Unmet aspirations as an explanation for the age U-shape in wellbeing. *Journal of Economic Behavior and Organization, 122*, 75–87.

Stone, A. A., Schwartz, J. E., Broderick, J. E., & Deaton, A. (2010). A snapshot of the age distribution of psychological well-being in the United States. *Proceedings of the National Academy of Sciences, 107*(22), 9985–9990.

Tellegen, A., Lykken, D. T., Bouchard, T. J., Wilcox, K. J., Segal, N. L., & Rich, S. (1988). Personality similarity in twins reared apart and together. *Journal of Personality and Social Psychology, 54*, 1031–1039.

Van Landeghem, B. (2012). A test for the convexity of human well-being over the life cycle: Longitudinal evidence from a 20-year panel. *Journal of Economic Behavior & Organization, 81*, 571–582.

Van Praag, B., & Ferrer-i-Carbonell, A. (2004). *Happiness quantified.* Oxford: Oxford University Press.

Wunder, C., Wiencierz, A., Schwarze, J., & Küchenhoff, H. (2013). Well-being over the life span: Semiparametric evidence from British and German longitudinal data. *Review of Economics and Statistics, 95*, 154–167.

Zimmerman, A., & Easterlin, R. (2006). Happily ever after? Cohabitation, marriage, divorce, and happiness in Germany. *Population and Development Review, 32*, 511–528.

Chapter 18
Happiness Amongst Teens in Australia

Tony Beatton and Paul Frijters

Abstract Richard Easterlin's lifetime happiness theory holds that people get less happy over the life-cycle as exaggerated expectations hit; this has been found to be true for the 20–50 age range in many Western countries. This paper looks at the implications for child happiness and asks: when does the 'disappointment with reality' start to bite in early life, i.e. when does happiness drop? We develop child-specific scales to measure the effect of personality and childhood life satisfaction domains. With an internet-based survey, we collect unique data from 389 Australian children aged 9–14. Adding to previous findings that satisfaction levels Australian life decline between age 15 and 23 by almost 0.7 on a ten-point scale, we find an even steeper decline before age 14. Using a decomposition method, we show that the *natural environment* domain has no significant effect on childhood life satisfaction, whilst the children's *school environment* and *interaction with friends* domains explain over 40% of the decline in childhood life satisfaction. This decline is steepest when the children transition to high school. As expected, extraverted children are happier, but unexpectedly, so are conscientious children.

18.1   Introduction

In 1974, Richard Easterlin alerted economists and social scientists generally to the failure of higher GDP to buy more happiness. Basing himself on 8 countries, and information for the US going back since the 1940s, he found no long-run relation between the growth of the overall economic pie and the average level of happiness in a country. He explicitly explained this with a simple theory of social comparisons

T. Beatton
The Institute for Social Science Research, The University of Queensland and the Queensland University of Technology (QUT), Brisbane, QLD, Australia
e-mail: d.beatton@uq.edu.au

P. Frijters (✉)
London School of Economics, London, UK
e-mail: p.frijters@lse.ac.uk

© Springer Nature Switzerland AG 2019
M. Rojas (ed.), *The Economics of Happiness*,
https://doi.org/10.1007/978-3-030-15835-4_18

wherein the amount of happiness that individuals get out of their incomes depends on what others earn: if the waters rise, all boats rise equally and none has grown relative to the others.[1]

In 2001, Richard then published a more detailed theory of how this might work over the life-cycle. He postulated that individuals are prone to a particular irrationality: they expect their incomes to grow over their life, but they expect their own ideas as to what they would need to be happy to remain the same. So they expect to end up with a lot of income relative to their benchmark level as determined in childhood, feeling happy about that prospect. As reality sets in, which includes people adapting their benchmark to what they earned in the recent past and what their neighbours earn, they get less happy as life goes on, particularly when their incomes grow less than originally anticipated.

Richard's elegant 2001 theory was of course highly stylised and by necessity did not capture all the nuances of real lives. It should thus not be taken too literally, but nevertheless has a couple of components worth confronting with data. One main one is of course whether or not people indeed adapt their material benchmarks. Richard Easterlin's 2005 paper used the small Roper Foundation surveys from 1978 and 1994, concluding "The evidence I have presented suggests that pecuniary or living level aspirations tend to change, on average, to about the same extent as actual circumstances. In contrast, aspirations with regard to marriage and number and quality of children appear to be more stable and vary less as actual circumstances change".

In this paper we want to look at the implications for child happiness that Richard's story implies. For one, his 2001 theory implies that people get less happy over the life-cycle. This has been found to be true for the 20–50 age range in many Western countries, though the consensus is now that this is followed by a late-life happiness wave: a retirement surge in happiness that only fades close to death. This perchance reflects a phenomenon that Richard probably was aware of but couldn't get to work in his 2001 model, which is a 'letting go' after retirement of the importance of previous aspirations, followed by a greater capacity to enjoy the lack of responsibilities of retired life.

But when does the 'disappointment with reality' start to bite earlier in life? Can we already see before the age of 20 whether children lose their innocent belief in a fantastic new future where they will be richer than their benchmark? More simply: when does the happiness downturn begin?

A related question is the issue of relative comparisons generally. Are children already affected by relative income comparisons and thus already on the 'hedonic treadmill' of socially determined wants? And if not, when does relative wealth become more important?

---

[1] An important question is of course why countries are so obsessed with higher national incomes. In Frijters and Foster (2013) it is argued that relative standing between groups is a prime motivator for the existence and cohesion of the nation state. This is partially from the (somewhat mistaken) belief of the population that it will make them happier, but it is also connected with military might (money can buy weapons) and hence with relative power.

And finally, is it true that children have inflated expectations of the future and their ability to achieve good outcomes in that future?

We will try to answer these questions, and some others, in a unique dataset that we gather in 2008 in Queensland, the North-Eastern state of Australia. We were lucky enough to then be invited to design a web-based survey for school children who attended exhibitions in a 'Smart Train' that went via several regional stations in Queensland. We ran a lottery to give a prize amongst those willing to participate in our survey and got some 400 responses from children aged 9–14.

This is not a huge survey. Neither is it very representative. And, in hindsight, we did not ask all the questions we would have liked to answer the questions above. Yet, happiness information on children is very rare and we know of no studies that look at relative income effects amongst children. Also, nothing on our dataset has been previously published, so using the dataset to look for information on the childhood implications of Richard's 2001 theory is our small contribution to celebrate the immense impact that Richard Easterlin has made on social science.

We first discuss the literature on childhood happiness, moving on to our survey, the results, and a discussion of those results.

18.1.1 The Literature on the Happiness of Children Versus Adults

The study of life satisfaction in adults has become a major area of research in the social sciences (Diener 1984; Stutzer and Frey 2012). Yet, as Heubner and Diener (2012, p. 383) conclude in their survey of the literature, "Research in children's school and life satisfaction is in its infancy". We add to the small literature on life satisfaction amongst children by looking at the changes in 9–14-year olds in a sample of 389 Australian school children.

From the few studies available, Heubner and Diener (2012, p. 379) state that "Global life satisfaction reports of children, above the age of 8, do not appear to differ significantly as a function of age". At the outset, we did not quite believe this: there are quite a few studies that report that children who are in early junior high school or in early adolescence experience an increase in mental health problems and a decrease in their satisfaction with school itself (Hirsch and Rapkin 1987; Huebner et al. 2000). This raises the possibility that sample sizes or other methodological issues have so far prevented a clear age-happiness profile to be found amongst children. We revisit this issue. Relevant to economists is also the question whether the very strong relation between life satisfaction and perceived relative wealth amongst adults (Headey and Wooden 2004; Clark et al. 2008) also shows up for children: does relative wealth buy childhood happiness?

Currently, the main information on life satisfaction in Australia comes from the Household and Income Dynamics Australia (HILDA 2013). In Fig. 18.1 we show the age-profile amongst the respondents, showing a drop in happiness of around 0.7

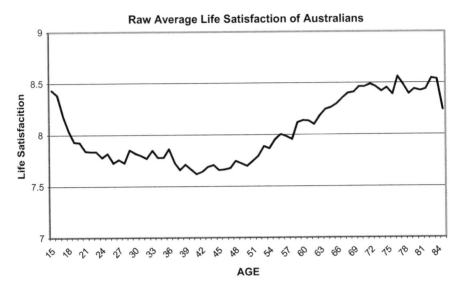

Fig. 18.1 Average Life satisfaction for 15 to 85-year-old Australians in waves 2–13 of the Household Income and Labour Dynamics in Australia Survey

between the age of 15 and 23 on a ten-point scale, leading to the question of what happens before then.

Childhood studies on global life satisfaction are infrequent in the economics literature but more prevalent in the psychological and other literatures, although still far fewer than the number of studies on the concept of subjective well-being (Diener and Suh 1998; Easterlin 2001; Seligman 2011).

In economics, children have usually been considered in the context of the negative (Stutzer and Frey 2006; White 2006) or positive (Tsang 2003) effect they have on adult happiness, not their own happiness. A typical example is Bruhin and Winkelmann (2009) who looked at the relationship between parents and their adult children's subjective well-being in a German panel, where the happiness of children was not measured. In a related vein, some economic studies have looked at the childhood predictors of adult life satisfaction (Flouri 2004; Frijters et al. 2011).

The few economic studies looking at the life satisfaction of children themselves have mainly looked at adolescents above 14 and their family. Bedin and Sarriera (2015) did a comparative analysis of the subjective well-being of parents and their 12 to 16 year-old adolescent children regarding gender, age and social class. Carlsson et al. (2014) looked at the intergenerational transmission of happiness in China between preadolescents and their parents. Ebner's (2008) longitudinal study used the European Community Household Panel data (ECHP 2015) to reveal that adolescents are happier when they make the decision to leave the family home. A study by Dockery (2005) used data from the (1997–2004) Longitudinal Surveys of Australian Youth (LSAY 2012) and wave 1 of the HILDA and found evidence of declining levels of happiness in adolescents during periods of unemployment. He also documents the importance of the quality and type of work to the happiness of adolescents. Ulker (2008), using the Australian HILDA data, found that adolescents become less happy when their parents' divorce. Other studies looked at school performance or aggregate changes amongst children over the age of 14 (Cheng and Furnham 2004).

A few studies in economics look at life satisfaction in the 9–14 age range. Powdthavee and Vernoit (2013) examined the longitudinal relationship between parental unemployment and 11–15 year-old British children's self-reported happiness with life scores over time. Fogle et al. (2002) cross-sectional study revealed a positive relationship between extraversion, social competence and life satisfaction among children aged 10–15 years from public schools in mid-sized cities in the South-East of the United States. A positive attitude, confidence in own abilities and the skills to interact with your peer group were found to be important to childhood happiness. Also focussing on school children, Huebner et al.'s (2005) cross-sectional study of public middle school students from South Carolina (U.S.A) proposed that family, friends, school and the environment in which children live and learn are important to childhood happiness. Lee and Oguzoglu (2007) longitudinal study of Australian youths ventured outside the school environment and found that income support payments contributed to childhood happiness. The main conclusion we draw from these is that personality, friends, and the school environment are prime candidates to explain change in the happiness of children over time and thus need to be included in the survey.

The literature in psychology and other social sciences on life satisfaction amongst adolescents older than 14 is much larger than in economics and has looked at a huge range of issues. The many topics looked at include the importance of academic success (Suldo et al. 2006), bullying (Moore et al. 2012), family structure (Levin et al. 2012), ethnicity (Campbell and Eggerling-Boeck 2006), obesity (Forste and Moore 2012), mental health (Ulker 2008; Dear et al. 2011; Antaramian et al. 2010), and low income (Levin et al. 2011).

If we look at the literature on global life satisfaction of children aged 9–14, there are far fewer studies, where the main finding relevant to the objectives of this paper is the lack of any clear change in life satisfaction level over age (Gilman and Huebner 2003). An early study is Huebner et al. (2005), who looked at 2278 public middle school students in the US and found that the influence of demographic variables in the level of happiness was limited, although middle school children were particularly dissatisfied with their school experiences. A later study by Antaramian et al. (2008) focused on the importance of family structure, finding that children in single parent or step-parent families were less satisfied with their lives. Heubner and Diener (2012) review roughly 20 papers that look at child satisfaction, which mainly deal with the development of proper measurement instruments and particular groups at risk of experiencing problems. These studies will be important in the next section dealing with data gathering.

18.2   Data and Survey Method

18.2.1   The HILDA Data

We use two data sets.[2] The first data set is the 15–93 year-olds from waves 2–13 of the 'Household, Income and Labour Dynamics in Australia' Survey (HILDA, 2013)[3] and underlies Fig. 18.1. The second is our own data from younger children.

18.2.2   Collecting Data from Children

Collecting data from children is fraught with ethical, logistical and truthful self-reporting roadblocks (Gilman and Huebner 1997, 2000; Haranin et al. 2007). To avoid the issue of untruthful reporting when confronted with outside survey collectors, our collecting procedures follow the literature by folding it into the children's normal teaching program, wherein school teachers took their classes to local railway stations to visit a 'Smart Train'[4] that went from urban Brisbane throughout regional Queensland, with carriages containing university research displays; one of which explained happiness. Upon returning to school, the children were requested to complete an internet-based 'Happiness' survey. To encourage response, teachers were provided with 'Happy Posters' to hang on classroom walls and 'Happy Teaching Guides' with instructions on how the children could use their school computers to respond to our *Childhood Happiness Survey.*[5]

To answer these questions, we gathered data on school children throughout Queensland, the north-eastern state in Australia, with the help of teachers and the Queensland Government. We measure various domains of life for these children, including school circumstances, social circumstances, the personality of the

---

[2]The HILDA data was extracted using the Add-On package PanelWhiz v3.0 (Nov 2010) for Stata. PanelWhiz was written by Dr. John P. Haisken-DeNew (john@panelwhiz.eu). The PanelWhiz generated DO file to retrieve the HILDA data used here and any Panelwhiz Plugins are available upon request. Any data or computational errors in this paper are my own. Haisken-DeNew and Hahn (2006) describes PanelWhiz in detail.

[3]This paper uses unit record data from the Household, Income and Labour Dynamics in Australia (HILDA 2013). The HILDA Project was initiated and funded by the Australian Government Department of Families, Housing, Community Services and Indigenous Affairs (FaHCSIA) and is managed by the Melbourne Institute of Applied Economic and Social Research (MIAESR). The findings and views reported in this paper are those of the authors and should not be attributed to either FaHCSIA or the MIAESR. We thank FaHCSIA & the Melbourne Institute director, Professor Deborah Cobb-Clark, and her staff for making the data available.

[4]More information on the 'Smart Train' is at: http://www.abc.net.au/local/photos/2008/05/09/2240428.htm

[5]After the 3-week survey response period, the Queensland Government, Department of Innovation, Tourism Industry Development randomly selected a student who received an individual prize of an Apple iPod and their school received $1000 to spend on science resources.

children, and their perceived relative wealth. After looking at the raw profile of happiness we apply techniques previously used in the economics literature (Frijters et al. 2004) to decompose the found changes in happiness as a function of changes in other variables.

18.2.3   Survey Questions

The meta-analysis of life satisfaction research with children and adolescents by Gilman and Huebner (2003) provides a summary of childhood happiness-affecting variables. Their list includes many factors, of which we choose the factors easiest to gather from the children themselves, including socio-economic variables that economists usually incorporate into their models of individual happiness (age, gender), as well as personality factors, life satisfaction domains, environment factors, and school variables. This means we did not gather variables that would require information of others, such as parental circumstances, medically assessed health and self-reflecting behaviour, which one would want to ask of teachers (such as asking whether the child causes problems for others).

18.2.3.1   The Happiness Question

The dominant happiness surveys are generally targeted at individuals 15 years and older. Since we wish to compare the findings for young children with these age ranges, we also use the *Global Life Satisfaction* question (Cummins 1996; Fordyce 1988; Wessman and Ricks 1966) wherein we ask children on a 1 (very unhappy) to 5 (very happy) scale:

All things considered in your life, how happy would you say you are usually?

The high response rate (100%) as well as the fact that these children had just seen exhibits on happiness research gives some confidence that children had an intuitive understanding of what was being asked.

18.2.3.2   Demographic Questions

In order to be able to ascribe changes in happiness to changes in circumstances, we wanted to have an array of demographic questions, which raised the issue of whether children as young as 9 would have a reasonable concept of such high-level circumstances such as their family's income. Researchers have long been concerned with inaccuracies in how adults report their income (Moore et al. 2000), which makes it likely that the problem of misreporting is even higher amongst children. As a result we more directly ask about relative wealth, since children do understand the concept of money as they swap it with others to get what they want (Leiser and Beth

Halachmi 2006). We furthermore suspected that relative comparisons are easier to understand than absolute levels: a child might not know what things cost or how much the family makes, but; will notice whose house is bigger, and; who is jealous of others for things they cannot afford. We thus asked:

> Would you say that your family is; wealthier; the same; poorer than others in the neighbourhood.

A drawback of asking children to complete the questionnaire at school was that we could not ask information about the parents, such as their employment, years of education, relationship status, and recent shocks.

18.2.3.3 Personality

Amongst adult happiness studies (Lischetzke and Eid 2006; Wilson 1967), the personality traits most related to happiness are extraversion and emotional stability. It is an open question whether that is also true of children and hence whether there is a role for agreeableness, conscientiousness, or openness to experience. However, the survey instruments measuring these Big-5 personality constructs (Goldberg 1990) are only suitable for adults and adolescents as young as 12 years (Muris et al. 2005); not the 9–11 year olds that formed part of our target population.

We thus adopt the Big Five Questionnaire for Children (BFQ-C) of Barbaranelli et al. (2003). Their analysis of the internal validity of this scale revealed a high positive correlation between the BFQ-C scale completed by the children and their parent's assessment of their child's personality using the adult Big-5 questionnaire. In support of its use, del Barrio et al. (2006) successfully used the BFQ-C scale to assess the personality of eight to 12 year old school children. More recently, the study of 13–14 year olds by Barbaranelli et al. (2008) used multi-trait methods and confirmatory factor analysis to assess the validity of the BFQ-C and found convergent validity was supported for all five personality factors.

We had to adapt the BFQ-C scale for our purposes because it had 65 questions; twelve or more questions per personality trait is lot of questions for an internet survey.[6] Using BFQ-C psychometric property/correlation results from Muris et al. (2005), we constructed a short-form Big Five Questionnaire for Children (SBFQ-C) by choosing six questions per personality trait.[7] After data collection, confirmatory factor and Cronbach's alpha analysis confirmed our chosen six questions per personality trait exhibited acceptable levels of convergence and scale reliability (Table 18.1).

---

[6]In middle childhood, children get bored and fail to complete surveys with too many questions, they also require literally worded questions that they can understand (de Leeuw et al. 2004).

[7]The HILDA socio-economic panel surveys adults with 5–8 questions per personality trait.

18.2.3.4 The Life Satisfaction Domain Measures

Huebner (1991, 1994, 1995), Natvig et al. (2003), Seligson et al. (2005) and Suldo et al. (2006) provide theoretical directions that identify domains considered to correlate with childhood happiness; *school environment, interaction with friends,* and, the *natural environment* life satisfaction domains. The wording of the survey questions we developed for each domain was based on this. For example, because sharing, friendly, communicative children who like to interact with their peers are happier we posed the questions; *I make friends easily, I like to talk to others, I like to help my classmates, I like to share with others,* and, *I am forgiving.* These were included for the *interaction with friends* life satisfaction domain. The rationale for including forgiveness is that it has been found to be positively associated with childhood life satisfaction (Gilman and Huebner 2003).

When it comes to the school environment life satisfaction domain, Huebner et al. (1999) found it important to know whether children understand what the teacher says, can concentrate, work hard, get bored, whether they participate in structured extracurricular activities, and aspects of their academic life (including achievement and learning with classmates).

In addition to the life satisfaction domain questions, the children were asked questions about their *natural environment.* We asked the children if they were engaged in discussions on their natural environment; if they were aware of environmental problems; what they were doing about them; whether it was an acceptable behaviour to pollute their river or a river in a neighbouring state; and the importance of animals and plants in their live. These questions were coded as dummy variables and summed to form the *natural environment* life satisfaction domain factor, where 1 is the lowest level of concern for the natural environment and 13 the highest level of concern for the natural environment.

Table 18.2 lists the questions posed on these three domains. Results from Cronbach's alpha test, and confirmatory factor analysis, revealed that all three life satisfaction domain factors offered an acceptable to high level of internal consistency and reliability.

Finally, we included a number of *fun* questions (on magic & handedness) to encourage the children to respond to our internet-based childhood happiness survey; see the *natural environment* and *fun* questions in Table 18.7.

18.3 Analyses

18.3.1 Summary Statistics

Of the 389 children who responded to the internet-based 'Happiness' survey, 327 visited the 'Smart Train' at one of 25 regional railway stations and 62 at the urban railway station (the state capital of Brisbane). There were 217 female and 172 male children (44%) respondents with an average age of 11.76 years.

Table 18.3 shows the summary statistics. Average life satisfaction for our 9 to 14-year-old sample is a very high 9.0 if we translate the scale to 0–10; 14% higher than the 7.91 we see in 15 to 23 year-olds in the HILDA and 12% higher than the average of 8.07 for the complete HILDA sample. Average happiness for female children in our sample (9.31) was 8% higher than for male children (8.60), a very significant difference ($t = 3.59$, $p = 0.0004$) that is commensurate with what is found later in life but which has not been in previous child studies (Heubner and Diener 2012). What drives this average difference in our data is the relatively low happiness of regional males versus regional females, which suggests that one of the reasons for the divergence with previous studies is that our data includes both urban and regional children.

Twelve per cent of the children self-reported as left-handed, a few percent more than the expected 10% (Johnston et al. 2009) and 47% reported a ring finger longer than their index finger; an indicator of the higher testosterone levels typical of males.

Turning to Table 18.7, which shows a summary of the natural environmental questions: children have a high awareness of environmental issues such as climate change (68%), and; water restrictions (59%), but; a much lower awareness of native animals dying out (42%); declining fish stocks (21%), and; land salinity (16%). Climate change (47%) and water restrictions (15%) were seen as the worst problems, with urban children showing more concern about climate change than regional children (61% versus 44%). We expected that regional children would show a higher awareness and concern for climate change and water restrictions, because the Millennium 2001–2010 series of droughts in Australia had such a severe negative economic effect on Australia's rural and agricultural communities (SoE 2011). This was not the case though with regional children showing less awareness and concern for the environment.[8] Perhaps the reason for this arises from the attitudes of their parents. In Australia, more than twice as many urban dwellers (58%) are of the opinion that humans are causing climate change; versus just 27% for primary producers in regional areas (Donnelly et al. 2009, p. 5).

Overall, the children are not just showing concern for the natural environment, they are acting on that concern. Fifty-nine per cent of the children are engaging in recycling and 65% have tried to reduce their water consumption, and, the numbers are even higher for urban children (Table 18.4); more urban children (81%) than regional children (62%) had tried to reduce their water consumption, and a similar urban-rural difference held for engaging in recycling (73% versus 57%). The children are also showing concern about the poor environmental behaviour of others; 98% of the children said it was wrong to pollute a river, even if that river was in another state (99%). Based on these results, Australia's next generation shows more concern for climate change and the natural environment than their parents, who answer the same questions 68% versus 53% (ABS 2010).

---

[8]Overall, regional children showed less concern for the environment; the average of the Natural Environment Life Satisfaction Domain factor for urban children was 14% higher than for regional children (Table 18.6).

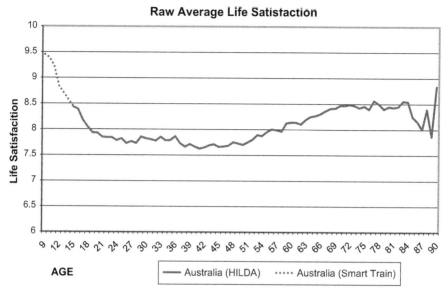

Fig. 18.2 Average Life Satisfaction for 9 to 14-year-old Australian children in the 'Smart Train' data and 15 to 93-year-old Australians in the 2002–2013 HILDA panel data

18.3.2   Extending Our View of Happiness over a Lifetime

We can now append the average happiness of the 9 to 14 year-olds from our 'Smart Train' sample to the graph of average happiness for the 15 to 93 year-old Australians from the HILDA (Figs. 18.2 and 18.3).

One thing one can notice is how well the lines match up from the data on the Smart Train with the HILDA data, which at least suggests that the sample is representative of the happiness of Australian children. The second thing we notice is that the steep happiness fall we previously saw in 15 to 23-year-olds extends back to 9-year-old children. Whilst 15 to 23 year-old Australians in the HILDA witness a 7.2% (−0.73 unit) decline in happiness, this is preceded by a further 9.3% decline (9.44–8.56, −0.88 units) between 9 and 14 years (dotted line in Figs. 18.2 and 18.3). The total fall in happiness from age 9 to age 23 is then 16.5% (−1.61 units).

In terms of the main Easterlin-related questions of the introduction, our first 'result' is hence that the decline in happiness starts at age 9 and 10, but becomes particularly pronounced from age 12 to 13, which coincides with the children's transition to high school and the onset of puberty.

This very strong decline raises the question as to the factors responsible; we look at that next.

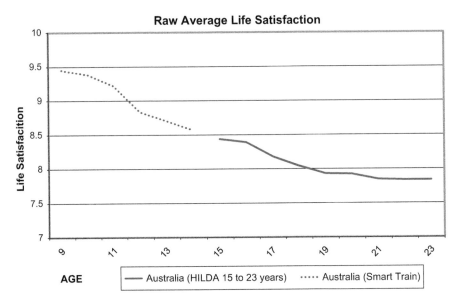

Fig. 18.3 Average Life Satisfaction for 9 to 14-year-old Australian children in the 'Smart Train' data and 15 to 23-year-old Australians in the 2002–2013 HILDA panel data

18.3.3 The Determinants of Life Satisfaction

In Eq. (18.1) we model life satisfaction of child (i) in age-group (t) as a linear function of the available variables:

$$LS_{it} = C + \beta_1 X_{it} + \beta_2 S_{it} + \beta_3 F_{it} + \beta_4 N_{it} + Z_i + \varepsilon_{it} \qquad (18.1)$$

where

LS_{it} Individual life satisfaction (happiness)
C Constant
X_{it} individual demographics (wealth, religion)
S_{it} *School environment* life satisfaction domain factor
F_{it} *Interaction with friends* life satisfaction domain factor
N_{it} *Natural Environment* life satisfaction domain factor
Z_i Personality and gender
ε_{it} error term

Here, childhood happiness (LS_{it}) is a function of a constant (C), time-variant socio-economic variables specific to the individual (X_{it}) and individual traits (Z_i). A child's happiness is further affected by the *school environment* (S_{it}), *interaction with friends* (F_{it}) and *natural environment* (N_{it}) life satisfaction domains, with unobservables manifest in an error term (ε_{it}).

Regression results for different specifications are shown in Tables 18.5 and 18.6, which progressively include more factors. Looking at Table 18.5, specification 1a, we see that girls are happier (+0.63) than boys and attending religious services more often is related to higher happiness (+0.09), much the same as what we see in adults. The children are unhappier the longer they are in the school system (we will look at this in more detail later).

Unlike adults, relative wealth has a non-significant and small effect on childhood happiness.

A possible reason for this is that the wealth question is poorly understood by children. Alternatively, there really is little relation at this age. One possibility to explore with richer data would be that parents manage to shield children from their own feelings about their relative wealth; keeping the rat-race away from their children when they are young.

In terms of our introductory motivation around Richard Easterlin's 2001 theory of how relative comparisons affect the national income-happiness relationship, our second main finding is thus that relative considerations are not yet that important for teenagers. That is, not amongst teenagers from within a relatively wealthy group that are all sufficiently well-to-do that their school has excursions to visiting exhibitions. Still, taken at face value, it would mean that Richard's story of disappointment with the disconnect between anticipated income trajectories and anticipated benchmarks are unlikely to be very relevant for young teenagers under 15-years. If such a dynamic is important, it is important in later life, perchance when individuals start earning money themselves.

Adding personality to the specification in Table 18.5 (specification 1b.), we see that extraverted children are happier whilst children with low emotional stability are less happy. We get an unexpected result for conscientiousness. For adults in the Australian socio-economic panel data (HILDA), conscientiousness has a significant negative effect on overall happiness (-0.33, t-$value = 2.22$).[9] For the 9–14 year olds in the 'Smart Train' data we get an opposite effect (0.066, t-$value$ 2.85). Unlike adults, Australian children who exhibit conscientious behaviours (orderly, systematic, efficient, neat, organised, and efficient) are happier, perchance because the rewards for such behaviour are higher for school children than for adults.

If we now also add domain factors to the demographics (Table 18.6, specification 18.2e), we can see that the effect from the *natural environment* domain factor[10] is non-significant, whilst, as expected, the *interaction with friends* and *school environment* domains both have a significant effect on childhood happiness.

---

[9]The personality traits are scaled 1–7 in the HILDA & 1–30 in this paper; the HILDA coefficient has been rescaled; 1–30. Regression tables relevant to this are available on request.

[10]If we look at the effect from the individual 'natural environment' questions in Table 18.7, we see that only one environment question (q17) had a significant effect on happiness. Children who perceived their family as wealthier than their friend's families are more likely to discuss environmental issues within their family (q17 was strongly positively correlated with wealth).

18.3.4 Decomposing Changes in Life Satisfaction

Many of the factors that affect life satisfaction, such as gender and personality, are constant or change little over time. The main areas that change over time for these school children are the three main life satisfaction domains, meaning we focus on Specification 2c of Table 18.6.

There is a large decline in the magnitude of these domain factors as the children move from one grade to the next. Between grade 5 and grade 10 the average for the *interaction with friends* domain declines from 4.21 in grade 5 to 3.92 in grade 8 then rises to 4.08 by the end of grade 10. The average of the *school environment* domain drops from 3.97 in grade 4 to 5 and continues to drop all the way to 3.24 in grade 10.

To see how much these changes in domain satisfactions can help explain the differences in life satisfaction between children of different school grades; we employ a standard decomposition of the difference in aggregate life satisfaction (*LS*) levels:

$$\left(\overline{LS^{grade9}} - \overline{LS^{grade4}} \right) = \sum_{k=1}^{k=3} \sum_{l=4}^{l=8} \left(\left(\bar{X}_{k,l+1} - \bar{X}_{k,l} \right) * \beta_k \right) \quad (18.2)$$

Where the childhood life satisfaction domain factors are:

$$k \begin{cases} \textit{School enviroment} \\ \textit{Interaction with friends} \\ \textit{Natural enviroment} \end{cases}$$

and the school grade transition is from a lower (*l*) to the next higher school grade (*l* + 1):

$$l,l+1 \begin{cases} l & to & l+1 \\ 4 & to & 5 \\ 5 & to & 6 \\ 6 & to & 7 \\ 7 & to & 8 \\ 8 & to & 9 \end{cases}$$

This decomposition shows the predicted life satisfaction difference across grades due to changes in domain factors. The formula shows the predicted difference between grade 4 and 9, but an analogue formula holds for the difference between any pair of grades.

Figure 18.4 shows the predicted changes in childhood happiness as children move through the state school system (grades 4–7) and then transfer to high school (grades 8–9).[11]

---

[11]Post this study, the transition to high school in Queensland now occurs in grade 7.

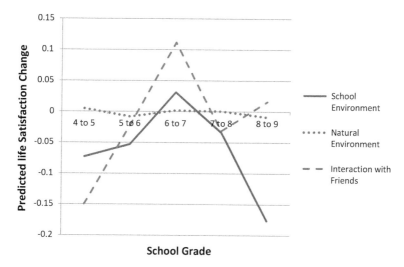

Fig. 18.4 Predicted grade-by-grade change childhood happiness from each domain factor as the children move up in school grade

This figure shows the predicted change from year to year due to changes in particular domain factors, which means one should add them up to arrive at a cumulative predicted change. Looking at Fig. 18.4 we see the negligible childhood happiness change arising from the non-significant *natural environment* domain factor (dotted line), less than a 0.012 happiness unit decline (−0.1%) if we add them up across these years. However, the predicted happiness change from the other two factors is both significant and large: when accumulated, the *school environment* and *interaction with friends* domains account for 44% (−0.39) of the −0.88 unit fall in childhood happiness for 9 to 14 year-old Australians we saw in the raw data depicted in Figs. 18.2 and 18.3.

Examining how each factor affects childhood happiness as the children progress through the school system, we see that the predicted change in childhood happiness arising from the *interaction with friends* domain (Fig. 18.4 dashed line) is −0.15 units as the children transition from grades 4–5; the predicted happiness change is almost zero (−0.02) as the children move from grades 5–6, and; there is an even smaller predicted positive change (+0.011) as the children transition through the last grades (6–7) in the lower grade school, potentially reflecting that this is their best year in terms of friendships.

Australian children are often not sent to their local high school but enrolled in public or private high schools that may be many kilometres from the lower grade school that a child attended. This may be a factor in the small (−0.03) decrease in life satisfaction as children move to high school (from grade 7–8). The big drop in happiness (−0.15) comes when the children transition to high school though, driven entirely by a marked drop in the school environment but not the interaction with friends.

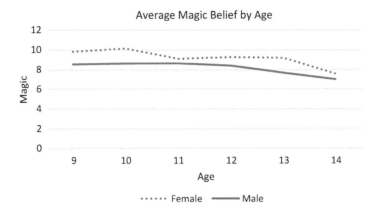

Fig. 18.5 Magic beliefs for children aged 9–14 years in the Smart Train dataset

Cumulatively, the largest predicted negative change in childhood happiness (−0.31) comes from the school environment, mainly occurring in the transition from grade 4–5 and from grade 8–9.

In terms of the Easterlin theory of income comparisons, these results suggest that other factors play their own role in declining happiness when young: puberty and perchance the increased pressures of school and society that are piled on during high school reduce happiness amongst children. Note though that even our 15-year old Queensland children are very happy compared to almost any group of adults anywhere in the world, leaving plenty to scope for income-comparison disappointments later in life to drag them down!

Finally, we address the third Easterlin-relevant component we want to answer with our data: do kids have unrealistic aspirations or beliefs and do they change in any way over time?

We asked about a particular form of high expectations and naivety: belief in magic. Table 18.6 lists the questions (q6, 7, 8, & 10) which we added together to arrive at a 0–12 index. We included them to capture something that many of us believed in as children, the magic in our lives (Woolley et al. 1999). In our results we see the expected the significant decline ($F = 15.66 \, p = 0.0001$) in magical beliefs for both females & males ($F = 2.49$, $p = 0.0309$) as the kids age (Fig. 18.5). The effect of magic on happiness is positive ($t = 0.019$, $p = 0.45$) but non-significant, and, reducing in age ($t = -0.14$, $t = -.1.57$).

We saw earlier that 98% percent of the kids did not think it was OK to throw garbage in a river, whilst only 65% of their parents though so, an indication that updating takes place on that later in life. We then look at the sum of the survey questions listed in Table 18.6 on the Natural Environment. We see that the kids' attitude to the environment does not significantly change by age ($F = 1.93$, $p = 0.0920$), but on average girls show significantly ($F = 4.47$, $p = 0.0351$) more

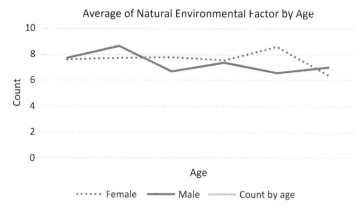

Fig. 18.6 Natural Environment attitude of 9 to 14-year-olds in the Smart Train dataset

concern for the environment than the boys (this result is consistent with recent research by Tranter and Skbris (2011). While kids may be concerned for the natural environment it does not have a significant independent effect on the happiness of the kids in our sample (Table 18.6, specification 2c, Table 18.7) (Fig. 18.6).

Another factor we examined was fairness, the impartial and just treatment of behaviour without favouritism or discrimination. Our fairness factor is the sum of the following three question, each measured on a 5-point Likert scale:

1. Imagine you are hiking in a remote desert. Only 10 bottles of water are available from a shop for $1 each. On a very hot day 20 hikers want to buy water. Is it fair if the shopkeeper makes everybody wait in line for their turn to buy water?
2. Is it fair if the shopkeeper flips a coin to decide if you will be sold a bottle of water? (reverse coded)
3. Is it fair if your hero buys all the water for $1 per bottle and sells it according to his/her own judgement? (reverse coded)

Looking at Fig. 18.7, we see no significant difference between the fairness attitudes of girls or boys ($F = 0.00$, $p = 0.9445$) nor was there any difference across ages ($F = 0.85$, $p = 0.517\ 5$).

However, when we look at the distribution of response for questions 2 & 3 that refer to the shopkeeper interfering in the supply and price of water we see a very emotive response by the kids. 85% of the kids said it was probably or completely unfair for the shopkeeper to monopolise the price of water or interfere in who was supplied water. It would appear that kids have strong expectations of how markets should operate, even at a young age. Fairness had a positive but non- significant effect on the kid's happiness (*0.033, t = 0.71*).

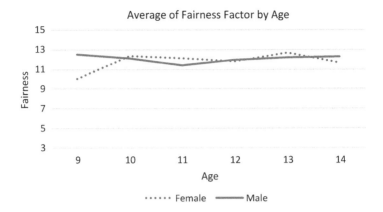

Fig. 18.7 Fairness attitude of 9 to 14-year-olds in the Smart Train dataset

In short, we find clear evidence for the idea that kids aged 9–15 are highly idealistic and naïve, but only become less naïve in this age range about the subject of magic.

We can mention that we had a quick look at changes amongst the 85 individuals in the HILDA aged 15–18 (compared to the rest, analysed in Headey and Wooden 2004). When Headey and Wooden (2004) looked at the effect of asset income on happiness for all ages in the HILDA, it is significantly positive, but when we ourselves look at asset income for ages 15 to 18 in the HILDA the asset income effect is still positive but non-significant at the 5% level. On top of this, in our Smart Train data, most kids (79%) thought their wealth was the same as those in their neighbourhood. Combined, this suggests that relative wealth comparisons are not yet that important for Australian children under 18 and that concerns for relative wealth become larger afterwards, i.e. when they also lose their naivety about fairness, and the environment.

18.4 Conclusions and Discussion

This paper contributed to our understanding of lifetime happiness by extending our view of happiness back to childhood. We developed an Internet-based happiness survey for 9 to 14-year-old Australian children. Analysis of the collected data with a model of childhood happiness revealed a large decline in happiness (−0.88 on a 0–10 scale) between the ages of 9 and 14. This solves a puzzle in the existing literature wherein it was previously found that early adolescence was marked with low school environment and higher rates of depression (Hirsch and Rapkin 1987; Huebner et al. 2000), but where there was not yet a clear finding that global life satisfaction levels decreased accordingly (Heubner and Diener 2012).

Another finding is that conscientious children are markedly happier, whilst we found for data amongst adults that the conscientious are less happy. Importantly, there was no found effect of relative wealth, whereas that factor is amongst the most important ones for adults. The kid's view of family wealth appears to be much removed from reality; 79% of the kids said their family wealth was the same as other families. This is very different from what we see in the Australian 2013–2014 wealth distribution data, where 53% of the wealth is in the top two percentiles (ABS 2015). Our wealth result might indicate that parents within the relatively rich demographic we have in our survey are successful in not transferring their own feelings about their relative wealth on to their children, effectively shielding them from the status race.

With other factors though, the determinants of child happiness were the same as those of adult happiness: girls were happier; the more religious were happier; and the more extraverted were happier.

When we decomposed the changes in life satisfaction amongst children we found that some (44%) of that change was attributable to worsening domain factors. Worsening of the school factors alone could explain 30% in the drop. These school factors include the interaction with the teacher (whether they understand what the teacher says; whether they get bored), items of school success (whether they learn easily, whether they start what they finish), and items of personal effort (whether they work hard, whether they help others and whether they concentrate). These aspects deteriorated markedly in our data from 9 to 10 years of age and 13 to 14 years of age.

What turned out to be unimportant for changes in life satisfaction was their social interaction (number of friends), as this did not decrease over time, nor whether the children were aware of environmental problems.

As to the main questions we started out with pertaining to Richard Easterlin's thoughts on happiness decline over age and the role of income comparisons therein, we end with 3 tentative conclusions from our study:

- Richard's hypothesised decline in happiness over age already starts at age 9, but, is particularly pronounced in the transition to high school.
- Children aged 9–15 have no trouble answering questions on relative wealth, but unlike our own expectations, these relative comparisons were largely irrelevant for happiness in this age group for this social demographic. Disappointment in income-comparisons simply do not appear yet to play a role, perchance because these children do not have to work for a living. The relative unimportance of relative wealth persists at least till 18.
- These children are highly idealistic, with 99% saying pollution of the waters flowing to another state is bad, whilst only 45% of their parents' generation say so. Similar naivety is found when it concerns fairness and magic, and only in the case of the belief in magic do we see a significant drop before the age of 15. So we do indeed find strong evidence for highly unrealistic expectations and beliefs amongst children, indeed at the same time as their happiness levels are extremely high.

Let us end with thanking Richard for his massive contributions to social science. Our paper does not quite prove him right on every point of his 2001 theory as it pertains to children, but at least we find them able to answer relative income questions and that the pressures of life do drag them down a bit in teenage years and much stronger after that. We cannot quite confirm his theory to be right on all counts, because our data is simply not rich enough for that, but, our findings are in line with Richard's thinking.

Acknowledgments We thank Dr. Markus Schaffner of the Queensland Behavioural Economics Group (QuBE); Leesa Watkin (QUT Smart Train Project Manager), and; Annie Harris (Department of Innovation, Tourism Industry Development, Queensland State Government) for their considerable technical, organisational, and financial assistance.

Appendices

Appendix A: Survey Questions

Table 18.1 The six questions per personality trait included in the Childhood Happiness Survey (selected from the 65 BFQ-C scale (Muris et al. 2005, p. 1762, Table 1)

Personality trait	Questions	Scale reliability[a]
Extroversion	I make friends easily	0.65
	I do many things so I don't get bored	
	I like to talk to others	
	I say what I think	
	I like to joke	
	I like to meet with other people	
Agreeableness	I trust others	0.73
	I share my things with other people	
	I understand when others need my help	
	I am kind to those who I dislike	
	If a classmate has some difficulty I help her/him	
	If someone hurts me I forgive them	
Conscientiousness	I keep my school things neat and tidy	0.78
	During class I concentrate on the things I do	
	I play only after I finish my homework	
	I work hard at the things I do	
	When I start to do something, I have to finish it at all costs	
	When I finish my homework, I check it many times to see if I did it correctly	

(continued)

Table 18.1   (continued)

Personality trait	Questions	Scale reliability[a]
Emotional stability	I am often sad	0.78
	I get nervous over silly things	
	I worry about things	
	I get offended easily	
	I cry often	
	I am impatient	
Openness to experience	When the teacher explains something, I understand immediately	0.78
	I am able to solve mathematical problems	
	I understand most things immediately	
	I like scientific TV shows	
	I easily learn what I study at school	
	I know many things	

[a]Cronbach's Alpha values of 0.6 to 0.8 are considered acceptable; greater than 0.8 are good

Table 18.2   Survey questions for the 'school environment', 'interaction with friends' and 'natural environment' life satisfaction domain factors

Life satisfaction domain	Survey question
School environment[1] (schoolenv)	When the teacher explains something, I understand immediately
	I do many things so I don't get bored
	During class I concentrate on the things I do
	I play only after I finish my homework
	I understand most things immediately
	I work hard at the things I do
	If a classmate has some difficulty I help her/him
	When I start to do something, I have to finish it at all costs
	I easily learn what I study at school
Interaction with friends[2] (friends)	I make friends easily
	I trust others
	I share my things with other people
	I like to talk to others
	I understand when others need my help
	I am kind to those who I dislike
	I like to meet with other people
	If someone hurts me I forgive them
Natural environment[3] (natenv)	Which of the following environmental problems have you noticed?
	Climate change
	Water restrictions
	Native animals dying out
	Declining fish stocks
	Land salinity

(continued)

Table 18.2 (continued)

Life satisfaction domain	Survey question
	Does your family talk about the environment much?
	Have you ever started a conversation about the environment?
	Have decided for environmental reasons to reuse or recycle something rather than throw it away?
	Have you tried to reduce water consumption for environmental reasons?
	Attended a meeting or signed a letter or petition aimed at protecting nature or the environment?
	Let's say that in your neighbourhood everyone throws their garbage in the river; would that be all right?
	Let's say that in New South Wales (the state next to the children's home state), a whole neighbourhood throws its garbage in the river; do you think it is all right for them to throw their garbage in the river?
	Do you think that throwing garbage in the river is harmful to the birds that live around the river?

Cronbach's alpha scale reliability coefficients: 0.86^1; 0.76^2; 0.65^3
Confirmatory factor analysis results: school environment: $X^2 = 2.84$ (5), p = 0.72; RMR = 0.02; RMSEA = 0.00; RFI = 0.99; CFI = 1.0; AGFI = 0.99; NFI = 0.99; GFI = 0.99. Interaction with friends: $X^2 = 0.13$ (2), p = 0.94; RMR = 0.003; RMSEA = 0.00; RFI = 0.99; CFI = 1.0; AGFI = 0.99; NFI = 1.0; GFI = 1.00

Appendix B: Descriptive Statistics

Table 18.3 Descriptive statistics for the Smart Train data; N = 389

	Mean	S. D.
Gender (female = 1)	0.56	0.44
Age (years)	11.76	1.04
School grade (4–9)	6.76	1.04
Urban resident (urban = 1)	0.16	0.37
Relative wealth (1 poorer; same; 3, wealthier)	2	0.45
Religious service attendance; (1 never to 8 more than once a week)	4.39	2.72
Personality factors (scaled 1–30)		
Extraversion	24.7	3.63
Agreeableness	23.71	4.07
Conscientiousness	21.85	5.23
Emotional stability	16.68	4.06
Openness to experience	21.8	5.05
Life satisfaction domain factors		
School environment (scaled 1–5)	3.71	0.74
Interaction with friends (scaled 1–5)	4.05	0.62
Natural environment (scaled 1–13)	7.44	2.23

Table 18.4 Descriptive statistics for the children's responses to the natural environment questions

	Urban	Regional	All
Which of the following environmental problems have you noticed?			
Climate change	74%	64%	65%
Water restrictions	90%	53%	59%
Native animals dying out	56%	39%	42%
Declining fish stocks	27%	20%	21%
Land salinity	24%	14%	16%
Which of these problems do you think is the worst?			
Climate change	61%	44%	47%
Water restrictions	21%	14%	15%
Native animals dying out	10%	29%	26%
Declining fish stocks	0%	6%	5%
Land salinity	8%	5%	5%
Loss of native fauna	0%	0%	2%
None of the above	0%	2%	0%
Relevance of plants and animals to the children			
Are animals an important part of your life?	90%	94%	93%
Are plants an important part of your life?	85%	81%	82%
The children's engagement in the environmental debate (yes = 1)			
Have you ever started a conversation about the environment?	73%	68%	68%
Does your family talk about the environment?	52%	50%	50%
Things that the children had done over the past 12 months to help the environment (yes = 1)			
Tried to reduce water consumption	81%	62%	65%
Have decided for environmental reasons to reuse or recycle something rather than throw it away	73%	57%	59%
Attended a meeting or signed a letter or petition aimed at protecting nature or the environment?	6%	9%	8%
None of the above	10%	14%	14%
Children's attitudes to pollution (yes = 1)			
Let's say that in your neighbourhood everyone throws their garbage in the river; would that be all right?	0%	2%	2%
Let's say that in New South Wales (the state next to the children's home state), a whole neighbourhood throws its garbage in the river. Do you think it is all right for them to throw their garbage in the river?	0%	1%	1%
Do you think that throwing garbage in the river is harmful to the birds that live around the river?	92%	93%	93%
Natural environment life satisfaction domain factor	8.48	7.45	7.44
(0: Lowest awareness of the environment to highest: 13)			
N	62	327	389

Appendix C: Regression Results

Table 18.5 The determinants of Life Satisfaction for children aged 9–14 years in the Smart Train dataset; OLS regression, N = 389

Variable	1a. Demographics		1b. Demographics personality		2a. School environment		2b. School environment interaction with friends	
	Coefficient	t-value	Coefficient	t-value	Coefficient	t-value	Coefficient	t-value
q1: Where did you visit the Smart Train?	−0.022	1.72	−0.013	1.05				
q2: Female = 1	0.632	3.44	0.645	3.51				
q4: School grade (age proxy)	−0.16	1.84	−0.125	1.52				
q5: Relative wealth	0.052	0.26	−0.066	0.34				
q9: Religious service attendance	0.092	2.72	0.05	1.5				
Personality factors								
Extraversion,			0.129	4.54				
Agreeableness			−0.049	1.5				
Conscientiousness			0.066	2.85				
Emotional stability			−0.089	4.17				
Openness to experience			0.003	0.14				
Life satisfaction domain factors								
School environment factor (schoolenv)					0.665	5.56	0.39	2.66
Interaction with friends factor (friends)							0.561	3.17
Natural environment factor (natenv)								
Constant	8.097	10.54	6.981	6.39	5.715	12.63	4.457	7.45
R^2	0.063		0.1969		0.0739		0.0974	
Adjusted R^2			0.1757				0.0927	

Table 18.6 The determinants of Life Satisfaction for children aged 9–14 years in the Smart Train dataset; OLS regression, N = 389

Variable	2c. School environment Interaction with friends, natural environment		2d. Natural environment		2e. Demographics school environment interaction with friends/natural environment	
	Coefficient	t-value	Coefficient	t-value	Coefficient	t-value
q1: Where did you visit the Smart Train?					0.01	0.79
q2: Female = 1					0.484	2.66
q4: School grade					−0.135	1.59
q5: Relative wealth					0.021	0.11
q9: Religious service attendance					0.052	1.5
Life satisfaction domain factors						
School environment factor (schoolenv)	0.382	2.54			0..378	2.46
Interaction with friends factor (friends)	0.557	3.11			0.421	2.22
Natural environment factor (natenv)	0.01	0.23	0.101	2.45	−0.003	0.07
Constant	4.434	7.3	7.429	23.24	5.333	5.71
R^2	0.0975		0.0153		0.1251	
Adjusted R^2	0.0905		0.0127		0.1067	

Table 18.7 Other determinants of Life Satisfaction for the children aged 9–14 years in the cross-sectional Smart Train dataset; OLS regression, N = 389

Variable:	coefficient	t-value
q1: Where did you visit the Smart Train?	−0.018	1.31
q2: Female = 1	0.733	3.4
q4: School year (age proxy)	−0.166	1.63
q5: Relative wealth	0.111	0.48
q9: Religious service attendance	0.091	2.3
Fun questions:		
q6: Good luck charms do bring good luck (1 definitely not true to 5 definitely true)	−0.107	0.83
q7: Do you have a lucky charm such as a mascot or a talisman? (yes = 1)	0.129	0.52
q8: Do you believe that a lucky charm can protect or help you? (1 definitely not true to 5 definitely true)	−0.032	0.25
q10: Some fortune tellers really can foresee the future (1 definitely not true to 5 definitely true)	0.053	0.53
q11: Is there someone who cannot be seen by others watching over you? (yes = 1)	0.032	0.12

(continued)

Table 18.7 (continued)

Variable:	coefficient	t-value
Natural environment:		
q15: Are animals an important part of your life? (yes = 1)	0.534	1.23
q16: Are plants an important part of your life? (yes = 1)	−0.089	0.3
q17: Does your family talk about the environment much? (yes = 1)	0.396	1.78
q18: Have you ever started a conversation about nature or the environment? (yes = 1)	0.034	0.14
q22: Let's say that in your neighbourhood everyone throws their garbage in the river; would that be all right? (no = 1)	−0.579	0.68
q23: Let's say that in New South Wales, a whole neighbourhood throws its garbage in the river. Do you think it is all right or not all right for them to throw their garbage in the river? (no = 1)	1.029	0.92
q24: Do you think that throwing garbage in the river is harmful to the birds that live around the river? (yes = 1)	−0.467	1.13
Handedness:		
q63: What hand do you write with? (left = 1)	−0.177	0.56
q64: Which finger is longer? (1 my ring finger is longer; 2	−0.032	0.27
My ring and index fingers are the same length; 3 my index finger is longer)		
Constant	6.723	2.75
R^2	0.089	
Adjusted R^2	0.042	

Huebner et al. (2000)

References

ABS. (2010). 4102.0 – Australian social trends, June 2010 (Previous ISSUE Released at 11:30 AM (CANBERRA TIME) ed.): Australian Bureau of Statistics.

ABS. (2015). 6523.0 – Household income and wealth, Australia, 2013–14E. Released at 11:30 am (CANBERRA TIME) 4 September 2015: Australian Bureau of Statistics.

Antaramian, S. P., Huebner, E. S., & Valois, R. F. (2008). Adolescent life satisfaction. *Applied Psychology: An International Review, 57*(1), 112–126.

Antaramian, S. P., Huebner, E. S., Hills, K. J., & Valois, R. F. (2010). A dual-factor model of mental health: Toward a more comprehensive understanding of youth functioning. *American Journal of Orthopsychiatry, 80*(4), 462–472. https://doi.org/10.1111/j.1939-0025.2010.01049.x.

Barbaranelli, C., Caprara, G. V., Rabasca, A., & Pastorelli, C. (2003). A questionnaire for measuring the Big Five in late childhood. *Personality and Individual Differences, 34*(4), 645–664. https://doi.org/10.1016/s0191-8869(02)00051-x.

Barbaranelli, C., Fida, R., Di Giunta, L., & Caprara, G. V. (2008). Assessing personality in early adolescence through self-report and other-ratings a multitrait-multimethod analysis of the BFQ-C. *Personality and Individual Differences, 44*, 876–886.

Bedin, L. M., & Sarriera, J. C. (2015). A comparative study of the subjective well-being of parents and adolescents considering gender, age and social class. *Social Indicators Research, 120*(1), 79–95. https://doi.org/10.1007/s11205-014-0589-7.

Bruhin, A., & Winkelmann, R. (2009). Happiness functions with preference interdependence and heterogeneity: The case of altruism within the family. *Journal of Population Economics, 22*(4), 1063–1080.

Campbell, M. E., & Eggerling-Boeck, J. (2006). What about the children? The psychological and social well-being of multiracial adolescents. *Sociological Quarterly, 47*(1), 147–173.

Carlsson, F., Lampi, E., Li, W., & Martinsson, P. (2014). Subjective well-being among preadolescents and their parents – Evidence of intergenerational transmission of well-being from urban China. *Journal of Socio-Economics, 48*, 11–18. https://doi.org/10.1016/j.socec.2013.10.003.

Cheng, H., & Furnham, A. (2004). Perceived parental rearing style, self-esteem and self-criticism as predictors of happiness. *Journal of Happiness Studies, 5*(1), 1–21.

Clark, A. E., Frijters, P., & Shields, M. A. (2008). Relative income, happiness, and utility: An explanation for the easterlin paradox and other puzzles. *Journal of Economic Literature, 46*(1), 95–144.

Cummins, R. A. (1996). The domains of life satisfaction: An attempt to order chaos. *Social Indicators Research, 38*(3), 303.

de Leeuw, E., Borgers, N., & Smits, A. (2004). Pretesting questionnaires for children and adolescents. In S. Presser (Ed.), *Methods for testing and evaluating survey questionnaires* (pp. 409–452). Hoboken: Wiley.

Dear, K., Henderson, S., & Korten, A. (2011). Well-being in Australia. *Social Psychiatry and Psychiatric Epidemiology, 37*(11), 503–509.

del Barrio, V., Carrasco, M. Á., & Holgado, F. P. (2006). Factor structure invariance in the Children's Big Five Questionnaire. *European Journal of Psychological Assessment, 22*(3), 158–167. https://doi.org/10.1027/1015-5759.22.3.158.

Diener, E. (1984). Subjective well-being. *Psychological Bulletin, 95*(3), 542–575.

Diener, E., & Suh, M. E. (1998). Subjective well-being and age: An international analysis. In K. W. Schaie & M. P. Lawton (Eds.), *Annual review of gerontology and geriatrics* (Focus on emotion and adult development) (Vol. 17, pp. 304–324). New York: Springer.

Dockery, A. M. (2005). The happiness of young Australians: Empirical evidence on the role of labour market experience. *Economic Record, 81*(255), 322–335.

Donnelly, D., Mercer, R., Dickson, J., & Wu, E. (2009). *Australia's Farming Future Final Market Research Report. Understanding behaviours, attitudes and preferences relating to climate change*. Sydney: Instinct and Reason.

Easterlin, R. A. (2001). Subjective well-being and economic analysis: A brief introduction. *Journal of Economic Behavior & Organization, 45*(3), 225–226.

Easterlin, R. A. (2005). A puzzle for adaptive theory. *Journal of Economic Behavior & Organization, 56*(4), 513–521.

Ebner, A. (2008). 'Nest-leaving' in Osterreich: Was beeinflusst die Wohnentscheidung junger Erwachsener? (Nest-Leaving in Austria: What Determines Young Adults' Housing Decisions? With English summary). *Wirtschaftspolitische Blatter, 55*(2), 407–423.

ECHP. (2015). *European community household panel*. http://ec.europa.eu/eurostat/web/microdata/european-community-household-panel

Flouri, E. (2004). Subjective well-being in midlife: The role of involvement of and closeness to parents in childhood. *Journal of Happiness Studies, 5*(4), 335–358.

Fogle, L. M., Huebner, E. S., & Laughlin, J. E. (2002). The relationship between temperament and life satisfaction in early adolescence: Cognitive and behavioral mediation models. *Journal of Happiness Studies, 3*(4), 373–392.

Fordyce, M. W. (1988). A review of research on the happiness measures: A sixty second index of happiness and mental health. *Social Indicators Research, 20*(4), 355–381.

Forste, R., & Moore, E. (2012). Adolescent obesity and life satisfaction: Perceptions of self, peers, family, and school. *Economics and Human Biology, 10*(4), 385–394.

Frijters, P., & Foster, G. (2013). *An economic theory of greed, love, groups and networks*. New York: Cambridge University Press.

Frijters, P., Haisken-DeNew, J. P., & Shields, M. (2004). Money does matter! Evidence from increasing real income and life satisfaction in East Germany following reunification. *American Economic Review, 94*(3), 730–740.

Frijters, P., Johnston, D. W., & Shields, M. A. (2011). *Destined for (Un)happiness: does childhood predict adult life satisfaction?* (IZA discussion paper series). Bonn: Institute for the Study of Labor.

Gilman, R., & Huebner, E. S. (1997). Children's reports of their life satisfaction: Convergence across raters, time and response formats. *School Psychology International, 18*(3), 229–243.

Gilman, R., & Huebner, E. S. (2000). Review of life satisfaction measures for adolescents. *Behaviour Change, 17*(3), 178–195.

Gilman, R., & Huebner, S. (2003). A review of life satisfaction research with children and adolescents. *School Psychology Quarterly, 18*(2), 192–205.

Goldberg, L. R. (1990). An alternative "description of personality", The Big-Five factor structure. *Journal of Personality and Social Psychology, 59*, 1215–1229.

Haisken-DeNew, J. P., & Hahn, M. (2006). *PanelWhiz: A flexible modularized stata interface for accessing large scale panel data sets*. Mimeo. Retrieved from http://www.panelwhiz.eu

Haranin, E. C., Huebner, E. S., & Suldo, S. M. (2007). Predictive and incremental validity of global and domain-based adolescent life satisfaction reports. *Journal of Psychoeducational Assessment, 25*(2), 127–138.

Headey, B., & Wooden, M. (2004). The effects of wealth and income on subjective well-being and ill-being. *Economic Record, 80*, S24–S33.

Heubner, E. S., & Diener, C. (2012). Research on life satisfaction of children and youth: Implications for the delivery of school-related services. In M. Eid (Ed.), *The science of subjective wellbeing* (pp. 376–392). New York: Guildford Press.

HILDA. (2013). *The household, income and labour dynamics in Australia (HILDA) survey, release 11*. Retrieved August 21, 2013, from https://melbourneinstitute.unimelb.edu.au/hilda

Hirsch, B. J., & Rapkin, B. D. (1987). The transition to junior high school: A longitudinal study of self-esteem, psychological symptomatology, school life, and social support. *Child Development, 58*, 1235–1243.

Huebner, E. S. (1991). Correlates of life satisfaction in children. *School Psychology Quarterly, 6*(2), 103–111.

Huebner, E. S. (1994). Preliminary development and validation of a multidimensional life satisfaction scale for children. *Psychological Assessment, 6*(2), 149–158.

Huebner, E. S. (1995). The Students' Life Satisfaction Scale: An assessment of psychometric properties with black and white elementary school students. *Social Indicators Research, 34*(3), 315.

Huebner, E. S., Gilman, R., & Laughlin, J. E. (1999). A multimethod investigation of the multidimensionality of children's well-being reports: Discriminant validity of life satisfaction and self-esteem. *Social Indicators Research, 46*, 1–22.

Huebner, E. S., Drane, W., & Valois, R. F. (2000). Levels and demographic correlates of adolescent life satisfaction reports. *School Psychology International, 21*(3), 281–292.

Huebner, E. S., Valois, R. F., Paxton, R. J., & Drane, J. W. (2005). Middle school students' perceptions of quality of life. *Journal of Happiness Studies, 6*(1), 15–24.

Johnston, D. W., Nicholls, M. E. R., Shah, M., & Shields, M. A. (2009). Nature's experiment? Handedness and early childhood development. *Demography, 46*(2), 281–301.

Lee, W.-S., & Oguzoglu, U. (2007). Income support and stigma effects for young Australians. *Australian Economic Review, 40*(4), 369–384.

Leiser, D., & Beth Halachmi, R. (2006). Children's understanding of market forces. *Journal of Economic Psychology, 27*(1), 6–19.

Levin, K., Torsheim, T., Vollebergh, W., Richter, M., Davies, C., Schnohr, C., Due, P., & Currie, C. (2011). National income and income inequality, family affluence and life satisfaction among 13 year old boys and girls: A multilevel study in 35 countries. *Social Indicators Research, 104*(2), 179–194. https://doi.org/10.1007/s11205-010-9747-8.

Levin, K. A., Dallago, L., & Currie, C. (2012). The association between adolescent life satisfaction, family structure, family affluence and gender differences in parent-child communication. *Social Indicators Research, 106*(2), 287–305. https://doi.org/10.1007/s11205-011-9804-y.

Lischetzke, T., & Eid, M. (2006). Why extroverts are happier than introverts: The role of mood regulation. *Journal of Personality, 74*(4), 1127–1162.

LSAY. (2012). *The longitudinal surveys of Australian youth.* Retrieved April 2, 2012, from National Centre for Vocational Education Research (NCVER). http://www.ag.gov.au/cca

Moore, J. C., Stinson, L. L., & Welniak, E. J. (2000). Income measurement error in surveys: A review. *Journal of Official Statistics, 16*(4), 331–361.

Moore, P. M., Huebner, E. S., & Hills, K. J. (2012). Electronic bullying and victimization and life satisfaction in middle school students. *Social Indicators Research, 107*(3), 429–447. https://doi.org/10.1007/s11205-011-9856-z.

Muris, P., Meesters, C., & Diederen, R. (2005). Psychometric properties of the Big Five Questionnaire for Children (BFQ-C) in a Dutch sample of young adolescents. *Personality and Individual Differences, 38*(8), 1757–1769. https://doi.org/10.1016/j.paid.2004.11.018.

Natvig, G. K., Albrektsen, G., & Qvarnstram, U. (2003). Associations between psychosocial factors and happiness among school adolescents. *International Journal of Nursing Practice, 9*(3), 166–175.

Powdthavee, N., & Vernoit, J. (2013). Parental unemployment and children's happiness: A longitudinal study of young people's well-being in unemployed households. *Labour Economics, 24*, 253–263. https://doi.org/10.1016/j.labeco.2013.09.008.

Seligman, M. (2011). *Flourish: A visionary new understanding of happiness and well-being.* New York: Free Press.

Seligson, J., Huebner, E., & Valois, R. (2005). An investigation of a brief life satisfaction scale with elementary school children. *Social Indicators Research, 73*(3), 355–374.

SoE. (2011). In A. S. o. t. E. Committee (Ed.), *State of the environment 2011.* Canberra: Department of Sustainability, Environment, Water, Population and Communities.

Stutzer, A., & Frey, B. S. (2006). Does marriage make people happy, or do happy people get married? *Journal of Socio-Economics, 35*(2), 326–347.

Stutzer, A., & Frey, B. S. (2012). *Recent developments in the economics of happiness: A selective overview* (IZA Discussion Series). Institute for the Study of Labour. Bonn, Germany. Retrieved from http://ftp.iza.org/dp7078.pdf

Suldo, S. M., Riley, K. N., & Shaffer, E. J. (2006). Academic correlates of children and adolescents' life satisfaction. *School Psychology International, 27*(5), 567–582.

Tranter, B., & Skbris, Z. (2011). *Attitudes toward global warming, climate change and other environmental issues among young Queenslanders.* eSpace, The University of Queensland. https://espace.library.uq.edu.au/view/UQ:269694

Tsang, L. L. W. (2003). the effects of children, dual earner status, sex role traditionalism, and marital structure on marital happiness over time. *Journal of Family and Economic Issues, 24*(1), 5–26.

Ulker, A. (2008). mental health and life satisfaction of young Australians: The role of family background. *Australian Economic Papers, 47*(2), 199–218.

Wessman, A. E., & Ricks, D. F. (1966). *Mood and personality.* Oxford: Holt, Rinehart, & Winston.

White, N. P. (2006). *A brief history of happiness.* Malden/Oxford: Blackwell Pub.

Wilson, W. R. (1967). Correlates of avowed happiness. *Psychological Bulletin, 67*(4), 294–306.

Woolley, J. D., Phelps, K. E., Davis, D. L., & Mandell, D. J. (1999). Where theories of mind meet magic: The development of children's beliefs about wishing. *Child Development, 70*(3), 571–587.

Chapter 19
Do Humans Suffer a Psychological Low in Midlife? Two Approaches (With and Without Controls) in Seven Data Sets

David G. Blanchflower and Andrew J. Oswald

Life satisfaction is stable across... age groups.
Diener et al. (1999)

Abstract Using seven recent data sets, covering 51 countries and 1.3 million randomly sampled people, the paper examines the pattern of psychological well-being from approximately age 20 to age 90. Two conceptual approaches to this issue are possible. Despite what has been argued in the literature, neither is the 'correct' one, because they measure different things. One studies raw numbers on well-being and age. This is the descriptive approach. The second studies the patterns in regression equations for well-being (that is, adjusting for other influences). This is the ceteris-paribus analytical approach. The paper applies each to large cross-sections and compares the patterns of life-satisfaction and happiness. Using the first method, there is evidence of a midlife low in five of the seven data sets. Using the second method, all seven data sets produce evidence consistent with a midlife low. The scientific explanation for the approximate U-shape currently remains unknown.

D. G. Blanchflower
Dartmouth College, Hanover, NH, USA

University of Stirling, Stirling, Scotland

NBER, Cambridge, MA, USA
e-mail: david.g.blanchflower@dartmouth.edu

A. J. Oswald (✉)
University of Warwick, Warwick, UK

IZA Institute for the Study of Labor, Bonn, Germany
e-mail: andrew.oswald@warwick.ac.uk

© Springer Nature Switzerland AG 2019
M. Rojas (ed.), *The Economics of Happiness*,
https://doi.org/10.1007/978-3-030-15835-4_19

439

19.1   Introduction

What is the pattern of mental well-being at different ages in the human life-course? This important question is relevant to scientific researchers across a wide range of disciplines. Nearly two decades ago, Diener et al. (1999) concluded that well-being and quality of life are essentially independent of age. They illustrated that view with a flat line (in their Fig. 19.3). Monographs at that time, such as Argyle (2001), were typically similar. To our knowledge, most textbooks in social psychology continue to teach students the same result.

How should this important topic be studied by economists and behavioural scientists? One way to tackle the question is to use longitudinal data sets in which different sorts of people are followed throughout their lives. This has many advantages. It also has the potential disadvantage that, at the time of writing, such data sets tend to be fairly small and not to extend over a long span of adult life. Moreover, some human beings may become disenchanted with being interviewed and, in a free country, cannot be forced to stay in a longitudinal sample. Those who drop out of a longitudinal survey may not do so randomly. If such attrition is then biased, in ways that are important to an investigator's inquiry, the patterns observed in the remaining sample of individuals will give misleading answers.[1]

Another way to study such a question is to use cross-sectional data sets. This is a snapshot approach (to use the term adopted in Stone et al. 2010). It has some advantages, including simplicity, and the ability to examine large cross-national samples. It has the disadvantages that it may be subject to year-of-birth cohort effects and that, more broadly, the statistical information about ageing then comes from cross-person rather that within-person observation. Such cohort effects are themselves, in principle, of scientific interest.

This paper argues that the traditional Diener et al. (1999) wellbeing-is-flat-through-life conclusion does not do justice to current evidence. We examine data on 1.3 million randomly sampled individuals across a large number of nations. The paper brings together seven cross-sectional data sets, treats them in a statistically consistent way, and plots the results. It implicitly argues that it is natural for researchers to try to understand the patterns in pooled cross-sectional data sets as well as those in longitudinal data set sets.

The background literature is large and, currently, a shade disputatious (Baird et al. 2010; Blanchflower and Oswald 2008; Carstensen et al. 2011; Charles et al. 2001; Easterlin 2003, 2006; Frey and Stutzer 2002; Frijters and Beaton 2012; Glenn 2009; Graham and Pozuelo 2017; Hellevik 2017; Hudson et al. 2016; Lachman 2015;

---

[1] As a related example that is topical at the time of writing, the longitudinal British Election Study Wave 9 asked UK respondents after the EU referendum on Brexit how they voted. In the survey a small majority of the respondents reported that they voted to leave – by a margin of 49.5%–50.5% for remain. This contrasted with the actual outcome of 51.9% for Leave. The head of the BES Professor Ed Fieldhouse told us in private communication that *"this is because a known bias in the sample which is that politically interested people are more likely to respond/remain in the study."*

Mroczek and Kolanz 1998; Mroczek and Spiro 2005; Shields and Wheatley Price 2005; Stone et al. 2010; Steptoe et al. 2015; Wunder et al. 2013; Schwandt 2016). Helliwell and Grover (2014) argue that married people have a slightly shallower U-shape dip than the unmarried. An unusual paper that is related to this literature, which uses data on three samples of great apes, also documents evidence of a U shape: Weiss et al. (2012).

Easterlin (2006) is a particularly important paper. Controlling for year of birth, the paper finds evidence of a hill-shape in well-being over the life cycle. It uses pooled General Social Survey data from the United States. Richard Easterlin's paper is one of a number of challenges to the early Diener et al. (1999) result. Debate in this area has recently been fierce. A modern review by Ulloa et al. (2013) goes as far as to draw the conclusion that "extant studies… show either a U-shaped, inverted U-shaped or linear relation between ageing and subjective well-being." Other studies, such as Lachman (2015), come close to arguing that there may be a midlife dip but that it may be too small to be significant.

19.2 Analysis

Within the cross-section tradition, two broad ways to analyze the paper's scientific issue can be found in the literature. Despite what is sometimes argued (such as in Glenn 2009 and Hellevik 2017), it is not natural to see either approach as the 'right' or 'wrong' one. The reason is that they measure different things.

One set of writings has attempted to study raw numbers on well-being and age. This might be called the descriptive approach. A second, including Blanchflower and Oswald (2008), has examined the patterns in regression equations for well-being (that is, adjusting for other influences). This might be termed the ceteris-paribus analytical approach. Methods of the latter kind are standard in epidemiology and economics, for example, where the tradition has been to try to understand the consequences of an independent variable (smoking, income, etc.) after adjusting for other influences on the dependent variable.

The descriptive approach measures the 'total', or reduced-form, effect of age. By contrast, the ceteris-paribus analytical approach measures the marginal effect of age after controlling for other socio-economic influences. For example, as people move from their 20s to their 50s, they typically become considerably richer. Say, for illustrative purposes, they also become happier. The descriptive approach would then ascribe the possible rise in their happiness over that period as due to age. The analytical approach would divide the possible rise in happiness into two components – that coming from income per se and any residual effect from ageing per se. In principle, neither of these approaches is better than the other. Which is the more appropriate, in a particular empirical setting, will depend on the exact research question being addressed by the investigator.

The paper's later analysis is an attempt to compare these two. It looks at:

- Estimates of the well-being-age relationship both with and without adjustments for the other influences on well-being;
- Samples of adults up to the age of 90 (after which extreme ill-health becomes prevalent: we are doubtful that many researchers believe that humans are happy in the final few years of life: Evidence is provided by Gerstorf et al. 2010);
- Estimates that do not adjust for people's incomes (that is, it is not one of the controls), partly to be comparable with most of the literature, and partly because in some of the seven data sets there are no data on earnings;
- Statistical analysis that uses a set of individual age-year dummy variables (more than 70 individual dummy variables), to ensure that the data are able to follow any pattern, so that no particular mathematical form is artificially forced on the data.

It will become apparent below that the well-known papers of Easterlin (2006) and Glenn (2009), which are sometimes taken as key ones that shed doubt on the idea of a midlife low, rely on the one data set out of the seven that is rather unrepresentative of patterns in others.

Analogously, there is also evidence that there is an inverted U-shape in unhappiness. Blanchflower and Oswald (2008), for example showed such a pattern in depression data for the UK, which maximized at around age 45. At the time of writing we also became aware of a recent Office for National Statistics publication for England and Wales which showed that drug poisoning deaths maximized at ages 40–49.[2] This age group had a mortality rate of 108.0 in 2016, versus in that year a rate of 43.7 for ages 20–29; a rate of 97.5 for ages 30–39; a rate of 39.4 for 50–69, and a rate of 10.7 for 70 and older. There is some evidence that the maximum had recently moved up. In 2015, the age 30–39 group had the highest rate. This arose because of a large increase for the 40–49 year olds' mortality rate from 95.1 in 2015 compared with a fall for the 30-30 group whose 2015 rate was 98.4.

The current paper's seven data sets provide information on more than one million randomly sampled citizens; each person is asked questions about happiness or life satisfaction. These data sets are, respectively, for the United Kingdom, the USA, 36 European countries, 32 European countries, 51 nations around the world, and (again) the USA. We take each in turn, and begin with two data sets collected by official government statistical agencies (the UK Office of National Statistics and the US Centres for Disease Control) in which the random sampling is presumably of reliable quality.

UK (Office for National Statistics Data)
Figure 19.1 plots life-satisfaction data for approximately 416,000 randomly sampled citizens of the United Kingdom. Well-being data are now collected annually as part of official government statistics by the UK Office for National Statistics (ONS). One

---

[2] 'Deaths related to drug poisoning in England and Wales: 2016 registrations', ONS, 2nd August 2017   https://www.ons.gov.uk/peoplepopulationandcommunity/birthsdeathsandmarriages/deaths/bulletins/deathsrelatedtodrugpoisoninginenglandandwales/2016registrations

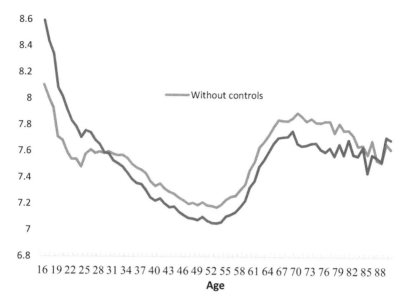

Fig. 19.1 Life Satisfaction Polynomial in Understanding Society ONS Data (United Kingdom; 416,000 observations). Years 2011–2015.This figure is based on data using the question *"Overall, how satisfied are you with your life nowadays?"* scored from zero to 10. To aid in understanding the size of the age effect, the coefficients on marital separation and unemployment in a life-satisfaction equation here are approximately −0.3 and −0.8. The figure is constructed by estimating a regression equation with approximately 74 separate age dummy variables. These curves are plots of the age coefficients. Because of the large sample sizes, levels of statistical significance in the paper are high, so for clarity the confidence intervals here, and later, are left off the paper's figures; they are available upon request

of those is a measure of citizens' overall life satisfaction. The details and sampling methods are discussed at website www.ons.gov.uk/well-being.

Figure 19.1, and each of the later figures in this paper, lays out two kinds of plots. One is for raw averaged life-satisfaction scores at different ages. This is the descriptive approach, advocated by, for example, Glenn (2009). The other, derived from a regression equation in which other covariates (so-called 'controls') are included, is the regression-adjusted level of life-satisfaction. This can be thought of as an estimate of the pure or 'marginal' effect of ageing. It can be seen in the Figure that the two curves are similar to one another, so in this case the adjustment for controls does not greatly affect the fundamental conclusions.

What comes out of Fig. 19.1 is a broad, and perhaps surprisingly smooth, pattern. Well-being starts high in youth; it then declines reasonably steadily (apart from a blip around the mid-20s) until approximately the age of 50; it then rises in a hill-like way up to approximately the age of 70; after that it declines slightly until the age of 90.

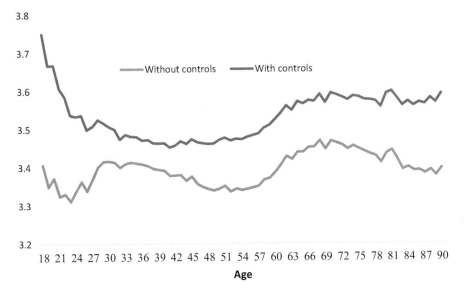

Fig. 19.2 Life Satisfaction Polynomial in BRFSS Data (USA; 427,000 observations). Year 2010. This figure is based on data using the question "In general, how satisfied are you with your life? Very dissatisfied ..., very satisfied." scored from 1 to 4. To aid in understanding the size of the age effect, the coefficients on marital separation and unemployment in a life-satisfaction equation here are approximately −0.3 and −0.3

The covariate controls in this case are gender, race, level of education, marital status, labor market status, region within the UK, and year dummies. The exact sample size is 415,589 and covers the years 2011–2015 inclusive.

USA (BRFSS Data)

Figure 19.2 plots life-satisfaction data for approximately 427,000 randomly sampled citizens of the USA. The data are from the Behavioral Factor Surveillance System, which is a survey run by the US Centres for Disease Control, available through www.cds.gov/brfss. The data are for 2010, which is the most recent year in which the BRFSS asked this question. As before, the Figure lays out two kinds of plots. One is for raw averaged life-satisfaction scores at different ages. The other, derived from a regression equation in which other covariates (so-called 'controls') are included, is the regression-adjusted level of life-satisfaction. It can be seen, as in Fig. 19.1 for UK data, that the two curves in Fig. 19.2 have some similarities to one another. There is apparently some form of midlife low, although now the adjusted nadir (that is, with controls) is closer to early-40s rather than approximately 50. However, the pattern across all ages in the no-controls case is more 'wavy' with an early dip at the start of people's 20s. Adjusted well-being in the USA starts high in youth, declines smoothly until the flat part in middle age; it then rises in hill-like way to approximately the age of 70; after that it runs roughly flat, or even fractionally up, until the age of 90.

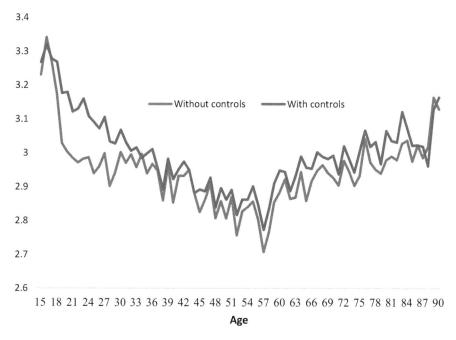

Fig. 19.3 Life Satisfaction Polynomial in Eurobarometer Data (36 nations; 32,000 observations). Year 2016.This figure is based on data using the question "On the whole, are you very satisfied, fairly satisfied, not very satisfied, or not at all satisfied with the life you lead?" scored from 1 to 4. To aid in understanding the size of the age effect, the coefficients on marital separation and unemployment in a life-satisfaction equation here are approximately −0.2 and −0.3

The controls in this case are gender, race, level of education, marital status, labor market status, disability dummy variable, number of children, and dummy variables for the state the person lives in within the US. The exact sample size is 426, 648.

19.2.1   Europe (Eurobarometer Data)

Figure 19.3 plots life-satisfaction data for approximately 32,000 randomly sampled citizens across a pooled set of 36 Europeans. The data are from the Eurobarometer Survey series, available through www.ec.europa.eu. Figure 19.3 has the previous form of double plot. One is for raw averaged life-satisfaction scores at different ages. The other is the regression-adjusted level of life-satisfaction. As in Fig. 19.1 for the UK, and to less extent in Fig. 19.2 for the USA, the two curves track each other. Thus, as before, in this case the adjustment for controls does not alter the fundamental result.

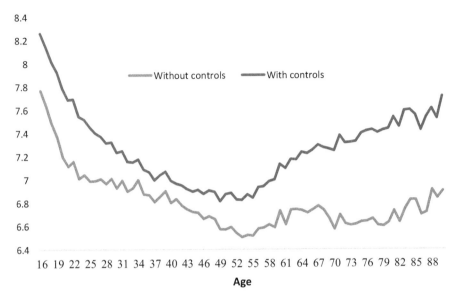

Fig. 19.4 Life Satisfaction Polynomial in ESS Data (32 European nations; 316,000 observations). Years 2002–2014. This figure is based on data using the question "All things considered, how satisfied are you with your life as a whole nowadays? Extremely dissatisfied, …, extremely satisfied." scored from zero to 10. To aid in understanding the size of the age effect, the coefficients on marital separation and unemployment in a life-satisfaction equation here are approximately −1.0 and −0.6

What comes out of Fig. 19.3 is a pattern very like the one in Fig. 19.1. Well-being starts high in youth; it falls in a fairly linear way to approximately the mid-50s; as an underlying trend, it then rises in a roughly linear way up to approximately the age of 90. The controls in this case are country dummy variables, gender, level of education, marital status, labor market status, and year dummies. The exact sample size is 32,857 and is for the year 2016.

19.2.2 Europe (ESS Data)

Using a different data set, Fig. 19.4 plots happiness data for approximately 316,000 randomly sampled Europeans. Here the data are from the European Social Survey, available from www.europeansocialsurvey.org. One curve is for raw averaged happiness scores at different ages. The other allows for controls in the equation for happiness. It can be seen in the Figure that the two curves have elements in common. However, allowing for controls gives a more pronounced V shape. Nevertheless, in both of the shapes within Fig. 19.4, well-being starts high in youth; it then drops until approximately the early 50; it then goes up quite strongly in the adjusted case and rather mildly in the raw-data case. The controls in the ESS regression are gender,

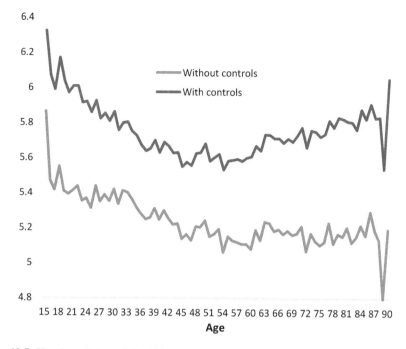

Fig. 19.5 Happiness Polynomial in ISSP Data (41 nations; 59,000 observations). Year 2012. This figure is based on data using the question "If you were to consider your life in general, how happy or unhappy would you say you are, on the whole? Completely happy, ..., fairly unhappy" scored from zero to 5. To aid in understanding the size of the age effect, the coefficients on marital separation and unemployment in a happiness equation here are approximately −0.5 and −0.5

level of education, marital status, labor market status, country dummy variables, and year dummies. The exact sample size is 316,509 and covers years 2002–2014 inclusive.

19.2.3   Multi-country (ISSP Data)

Figure 19.5 plots happiness data for just over 59,000 randomly sampled citizens from 45 nations of the world. The data come from the International Social Survey Program, available through www.issp.org, and the 41 countries are as follows (Argentina, Australia, Austria, Belgium, Bulgaria, Canada, Chile, China, Taiwan, Croatia, Czech Republic, Denmark, Finland, France, Germany, Hungary, Iceland, N-India, Ireland, Israel, Japan, South Korea (South), Latvia, Lithuania, Mexico, Netherlands, Norway, Philippines, Poland, Portugal, Russia, Slovakia, Slovenia, South Africa, Spain, Sweden, Switzerland, Turkey, United Kingdom, United States and Venezuela). Here the unadjusted curve takes a slightly different form: it falls in the usual way until around age 50, but then it runs essentially flat into older age.

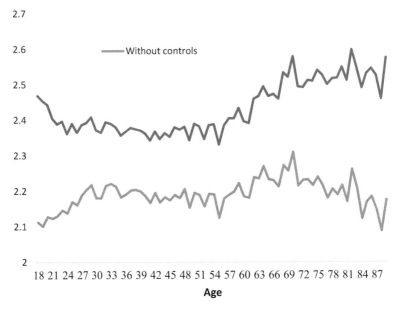

Fig. 19.6 Happiness Polynomial in the GSS Data (USA; 54,000 observations). Years 1972–2014. This figure is based on data using the question "Taken all together, how would you say things are these days – would you say that you are very happy, pretty happy, or not too happy?" scored from 1 to 3. To aid in understanding the size of the age effect, the coefficients on marital separation and unemployment in a happiness equation here are approximately −0.3 and −0.4

Despite the evident irregularities, it can be seen in the case with controls that, once more, well-being starts high in youth; it then declines fairly systematically until approximately the age of 50; from then on it rises in a reasonably linear way up to approximately the late 80s. The controls in this case are country dummies, gender, years of education, marital status, and labor market status. The exact sample size is 59,156 and is for the year 2012.

19.2.4   USA (GSS Data)

The sixth data set is described in Fig. 19.6. It plots happiness data for approximately 54,000 randomly sampled citizens of the USA. The data are from the long-running General Social Survey of the United States, available at www.gss.norc.org.

   In Fig. 19.6, there is a marked difference in shape between the adjusted and unadjusted curves. In the no-controls case, there is almost no sign of a U shape. Instead, the data are more consistent with a flat line (with uneven jumps in it). However, what emerges from Fig. 19.6 once controls are allowed for is a version of a more familiar pattern. There is some sign of a U shape (of a shallow kind) and then a climb up in well-being from approximately the early 50s until the early 70s, after

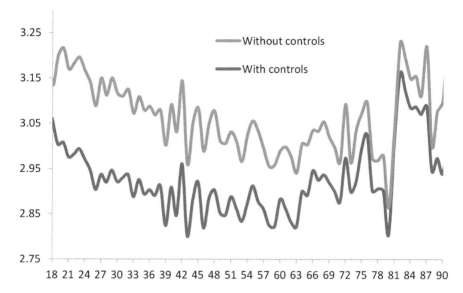

Fig. 19.7 Life Satisfaction Polynomial in the Latino Barometer Data (18 nations; 43,000 observations). Years 2013 and 2015 pooled. This figure is based on data using the question "Generally speaking, would you say you are satisfied with your life?" scored from 1 to 4. To aid in understanding the size of the age effect, the coefficients on marital separation and unemployment in a happiness equation here are approximately −0.1 and −0.2

which the trend is nearly flat. The controls in this case are gender, race, level of education, marital status, labor market status, and year dummies. The exact sample size is 54,532 and covers the years 1972–2014 inclusive.

19.2.5   Multi-country (Latino Barometer Data)

Figure 19.7 plots life satisfaction data for approximately 43,000 randomly sampled citizens from 18 Latin American nations of the world. The data come from the Latino Barometer Program, available through www.latinobarometro.org, and the 18 countries are Argentina, Bolivia, Brazil, Canada, Chile, Colombia, Costa Rica, Dominican Republic, Ecuador, El Salvador, Guatemala, Honduras, Mexico, Nicaragua, Panama, Paraguay, Peru and Venezuela.

Here the unadjusted curve takes a broadly U-shaped, but slightly irregular, form: it falls in the usual way until midlife, and rises somewhat jerkily into older age. It can be seen in the case with controls that once more well-being starts high in youth; after that it declines; the pattern then rises in a nonlinear way up to approximately the late 80s.

The controls in this case are country dummies, gender, years of education, marital status, and labor market status. The sample size is 42,913 and covers years 2013 and 2015.

19.3 Discussion

Five points seem relevant. First, it is natural to emphasize that, as in most writings in the literature, the data used in this paper are cross-sectional. It might be argued that longitudinal data are, in principle, the desirable kind of testbed. How serious a concern is that? A well-known early paper by Mroczec and Spiro (2005) concludes that well-being is hump-shaped in age, and is thus sometimes quoted as longitudinal evidence against a U pattern, but in fact its data begins from midlife, so an initial rise might be expected. There is a correction for cohort effects in Blanchflower and Oswald (2008), and there are emerging panel results, such as Cheng et al. (2017), in which in four longitudinal data sets a U shape is found. Perhaps the most effective longitudinal evidence against a midlife low is the potentially important work of Galambos et al. (2015) on Canadian data. It is not currently possible to know why the small number of modern longitudinal studies do not currently agree with one another.

However, there is an important case to be made against the sole use of longitudinal data. What has not often been pointed out in the literature is that longitudinal data sets have a drawback. They face the problem of non-random attrition. In the case of Galambos et al. (2015), for example, half of the sample drop out through time in the study. It remains an open question whether that allows reliable inferences to be drawn (if, as seems plausible, unhappy people decline to answer survey questionnaires, for example).

Moreover, there remains the intriguing intellectual question: why do so many pooled cross-section data sets produce a U shape? It therefore seems appropriate to treat large cross-sectional samples, of the sort used in this paper's analysis, as offering one form of evidence that will eventually have to be understood.

Second, perhaps the midlife decline is substantively tiny, even if statistically significant? If so, the data can in practice be viewed as approximately flat through the course of life. That view does not appear to be correct. In our seven data sets, as explained in the Figures, the size of the drop in well-being to the low point in the late 40s *is equivalent in magnitude to the influence of a major life event* like unemployment or marital separation.

Third, it might be argued, as by Glenn (2009), that it is inappropriate to include covariate controls. It is hard to see why that methodological position – one that is the opposite of standard practice in some disciplines – is an inevitable one (the issues is discussed in Blanchflower and Oswald 2009). In general, scientific researchers do not wish solely to describe the patterns that are observed in the world. This paper suggests that two approaches – descriptive and analytical – are possible, that neither is the right one, and that both have their place and, ultimately, have to be reconciled.

Fourth, perhaps a U form is found only for 'evaluative' measures of well-being, and those do not do justice to the complexity of human feelings? Large-scale data sets on experiential or eudemonic measures are rare; more research is needed here. Nevertheless, the Appendix shows in Fig. 19.8 that, for a question in the United Kingdom for Worthwhileness of Life, there is again a U-shaped pattern.

Fifth, perhaps the putative midlife low is due to cohort effects? However, it is not easy to see why cohort effects would work in such a similar way in different countries and time periods, and there is other evidence, including some longitudinal, against any simple version of such an explanation. Moreover, any such cohort effects would themselves presumably be important to document and understand.

19.4   Conclusions

There is much evidence, in Figs. 19.1, 19.2, 19.3, 19.4, 19.5 and 19.6, that humans experience a midlife psychological 'low'. The decline in well-being is apparently substantial and not minor (see the notes below each Figure, which compare to the coefficients on major life events). Our own view is that these kinds of plots of happiness and life satisfaction should be shown – with a discussion of appropriate caveats – to all young psychologists and economists. However, in the interests of scientific completeness, it is important to note exceptions to this conclusion; the paper documents two cases out of seven where if all controls are omitted the dip is not found. Finally, the Appendix offers evidence of a U shape for a measure of 'worthwhileness of life', so the idea of a midlife low does not rest solely on happiness or life-satisfaction data.

In the descriptive approach, in which raw data are plotted, five of the seven data sets suggest evidence of a midlife low and some form of U-shape. In the ceteris paribus approach, all seven data sets point to the existence of a midlife low and a U-shaped curve. In this latter case, the regression equations allow for confounding influences – including education and marriage – upon happiness and life satisfaction. In this paper, we have studied data up to the age of 90. Sample sizes after this point become small, and non-random, and it would presumably not be sensible to believe that human beings tend to be happy in the few years before they die. We are not able to say why the General Social Survey data set is so different, in its raw patterns than the others. After adjustment, it traces out the same kind of U shape as other sources. The important work of Easterlin (2006) and Glenn (2009), which uses the GSS, has had considerable influence, and is often cited by critics of the idea of U-shaped well-being. It therefore seems important for researchers to know that the pattern in the General Social Survey appears to be unrepresentative of most modern data sets.

Much remains to be understood in this intriguing area of quantitative social science – one in which Richard Easterlin has been an immense intellectual figure.

Appendix

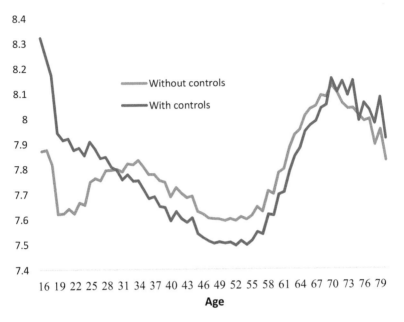

Fig. 19.8 Worthwhileness-of-Life Polynomial in Understanding-Society ONS Data (United Kingdom; 416,000 observations) Years 2011–2015. This figure is based on data using the question "Overall, to what extent do you feel the things you do in your life are worthwhile?" scored from zero to 10

References

Argyle, M. (2001). *The psychology of happiness* (2nd ed.). London: Routledge.

Baird, B., Lucas, R. E., & Donovan, M. B. (2010). Life satisfaction across the life span: Findings from two nationally representative panel studies. *Social Indicators Research, 99*, 183–203.

Blanchflower, D. G., & Oswald, A. J. (2008). Is well-being U-shaped over the life cycle? *Social Science & Medicine, 66*, 1733–1749.

Blanchflower, D. G., & Oswald, A. J. (2009). The U-shape without controls: A response to Glenn. *Social Science & Medicine, 69*, 486–488.

Carstensen, L. L., Turan, B., Scheibe, S., Ram, R., Ersnser-Hershfield, H., Samanez-Larkin, G. R., Brooks, K. P., & Nesselroade, J. R. (2011). Emotional experience improves with age: Evidence based on over 10 years of experience sampling. *Psychology and Aging, 26*, 21–33.

Charles, S. T., Reynolds, C. A., & Gatz, M. (2001). Age-related differences and change in positive and negative affect over 23 years. *Journal of Personality and Social Psychology, 80*, 136–151.

Cheng, T., Powdthavee, N., & Oswald, A. J. (2017). Longitudinal evidence for a midlife nadir: Result from four data sets. *Economic Journal, 127*, 126–142.

Diener, E., Suh, E. M., Lucas, R. E., & Smith, H. L. (1999). Subjective well-being: Three decades of progress. *Psychological Bulletin, 125*(2), 276–302.

Easterlin, R. A. (2003). Explaining happiness. *Proceedings of the National Academy of Sciences, 100*, 11176–11183.

Easterlin, R. A. (2006). Life cycle happiness and its sources: Intersections of psychology, economics and demography. *Journal of Economic Psychology, 27*, 463–482.

Frey, B. S., & Stutzer, A. (2002). *Happiness and economics*. Princeton: Princeton University Press.

Frijters, P., & Beaton, T. (2012). The mystery of the U-shaped relationship between happiness and age. *Journal of Economic Behavior & Organization, 82*, 525–542.

Galambos, N. L., Fang, S., Krahn, H. J., Johnson, M. D., & Lachman, M. E. (2015). Up, not down: The age curve in happiness from early adulthood to midlife in two longitudinal studies. *Developmental Psychology, 51*, 1664–1671.

Gerstorf, D., Ram, N., Mayraz, G., Hidajat, M., Lindenberger, U., Wagner, G. G., & Schupp, J. (2010). Late life decline in well-being across adulthood in Germany, the United Kingdom and the United States: Something is seriously wrong at the end of life. *Psychology and Aging, 25*, 477–485.

Glenn, N. D. (2009). Is the apparent U-shape of well-being over the life course a result of inappropriate use of control variables? A commentary on Blanchflower and Oswald. *Social Science and Medicine, 69*, 481–485.

Graham, C., & Pozuelo, J. R. (2017). Happiness, stress, and age: How the U curve varies across people and places. *Journal of Population Economics, 30*, 225–264.

Hellevik, O. (2017). The U-shaped age-happiness relationship: real or methodological artifact? *Quality & Quantity, 51*, 177–197.

Helliwell, J., & Grover, S. (2014). *How's life at home? New evidence on marriage and the set point for happiness* (NBER Working Paper #20794). Cambridge, MA: National Bureau of Economic Research.

Hudson, N. W., Lucas, R. E., & Donellan, M. B. (2016). Getting older, feeling less? A cross-sectional and longitudinal investigation of developmental patterns in experiential well-being. *Psychology and Aging, 31*, 847–861.

Lachman, M. E. (2015). Mind the gap in the middle: A call to study midlife. *Research in Human Development, 12*, 327–334.

Mroczek, D. K., & Kolanz, C. M. (1998). The effect of age on positive and negative affect: A developmental perspective on happiness. *Journal of Personality and Social Psychology, 75*, 1333–1349.

Mroczek, D. K., & Spiro, A. (2005). Change in life satisfaction during adulthood: Findings from the veterans affairs normative aging study. *Journal of Personality and Social Psychology, 88*, 189–202.

Schwandt, H. (2016). Unmet aspirations as an explanation for the age U-shape in well-being. *Journal of Economic Behavior & Organization, 122*, 75–87.

Shields, M. A., & Wheatley Price, S. (2005). Exploring the economic and social determinants of psychological well-being and perceived social support in England. *Journal of the Royal Statistical Society, Series A, 168*, 513–537.

Steptoe, A., Deaton, A., & Stone, A. A. (2015). Subjective wellbeing, health, and ageing. *Lancet, 385*, 640–648.

Stone, A. A., Schwartz, J. E., Broderick, J. E., & Deaton, A. (2010). A snapshot of the age distribution of psychological well-being in the United States. *Proceedings of the National Academy of Sciences of the USA, 107*, 9985–9990.

Ulloa, B. F. L., Moller, V., & Sousa-Poza, A. (2013). How does subjective well-being evolve with age? A literature review. *Journal of Population Ageing, 6*, 227–246.

Weiss, A., King, J. E., Inoue-Murayam, M., Matsuzama, T., & Oswald, A. J. (2012). Evidence for a midlife crisis in great apes consistent with the U-shape in human well-being. *Proceedings of the National Academy of Sciences USA, 109*, 19949–19952.

Wunder, C., Wiencierz, A., Schwarze, J., & Küchenhoff, H. (2013). Well-being over the life span: Semiparametric evidence from British and German longitudinal data. *Review of Economics and Statistics, 95*, 154–167.

Chapter 20
Happiness at Different Ages: The Social Context Matters

John F. Helliwell, Haifang Huang, Max B. Norton, and Shun Wang

Abstract This paper uses a variety of individual-level survey data from several countries to test for interactions between subjective well-being at different ages and variables measuring the nature and quality of the social context at work, at home, and in the community. While earlier studies have found important age patterns (often U-shaped) and social context effects, these two sets of variables have generally been treated as mutually independent. We test for and find several large and highly significant interactions. Results are presented for life evaluations and (in some surveys) for happiness yesterday, in models with and without other control variables. The U-shape in age is found to be significantly flatter, and well-being in the middle of the age range higher, for those who are in workplaces with partner-like superiors, for those living as couples, and for those who have lived for longer in their communities. A strong sense of community belonging is associated with greater life satisfaction at all ages, but especially so at ages 60 and above, in some samples deepening the U-shape in age by increasing the size of the life satisfaction gains following the mid-life low.

An earlier version of this chapter appeared as NBER Working Paper 25121, October 2018.

J. F. Helliwell (✉) · M. B. Norton
Vancouver School of Economics, University of British Columbia, Vancouver, BC, Canada
e-mail: john.helliwell@ubc.ca

H. Huang
University of Alberta, Edmonton, AB, Canada
e-mail: haifang.huang@ualberta.ca

S. Wang
KDI School of Public Policy and Management, Sejong, South Korea
e-mail: swang@kdis.ac.kr

© Springer Nature Switzerland AG 2019
M. Rojas (ed.), *The Economics of Happiness*,
https://doi.org/10.1007/978-3-030-15835-4_20

455

20.1 Introduction

A variety of research has shown that life satisfaction in many countries shows a U-shape over the life course, with a low point about the age of 50.[1] But there is a lot of variability too, with some countries showing little or no tendency to rise after middle age,[2] while elsewhere there is evidence of an S-shape, with the growing life evaluations after middle age declining again in the late 70s.[3] The existence and size of these trends depend on whether they are measured with or without excluding the effects of physical health, which by both clinical and subjective measures[4] declines steadily over the life course. Rises in average life evaluations after middle age are seen in some countries even without excluding the increasing negative effects due to health status, which gradually worsens with age. Because the U-shape in age is quite prevalent, some researchers have thought that it might represent something beyond the scope of human life experiences, since it has been found in a similar form among great apes.[5] Studies using longitudinal panels have sometime failed to produce significant U-shapes.[6]

This paper builds upon two of Richard Easterlin's important contributions: his early emphasis on the social determinants of happiness, and his later analysis of well-being over the life course. In his life-course analysis he made two primary contributions.[7] First, he broke new ground in using synthetic panels constructed from repeated cross-sections to separate life-course and cohort effects.[8] He was able to show, as recently confirmed by Clark (2018) using panel data with individual fixed effects, that the age pattern of life satisfaction is not primarily due to cohort effects. Second, he compared life-course patterns for several different measures of domain satisfaction, and found different shapes for each. He then concluded that the time-shape of life satisfaction was likely to represent the net impact of what was going on in different aspects of people's lives.

Easterlin found, using data from the US General Social Survey (GSS), that life satisfaction had a hump shape in age, with a peak where many other studies have found a trough. Subsequent research has shown his GSS data and results to differ from most other surveys for the United States and for most industrial countries, as

---

[1]For example, see Latten (1989), Clark and Oswald (2006), Van Landeghem (2012), Cheng et al. (2015), and Blanchflower and Oswald (2004, 2008, 2009, 2016, 2018).

[2]See Steptoe et al. (2015) and Fortin et al. (2015).

[3]See Bonke et al. (2017), Wunder et al. (2013), and Laaksonen (2018).

[4]For example, Steptoe et al. (2015, Figures 18.1 to 18.4) show self reports of experienced pain to become steadily more frequent as age increases in all four major groups of countries reviewed.

[5]See Weiss et al. (2015).

[6]See Fritjers and Beatton (2012) and Kassenboehmer and Haisken-DeNew (2012).

[7]See Easterlin (2006).

[8]If the sequence of cross-sections is large and frequent enough, this procedure provides a promising way to solve the age/cohort separation problems raised in the U-shape context by De Ree and Alessie (2011), Schilling (2006) and others.

surveyed and extended most recently by Blanchflower and Oswald (2018), almost all of which show U-shapes in age with or without adjusting for a variety of control variables. While we also find, using several different data sources, a U-shape in life satisfaction in many but not all countries, we agree with and implement Easterlin's suggestion that the U-shape, or any other given shape, is not inevitable, but instead reflects the evolution of important aspects of each person's life.[9]

We pay special attention in this paper to social conditions in the workplace, the home, and the community. In all three cases, we expect to find that life satisfaction is higher in those age ranges where the relevant social context is more important and more supportive. Although our analysis is mainly across individuals living in the same country, we would expect to find that cross-national differences in the quality of the institutions providing social support might also help determine cross-national differences in the U-shape in age. That must remain a topic for future research.

Our particular hypothesis is that various aspects of each individual's social context help to explain their life satisfaction at different ages. We initially test this by simply comparing average happiness values at different ages for respondents in different subgroups where we expect to see possible differences. There are two reasons for starting with this simple approach. First, it avoids debates[10] about whether the specific choice of control variables affects the conclusions about the U-shape without explaining why. Second, Blanchflower and Oswald (2018) and Stone et al. (2010) show that the usual sets of control variables neither create nor eliminate the prevalence of a U-shape in their data samples. However, to increase the robustness of our findings, and because our social variables are likely to be correlated with some of the standard control variables, we undertake the main body of our analysis using otherwise comparable econometric specifications with and without control variables. Our methods are exactly the same as theirs, with one critical difference. Their analysis treats each of the variables as independent, while we hypothesize that some key social relationships might in fact interact with age. After this initial survey, we shall then test our hypotheses more explicitly within a matched pair of models, one without and the other with standard sets of control variables used in modelling individual-level data for subjective well-being.

If we are right to suppose that the age patterns found for subjective well-being are often reflections of a changing pattern of social relationships, then they are likely to appear in some places and not in others, and for some people but not others, depending on the social circumstances in which they live. As the empirical science of well-being has developed, and as the available data become richer, it is becoming natural to consider not just the possible separate effects of, e.g. age, marriage, employment, income, and the social context, but also to consider the quality and complexity of their interactions. The primary contribution of this paper is to test for interactions that are usually left untested. Most previous analyses of these data have

---

[9]For example, Schwandt (2016), using German panel data, argues that the U-shape is more prevalent among those respondents with unmet expectations for the evolution of their happiness.

[10]For example, see the exchange between Glenn (2009) and Blanchflower and Oswald (2009).

presumed linear independence, with the exceptions of a log-linear form for income and a non-linear form for age itself. Age is sometimes modelled by age groups but more usually by a quadratic form including both age and age-squared, with an expected negative sign on age and a positive sign on age-squared, as would be implied by a U-shape in age. In this paper we prefer the greater generality provided by the use of population age groups, thus permitting us to see at which particular ages the social context effects are most evident. In the following sections we consider interactions between age and specific measures of the social context on the job, at home, and in the community. All of these measures of the social context have been found previously to have positive effects on life evaluations. By including interaction terms, we are now able to show that these effects vary by age group, with the better social context having its largest effects in the middle age groups, thereby lessening the U-shape in age. We also do parallel analysis using an affective measure relating to each respondent's feelings of happiness on the previous day when our data sources permit it.

20.2   Assessing the U-Shape Consequences of the Workplace Social Context

Our general hypothesis is that the social context is a first-order determinant of subjective well-being to an extent that varies with the age of the respondent. For instance, in this section, we hypothesize that workplace social quality is more important for subjective well-being in mid-life than elsewhere, since mid-life years are for many people a time of stress created by competing demands from their work and family lives, and since these pressures are more easily reconciled when the workplace environment is more congenial and supportive.[11] Our primary data for testing this hypothesis come from large samples of employed respondents to the Gallup-Healthways Daily Poll, comparing those who regard their immediate work superior as a partner with those who instead think of their supervisor as a boss. Figure 20.1 shows the average ladder scores for the two groups of respondents. Those who regard their supervisor as a partner have at all ages life evaluations that are significantly higher than for those with boss-like superiors. The vertical lines show the 95% confidence intervals for the estimates of the subgroup means. The tightness of these intervals reflects the fact that the samples are very large in both

---

[11]We find evidence for this from a sample combining several waves of life satisfaction data from the Canadian General Social Survey. Regressions of individual SWL on work/life balance, marital status and length of tenure in one's neighbourhood, done separately for the population divided into three age groups, show that the impact of the self-assessed quality of work/life balance is ten times greater for those in the 45–54 age group than for older workers. It is 50% greater than for younger workers. By way of comparison, the coefficients for marital status and length of tenure in the neighbourhood are the same for middle-aged and older workers, while being less for younger workers.

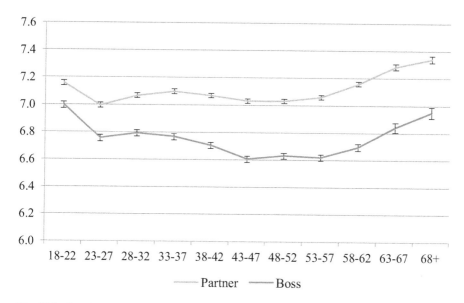

Fig. 20.1 Cantril ladder for US employees of different ages with different types of supervisor, US Gallup-Healthways Daily Poll

cases, while the big vertical distance between the two lines shows dramatically different life evaluations for the two groups of US workers. In the middle of the age range, from ages 43–47, the difference favours those with partner-like supervisors by just over 0.4 points on the 0–10 scale used for the Cantril ladder. This is a very large difference, equivalent in life satisfaction terms to more than a doubling of household income. The fact that the confidence regions are larger for those who select the 'boss' alternative shows that in the large US samples there are more partners than bosses in US workplaces, by about a two to one margin.

The most important feature of Fig. 20.1, for our current purposes, is that those with partner-like bosses show no significant drop in life evaluations between the late 20s and the early 50s, while for those with boss-like supervisors there is a large drop, about 0.2 points on the 0–10 scale. Both groups of workers show similarly large gains in life evaluations from mid-50s to age 70. Thus there is a significant U-shape for those with bosses, while for those in partner-like settings there is no mid-life dip.

Figure 20.2 shows parallel results from a question asking workers about their happiness yesterday, a measure of positive affect answered in this case on a binary scale. The figure shows the proportion of the sampled populations who described themselves as being frequently happy on the previous day. In proportionate terms, the differences between the boss and partner groups are roughly of the same size for positive affect as for life evaluations, but the time pattern is different in two

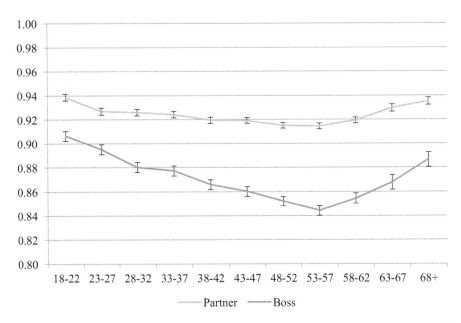

Fig. 20.2 Happiness (yesterday) for US employees of different ages with different types of supervisor, US Gallup-Healthways Daily Poll

important ways.[12] First, it can be seen by comparing Figs. 20.1 and 20.2 that the happiness drops for those with boss-like supervisors are larger and longer lasting than they are for life evaluations. There is essentially no drop in happiness for those with partner-like supervisors. For those with boss-like supervisors, however, the proportion reporting happiness yesterday drops from 0.90 at age 27 to just over 0.84 in the 53–57 age range.[13]

The second difference relates to weekend effects. We can separate the responses to the life evaluations and positive affect questions according to the day the survey was taken. We divide them into two groups, split according to whether or not the preceding day was a regular workday or not.[14] We do not know the work schedules for individual respondents, so our sample split is instead based on the fact that Mondays to Fridays are more frequent workdays than are Saturdays and Sundays. Figure 20.3 shows that there are no weekend effects for life evaluations. Regardless of the day on which the question is asked, respondents with boss-like supervisors have lower life evaluations than those with partner-like supervisors, while within

---

[12]Xing and Huang (2014) also find U-shapes that vary for different measures of subjective well-being, in their case based on Chinese data.

[13]Stone et al. (2010), using an earlier and smaller sample of data from the same Gallup Daily Poll, also show a later trough for positive affect than for the ladder, in their case looking at the whole population.

[14]The data and procedures are explained more fully in Helliwell and Wang (2015).

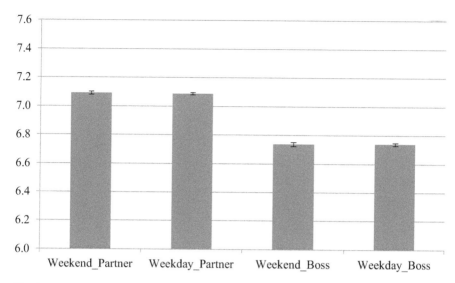

Fig. 20.3 Cantril ladder on weekends and weekdays for different types of supervisors in US, US Gallup-Healthways Daily Poll

each respondent group, no significant change occurs between weekdays and week-ends. This lack of change is reassuring evidence of the quality of life evaluations, which are intended to relate to life as a whole, and not to a particular day. But our data also provide assurance against another possible source of scepticism: that happier people will think better of everyone, so that their partner/boss responses reflect their personalities rather than their workplaces. The answers for the question about happiness yesterday eliminate the grounds for such a possibility, because they show, as can be seen in Fig. 20.4, very pronounced weekend effects that are much larger for those with boss-like supervisors. If the workplace environment, rather than personality differences, is the underlying cause of the different answers, then we should expect to see the relief at being off work being much greater for those in less congenial workplaces. And that is indeed what we find. On the other hand, if happier people are more likely to rate their supervisors as partners, then they would be equally happy every day, and not just on weekends away from their boss-like supervisors.

   If the U-shape in age is largely a consequence of the social contexts of different aspects and times of life, then we might also expect to find differences across nations and cultures, and possibly over time as well. That is indeed the case, as shown by Fig. 20.5 showing population-weighted U-shapes for each of nine major global regions. While every region shows at least some drop from the young to middle ages, only two regions have well defined recoveries after middle age, and there are also considerable differences in the steepness of the drop from youth to middle age. Finding a role for the workplace social context in explaining these differences is complicated by the fact that the boss-partner question has only been asked in some countries of the Gallup World Poll, and the samples are in any event far smaller than

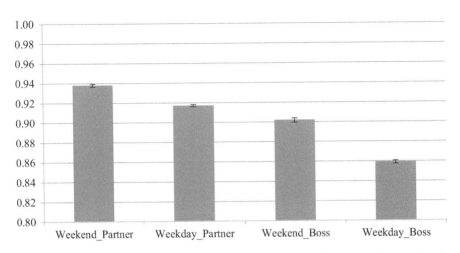

Fig. 20.4 Happiness (yesterday) on weekends and weekdays for different types of supervisors in US, US Gallup-Healthways Daily Poll

available from the Gallup-Healthways Daily Poll. If we combine the responses from employed workers in those countries in which the boss-partner question has been asked more than 100 and up to about 1000 times, we get a sample of 38,000 from 114 countries including some representation in all regions.[15]

Figure 20.6 divides the employed respondents by boss vs partner and into younger (<45), middle-aged (45–55) and older (>55) workers. Everywhere and at all ages, respondents with partner-type bosses have systematically higher life evaluations. Although there is no universal evidence of a U-shape linking the different age groups, the central element of our buffering hypothesis is supported by these international data – where midlife evaluations are compared to those of younger workers in similar job situation, the midlife evaluations fall less for those in partner-type job environments.

The results above are obtained simply by dividing the data samples for each age group according to whether they have partner-like or boss-like supervisors. We now need to ensure that these results still hold when due account is taken of all of the other variables often used to explain individual-level subjective well-being. This is advisable because many of these other variables may be correlated with answers to the partner/boss question, with estimates of the latter effect being falsely high or low, depending on the nature of the correlations. Our econometric analysis is conducted by estimating two different models in the US Gallup-Healthways Daily Poll, which has a much bigger usable sample than the international Gallup World Poll. The simpler model explains well-being using age categories, a dummy variable for a

---

[15]We exclude the larger samples from Russia, Germany and the United Kingdom (roughly 2000, 9000 and 10,000, respectively) because they are sufficient for separate analysis and are large enough to affect the overall findings from a pooled sample.

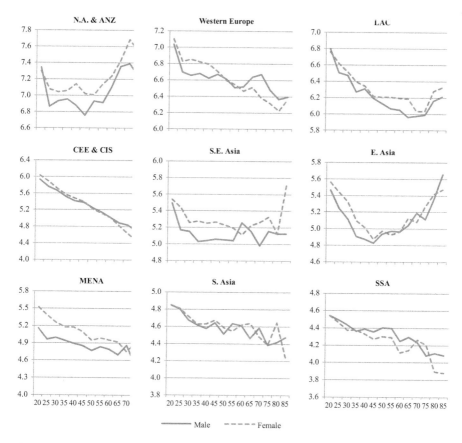

Fig. 20.5 Cantril Ladder by Gender in 9 World Regions, Gallup World Poll

partner-like supervisor, a full set of interaction terms between the partner variable and the age groups, plus dummy variables to capture state and year fixed effects. The second model adds a number of individual-level control variables.

More specifically, the base model for the working environment, estimated using data for employees only, is:

$$SWB_{ijt} = \alpha_0 + Agec_{ijt}\boldsymbol{\beta_1} + Agec_{ijt}Partner_{ijt}\boldsymbol{\beta_2} + \gamma_1 Partner_{ijt} + \mu_t + \rho_j + \varepsilon_{ijt} \tag{20.1}$$

where SWB_{ijt} indicates a subjective well-being measure of individual i in state j in year of survey t, $Agec_{ijt}$ is a vector of age groups (omitting the 18–22 base age group), $Partner_{ijt}$ is a dummy variable for supervisor being more like a partner than a boss, μ_t is a year fixed effect, ρ_j a state fixed effect, and ε_{ijt} is the error term.

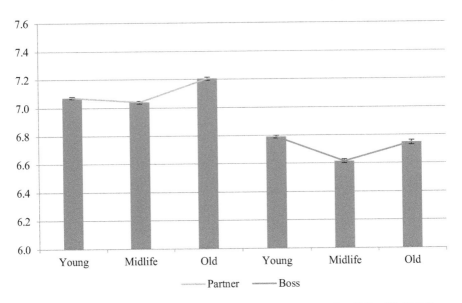

Fig. 20.6 Cantril ladder for different types of supervisors in 114 countries, Gallup World Poll

The corresponding model with controls added is:

$$SWB_{ijt} = \alpha_0 + Agec_{ijt}\beta_1 + Agec_{ijt}Partner_{ijt}\beta_2 + \gamma_1 Partner_{ijt} + X_{ijt}\theta + \mu_t + \rho_j + \varepsilon_{ijt} \tag{20.2}$$

where X_{ijt} is a vector of individual and household covariates, including gender, marital status, number of children, four levels of education (vs less than high-school completion), log of household income (with a dummy variable for those with income not reported), and full-time employment status (vs part-time).

The full results of the estimation are available in the online appendix materials, along with more detailed descriptions of the variables. The key results for this section of the paper relate to the coefficients for having a work supervisor regarded by the respondent as a partner rather than a boss. This is the case for about two-thirds of the employed US respondents to the Gallup-Healthways Daily Poll. In the base group, aged 18–22, having a partner-like supervisor is associated with a Cantril ladder score that is 0.166 points (t = 11.1) higher on the 0–10 scale. As shown in Fig. 20.7, this difference grows until middle age, and then declines, delivering a U-shape in age that is more pronounced for those with less congenial working environments. The red line in Fig. 20.7 shows the sum of the estimated β_1 and β_2 for each of the age group other than the omitted group (age 18–22). The lower line shows the estimated β_1. Thus the vertical gap between the two lines illustrates the magnitude of the estimated β_2 for each of the age groups. A wider gap indicates a greater positive impact on well-being of having a partner-like superior. We use an identical or similar thematic design for all of our subsequent figures.

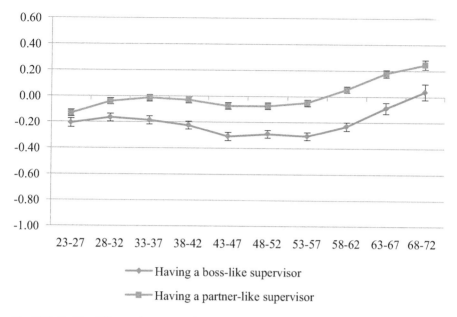

Fig. 20.7 Ladder difference between each age group and the youngest age group (18–22), partner vs boss, in the model without controls, US Gallup-Healthways Daily Poll

How well do these results hold up when we include the usual set of individual-level control variables? Our second model is essentially a conventional estimation for an individual-level subjective well-being equation, except that we add interaction terms for age and job quality. In most happiness equations, such interactions are assumed to be zero. Our alternative hypothesis is that the coefficients on the interaction variables will be significantly positive, with the departures from linearity being greatest in middle age. Figure 20.8 plots the U-shape results with control variables. For the youngest age group, the effect of having a partner-like supervisor is essentially unchanged, 0.162 (t = 10.8). For higher age groups, at least up to middle age, the effects are significantly greater, but by a smaller multiple than in the simpler model. Thus for those in the 43–47 age group the effects of having a partner-like supervisor are 0.143 points (t = 7.1) greater than for the youngest age group. Both the size and significance of the U-shape remains very large, even if smaller in magnitude than that in the simpler model. In the simple model, the effects of having a partner-like supervisor are 140% larger for the typical respondent in the 43–47-year category than for those aged 18–22. In the model with controls, the partner-like supervisor is associated with a life evaluation premium that is 88% larger for the 43–47 age group than for those aged 18–22. Hence we reject the null hypothesis that that partner premium does not vary with age.

This analysis is repeated for happiness yesterday in Figs. 20.9 and 20.10. With or without the inclusion of control variables, the maximum positive interaction effects appear at a later age, 53–57 for happiness yesterday compared to 43–47 for the

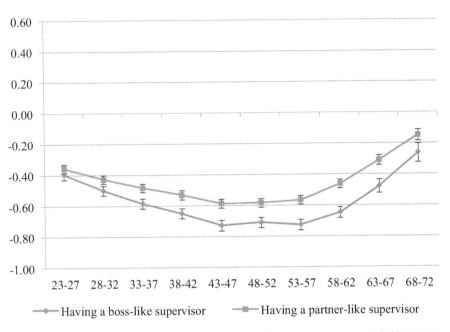

Fig. 20.8 Ladder difference between each age group and the youngest age group (18–22), partner vs boss, in the model with controls, US Gallup-Healthways Daily Poll

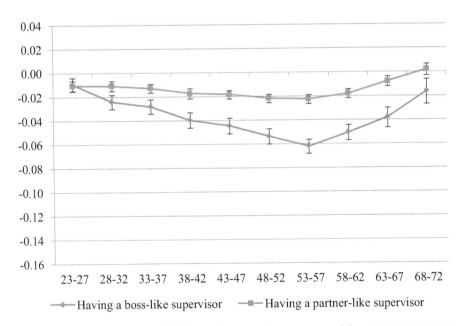

Fig. 20.9 Happiness (yesterday) difference between each age group and the youngest age group (18–22), partner vs boss, in the model without controls, US Gallup-Healthways Daily Poll

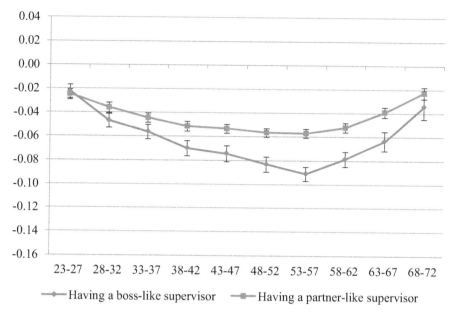

Fig. 20.10 Happiness (yesterday) difference between each age group and the youngest age group (18–22), partner vs boss, in the model with controls, US Gallup-Healthways Daily Poll

Cantril ladder. The happiness-yesterday effect of a partner-like supervisor is 0.023 in the simple model and 0.057 with controls (t = 10 in both cases). In proportionate terms, this is larger than for the life evaluations, although such comparisons are difficult to make, since the individual answers to the life evaluation question are on a 11-point response scale running from 0–10, while the happiness yesterday question offer only a binary yes/no response possibility. The age-group interaction effects are proportionately roughly the same for happiness as for life evaluations, except for the different age pattern already noted.

20.3   The U-Shape Is Flatter for Those Who Are Married

We turn now to consider the U-shape effects of marriage, both with and without control variables, and then return to consider interactions between the social contexts at home and at work. We hypothesize the U-shape in age is significantly less for those who are married than those who are not.[16] This supposes that together spouses can better shoulder the extra demands that may exist in mid-life when career and other demands coincide. This was found in earlier studies of adaptation to marriage, which showed that although it was true in longitudinal data sets from several

---

[16]See Grover and Helliwell (2017).

countries[17] that those who married often return to their baseline life evaluations after a few years, they were nonetheless significantly happier than their unmarried matched counterparts, whose happiness was following a steady decline. Thus marriage provides a buffer against what otherwise would have been a U-shaped decline into middle age.

So we hypothesize that, at least in some countries, a happy home life can flatten the U-shape, just as we have shown for happy workplaces. We do our main marriage analysis using US data for approximately 240,000 respondents to the Gallup-Healthways Daily Poll, more than twice the previous sample, which was restricted to paid employees.

The base model for marital status is:

$$SWB_{ijt} = \alpha_0 + Agec_{ijt}\boldsymbol{\beta_1} + Agec_{ijt}Marr_{ijt}\boldsymbol{\beta_2} + \gamma_1 Marr_{ijt} + \mu_t + \rho_j + \varepsilon_{ijt} \quad (20.3)$$

where SWB_{ijt} indicates subjective well-being measure, $Agec_{ijt}$ is a vector of age groups (omitting the base age group), $Marr_{ijt}$ is a dummy variable for marriage or common law, μ_t is year fixed effect, ρ_j is state fixed effect, and ε_{ijt} is the error term.

The model for marital status with controls is:

$$SWB_{ijt} = \alpha_0 + Agec_{ijt}\boldsymbol{\beta_1} + Agec_{ijt}Marr_{ijt}\boldsymbol{\beta_2} + \gamma_1 Marr_{ijt} + X_{ijt}\theta + \mu_t + \rho_j + \varepsilon_{ijt}$$
$$(20.4)$$

where X_{ijt} is a vector of individual and household covariates including employment status, gender, log of household income, level of education, and number of children.

Figures 20.11 and 20.12 compare the life evaluation U-shapes for married and unmarried respondents. Whether or not control variables are included, the life evaluations for the 18–22 age group are the same whether the respondents are married or not. Thereafter the coefficients on the interactive age variables (i.e. the vertical difference between the line for the married and the unmarried in Figs. 20.11 and 20.12) show an increasing pattern, with a peak in the 53–57 age category, of 0.78 (t = 31) in the simple model and 0.52 (t = 23) in the model with controls. With or without controls, the U-shape is much shallower for the married than the unmarried, to an extent that is quantitatively large and statistically very significant.

Figures 20.13 and 20.14 show the corresponding results for answers to the happiness yesterday question. The reduction in the depth of the U-shape is very large and significant in both cases. The coefficients on the age-marriage interaction terms in the 53–57 age group are +0.110 (t = 28) without controls and + 0.085 (t = 28) with controls.

Previous research using UK longitudinal data has shown marriage to be associated with substantially higher life evaluations even when pre-marriage life satisfaction is taken into account (Grover and Helliwell 2017). Additionally, large samples

---

[17]These included the United Kingdom (Yap et al. 2012), Switzerland (Anusic et al. 2014a) and Australia (Anusic et al. 2014b).

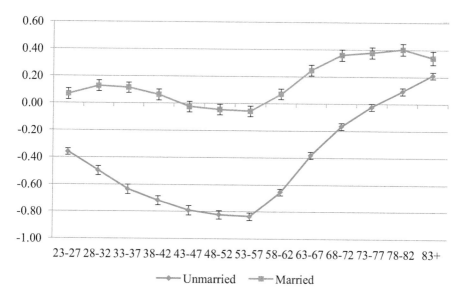

Fig. 20.11 Ladder difference between each age group and the youngest age group (18–22), married vs not, in the model without controls, US Gallup-Healthways Daily Poll

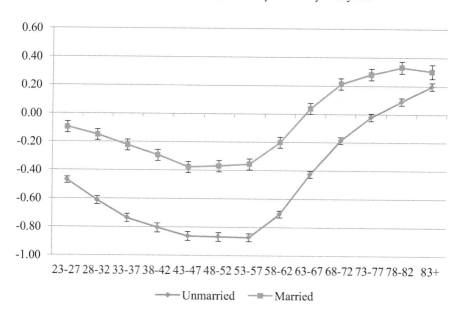

Fig. 20.12 Ladder difference between each age group and the youngest age group (18–22), married vs not, in the model with controls, US Gallup-Healthways Daily Poll

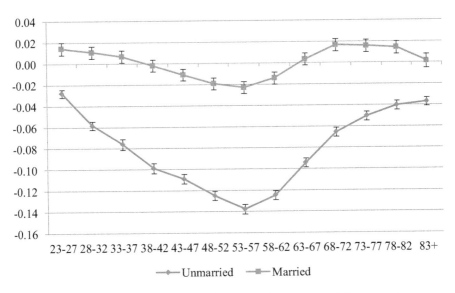

Fig. 20.13 Happiness (yesterday) difference between each age group and the youngest age group (18–22), married vs not, in the model without controls, US Gallup-Healthways Daily Poll

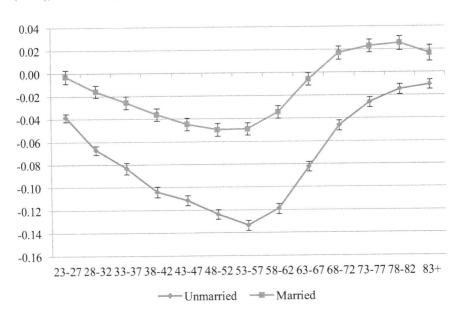

Fig. 20.14 Happiness (yesterday) difference between each age group and the youngest age group (18–22), married vs not, in the model with controls, US Gallup-Healthways Daily Poll

of cross-sectional data from the UK's Annual Population Survey (APS) showed the U-shape in age to be much flatter for the married, even when the comparison is done between the ever-married and the never-married to remove the selection out of marriage by separation and divorce (Grover and Helliwell 2017, Fig. 3). Because the UK APS asks about life satisfaction and about happiness yesterday, using identical 0–10 response scales, we can compare the U-shape consequences for life satisfaction and for happiness yesterday more consistently than is possible with the US data. We therefore repeated the analysis shown in Figs. 20.11, 20.12, 20.13 and 20.14 using the UK data, as reported in the statistical appendix. With or without controls, the U-shape is much shallower for the married than the unmarried for both life satisfaction and happiness yesterday. The coefficient on the age-marriage interaction term for life satisfaction in the 48–52 age group, which is at the bottom of the U-shape, is 0.46 points higher (t = 9.7) for the married than for the unmarried, with or without controls, relative to a comparison group comprising those aged 18–27. This is just slightly lower than was found in the model with controls applied to the US Gallup data in Figs. 20.11 and 20.12. For happiness yesterday, on the same 0–10-point scale, the interaction coefficient is +0.35 points (t = 6.2). Thus the U-shape effects of marriage in the UK data are somewhat greater for life satisfaction than for happiness yesterday, while being large and statistically significant in both cases.

20.4 Assessing the Combined Effects of the Social Context at Work and at Home

We now use the large data samples provided from the US Gallup Daily Poll to show the U-shape differences for two-way interactions between the social context of the working environment and marriage with and without the use of the fuller sets of controls frequently used in the explanation of subjective well-being. Once again, we do this using both the Cantril ladder and happiness yesterday as alternative measures of subjective well-being.

The base model for two-way interactions between working environment and marital status is:

$$
\begin{aligned}
SWB_{ijt} = {} & \alpha_0 + Agec_{ijt}\beta_1 + Agec_{ijt}Marr_{ijt}\beta_2 + Agec_{ijt}Partner_{ijt}\beta_3 \\
& + Agec_{ijt}Marr_{ijt}Partner_{ijt}\beta_4 + \gamma_1 Marr_{ijt} + \gamma_2 Partner_{ijt} \\
& + \gamma_3 Marr_{ijt}Partner_{ijt} + \mu_t + \rho_j + \varepsilon_{ijt},
\end{aligned}
\tag{20.5}
$$

The model for two-way interactions between working environment and marital status with controls is:

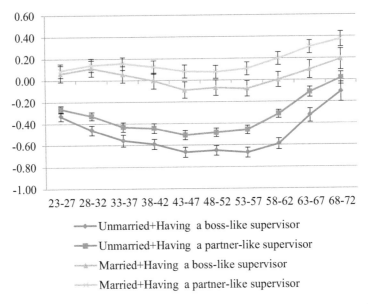

Fig. 20.15 Ladder difference between each age group and the youngest age group (18–22), combined, in the model without controls, US Gallup-Healthways Daily Poll

$$
\begin{aligned}
SWB_{ijt} = {} & \alpha_0 + Agec_{ijt}\boldsymbol{\beta_1} + Agec_{ijt}Marr_{ijt}\boldsymbol{\beta_2} + Agec_{ijt}Partner_{ijt}\boldsymbol{\beta_3} \\
& + Agec_{ijt}Marr_{ijt}Partner_{ijt}\boldsymbol{\beta_4} + \gamma_1 Marr_{ijt} + \gamma_2 Partner_{ijt} \\
& + \gamma_3 Marr_{ijt}Partner_{ijt} + X_{ijt}\theta + \mu_t + \rho_j + \varepsilon_{ijt}
\end{aligned}
\tag{20.6}
$$

The coefficient γ_3 estimates the interaction effects between marriage and the social context on the job for respondents in the 18–22 age group, while the coefficients $\boldsymbol{\beta_4}$ show the corresponding interaction effects for each age group. Almost universally, these interaction effects are small and statistically insignificant, for both life evaluations and happiness yesterday, and for equations with and without control variables. We nonetheless include these small effects in the calculations shown in Figs. 20.15, 20.16, 20.17 and 20.18. The estimation sample is essentially the same as was used for the workplace equations, so that the marriage results are now those for employed workers, rather than the full population sample used for the earlier marriage results. By comparing the marriage effects in the two samples, we find that the U-shape effects of marriage are less for the sample of employed workers than they were previously found to be for the larger sample including the self-employed, the unemployed, and those not in the labor force. For the 53–57 age group, the marriage coefficient is about 10% smaller in the employed sample, while for happiness yesterday it is about 25% smaller. Thus, while the marriage premium appears to be independent of work quality, it is not independent of employment status in general.

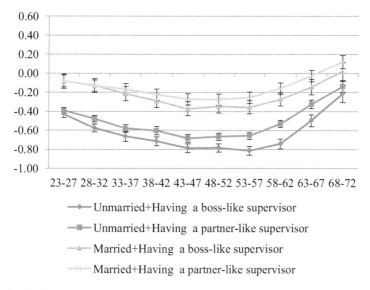

Fig. 20.16 Ladder difference between each age group and the youngest age group (18–22), combined, in the model with controls, US Gallup-Healthways Daily Poll

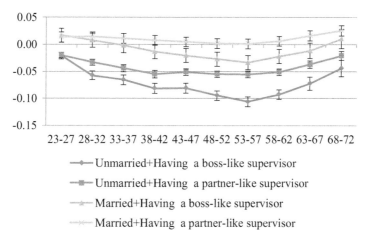

Fig. 20.17 Happiness (yesterday) difference between each age group and the youngest age group (18–22), combined, in the model without controls, US Gallup-Healthways Daily Poll

Looking at the employed sample, we can compare the relative sizes of the marriage and workplace effects. These comparisons are not exact, of course, as the marriage effect is not showing the effects of marriage quality, but just whether the respondent is married or not. Previous research[18] using UK data showed that the

---

[18]See Grover and Helliwell (2017).

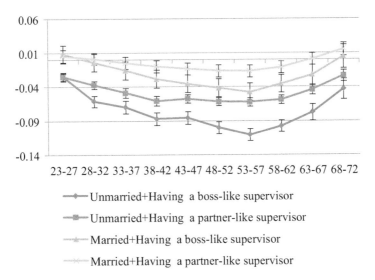

23-27 28-32 33-37 38-42 43-47 48-52 53-57 58-62 63-67 68-72

        Unmarried+Having a boss-like supervisor

        Unmarried+Having a partner-like supervisor

        Married+Having a boss-like supervisor

        Married+Having a partner-like supervisor

Fig. 20.18 Happiness (yesterday) difference between each age group and the youngest age group (18–22), combined, in the model with controls, US Gallup-Healthways Daily Poll

marriage effects were twice as large for those who also regarded their spouse as their best friend, a reasonable measure of the quality of a marriage in terms of happiness. For the social context of the job we are looking solely at job quality, but using only one measure among many possible. Previous research has shown a large life satisfaction premium for being employed rather than unemployed, in both cross-sectional and longitudinal data samples.

Looking first at the two parts of Figs. 20.15 and 20.16, the life evaluation effects of marriage on the U-shape are about twice as large as those for having a partner-like supervisor in the simple model, and about three times as large in the model with controls. Using the results from the model with controls, what can we conclude about the combined effects of marriage and the workplace social context? From Fig. 20.16, we can see that employed workers aged 53–57 who are unmarried and have a boss-like supervisor have life evaluations that are lower by 0.82 points than those in the youngest age group with the same job and home characteristics. For those who are married and have partner-like supervisors, there is still some evidence of a U-shape, about 0.28 points, about one-third as large as for those who are unmarried and in jobs with boss-like supervisors.

The results in Figs. 20.17 and 20.18 for happiness yesterday have the same general pattern, while showing even larger proportionate reductions in the U-shape for those who are married and partner-like supervisors. Looking at the results with controls in Fig. 20.18, the U-shape for the married in good jobs is less than one sixth as large as for those who are unmarried and with boss-like supervisors. For those in the 53–57 age group, for example, the reported frequency of happiness yesterday is lower by 0.02 for the married in good jobs, compared to 0.11 for those who are unmarried and with boss-like supervisors.

20.5 The U-Shape Is Also Flatter for Those Who Have Lived Longer in Their Communities

If the U-shape in age is importantly based on the quality of the social context, we might also expect to find the U-shape to be less for those who have lived for longer in their local communities, since social foundations take time to build. Danish researchers calculated age distributions of life satisfaction separately for those who have lived for more or less than 15 years in their communities, and found there was a U-shape for both groups, but much deeper for those who were recently arrived in the community.[19] We find that the same pattern appears in large samples of pooled data from several waves of the Canadian General Social Survey (GSS). In the Danish case, the U-shape drop from early to middle ages is significantly less (by about 0.25 points on the 10-point life satisfaction scale used in both countries) for those whose have lived longer in their neighbourhoods.

In the Canadian case the GSS data have separate measures for time in the neighbourhood and time in the "city or local community," with 10 years being in both cases the dividing line between short-term and long-term residence. The most transient of the population groups are the 25–34 year olds. In this group, only 10% have lived for more than 10 years in their current neighbourhood, and 33% in their city. These percentages rise thereafter with age, to 37% and 69% for those aged 45–54, and 84% and 85% for those over 75. As was found with the Danish data, the U-shape in age is shallower for those who have lived for longer in the neighbourhoods.

We estimate the interacted effect of age and time in residence using two econometric models that parallel the models without and with standard control variables used in the previous sections. The simpler model explains well-being using age categories, a dummy variable for long-term residence, a full set of interaction terms between the residence variable and the age groups, plus dummy variables to capture province and year fixed effects. The second model adds a number of individual-level control variables, as shown in the statistical appendix. The figures reported in this section reflect the results for the model that includes the additional controls.

More specifically, the base model is:

$$SWB_{ijt} = \alpha_0 + Agec_{ijt}\boldsymbol{\beta_1} + Agec_{ijt}Residence_{ijt}\boldsymbol{\beta_2} + \gamma_1 Residence_{ijt} + \mu_t + \rho_j + \varepsilon_{ijt}$$

$$(20.7)$$

where SWB_{ijt} indicates a subjective well-being measure of individual i in state j in year of survey t, $Agec_{ijt}$ is a vector of age groups (omitting the 15–24 base age group), $Residence_{ijt}$ is a dummy variable for long-term residence, μ_t is a year fixed effect, ρ_j a province fixed effect, and ε_{ijt} is the error term.

The corresponding model with controls added is:

---

[19]See Bonke et al. (2017, Figures 18.9 and 18.10).

$$SWB_{ijt} = \alpha_0 + Agec_{ijt}\boldsymbol{\beta_1} + Agec_{ijt}Residence_{ijt}\boldsymbol{\beta_2} + \gamma_1 Residence_{ijt} + X_{ijt}\theta$$
$$+ \mu_t + \rho_j + \varepsilon_{ijt} \tag{20.8}$$

where X_{ijt} is a vector of individual and household covariates, including gender, marital status, three levels of education (vs less than high-school completion), and six household income brackets (with a dummy variable for those with income not reported).

Using the model with a full set of controls, Figs. 20.19 and 20.20 show the U-shapes separately for those who have lived for more and less than 10 years in their current neighbourhoods.

The results are very like those for Denmark, with the age U-shape being less pronounced for those who have lived for longer in their current neighbourhoods. Except for those aged over 75, the well-being improvement effects are largest for those in the 45–54 year age group, where satisfaction with life is 0.189 points higher (t = 3.3) for those with more than 10 years in the same community than it is for more recent arrivals. Both the size and the shape of this effect are the same as found in Denmark, in both cases about one-quarter of a point on the 10-point scale.

The Canadian GSS provides additional information that lets us check the nature and some possible sources for the community-based U-shape effects. First, we now have the capacity to see whether the results are specific to time living in the neighbourhood, or more generally to time spent in the same city. This distinction is possibly important, as if the U-shape advantages are derived from friendly neighbours, then neighbourhood tenure might be more important than city tenure. On the other hand, if the support is coming from broader networks of friends in the same activities, then time in the same city might be equally or more important. As was seen from the averages, moves between neighbourhoods in the same city are more frequent than moves from one city to another, such that for the whole sample 34% have lived for more than 10 years in their current neighbourhood, compared to 62% in the same city. Although the averages are different, and move differently between generations, the

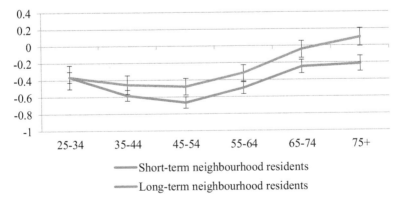

Fig. 20.19 Satisfaction with life difference between each age group and the youngest age group (15–24) in the model with controls, by time in neighbourhood, Canadian General Social Survey

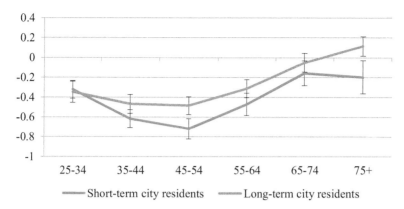

Fig. 20.20 Satisfaction with life difference between each age group and the youngest age group (15–24) in the model with controls, by time in city, Canadian General Social Survey

correlation between these two measures of permanency is quite high (+0.74), making it less surprising that the U-shape effects of the two measures are also very similar, as shown by comparing Figs. 20.19, 20.20, 20.21 and 20.22.

Figure 20.20 shows the corresponding results for time spent living in the same city, just as Fig. 20.19 does for neighbourhood tenure. In both cases long-term residence lessens the life satisfaction drop from youth to middle age, and increases the subsequent improvements. By flattening the left-hand side of the U-shape and increasing the steepness of the right-hand side, the net effect is to increase life satisfaction significantly for those in the highest age groups.

The Canadian GSS also includes a subjective measure of community belonging, thereby permitting us to see if the U-shape effects of time in place are working through an enhanced sense of belonging to the community. Overall, for all the roughly 60,000 observations in the pooled GSS sample, strong vs weak sense of belonging in the community is positively, but fairly weakly, correlated with both time in the neighbourhood (+0.13) and time in the city (+0.11). When we fit the life satisfaction model, with controls, to the sense of community belonging at different ages using the community belonging variable in precisely the same way as previous described for the long-term residence variable, we find that a sense of community belonging has very strong effects on life satisfaction, and that these effects are essentially the same for people in all of the younger age groups. We illustrate this result in Fig. 20.21, where we show two different U-shapes separated only by the effects of strong vs weak sense of belonging to the local community. Those with a strong sense of community belonging have substantially higher life satisfaction at all ages, by 0.71 points (t = 15.2) for the 15–24 year olds, and statistically similar amounts at other ages. Only for the age group 75 years and older is there any suggestion of a greater effect, by 0.14 points (t = 1.6).

The much larger Canadian Community Health Survey (CCHS) has the same life satisfaction and community belonging questions, so that it is possible (a) to see if the GSS community belonging result of a similar-size life satisfaction premium associated with community belonging for most age groups is replicated with finer age groups and

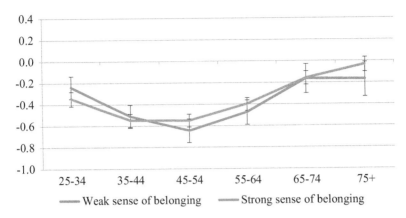

Fig. 20.21 Satisfaction with life difference between each age group and the youngest age group (15–24) in the model with controls, by belonging, GSS sample

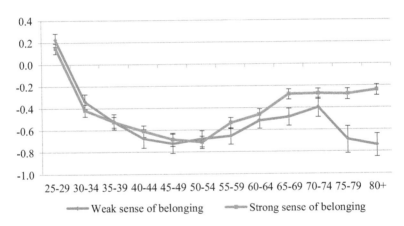

Fig. 20.22 Satisfaction with life difference between each age group and the youngest age group (20–24) in the model with controls, by belonging, CCHS sample

a sample size exceeding 400,000, and (b) to test the hypothesis that community belonging is especially valuable in the oldest age groups. This is done in Fig. 20.22, which indicates a positive answer to both questions. As in the GSS, the effects of community belonging are also large and strongly significant (+0.56 points, t = 26.6), and roughly equal in all the younger age groups. Only after age 55 do significant U-shape effects appear, and become greatest at very high ages, being +0.41 (t = 6.3) in the 75–80 year group and +0.50 (t = 8.7) for those over 80 years of age.

Thus the Canadian evidence suggests that the U-shape effects of length of residence and of community belonging have different age patterns. Time in residence dampens the drop in life satisfaction from young to middle ages while community belonging only acquires significant U-shape influence at higher ages. The greater impact of community belonging for those of greater ages may reflect changing patterns of life, with less time on the job and more in community settings. Those in the oldest age groups are also more likely than those in younger groups to be living alone, whether through divorce or widowhood. This lower prevalence of supportive networks on the job or at home thus may be what elevates the relative importance of the community as a source of social engagement and support.[20]

For both Denmark and Canada, neighbourhood-level social capital, insofar as it is fostered by time spent living in the neighbourhood, dampens the onset and lessens the depth of the U-shape decline in life evaluations from youth to middle ages. The Canadian evidence from two different surveys shows community belonging to be a strong support for life evaluations at all ages, with U-shape ramifications mainly at higher ages. The CCHS in particular, with its much larger sample sizes, shows that those with a weak sense of community belonging do not have the same rise in life satisfaction at higher ages enjoyed by those with a strong sense of community belonging.

If we estimate a model that includes both time in residence and community belonging, and the interactions between them, we find some evidence that these two measures of local social capital are not independent. In particular, the average life satisfaction gains from living more than 10 years in the neighbourhood and having a strong sense of belonging are about 12% less than the sum of the estimated effects when we model the two separately.

20.6 Conclusion

Although many researchers have found a U-shape for happiness over the life course, others have noted that the shape appears in some times and places, and not in others.[21] We argue that the social context is likely to be a key determinant of life satisfaction at all stages of life, and in particular that a supportive social context is likely to ameliorate or even remove the mid-life low that is characteristic of the U-shape, and to augment the typical life evaluation increase after middle age. Although much of our emphasis has been on the front part of the U-shape, the drop from younger ages into middle age,[22] our study of the effects of community belonging suggests that its power lies mainly in delivering a supportive social context at ages when the workplace become less relevant as working time decreases with age. Our results for the community context suggest it to be most important in the later stages of life, when it comes to replace the workplace as the centrepiece of daily life.[23]

---

[20]This is consistent with Van Willigen's (2000) longitudinal analysis showing that the life satisfactions gains from volunteering were larger for elderly than for middle-aged subjects.

[21]As emphasized by Graham and Pozuelo (2017).

[22]This is also the focus of Piper (2015) using UK data.

[23]See Gwodz and Sousa-Poza (2010), Schilling (2006), Mroczek and Spiro (2005), Steptoe et al. (2015), and Ulloa et al. (2013).

Our evidence relates specifically to workplace congeniality, marriage, time spent living in the same neighbourhood and city, and a sense of community belonging, all of which are associated with higher subjective well-being in general, and especially so for those in the middle or later stages of life. We find that the U-shape in age is significantly shallower, and rises more in the higher age groups, for those with the most supportive workplaces, families, neighbourhoods, and cities. Our evidence is based almost entirely on large samples of cross-sectional data, large enough to show highly significant patterns, but adequate only to suggest, not demonstrate, causal connections. The power and prevalence of these associations suggest to us that more experimental methods and evidence are also likely to demonstrate the power of good social relations to support higher life evaluations, and to provide resilience against the stresses of mid-life, or indeed other problems that people may face.

Acknowledgements The authors thank the Gallup Organization and Statistics Canada for access to data, and the Canadian Institute for Advanced Research for research support. Wang is grateful to the KDI School of Public Policy and Management for financial support. We acknowledge helpful comments from readers and conference participants, especially Andrew Oswald and Arthur Stone.

References

Anusic, I., Yap, S. C., & Lucas, R. E. (2014a). Testing set-point theory in a Swiss national sample: Reaction and adaptation to major life events. *Social Indicators Research, 119*(3), 1265–1288.

Anusic, I., Yap, S. C., & Lucas, R. E. (2014b). Does personality moderate reaction and adaptation to major life events? Analysis of life satisfaction and affect in an Australian national sample. *Journal of Research in Personality, 51*, 69–77.

Blanchflower, D. G., & Oswald, A. J. (2004). Well-being over time in Britain and the USA. *Journal of Public Economics, 88*(7–8), 1359–1386.

Blanchflower, D. G., & Oswald, A. J. (2008). Is well-being U-shaped over the life cycle? *Social Science & Medicine, 66*(8), 1733–1749.

Blanchflower, D. G., & Oswald, A. J. (2009). The U-shape without controls: A response to Glenn. *Social Science & Medicine, 69*(4), 486–488.

Blanchflower, D. G., & Oswald, A. J. (2016). Antidepressants and age: A new form of evidence for U-shaped well-being through life. *Journal of Economic Behavior & Organization, 127*, 46–58.

Blanchflower, D. G., & Oswald, A. J. (2018). Do modern humans suffer a psychological low in midlife? Two approaches (with and without controls) in seven data sets. In M. Rojas (Ed.), *The economics of happiness*. Cham: Springer.

Bonke, J., Mortensen, L. H., Ploug, N., & Hansen, A. V. (2017). *Explaining inter-area variation in life satisfaction-matched survey and register data*. Copenhagen: Statistics Denmark. (revised version of paper presented at the OECD-LSE conference on subjective well-being over the life course, London, December 2016).

Cheng, T. C., Powdthavee, N., & Oswald, A. J. (2015). Longitudinal evidence for a midlife nadir in human well-being: Results from four data sets. *Economic Journal, 127*(599), 126–142.

Clark, A. E. (2018). Born to be mild? Cohort effects don't (fully) explain why well-being is U-shaped in age. In M. Rojas (Ed.), *The economics of happiness*. Cham: Springer.

Clark, A. E., & Oswald, A. J. (2006). *The curved relationship between subjective well-being and age* (PSE Working Papers No. 2006–29).

De Ree, J., & Alessie, R. (2011). Life satisfaction and age: Dealing with underidentification in age-period-cohort models. *Social Science & Medicine, 73*(1), 177–182.

Easterlin, R. A. (2006). Life cycle happiness and its sources: Intersections of psychology, economics, and demography. *Journal of Economic Psychology, 27*(4), 463–482.

Fortin, N., Helliwell, J. F., & Wang, S. (2015). How does subjective well-being vary around the world by gender and age? In J. F. Helliwell, R. Layard, & J. Sachs (Eds.), *World happiness report 2015* (pp. 42–75). New York: Sustainable Development Solutions Network.

Frijters, P., & Beatton, T. (2012). The mystery of the U-shaped relationship between happiness and age. *Journal of Economic Behavior & Organization, 82*, 525–542.

Glenn, N. (2009). Is the apparent U-shape of well-being over the life course a result of inappropriate use of control variables? A commentary on Blanchflower and Oswald (66:8, 2008, 1733–1749). *Social Science & Medicine, 69*(4), 481–485.

Graham, C., & Pozuelo, J. R. (2017). Happiness, stress, and age: How the U curve varies across people and places. *Journal of Population Economics, 30*(1), 225–264.

Grover, S., & Helliwell, J. F. (2017). How's life? New evidence on marriage and the set point for happiness. *Journal of Happiness Studies*, 1–18. https://doi.org/10.1007/s10902-017-9941-3.

Gwozdz, W., & Sousa-Poza, A. (2010). Ageing, health and life satisfaction of the oldest old: An analysis for Germany. *Social Indicators Research, 97*(3), 397–417.

Helliwell, J. F., & Wang, S. (2015). How was the weekend? How the social context underlies weekend effects in happiness and other emotions for US workers. *PLoS One, 10*(12), e0145123.

Kassenboehmer, S. C., & Haisken-DeNew, J. P. (2012). Heresy or enlightenment? The well-being age U-shape effect is flat. *Economics Letters, 117*(1), 235–238.

Laaksonen, S. (2018). A research note: Happiness by age is more complex than U-shaped. *Journal of Happiness Studies, 19*(1), 471–482. https://doi.org/10.1007/s10902-016-9830-1.

Latten, J. J. (1989). Life-course and satisfaction, equal for every-one? *Social Indicators Research, 21*(6), 599–610.

Mroczek, D. K., & Spiro, A. (2005). Change in life satisfaction during adulthood: Findings from the Veterans Affairs Normative Aging Study. *Journal of Personality and Social Psychology, 88*, 189–202.

Piper, A. T. (2015). Sliding down the U-shape? A dynamic panel investigation of the age-well-being relationship, focusing on young adults. *Social Science & Medicine, 143*, 54–61.

Schilling, O. (2006). Development of life satisfaction in old age: Another view on the 'Paradox'. *Social Indicators Research, 75*(2), 241–271.

Schwandt, H. (2016). Unmet aspirations as an explanation for the age U-shape in wellbeing. *Journal of Economic Behavior & Organization, 122*, 75–87.

Steptoe, A., Deaton, A., & Stone, A. A. (2015). Subjective wellbeing, health, and ageing. *Lancet, 385*(9968), 640–648.

Stone, A. A., Schwartz, J. E., Broderick, J. E., & Deaton, A. (2010). A snapshot of the age distribution of psychological well-being in the United States. *PNAS, 107*(22), 9985–9990.

Ulloa, B. F. L., Møller, V., & Sousa-Poza, A. (2013). How does subjective well-being evolve with age? A literature review. *Journal of Population Ageing, 6*(3), 227–246.

Van Landeghem, B. (2012). A test for the convexity of human well-being over the life cycle: Longitudinal evidence from a 20-year panel. *Journal of Economic Behavior & Organization, 81*, 571–582.

Van Willigen, M. (2000). Differential benefits of volunteering across the life course. *The Journals of Gerontology Series B: Psychological Sciences and Social Sciences, 55*(5), S308–S318.

Weiss, A., King, J. E., Inoue-Murayama, M., Matsuzawa, T., & Oswald, A. J. (2015). Evidence for a midlife crisis in great apes consistent with the U-shape in human well-being. *PNAS, 109*(49), 19949–19952.

Wunder, C., Wiencierz, A., Schwarze, J., & Küchenhoff, H. (2013). Well-being over the life span: Semiparametric evidence from British and German longitudinal data. *Review of Economics and Statistics, 95*(1), 154–167.

Xing, Z., & Huang, L. (2014). The relationship between age and subjective well-being: Evidence from five capital cities in mainland China. *Social Indicators Research, 117*(3), 743–756.

Yap, S., Anusic, I., & Lucas, R. (2012). Does personality moderate reaction and adaptation to major life events? Evidence from the British Household Panel Survey. *Journal of Research in Personality, 46*(5), 477–488.